The Making of American Society

D1572941

An Institutional and Intellectual History of the United States

The Making of American Society

second edition
Volume I to 1877

Edwin C. Rozwenc
Thomas Bender
New York University

Alfred A. Knopf New York

For Harriet who always kept faith   EDWIN C. ROZWENC

For David who this year begins an
American life   THOMAS BENDER

THIS IS A BORZOI BOOK
PUBLISHED BY ALFRED A. KNOPF, INC.

Second Edition
987654321
Copyright © 1972, 1978 by Alfred A. Knopf, Inc.

Originally published by Allyn and Bacon, Inc.

Library of Congress Cataloging in Publication Data

Rozwenc, Edwin Charles, 1915–1974.
　The making of American society.

　Includes bibliographies and indexes.
　CONTENTS: v. 1. To 1877.—v. 2. Since 1865.
　1. United States—History. I. Bender, Thomas,
joint author. II. Title.
E178.1.R73 1978　　973　　78–1988
ISBN 0–394–32177–4 (v. 1)
　　　0–394–32178–2 (v. 2)

Preface to the Second Edition

In revising this text I have endeavored to maintain the basic integrity and thrust of the late Edwin Rozwenc's original edition. Although nearly every chapter has been affected by the revisions, the basic presentation of topics has not been changed. Where appropriate, however, changes have been made to take account of important new scholarship and new perspectives on the past. The second volume, moreover, has been brought up to date.

The emphasis on major ideas, thinkers, and institutions remains, but in this edition more attention is devoted to the broader social context of these intellectual and institutional developments and to the ideas and institutions of those groups who, in varying degrees, dissented from or were excluded from the dominant patterns of American public culture. Blacks in slavery and freedom, native Americans, women, and immigrants appear more frequently, therefore, in this edition than in the first.

Major changes have been made in the visual essays. All have been reworked completely; some that appeared in the first edition have been deleted in this one. Some completely new essays have been developed. The basic intention, however, has remained to use materials drawn from the arts and popular culture to probe the perceptions, fears, and hopes of earlier generations of Americans. The essays are formulated in a manner that will raise questions and suggest new perspectives rather than argue a single thesis.

THOMAS BENDER
New York City
August 1977

Preface to the First Edition

If we assume that man is the most interesting of all natural creations, we should also recognize that societies are the most interesting of all human creations. To some this may seem to be an exaggerated claim, but at least they might be willing to grant George Herbert Mead's assertion, made some years ago, that our personalities are formed in societies; it is through adopting, playing, and imaginatively constructing social roles that we develop our human selves. If we believe this, then we can assume that self and society are intimately connected; to know ourselves, we also need to know something of the society in which we act our acts, think our thoughts, and feel our feelings.

The idea of such an intimate connection may seem distasteful, especially at a time when many of us are tempted to think of society as a set of external and constraining (and even evil) social forces. We tend to share the Freudian notion that the constraints of civilized societies inevitably generate individual discontents. But we should also remember that Freud could never have written a book like *Civilization and Its Discontents* if he had not participated in the rich network of symbolic communication that constituted the society in which he lived.

In its most fundamental sense, a society consists of a variety of mechanisms to establish communication for shared definitions of the world and for the social goals of the human beings who compose it. But a genuine consensus of beliefs and goals is rarely, if ever, achieved in large human groups, because the complexity and diversity of such large groups provide individuals with a broad range of options in developing their personal definitions of the world and the goals that they seek. Hence a society attempts to obtain a satisfactory degree of compliance from its members by organizing an institutional order to teach and enforce the rules that will implement its beliefs and goals. In short, society and culture are closely intertwined; every society is an institutional order which embodies a set of cultural beliefs.

Because society has a life span that precedes and goes beyond that of any of the individuals who compose it, it is an institutional order that is inescapably rooted in history. But to say that institutions are rooted in history does not necessarily endow them with a static character. If societies have longer life spans than individuals, we must also recognize that each new generation of individuals constitutes a potential threat to the settled character of the institutional order as well as the cultural ideals which it embodies. Hence institutions, by themselves, cannot define the boundaries of social experience; they can be altered or even discarded by the forces of change that come with the continual birth of new generations of humans. Consequently, societies cannot be sufficiently understood if they are photographed as still pictures; they must be photographed in movement as in a motion picture film in order to recapture human actions, thoughts, and feelings in a variety of situations.

If this is so—if society is a human process and not simply a static system of external constraints—then a crucial variable in the study of societies is the event or the happening. It is in the events of social experience that we can see the interplay between established institutions and claims in behalf of new cultural ideals and new visions of reality. The study of history, therefore, is an indispensable way of learning about any society. If to know one's society is the way to knowledge of oneself, then a knowledge of the history of one's society is a bridge that must be crossed along that way.

This book attempts to examine and explain the relationship between institutions and ideas over some three hundred and fifty years of American social experience. Its main focus is on the institutions that Americans fashioned for their social order and on the forces that brought about changes in major institutions and the cultural beliefs which sustained them. Underlying my interpretation is the assumption that this social experience has been a dynamic process and that any explanation that views American history as "frozen" or "locked" is deficient in historical understanding.

Because American society has been fashioned in a period of world history when men (European men) were resorting more and more to political and legal processes to implement their social goals, my history of the making of American society gives heavy emphasis to political institutions. But the shaping and reshaping of political institutions cannot be understood without examining other aspects of the social order—economic organizations, class and status systems, religious and educational institutions, and the cultural media by which ideas and values are communicated to the people. Indeed, these other aspects of the social order gave form to the human needs and discontents which endlessly reshaped the drama of American politics in all of its aspects: the frameworks for action, the roles of the actors, and the culminating events.

Consequently, the events and happenings which are examined in this book are chosen largely because they can help us understand these relationships between institutions and ideas, between order and change. I have chosen the human actors and thinkers who appear in the following pages for the same purpose, and not because of some other interesting facets of their personalities or life histories. It will also be apparent to readers that I have chosen the writings of prominent persons—political and social thinkers, theologians, philosophers, scientists, historians, poets, and novelists—as a way of explaining the cultural beliefs of Americans. Although this method may seem to neglect popular culture, I believe that it does give us some insight into popular attitudes and beliefs because, as Tocqueville observed in his classic commentary on American democracy, Americans learned very early to develop a flourishing trade in literature. In any case, I believe that visual materials may offer us another and possibly better way of understanding significant aspects of the popular consciousness. The visual essays prepared for this book, using the splendid pictures selected by Judith Mara Gutman, are designed to suggest the rich possibilities of analyzing popular conceptions through the non-verbal images created by successive generations of Americans.

While a synthesis of institutional and intellectual history provides the essential framework for this general history of American society, many fascinating aspects have been left unexplored. But my students have taught me that they can understand the anatomy of a society better if we peel away some of its features, however fascinating they may be. Indeed, I owe a considerable debt to my students at Amherst College who, unknowingly in most cases, have encountered the ideas in this book in my lectures and colloquia. Their boredom often forced me to search for new strategies of explanation, and their questions led me to reconsider the logic or the relevance of my own interpretations. Above all, my experience with them has convinced me that a comprehensive history of the United States is indispensable to an understanding of American society. Tunneling into a few special time periods or specialized areas traps the historical imagination in a labyrinth of cul-de-sacs.

No one could possibly write a comprehensive history of the sort that appears in the two volumes of this book without the aid of monographs, journal articles, and other special studies. Although professionalization and specialization are often attacked as stultifying and socially harmful aspects of historical scholarship, I can only hope most fervently that writings of that kind will continue to pour forth with a generous abundance. Such special studies provide the building blocks for larger syntheses of American history and sometimes they can provide indispensable support for new interpretative strategies. I am also grateful for the continuing vitality of American historical enterprise, particularly those writings that have made successful use of the conceptualizations of the modern social sciences. Such works, as well as assiduous special studies, have informed my writing at every point, and my listing of titles in the bibliographies of these volumes is a very inadequate way of acknowledging my indebtedness.

EDWIN C. ROZWENC

Contents

Contents

Visual Essays

chapter one

The European Discovery of America

From Part I in Theodore DeBry's America. *Rare Book Division. The New York Public Library. Astor, Lenox and Tilden Foundations.*

The New World

When Europeans arrived in the New World, a large population of Americans, living in diverse and complex cultures, was already there. The history of human society in the New World began well before the voyage of Columbus. How long before? Anthropologists who have analyzed surviving objects of their material culture (pots, tools, and the like) with carbon-14 dating techniques estimate that these first Americans had come perhaps 40,000 years earlier, and maybe even before that. They had migrated from Asia, crossing a landbridge that once connected Siberia with Alaska.

The First Americans

Over many thousands of years these men and women spread across the North and South American continents. Out of this migration and the resulting differential cultural development, encouraged largely by adaptation to varying ecological settings, there emerged a rich diversity of tribal cultures. In fact, as many as two thousand languages were spoken by native Americans by 1492. Although it is difficult to generalize about so many diverse cultures, it is important to note that many of them, including those in the area that would become British North America, had passed through or were passing through the agricultural revolution, just as had many societies in many parts of the world over the course of world history. What this meant was that a sedentary as opposed to a nomadic existence was possible for these peoples. Substantial populations, in other words, lived in settled villages and practiced agriculture at the time of European contact.

When we recognize the populousness and vigor of these tribal cultures, the meaning of the European "discovery" takes on a quality not suggested when 1492 is used as the beginning date for American history. The discovery was really an invasion. And the first years of European settlement have to be seen as a process of cultural interaction—and as a failure in cultural coexistence. The tribal cultures were eventually eclipsed by the ever-expanding Euro-American culture, but it is well to remember that at the beginning the Europeans represented only one more culture in a land marked by remarkable cultural diversity.

For Europeans, however, the discovery of the New World gave reality to myths that had existed for centuries in the European imagination. In the words of a modern Mexican poet, the appearance of America as an actual place had been anticipated in mythology and poetry "as if it were a form necessary to the minds of Europeans." More than two thousand years before Europeans correctly perceived the existence of the large continental land mass in the Western Hemisphere, Plato wrote of a great and populous island in the outer (Atlantic) ocean which had been swallowed up by a tidal sea. Plato's tale was a philosophic romance, but it led countless generations to accept the story of Atlantis as a historical account of a real place. One finds other accounts of a new land in the works of later Christian writers. The most famous of these was, perhaps,

The Beckoning Myth

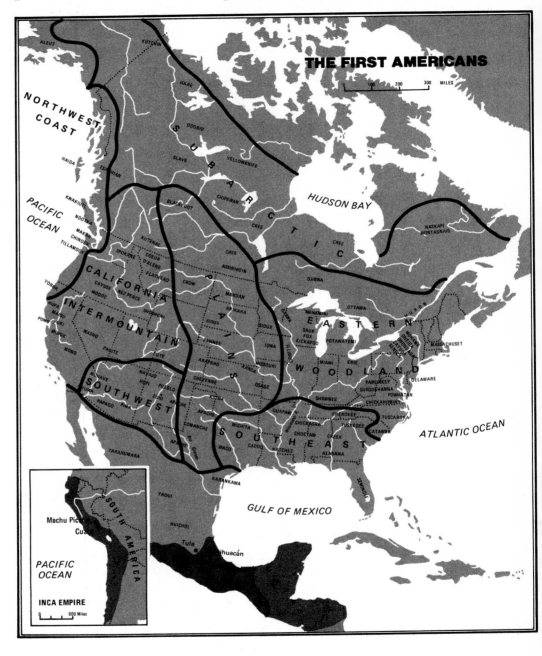

THE FIRST AMERICANS

that of the Irish monk, St. Brenden, who described a fabulous land of promise that he had reached by sailing west of Ireland. The tales of Norse voyages to the New World, no doubt growing with the telling and retelling, fed these European fantasies.

By the end of the fifteenth century, this vague geographical consciousness, nourished by Hellenic, Christian, and Norse imaginings and legends, had been transformed into a stupendous realization that a vast New World did indeed exist across the Atlantic Ocean. Although Europeans looked out on the expansive Atlantic with some fear, they also felt that it might lead to the fulfillment of a promise nourished by two thousand years of myth. The promise of the New World, now Christianized, expressed the possibility of extending God's word to a whole new hemisphere. And there were other possibilities that increasingly caught up the hopes and dreams of Europeans: wealth, glory, adventure, power.

The Gathering Forces of European Expansion

Yet myth alone could not entice European explorers into the western waters of the Atlantic Ocean. The ancient legends repelled as much as they beckoned because the mythical tableau of the Atlantic Ocean was also embellished with dreadful sea monsters, diabolical sea currents, and death-delivering winds. The discovery of America was more particularly the consequence of new scientific knowledge and of new forms of social organization. When the Norsemen were making their voyages to the New World, Europeans lacked the knowledge and the techniques to explore and to settle continents larger than their own. They lacked the means to sustain and govern colonies across several thousand miles of ocean; indeed they lacked administrative resources for maintaining effective economic and political control over anything more than small domains on the European continent. A considerable evolution of social institutions and scientific knowledge had to take place before voyages across the Atlantic Ocean could produce anything more than an enlarged body of mythological lore.

In the first place, Europeans had to break out of the feudal system *Feudal Europe* which had risen from the chaos after the fall of Rome. The feudal manor and the feudal town had become the foci of productive activity and in both these forms of social organization, the primary social goal was a maximum degree of self-sufficiency in the production of food, clothes, tools, furnishings, as well as weapons of defense. In the political sphere, feudal lords administered their little principalities and maintained their power and prestige by petty wars, by strategic marriages, and by individual exploits in the joust and hunt. Even the Roman church, which strove to preserve the catholicity of the Christian faith, had to leave the majority of ecclesiastical functions in the hands of bishops and abbots who presided over their religious principalities using methods similar to

*The Revitalization
of Western Europe*

those of lay lords. Indeed, in their pursuit of power and prestige, the lords spiritual could not easily be distinguished from the lords temporal.

Nevertheless, the political anarchy of the ninth and tenth centuries was not self-perpetuating. The later decades of the tenth century witnessed an interesting revival of political energy. This revitalization of Western Europe that occurred after the tenth century transformed every aspect of political and social life and generated a new dynamism that was to have profound consequences for world history for a thousand years. An agricultural revolution based upon three new techniques—the use of the heavy wheeled plow equipped with a moldboard, the employment of horsepower, and the development of the three field system of crop rotation—led to the production of more food which served to stimulate the growth of population. The increase in population became, in turn, a stimulus for the cultivation of new lands. A remarkable internal expansion or "colonization" took place in large hitherto uninhabited areas of Western Europe. Forests and marshes were cleared and placed under cultivation; entire new villages and towns sprang up.

The increase in the supply of agricultural products and the growth of the population stimulated trade and commerce. This revival of economic life based on internal aspects of the Western European economy quickly became linked to a resumption of long-range trade with the East through the entrepots of the eastern Mediterranean. The upsurge of political and religious energies which had checked the barbaric invasions in the tenth century was transformed into a form of politico-religious expansionism in the crusades against the Saracens in the Holy Land. The crusading expeditions, in turn, intensified and magnified the new social forces stirring in Western Europe. Genoese, Pisan, and Venetian merchants furnished ships and supplies to the crusading expeditions and established trading posts in Syria, Palestine, and Constantinople. Commerce in the silks, sugars, and spices of the East began to flourish, and cities along the favorable routes of commerce—not only in Italy but as far north as the Flemish towns of Ghent, Bruges, and Lille—began to grow in population and wealth.

More particularly these rapidly growing cities created an urban middle class quite unlike any which had existed before. The urban bourgeoisie—merchants, skilled craftsmen, and shopkeepers—displayed an innovating spirit that paralleled the political ambition of powerful feudal princes. The urban middle classes promoted industrial growth characterized by a more complex division of labor and higher skills. As trade increased with the Moslem states of the eastern Mediterranean, the merchants of the medieval cities learned to build larger and better ships and to improve the arts of navigation. More important, they learned to develop more advanced forms of economic organization. They also formed associations for trade over long distances in order to mobilize larger amounts of capital and to spread the risk of such large undertakings. The more successful capitalists became money-lenders and helped to develop the techniques of banking as an indispensable aid to the expanding economic activities of medieval cities.

The emergence of a money economy associated with the expansion of commercial activity gave added impetus to the transforming forces in feudal society. Peasants began to receive money for surplus farm products sold in local markets and gradually were able to change their feudal obligations from payments in kind or in services to payments in money. The cities lured the more adventurous serfs from the feudal manors to perform the new skills and to partake of the greater comforts and delights of city life. In this world of new economic appetites and changing economic relations, serfdom began to lose viability and various forms of freer status began to appear first in the cities and then among the peasantry in the country districts. If the cities enhanced the possibilities for individual liberty, they also magnified the possibilities for organizing political power. Ambitious princes learned the wisdom of making alliances with the wealthy bourgeoisie. The creation of new military forces, financed by the urban bourgeoisie and recruited from the

From Joseph Strutt's A Biographical Dictionary. *London, 1785. Henry E. Huntington Library and Art Gallery.*

lower classes, enabled the aspiring "new monarchs" to overpower the feudal barons and weld their feudal principalities into unified nation states.

These new forms of social experience stimulated new modes of thinking and new ways of looking at the world. The crusaders and the merchants discovered that the culture of the East was more advanced than their own in many respects. Contacts with Moslem scholars in Spain, Sicily, and North Africa enabled European scholars to rediscover the natural history and geography of Aristotle and Ptolemy. Bold commercial travellers like Marco Polo in the thirteenth century added new data to the renaissance of geographical study in Europe. By this time most of the scholars of the medieval universities had come to accept the Greek theory of a spherical earth divided into climatic zones.

Roger Bacon, who displayed the new scientific spirit better than any of the university scholars of the thirteenth century, accepted not only the theory of a spherical earth but also the Aristotelian assumption that there was a relatively short westward sea passage to India. This conception of a short westward passage to India was repeated in Pierre d'Ailly's widely-read world geography, *Imago Mundi,* and among the avid readers of this work was Christopher Columbus. The marginal notes in Columbus' personal copy of the *Imago Mundi* indicate that he was fully persuaded to believe that "water runs . . . between the end of Spain and the beginning of India" and that "the end of Spain and the beginning of India are not distant but close." The close link between the man of science and the explorer was a crucial element in the discovery of America.

But the recovery of Greek geography was only a part of the new scientific spirit. More important was the empirical and pragmatic way in which European thinkers began to conceive of the world of nature and of man. By the end of the fifteenth century, Leonardo da Vinci, artist and inventor, was puzzling over problems of mechanical movement and of human anatomy. Although he lacked the ability to formulate the abstract concepts of gravitation, momentum, and energy that later scientists used to explain the underlying unities of Nature, Leonardo was a man who looked into the details of natural phenomena for the meaning of things. With a similar scientific perspective, his contemporary, Niccoló Machiavelli, began to look at how society was run and how people actually behaved in order to develop his conceptions of government and the uses of power.

To be sure, another full century of inquiry and experimentation was necessary before something like a "scientific revolution" could be clearly identified in European thought. Nevertheless, there is abundant evidence that Europeans who were close to the centers of commerce and culture were beginning to move away from traditional conceptions toward new perceptions of reality. The mythical conception of a world peopled by demons and spirits—both good and evil—was no longer satisfying. The "new men" of the cultural renaissance were ready to believe that all the phenomena of the world could be identified and classified, and that their underlying unities could be explained and used for the benefit of mankind. This belief in the possibility of understanding the forces of nature and society undoubtedly nourished a growing eagerness to explore and master the world.

Explorers and Conquistadors

Portugal, the first of the newly risen nation states to launch voyages of exploration into the Atlantic, exhibited all the new forms of social energy to a remarkable degree. John of Avis led a struggle for a unified national monarchy at the turn of the fifteenth century with the full support of the merchant guilds of Lisbon. Victorious in arms against a factious nobility as well as the Moslems, King John created an efficient administration staffed with leading men of the guilds of Lisbon which replaced the feudal court as the center of Portuguese life and politics.

King John was able to bequeath a firmly established national monar- *The Portuguese*
chy to his sons, and his third son, known to history as Prince Henry the *Explorations*
Navigator, was able to strengthen the commercial power of the new nation state by organizing the discovery of new territories and new sea routes to the south of Portugal. Prince Henry, to be sure, retained the passion for religion that had sustained the Portuguese in the long struggles with the Moors in the Iberian peninsula; he was anxious to discover whether there were Christian peoples in Africa, for a medieval legend had told of a Christian king, Prester John, whose kingdom lay somewhere in the heart of Africa. But Henry's mythical perceptions were combined with a strong scientific bent. His interest in learning is testified by his close attention to the welfare of Lisbon University where Portuguese scholars, like the Spaniards, had absorbed much of the scientific teaching of Moslem scholars. Prince Henry established an academy at Sagres, the southwestern tip of Portugal, and there he gathered an able group of cosmographers, astronomers, and physicians, many of them Jews and Spanish Moors; there, he selected his captains and pilots; and, there the impulse to discovery was nourished and made systematic.

Two great technical advances came from the Sagres academy which were to make the Portuguese pre-eminent in exploration in the fifteenth century—the art of shipbuilding and the art of map-making. The caravels of Portugal were the best ships afloat for sailing the stormy and fearsome waters of the Atlantic, and Portuguese captains led the way in the intelligent use of sea charts. Prince Henry's sea captains discovered and colonized the Canary Islands and the Azores; by the time of his death in 1460, Portuguese expeditions had rounded the great bulge of Africa. In the forty years after Henry's death, the Portuguese gained the full measure of wealth and glory made possible by the knowledge so carefully assembled in the Navigator's time. In 1487 Bartholomew Dias sailed around the southern end of Africa. Eleven years later Vasco Da Gama fulfilled the long-awaited Portuguese dream by sailing around the Cape all the way to Calicut on the west coast of India. In the next few years, the Portuguese developed the greatest trading empire in the world, adding bases at Goa and Diu in India to those already established in West and East Africa.

The Portuguese discoveries helped to change the picture of the world in men's minds and stimulated the more daring to attempt other voyages of discovery. The wealth that poured into Portugal from the oriental trade aroused the admiration and envy of other new monarchs in the nation states of Europe. Among these were the monarchs of Spain who were concluding the reconquest of the larger portion of the Iberian peninsula from the Moors.

The Westward Voyages of Columbus

Spain had developed a hardy sea-faring population in the Andalusian harbors near Gibraltar. Spanish sailors had fished and traded all along the coasts between the Bay of Biscay and the Gulf of Guinea and as far west as the Canary Islands, despite Portuguese pre-eminence in those waters. Thus Spanish seamen had some experience with voyages in the Atlantic when Columbus came to the Spanish court seeking support for his scheme for a western voyage of exploration.

Christopher Columbus supplied the monarchs of Spain with an organizing idea for exploration. Born in Genoa in 1451, Columbus had spent many years as a sailor in Genoese trading voyages to the eastern Mediterranean. He had served eight or nine years under the Portuguese and had probably made several voyages down the West African coast. There is some reason to believe that he had sailed in a Portuguese voyage to the British Isles and as far north as Iceland. He married the daughter of the hereditary captain of Porto Santo in Madeira Island and during his residence there developed his single-minded vision of a westward voyage across the Atlantic. Thus, when Columbus offered his services to Spain, he was a deep-water navigator, thoroughly experienced in the Portuguese techniques of nautical science.

Columbus' conception of "the enterprise of the Indies" was based upon the two modes of imaginative experience that furnished much of the dynamism for the impulse to discovery in the fifteenth century. He believed in the mythical islands of the Atlantic. At the same time, he had read some of the new cosmography of his day such as the *Imago Mundi* and had corresponded with Paolo Toscanelli, the celebrated Florentine scholar and geographer. D'Ailly's *Imago Mundi* and Toscanelli's letters strengthened his conviction that a western sea route to the Indies would be a relatively short one. The mixture of myth and science in his mentality produced in Columbus a vision and a purpose of great intensity.

Columbus' attempts to win support for his project from the king of Portugal were fruitless; the Portuguese were still preoccupied with the grand enterprise of a passage to India around Africa. Columbus then

demons

What did Europeans expect to find in the New World? Did they really expect, as in this engraving from Theodore DeBry's Voyages and Travels, *to have the "wretchedness and fury" of Kaagere and Aygnan, two classic gods, ravage and envelop them?*

From the title page of Part IV in Theodore DeBry's America. *Rare Book Division. The New York Public Library. Astor, Lenox and Tilden Foundations.*

Did they believe that beastly creatures with the frenzy of a savage would greet them as they stepped off the boats in which they had travelled for months? Did these fearful images that they created depicting the New World and its peoples reflect deeply seated fears in European consciousness? Or were they stimulated by some specific aspects of life in the New World?

Whatever the source of it, European perception of the demonic spirit wound itself into the movement and shape of the Indians. Their hands were drawn as claws, while their testicles were portrayed in a devilish mask.

Were the Indians the devil incarnate? Were they furious and violent? Sir William Strachey, a sixteenth-century English explorer, was certain that the Indians' "chief god is no other indeed than the Devil." Might such images help justify European invasion of the New World and the violence and fury directed against the Indians? Does this picture tell us about a murderous impulse within New World or European cultures?

The written and visual records left by Europeans in the Age of Exploration reveal that the New World had multiple and complex images and feelings for them. The European mentalities that formed these images are at the base of the American heritage.

From F. M. Guazzo's Compendium Maleficarum. *Milan, 1626. Rare Book Division. The New York Public Library. Astor, Lenox and Tilden Foundations.*

Demons, we should recall, were not new to the minds and lives of Europeans. The iconography of European civilization offers images of the devil in various guises. The forests and thrones of Europe provided images of monsters and demons before and during the time of European discovery of the New World. The mysterious powers possessed by demons were even occasionally associated with the power of priests and monks.

If the iconography of the age of discovery discloses an irrational fear of demons, it is also marked by symbols of religious faith and those of science. Men saw God in nature, and they developed new technologies and scientific instruments to study and to conquer nature. The astrolabe and the magnetic compass eased exploration of the seas, while Galileo used a scientific method and a telescope to explore the heavens and the laws of nature.

If science gave men confidence and a sense of power, so did the cross. Where the compass and astrolabe directed explorers, the cross followed.

Plate 9 in Part IV of Theodore DeBry's America. *Rare Book Division. The New York Public Library. Astor, Lenox and Tilden Foundations.*

Live, *ever mindfull of thy* dying;
For, Time *is alwayes from thee flying.*

An allegorical emblem from
George Wither's A
Collection of Emblems,
1635. From the Spencer
Collection. The New York
Public Library. Astor, Lenox
and Tilden Foundations.

For all the power of science and faith, death was a constant fact of life. If the idea of death is today banished from our daily lives, it was ever present in earlier periods of Western history. Can this account, perhaps, for the somberness of many of these images? And can it account for the preoccupation with devils and mysterious demonic forces? Was the devil death? Was the devil that which was unknown or strange? Did the devil inhabit the New World? Brave settlers feared it did.

From Bellegardex and
DuPerier's A General History
of all Voyages and Travels
Throughout the Old and
New World. *London, 1708.
American Antiquarian
Society.*

From Part VI of Theodore
DeBry's America. *Rare Book
Division. The New York
Public Library. Astor, Lenox
and Tilden Foundations.*

*Of course explorers did not think all demons were evil. Sometimes
they saw them as mysterious forms wielding a power without
damning a person to death or threatening his life; some even saw
this demonic power granting a health and happiness. When travelers
stopped at one of the Canary Islands on their trip west and saw a
tree like this they knew that an unseeable power maintained life on
the island. With no "Spring, River, Fountain, Rain, or other water"
on the whole island, some controlling hand rebalanced life and
"made amends" for the lack of water. Fogs and clouds continually
hung over the top of the tree dropping water into a "cistern or
bason" under the tree. Sometimes, as in this same scene from
DeBry's account, one saw the water actually dripping. Yet for every
dark and somber image of the New World, there are others that are
light and cheerful.*

How can we account for this? Did pessimistic world views produce more fearful images of the New World? The Puritan John Winthrop lived by a philosophy and religion that directed attention to the evils of the world. And he believed that the wilderness of the New World threatened the order of the Godly community and thus encouraged an ungodly liberty more like that of the beast than of a Christian. Perhaps, as this early eighteenth-century woodcut suggests, settlers in New England succumbed to the demonic forms that the explorers first expected? Or was the threat really from within?

The Age of Exploration also produced Edenic images of the New World. If America were a land of fruit and honey, could settlers dispense with the fears of moral corruption that preoccupied Puritan settlers?

While surely less fearful than the demonic images of the New World, the notion of easy living in an Edenic paradise also posed a moral threat. Perhaps it would encourage moral degeneracy associated in the minds of European moralists with laziness, ease, and luxury. Were settlers morally trapped between the dangers of barbarism in a wilderness on the one hand, and indolence in a fruitful garden on the other?

Were these extreme images reflective of reality? Must one choose between demonic and Edenic images of life in either the Old World or the New? How different was the actual character of life in America? More particularly, how different was the village life of Englishmen from that of Indians? Was one a model of moral and social order with the other totally lacking these qualities?

Jamestown Reconstruction.
*Photo by Thomas L.
Williams.*

What of the material quality of life? How did the physical village of Jamestown, shown below in a reconstruction, differ from Indian villages? Is there reason to believe it contained a morally superior way of life?

Indian village in Virginia. From Part I, Plate XX in Theodore DeBry's America. *Rare Book Division. The New York Public Library. Astor, Lenox and Tilden Foundations.*

Many Europeans thought that Indians were living without culture, tradition, and restraint. Is such a condition suggested in this contemporary representation of an Indian village? How different is this village as a container of human life from what the English established at Jamestown? If the Indian village depicted here seems to reflect a complex and well-ordered society, why did Europeans so often assume that Indians lacked order in their way of life? Was it perhaps because these were issues that troubled Europeans in respect to their own lives?

A schoolmaster attributed to the eighteenth century American School. Frick Art Reference Library.

The settlers could not, or at least did not, understand the order of tribal cultures. Perhaps this worsened their fears about their own internal impulses to disorder. The terror of life without restraint, the terror of strangeness were real. This made the seventeenth century a century of authority. Authority would be nourished, British colonists believed, in the institutions of the community. In these institutions, including the school, Satan, that old deluder, would, they hoped, meet his match.

turned to Spain for support and, after seven years of petitions and intrigue at the court of Ferdinand and Isabella, he was finally empowered by Queen Isabella to equip a small fleet for his westward expedition. The royal commission conferred upon Columbus the title of "Admiral of the Ocean Sea" and "Viceroy and Governor" of any islands or countries (presumably Japan and China) that he might occupy or possess.

Armed with this royal commission and a large subsidy from the royal treasury, Columbus proceeded to Palos, a small Andulasian port whose seamen had had an active part in voyages to West Africa. Columbus won over to his project an important local family of ship captains who helped procure the caravels and crews for this first voyage of exploration. On August 3, 1492, the fleet of three ships put out to sea and two months later on the night of October 12, 1492, the lookout on one of the vessels saw something like a white sand cliff gleaming in the moonlight. In this moonlit moment, the first island of the New World was sighted by Columbus—San Salvador (or Watling's Island) in the Bahamas.

Columbus, however, did not assume that San Salvador was a part of a new world; he believed that it was an island near Cipangu (Japan). The day following his landfall, Columbus recorded hopefully in his journal that he would depart the next day "to go and see if I can find the Island of Japan." All the rest of his first voyage was a search for gold and Cipangu. Each of the larger islands reached in this voyage, Cuba and Hispaniola, Columbus hopefully identified as Japan but no ivory and alabaster cities came into view, only "beautiful and green trees," "birds which sang very sweetly," and "naked people" living in primitive dwellings.

Three more voyages—touching Yucatan (1493–1496), the eastern side of the Isthmus of Panama (1498–1500), and the mouth of the Orinoco River (1502–1504)—produced much the same kind of evidence for his eyes over a wide area of the Caribbean Sea. Yet Columbus continued to identify these new lands with the Indies of Asia. Whatever scientific sense he had once had became increasingly buried in mystical conceptions by his last two voyages. To justify his geographical conceptions he began to argue that the earth had "the form of a pear . . . upon one part of which is a prominence like a woman's nipple." After his third voyage, he developed the fantasy that the "terrestial paradise" spoken of in the Holy Scriptures lay beyond the mouth of the Orinoco. Columbus died a disappointed man who had earned the contempt of the majority of Spaniards for his false claims and wild imaginings concerning the meaning of his explorations. The tragedy of Columbus was not his failure to reach Japan and China; the tragedy lay in his inability to conceive of a more correct identification of his geographical discoveries.

In due course, the scientific imagination of Europe's cosmographers prevailed over the conceptions of medieval mythology. Peter Martyr d'Anghiera, the earliest historian of America and a sophisticated Italian thoroughly imbued with Renaissance humanism, was among the first to suspect the true meaning of Columbus' voyages. Peter Martyr lived most

The Naming
of the New World

of his life at the Spanish court where he tutored young nobles and filled various diplomatic appointments. He had met Columbus in Barcelona after the first voyage and continued to follow the later expeditions of Columbus with great interest. Indeed, when Columbus left for his second expedition, Peter Martyr determined to devote himself to a lifelong task of recording the history of the voyages of discovery by others as well as Columbus. Peter Martyr's *Libretto,* written at the time of the second voyage, spoke of "a new world" and a "Western Hemisphere" although the words were still largely metaphorical in meaning.

The true possibilities of these metaphors became clear with the publication of a Latin tract in Florence in 1503 purporting to be the translation of a letter written by a Florentine, Amerigo Vespucci, to Lorenzo de Medici describing a voyage he had made in the service of the king of Portugal for the discovery of lands in the southwest. In this letter and others which followed, Amerigo Vespucci gave accounts of four voyages which he had made on Portuguese expeditions to the northern shores of South America and the hump of Brazil including the Amazon River area. He contended that a large continental land mass existed in the western hemisphere—a truly "new world" unknown to the ancients which lay between Europe and Asia.

Many editions of such *Mundus Novus* letters circulated in Europe in the first decade of the sixteenth century, and historical scholars have argued for many centuries about the authenticity of the letters and the actuality of the voyages imputed to Amerigo Vespucci. But what is

Waldseemüller's globe map of the world with "America" printed on it. From Seiner Durchlaucht dem Fürsten, Franz von Waldburg zu Wolfegg-Waldsee. Rush Rhees Library. The University of Rochester.

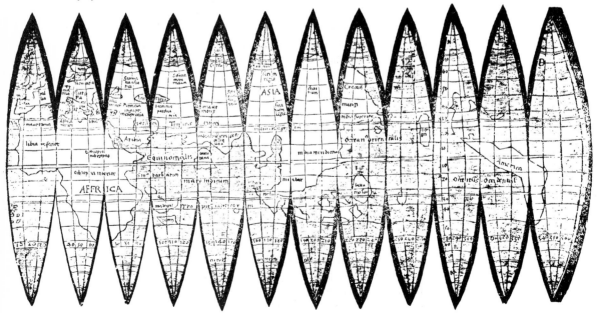

authentic, beyond dispute, is that these letters paved the way for the correct identification of a new world in the western hemisphere by European cosmographers—the true "discovery of America." Martin Waldseemüller, a geographer at the monastery of St. Dié in the Vosges mountains, included the original *Mundus Novus* letter in his *Cosmographiae Introductio*, published in 1507 together with a map of the new lands as then known. That Waldseemüller's work went through six or seven editions in a single year is significant evidence of the exciting impact of this idea in the European imagination.

In his essay on the voyages of discovery to the New World, Waldseemüller made this interesting proposal: "Today three parts of the world (Europe, Africa and Asia) have been more fully explored, and a fourth part has been discovered by Americus Vesputi . . . Since Europe and Asia have received the names of women, I see no reason why we should not call this other part 'Amérigé,' that is to say, the land of Americus, or *America* after the sagacious discoverer Americus." The contemptuous conclusion of Ralph Waldo Emerson that Vespucci was "a pickle dealer who managed in this lying world to supplant Columbus and to baptize half the earth with his own dishonest name" should not blind us to the significant intellectual achievement in the discovery of America. Men like Martyr, Vespucci, and Waldseemüller were able to imagine an America. Columbus could not.

Another two centuries of exploration were necessary before the American continents were revealed in their geographical fullness to the princes and philosophers of Europe. Something of their magnitude was suggested in 1522 when Magellan's crew, on the ship *Victoria,* completed the circumnavigation of the globe after suffering incredible hardships and the loss of their heroic leader in the Philippine Archipelago. But the task of penetrating the mysteries of the continental land mass of America could not be done by sea captains. A new type of explorer was necessary and Spain was the first to create him in the form of the *conquistador*—the soldier-knight of the Cross—ready to confront appalling natural obstacles of jungles, deserts, and huge mountains, and to fight in small bands against the heathen and hostile Indians even in their greatest centers of power and culture.

Spain's Empire in America

At the opening of the sixteenth century, Spain was ready for the conquest of America. The reconquest of Spain from the Moors had produced soldiers with a crusading zeal, admirably fitted by training and temperament to create an empire in America. Politically, Spain was refashioned by Ferdinand and Isabella into a strong feudal monarchy. Royal courts—*audiencias* and *chancellerias*—were established; *visitadores* travelled through the kingdom and examined the administration of justice and finance; municipal councils were subjected to royal control through *corregidores* sent out to inspect the activities of the town councils. The Catholic kings reorganized the Inquisition and made it a powerful instrument of religious unity within the Spanish dominions.

For two hundred years surprisingly few additions were made in the institutional structure which they had set up. And this institutional stability provided a firm base which could sustain the tasks of governing a huge empire across several thousand miles of ocean.

Nevertheless, the recital of Spain's institutional advantages seems pallid when compared to the marvellous feats of the conquistadors. The conquest of Mexico by Cortés established the prototypal pattern of heroic conquest and exploration. In 1519, Hernando Cortés led a band of 550 men from Cuba into Mexico and conquered the rich and powerful Aztec empire. With the help of Indian allies and aided by Aztec legends that prophesied the return of a white god (Quetzalcoatl), Cortés and his men entered the great Aztec city of Tenochtitlan without a fight. But it took another year of perilous diplomacy and fierce fighting before Cortés was able to destroy Aztec power and make himself the complete master of the Aztec empire and of Montezuma's treasures of gold and precious jewels. The romance and the greatness of Cortés' achievements equalled, if they did not exceed, the conceptions of glory and great deeds that were firmly rooted in the Spanish imagination by the Castilian epic of *The Cid.*

Elsewhere the role of the conquistador was not so brilliant and only in Peru was it more rewarding in the accumulation of stores of precious metals. But the marches of the conquistadors opened vast stretches of the New World to the vision of the Europeans. Francisco Pizarro penetrated the Inca strongholds in the mountains of Peru; Gonzalo Jiménez de Quesada fought his way up the steaming Magdalsna Valley against hostile Indian tribes and founded the town of Bogotá; Ponce de Leon explored Florida; Hernando De Soto discovered the lower Mississippi Valley; and Francisco de Coronado penetrated the Rocky Mountain area of North America. By the middle of the sixteenth century, equally daring Spanish adventurers had explored the great basin of the Rio de la Plata in the further reaches of South America, had ascended the Paraguay River, and then crossed the Andes into Peru. In an ordinary man's lifetime, the conquistadors had ranged over and claimed for Spain a vast area stretching from the heart of the North American continent to the mountains of Chile and the plains of Patagonia.

These remarkable achievements were characterized by an essentially feudal style. The conquistadors and their successors were rewarded with titles of nobility. Cortés was honored with the title of the Marquis del Valle de Oaxaca and granted a vast estate of thousands of square miles of the richest land in Mexico. The monarchs of Spain extended the system of government already established in Spain to the New World. The larger dominions such as Mexico and Peru were placed under the control of viceroys; the small dominions like Guatemala and Chile were governed by captains-general. Within the areas under his control, the viceroy or captain general served as commander-in-chief of the army, acted as vice-patron of the church, and presided over the *audiencia* or supreme court which had judicial, advisory, and administrative func-

From Part IV, Plate XVII in Theodore DeBry's America. *Rare Book Division. The New York Public Library. Astor, Lenox and Tilden Foundations*

tions. The economic life of the new lands was based on a system of *ecomiendas* by which land titles were granted to favored conquistadors, including the right to take tribute from the Indians and the legal privilege of using their labor. Thus a new feudal order using a new form of servile labor was established as a primary institutional creation of Europeans in the New World.

While much of the black legend of Spanish cruelty to the Indians is largely an Anglo-Saxon and a Protestant invention the forced labor system was unquestionably harsh. Both the Crown and the Church sought to limit the dangerous power of the encomenderos and to mitigate the brutality of their exploitation of Indian labor. The mendicant friars who undertook the task of Christianizing and civilizing the Indians led the battle for more humane treatment of Indian laborers. Bartolomé de las Casas, a compassionate and learned Dominican monk, attacked the injustices done to the Indians and declared that Spain was entrusted by God to convert the Indians to the true faith and to all the civilized virtues. He firmly believed that "no nation exists today, or could exist, no matter how barbarous, fierce, or depraved in its customs, which may not be attracted and converted to all political virtues and to all the humanity of domestic, political, and rational men."

Las Casas' declaration of the essential equality of all men and all races represents one of the important expectations generated by the encounter between men of the Old World and the New. Indeed, the Dominicans were able to wield enough influence with the Council of the Indies in Spain to induce the Council to promulgate in 1542 the famous code known as *The New Laws of the Indies for the Good Treatment and Preservation of the Indians.* But these new laws were ineffective because every part of the economic structure of the Spanish empire in the New World depended upon the labor of the Indians. A further decree of the Spanish Crown in 1601 sought to limit the use of forced Indian labor in the fields, mines, and transportation routes of the New World. But, since the decree of 1601 urged the substitution of black slave labor, the use of servile labor was increased by the addition of another subservient race.

Such conditions preserved a feudal spirit in the governing class in the Spanish dominions. There was little to encourage the devotion to industry and frugality or the entrepreneurial zeal that marked the rising bourgeoisie of the European cities. Indeed, the strict regulation of trade in Spanish America by the Spanish Crown and the heavy contributions levied on nearly every form of business enterprise made life more difficult for the nascent middle class in Spanish American towns than in the urban centers of the mother country. Smugglers and buccaneers became the only entrepreneurs worthy of the name, but they were hardly in a position to develop a legitimate institutional life in Spanish America.

Spain's Imperialist Rivals

Much of the destiny and the culture of the larger portion of the New World is still shaped today by the consequences of the remarkable achievements of sixteenth-century Spain. Yet Spanish physical and spiritual resources were not great enough for the gigantic task of mastering two continents. At the end of the sixteenth century, large areas of the interior of South America were still beyond the reach of the boldest conquistadors and the most dedicated friars, while the greater part of North America was untouched and unknown by Europeans. The expansionist energies of Spain not only were slowed down by the sheer magnitude of the spatial demands of the New World, but also were drained away by the prolonged struggle to defend the Spanish monopoly against the expansive thrusts of imperial rivals.

Immediately after Columbus' first voyage, the Spanish monarchs had tried to legitimize a monopoly over all newly discovered lands. In 1493, the Spanish Pope, Alexander VI, issued *Bulls* which gave sanction to a division of the whole unexplored world into Spanish and Portuguese spheres of influence. Subjects of other Christian princes were forbidden to enter territory legally held by the Christian sovereigns of Spain and Portugal. The geographical meaning of these papal Bulls was specified in the Convention of Tordesillas agreed to by Spain and Portugal in Portugal in 1494. The Treaty established a line of demarcation, running north and south 370 leagues west of the Azores, which gave Spain all of the yet undiscovered New World except for the hump of Brazil.

Nevertheless, the Catholic kings of France refused to acknowledge the legitimacy of the papal line of demarcation. During the sixteenth century Jacques Cartier and Samuel Champlain explored the rivers and lakes of the northern sector of the North American continent and, by 1608, the French were ready to establish their first permanent settlement on the rock of Quebec. The revolt of the Dutch provinces against their Spanish rulers in the closing decades brought an even greater challenge to the Spanish Empire. Since the Dutch were Protestant in religion they had an additional incentive to ignore the papal Bulls.

The Dutch offered a more serious threat to the Spanish and Portuguese monopolies because they learned very quickly to coordinate their political, military, and trading efforts through the creation of powerful trading corporations. The Dutch East India Company, founded in 1602, was granted extensive political and commercial powers and, within a few years, had established important trading posts along the African and Asian coasts and in the Spice Islands of the Malay Archipelago. Between 1602 and 1615, bold Dutch sea captains captured more than 500 Spanish and Portuguese ships and succeeded in ousting the Portuguese from much of the spice trade. The Dutch West India Company, founded in 1621, was granted similar rights in American trade and soon the Dutch were menacing the Spanish trading empire in the New World from footholds on the northern coast of Brazil and in several Caribbean islands. Dutch ships seemed to be as ubiquitous in the New World as in the waters of Africa and Asia. One of the more enterprising Dutch sea captains, Henry Hudson, ventured far into the northern waters of the New World where a strategic river and a great bay still bear his name in the maps of the world.

England's Expansionist Impulses

At the opening of the seventeenth century, the Dutch and French must have looked like the powers that would shape the destiny of North America. Certainly few men at that time would have dared to predict that in the next two hundred years much of the destiny and culture of North America would be shaped in an Anglo-Saxon mold. Indeed, during much of the sixteenth century, England was still a backward province in the political affairs of Europe; and at no time during that important century of European exploration and expansion did the English obtain a firm foothold either in the New World or in the trading centers of Africa and Asia.

Although England was left behind in the efforts of discovery and colonization during the sixteenth century, there was a great outpouring of creative energy within the English realm that was preparing its people for a remarkable role in the New World. One of the significant manifestations of this new vigor was the astonishing richness and variety of intellectual activity which reached a crescendo of productivity in the

Elizabethan generation. When we think of names such as Thomas More, Edmund Spenser, William Shakespeare, Christopher Marlowe, Ben Jonson, and Richard Hakluyt, we can readily understand that there were forces at work in English society that called forth and rewarded extraordinary efforts of intellect and imagination.

The Utopian Impulse

If the English did not excel in the exploration of America during most of the sixteenth century, there is abundant evidence that the idea of America aroused the imagination of leading Englishmen. Sir Thomas More's famous work, *Utopia,* was influenced in part by the exciting possibilities for mankind created by the discovery of a New World hitherto unknown to Europeans. His description of a Utopia, completed in 1516, is based upon a supposed conversation with a Portuguese philosopher who had sailed with Amerigo Vespucci on the last three of his four voyages. The ideal commonwealth, therefore, has its imaginary existence as an island situated somewhere in the ocean sea of the New World.

An early map of Virginia. Collection of j mara gutman.

More's Utopia is a land where one finds "the ayre softe, temperate,

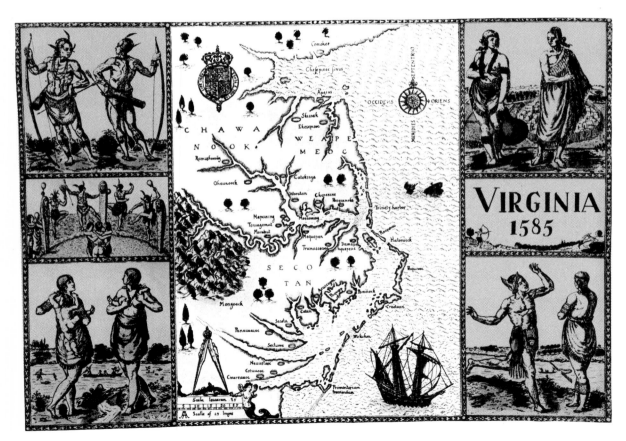

and gentle. The grounde covered with grene grasse [and] Lesse wild-ness in the beastes." In this arcadian landscape, there are "large and faire cities, or shiere towns," none of them more distant from the next than one day's journey on foot. Economic activity is so organized that city-dwellers and farmers change occupations every two years. Hence, all citizens of Utopia have a common knowledge of husbandry in addition to a training in some particular craft useful to the life of the community. All citizens labor only six hours a day; hospitals for the sick are provided by the community; all children are provided with free education; and both men and women continue to give much of their leisure hours to learning throughout their adult lives. The citizens of Utopia detest warfare as "a beastly thing," yet they "practise and exercise themselves in the discipline of warre" to defend their country if need should require. Government is carried on by elective officers with yearly elections except for the prince, who is chosen for life—yet even he may be deposed for "suspition of tyranie." In sum, the citizens of Utopia define "vertue" to be "life ordered according to nature, and that we be hereunto ordeined of God."

Something of this utopian impulse is evident in the intentions of more practical Englishmen. When Walter Raleigh and Humphrey Gilbert

A settlement of Virginia Indians. From Part I, Plate XX in Theodore DeBry's America. *Rare Book Division. The New York Public Library. Astor, Lenox and Tilden Foundations.*

speculated—and acted—on proposals for a "western planting," their rhetoric had utopian overtones. Gilbert tried to establish colonies in Newfoundland and New England, but he failed, losing his life in the process. Raleigh, a court favorite under Elizabeth, did not himself embark upon a colonial adventure, but he organized and promoted a colony established at Roanoke Island in Virginia in 1585. The plantations of Gilbert and Raleigh were intended to serve as an English and Protestant counteroffensive in the New World to save mankind, including the Indians, from the tyranny of Catholic Spain. A colony, moreover, would provide a new opportunity for the poor of England, perhaps reforming them into more productive workers, while offering a base for liberating the red and black peoples enslaved in the Spanish colonies. It was a utopian vision that nicely wedded English imperial interests with humanitarianism. The image of life in the proposed colony that comes through this rhetoric is compelling: it portrays a peaceful cooperation of Englishmen and Indians, all the while supposing that the Indians would be improved by their contact with English Christians.

In the long run, of course, contact with the English proved disastrous for the Indians. But even in the short run matters turned out differently from what was envisioned. The colony was immediately beset by troubles, and it failed by 1589, when the settlers disappeared—a disappearance that historians still cannot explain with certainty. The noble dream of economic prosperity and inter-racial harmony collapsed with this failure. Later English efforts lacked this utopian quality, and soon a pattern of mutual suspicion and conflict marked Indian-white relations.

The most influential English colonial thinking stressed complex economic and political purposes. The key spokesman for this important perspective was Richard Hakluyt, an indefatigable Elizabethan propagandist for overseas expansion. He argued in his *Discourse on Western Planting* (1584) that a North American colony would gain much for England even if gold and silver were not found. In North America, England would find many of those products which had to be imported from other countries, or which had to be obtained at second or third hand from the Portuguese or Spanish. By establishing a plantation type of settlement, English colonists could be sent overseas to produce sugar, wine, silk, hides, olive oil, dyes, and other staples. This would also end unemployment in England and open up new markets for English manufacturers. Moreover, a North American colony would provide a base for striking at both the Spanish treasure fleets in the West Indies and the foreign fishing fleets at Newfoundland.

English Conceptions of New World Expansion

Hakluyt's conception of "western planting" was closely related to fundamental social changes that had taken place in sixteenth-century England. When Henry VIII broke England's religious ties to Roman Catholicism, large amounts of church lands were confiscated. The resulting widespread redistribution of landed property stimulated speculative appetites of landlords. Older feudal attitudes toward the land were altered as landowners sought to maximize their profits by raising rents for peasant tenants and enclosing lands in order to raise sheep for the wool trade. The capitalistic drive of the English gentry made them increasingly eager to support colonizing ventures in the New World where landed estates might be multiplied cheaply and quickly for the benefit of their land-hungry younger sons.

The Sinews of English Enterprise

The break-up of English rural society also created a growing number of landless tenants and laborers. The Parliaments in Elizabeth's reign tried to control the problem of unemployment and pauperism by means of a system of poor relief which was codified in the Poor Laws of 1597 and 1601. These laws placed the burden of poor relief upon the local parishes and financed the various relief and work activities by a compulsory rate levied upon householders. Since the landed gentry were leaders in local government, they were all the more eager to support colonizing ventures as a way to rid England of the burdens of unemployment and pauperism.

Important changes were also taking place in English commercial life; above all, London grew to be a great trading city under the Tudors. The price revolution in the entire European trading area resulting from the inflow of Spanish treasure, the growth of the cloth trade with the

Netherlands, and the expansion of coal and mineral mining were important stimulants in the notable economic growth of England in the sixteenth century. Moreover, trade and industry were encouraged by the royal licensing of monopolies particularly in Elizabeth's reign.

In addition, English merchants were perfecting techniques for mobilizing larger amounts of capital and for spreading the risks involved in large-scale enterprises. The joint-stock principle already used for single voyages by merchants in the medieval cities was extended into a more permanent system of capital formation by which men kept their stock in an enterprise and drew periodic dividends from the continuing ventures of the company.

Such joint-stock companies were often protected by the privilege of a royal monopoly. Indeed, it is doubtful whether the search for new trade routes or the planting of colonies would have been undertaken without such government aid. In any case, the great merchants of London gave their initial support to the formation of the Muscovy Company in 1555 in order to outflank the monopolistic position of the Hanseatic League in the Baltic by a trade route to Russia through the White Sea. At the same time, the promoters of the Muscovy Company were eager to explore a possible northeast passage to the trading centers of China. Similarly, in 1581 the Levant Company was organized to develop new trade in the Mediterranean; and in 1583 one of the first English voyages around the Cape of Good Hope was financed by London merchants to establish the contacts with trading centers in India and the Malay Peninsula that would lead to the eventual formation of the East India Company.

These enterprises seemed to promise more immediate advantages to London merchants. If any London merchants were interested in the New World, they were more likely to seek quicker and richer returns by taking a share in one of the semi-piratical expeditions led by Hawkins or Drake. The prolonged Anglo-Spanish War following the defeat of the Armada in 1588 made the risk of any investment in colonizing ventures look prohibitive. Only with the ending of the war with Spain in 1604 did the merchants of London become seriously interested in America.

The Protestant Spirit   New forms of religious conflict gave added impetus to the English thrust toward the New World. The sixteenth century was an era of religious reformation in England and conflicts over doctrine and the dividing line between spiritual and temporal powers aroused the deepest loyalties and sentiments of Englishmen.

When Henry VIII broke with the Church of Rome in the 1530's, there were many English Catholics who were willing to die rather than to accept the king as supreme head of the church. Many did die when Henry suppressed the Pilgrimage of Grace, as the rebellion led by the Catholic nobility of the north of England was called. In the brief reign of Henry's son, Edward VI, the English Church was reformed in a more radically Protestant way. A new Prayer Book was adopted, the sacramental doctrines were changed, priestly vestments were modified, and altars were replaced by communion tables. The persecution of Catholics which was carried out by Edward's ministers came to a sudden end when the early death of Edward brought his sister Mary, a Catholic, to the throne. In the five years of Mary's reign, it was the Protestants who were burned at the stake and driven into exile.

Not until the long reign of Elizabeth was it possible to arrange something like a permanent religious settlement for the Church of England. A new act of supremacy enforced a renewed break with Rome, and the Queen became the "supreme governor" of the Church of England. An act of uniformity was approved by Parliament enforcing reformed doctrines and practices, not quite as extreme as those of Edward's reign, but clearly Protestant in character. Catholics were forbidden to hold offices in the government, the Church, or the universities. To attend Mass or to advocate the ecclesiastical or doctrinal claims of the Catholic Church was punishable by fines and imprisonment. When the war with Spain began, the anti-Catholic measures of Elizabeth's reign became more stringent. Catholics who refused to take the oath of supremacy and who by word or deed supported the claims of the Church of Rome would suffer confiscation of property and, in flagrant cases, execution for treason.

But it was not the Catholics who offered the greatest threat to Elizabeth's religious establishment. The more extreme Protestants in the Church of England, known as Puritans, were much more troublesome and were located in strategic positions in English society. These Puritans wished to purify the Church of England by carrying out a thoroughgoing reformation in greater accord with the Protestant movement which had been under way for a longer time on the continent. Moreover, the anti-Catholic feelings of the English people after the attack on England by the Spanish Armada made Puritans look like the most ardent defenders of Protestant England in its life and death struggle with Catholic Spain. Queen Elizabeth opposed Puritanism to the end of her reign, but the Puritans found important allies in Parliament and in the press. Puritan pamphlets and manifestos flooded the country, and every meeting of Parliament offered an opportunity for airing Puritan views and putting forth Puritan bills for reform. The Queen and her bishops were successful in driving Puritan ministers from official places in the Church, but Puritan clergymen found other places for their ministry in London and in counties where Puritan sentiments were strong.

By the 1580's more radical deviations were appearing among these religious reformists. Robert Browne, a preacher and pamphleteer of great ability, began to agitate for a congregational system of church organization. The majority of the Puritans had always clung to the idea of working within the Church of England and of purifying it in liturgy and polity. Robert Browne and his followers, however, believed that true believers should separate from the Church of England "without tarying for anie." Although the original group of Brownists were driven into exile at Middleburgh in Holland, other Separatist groups appeared in England. While they were never numerous under Elizabeth, their influence was to grow under her Stuart successors, and in the Puritan Revolution of the seventeenth century their spiritual heirs—the Independents—were to dominate the government under Cromwell.

Thus English Puritanism was increasingly infected by the militant spirit of Calvinism. In particular, English Puritans accepted and taught the central doctrines of Calvinism—predestination and personal regeneration. God chose whom he would for salvation and the freely given grace of God was a call to action. As expressed by one Puritan writer early in the seventeenth century, "A Christian faced with this spiritual life, can see Christ and glory beyond all things of this life . . . he hath strength of reasons beyond all the apprehensions of reason: he is a man of strong working." John Bunyan's *Pilgrim's Progress,* which was to become the epitome of Puritan allegory in the seventeenth century, is notable for its fierce insistence on individual spiritual striving.

While there were no Puritans before the Puritan Revolution who openly challenged the established order of rank and class, many of them were middle-class men whose attitudes toward rank and social pretension, particularly as exemplified by the court, were profoundly affected by Calvinist teachings that stressed the inner worth of the regenerated Christian. Although Puritan political ideas stressed communal solidarity and acknowledged the hierarchical arrangement of society, there was a continual tension between the inward impulses of Puritanism and the requirements of the social order.

The First English Settlements

By the opening of the seventeenth century, England was ready for expansion. The long war with Spain had strengthened English sea power and had inflated the dreams of glory among the English gentry. The daring, semi-piratical expeditions of the Elizabethan sea dogs whetted the economic appetites of the English merchants and taught them to take greater risks in the pursuit of greater gains. An irrepressible Protestant spirit toughened the aggressive traits in the English character and fostered the myth of individual striving within a community of believers.

The Planters of Virginia   The first successful colonizing venture resulted from an interesting conjuncture of the more dynamic forces in English society. Much of the initiative came from the great merchants of London and reflected the growing skills in capitalistic technique that had been developing in England's leading mercantile community. In particular, the leadership of Sir Thomas Smith, London's greatest merchant prince, contributed greatly to the growing influence of the London merchants in the Virginia Company. But the Virginia Company was not simply a joint-stock company composed of merchants and tradesmen; it was a company chartered by the Crown to serve national goals as well as to encourage the pursuit of private profit. The national interest had already been fully defined by Richard Hakluyt in his *Discourse of Western Planting,* and it should not surprise anyone to discover that Hakluyt was one of the patentees named in the original charter of the Virginia Company.

Issued on April 10, 1606, the charter of the Virginia Company recognized two groups of adventurers. One was made up of "certain knights, gentlemen, [and] merchants" with headquarters in London who planned a settlement in the southern part of Virginia. Three years later, the members of this London group included more than one hundred merchants, one hundred and fifty knights and gentlemen, twenty-one peers of the realm, and more than fifty companies of tradesmen and artisans. The second group was made up of representative merchants in Bristol, Exeter, and Plymouth, who planned to establish a colony in the more northern part of Virginia. According to the charter, the London Company was to establish its colony somewhere between 34° and 41° north latitude, roughly between Cape Fear on the Carolina coast and the Hudson River; the Plymouth Company, as the second group is often described, was to establish its colony somewhere between 38° and 45° north latitude, that is to say, between the area of the Potomac River and the middle of the present state of Maine. Although the charter appeared to provide a confusing overlapping of claims, both companies were to operate under the supervision of a special royal council whose members were resident in England. This Virginia Council was to act with and for the king in the exercise of broad powers of government in the colony.

The lawyers on the Virginia Council who drew up the instructions for the government of the colony set forth the manner and form in which "all goods, wares and merchandizes . . . shall be brought into and taken out of the several magazines or storehouses of the colony" and provided for the appointment of a treasurer or "cape-merchant," to take charge and management of the trade in all the goods and commodities which were to be sent to England. In addition, the instructions for colonies to be established in Virginia provided that, "for the good government of the people to be planted in those parts," all cases at law arising there should be tried "as neer to the common lawes of England, and the equity thereof as may be." Moreover, the colonists and their children were expressly guaranteed all the "liberties, franchises and immunities," which Englishmen were at the same time enjoying at home. These included trial by jury, benefit of clergy, and all the rights of possession and inheritance of land. In the long run these legalistic conceptions of laws and liberties were to prove fruitful to the hopes of men in the New World; in the first years of the colony planted in Virginia, however, these conceptions were largely meaningless.

Approximately one hundred men and four boys sailed from London at the end of 1606 in three small ships to become the first planters of

The Jamestown Settlement

Virginia. The location chosen for a fort and settlement was a peninsula about 30 miles upstream of the river now known as the James River. The low-lying, marshy land was not a particularly healthy site. In the first year (1607) the men at Jamestown suffered terrible hardships. Daily food rations were wretched, often consisting of a pint of worm-eaten barley and wheat boiled in water; the summer heat and mosquitoes added to their misery. Chronic sickness made the men weak and irritable and sporadic attacks by the Indians kept them in a state of constant fear. According to Captain George Percy, "Our men were destroyed with cruel diseases, as swellings, fluxes, running fevers, and by warres; and some departed suddenly; but for the most part they died of meere famine." When the second shipload of supplies and settlers arrived at Jamestown in January, 1608, only 38 of the original group of settlers had survived.

Those who survived owed much to the energetic leadership of Captain

John Smith who claimed in *The True Relation* that "by his owne example, good words, and faire promises, set some to mow, others to bind thatch; and some to build houses, others to thatch them; himself alwaies bearing the greater taske for his own share." Captain Smith was particularly skillful in trading with the Indians for corn and Powhatan, the Indian "Emperor," even went so far as to send some of his men to teach the settlers how to plant corn and to make fish traps.

Smith was almost unique among the Virginians in his acceptance of work as a way of life. The high-born "gentlemen-adventurers" had come for gold and glory, not for work. The lowly laborers brought along were no more anxious to work. With the exception of Smith, the settlers were not drawn from the hard-working yeoman classes of England. Faced with such a labor force, Smith complained that "in Virginia a plaine Souldier that can use a pickaxe and spade, is better than five Knights." Although they lived in a society where only labor could provide wealth—indeed survival—the early Virginians were unwilling to work. Without the food supplied by the Indians even fewer would have survived than did. After Smith returned to England a succession of governors and stern laws to maintain better work discipline were tried, but to no avail. After a decade marked by much death and misery there were in Virginia, according to John Rolfe, only "three hundred and fifty-one persons—a small number to advance so great a work."

Until 1619 life in Virginia had been more like a labor camp than a society. The settlers owned no land and had to labor for the company. When the seven-year term of service of the first settlers expired, they were offered three acres of land each, to be worked as tenant farms on a sharecropping basis. These were hardly attractive conditions, and some settlers returned to England. Others remained to try their luck. Many of these found success after John Rolfe discovered in tobacco a crop that could be exported with profit.

The year 1619 was important in Virginia's history. The severe, almost martial laws governing the colony since 1610 were replaced by a more attractive system of government that, it was hoped, would encourage settlement. On July 30, 1619, a general representative assembly, consisting of 22 burgesses elected by the voters of their local districts, convened for its first session. In retrospect, this event is a key benchmark in the history of American political institutions. But no such significance was imagined at the time.

At about the same time the colonists learned that the land policies were being altered—an event that was of supreme importance to them. All older settlers who had completed their terms of service were granted 100 acres of land in individual ownership. And a "headright" system was introduced by which 50 acres of land would be granted to new emigrants who came over at their own expense, with an additional 50 acres for each dependent or servant he might bring with him. The emphasis was now on settlement and agricultural development, and the prospects for

Virginia had brightened considerably. Indeed, the production of tobacco was generating a remarkable economic boom.

During the boom years produced by tobacco, private enterprise operated seemingly without check. The result was a vicious system of labor that treated human beings as things. At first it was Englishmen who suffered under this pattern of economic life, but the ultimate solution to the problem of labor in Virginia was the importation and enslavement of Africans. The first blacks, apparently offered for sale by Dutch traders, were imported into Virginia in 1619. It is difficult to determine just when lifetime hereditary slavery based upon race became an established institution in colonial Virginia. Prejudice and discrimination were present from the beginning, but the formal institution of slavery evolved slowly over the years. Before the end of the seventeenth century, however, the transition to a slave labor system had been made. This degradation of black men and women into slavery was, paradoxically, the foundation for an elevation of whites. American slavery and American freedom thus grew out of the sordid relations of blacks and whites in the first years of the Virginia colony. It is out of this complex background that later Virginians who were slaveholders, like Jefferson, could speak in behalf of freedom and equality.

The development of tobacco as a major money crop meant new demands for land which in turn upset already delicate relations with the Indians. When the English had first arrived, Powhatan, the chief of the coastal Indians, had welcomed them as potential allies against his own inland enemies. Yet Indian-white relationships were always tense and often violent. Finally, in 1622, after Powhatan's death, the Indians, worried about aggressive English expansion, attacked several white settlements, wiping out perhaps one-third of the white population. Ironically, this disaster was interpreted by the English as an opportunity; they need no longer restrain their aggressive impulses. Almost with glee, one Englishman wrote: "Our hands which before were tied with gentlenesse and faire usage, are now set at liberty by the treacherous violence of the Sauvages." From this date relations grew worse between whites and Indians. The actual and relative strength of the Indians decreased rapidly; interaction with the English had been devastating for the tribal cultures of the Chesapeake. Six decades after the initial settlement, the original twenty-eight tribes of the area had decreased to eleven, and the total number of Indians fell even more dramatically, from about 30,000 to less than 2,000.

Meanwhile in England a very different body of men were preparing to plant a colony in America. This small band of religious separatists, known in American history as Pilgrims, came from Nottinghamshire's village of Scrooby, where their Elder, William Brewster, was postmaster. When King James came to the throne of England, he was determined to deal with Puritan dissenters more forcefully than had been the case in Elizabeth's long reign. "I will make them conform," he declared in 1604, "or I will harry them out of the land." In the face of the relentless policy of persecution pursued by the King and by the bishops of the Anglican church, the Scrooby Separatists fled to Holland between 1608 and 1609. There they remained for some years, living the life of exiles in a country where there was religious toleration but also much economic hardship and the usual difficulties of adjusting to a new language and new customs.

In time the members of the congregation in Leyden decided to go to the New World to escape the oppression of their heavy labors in Holland and to lay "some good foundation, or at least to make some way thereunto, for ye propagating and advancing ye gospell of ye kingdom of God in those remote parts of ye world." This decision, as William Bradford was to emphasize in his famous history of Plymouth Plantation, was taken by the Pilgrims "not rashly or lightly, as many have done, for curiosite, or hope of gain, etc. . . . their ends were good and honorable; their calling lawfull and urgente; and therefore they might expect the blessing of God in their proceeding."

Two agents were sent to the London adventurers in the Virginia Company to see if they might not secure a patent for the Pilgrims to settle in Virginia under the liberalized land policy that was being established. The Virginia Company was anxious to recruit new colonists and the treasurer of the Company, Sir Edwin Sandys, had strong Puritan sympathies. But the Pilgrims were not able to obtain satisfactory assurances that they would not be persecuted for their religious beliefs among the Anglicans of Virginia. At the same time, moreover, Sir Ferdinando Gorges and other enterprisers were seeking a charter for a Council of New England, to replace the moribund Plymouth Company, and to have title to the northern half of the lands originally granted to the Virginia Company.

A group of London merchants offered to provide financial backing to the Pilgrims if they would agree to work seven years for their creditors. The Pilgrims had no choice but to accept such hard terms because they lacked sufficient resources of their own to make the voyage. Their financial backers hoped to get a patent for settlement from the Council of New England but ran into so many legal delays that the Pilgrims decided not to linger any longer. Hence they proceeded to America without waiting for any clear title to any lands that they might settle and not even sure where they might establish their settlement.

On September 16, 1620, the *Mayflower* set sail with 102 passengers, 41 of whom were the close-knit group of Separatists who had been at Leyden; the rest were ordinary men and women seeking to improve their lot in the New World. After a stormy voyage, they sighted land near the tip of Cape Cod and, following a brief halt there, made their way across the bay to a place "fit for situation" which they named Plymouth.

Although the first winter at Plymouth was a terrible tale of death and hardship—half of the colonists died—Plymouth was a more stable society in the beginning than Jamestown. Perhaps the presence of their women and their families helped to preserve decency and good order in the community. Despite the "discontents and murmurings" of many of the colonists who were not "pilgrims," the intensity of religious faith of the Pilgrim leaders gave the colony an inner discipline and morale that had been lacking among the first settlers at Jamestown or the short-lived settlement at Sagadahoc. Already toughened by the experiences of exile, the Pilgrims had a more serene sense of the larger meaning of their enterprise. Governor Bradford expressed this view of life in the beautifully balanced prose of his history when he wrote:

All great and honorable actions are accompanied with great difficulties and must be both enterprised and overcome with answerable courages. It was granted the dangers were great but not desperate. The difficulties were many but not invincible. For though there were many of them likely yet they were not certain. It might be sundry of the things feared might never befall; others by provident care and the use of good means might in a great measure be prevented; and all of them through the help of God by fortitude and patience, might either be borne or overcome.

The Pilgrims were fortunate to have the help of Squanto, a sympathetic Indian who taught them to catch fish and plant corn. Moreover, they were able to avoid serious clashes with the Indians since the Indian tribes had deserted the area around Plymouth a few years earlier because of a plague that had decimated the Indian villages in the vicinity. By the use of diplomacy and the military skill of Myles Standish, the Pilgrims were able to develop a flourishing trade in beaver skins with the Indians of Massachusetts and Maine. This gave them the means to reduce their indebtedness to the London merchants more rapidly.

After ten years, the Plymouth colony was no larger than the Virginia colony had been in the same interval of time, but several important institutional patterns had developed which were to have great significance in the further history of American society. When the *Mayflower* was anchored off Cape Cod and before an actual site for settlement had been chosen, the Pilgrim leaders signed a covenant known as the Mayflower Compact. By this compact, they agreed to "combine ourselves together into a civil body politick . . . and by virtue hereof to enacte, constitute, and frame such just and equal laws, ordinances, acts, constitutions, and offices, from time to time, as shall be thought most meete and convenient for ye generall good."

In accordance with this covenant, the colonists organized a simple structure of government. A governor and a council of assistants were elected annually by the freemen to enact laws and administer justice. The system established by the Pilgrims, however, should not be taken as evidence of a special concern to create democratic institutions. Bradford's *History* tells us frankly that the Mayflower Compact was "occasioned partly by the discontented and mutinous speeches that some of the strangers amongst them had let fall from them in the ship; that when they came ashore they would use their owne libertie; for none had power to command them"—thus the signers of the compact were more concerned to establish authority than to guarantee liberty.

Nevertheless, the adjustment between authority and liberty which was instituted in the political system of Plymouth was democratic in spirit, certainly more so than in the governmental system of England. And when other towns grew up in the colony, a system of representation whereby the freemen of each town elected deputies to the "General Court" preserved the liberal features of the Plymouth government. In actuality, the Pilgrims had formed the kind of "social contact" resting on the consent of the governed that seventeenth-century philosophers like John Locke were to imagine as the rational basis for all civil government.

Moreover, the Pilgrims quickly established an equivalent freedom in their economic life. The Pilgrim leaders never liked their original contract with the London adventurers which bound them so strictly to work for the common account of the venture and left little room for individual incentive. A new agreement was made with the London merchants in 1623 which ended the obligation to work only for the "common cause and condition" and assigned to every family and individual freeman a parcel of land. William Bradford observed in his history that "this had very good success, for it made all hands very industrious, so as much more corn was planted than otherwise would have been." By this time, also, the Pilgrims had acquired legal title to their lands from the Council of New England.

The little Commonwealth of Plymouth was soon to be overshadowed by the more rapid growth of the colonies of Massachusetts Bay and Connecticut. But much of the Pilgrim story has moved into American mythology and still exercises a powerful influence on the minds of Americans even in the complex conditions of twentieth-century life so totally removed from the simple village life of Plymouth.

Society-Building in a Virgin Land

The Great Migration

The record of English emigration reveals that only a small number of Englishmen were lured to risk their lives and their fortunes in the New World before 1625. The terrible hazards of the American wilderness were only too plain. A special commission of enquiry appointed by the Privy Council in 1623, after a particularly destructive outbreak of Indian warfare, reported that only twelve hundred colonists remained alive in Virginia after fifteen years of colonizing effort. According to population estimates for this period, there were scarcely two hundred colonists in the small colony at Plymouth in 1625.

But, between 1625 and the beginning of the civil war in England in 1642, a great flow of migration carried at least 80,000 Englishmen across the Atlantic. It was in this decade and a half that a vital and viable colonial society was established in English America. And in another four decades the total population of English America would number 200,000 inhabitants.

Some historians have attributed this flow of migration from 1625 to 1642 almost wholly to the influence of religious motives and speak of this great migration only in reference to Puritan Massachusetts. A closer analysis, however, suggests that other influences were also stimulating this large movement of population. Certainly not all of the migrants went to Puritan New England; large numbers were also going to the Chesapeake Bay region. Estimates of the population of Massachusetts Bay Colony in 1643 indicate a population of 15,000 inhabitants. A similar estimate for Virginia, in 1648, claimed a population of 15,000 Englishmen and 300 black servants.

In the light of the major events of English historical experience in the 1620's and 1630's, we can assume that an unusual accumulation of discontents created the urge to migrate among such large numbers of Englishmen. Certainly the widespread dissatisfaction with the policies of the Church of England was a compelling motive in such centers of Puritanism as London and the eastern and southern counties of England. William Laud, whom Charles I made Archbishop of Canterbury in 1633, pursued a policy which deprived Puritan ministers of their pulpits and moved the Church of England closer to Rome in its ceremonies and vestments and in the decoration of churches.

Social Discontents in England

But it is also important to remember that the economic discontents of various classes of Englishmen had reached a critical point. Most of the earlier Elizabethan laws which sought to protect English peasants by limiting the enclosure of agricultural lands were repealed by Parliament in 1624 and the competitive struggle for capital investment in agriculture was greatly intensified. As a result there were minor revolts among unemployed agricultural workers from 1628 to 1631; and antienclosure riots took place over large areas of England from 1640 to 1643.

At the same time, the royal policy of granting monopolies in trade and industry reached its height in the 1620's. There were alleged to be seven hundred of these monopolies in 1621 and almost every article of common use—salt, soap, herrings, wine, paper, glass, coal, iron, leather, lace, linen, etc.—was under the control of favored trading companies or of privileged guilds of producers. Since small capitalists were cut off from opportunities of personal enterprise by the rigid, monopolistic structure of the English economy, there was a marked slackening of new capital investment in the commercial and industrial sectors of the economy.

These mounting economic difficulties were compounded by the efforts of Charles I and his ministers to increase the royal revenues. In order to tighten the system of collecting royal dues and rents, the king began to delegate to syndicates the privilege of collecting such taxes. And when the English gentry began to oppose these intensified royal exactions, King Charles used arbitrary arrest and martial law to enforce compliance. By 1628, Parliament was ready to challenge the authority of the king. A Petition of Right was adopted complaining of arbitrary taxes and arbitrary arrests.

The conflict between king and Parliament reached a crisis in 1629 when Charles I dissolved Parliament and imprisoned some Parliamentary leaders. In the 11 years of personal rule that followed, Charles and his ministers resorted to a variety of financial expedients to raise money without calling a new Parliament. Old feudal dues were revived and reassessed in higher values, special fines were levied for enclosures and encroachments on royal forests, and forced loans were exacted of the newly rich capitalists of London and other cities. English enterprise in agriculture, trade, and industry was plunged into a state of uncertainty in the face of fluctuating and arbitrary government policies. All men of capital must have longed for a political system which would restore stability, regularity, and confidence. They undoubtedly shared the complaint of one London merchant who said, "The merchants are in no part of the world so screwed and wrung as in England."

Feudal Dreams   If such conditions encouraged migration, or pushed Englishmen toward the colonies, other factors pulled them back. For merchants and farmers North America offered new opportunities in the form of commerce and land. For another group, aristocrats and court favorites, the English colonies offered a chance to create great feudal estates populated by tenants paying highly profitable quitrents, or annual dues. They projected onto the New World a vision of society drawn from the English past, a vision that could no longer work in England itself. Nonetheless, attempts to establish feudal patterns of landholding were made in all parts of English North America. George Calvert, the Catholic Lord Baltimore, persuaded King Charles to grant to him proprietorship of an immense expanse of land on the north side of the Chesapeake, and his son, Cecilius Calvert, laid the foundations for a feudal system of land tenure in Maryland in 1634. Eight powerful lords and gentlemen were granted proprietary authority in Carolina by Charles II in 1663, while Sir George Carteret and Lord Berkeley were given similar authority in New Jersey. In New York large feudal estates known as patroonships were established along the Hudson River by the Dutch, and this pattern was followed by the English. Farmers in each case were expected to work the land and pay the landlord an annual rent. But matters worked out differently. The dominant pattern of landholding, already evident by the end of the seventeenth century throughout the colonies, became that known as *fee simple*—that is, without the burden of perpetual quitrents and with full rights of transfer. A combination of abundant land and the ambitions, values, and purposes of the migrants nullified the dreams of would-be feudal lords.

Puritan New England

The settlement of New England by the Puritans proceeded from a very different vision. Puritanism was a religious reform movement hostile to the remnants of Catholicism in the English Church. It was also a response to long-range social and economic changes. Traditional institutions were becoming unhinged by the first stages of what social scientists now refer to as "modernization." The pace and extent of economic activity was increasing and the spirit of capitalism was making itself apparent. To those who called themselves Puritans, these changes signified a dangerous disintegration of society and proper authority. Puritans found comfort in this disorderly world by stressing commitment to one's "calling," one's earthly task. They also established churches that were communities of visible saints. When they migrated to America, however, they grasped at the chance to build a whole social order based upon the notion of a Christian community.

In 1629 a group of disaffected Puritans obtained a crown charter that created the Massachusetts Bay Colony. The project was able to enlist a number of prominent and well-established men, including John Winthrop, an attorney and landowner who became the leader of the colony. Beginning in 1630, the Puritan migration counted more than one thousand settlers before the first year was out. By 1643, when the Civil War in England considerably dampened the migratory flow, over 20,000 Englishmen had come to New England.

Originally the Puritans had intended to form a single settlement, but the flood of emigrants was too rapid and diverse. Boston became the metropolis for a series of smaller communities. The town became the focus of Puritan life, and towns multiplied across the New England landscape to absorb the influx of new settlers. The town, like the church, was based upon a covenant among its members. In both the church and town Puritans stressed mutual watchfulness in the work of salvation. The Puritan dream of a tightly organized and cohesive community, deriving in part from medieval memories and in part as a reaction to the social disorder of England at the beginning of the seventeenth century, was

The Quest for Community

John Winthrop. *Courtesy,*
The American Antiquarian
Society, Worcester, Mass.
Copy by Marvin Richmond.

given compelling expression by John Winthrop. In a lay sermon delivered to his fellow Puritans as they arrived off the coast of Massachusetts, he told them that they "shall be as a city upon a hill." Their mission was to live together in a loving, Godly community. Their example would, he believed, start a more general reformation back in England. "We must," he urged his followers, "be knit together as one man. We must entertain each other in brotherly affection; we must be willing to abridge ourselves of our superfluities, for the supply of others' necessities; . . . We must delight in each other, make others' conditions our own, rejoice together, mourn together, labor and suffer together . . ."

Winthrop's sermon represents one of the clearest and most powerful calls for community in American history, and to a remarkable degree it was achieved in the towns established by the Puritans. Each of these towns was created through the signing of a covenant. The head of every household affixed his name to this founding document which expressed the dream of community. The communal quest is evident in a covenant drawn up for a Massachusetts town in 1636: "We whose names are here unto subscribed to, in the fear and reverence of our Almighty God, mutually and severally promise amongst ourselves and each other to profess and practice one truth according to the most perfect rule, the foundation whereof is everlasting love." These communities were utopian in the sense of striving for absolute perfection according to the single truth of God's Word. Members of the community proposed to "keep off from us all such as are contrary minded." This corporate exclusiveness provided the homogeneity and consensus necessary for the harmony sought in the Puritan town. By joining the town and by being accepted, the individual subordinated his individual interests to those of the town as a whole.

The village, the built-up part of the town, was located at the center. Here the meetinghouse and the village green marked the center. Everyone had a houselot in the village; they walked each day to the fields, woods, and common lands where they worked. The tract of land that made up the township was granted to the town by the Massachusetts legislature or General Court. One obtained land as a member of a town, not as an individual. More precisely, it was as the head of a family in a town that one gained rights to land. The head of every family admitted into the town was given a houselot, agricultural land, and rights to the common lands. This is not to say, however, that everyone got the same amount of land. The Puritans, like other Englishmen of their time, were not egalitarians. Men of eminence who carried high status with them from England received larger parcels of land than others. Adjustments were also made for those with large households to support. But all had enough land, and by later American standards the gap between the wealthiest and poorest was narrow.

The New England Town

Decisions within the town were made by the freemen of the town gathered as a group, similar to a town meeting. They might decide where to locate the meeting house, how streets ought to be laid out, land allotted, and crops planted. Certain elite members dominated town offices; no doubt they dominated the discussions that led to a community consensus on these issues. The records indicate that decisions were made by "general agreement"; the notion of vote tallies and numerical majorities went against their idea of a consensus on a single truth. Persuasion, it was hoped, would make each town a peaceable kingdom.

Under the general umbrella of Puritan ideology and with some practical oversight from the General Court, life in Puritan New England was lived and centered in the family and the town. Here was the locus of religious experience, political power, and economic opportunity. The idea of pursuing one's individual interest independently of one's family

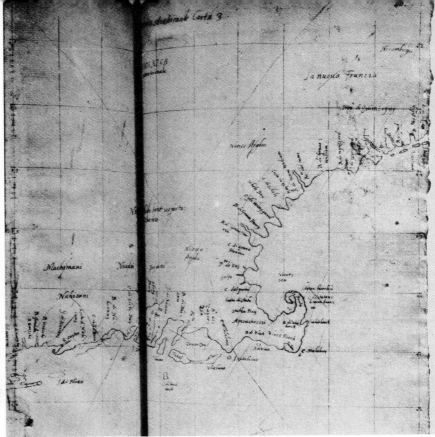

The many settlements of New England. From I. N. Phelps Stoke's Iconography of Manhattan Island, *Volume II. Robert Dudley map, 1636. Collection of j mara gutman.*

and community went against clearly articulated and strongly held Puritan beliefs during the first half of the seventeenth century. The constraint imposed on economic ambition in Massachusetts by community ties and moral prescription contrasted with the unrestrained economic exploitation that characterized early Virginia.

Diverse Patterns of Economic Opportunity

The migrants who came to America in such large numbers after 1625 brought with them the attitudes of seventeenth-century Englishmen toward the pursuit of private gain. The inexorable spread of the enclosure movement in the English countryside revealed the growing strength of capitalistic motives in English agriculture. At the same time, the continued expansion of English commerce demonstrated that other forms of wealth besides landed estates offered alluring possibilities for the rapid accumulation of private wealth and prestige. Indeed, the older gentry as well as the new men of wealth were drawn into the profitable expansion of such forms of enterprise as coal production and cloth production. Hence the Englishman who came to America knew in his bones that the way to wealth lay in the new techniques of investment and organization associated with a rapidly developing capitalistic economy.

In addition, English Protestantism, particularly as expressed by the more militant carriers of the Protestant spirit—the Puritans and the Quakers—provided ethical support for individual striving in the new economic order. The Puritan believed that a regenerate man was obliged to strive mightily to please God in every aspect of his life."We teach that only Doers shall be saved," an English Puritan stated emphatically,"and by their doing though not for their doing. . . . The profession of religion is no such gentleman-like life or trade whose rents come in by their stewards whether they sleep or wake, work or play." The symbols of self-discipline and striving are obvious enough in such statements, but the conception of the calling of a Christian was an equally explicit aspect of the Puritan ethic. A Christian's occupation was an important part of his offering to God. "As soon as ever a man begins to look toward God and the way of His grace," declared John Cotton, a leading minister in Massachusetts Bay Colony, "he will not rest til he find out some warrantable calling or employment."

The Ethic of Individual Enterprise

Although the basic religious conceptions of the Quakers were quite different from those of the Puritans, they developed a similar pattern of social ethics. The Quakers were particularly opposed to the vices of ostentation and vanity in clothing, furniture, and other aspects of living. And many of their ethical teachings, which stemmed from their concern with the vice of vanity, reinforced the models of behavior that were appropriate to the growth of a capitalistic economy. "Be plain in clothes, furniture, and food, and the coarser the better; the rest is folly and a snare," said William Penn to his children. But he also maintained that good Quakers should practice diligence in all that they do: "Diligence is [a] Virtue laudable and useful among Men . . . It gives great Advantages to Men. It loses no Time, it conquers Difficulties, recovers Disappointments, gives Dispatch, supplies Want of Parts . . . The diligent Hand makes Rich. . . ."

To be sure, the Puritans and the Quakers never gave approval to unrestrained acquisitiveness. Puritan leaders in Massachusetts were faithful to Calvin's preachments against usury and avarice. This was evident in their concept of the "just price," as John Cotton stated clearly when he wrote, "A man may not sell above the current price, i.e., such a price as is usual in the time and place. . . ." As for the lending of money, Cotton affirmed the rule: "Noe increase to be taken of a poore brother or neighbor for anything lent unto him." Puritan preachers also asserted that although private wealth may well be a sign of God's favor, the wealth given to men must be improved for God's glory. "Freemen," said Roger Williams, "are not free Lords of their owne estates, but are onely stewarts under God." Cotton Mather summed up this basic Puritan doctrine later in the seventeenth century when he wrote, "All that we have is but a Loan from the Great God unto us," and concluded that the proper uses of wealth should include "giving and forgiving" as well as "paying and lending." A similar conception of Christian stewardship may be found in Quaker thought. William Penn continually urged the monthly meetings of the Friends "to supply the wants of the poor" and to care for "widows and orphans and such as are helpless."

Economic Opportunities in Agriculture

However effective such social constraints may have been, the ways to wealth were certainly many and diverse in the broad expanse of territory from Maine to the Carolinas. Everywhere in seventeenth-century America, land was the great economic resource. Between 90 and 95 per cent of the settlers were engaged in agriculture. In New England and the middle colonies of New York, New Jersey, and Pennsylvania, the farmers lived and worked in a diversified economy centering in grain production, livestock-raising, and household manufactures.

The region between the Hudson and the Potomac possessed natural advantages of soil and climate that quickly made it an outstanding area for the production of foodstuffs. Wheat became the most valuable staple crop, but rye, corn, oats, and barley were also raised in abundance. By the end of the century, the middle colonies were clearly the "bread colonies" of English America. Flour and other foodstuffs made from wheat were processed for foreign sale. At this time the manufacture of flour and bread was the chief industry of New York City and a source of wealth to local merchants. Philadelphia, too, began to develop rapidly as an exchange center for the flour and meat products produced in the Delaware River region—western Jersey, eastern Pennsylvania, and northern Maryland.

In the South, where tobacco had very early become a great staple crop, farming was much more of a capitalistic enterprise. The planter raised his specialized crop for export and the possibilities for quick profits were high because smoking became a craze in Europe in this century. In 1615, England exported £ 200,000 in specie to buy foreign tobacco, primarily from Spain; thereafter, Virginia and other southern colonies in English America were able to supply the English market and to furnish a surplus that could be used in England's foreign trade. By 1627 Virginia's exports amounted to 500,000 pounds, and the colony began to prosper. It was said that a Virginia planter could make five or six times more from tobacco than from any other crop. In the 1630's Maryland became a producer of tobacco, and the northern section of Carolina followed in the 1660's. By the turn of the century, 35,000,000 pounds of tobacco a year were being exported to England.

The prospects of easy wealth in tobacco production stimulated the acquisitive appetites of ambitious men. Some, possessed of larger capital or greater business acumen, were able to create very large tobacco plantations. By 1700 there were 50 planters in Virginia whose wealth amounted to several hundred thousand dollars as calculated by the values of our own time. Robert Beverly owned at least 37,000 acres of land and William Byrd over 15,000 acres, although the average large holding in

Virginia was about 5,000 acres. Although tobacco was king in the three large southern colonies, a considerable number of planters in the Charleston region of South Carolina developed profitable rice and indigo plantations.

Yet we must not assume that the large plantation was the typical farming unit in the southern colonies. The overwhelming portion of the population in Virginia, Maryland, and the Carolinas was composed of yeoman farmers whose holdings varied from 50 to 600 acres. Many of them raised tobacco in the hope of increasing their private wealth as the leading planters had done, but large numbers of them also raised foodstuffs in a pattern of diversified farming which was characteristic of the yeoman farmer everywhere in seventeenth century America. They raised Indian corn, wheat, beans, peas, hogs, poultry, and fruits; and the woods provided venison, partridge, turkeys, and other game.

In contrast to the other colonies, farming in New England was not likely to be an avenue to wealth. Little of the land in the New England colonies was especially fertile and early frosts frequently plagued the farmers. Much of the land was hilly and mountainous and in many areas it was strewn with boulders. Yet the village life of New England supported a sufficient degree of crude comfort. The home lots contained the house, barn, garden, and orchard; the arable fields outside the village center were used for growing grain; the cattle were taken to graze in the meadows or hillside pasture; and the woodlands furnished wood for fuel and materials for household furnishing and utensils.

If the village provided the basic context for most people's lives, some enterprising men of wealth found opportunities in urban commercial activities. These rising merchants oriented their lives to the urbane world of Atlantic trade, and this compromised their attachment to the village and its ways. Puritan leaders recognized the threat, but they knew that commerce was necessary for the colony's survival. New England thus had to live with a tension between those holding to the traditional village ethic and those subscribing to an emerging urban commercial ethic.

Commerce as a Way to Wealth

The fishing trade became the keystone of New England's commercial development. The waters off New England abounded in a variety of fish—haddock, halibut, mackerel, and the chief profit-maker, the cod-fish, which was larger and more numerous than those in the waters off Newfoundland. Furthermore, the New England fishermen operated throughout the year and New England fish sold at higher prices in Europe because "tis taken all winter and in cold weather it is better cured."

Even more important was the expansion of the fishing trade into broader forms of mercantile activity. New England merchants began to establish close trading contacts with London merchants who were buying shiploads of fish to sell in the markets of southern Europe, in the Wine Islands, and in the West Indies. These arrangements introduced New England merchants to the larger world of English trade and it was not long before they began to trade directly with Spain, the Canary Islands, and the West Indies without relying on the London merchants. By 1660 the New England merchants had become an active and dynamic group in the complex network of the English commercial system. They had thoroughly established themselves in the great criss-crossing patterns of triangular trade with New England, the British or Spanish ports, and the West Indies forming the main points of the triangular circuits.

These developments in fishery and commerce stimulated a remarkable growth of the shipbuilding industry in New England. The shipbuilders of Massachusetts were particularly resourceful and as early as 1633 they were building their own fishing shallops; in 1641 a 50-ton vessel built in the Bay Colony put out to sea, and in 1650 a 300-ton ship was constructed. Because of the abundance of timber in New England, shipbuilding costs were 20 to 50 per cent lower than in England. Colonial shipbuilders soon began to supply English merchants as well as those of New England with vessels. By 1670 Massachusetts shipbuilders had turned out more than 700 vessels, and between 1696 and 1713 over 1000 vessels were constructed averaging about 62 tons.

During the seventeenth century more than one-half of the vessels constructed in New England were made in Boston; Salem and Scituate were also important shipbuilding centers. Other seaport towns in Maine, Rhode Island, and Connecticut also engaged in shipbuilding to a lesser extent. Much of the capital for shipbuilding was contributed by English merchants who placed large orders for vessels in advance of construction. And the net effect was to stimulate the growth of colonial merchants and colonial shipwrights who had taken this lucrative road to the accumulation of private wealth.

New England led all other areas of English America in developing a merchant class and far-flung commercial operations, but other northern colonies displayed an increasing initiative in this type of economic activity. New York and Philadelphia also contained a growing number of merchants who traded in their own vessels. During this century, however, Boston ranked first in the importance of her commerce, New York was second, and Philadelphia third. Indeed, before 1700 New York and Philadelphia were commercial satellites of Boston, and Philadelphia, to a certain extent, was a satellite of New York. In the southern colonies, most capital and labor were attracted by the profits of tobacco production and the planters of Virginia, Maryland, and the Carolinas relied on London merchants or the merchants of New England to handle their exports of tobacco, naval stores, rice, and indigo.

The expanding commerce stimulated a host of manufacturing activities in the hinterlands of such great exchange centers as Boston, New York, and Philadelphia. In New England, saw mills sprang up everywhere to produce masts and ship timbers, building lumber, and barrel staves. In the middle colonies especially, flour milling overshadowed all other types of manufacture. Most seventeenth-century grist mills were small, local establishments grinding 10 to 20 barrels of flour a week, but by the end of the century the flour milling industry began to develop clear tendencies toward concentration of capital and equipment in the hands of merchant capitalists in larger centers of trade like New York and Philadelphia.

Everywhere there was unmistakable evidence of a dynamic colonial capitalism. The rapid growth of tobacco production, the remarkable expansion of New England's commerce and shipbuilding, the mushroom growth of flour milling and saw mills throughout the northern colonies, all testified to the avid pursuit of private gain by colonial Americans in the seventeenth century. There were plenty of hardships and many setbacks caused by bad harvests, shipwrecks, the menace of Indian warfare, and the disruption of commerce by England's civil and foreign wars; but the long-run possibilities continued to favor the opportunities for economic growth. The American appetite for material gain was being whetted, and no one in the English government could afford to ignore the potency of these expectations in the minds and hearts of colonial Americans.

Distinctions of Class and Status

Although the rapid development of economic opportunities in English America created greater possibilities for social mobility than were present in the structure of English society, it would be naive to assume that American society was born free of the encumbrances of a class system. By the end of the century distinctions of rank and status were plainly evident in every one of the colonies. To be sure, the conditions of the American social environment guaranteed a considerable degree of "openness" in the American class system, but the reality of social distinctions was an essential component of the major institutions of this society. Politics, trade, religion, and education were all enmeshed in the constraining net of class relations.

The openness of the class system in English America cannot be explained simply as a response to the conditions of the American environment. The Englishmen who migrated to America in the seventeenth (or eighteenth) century came from a society that was becoming increasingly fluid. There was a graded hierarchy of status in the English social structure but without the mutually hostile layers of a class system that was to be depicted later in the writings of the classical economists and Karl Marx. Indeed, William Blackstone, the great English legalist of the eighteenth century, noted some 40 different status levels, each blending into a continuum of social distinctions usually spoken of as "ranks," "degrees," and "orders."

At the top of the social order were the peers of the realm, the greater nobility of England. This was an expanding class largely because new peerages were created in every reign, and King James I created an

The English Social Order

unusually large number of them in the opening decades of the seventeenth century. Hence many of the greater nobility were new men of wealth and power, rather than noblemen who belonged to ancient families located on ancestral feudal estates.

Also included in the aristocratic order was the gentry, consisting of knights of the shire and squires who had the right to bear a coat of arms. These lesser gentry drew most of their income from the rents of their tenants, although many of them farmed their own lands using a bailiff as a manager or overseer. A considerable number of these country gentlemen favored a style of life that included much leisure and merriment. A typical day's recording in the diary of one of these was simple and to the point: "ate, drank wine, and was merry, and to the field again." This class was heavily reinforced in the seventeenth century by an influx from the professional and mercantile classes. Lawyers, government officials, and successful merchants bought landed estates not only to increase their income but also to better their social standing. This new group of squires, however, seemed to be less disposed to favor fox-hunting and dancing. They brought with them a sterner code of self-discipline formed by the habits of trade and professional service; many, indeed, were Puritans. This broadening squirearchy of England testified to the growth, in numbers and in influence, of the English middle class.

Next in the English social order came the yeoman farmers; these were usually freehold farmers, although some might be more successful leaseholders. Modern historians are uncertain about the size and composition of the English yeomanry; but Gregory King's famous estimate of income distribution, made in 1696, indicates that they made up about two-thirds of the "middle ranks" in English society. In addition, the English yeoman farmer is usually pictured as a man who worked hard on the land, manned the militia, and took an active part in local affairs.

Forming the broad base of the English social pyramid was the largest class of them all—"the lower orders"—who formed perhaps as much as three-quarters of the population. This class included cottagers and agricultural laborers in the country, apprentices and unskilled laborers in the towns and cities. Many of the wage-earning classes lived a poor and miserable life; many were unemployed vagabonds and beggars who could be seen everywhere on the roads of England. Upward mobility from the ranks of the common people was rarer but not impossible. The usual routes to a better life were by means of apprenticeship in a craft or mercantile enterprise, or occasionally through military service or, for a bright boy, through the church.

Although upward social advance was possible at the several levels of the English social order, America offered greater and more rapid prospects of economic and social betterment, especially to the lower classes. Yet, if we assume that the seventeenth-century Englishmen who came to America were seeking greater economic opportunities, it is also reasonable to assume that they should wish to translate their economic

success into the honorific distinctions that had symbolized success in English life. Private wealth can command considerable respect and power, but rarely in the modern history of the Western world has wealth alone been sufficient to establish an acceptable basis of social esteem. Other ingredients are necessary to secure the ready recognition of superior rank—a tasteful style of living, a family tradition, a grand manner, and a cultivation of knowledge and culture.

The evidence for such social motives in the evolution of a social order in Virginia, for example, is unmistakable. Though many modern historians perceived in Virginia some seeds of American democratic institutions, Virginia also produced an elite of wealthy planters who created a style of life modelled after that of the English gentry and who wielded an oligarchical power over the colony as great as that of the peers in the realm of England.

The nineteenth-century descendants of this early Virginia elite found it useful to develop the romantic notion that the Virginia gentry came from a select group of rich and dashing Cavaliers who had lived in feudal splendor in England and had transferred their furniture and finery to the New World. But modern studies of Virginia social structure indicate that some of the most enterprising and prominent of the Virginia families of the seventeenth century were descended from merchants and tradesmen, and it does not take a great effort of historical imagination to assume that the familiar English linkage of economic success with yearnings for the social status of the gentry was being transferred to the New World.

Although the great Virginia planter capitalists were diligent and

From George Bickham's Universal Penman. *London, 1733. Rare Book Division. The New York Public Library. Astor, Lenox and Tilden Foundations.*

Social Structure in Virginia and Southern Colonies

industrious in the management of their estates, they sought to give grace and dignity to their lives by imitating the living style of the older English gentry. The Virginia gentlemen were lavish in their hospitality and great lovers of sports and other pastimes such as hunting, fishing, horse racing, cock fighting, and card playing. They maintained a family pride by collections of portraits and the display of coats of arms. The best libraries in Virginia were the private collections of Virginia planters. In this and other ways, the first gentlemen of Virginia cultivated the outward manifestations of gentility and taught their children the social graces.

The Virginia gentry was only a small minority of the population. Below them in rank were the yeoman farmers who were the largest class in the colony. The tax records of Virginia indicate that approximately three-fifths of the population was composed of yeoman farmers and their families. Such sources of information also reveal that Virginia was divided into hundreds of small farms varying in size from 50 to 600 acres, with here and there a plantation of from six hundred to five thousand acres, some of them representing portions of the scattered holdings of the wealthiest planters. Probably two-thirds of the yeoman farmers owned no servants or slaves; the rest owned only a few.

The Virginia yeomanry was undoubtedly a more prosperous group than their counterparts in England. Land was abundant and cheap in the New World and an enterprising farmer could create a comfortable life for himself and his family. The more successful yeoman farmer might even hold office in the county government or serve in the House of Burgesses. Furthermore, most of the yeoman farmers had already achieved social advancement; probably the larger portion of them had come to Virginia as indentured servants and had risen to the status of freehold farmers.

Indentured servitude provided the most effective means of developing a labor supply in Virginia and other colonies during much of the seventeenth century. During this time, Virginia alone imported approximately 1500 servants a year. Indentured servants were workers who served under a labor contract in return for their transportation to America. Sometimes the planters or their agents paid for the immigrant's passage to America and he, in return, bound himself to make good the sum by working for the planter. Some immigrants made bargains with ship captains or merchants for their passage to the colonies with the understanding that if the servant could not find a planter who would pay his transportation costs, the ship captain could auction him off to the highest bidder when the vessel arrived in port. After a stated term of service, the indentured servant became a freedman, privileged to go where he pleased and to hold land as a freeholder. The common term of service in Virginia and the neighboring colonies of Maryland and Carolina was four years. In 1625 indentured servants composed 40 per cent of Virginia's population; by the end of the century they amounted to about 16 per cent of the whole.

The life of an indentured servant was not an easy one. He had to work hard for his master; he could be punished by whipping or by extension of the period of indenture. He could not marry without his master's consent, nor could he leave his master's premises without permission. He could not stay out late at night, or buy liquor, or frequent taverns. On the other hand, the legal codes of most colonies were much like that of Maryland where penalties were imposed on any master who failed to supply sufficient "meat, drink, lodging, and clothing." Moreover, the fact that the term of service was relatively short was of great significance for the class system of Virginia and other colonies. The freed servants furnished a steady supply of recruits for the growing class of yeoman farmers.

Yet the system of indentured servitude had important limitations for the wealthy planters. The term of service was relatively short and it was obvious to everyone before the end of the seventeenth century that the industrious servant, when he achieved his freedom, was likely to use the "headright" system to obtain his own land rather than become a tenant farmer working the land of his former master. Furthermore, as tobacco production expanded, tobacco prices declined and competition among tobacco producers increased in intensity. This fierce competition for profit favored larger units of production because the wealthy planter was able to get better advantages in credit and transportation. In the economic pressures of this situation, the large planters were more anxious than ever to find a steady supply of forced labor. Thus, the gentry of Virginia and of the other southern colonies moved readily and irrevocably toward a system of slave labor.

For much of the seventeenth century, the blacks in Virginia and Maryland were probably kept in a status of servitude similar to white indentured servitude. Some of these earlier black "servants" gained their freedom after serving a term of years, or after conversion to Christianity. Gradually, however, by custom and then by law, distinctions between black "servants" and white servants began to evolve. It was easy enough for the planters to justify the creation of a separate status for blacks; they

Plan for English Slave Ship. New York Public Library, Rare Book Division, Astor, Lenox and Tilden Foundations.

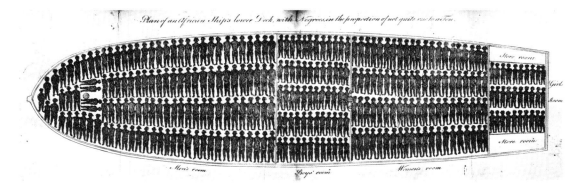

were brought into the country without the protection of written indenture contracts and well-established English racial attitudes provided additional excuses for placing them in a more permanent servitude. Thus, in the 1660's, Virginia and Maryland began to make important legal distinctions between white and black servants. A Maryland law of 1663, for example, stated that "all negroes or other slaves within the province, and all negroes and other slaves to be hereafter imported into the province shall serve *durante vita* (for life); and all children born of any negro or other slave, shall be slaves as their fathers were for the term of their lives." Further distinctions were developed in the later statutes of Virginia and Maryland which provided that black children were to inherit the condition of the mother in the case of marriage between freed blacks and slave women; and that Christian baptism should not change a black's status. The full details of a genuine slave code in Virginia and other colonies were developed in a later period, but it is clear that custom

The tobacco manufactory in different branches. Arents Collection. The New York Public Library. Astor, Lenox and Tilden Foundations.

and law had laid the foundations of human slavery in seventeenth-century America.

In many ways, then, Virginia set the pattern for the class structure of the southern colonies. Despite differences in local circumstances, the social hierarchy that developed in Maryland and the Carolinas was, in basic outline, like that of Virginia. And the Virginia pattern represented the most successful effort to transplant the English class system to America. The Virginia gentry imitated the style of life of the English gentry and opened its ranks just as readily to the sons of successful tradesmen or enterprising men of lower social origin who had achieved wealth and economic power. The southern yeomanry resembled the same class in England, but it was a rapidly expanding class with a brighter future than that of the English yeoman. Likewise, the indentured servant had better prospects for a good life than his counterparts in England who lived close to the brink of unemployment and vagabondage. Only in the development of black slavery did the southern colonials make a radical departure from the evolution of English law and custom.

If the southern colonies came close to reproducing the social hierarchy of England—with the obvious and spectacular difference created by slavery—the social structure of New England produced an unusually broad rural middle class. The agricultural economy of New England was not favorable to the establishment of large landed estates or the creation of a landed gentry. But such an aristocratic social order was not the intention of the Puritans. By the end of the seventeenth century, however, commercial development had produced a class of urban merchants whose wealth and style of life clearly distinguished them in this predominately middle-class society.

Class and Status in Puritan New England

There was an important sense in which Puritanism undercut conventional pretensions to status. There is, therefore, a certain fit between Puritanism and middle-class society. In the Puritan scale of values, the regenerate man deserved more social approval than the unregenerate man—whatever the income or style of life of either might be. A regenerate man, after all, was a man who had received some sign of God's grace, some sign that he might be one of the few predestined to salvation. In the Puritan vision of life, there was no higher status than to be one of God's elect.

It must be acknowledged, of course, that the Puritan system of thought challenged the worldly values of any and every class in the English social hierarchy. Any man, whether he was a gentleman of high rank or a lowly cottager, was a captive of sinfulness destined for damnation if he did not experience a spritual rebirth. Yet, we must also recognize that the Puritan emphasis on regeneracy was particularly subversive of the values of the old English gentry. In theory, at least, any cottager or any apprentice who had experienced the redemptive power of God's grace deserved more social approval than the wealthy gentleman who persisted in the enjoyment of his worldly wickedness.

On the other hand, the Puritan ethic contained a marked predisposition toward achievement. The regenerate man was expected to be a "Doer." The doctrine of the Christian calling emphasized the importance of diligent and industrious application to one's occupation. Moreover, since the Puritan believed in the reality of providential intervention in all human events, the achievement of wealth by a regenerate man could be taken as a sign of God's favor. Thus Puritan social theory contained ample means for justifying distinctions of status in a Puritan commonwealth; but the status system was more likely to favor middle-class values than aristocratic values.

In the very beginning, the socially visible criteria of status in seventeenth-century New England were strongly Puritan. The dominant class of Massachusetts, for example, was composed largely of Puritan ministers and magistrates. Also, many of the magistrates came from the newer English gentry, representing the mercantile and professional families which had acquired country estates and gentility. John Winthrop, first governor of the colony, was the grandson of a master draper who had purchased a manor in East Anglia and the son of a successful lawyer who had practiced in London for a time. Thomas Dudley, first deputy-governor, had been the steward or business manager for the Earl of Lincoln. Richard Saltonstall, Jr., a leading member of the Council of Assistants, was in the direct line of inheritance of a Lord Mayor of London who had also been Master of the Worshipful Company of Skinners (a guild of hide and leather manufacturers). Such men were used to social distinctions based on wealth and education and quickly became the natural leaders of the Puritan society of Massachusetts. The ministers of Massachusetts enjoyed a higher status than they had at home; their relative social position was akin to that of bishops and archbishops in England.

Since the ways to wealth in New England were more favorable in mercantile pursuits, the upper class in the New England colonies was expanded steadily by the addition of a growing number of newly rich merchants. By 1670, there were 30 merchants in Massachusetts with estates valued at £10,000 to £30,000. Smaller but no less prosperous groups of merchants were laying the foundations of commercial greatness in Newport, Rhode Island, and in the lesser ports of New England like Salem and New Haven. By the end of the century, the New England merchants were clearly overshadowing all other social types—even the Puritan clergy—in social influence. Indeed, many of the sons and daughters of the Puritan clergy were joined by ties of marriage and kinship to the rising merchant class.

Below this elite group in the social hierarchy of New England were the skilled artisans of the towns and the freeholders of the villages. Sturdy, intelligent, and hardworking, they were the largest social group and were the backbone of New England life in the affairs of church and town meeting. The lower levels of society were composed of wage workers, unskilled laborers, and indentured servants. Indentured servitude in New England, as elsewhere in America, was usually a temporary condition on the way toward the independent status of a freeholder or craftsman. There were a few slaves, Indian and black, but they served largely as household servants and were a symbol of upper-class status rather than an essential element of New England's labor force.

Class differences in New England were kept socially visible in a variety of ways. The forms of address, in particular, helped to define the boundaries of status. Wealthy merchants and landowners were addressed as "esquire" or "gentleman." "Master" was used for clergymen and "mister" for landowners and merchants of substance. "Goodman" was used for ordinary yeoman farmers and artisans. The lower orders were addressed simply by their family or given names. Furthermore, many towns assigned church pews according to social status, and the names of students in the student register at Harvard were listed not in alphabetical order, but according to their "dignities."

The middle colonies of English America stood somewhere between New England and the southern colonies in social structure just as they did in geography. In New York a landed gentry somewhat similar to the planter gentry took form in the seventeenth century. Englishmen, who brought with them considerable wealth, created vast landed estates in the Hudson River Valley side by side with the patroonships of the older Dutch families. These great Dutch and English families composed the aristocracy of New York—the Van Rensselaers, Schuylers, Morrises, Livingstons, Van Cortlandts, and Phillipses. Their vast estates were farmed by tenants in feudal style. Rensselaerswyck, near Albany, included 700,000 acres, while other family domains ran from 140,000 to 240,000 acres.

Class and Status in the Middle Colonies

In Pennsylvania, the Penn family retained large holdings of land as an important part of their proprietary rights, but the rise of a Quaker elite was primarily the consequence of the commercial growth of Philadelphia. William Penn had once fondly imagined that the "great men" of his colony would be country gentlemen who would live on their broad acres and visit Philadelphia only to transact necessary business. On the other hand, Penn himself inhibited the growth of a class of great landowners by limiting the amount of land that a purchaser could obtain to one thousand acres. Hence, the men who rose to dominate the social and political life of Pennsylvania were the Quaker merchants of Philadelphia. Mercantile pursuits were an important avenue to wealth because the possibilities for profit were very high in Philadelphia. One observer noted in 1686 that "merchants find themselves encouraged by the profit which is seldom less than 50 percent, the which is a great advance." By the end of the century, such Quaker merchants as Samuel Carpenter, Edward Shippen, Isaac Norris, and Robert Turner had already gained considerable wealth and prominence.

As with the Puritans, Quaker religious and social theory was antipa-

Depiction of William Penn
Signing Treaty with
Delaware Indians. *Courtesy
of the Pennsylvania
Academy of the Fine Arts,
Joseph & Sarah Harrison
Collection.*

thetic to aristocratic values. The Quaker refused to uncover his head in
the presence of magistrates or even the king. The Quaker said *thou* to all
men regardless of rank or title. "The World's Respect is an empty
ceremony, no Soul or Substance to it," William Penn once wrote. Yet a
closer reading of Quaker social thought indicates that the Quakers did
not really wish to destroy social distinctions; they proposed instead to
develop new ways of showing love and respect within the existing social
order. Robert Barclay, a leading Quaker thinker, whose *Apology For True
Christianity Divinity* was read in many Quaker homes in Pennsylvania
stated in that book, "I would not have any judge that . . . we intend to
destroy the mutual relation that either is between *Prince* and *People,
Master* and *Servants, Parents* and *Children;* nay not at all: We shall
evidence, that our Principle . . . hath no such tendency, and that these
Natural Relations are rather better established, than any ways hurt by
it. . . ."

Thus, it can hardly be said that the American forest or the abundant
economic opportunities of America prevented the development of distinctions of class and status. A class structure emerged with remarkable

rapidity at this time. Yet there were important forces at work which foreshadowed the continued growth of an open class system. The competitive economic growth of the colonies encouraged the widespread adoption of fee simple land tenure, and the resulting expansion of the class of freeholding farmers in America encouraged attitudes of independence and moral equality. The appearance of a vigorous mercantile capitalism in the northern colonies strengthened the development of a social structure that was conditioned by a middle class rather than an aristocratic ethic. Both the capitalistic ethic and the Protestant ethic emphasized the efficacy of individual effort: that any man, by God's grace and his own industry, was capable of spiritual regeneration and social betterment. The revolutionary dynamism of seventeenth-century England was an essential part of the social energy that was overspreading the virgin land of English America.

chapter three

The Political Culture of
Seventeenth-Century America

The Instruments of Authority

Historians of the English constitutional system never fail to remind us that the English constitution cannot be found in any single document or group of documents. Only if we recognize that the English constitution consists of a great body of law and custom with a continuously evolving series of precedents and established procedures can we begin to understand the process by which the instruments of political authority were shaped and reshaped in English America. Any analysis of the political institutions that were created in seventeenth-century America is all the more intricate because, in every period of history, the English people have always had a way of giving new meanings to old forms and precedents. Consequently, the keys to an understanding of the forms of government that were originally established in America must be sought for in the new relationships of form and meaning as they existed in the English political system when the American colonies were founded.

At the opening of the seventeenth century, the king was the focus of loyalty and power in the English constitutional system. He was an exalted figure to whom all classes of men, high or low, gave devotion and service. His court was made up of lords and ladies-in-waiting and he could, at his pleasure, create new peers of the realm from among his favorites and his friends. He also controlled a valuable royal patronage in the many posts of dignity and influence that he could bestow in his royal administration. The king was also the fountain of justice through his power to name judges of the royal courts. In addition, he was the supreme governor of the established Church of England; archbishops, bishops, and lesser church officials owed their appointments and their considerable incomes to him.

The English Kingship

The early Stuart kings, James I and Charles I, were particularly jealous of their primacy and their royal prerogatives. They resented all attempts by Parliament to interfere in such matters of royal prerogative as the conduct of foreign affairs, the granting of monopoly patents, or the supervision of the liturgy and polity of the English church. It was King James, after all, who turned out a book entitled *The Trew Law of Free Monarchies* in which he upheld the doctrine of the "divine right" of kings.

To assist in the administration of the affairs of the realm, there was a Privy Council composed of nobles and members of the gentry who were chosen to be associated with the king in the exercise of his powers. Under James I and Charles I, the Privy Council was made up of over 40 members, although many members did not attend regularly and most of the work was done by about 15 or 20 men. For the more efficient conduct of business, the Privy Council found it necessary to appoint committees to deal with special areas of royal administration. These committees kept a close watch on such matters as foreign affairs, trading companies, colonizing ventures, and the development of the economic strength of the nation through such industries as the cloth or mining industries. The Privy Council also kept a close watch on Parliament for the king. Many Privy Councillors were members of the House of Commons and it was their duty to promote such legislation as the king desired, especially the voting of taxes and financial subsidies for the support of the royal administration.

The English Parliament

The English Parliament of this century represented the propertied classes exclusively. The House of Lords was composed of the biggest landowners of the realm together with the bishops of the Church of England. Under James I and his son, Charles I, the numbers in the peerage were greatly increased by the sale of titles; and this added many new men of wealth to the House of Lords. Even the House of Commons represented the propertied classes of the country for their members from the counties of England were elected on the basis of an electoral franchise that was restricted to men holding freeholds with at least 40 shillings a year in income. This excluded smaller freeholders, leaseholders, cottagers, and agricultural laborers—all together composing about 80 per cent of the rural population. In the larger towns and cities, the franchise was more varied. In some towns it was vested in the corporation (or town council), in others in all the rate payers, in still others in all the freemen. But in most towns, the minority of propertied men had the decisive voice in choosing members of the House of Commons.

Consequently, it may be said that, if the upper house of the English Parliament represented the lords and bishops, then the lower house spoke for the prosperous gentry and merchants. "We be the gentry" said a member of the House of Commons in 1610 and no one would have questioned the truth of his observation. Three decades later, Sir Thomas Ashton, the author of a "Remonstrance against Presbytery," asserted the same principle when he wrote, "the Primates, the Nobiles, with the *minores nobiles,* the gentry, consult and dispose the rules of government; the plebeians submit to and obey them."

Imperial control through merchant power. Copyright British Museum.

The House of Commons, in particular, was watchful of its privileges and liberties gained over a long period of time; their most cherished privileges were immunity to arrest and the right to uncensored discussion within the House. "Our privileges and liberties," the House declared to James I in 1604, "are our true right and due inheritance, no less than our lands and goods." In this statement of the House of Commons to the king, it is possible to see how closely the conceptions of liberty and property were intertwined in the minds of seventeenth-century Englishmen. Liberty was a right like that of the ownership of lands or goods. "He that hath no property in his goods," said a member of Parliament in 1624, "is not free."

The Liberties of the Commons

In consequence, the members of the House of Commons who defended their liberties against encroachments by the king were proud men of property and of sufficient learning to think of ways to challenge the doctrine of divine right which had been expounded in *The Trew Law of Free Monarchies*. When King Charles I dissolved Parliament in 1629 and imprisoned the leaders of his opposition in the House of Commons, Sir John Eliot used the remaining days of his life in the Tower of London to compose a treatise, *De Jure Majestatis* (On the Rights of Sovereignty). In this treatise, Eliot asked the question, Who is sovereign in England? His answer was, The king in Parliament. To be sure, Sir John was unable to express in theoretical form any clear idea of what should happen if king and Parliament should disagree. No one could answer such a question clearly before the Civil War—and, indeed, the eventual answer came out of the events of the Civil War. But many Englishmen felt in their bones that, somehow, king, Lords and Commons were jointly sovereign or that the common law itself was sovereign. Sir Edward Coke, the Lord Chief Justice of England, expressed this theory very simply when he said, "Magna Carta is such a fellow that he will have no sovereign."

The political upheavals in England during the seventeenth century made the organic relationships of form and meaning in the English constitution more uncertain than ever. Nevertheless, the filaments of continuity and change are visible enough in the transplanting of English law and government in America. They can be traced in the charters issued to corporations and proprietors by the king and they can be followed in the later relations of the colonial governments to the king and Privy Council. It may seem odd to modern Americans but it is true, nevertheless, that the king and not Parliament, or even the king in Parliament, was the fountainhead of authority for the governments of English America.

The original charter granted by the king to the Virginia Company provided that a resident council, consisting of 13 members and with a president elected by themselves, should serve as the sole governing board of the colony. This council residing in Virginia was to be under the general supervision of a royal council in England whose members were

The Virginia Charters

appointed by the king, whereas those of the resident council were appointed by the merchants and gentlemen associated with the Virginia Company. In actual practice, however, the Virginia Company in London and its resident council exercised control over the affairs of the Virginia settlement without much interference from the royal council.

By successive revisions of the charter in 1609 and 1612, the supervisory royal council was eliminated and full governing powers were granted to the Virginia Company. The governors who were sent to Virginia after 1610 were authorized to exercise virtually dictatorial powers with the advice and assistance of an appointed council. It was hoped that these stern measures would bring to an end the violence and factious quarrels that had caused so many troubles for the infant colony.

The harsh uses of authority by governors sent out between 1611 and 1618 effectively restrained the lawless elements among the Virginia settlers, but they did not increase the prosperity of the settlement or make the people more contented. To become profitable, the Virginia colony needed a growing, industrious, and satisfied population. Hence the promoters of the Virginia Company found it necessary to liberalize their land policy and to encourage private ownership as a means of luring more settlers. In addition, a charter of liberties was drawn up for the colonists as a means of increasing the attractiveness of settlement in the New World.

The Virginia Assembly   A leader in the experiment of creating greater liberty for the freemen of Virginia was Sir Edwin Sandys, a liberal-minded and far-sighted member of the Company. He realized that success for the Virginia venture was possible only if the colony were enriched materially and morally by better colonists, and by the introduction of such civilizing institutions as churches, schools, and hospitals. He believed that such institutions might develop more rapidly if a popular government existed in Virginia. The influence of Sandys and other progressive leaders was great enough to cause a new governor to be sent to Virginia in 1619 with a commission to provide for the holding of yearly meetings of a general assembly "freely to be elected by the inhabitants thereof; this assembly to have power to make and ordaine whatsoever lawes and orders should by them be thought good and profitable. . . ." By this grant of liberty, the governing power in Virginia was to be shared by the governor and his Council with a House of Burgesses composed of two burgesses chosen by each town or hundred.

The plans of men like Sandys to resuscitate the economic prospects of the Virginia Company proved to be too ambitious. Further financial difficulties and the Indian massacre of 1622 brought the Company to ruin and bankruptcy. An order from the court of King's Bench dissolved the Company in 1624, and King James declared that "the government of the colonies of Virginia shall immediately depend on Our Selfe." Thereafter, the governor and Council of Virginia were appointed by the king and held office during his pleasure.

Yet, even though Virginia had become a royal colony under the direct supervision of the king and Privy Council, the form of popular government introduced in 1619 continued to demonstrate a capacity for growth and vitality. When the charter of the Virginia Company was dissolved, a petition was forwarded to England requesting the Privy Council not to entrust the royal governors with arbitrary power over them. "The governor," said the Assembly in its entreaty, "shall not lay any taxes or ympositions upon the colony, their lands or commodities other way than by the authority of the General Assembly, to be levyed and and ymployed as the said assembly shall appoint."

In view of the conflict between king and Parliament in England, the preservation of a popular assembly in Virginia is truly remarkable. King Charles, who disliked Parliaments even more than his father, was very chary of instructing his governor to Virginia to summon a meeting of the House of Burgesses. The first such meeting of the Burgesses in his reign, called in 1628, was severely restricted in the matters which could be debated. The future for the House of Burgesses looked even more uncertain when King Charles dissolved the English Parliament in 1629 and began the 11 years of personal government that would lead to the outbreak of civil war in England.

During those years, however, when there was no Parliament in England, the General Assembly of Virginia continued to meet. King Charles gave no sign that he approved of these assemblies or that he was willing to authorize his governor to call them. Even so, between 1629 and 1639, the House of Burgesses met every year except for one and continued to pass laws which had force in the colony. So far as can be determined, only a few of these laws were ever sent to England for confirmation, and not one of them was ever approved by the Privy Council.

By keeping the Assembly alive in this extra-legal fashion, the Virginians were helping to create a predisposition toward self-government in America. In the English political system, custom and precedent had great potency in shaping the instruments and conceptions of government. It should not require much historical imagination to assume that similar political habits would continue to operate in the New World. The Virginians were giving life and meaning to the precedents according to which the freemen, even in a royal colony, were assured of a right to choose representatives for the making of laws and the levying of taxes.

In Massachusetts, on the other hand, the pathway to representative government was more direct and more rapid than in Virginia. The Charter of 1629, granted by the king to the Massachusetts Bay Company, was unusual in several respects. In its form, the Massachusetts Bay Company resembled a typical trading company but, in tone and in detail, the Charter of 1629 revealed much larger aims than those of trade and profit. The promoters of the Company were more than men of capital; they were dedicated Puritans as well. The strength of their Puritan

The Massachusetts Bay Company Charter

convictions led them to insist upon the incorporation of religious purposes in the legal phrases of the charter. The Massachusetts Bay Company, according to one of these phrases in the charter, was being set up

for the directing ruling and disposeing of all matters and things whereby our said people, Inhabitants there, maie be soe religiously, peaceablie and civilly governed, in their good life and orderlie conversacion, . . . and the Christian fayth, which in . . . the Adventurers free profession is the principall ende of this Plantacion.

The organization of the Company also contained some unusual features. The charter established a group of 26 men as a corporation possessing the right as a corporate body to rule and administer an extensive territory in New England. The governing body of this corporation was to consist of a governor and 18 assistants; the names of the first assistants were inserted in the text of the charter but, thereafter, all officers were to be elected by the freemen—that is to say those who had been admitted as members of the Company. These members were to be called together in an assembly known as a General Court four times a year for such various purposes as the admission of new members, the election of officers, and the making of laws and ordinances for the welfare of the company and the colony. In the light of the religious purposes stated in the charter, this political structure foreshadowed the transformation of what was ostensibly a trading company into a Puritan commonwealth.

The Puritan Commonwealth

The first extraordinary step in the evolution of the Puritan commonwealth occurred four months after the granting of the charter. This was a decision to remove the corporate body of the Company to New England instead of maintaining its legal presence in England as was the case with all such companies chartered by the Crown. This daring action was a direct consequence of the consultations of Puritan leaders inside and outside of the Massachusetts Bay Company. In particular, the members of the Company persuaded John Winthrop, a leading Puritan in East Anglia, to play a major role in organizing a Puritan migration to New England. Winthrop, as well as other Puritans, was greatly disheartened with the state of affairs in England after the dissolution of Parliament by King Charles; all were also troubled by the anti-Puritan measures of Bishop Laud and other religious advisers close to the king. Consequently, at a secret meeting of a small group of the members of the Massachusetts Bay Company it was proposed that the corporation with all of its governing powers should be transferred to New England. Such an action would have the effect of removing the proposed Puritan colony from any effective interference by the king or by the bishops of the Church of England.

Despite the doubtful legality of such a transfer of the Company and its

charter to New England, the necessary reorganization of the Massachusetts Bay Company was accomplished speedily. Some of the earlier subscribers withdrew, and new members were added from among those Puritans anxious to create a New Zion in America; at the same time, an election of new officers took place which brought John Winthrop to the high post of governor. After months of strenuous effort and the expenditure of large sums of money, 17 ships containing about a thousand men, women, and children departed for Massachusetts in 1630. And this was only the beginning of a large and well-financed exodus; it is estimated that between 1630 and 1643 nearly two hundred ships left England for New England at a cost of £200,000 and carried not less than 20,000 people.

The transformation of the charter of the trading corporation into the constitution of a Puritan commonwealth occurred in several stages during the first years of settlement in Massachusetts. In the beginning Governor Winthrop and the assistants exercised more powers than a strict interpretation of the charter allowed because the necessitous conditions of the first stages of settlement seemed to require a *de facto* concentration of legislative, as well as executive and judicial, power in the hands of leaders whose authority could not easily be challenged. Thus, in the first four months after Winthrop arrived in Massachusetts, the governor and assistants met four times and exercised authority in a variety of ways: they provided for the housing and support of ministers and military captains; they regulated trade with the Indians; they set up the process by which towns should be named and their officials elected; they regulated wages and prices; they levied a tax; they arrested wrongdoers; and they conducted judicial business.

Although there seemed to be a general acquiescence in such a concentration of power during the first years of settlement, it must also be recognized that the Puritan magistrates were not abashed to wield such sweeping authority. Governor Winthrop, in particular, had a stiff-necked attitude about authority. He firmly believed that, in matters of government, the people at large were unfit to rule. "The best part of the community," he wrote, "is always the least and of that least part the wiser part is always the lesser."

For a time, the magistrates clearly overshadowed the freemen in meetings of the General Court. At a General Court held in May, 1631, the freemen exercised their right to elect the governor and deputy governor for the first time since the charter had been transferred to Massachusetts. But the magistrates continued to exercise the same broad powers; most legislative orders for the next two or three years still came from the governor and council of assistants. Their predominant influence was evident when the freemen of the General Court, held in May, 1631, adopted the momentous rule proposed by the magistrates that, henceforth, "noe man shalbe admitted to the freedom of this body politicke, but such as are members of some of the churches within the limits of the same." This action placed the government of Massachusetts upon the religious foundation that was intended by the Puritans who had first obtained the charter for the Massachusetts venture.

Gradually, however, the freemen of Massachusetts began to become restive under the plenitude of power which was being wielded over them by Governor Winthrop and the magistrates. In 1632, the pastor and elder of the church at Watertown, supported by a meeting of the inhabitants, protested against the imposition of a tax by the council of assistants for the purpose of constructing a palisade around the new town of Cambridge. The objectors declared that it was not safe to pay taxes which had not been assented to by the majority of the freemen "for fear of bringing themselves and their posterity into bondage." Winthrop conceded the basic principle of the protestors when he explained that the body which levied the tax was like a Parliament since it had been chosen by the freemen "who had the power likewise to remove the assistants and put in others . . . at any general court."

Nevertheless, it may have been because of this incident that, at the next General Court held in May, 1632, 16 persons, two from each of the eight towns, were appointed to advise the governor and assistants about a system of taxes and assessments. And in 1634, the freemen voted that only the General Court should have the right "to rayse money and taxes."

By this time, a revolt which had been brewing for a long time against the authoritarian leadership came to a head. The meeting of the General Court in 1634 was stormy and long and, in the end, the freemen won a notable victory. It was voted that only the General Court should have authority to raise money and taxes, dispose of land, and confirm titles. It was also voted to restore to the towns the right to assess every man according to his property and not according to the number of persons in his family as the council of assistants had done. Finally, it was voted to set up a representative system of government whereby the freemen of the towns were to elect two deputies from each town to sit in the General Court in order to "make and establish laws" and "deal in all other affairs of the commonwealth wherein the freemen have to do."

Eventually, after 1644, the General Court came to be two separate legislative houses. Until then the governor, deputy governor, assistants, and the deputies of the freemen sat together as one General Court to make laws and decide issues of administration and justice. The separation of the assistants and the deputies came over a seemingly trivial case—a lawsuit of Richard Sherman against Robert Keayne concerning the ownership of a white sow. The plaintiff was a poor man in whose name the suit was brought by his wife. Keayne, the defendant, was a wealthy merchant and moneylender who was known to charge usurious rates of interest. An inferior court at Boston had heard the case, and, on the basis of the evidence, awarded the sow to Robert Keayne. Popular sympathy was with Sherman, however, and the matter became much more than a dispute over the ownership of a pig after it was appealed to the General Court because a majority of the assistants favored Keayne's claim, whereas a majority of the deputies was for Sherman.

As a way out of the deadlock, the magistrates insisted on their privilege of acting by themselves and thus to veto the decision of the deputies. Although the case was settled in Keayne's favor by use of the established precedent of "the negative voice" of the magistrates, the political crisis continued. The deputies of the freemen were convinced that a negative voice for the magistrates alone did not contribute to the welfare of the commonwealth. Because they were able to win support of three liberal-minded assistants, the deputies won their point. In 1644, a motion prepared by the deputies was adopted ordering "that the (General) Court should be divided in their consultations, the magistrates sitting by themselves and the deputies by themselves, what one agreed on they should send to the other, and if both agreed then to pass, etc." This decision provided Massachusetts with a two house legislature; within the legislature, the magistrates and the deputies of the freemen were each to have a negative voice over the other.

The pattern of government which emerged in Massachusetts became the model for other colonies in New England. The "Fundamental Orders" of Connecticut adopted by the settlers of Hartford, Windsor, and Wethersfield in 1639 stipulated that once a year the freemen were to assemble in a court of election to choose a governor, a council of assistants, and four deputies from each town to meet together as a General Court for the making of laws, the admission of new freemen, the granting of lands, etc. The assistants initially had a negative voice as in Massachusetts; but, by the end of the seventeenth century, the assistants and the deputies sat as separate houses. In Rhode Island, the four towns of Providence, Newport, Portsmouth, and Shawomet united under a common government in 1647. The freeholders of each town, after 1650, elected deputies who met with an elected governor and council of assistants to form a general assembly. For a time, however, any of the four towns in Rhode Island had the right to refuse to accept for itself any of the enacted laws of the general assembly. Otherwise, the institutions of government functioned much like those of Massachusetts.

The evolution of these forms of representative government in New England, as in Virginia, were tremendously important for the creation of the instruments of authority at this time. The political experience resulting from the growth of such political institutions generated conceptions of "liberty" which included more than the legalistic "liberties and immunities" that were guaranteed in the charters—including trial by jury, benefit of clergy, and the rights of ownership and inheritance. The conception of liberty had been expanded to include the freedom to choose representatives to a general assembly whose assent was necessary for the making of laws and the levying of taxes. In the competitive

Representative Government in other New England Colonies

race to promote colonies in the seventeenth century, no other colonies could afford to ignore the expectations aroused by the examples of Virginia or Massachusetts.

*Government in
the Proprietary Colonies*

This was particularly important because the proprietary charter became a favorite device of the Crown for the further development of colonies in America, particularly after the dissolution of the Virginia Company and the strange transubstantiation of the Massachusetts Bay Company. The proprietary grants, it should be remembered, threatened to create a wholly different political order in America. The Maryland charter, for example, was modeled on the medieval charter granted to the Bishop of Durham. making the lord proprietor of Maryland something like a king there according to the ancient formulation, "What the king has without, the bishop [of Durham] has within." Within the boundaries of Maryland, Lord Baltimore was to be a monarch with complete control over the administration, defense, and development of his province. All writs were to be issued in his name and not that of the king; the confirmation of all laws and all judicial appeals were in the control of the proprietor and his courts.

Since Lord Baltimore was never able to join his colony in America, the actual governorship of the colony was placed in the hands of his brother, Leonard Calvert. But Maryland's proprietor was not wholly unaware of the expectations of English colonists in America. As a consequence he commissioned his brother in 1637 to assemble the freemen of the province or their deputies to secure their advice and consent to the laws of the proprietor. Such an assembly was held in 1638, but it was clear that the representatives of the freemen were not to have the right to originate laws or to alter those which had been sent over by the proprietor. Governor Calvert also let it be known that he possessed the power to adjourn and prorogue the assembly and that he would be accountable to no man for such decisions. Furthermore, the assemblies were not to meet regularly, but only when summoned by the governor as was the case with king and Parliament in England.

Such high-handed policy proved to be impossible to maintain in the New World. Indeed, events in the Old World added strength to the claims of the Maryland Assembly when Parliament came into open rebellion against King Charles after 1641. Influenced, perhaps, by the example of Parliament, a Maryland Assembly, called in 1642, resolved that it could not be prorogued or adjourned without its consent. At about this time, also, a considerable number of Puritans were migrating to Maryland and bringing with them their customary religious and political zeal. In 1650 the proprietary governor made several important concessions to a meeting of the General Assembly. The delegates elected by the freemen won the right to sit as a separate house, and it was enacted that all laws passed by a majority vote in each house (the Council and the House of Delegates) and ordered by the governor should be as truly binding "as if they were advised and assented unto by all the freemen in the province personally."

In one way or another, the proprietors of another proprietary colonies were forced to assent to the establishment of similar forms of representative government before the end of the seventeenth century. In the Carolinas, the legislatures of North and South Carolina consisted of the governor at Charles Town, and a deputy governor in North Carolina, the members of a proprietary Council, and delegates elected by the freeholders. At first, the delegates could consider only the measures presented to them by the Council but, in 1693, the proprietors conceded to the delegates the right to prepare and enact bills of their own. Soon afterwards, the delegates were also granted the right to sit as a separate house. In Pennsylvania, William Penn tried for a time to maintain a "frame of government" which centered the greater legislative power in the hands of a governor's council. Between 1683 and 1696, however, Penn instituted successive "frames of government" which moved toward a system that placed full legislative power in the hands of an elected assembly, confined the governor's council to executive and judicial functions, and endowed the governor with a veto power.

Everywhere in America, the instruments of government were shaped by the conceptions of representative government that were derived from the evolution of the English Parliament. The free-born Englishmen of the seventeenth century were still wrestling with the perplexing problems of the competing claims of king and Parliament in their definitions of sovereignty, but the majority of them knew that the principle of representative government must be an essential element of the process of making laws. For the Englishman who came to America, this principle had a greater and more immediate urgency. The creation of viable settlements and the bringing into existence of the institutions of a civilized society was possible only with colonists who were possessed by a belief that they could shape their own destiny in the New World. Next to the right of possession in a freehold tenure, the right to be governed by representatives of their own choosing stimulated the energy and morale which guaranteed success for building a society in the wilderness of English America.

Conceptions of Authority

If the creative genius of the English people was expressed most notably in poetry and drama in the Elizabethan age, one can say that an equally remarkable creativity in political theory occurred in England in the seventeenth century. In that century of political turmoil and civil war, Englishmen could not escape the necessity of re-examining their political loyalties; they needed to understand the source of the sovereign authority which they chose to obey; and, since obedience to either king or Parliament became a dangerous choice that involved great personal risk, they needed to find satisfactory ways of defining the legitimate uses of power. The great out-pouring of polemic literature that accompanied the Puritan Revolt and the Civil War filtered and refined the basic assumptions of the Cavaliers and the Puritans. Out of this refining experience came the political speculations of Hobbes, Milton, Harrington, Filmer, and Locke.

English Political Theories

In particular, the *Leviathan* of Thomas Hobbes, published in 1651, and the *Two Treatises of Government* of John Locke, published in 1690, represent the highest points of seventeenth-century English political speculations and provide the modern student with classic statements of two contrasting political philosophies. Hobbes' view of human nature is the more pessimistic: men are brutal and selfish and constantly at each other's throats; therefore, it is necessary to concentrate the sovereign power. The only way for Englishmen to defend themselves from the injuries of one another is "to confer all their power and strength upon one man, or upon one assembly of men, that may reduce all their wills, by a plurality of voice until one will." Locke's view of human nature was more optimistic: men are born rational and most of them possess the natural and rational disposition to control their passions; consequently all that is needed for a stable society is a reasonable government based upon the consent of the governed.

These speculations were to have an important influence on American political thought at a later time. But they did not enter into the thinking of seventeenth-century Americans; very likely only a few Americans knew these works or read them at the time they were published. Furthermore, the larger number of colonists who had come with the great migration before the Civil War missed the fullness of the political dialogue which engaged the attention of Englishmen for the rest of the century.

Only in New England were political ideas expressed with an intensity that paralleled the experience of England. The Puritan commonwealth of Massachusetts, after all, was a precursor of the short-lived Puritan commonwealth in England. It seems reasonable to assume, therefore, that the magistrates and ministers of Massachusetts felt a similar need to explain and to justify the nature of the authority which they were exercising.

Puritan Theories of Governance

The Puritan conception of governance began with the doctrine of original sin. Since men were corrupted by the sin of Adam, it was necessary for mankind to have some sort of corporate power to enforce obedience and to inflict punishments on the crimes of men. The entire system of Puritan political thought, therefore, rested on the assumption that the commandments of God as revealed in the Scriptures were the primary source of legitimate authority. The ministers

Magnalia Chrifti Americana :

OR, THE

Ecclefiaftical Hiftory

OF

NEVV-ENGLAND,

FROM

Its Firft Planting in the Year 1620. unto the Year
of our LORD, 1698.

Title page from Cotton Mather's Magnalia Christi Americana. *Rare Book Division. The New York Public Library. Astor, Lenox and Tilden Foundations.*

and the magistrates were equally vice-regents of God and should work together to administer the justice of God among men.

There was also a strong predisposition toward an authoritarian form of government in the minds of the Puritan leaders of Massachusetts. John Cotton, who embodied the Puritan ideal in the ministry of the colony, stated the case for theocratic authority with these words in 1636:

Democracy, I do not conceive that ever God did ordeyne as a fitt government eyther for church or commonwealth. If the people be governors, who shall be governed? As for monarchy and aristocracy, they are both of them clearly approved and directed in scripture—and setteth up theocracy in both, as the best form of government in the commonwealth, as well as in the church.

Governor John Winthrop, who embodied the Puritan ideal in the magistracy, expounded a similar view when he wrote:

Where the chief Ordinary powr & administration thereof is in the people, there is a Democratie—the Deputies are the Democraticall p'te of o'r Governm't. Now if we would change from a mixt Aristocratie to a meere Democratie: first we should have no warr'nt in scripture for it—2: we should heerby voluntaryly abase o'rselves—for a Democratie is, among most Civill nations accounted the meanest & worst of all formes of governm't—

It would be wrong to assume, however, that the justifications of theocratic authority as expounded by men like Cotton and Winthrop represented claims to the exercise of unlimited power for the magistrates and ministers of Massachusetts. Winthrop recognized the claims of liberty in a "little speech" which he delivered to the General Court in 1645. Liberty, he insisted "is a liberty to [do] that only which is good, just, and honest—it is of the same kind of liberty wherewith Christ has made us free." Yet while he placed weighty moral constraints upon liberty, he also acknowledged the limit upon his authority by saying,

The covenant between you and us is the oath you have taken of us, which is to this purpose, that we shall govern you and judge your causes by the rules of God's laws and our own, according to our best skill. When you agree with a workman to build you a ship or a house, etc., he undertakes as well for his skill as for his faithfulness . . . and you pay him for both. But when you call one to be a magistrate, he doth not profess nor undertake to have sufficient skill for that office—therefore you must run the hazard of his skill and ability. But if he fail in faithfulness, which by his oath he is bound unto, that he must answer for.

Other leaders were less grudging than Winthrop in acknowledging the proper basis of authority in a Puritan commonwealth. Thomas Hooker, one of the founders of Connecticut, preached an election sermon in Hartford in 1638 in which he reasoned about the nature of authority. His argument emphasized that the privilege of election of public magistrates belonged to the people "by God's own allowance" and that those who have the power to elect officers and magistrates can also "set the bounds and limitations of the power—unto which they call them." In actual practice, however, the government of Connecticut did not differ much from that of Massachusetts.

Of course, the incessant intellectual activity of the Puritans in seventeenth-century New England never produced a single systematic work of political theory that could be compared to the efforts of such English philosophers as Hobbes or Locke. That would be too much to expect of men who had to give the greater part of their energies to constructing civilized communities in the American wilderness. Of necessity much of the Puritan thought in New England was articulated not in abstract works of theory but in preachings and disputations close to practical events and practical situations. Yet, when a modern student reads the considerable body of sermons, diaries, and histories, he can see that Puritan political thought had a tightly knit structure.

The only authority which the Puritan would recognize as legitimate was an authority which was based on a covenant between God and the people; more specifically, a true covenant was a compact between God and a regenerate community. Hence the liberties of suffrage and officeholding in Massachusetts were restricted to church members, that is to say, to those who had given acceptable testimony of a conversion experience. In this dictatorship of the regenerate, the magistrates were bound by their oaths to be faithful to the covenant; if they transgressed the limits of their authority in the administration of God's justice they were accountable not only to the people but to the wrath of a just God.

Aristocratic Theories of Governance

Elsewhere in America there were fewer disputations about the nature of authority. The dominant class in Virginia or in the proprietary colonies did not share the peculiar intellectual urges that shaped Puritan political thought. Those who imitated the style of life of the English gentry cultivated learning in their own gentlemanly ways. They enjoyed the works of classic authors and contemporary books on law, history, biography, or belles-lettres; but they had no taste for the doctrinal dialectics and the paradoxical reasoning which was so characteristic of the writing of New England Puritans. The gentry of the New World like the older gentry of England preferred to rely on old habits and loyalties as the surest foundation of their political ideas—"Fear God and serve the King" was a sufficient conception of the nature of authority.

Sir William Berkeley, who served as governor of Virginia almost continuously from 1641 to 1677, probably expressed the conservative prejudices shared by the gentry as well as any member of his social class. During the English Civil War, Berkeley urged all good Virginians to adhere to their loyalty to the king and the established order of things. "Consider yourselves," he said to the members of the General Assembly in 1651, "how happy you are, and have been, how the gates of wealth and honour are shut on no man—What is it can be hoped for in a change, which we have not already?—But Gentlemen, by the grace of God, we will not so tamely part with our King, and all these blessings we enjoy under him. . . ."

Somehow, America seemed to call forth some of the sterner conceptions of authority at the same historical moment that the English political system was being liberalized by revoltuionary change. The "Fundamental Constitutions" of Carolina reveal this tendency to an extraordinary degree. In 1669, Lord Ashley, a liberally-educated peer who had just been elevated to the post of Chancellor of the Exchequer in England, assumed a leading role among the proprietors of Carolina. One of his first steps was to prepare a plan of government for this great province in the New World and, to aid in this task, he persuaded his young friend John Locke to become secretary to the Lords Proprietors of Carolina. Thus the young man who was to become one of England's great political philosophers collaborated with Lord Ashley in framing "Fundamental Constitutions" which proposed to create a pyramided structure of social and political power for the colony of Carolina. At the top of the pyramid were eight seignories representing the eight proprietors' rights to land and rents; next in order came sizeable "baronies" granted to "landgraves" and "caciques," and then came "colonies" of land apportioned among freemen. The landgraves and caciques were to compose the hereditary nobility of Carolina with hereditary seats in the legislature. All others in the province were to be commoners with the right of suffrage restricted to freeholders possessing at least 50 acres of land. The basic political philosophy which lay behind the Fundamental Constitutions was stated frankly in a preamble. This elaborate structure of privilege and power was being created so "that the government of the Province may be made most agreeable to the Monarchy under which we live—and that we may avoid erecting a numerous democracy. . . ." Of course, the political and social order proposed for Carolina proved to be artificial and unworkable in practice.

By and large, the conceptions of authority that were held by all governing groups in the colonies of English America were closer in spirit to Hobbes than to Locke. Democracy was condemned as a form of civil tumult, and liberty was defined as obedience to the just commands of those who possessed governing power. The only notable exception to such views so widely shared by the governing elites of seventeenth-century America was the simple political philosophy of William Penn, the Quaker proprietor of Pennsylvania. In the preface to the first "Frame of Government for Pennsylvania," issued in 1682, Penn summed up his notion of rightful authority with these words:

I know what is said by the several admirers of monarchy, aristocracy and democracy . . . when men discourse on the subject . . . But, lastly, when all is said, there is hardly one frame of government in the world so ill designed by its first founders, that, in good hands, would not do well enough . . . wherefore governments rather depend upon men, than men upon governments. Let men be good, and the government cannot be bad; if it be ill, they will cure it. But, if men be bad, let government be never so good, they will endeavor to warp and spoil it to their turn.

In actual practice, however, the government of Pennsylvania did not operate according to the precepts of this benign philosophy—the simple belief that good governments depend upon good men. Pennsylvania, like every other colony, developed its forms and hierarchies, its social classes and structures of power.

In the long run, the prevailing conceptions of authority could be modified only by the political struggles of those who felt deprived of a due share in the uses of political power. Such political resistance was rarely successful in the seventeenth century, but the protests of dissenting and rebellious men undoubtedly helped to prepare the minds of Americans for their later acceptance of Locke's political philosophy as the only adequate explanation of the nature of authority that seemed to fit the conditions of the New World.

Religion as an Instrument of Governing Power

Governing power in seventeenth-century America was largely in the hands of an upper–class elite. The political leaders who made the key decisions and who administered the affairs of particular colonies were recruited largely from the highest ranks of wealth and social station. Just as social dignity was linked to the accumulation of property, so, too, did power and property go hand in hand. To be sure, not all men of wealth had direct access to the higher posts of government, but there were many and varied interlocking arrangements which tied together wealth, status, and power. In Virginia and the southern colonies, a leading role in politics was an essential form of conduct for the complete gentleman. In those colonies, too, the important posts in the government of the colony and the local counties were held by the gentry. In New England, the merchant capitalists could not claim the privileges of leadership and power by virtue of their wealth alone; they needed the badge of regeneracy as well. Nevertheless, the interlocking patterns of marriage and kinship helped to pave the way for the substitution of wealth and class for the Puritan criterion of church membership as the acceptable basis of leadership and power. In Pennsylvania, too, the emergent forces of wealth and class were proving stronger than religious definitions of social value. The rapid rise of a Quaker elite, in whose hands political power and social prestige were concentrated, challenged the truth and relevance of Quaker principles of humility.

Nowhere, of course, did the colonial upper class retain a complete monopoly of power. The growth of representative institutions of government in the seventeenth century is evidence of the degree to which the colonial oligarchies were compelled to share power with a rising class of freeholders. At the same time, however, there was no colony in which the commoners or the small freeholders were able to establish a significant degree of control over the instruments of authority. Theoretically this would have been possible in New England where the majority of the regenerate were men of modest means and ordinary social rank. But the superior learning and political skill of the magistrates and ministers made it possible to retain decision-making power in the hands of a select group. The commoners and freeholders won the right to check the exercise of arbitrary power, but the preponderance of power was in the hands of those who possessed the advantages of superior wealth and social station.

The evidence is unmistakable that the governing classes in America were jealous guardians of their privileged positions of power. They sought after and generally obtained for their policies the acquiescence of the elected representatives of the freemen. Furthermore they expected obedience as they administered those policies; dissenters and troublemakers were dealt with harshly. By and large, English America was not yet a place in which the habits of political tolerance had developed, or in which open and continuous criticism of the government was accepted as a necessary and valuable aspect of the political process.

Massachusetts offers a particularly instructive example of the uses of political power at this time. The policies of the ruling magistrates were challenged openly several times in the early history of the colony, and the unhappy consequences experienced by these political and religious objectors reveal how liberty was limited in the Puritan commonwealth.

In 1633 Governor Winthrop and the assistants became alarmed at reports of "divers new and dangerous opinions" which were being expressed by Roger Williams in the church at Salem. Williams, a young minister who was greatly admired by his congregation, had attacked in his preaching certain fundamental aspects of the religious and political system of Massachusetts. In some respects, he was a more zealous

Established Churches as Instruments of Authority

Puritan than the leading ministers of Massachusetts: he openly attacked the Church of England and urged the members of his congregation to make a personal renunciation of any ties between the churches of New England and England. Furthermore, he had publicly avowed his belief that the magistrates had no authority to punish anyone for breaches of the first table of God's law as given in the Ten Commandments. That is to say, Williams denied the right of the civil government to punish idolatry, blasphemy, perjury, and sabbath-breaking.

Equally troublesome was Williams' criticism of the charter of Massachusetts. He took the position that the king had no right to grant title to any land in the New World; the only ethical basis for any land titles was through purchase agreements made with the Indians. He even went so far as to call the patent granted to the Massachusetts colony by the king "a solemn public lie."

The magistrates of Massachusetts were horrified by these public utterances. They were particularly fearful that such assaults on the king's name and on the charter might invite a royal investigation and encourage the legal attacks being made on the charter by their enemies in England. The charter was the legal basis of their authority and an attack on the charter was, in effect, an attack on the constitution of the colony.

Moreover, the magistrates and ministers alike were deeply disturbed by Williams' religious teachings and feared that his ideas would disrupt the uniformity of belief and worship which they believed was necessary for a covenanted community of regenerate men. John Cotton, the leading minister in the colony, recommended that Williams should be led away from his errors by the method of admonition. He assured Winthrop and the magistrates that Williams' "violent course did spring rather from scruple of conscience than from seditious principle."

The conscience of Roger Williams proved to be more of a problem than Cotton had imagined. Williams appeared before the members of the General Court and seemed to accept their admonitions in a satisfactory fashion, but, in 1635, he was summoned to appear again because of his continued attacks on the policies of the magistrates. Particularly serious was his public criticism of the requirement that all inhabitants of Massachusetts should take the "resident's oath," swearing allegiance and submission to "the government—of this commonweale." Williams argued that oath-taking was an act of worship and a magistrate should not tender the oath to any unregenerate men. Such ideas threatened to undermine the authority of the magistrates over the large number of inhabitants who were not church members.

In the summer of 1635, Roger Williams was summoned before the General Court to answer a full list of charges against him. After a prolonged debate, in which ministers also took part, his opinions were unanimously adjudged to be erroneous and dangerous. The Salem church was asked to rescind its call to Williams as a teacher of the church and considerable political pressure was brought to bear in order to get the members of the Salem church to yield. At a succeeding meeting of the General Court, Thomas Hooker, who held a leading position among the ministers of Massachusetts before he moved to Connecticut, was appointed to make a final attempt to persuade Williams to recant. And, when it was clear that Hooker "could not reduce him from any of his errors," the governor pronounced a sentence of banishment. In the winter of 1636, therefore, Roger Williams went into exile in the wilderness region of Narragansett Bay.

Williams' banishment, however, did not make the religious establishment of Massachusetts safe and secure. After all, his religious ideas sprang from Puritan logic; and the Puritan emphasis on the centrality of a personal conversion experience could breed other dangerous forms of religious reasoning. Such dangers came to plague the Puritan leaders again only a short time after the banishment of Williams. This time the trouble came from Anne Hutchinson. A friend and disciple of John Cotton, Hutchinson possessed an intellect second to none, and she did not hesitate to use it to challenge the leading men of the colony. Winthrop, in turn, described her as "of haughty and fierce carriage, of nimble wit and active spirit and a very voluble tongue."

She arrived in 1634 as the wife of a prominent merchant and served the community as a midwife and spiritual counselor. She devoted herself to leading religious discussions at which she dissected the sermons of the previous Sunday. Hutchinson maintained that religious truth could be apprehended by direct inspiration from God. According to this "Antinomian" position, a Christian who was truly filled with the Holy Spirit did not need the teaching of ministers or the laws that govern ordinary people. This emphasis on the "covenant of grace" as the sole authority for the divinely inspired Christian was a dangerous doctrine in the view of the colony's leaders. It threatened any uniformity or orthodoxy of belief; it subverted the authority of the laws of the commonwealth. The ministers and magistrates were, therefore, quick to act. Early in 1637, John Cotton, whose own teachings bordered on Anne Hutchinson's supposed heresy, was persuaded by a synod of the clergy to see the orthodox light; some months later the General Court found Hutchinson guilty of "traducing the ministers." Ordered out of the colony, she fled in winter to Rhode Island where Williams had established religious freedom.

The defeat of the Antinomians tightened the control of the ministers and magistrates over the government of Massachusetts. Thereafter it was clear that religious orthodoxy was to be defined by the ministers and enforced by the magistrates of the covenanted community. The Congregational Church of the Puritans became the established Church of Massachusetts and received all local taxes collected for the support of religion. Furthermore, the web of secular and religious authority was

woven together in a codification of the laws of Massachusetts in 1648 officially entitled the *Body of Laws and Libertyes.*

The *Body of Laws and Libertyes* was a blend of Mosaic law, the laws of the colony, and the common law of England designed to fit the peculiar needs of governance in Massachusetts. The "lawfull liberties" of the people were enumerated, including trial by jury, the rights of fee simple landownership, and the right of the freemen of each town to elect deputies to the General Court. But the enumeration of capital crimes included idolatry, witchcraft, blasphemy, murder, bestiality, sodomy, man-stealing, false witness, and treason. Thus matters of conscience and private belief were included among the most heinous offenses, and with this legal weapon the leaders of Massachusetts were able to suppress any form of religious dissent considered dangerous. The *Body of Laws and Libertyes* became a model afterward followed in New Haven and Connecticut.

Much of the political history of Massachusetts in the succeeding decades is a dreary tale of religious persecution. In 1647 five Presbyterian leaders were fined and imprisoned. In 1651 several Baptists were sentenced to be fined and "well whipped." Several Quakers, including a woman, were put to death from 1659 to 1660 for continuing to bear witness against the laws of Massachusetts. Since Quakers did not appear to be daunted by such executions, the leaders of Massachusetts began to hesitate about the wisdom of their harsh policy. With a peculiar show of leniency, a new law was adopted in 1661 which stated that Quakers who came into the colony should be whipped at the cart's tail from town to town all the way to their expulsion at the border. If any Quaker should return again as many as three times, he was to receive the same treatment each time and might also be branded if the court so chose. Any Quaker who returned a fourth time might be sentenced to death.

Influential Quakers in England were so aroused by the continuing harshness of Massachusetts toward their coreligionists that they sought and obtained a royal order commanding that any Quakers imprisoned in Massachusetts should be sent to England for trial. Unwilling to provoke the possibility of further royal intervention, the General Court of Massachusetts resolved that the death penalty and corporal punishment should not again be used against the Quakers.

Although Massachusetts surpassed all other colonies in the cruelty of its system of enforced religious conformity, established churches also held sway in the most populous colonies of the seventeenth century. In Connecticut taxes were levied for the support of the Congregational Church, and the towns admitted to the rights of freemen only those who were certified to be of "peaceable and honest conversation." In actual practice, the body of freemen in Connecticut consisted largely of Church members. In Virginia and the Carolinas, the Anglican church became the established church as in England. Each local parish in Virginia was required to furnish a minister with a two hundred acre allotment of land known as a "glebe," and a tithe or tax was imposed on all inhabitants for the support of the Church. Although the Carolina proprietors were more tolerant of religious dissenters, the Fundamental Constitutions declared that the Church of England "being the only true and orthodox, and the national religion of all the King's dominions, is so also of Carolina, and therefore it alone should be allowed to receive public maintenance." Hence organized parishes with glebes and tithing laws began to grow up among the early settlements of South Carolina.

The religious situation in Maryland was complicated by the fact that Baltimore, the Lord Proprietor, was a Roman Catholic. The interest of the Lord Proprietor in the development of his province required him to develop a policy of toleration and compromise in religious matters. As a Roman Catholic, he was anxious to provide a secure haven for his coreligionists in English America; yet he knew that he could not establish a state church in Maryland contrary to the laws of England. Moreover, the number of Catholic settlers who went to Maryland was always very small so that Baltimore had to offer religious toleration to Anglicans and other Protestants if he wished to obtain settlers for his province.

The Seeds of
Religious Liberty

Hence, in 1649, Lord Baltimore sent to Maryland from England a bill which became the Toleration Act of 1649. This Act granted freedom of conscience to all Christians and imposed fines and penalties on any who would disturb a Christian in his chosen worship or malign other Christians with offensive names—"papist," "heretic," "idolator," and the like. Baltimore's policy of toleration had only a limited degree of success. A Puritan majority in the Assembly in 1654 withdrew protection from Roman Catholics in their worship and, even though a policy of toleration was resumed in 1660 after the restoration of the monarchy in England, pressures continued to grow in the colony for the establishment of the Anglican religion. By the end of the seventeenth century, the

Anglican Church was officially established in Maryland and, from that time forward, Roman Catholics suffered many religious and civil disabilities.

Although the system of established churches took root in America more successfully than other Old World institutions, there were significant advances toward new ways of organizing the relations between church and state. In this respect, the efforts of Roger Williams in Rhode Island are particularly noteworthy. Williams articulated a new conception of the proper relation between religion and civil authority in one of his most important writings, *The Bloudy Tenent of Persecution for the Cause of Conscience,* printed in 1644. In this tract he likened a church or a company of worshippers to a college of physicians, a joint-stock company of merchants, or any other private society. Such companies or private groups can hold meetings, keep records, hold disputations, divide, and even break up and dissolve, and yet the peace of the civil society will not be impaired or disturbed. Williams argued that the weapons of civil government are not only improper but also unnecessary in judging questions of spiritual truth and error,

To batter downe *Idolatry, false worship,* heresie, *schisme, blindnesse, hardnesse,* out of the *soule* and *spirit,* it is vaine, improper and unsuitable to bring those weapons which are used by *persecutors,* stocks, whips, prisons, swords, *gibbets,* stakes, etc. . . . but against these *spirituall* strong holds in the soules of men, *Spirituall Artillery* and *weapons* are proper, which are mighty through *God* to subdue and bring under the very *thought* to obedience. . . .

Williams labored mightily to make thought and persuasion the sole basis of religious truth for all men in Rhode Island. Under his leadership a civil code was drawn up in 1647 guaranteeing complete religious freedom. Furthermore, a charter issued to the colony by the king in 1663 confirmed the full liberty of conscience which existed in Rhode Island.

In the middle colonies the great diversity of religious groups encouraged a policy of toleration. William Penn welcomed all kinds of religious sects to Pennsylvania in order to carry out his desire to establish a "free colony for all mankind that will come hither." Although the Quakers made up the dominant class in Pennsylvania, no effort was made to establish a privileged position for the Quaker religion, but there were religious tests for officeholding which favored Protestants. In New York the Duke of York granted toleration to the larger Protestant sects, Dutch and English, already located in the province, but all ministers had to be approved by the governor before they could carry on their religious duties. In New Jersey a considerable measure of religious freedom was granted by the proprietors in order to encourage settlement, but Roman Catholics were specifically excluded from the benefits of this liberty.

Thus, the development of religious liberty in most parts of English America was less the result of theory than of pragmatic adjustment to the realities of colonization. The policies of toleration in the proprietary colonies were essentially practical solutions to the problems of promoting settlement and of maintaining peaceful coexistence among diverse religious groups. Roger Williams, who himself came to believe that the only acceptable church was the individual, stands virtually alone in the seventeenth century as a principled believer in religious freedom. One must be careful, however, not to interpret Williams as a modern liberal. His position was grounded on religious belief and must be distinguished from the later Enlightenment insistence on the separation of church and state. For Williams, the separation was intended to keep the church free of taint; for more secular Enlightenment theorists, like Jefferson, the logic would be reversed: it was the state that was to be freed from the taint of organized religion. The ultimate accomplishment of full religious freedom and the separation of church and state that was written into the Constitution and the Bill of Rights grew out of a confluence of Enlightenment liberalism and religious pietism.

Bacon's Rebellion

In 1676 armed rebellion broke out in Virginia. This conflict, known as Bacon's Rebellion, after Nathaniel Bacon, the leader of the rebels, reveals the complexities of wielding power in colonial America. Although this was a rebellion within the white community, by settlers who felt that an old elite was monopolizing opportunity and power, Indian-white relations provide the essential background for it.

In 1646, at the end of a second general war between settlers and Indians, a treaty was signed guaranteeing the Chesapeake tribes the territory north of the York River. Both sides recognized that peace between the two cultures required this sort of separation and exclusive use within designated areas. The policy was largely successful, and both Indians and whites benefitted from a profitable fur trade that grew up during the ensuing three decades of relative peace. But the growth of English population in Virginia, to about 40,000 by 1670, complicated matters. As the population of Virginia grew, pressure mounted on Governor Berkeley to open the area north of the York River for white settlement. Newcomers and those who were now completing their indentures faced hard times, and they felt that more land should be available to them. When Berkeley refused to act, frontiersmen rebelled. They supposed that Berkeley's motives were in part selfish. The governor and his associates in the established elite merely wanted to preserve their own advantages. The frontiersmen suspected, moreover, that the established leaders were more interested in preserving their lucrative fur-trading relationship with the Indians than they were in helping white settlers.

Indian-White Relations

A small event sparked the actual uprising. In July of 1675 a group of Indians, angered by the failure of a planter to pay for goods they had traded, tried to steal his hogs. The Indian plan failed, and several Indians were killed by Englishmen. This began a pattern of attack and retaliation instigated by both sides, with the level of violence mounting with each round. The frontiersmen quickly recognized that the Indians, whose numbers had dwindled to perhaps a thousand, were extremely vulnerable. Land hungry settlers grew more aggressive with the realization that they could solve their grievances by literally wiping out the Indians. Their resentments against leaders within white society fueled the frontiersmen's racist hatred of Indians.

Bacon's Leadership   By May of 1676 Nathaniel Bacon, a young, well-connected gentleman who had arrived in Virginia two years earlier, had assumed leadership of the frontiersmen. When Bacon first landed in Virginia, Berkeley, who was related to him by marriage, took him into his circle and appointed him to the Council. But in 1676 they were already at odds. The ambitious Bacon had identified himself with the frontiersmen and their aggressive Indian policy, while Berkeley denounced the "savagery" of the mounting English attacks. His official response was to build a string of forts. He proposed, in short, a defensive policy. For all his royal authority, however, Governor Berkeley was unable to control the frontiersmen who wanted an aggressive policy and who resented the taxes they would have to pay to build the forts—money that would go into the pockets of contractors who would surely be Berkeley's favorites. This possibility touched off loud complaint about what the rebels saw as a long-standing grievance with Berkeley and his established associates. "Let us . . . see," they demanded in their "Manifesto," "what sponges have sucked up the public treasure and whether it hath not been privately contrived away by unworthy favorites and juggling parasites whose tottering fortunes have been repaired and supported at the public charge." Berkeley, however, was not the only leader to find his authority eroded in the crisis. The Indian chiefs with whom he might negotiate a peace treaty, pressed by rival inland tribes as well as by white settlers, were equally unable to control their warriors. The result of this collapse of both the white and Indian political systems was spiraling violence.

Seeking to restore order, Berkeley charged Bacon with treason. Bacon's response was to march on Jamestown, demanding a commission to legitimize his attacks on the Indians. The conflict between the frontiersmen and the Indians was now exposing its other dimension: political conflict internal to the white society. Berkeley had ordered the election of a new House of Burgesses to deal with the crisis, and he was unable to control the men who were elected. Bacon, elected from his home county, threatened the Governor, the Council, and the Burgesses with "fyer and sword" if he did not receive his commission. "God damme my blood," he shouted, "I came for a commission, and a commission I will have before I goe." The Burgesses gave Bacon his commission; they also passed a number of laws, known as "Bacon's Laws" even though he was not responsible for them, that were designed to correct the political abuses bothering many of Bacon's followers. An act was passed, for example, that required a yearly rotation of the office of sheriff; another forbade anyone to hold more than two important county offices; another provided penalties for excessive fees charged by justices of the peace and other public officials. But when Bacon returned to the frontier with his army, Berkeley raised an army of his own and marched after the man he now denounced as a traitor and rebel. Berkeley's frantic reports of the collapse of authority were sufficiently alarming to bring. the dispatch of a thousand royal troops from England, but things had settled down before the troops arrived in January, 1677. With the Indians crushed, Bacon's supporters wanted to return home. Bacon himself died of swamp fever, and his rebellion simply faded away.

Yet the rebellion had several facets worth remembering. It was a revolt of ambitious men on the make against established authority. Bacon's followers resented the tight grip on power and the best land possessed by Berkeley and his established associates. Yet when it was over, the great planters retained disproportionate wealth and power in Virginia. In fact, the class conflict dimension of the rebellion got lost in the racist preoccupation with Indian land. Bacon's attempt to use anti-Indian racism to unify the settlers into a political movement failed, largely because of Berkeley's resistance, but it was a premonition of what was achieved after 1676. The racist hatred that Bacon and his followers directed toward the Indians was shifted toward blacks, who were being enslaved in dramatically increasing numbers in the years following the rebellion. With this development we find the paradoxical union of slavery and freedom that characterized eighteenth-century Virginia, where whites were united through their common possession of freedom that was denied to enslaved blacks. The rebellion also marks a turning point in Indian-white relations. The last remnants of tribal culture were destroyed in the course of the crisis; effective Indian resistance to white expansion was at an end. Perhaps even more important, the rebellion showed that the colonial political authorities could not control the settlers' land hunger.

The Yoke of Imperial Authority

Although the king was the fountainhead of all governing authority in seventeenth-century America, the colonial governments acquired a considerable degree of self government. The autonomous position of the colonial governments resulted from the isolation of America—an isolation that was both physical and legal. Communication between England and the colonies depended upon wooden sailing ships beating their way across three thousand miles of ocean. Even an efficient imperial administration would have been limited by delays of six months or more in the transmittal of messages and instructions between England and the colonies. In this century, however, there was no efficiently organized colonial administration. The Stuart kings preferred to operate with indirect means of control and with occasional commissions of investigation—a method of administration which multiplied and extended the delays already built into the system by geographical isolation.

Problems of Imperial Control

To be sure, the charters which granted governing authority to proprietors and corporations were an attempt to control the colonies by a basic form of royal instruction. But a charter, after all, is only a general frame of government; it is the day-to-day process of law-making and administration that really shapes the course and character of a government. The charters, indeed, were often used as shields against the Crown's attempts to regulate matters of law and administration in the colonies. The dissolution of the Virginia Company, for example, came only after several years of complicated investigative and judicial proceedings. Furthermore, even after Virginia became a royal colony whose royal governors operated with instructions directly from the king in Privy Council, the Virginia Assembly was able to carry on in an autonomous fashion.

In Massachusetts, the charter was an even more effective obstacle to royal interference. Responding to pressures from a Privy Council Commission, the Court of King's Bench in 1637 ruled that the charter of the Massachusetts Bay Company was without warrant and ordered the return of the grant into the king's hands. But the Court's judgment lacked clear legality since both the charter and the officers of the Massachusetts Bay Company were not present to be heard and judged. For the next few years, the governing authorities of Massachusetts put off all orders from England for the return of the charter with petitions, delays, or refusals to reply. The political crisis in England that preceded the outbreak of civil war ended the efforts to enforce the judgment of the court of King's Bench.

The English Civil War strengthened further the forces of isolation and autonomy in colonial political affairs. The energies of English leaders were so completely absorbed in the struggle between king and Parliament that the American colonies had to make their own way in the 1640's and 1650's. It made little difference whether the dominant sympathies in a colony were royalist or Puritan—the universal consequence seemed to be a greater degree of local autonomy.

Virginia, for example, remained loyal to the king and actually made preparations to revolt against Cromwell's government. A parliamentary commission was sent to Virginia to secure obedience to parliamentary authority with threats to cut off all trade if Virginia did not submit. As a consequence, the General Assembly of Virginia agreed to acknowledge the authority of Parliament but, at the same time, the Assembly acquired a greater degree of authority than ever before. In Maryland also, the General Assembly acquired considerable freedom from the control of the proprietor during the years of Cromwell's government.

The New England colonies moved even further toward a state of quasi-independence. When war broke out between the king and Parliament in 1642, the Massachusetts government immediately dropped all reference to King Charles in the oath of allegiance required of the magistrates. No pledge of loyalty to Parliament was substituted either. Instead, Governor Winthrop and his fellow magistrates steered an independent course. Massachusetts claimed full jurisdiction over all trade and navigation in the waters of Massachusetts Bay. In 1643 the three smaller colonies of Connecticut, New Haven, and Plymouth were invited to join Massachusetts in forming the New England Confederation. Commissioners from the four plantations met in Boston under the presidency of Governor Winthrop and agreed to plan and fight all future wars together against whatever foes—the Indians, the French in Nova Scotia, and the Dutch in the Hudson River area. Thus the New England colonies were boldly pursuing an independent foreign policy at least in so far as their region was concerned.

Cromwell's government, nevertheless, began to shape a new colonial policy that was to have enduring effects on imperial administration in English America. During the disruptive years of the Civil War, much of the commerce of the colonies had been taken over by the merchants of other nations, particularly the Dutch. In 1650, Parliament enacted a navigation act that prohibited the vessels of any foreign country in the trade of the English colonies. This and other measures to exclude the Dutch from English trade led to a war between England and Holland— largely a naval conflict—in which England made the larger gains. The vigorous foreign policy carried on by Cromwell reflected the avid interest of English merchants in the colonial trade as a source of profit to themselves and to England.

England's New Commercial Policies

The return of Charles II to the throne of England with the restoration of the English monarchy in 1660 made further readjustments necessary in the use of imperial authority. Although Charles II immediately re-established such ancient institutions of the realm as the House of Lords and the Church of England, he was shrewd enough to recognize the strength of the new economic forces that had grown up in English life in the seventeenth century. In particular he consented to enlarge the commercial policy that the London merchants had pressed for so eagerly during the years of Cromwell's rule.

This policy was embodied in the Acts of Trade and Navigation which were to be the chief cornerstones of England's colonial system for the next hundred years. The Navigation Act of 1660, re-enacted in 1661 by the first elected Parliament under Charles II, was the first of these important laws. According to this Act, all trade of the colonies had to be carried in English ships; such vessels had to be built and owned by the subjects of the king in England, Ireland, or the colonies; and they had to be commanded by a captain and manned by a crew who were English subjects living in the realm of England, Ireland, or the colonial plantations. The Act of 1661 also stipulated that certain enumerated commodities produced in the colonies could be exported only to England, Ireland, or other English colonies—commodities such as sugar, tobacco, cotton, indigo, ginger, and various dyewoods. In 1663 this commercial policy was rounded out by the Staple Act which provided that any goods produced or manufactured in Europe that were being sent to the English colonies should first be shipped to England and landed there before reshipment to America. Exceptions were made to meet certain obvious colonial needs: servants, horses, and provisions from Scotland could be shipped directly; the same was true of wine from Madeira and the Azores, and salt from the southern countries of Europe.

These Acts of 1661 and 1663 injured Dutch trade even more than the policies of Cromwell; as a result, a second Anglo-Dutch naval war broke out in 1664. A notable gain for the English in that war was the conquest of New Netherland which gave the English control of the strategically important Hudson River region. A third naval war was fought with Holland in 1672 before the Dutch were willing to give up the attempt to disrupt England's closed system of imperial trade in North America.

Thus, there were powerful groups in England which favored a closer system of imperial control than had been exercised over the colonies during the first half of the seventeenth century. The great migration to the colonies had greatly stimulated economic growth in America. For the first time, the profitableness of colonies for English merchants had

State House of New York in 1679. The harbor came right up to the city, the Flemish architectural style predominating in official government buildings as well as residences. From I. N. Phelps Stokes's Iconography of Manhattan Island, Volume I.

become a genuine possibility instead of a theory publicized by zealous colonial promoters. The acts of trade and navigation also strengthened the position of colonial merchants, especially in the New England colonies. When the Dutch merchants were driven out of the North American trade, New England merchants stepped in rapidly and eagerly to take their share of the market. And, since they enjoyed the protection of the closed imperial market on an equal basis with English merchants, they became the chief competitors of the London merchants for a major share of the colonial trade.

Furthermore, the absence of a sufficient force of customs officials encouraged New England merchants to evade the requirements of the Staple Act and the enumerated commodities clause of the Navigation Act. This illegal trade made it possible for them to undersell English merchants in foreign markets and in the colonies. To stop this practice, Parliament enacted another trade act which placed a "plantation duty" on all enumerated commodities exported from one colony to another. Thus, if a ship captain should try the trick of pretending to take a cargo of tobacco from Virginia to Boston but sailing directly to Europe instead, he would already have paid a duty equivalent to what would have been levied on his cargo if he had obeyed the law and landed his enumerated commodities in England first. It must be remembered, however, that there were many New England merchants who did not rely on illegal trading methods and who began to see the economic advantages of the imperial trading system.

The new acts of trade and navigation led to greater centralization in colonial administration. A new Privy Council committee was created in 1675—the Lords of Trade and Plantations—with broader authority and a more effective organization than any previous council which had been set up to administer colonial affairs. As their title suggests, the Lords of Trade regarded the colonies as important for the expansion of the English economy through the regulation of overseas trade. At the same time, the Lords of Trade were determined to reduce the autonomous powers of the charter and proprietary colonies which were becoming troublesome obstacles to imperial regulation. Indeed, there is some evidence that their ultimate objective was the destruction of all colonial charters.

New Methods of Colonial Administration

The first and most important step in such a policy was to reduce the quasi-independence of New England. A peremptory royal letter was drafted, ordering Massachusetts to send agents to England to answer charges against the colony. A special agent, Edmund Randolph, was appointed to carry the letter and to gather further information about the laws and administration in the New England colonies. Randolph represented the new style of professional civil servant that was appearing in the royal bureaucracy. He was hard-working, intelligent, and absolutely devoted to making the royal administration more efficient. He was more than a match for the Puritan magistrates, and the Lords of Trade recognized this by appointing him collector of the king's revenue in Boston two years later.

For the next half-dozen years, Randolph was the relentless watchdog of English trade and English authority in New England. The leaders of Massachusetts attempted to defeat his efforts with all the old-time tactics of obstruction and delay, but he doggedly and persistently gathered evidence for an impressive compilation of charges against the Massachusetts authorities. He accused the Puritan leaders of permitting flagrant violations of the navigation acts; he charged them with an open usurpation of the king's prerogative through their operation of a mint for coinage; he reported that local juries refused to convict merchants accused of illegal trade; he revealed that the religious policies of Massachusetts discriminated against Anglicans by forcing them to pay taxes for the support of Puritan churches; above all, he accused the Puritan leaders of a lack of loyalty because they refused to require an oath of allegiance to the king. On the basis of these and other detailed charges, the Privy Council brought suit in the Court of Chancery against the Massachusetts Bay Company. The court ruled that the Company had abused its charter privileges and declared the charter vacated in October, 1684.

The destruction of the Massachusetts charter opened the way to a new experiment in imperial administration. This administrative purpose was re-enforced when James II succeeded his brother on the throne of England in 1685. As Duke of York, James had acquired some familiarity with colonial affairs in his role as proprietor of New York; as king of England, he was determined to rule with a strong hand both at home and in the colonies. The Lords of Trade, acting on the advice of Randolph, had already proposed a new government for Massachusetts, headed by a royal governor and an appointed council.

The Dominion of New England

In many ways, the success of the new experiment in imperial administration depended on Sir Edmund Andros, whom James II appointed as governor in 1686 with autocratic powers over all the New England area except Rhode Island and Connecticut. Andros and his council, whose members were appointed by the king, were given power to levy taxes, enact laws, erect courts, and grant lands in the name of the king. All laws had to be sent to the king for final approval, and all judgments of local courts involving more than £300 might be appealed to the Privy Council. All land grants made under the new government were to be subject to a quitrent of two shillings and six pence per acre.

More sweeping acts of centralization followed very quickly. Shortly after Andros arrived in Boston, Connecticut and Rhode Island were brought into the Dominion of New England, although their charters had not been legally annulled. In 1688 James II extended Andros' power by making him the governor of all of New England, New York, and New Jersey.

Andros was a strong-willed man whose actions antagonized important groups in New England. He took away the legal privileges of the Puritan church; the Puritans were even compelled to allow Anglicans to use one of their churches in Boston for purposes of worship. Andros' ruthless enforcement of the acts of trade and navigation aroused fear and uncertainty among merchants. Even though he did not seriously disturb existing land titles, all property rights in New England were placed in jeopardy by being made subject to the possible exercise of arbitrary power by the governor. To raise revenue, Andros and his council levied taxes without attempting to win the consent of the elected representatives of the freemen. And when John Wise, a liberal-minded minister, led the town of Ipswich in protest against such levies, 30 "rebels" were arrested, of whom six were fined and imprisoned.

The situation in New England soon paralleled in miniature that of England during the brief reign of James II between 1685 and 1689. Andros, like James, carried on in such a highhanded fashion as to alienate those classes of society accustomed to a larger share of political power. King James broke with Parliament in England, while Andros tried to govern without a representative assembly in New England. James II aroused the fears of Anglicans and other Protestants by his appointment of Catholics to high office; Andros alarmed the Puritans by fostering the Anglican Church in Boston. James threatened his opposition with a large standing army, and Andros flaunted a troop of red coats in Boston.

On both sides of the Atlantic, these unpopular governments were overthrown by bloodless revolutions. In December, 1688, James II fled into exile in France and, when the news of this "Glorious Revolution" reached Massachusetts, a well-organized mob seized and imprisoned Randolph, Andros, and other officials in April, 1689. In both revolutions, there was no popular upheaval; the revolutions were carefully managed by those who were seeking to protect their established positions of wealth, status, and power—the aristocratic landholders and merchants of England, the Puritan ministers, and merchants in New England.

The Overthrow of the Dominion of New England

The successful overthrow of the Dominion of New England did not bring a return to the old New England way. Some of the older Puritan leaders hoped for a restoration of the old Massachusetts charter, but the coalition of leaders that seized power from Andros in the bloodless revolution of 1689 included many new men closely affiliated with Boston merchants who had not previously held significant public offices. Such men sensed the need for a reconstruction of imperial relations even though they could not accept the extreme forms of centralization attempted in the Dominion of New England. Their experience with the expanded trade of the English empire made them ready to accept more direct royal administration provided that their property interests and their accustomed liberties were properly guaranteed.

chapter four

Learning and Literature in Seventeenth-Century America

Detail from an engraving by Peter Maverick, Genius of Penmanship. *Prints Division. The New York Public Library. Astor, Lenox and Tilden Foundations.*

The Transplanting of Educational Institutions

Education involves the transmission of culture across generations. In any society there are innumerable beliefs, values, and specific skills that must be learned by the young before they can fully participate in the society. The basic mechanism for such education in seventeenth-century England and her colonies was the family, and both church and state impressed this educational responsibility on parents. There were, however, a variety of other institutions supplementing the family's work. Some of these institutions were transferred intact from England to the colonies, others were changed, and yet others never made the crossing.

The educational system which was improvised in Virginia became a significant aspect of the quest for gentility by the larger landowners. The gentry of Virginia realized that their children needed to have a sufficient education to enable them to take care of their estates and to cultivate the manners of gentlemen. Consequently, they provided tutors and plantation schools according to their means, and, in rare cases, wealthy planters sent their children to England. In general, the system of hiring tutors made education available only to the children of well-to-do planters and to the children of such immediate neighbors who might be permitted to have a share of the tutor's time. Most other children were beyond the reach of any school.

Education in Virginia

To be sure, there was no Machiavellian intent on the part of the Virginia gentry to keep for their own class the very considerable advantages of status and power that education might bring. Most Virginia planters probably did not go so far in their aristocratic prejudices as Governor William Berkeley when he thanked God that there were no free schools and printing in Virginia because learning would only teach the people disobedience and heresy. As a matter of fact, some charitable-minded planters attempted to establish free schools in the colony. The earliest free school in Virginia was established in 1635 when Benjamin Symmes, a successful planter, provided in his last will and testament that two hundred acres of land together with the increase and milk of eight cows should be given out of his estate for the education of the children of his own and neighboring parishes. Other planters from time to time provided endowments for free schools or for the education of the children of the poor in the parish. But these efforts to broaden educational opportunities in Virginia were never very substantial; the lack of towns in the plantation economy made it difficult to mobilize the financial support needed to continue such schools.

The Reverend James Blair, sent by the Bishop of London to investigate matters of religion and education in Virginia, described the state of affairs in 1697 in very censorious terms: "for well-educated children, for an industrious and thriving people, or for a happy government in church and state, and in short for all the other advantages of human improvements, it is certainly . . . one of the poorest, miserablest, and worst countries in all America that is inhabited by Christians." The efforts of Blair were largely responsible for obtaining the necessary financial aid from the English government and the wealthy planters of Virginia to establish the College of William and Mary. Although the cornerstone of the first building was laid in 1695, the college was little more than a grammar school for the first 10 years after its foundation.

Education in New England

The educational system of Virginia lagged behind that which was established in New England. The Puritan leaders of Massachusetts were particularly zealous in creating such civilizing institutions as churches and schools. Many of them were well-educated men; indeed, no other colony had such a high proportion of university graduates among its leaders. Moreover, the closely knit pattern of community life which was established in Massachusetts made it easier to organize and support schools for the education of the children.

A number of leading towns in Massachusetts took measures to establish schools very soon after they were settled. Boston hired a schoolmaster in 1635, and took up a private subscription for his support. In 1636 Charlestown voted to hire a graduate of an English university "to keep a schoole for twelve monthe" and provided him with £40 a year out of town taxes. Dorchester in 1639, Ipswich in 1642, and Dedham in 1643 established schools with varying methods of financial support.

This remarkable effort to create schools in the infancy of the colony was crowned by the establishment of the first colonial college in English America. The General Court of Massachusetts, in 1636, appropriated £400 "towards a schoole or colledge." In the following year, a Board of Overseers, consisting of magistrates and ministers, was appointed to administer the college; a house was purchased in Cambridge, a professor was hired, and the first class of students began their studies in 1638. In September of that same year, John Harvard, a Cambridge University graduate and teaching elder in the church at Charlestown, died and left his library of four hundred volumes and half of his estate amounting to nearly £800 to the college which was then named after him.

Massachusetts also took the lead among the colonies in enacting laws for the compulsory maintenance of schools on the part of all towns of a certain size. In 1647 the General Court passed an act which provided that all towns of 50 householders should appoint a teacher for "all such children as shall resort to him to write and read." The teacher was to be paid "either by the parents or masters of such children, or by the inhabitants in general . . . as the major part of those that order the prudentials of the town shall [decide]." The same act required further that "when any town shall increase to the number of one hundred families or householders, they should set up a grammer school, the master thereof being able to instruct youth so far as they may be fitted for the university." Thus, Massachusetts was the first and only colony in the seventeenth century to establish a complete educational structure from the elementary forms of instruction to the higher learning offered at Harvard College.

Other New England colonies initiated some of the basic features of the educational system of Massachusetts. The Connecticut General Court copied the Massachusetts Act of 1647 almost verbatim in its school law of 1650; and when New Haven was annexed to Connecticut in 1665 the Connecticut Act became operative in the area of the old New Haven colony as well. Plymouth colony in 1658 recommended that schoolmasters be secured in each town to teach the children to read and write and, in 1677, allotted some of the proceeds of the Cape Cod fisheries to help support grammar schools in the larger towns. Of course, there is evidence to indicate that some New England towns failed to comply with these laws, particularly with the requirements to maintain grammar schools. But the larger number of towns seem to have made a serious effort to support the schools that were required by law.

Elsewhere in seventeenth-century America, there were varying patterns of public and private support for book learning or training in useful skills. William Penn's second frame of government, accepted in 1683, required all parents in the province of Pennsylvania to instruct their children in reading and writing. Subsequently, it was further provided that "the Governor and Council shall erect and order all public schools and encourage and reward the authors of useful science and laudable inventions. . . ." The first Public School in Philadelphia was started in 1689 and chartered by the Council in 1697. Several associated charity schools were added later under the provisions of the charter. Such efforts of the Quakers were matched occasionally by other religious denominations in the middle colonies, particularly the Dutch Reformed Church in New York. Otherwise, the effort to create schools in the middle colonies was not significantly better than that of Virginia and the southern colonies.

Class Character of Education

The only responsibility of the state toward education that was universally accepted by all of the colonies resulted from the imitation of the apprenticeship laws of England. Beginning in 1642, the Virginia Assembly passed several acts during the century which provided that orphans and children of the dependent poor should be taught a useful trade and the rudiments of reading and writing. Such laws, however, applied only to a relatively small number of dependent poor and were designed to prevent pauperism and to increase the industrial skills within the colony. Every other colony enacted similar laws in the seventeenth century with substantially similar social motives.

Everywhere the colonial educational systems reflected the status differences which were emerging in English America. In the middle and southern colonies, the book learning taught by schoolmasters or private tutors was limited largely to the upper classes. The yeoman farmer taught his own sons with occasional help from the parson of his church, while the apprenticeship system was designed for sons of tradesmen and the dependent poor. Even in New England, where the system of town support for education was most fully developed, the upper classes enjoyed superior advantages. Most children still had to pay tuition charges in addition to whatever the towns appropriated for the support of a teacher. There were no grammar schools in the smaller and more remote villages and, even in the larger towns, the children of the poor were usually apprenticed to learn a useful trade. The Latin grammar schools, after all, were designed to prepare students for the university, and such educational opportunities were available only to a few well-to-do families. The importance of education as a symbol of superior social station is clearly evident in the laws which permitted silk, laces, and gold buttons only for "persons of greater estates, or more liberal education." The evidence is unmistakable, therefore, that the schools of seventeenth-century America were not created to open doors to political and social opportunity, but rather to re-enforce the prevailing pattern of social arrangements.

Schooling and The Social Order

The Puritan Theory of Education   The Puritan leaders of New England, above all others, looked to education as a powerful aid to the preservation of order. They thought "the good education of children is of singular behoof and benefit to any commonwealth." Moreover, this conception of the importance of education for the well-ordered state was to be developed within the particular framework of the Puritan vision of life. Thus, the preamble to the Massachusetts law of 1647 stated that the establishment of schools was necessary because "it [was] one object of that old deluder, Satan, to keep men from the knowledge of the Scriptures."

The Puritan theory of education emphasized reverence and the fear of God, obedience to His commandments, and obedience to authority. John Cotton, the influential spokesman of Massachusetts Puritanism, wrote a short catechism for children entitled *Spiritual Milk for American Babes Drawn Out of the Breasts of Both Testaments for their Souls Nourishment.* Published in the 1640's, this catechism was memorized by many generations of children inasmuch as it became part of the *New England Primer*—an early schoolbook which has been aptly described as "the Little Bible of New England" because it was used in almost all schools. In this catechism the child learned that he was conceived in sin and that without God's saving grace, his corrupt nature would lead him to continued transgressions of God's commandments and to eternal damnation. In interpreting the Ten Commandments to the child, Cotton emphasized that the fifth commandment—Honor thy father and thy mother—meant obedience to all the forms of authority in the family, the school, the church, and the state.

When children learned to spell words and read sentences couched in the conceptions of the *New England Primer,* they were ready to read the Psalter and the Old and New Testaments. To further enrich the educational diet of those who had mastered the skill of reading, a poetic description of sinners facing the last judgment was written by Michael Wigglesworth, a teacher at Harvard College. This work, entitled *The Day of Doom,* was read widely after its publication in 1662. It was an epic of religious horror that has not been outdone, at least in intensity of imagination, by the horror comic books of our own time. Particularly poignant are the verses which tell of children who had died in infancy before baptism and regeneration. When brought before God's judgment, these infant children pleaded for mercy since they had had no chance to sin, only to receive the judgment that their natures were depraved as the result of the original sin of Adam and that they must, therefore, suffer the punishment decreed for all unredeemed sinners. Wigglesworth softened his poetic logic only to the extent of holding out the hope that such children might have the "easiest room in Hell."

Bible box. From Index of American Design. National Gallery of Art.

The Puritans, however, were never satisfied to leave such matters to the language of poetry. The practical application of such doctrines to the duties of everyday living were expressed more completely by Cotton Mather in a tract entitled *A Family Well-Ordered,* published in 1699. This handbook of family duties was divided into two parts—one for parents and the other for children. Parents were admonished to have their children baptized, to teach them to pray and obey, and to lead them to salvation by means of Bible reading and attending church.

The children were urged by Mather to remember their duties to their parents—not only their natural parents but their political parents (the

The Day of Doom:
OR, A
DESCRIPTION
Of the Great and Last
Judgment.
WITH
A SHORT DISCOURSE
ABOUT
ETERNITY.

Ecclef. 12. 14.

For God ſhall bring every work into Judgment, with every ſecret thing, whether it be good, or whether it be evil.

LONDON,

Printed by W. G. for John Sims, at the Kings-Head at Sweeting-Alley-end in Cornhill

(1)

The Day of Doom.

I.

STill was the night, ſerene and bright,
   when all men ſleeping lay;
Calm was the ſeaſon, and carnal reaſon
   thought ſo 'twould laſt for ay.
Soul take thine eaſe, let ſorrow ceaſe,
   much good thou haſt in ſtore;
This was their ſong their cups among,
   the evening before.

II.

Wallowing in all kind of Sin,
   vile Wretches lay ſecure;
The beſt of men had ſcarcely then
   their Lamps kept in good ure.
Virgins unwiſe, who through diſguiſe
   amongſt the beſt were number'd,
Had cloſ'd their eyes; yea, and the Wiſe
   through ſloth and frailty ſlumber'd.

III.

Like as of old, when men grew bold
   Gods threatnings to contemn,
(Who ſtopt their ear, and would not hear
   when mercy warned them:
But took their courſe, without remorſe
   till God began to pour
Deſtruction the World upon,

Michael Wigglesworth. London, 1673. Rare Book Division. The New York Public Library. Astor, Lenox and Tilden Foundations.

magistrates), their ecclesiastical parents (the ministers), and their scholastic parents (the teachers). The undutiful child, he emphasized, would almost certainly come to a bad end in life to be followed by the eternal punishment in the darkness of Hell.

Of course, the grammar schools and Harvard College pursued a more liberal conception of intellectual experience. In the grammar schools the faithful scholars could read such Latin authors as Cicero, Caesar, Livy, Virgil, and Horace. In the college, or in such grammar schools where Greek was taught, they might read Plato, Aristotle, and the Greek poets. Charles Chauncey, while president of the College, delivered a sermon in 1655 in which he defended the use of the "heathen" writers of Greece and Rome in the curriculum. A proper education, he declared, includes "the doctrine of God's works, which is called *Philosophy.*" In Chauncey's view, "the knowledge of Arts and Sciences is useful and expedient" for a true understanding of the works of God.

Educational Ideals of the Virginia Gentry

Elsewhere in seventeenth-century America, other values besides obedience and reverence were taught to the young. In the Virginia style of education, the ideals of the Virginia gentry had an unmistakable influence. The first student orations delivered at William and Mary College in 1699 praised learning as a means of attaining gentility. With the help of higher learning, one of these student orations emphasized, Virginians would be able to converse with such excellent men of past ages as Plato, Aristotle, Seneca, Cicero, Livy, and Tacitus and from them learn the lessons of wisdom and virtue. Another student orator emphasized, however, that the Virginia ideal of education did not propose to develop "mere scholars, which make a very ridiculous figure, made up of pedantry, disputativeness, positiveness, and a great many other ill qualities which render them not so fit for action and conversation."

A Quaker Conception of Education

More than any other group, the Quakers developed conceptions of education which were free of religious dogma or the pretensions of social station. William Penn's theory of education stressed practical and useful knowledge rather than the classical curriculum which had such a central place in both the aristocratic and the Puritan conceptions of education. He wrote

The first Thing obvious to Children is what is sensible; . . . We press their Memory too soon, and puzzle, strain and load them with Words and Rules: to know *Grammar* and *Rhetorick,* and a strange Tongue or two, that it is ten to one may never be useful to them; leaving their natural Genius to *Mechanical* and *Physical* or natural Knowledge uncultivated and neglected: which would be of exceeding Use and Pleasure to them through the whole Course of their Life. To be sure, Languages are not to be despised or neglected. But Things are still to be preferred.

And although Penn's conception of education seems close to modern characteristics of American education, the Puritan educational system demonstrated the greatest vitality and productivity of any in seventeenth-century America. And if it takes many generations of intellectual activity to thicken the texture of thought in a society, then the ministers and scholars of New England labored mightily to create the necessary accumulations of culture, not only in theology, but also in science and in literature. Much of the intellectual history of America has proceeded in dialectical process by which the initial propositions of Puritan thought were dismantled or modified.

Science and Other Special Providences

The seventeenth century brought an intellectual as well as a political revolution to Englishmen. At the same time that Puritans and Parliamentarians were challenging traditional authority in the political sphere, men of learning were questioning the authority of ancient ideas—the ideas of Aristotle in philosophy, of Galen in medicine, of Ptolemy in geography and astronomy. Sir Francis Bacon, in his various works on "the advance of learning," urged men to throw aside the authority of scholastic speculations. "For what purpose," he asked, "are these brain-creations and idle display of power . . . All these invented systems of the universe, each according to his own fancy (are) like so many arguments of plays—every one philosophizes out of the cells of his own imagination, as out of Plato's cave." Bacon called upon men to study nature and experiment with the activities and operations of natural phenomena. "The secrets of nature," he wrote, "betray themselves more readily when tormented by art than when left to their own course."

The Scientific Revolution

To be sure, Bacon was never able to free himself completely from the older modes of Aristotelian thought and he was often mistaken in his methods of experimentation; but he did express as clearly as anyone in his time the new spirit of scientific inquiry. And out of these new uses of experiment and speculation came the first great achievements of English science. William Harvey's discovery of the circulation of blood, Robert Boyle's contributions to the science of chemistry through his experiments with changing volumes and pressures of gases, and Newton's theories dealing with space, matter, and motion are great landmarks in the development of modern science. The Englishmen who came to America brought with them the influences of this intellectual revolution as well as the political revolution of seventeenth-century England.

The pre-eminence of New England in the organized institutions of learning made it the first important center of scientific thought and activity in America. This may seem strange in the light of the Puritan's belief in the power of God to intervene directly in human affairs through earthquakes, floods, drought, pestilence, and warfare. Moreover, in the Puritan scale of values, regeneration and the salvation of the soul were more important than the study of natural things. On the other hand, there were aspects of the Puritan mentality which responded quite readily to the new learning. The Puritan doctrine of providence opened

Puritans and the New Science

the way to the study of nature. The natural world was God's creation and hence deserved to be studied as part of God's works. Indeed, John Cotton argued that the investigation of nature was a positive obligation: "To study the nature and course, and use of all God's works, is a duty imposed by God upon all sorts of men; from the King that sitteth upon the Throne to the Artificer."

Consequently, the Puritans were not hostile to the teachings of the new science in seventeenth-century New England; they never went the whole way with the ideas of men like Bacon—they never abandoned the assumption that God was sovereign with the power to reverse or interrupt the laws of nature. God, they believed, could make the sun stand still or the Red Sea divide. Nevertheless, the Puritans were disposed to place more emphasis on God's operation of natural laws than on the use of miracles. "God can work miracles," a preacher in Boston declared in 1678, "but when ordinary means may be had, he will not work miracles." John Richardson, a minister at Newbury, stressed an even more limited view of the uses of divine power. The faithful children of God, he argued, can no longer expect him to divide the Red Sea—"we in these days, have no promise of such a miraculous and immediate assistance; God works now by men and means, not by miracles."

By such reasoning, the Puritans maintained a balance between the new formulation of the laws of nature and their conception of special providences through which men were punished by fire, flood, and earthquakes, or rewarded with beneficial rains and bountiful harvests. They were not far from the Newtonian conception of necessary and inviolable natural laws which God Himself obeys, except that they preferred to think of natural law as a remarkable example of God's skillful management of causes to produce proper effects in natural and human events. In this way, they were able to preserve the symbolic value of nature as a source of moral meaning. The facts of nature were not

Plate 4 in Edmund Vincent Gillon, Jr.'s Early New England Gravestone Rubbings. *Dover Publications, Inc., New York, 1966.*

interesting as facts only, but as signs of divine purpose in the ceaseless communication between man and God.

Thus, many educated Puritans busied themselves with matters of science in the seventeenth century. John Winthrop, Jr. is an outstanding example of a Puritan who was moved by an eager and persistent scientific curiosity. A graduate of Trinity College in Dublin, Winthrop found time outside of his duties as governor of New Haven colony to pursue his studies of science. He was a self-taught physician who experimented with chemical drugs made from herbs and minerals. Much of his experimentation was crude and simplistic but it did follow the path of chemical theory that represented the early efforts among English physicians to break away from the ancient teachings of Galen. Winthrop also investigated the composition of plants and minerals on a scale broader than that required for his medical experiments and communicated his findings to the Royal Society of London, in which membership was approved only for substantial scientific achievements. Winthrop, indeed, was chosen a fellow of the Royal Society in 1663.

No other New Englander was chosen to be a member of the Royal Society in the seventeenth century but a Philosophical Society, in imitation of the Royal Society, was founded in Boston in 1683. Its meetings contributed to the stimulation of scientific imagination as well as to the accumulation of scientific information. Harvard College, however, became the principal nursery of science in this century. In 1672 Harvard College received a gift of a three-and-one-half-foot telescope from John Winthrop, Jr. to encourage further studies relating to astronomy, and in 1686 Harvard adopted, for use by students, a compendium of physics which contained much of the new science of the time.

Such scientific stirrings were not enough to save the Puritans from the afflictions of a witchdraft hysteria at the end of the century. Even in their scientific inquiry, Puritans were particularly susceptible to delusions concerning human and natural events because such events might be signs of God's purpose. The great hardships of life encountered in their struggle to create a civilization in the American wilderness kept them in a continual turmoil of exaggerated hopes and fears. And their fears often outweighed their hopes in the later decades of the century. A major Indian war—King Philip's War—in the 1670's, and the troubles associated with the Andros regime and the recreation of the Massachusetts charter, strengthened the conviction that unseen forces were deviling the destiny of New England.

In 1688 a witchcraft case occurred in Boston. Four children were seized with fits and accused an old woman of bewitching them. The old woman was found to have a witch's collection of rag dolls which she stroked or pinched to cast the appropriate spells, and she confessed that she had made a pact with the devil. The woman was tried, found guilty, and executed for witchcraft according to the uses of seventeenth-century law. Since the children continued to exhibit symptoms of nervous disorders,

Science and Witchcraft

Cotton Mather, then a minister in Boston, took the oldest of the girls into his family, prayed with her and talked with her for weeks, until she was cured of her nervous affliction. Mather was so pleased with his success that he immediately published an account of his efforts in a book entitled *Memorable Providences Relating to Witchcraft and Possessions* (1689). His father, Increase Mather, had published *An Essay For the Recording of Illustrious Providences* in 1684, and now father and son had become New England's outstanding authorities on witchcraft.

Cotton Mather had written his book with an interest that was scientific as well as priestly. Witchcraft in this century, it must be remembered, was one of the numerous classes of natural phenomena like comets, lightning, herbs, and minerals that men of science were investigating. Mather observed all the child's symptoms and actions with intense interest and recorded them with meticulous care.

Cotton Mather undoubtedly intended to demonstrate to his readers how God's power had worked through him to a triumph over the Devil and the powers of darkness, but apparently the lurid details of the case described so vividly in the book inflamed the imaginations of the more emotionally unstable people in eastern Massachusetts. In 1692 a group of girls in Salem Village began to exhibit the same fits and jerks that had been manifested by the Boston children a few years before. This time there was no Cotton Mather to assist in a rapid cure of their nervous disorders. The whole situation quickly got out of hand; a vicious cycle of accusations, hysterical confessions implicating others in order to escape the gallows, special trials, and public executions took place. Within six months, 19 persons and two dogs had been hanged as witches, and a

Cotton Mather in . . . On Witchcraft . . . Mt. Vernon, New York, 1950. Rare Book Division. The New York Public Library. Astor, Lenox and Tilden Foundations.

The Tryal of G. B. at a Court of
OYER AND TERMINER,
HELD IN SALEM, 1692

man had been pressed to death for refusing to plead guilty or not guilty to such charges.

At first, the intellectual leaders of Massachusetts maintained a public silence that Samuel Eliot Morison has characterized as "cowardly." Certainly they knew that English law, available to the special court set up for the Salem trials, advised that "spectral evidence" was not enough to convict a person accused of witchcraft. Yet many of the accused in the Salem trials were convicted on the basis of testimony by alleged victims that they had seen the likeness of the accused in some "spectral" form. The frenzy of executions was halted, however, when Increase Mather, the president of Harvard College, prepared a treatise in which he attacked the use of "spectral evidence." The manuscript stating his opinion was signed by 13 ministers and presented to Governor Phips who, thereupon, dissolved the special court and ordered "spectral evidence" to be ruled out by Massachusetts courts in the future. By his action, New England was spared an even greater number of judicial murders because more than 150 persons were in prison awaiting trial and at least two hundred more had been accused of witchcraft.

The Salem witchcraft episode was a lesson not only in the rules of evidence at law, but also in the use of scientific evidence as well. Later in the decade, a Boston cloth merchant, named Robert Calef, wrote a stinging criticism of the witchcraft trials. Moreover, he went so far as to blame Increase and Cotton Mather for stimulating the hysteria by means of their writings on "memorable providences" and "wonders of the invisible world." His book, satirically entitled *More Wonders of the Invisible World* (1700), demolished many of the Mathers' explanations of "remarkable providences" with plain common sense. No printer in Boston dared to publish the book for fear of antagonizing such important personages as the Mathers, but Calef had it printed in London. The effort to suppress the book in Boston simply made more people eager to read it.

The Mathers, of course, were outraged by the book and published a reply to what they conceived to be false and scandalous charges. But, thereafter, no one, not even the Mathers, could take witchcraft so seriously as they had earlier.

Colonial Interest
in Natural History

Apart from New England scientific activity was less intense. Only in Virginia was there a sufficient cultivation of books and learning to generate a higher degree of scientific curiosity. William Byrd, one of the great planters of Virginia, built up a considerable library of books which included works on natural history. Byrd took great pleasure in his gardens and his flowers; botany, therefore, became an intellectual interest in which he had some knowledge and proficiency. This family heritage of scientific curiosity was carried on by his son, William Byrd II, who in 1699 was elected a member of the Royal Society of London. William Byrd II, like John Winthrop, Jr., fancied himself a physician and experimented with herbs with a view to developing new methods of chemical treatment. His first contribution to the Royal Society, however, was a paper entitled, "An Account of a Negro Boy That is Dappled in Several Places of His Body with White Spots."

In these early manifestations of scientific interest in seventeenth-century America, there was an overwhelming preoccupation with natural history. The environment of the New World was full of curiosities that excited the interest of Englishmen who were eager to compare and contrast the flowers, trees, birds, animals, rocks, and minerals of America with those that were known in England and Europe. This scientific activity was, for the most part, outside of the main currents of scientific thought and experimentation that were flowing from the work of Robert Boyle or Sir Isaac Newton. The men of intellect in English America were aware of the work of Boyle and Newton in charting new laws of physics but they lacked the mathematical competence to share in such activities. Hence, seventeenth-century American science had to be limited to fact-gathering and descriptions of the more obvious phenomena in the rich and exciting natural environment of America.

The First Fruits of Literature

Early Narratives
of America

Even while carrying on the tremendous tasks of clearing a wilderness and producing the necessary means for survival—food, shelter, and clothing—the first generations of Americans found time to express themselves in various forms of literature. The earliest writers, as one might expect, were explorers or settlers who were moved to describe the strange sights and remarkable occurrences that they experienced in America. Even after a full century of Spanish exploration and colonization, Europeans were still fascinated by the New World and eager to hear all that might be told about the possibilities of life in the great land across the Atlantic Ocean.

Captain John Smith, although he lived in America for only two years, shaped a story that persists in our literature by means of the dramatic tale of his rescue by Pocahontas. Historical scholars have often debated whether the Pocahontas story is fact or fiction since there was no mention of it in Smith's earliest account, *A True Relation of Occurrences and Accidents in Virginia,* published in 1608; the romantic episode was added in an expanded version of his experiences, published in 1624, under the title, *General Historie of Virginia, New England and the Summer Isles.* Most Americans, therefore, have forgotten how much useful information there is in Smith's writings about the geography of various regions of English America, about Indian life and customs, and about problems of settlement. On the other hand, the "brave encounters" between white men and the Indians which are part of the Pocahontas story struck deep roots in the American consciousness. Captain John Smith is the originator of a vast body of American fiction dealing with Indian-fighters and frontiersmen.

Our understanding of the early history of New England is greatly influenced by the chronicles of Plymouth and Massachusetts Bay written by their outstanding governors. William Bradford's *Of Plymouth Plantation* is a full account of Plymouth during the first three decades after the landing of the Pilgrims. Similarly, Governor John Winthrop's famous *Journal* is a record of occurrences in Massachusetts from 1630 to 1649. Both men wrote in the "plain style" that was highly valued in the Puritan literary culture.

Puritan Literature

William Bradford's *Of Plymouth Plantation* has many well-constructed passages made up of commonplace speech and homely images. The imagery of Bradford's historical narrative is close to the life of the village and the soil and conscious of changes of wind and weather. A modern student can readily respond to the power of Bradford's writing as he describes the plight of the Puritans when they first landed at Cape Cod:

Being thus passed the vast ocean, and a sea of troubles before in their preparation . . . they now had no friends to welcome them nor inns to entertain or refresh their weatherbeaten bodies; no houses or much less towns to repair to, to seek for succour . . . And for the season it was winter, and they that know the winters of that country know them to be sharp and violent, and subject to cruel and fierce storms, dangerous to travel to known places, much more to search an unknown coast—For summer being done, all things stand upon them with a weatherbeaten face, and the whole country, full of woods and thickets, represented a wild and savage hue. If they looked behind them, there was the mighty ocean which they had passed and was now as a main bar and gulf to separate them from all the civil parts of the world . . . What could now sustain them but the Spirit of God and His grace?

Even though modern Americans are far removed from the conditions of a primitive village life, Bradford's *History* can still be read with full appreciation of the strength of his "simple and sinewy" prose. Furthermore, no modern historian could possibly recreate with such clarity and certainty the impressions and the emotions of the Pilgrims at their first sight of America.

John Winthrop is as readable and quotable today as Bradford because of the simplicity and clarity of his prose. There are few expressions of political ideas in seventeenth-century writers that can match the directness of Winthrop's well-known "little speech" on authority and liberty given to the General Court in 1645. But Nathaniel Ward of Ipswich, the author of *The Simple Cobbler of Aggawam* (1647) and one of the chief compilers of the Body of Liberties for Massachusetts, equalled Winthrop in the economy of words and exceeded him in the liberality of his political ideas. "Authority," Ward stated simply, "must have power to make and keep people honest; People, honesty to obey Authority; both a joynt-Councell to keep both safe—He is a good King that undoes not his subjects by any one of his unlimited prerogatives: and they are good People, that undoe not their Prince, by any one of their unbounded Liberties—I am sure either may, and I am sure neither would be trusted, how good soever. . . . "

Occasionally, also, the poetry of the New England Puritans achieved such simplicity of language and imagery. This is apparent in the poetry of Edward Taylor of Westfield, whose poem "Huswifery" opens with the following lines:

> Make me, O lord, thy Spinning Wheele compleat.
> Thy Holy Words my Distaff make for mee.
> Make mine Affections thy swift Flyers meate
> And make my Soule thy holy Spoole to bee
> My Conversation make to be thy Reele
> And reele the yarn thereon Spun of thy Wheele . . .

The fact that Anne Bradstreet, a woman, could write poems made some of her contemporaries marvel. She wrote on topics ranging from physics to history, but her best poems were highly personal, such as the one written "Before the Birth of one of her Children." The following lines from that poem reveal the ever present awareness of the link between childbirth and death:

> And if I see not half my dayes that's due,
> What nature would, God grant to yours and you;
> The many faults that well you know I have,
> Let be interr'd in my oblivions grave;
>
> . . . .
>
> And when thy loss shall be repaid with gains
> Look to my little babes my dear remains.
> And if thou love thy self, or loved'st me.
> Those O protect from step Dames injury.

The poets who were particularly esteemed in seventeenth-century New England were those who used their verses for edification. Thus Michael

Wiggleworth's *The Day of Doom,* or *God's Controversy with New England* were best selling works because they were thoroughly didactic.

Eventually the successful use of the plain style by the first comers to Plymouth and Massachusetts gave way to more complicated and pretentious writings. This more elaborate style was taught to successive generations of students who passed through Harvard College, and the writing of leading Puritan intellectuals became more intricate, and more likely to flaunt impressive-sounding allusions, citations, and quotations. The supreme example of this tendency toward rhetorical embellishments and overabundant citations is to be found in the writing of Cotton Mather, particularly his *Magnalia Christi Americana.*

The *Magnalia,* however, is a significant summation of Puritan thought at the end of the seventeenth century, and it established an archetypical literary form that shaped discussions of American national identity long after Mather's death.

Cotton Mather's Magnalia

It is significant that this work is a history, for next to the sermon, the history was the most valued form of literature in Puritan New England. Since the Puritan believed that everything that had happened, disaster as well as triumph, even the minutest event, had been under providential management, the historian's task went beyond telling what happened to the fathoming of God's purpose as revealed in events. In this way, history became a means of instructing humans to live godly lives.

The *Magnalia,* completed in 1679 and published in 1702, was the most ambitious piece of historical writing produced in English America up to the end of the seventeenth century. Previous works of history had been much more limited in scope and technique. Edward Johnson's *The Wonder-Working Providence of Sion's Saviour in New England* (1654) was more allegory than history. Johnson's book reiterated the Puritan belief that the founding of New England was an important manifestation of God's plan for mankind, but it departed from the accepted Puritan technique of writing history by staying close to particular happenings or episodes.

A large portion of the *Magnalia Christi Americana* is made up of biographical sketches of the "fathers" of New England. For the Puritans, exemplary biographies were an essential part of history; they read the biographies of righteous men because such examples strengthened their faith and their resolve to live godly lives. Cotton Mather hoped that the exemplary lives of Bradford, Winthrop, Cotton, and others which were recorded in the *Magnalia* would cure the "degeneracy" which seemed to be afflicting the children of New England. Each year fewer adults seemed willing to seek membership in the church by testifying to a personal experience of regeneration. This raised a serious problem for the future of the church since only the children of church members could be baptized. "I hope," Cotton Mather asserted concerning his biographies of the founding fathers, "the plain history of their lives will be a powerful way of propounding their fatherly counsels to their posterity."

Nevertheless, the *Magnalia* is more than a jeremiad that laments the degeneracy of the children of the illustrious fathers of New England. Cotton Mather did not abandon the conviction that the Puritans were a chosen people and that New England was the culmination of world history, the ultimate manifestation of God's purpose as revealed in the events of human history. He had a grand vision of America's destiny which gave further point and meaning to the exemplary lives recorded in the *Magnalia.* The very first words of the *Magnalia* expressed this larger vision: "I write of the *Wonders* of the CHRISTIAN RELIGION, flying from the depravations of *Europe,* to the *American Strand."*

Cotton Mather believed that the hemisphere of America had been concealed from the eyes and minds of Europeans until the providence of God was ready to reveal it: "When the fulness of time was come for discovery." In his view, the English people were the chosen people for God's purposes in this new "ballancing half" of the globe. The vast efforts of the Spaniards and the French were dismissed by him because they had failed to participate in "the Reformation of Religion." Hence, in Mather's vision of America's destiny, "God sifted three nations that he might bring choice grain into this Wilderness."

In the historical imagination of Cotton Mather, the America which was encountered by the first comers to New England was a "rough wilderness" and "a desert full of dismal circumstances." The dominant theme in the Puritan epic as developed by Mather was the triumph of the Puritans over the inexpressible hardships of a wilderness where frost, hail, and the snows of harsh winters assailed them, and "bloody savages" were round about them like "wolves" in "every corner of the country." Yet "The God of Heaven," Mather made bold to assert, "so smiled upon the Plantacion—that no history can parallel it—an *howling wilderness* in a few years became a *pleasant land."*

Cotton Mather's *Magnalia Christi Americana* was the only general history of New England produced in the seventeenth century, but it was not the only historical work in English America that looked backward

tradition

Settlers came to the New World, but their lives did not begin completely anew. They brought with them the beliefs and expectations of the cultures they left. In time they would create a new kind of society and pattern of cultural values; at first, however, many expected to replicate the best of what they left. Family and wealth, signified in a coat of arms, were expected to provide the basis for the new society as they had in the old. But can traditional principles of stratification and symbols of status perform their accustomed function in a new society with an abundance of land?

Are these coats of arms themselves prophetic of change? What does it mean to see the traditional lion sharing space with the beaver, a prime symbol of the New World's natural resources?

Coats of Arms, New Netherlands. Manuscript Division. The New York Public Library. Astor, Lenox and Tilden Foundations.

Americans did not abandon the traditions and social conventions they brought with them from Europe, but they were subtly transformed as Americans used them to give order to their lives in a wilderness. The confrontation of inherited civilization and the virgin land is especially clear in this engraving depicting the orderly laying out of Savannah in the midst of the forest in 1734.

View of Savannah, 1734. *Library of Congress.*

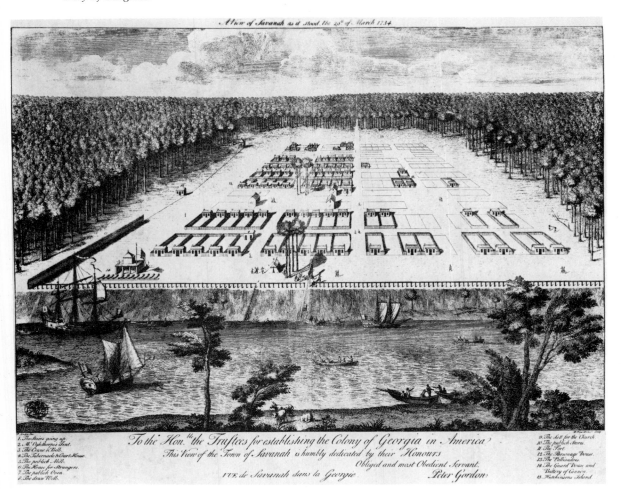

Settlement in the New World was a challenge for European culture. Many old goals were transformed and old restraints lightened. New energies were unleashed in the process and the way was opened for innovation, but the broad outlines of tradition remained firm.

Doe not the golden Meane, exceed,
In Word, in Passion, nor in Deed.

While adventurers felt the impulsive lusts that this woman teased out of life, they accepted the rules of behavior that encircled and constrained desire.

Parish Church, Atcham,
Shropshire England. *Courtesy, William H. Pierson, Jr.*

St. Luke's Church, Isle of
Wight County, Virginia,
1632. *Courtesy, Historic St.
Luke's Restoration. Photo by
Ken Cassell.*

Sometimes the appearance of cultural continuity was deceptive. Outward similarities in church architecture in England and Virginia mask vast differences in the church as it operated in the mother country and in the colonies. If the English church was supported by endowments of land and gifts, the Anglican church in Virginia had to resort to taxation. The territory covered by the Virginia parish was unworkably large by English standards, and the ministry poorly prepared and grossly underpaid. Most revealing of all, the church hierarchy in Virginia was frightfully weak by English standards; the churches in Virginia were controlled by the lay vestries rather than by traditional ecclesiastical officers.

Perhaps the sense of continuity provided by architecture made it easier for the English in the New World to cope with the social innovations forced upon them by circumstances. When members of the colonial elite, such as the Byrds of Virginia, built manor houses after the English fashion, the continuity of visual experience may well have supplied a sense of order and tradition for their lives.

Westover, *residence of the Byrd Family. Library of Congress.*

A planned landscape also provided a context of order for Europeans and Americans. If the nineteenth century celebrated the lightly restrained spontaneity and informality of the natural landscape park, the seventeenth and eighteenth centuries emphasized a formal classical order in their gardens.

Plate from Richard Blome's Gentleman's Recreation. London, 1686. Rare Book Division. The New York Public Library. Astor, Lenox, and Tilden Foundations.

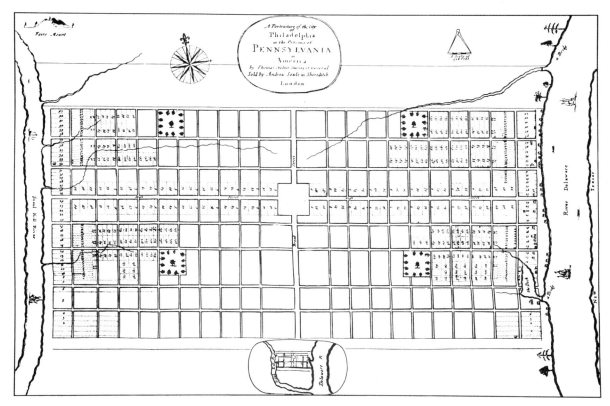

A portraiture of the city of Philadelphia. Cornell University Library.

When William Penn founded Philadelphia, he drew up a plan that would distinguish the order of civilized society from the natural landscape. In a city to be surrounded by wilderness he also provided for four parks. Why? Were Englishmen a bit afraid of the American wilderness and its dangerous potential for disorder? Is the urban park perhaps nature given order and rendered less threatening?

Clothes provided conventional symbols that gave order to social relations. In Europe the different classes of society could be identified by their dress. This tradition was brought to America, but in the fluid social structure men and women sometimes dressed above their class. It was no accident, therefore, that lower-class Virginians were fined for wearing the dress of upper-class gentle folk in the eighteenth century.

Etching called The Interview *in* Boston Magazine *for November, 1783. The Metropolitan Museum of Art, bequest of Charles Allen Munn, 1924.*

Were these traditional notions of dress compatible with Republicanism? Was there an important connection between dress, status, and power? Could dress shape—or reveal—one's identity? This merchant, ready to set sail a year before the minutemen fought the British army at Concord, conceived of himself and dressed in the style of an eighteenth-century, upper-class man. Did the success of the Revolution imply new conventions of dress?

Engraving in the Royal American Magazine *for March, 1774. Boston, 1774. Rare Book Division. The New York Public Library. Astor, Lenox and Tilden Foundations.*

The creation of a new nation and the projection of a distinctive national self-image or identity went hand in hand. Who was this new man, this American? What ought he strive to become? How were Americans related to Europeans and European traditions? Was there an American style or character? How did it differ from Europe's? What traditions—whether in dress or politics—were available to Americans? How did they transform these traditions? Hector St. John de Crèvecoeur, a Frenchman living in America on the eve of the Revolution, speculated on these questions in his book, Letters from an American Farmer, *but for most Americans it was a practical problem of how to act and even dress as an American.*

Portrait of Benjamin Franklin in William S. Baker's American Engravers and Their Works. *Philadelphia, 1875. The Henry E. Huntington Library and Art Gallery.*

Benjamin Franklin, who in his Autobiography *provided the essential image of the self-made American, expressed, almost caricatured, republican manners in the court of France with his affectation of frontier habits and by wearing a fur cap. But what of Franklin's upper-class contemporaries?*

However much wealthy Americans in the eighteenth century might have aped patrician dress, the American elite was different from traditional European aristocrats. If the American patrician indeed wore silk, we are reminded by this illustration from a schoolbook that there was no elite leisure class. The merchant is here at work, actively supervising workers on a dock. Again, visual similarities turn out to be superficial guides to the continuity of tradition. Beneath the appearance of aristocratic dress, one finds a working elite in America.

American merchant.
American Antiquarian
Society.

Portrait of Captain Samuel Chandler *by Winthrop Chandler. Gift of Edgar William and Bernice Chrysler Garbisch, 1933. National Gallery of Art, Washington, D.C.*

The formal patterns imitated by Americans were transformed into more generic American forms. Captain Samuel Chandler in this portrait sat in silken clothes, but he appears nonetheless roughhewn.

Did women's fashion also reveal the combination of patrician aspirations and active participation in a new and unfinished society with no true leisure class in the traditional sense? Did this provincial contradiction of English traditions make Americans appear a bit awkward in aristocratic poses?

Mrs. Josiah Martin, *Robert Feke, American, ca. 1705–1750. Oil on canvas. $50^1/_2'' \times 40^1/_2''$. Gift of Dexter M. Ferry, Jr. Courtesy of the Detroit Institute of Arts.*

Painting called The End of
the Hunt. *Artist Unknown.
Gift of Edgard William and
Bernice Chrysler Garbisch.
National Gallery of Art,
Washington, D.C.*

*The sporting tradition, just like dress, has often served to define an
elite and to reenforce the lines of social stratification. Was such the
case in colonial America? The patrician tradition of the hunt was
imported to America, but again there were suggestive differences.
The clear lines of class seem to be muted in this painting and
traditional expectations confounded. Does the dark tone of the
painting intentionally blend the whiteness of formal attire into the
background? And what are we to make of the rather ordinary
buildings we see? Would not an Englishman expect fine estate
houses in the background of an English hunt? Finally, we might ask
whether the plenitude of wild animals in America confused the
traditional rules of the hunt. When everyone could slay a deer, did
that mean that the hunt ended with everyone standing together as
equals?*

The Dinner Party, *Henry
Sargent. Courtesy, Museum
of Fine Arts, Boston. Gift of
Mrs. Horatio A. Lamb in
memory of Mr. & Mrs. Win-
throp Sargent.*

*Yet colonial America was undeniably a class society in which the
clothes, dwellings, possessions, and social life of the individual
closely correlated with class standing. And by the time of the
revolution, as American society matured, these differences were
quite sharp—to the point of stark contrasts. The immediate
environment of the elite was rich and elegant . . .*

. . . while the affairs of ordinary men and women were conducted in far plainer circumstances. Hence traditional ways of defining society—whatever their occasional ambiguities in America—remained important in the new republic.

Merrymaking at Wayside Inn. *The Metropolitan Museum of Art, Rogers Fund, 1942.*

from the perspective of the end of the century in an effort to discern a meaning in the American experience. In Virginia, too, there was a sufficiently long period of historical experience to supply materials and motives for creating a larger vision of America.

Unlike Massachusetts, however, Virginia had no well-developed literary tradition. The planters collected libraries and gave much time to reading, but they did not create a considerable literature of their own. The lack of a college deprived them of the stimulus of such an intellectual center. The Anglican clergymen who came to the colony were undistinguished in piety or learning. Thus, Virginia had been in existence for nearly a century before it produced a native historian. In 1705, Robert Beverley's *The History and Present State of Virginia* appeared in London, and from the pages of this work the modern student can obtain some idea of the quality of mind as well as the aspirations and values of a young Virginia aristocrat.

Beverley was the son of one of the wealthiest planters of Virginia who left an estate in excess of 50,000 acres. Robert Beverley, together with his

*Robert Beverley's
History of Virginia*

*Title page from Robert
Beverley's* The History and
Present State of Virginia.
*London, 1705. Rush Rhees
Library. The University
of Rochester.*

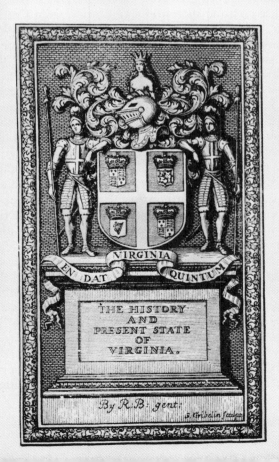

THE

HISTORY

AND

Present STATE

OF

VIRGINIA,

In Four PARTS.

I. The HISTORY of the First Settlement of *Virginia*, and the Government thereof, to the present Time.

II. The Natural Productions and Conveniencies of the Country, suited to Trade and Improvement.

III. The Native *Indians*, their Religion, Laws, and Customs, in War and Peace.

IV. The present State of the Country, as to the Polity of the Government, and the Improvements of the Land.

By a Native *and* Inhabitant *of the* PLACE.

LONDON:

Printed for R. *Parker*, at the *Unicorn*, under the *Piazza's* of the *Royal-Exchange*. MDCCV.

brothers, was sent to school in England, presumably the Beverley
Grammar School in Yorkshire. He married a daughter of William Byrd
and thereby became linked to another of the great families of Virginia. In
addition he was noted for his hard-headed and ceaseless pursuit of
wealth through the management of his plantation and through his land
speculations. In short, his whole life was shaped by the values and the
living style of the rising Virginia gentry.

Beverley's *History* is completely different in style and in method from
the works of New England historians like Cotton Mather. Anyone who
reads *The History and Present State of Virginia* will quickly discover that
Beverley is largely a secular historian with a pragmatic interest in the
affairs of this world and in the more materialistic motives of men. His
account of Bacon's Rebellion betrays the bias of Virginia's wealthy
planters, for he disparages the young rebel as a bold demagogue who
"was every way qualified to lead a giddy and unthinking Multitude."
Even so, Beverley recognized that the rebellion was a complex historical
event and his analysis of the fundamental causes of the rebellion displays
a remarkable perception of the interplay of political and economic factors
including the low price of tobacco, the tyranny of the English merchants,
the unfair tax policies, and the Indian disturbances.

The conception of America that is created by Beverley is strikingly
different in its physical aspect and its moral signification from Cotton
Mather's representation. Beverley's America is never a "howling wilderness"; nature, after all, was kinder in Virginia than in New England.
Beverley wrote many passages that expressed his delight with the
wonderful world of nature which he found in Virginia. He lingered over
descriptions of fishing hawks preying upon fish on a fair day in summer,
or of the odd shapes of flowers along a pasture fence, or of the delicious
taste of the red meat of a streaked watermelon. Indeed, he believed that
all men may be regenerated by the influence of America's idyllic
environment. "The clearness and brightness of the Sky add new vigour
to their Spirits, and perfectly remove all splenetick and sullen
thoughts . . . Here all their senses are entertained with an endless
Succession of Native Pleasures. . . ." Furthermore, Beverley even looked
back wistfully to the original state of nature in Virginia, "which the
native Indians enjoy'd without the Curse of Industry, their diversions
alone, and not their Labour, supplying their Necessities."

Like Cotton Mather, however, Beverley could not overcome a basic
ambivalence in his vision of America. On the one hand, he exalted the
virtues of a life lived close to "a Simple state of Nature;" on the other
hand, he lamented the laziness and stupidity of his compatriots amidst
the mild climate and easy abundance of Virginia. In the final pages of *The
History and Present State of Virginia,* therefore, he called upon Virginians
to redeem themselves by "Improvements." Men must improve the "gifts
of Nature" by a superior use of "Art and Industry"—by raising commodities other than tobacco: grain and provisions, flax, hemp, cotton

and silk; and even by intelligent experiments in wine-growing. Thus, Beverley's urges toward material success were a constant counterpoise to his effort to find a moral meaning for America in the simplicity of nature.

Cotton Mather and Robert Beverley are prime examples of the heritage of thought which was transmitted by seventeenth-century Americans to the further development of intellect and imagination in America. Cotton Mather's *Magnalia* was read by successive generations well into the nineteenth century. Hawthorne, Longfellow, and Whittier read and reread the *Magnalia* and Hawthorne, particularly, found materials and ideas there for his literary creations. Beverley's *History,* on the other hand, had fewer readers in America even in Virginia. Nevertheless, if one compares Jefferson's *Notes on the State of Virginia,* written in 1785, with Beverley's *History and Present State of Virginia,* a common tendency to blend history and natural history can be discerned. Neither Beverley nor Mather had a fully developed consciousness of being Americans—their perspectives are quite parochial—but their attempts to define a moral meaning for the American character were destined to reappear in many guises in the further history of American thought.

chapter five
The Course of Empire

*From Part IV in Theodore
DeBry's* America. *Rare Book
Division. The New York
Public Library. Astor, Lenox
and Tilden Foundations.*

Along the Imperial Way

The religious and political conflicts that agitated English society in the seventeenth century did not diminish the capitalistic spirit of Englishmen. Although the possession of landed property continued to be the symbol of social pre-eminence, the mercantile class was clearly the most dynamic group in English society. The century from 1660 to 1760 was an era of commercial and industrial growth in England, an era when the great mercantile houses of London and the lesser ports organized and channelled the output of the manufacturers of the midlands and the south of England into the avenues of foreign trade. At the beginning of the eighteenth century, England's population was less than 25 per cent urban, but agriculture was clearly declining in economic importance, and commerce and trade had become salient factors in the economic growth of the nation.

The Mercantilist Ideology

In the public dialogue during the latter decades of the seventeenth century, the advocates of mercantilist policies gained more and more prominence and won a respectful attention from the English government. The praise of trade was sounded again and again by the mercantilist pamphleteers such as George Phillips *(The Interest of England in the Preservation of Ireland, humbly presented to the Parliament of England, 1689)* who stated,

Trade is the glory, strength and security of the English nation, the fountain and source of the Riches, Wealth and Plenty, which render it the envy and astonishment of all the neighboring Kingdoms, and without which it were impossible to provide sustenance for the innumerable company of inhabitants wherewith the country is sufficiently furnished and the cities and towns are absolutely crowded.

Daniel Defoe, the editor for a time of a newspaper called *The Mercator,* and the author of *A Plan for English Commerce* (1728), as well as of numerous works of fiction, conceived of commerce as the essence of the English soul and society when he wrote,

England is a trading nation, the wealth and opulence of the nation is owing to trade, the influence of trade is felt in every branch of the government, in the value of its land, and the blood of trade is mixed and blended with the blood of gallantry, so that trade is the life of the nation, the soul of its felicity, the spring of its wealth, the support of its greatness, and the staff on which both king and parliament must lean, and which (if it should sink) the whole fabric must fall, the body politic would sicken and languish, its power decline, and the figure it makes in the world grow by degrees contemptibly mean.

To be sure, English mercantilism never became a rigid system of thought and policy. The mercantilist writers were often far from agreement as to problems and remedies in many aspects of economic development. They debated about questions of coinage, credit, exchange, banking, and interest; and they argued about the causes and cures for poverty and unemployment. Sometimes they disagreed about very fundamental questions of trade policy—whether to permit the importation of luxuries from France or whether to allow the importation of colorful calicoes from the East. By and large, however, there was widespread agreement that the American colonies existed primarily to benefit the mother country.

In view of such considerations, the merchant capitalists of England became less and less disposed to favor the earlier policy of developing colonies as private undertakings—either as proprietary or corporate colonies. They began to see the advantage of centralization—of disestablishing private colonies and placing them under the control of the royal bureaucracy. Most English mercantilists saw only two alternatives regarding the American colonies: either to keep them in a state of dependence and to monopolize their trade, or to give them a commercial liberty which might allow their trade to fall into the hands of some rival country like France. To most Englishmen, the latter alternative seemed almost unthinkable.

Imperial Rivalry of England and France

Since Englishmen were ready to believe that trade was the life of the nation, they were willing to make great sacrifices of blood and treasure to safeguard the source of their social health and strength. Hence, the relationship between trade and warfare became increasingly close in the eighteenth century. The English had already fought three naval wars with the Dutch in the seventeenth century to protect their imperial trading system. The consequence of these wars was the elimination of any serious threat of Dutch competition in England's North American trade. But, when France loomed as an even more serious rival than the Dutch had ever been, England fought four major wars with France between 1689 and 1763 to protect and enlarge the imperial system of trade and navigation.

Of course, there were other motives involved in the long years of warfare between England and France, but mercantilist considerations always occupied a central place in English policy. The accession of William III, head of the Dutch House of Orange, to the English throne in 1688 plunged England into a European war that had already broken out earlier in the year. King Louis XIV, because of his overweening ambition to conquer the Spanish Netherlands, had provoked William of Orange, the stadtholder of Holland, to form an alliance with Spain, Austria, and several German states to resist the armies of France. In accepting the English Crown, William of Orange sought to uphold the legitimacy of the royal succession in England since his wife was a daughter of the deposed James II but, at the same time, he accomplished his primary object of bringing England into the war against France. Moreover, the English merchants had been alarmed by the French colonizing ventures in North America. Consequently, they rallied around King William III in support of the war.

France was, indeed, a powerful commercial and colonial rival. Under the guidance of Jean Colbert, the great finance minister of Louis XIV between 1661 and 1683, a thoroughly mercantilistic policy had been developed which stimulated the growth of French industry and trade. Colbert had encouraged the establishment of colonies as producing areas rather than following the Dutch policy of using colonies primarily as trading posts. In the long run, therefore, Colbert's imperial scheme was more dangerous to England than the competition of the Dutch had ever been. Colbert envisioned an integrated empire in which France would produce manufactured goods, capital, merchant services, and shipping. The colonies of France in the West Indies would supply essential articles of consumption and raw materials—sugar, tobacco, cotton, ginger, dyewoods—in exchange for the manufactured goods of the mother country. Another purpose in his ambitious scheme was the establishment of slave trading stations in Africa, whence slaves might be shipped to the West Indian plantations. And finally, Canada and the Mississippi Valley were to supply furs to the French home market and serve as a

A French view of North America. 1690. Collection of j mara gutman.

market for French manufactured goods; in addition, Canada would be a source of foodstuffs and lumber products needed in the West Indies. Thus, the French colonial system threatened the English merchants at every point of the great triangular trading system which they had developed between the continents of Europe, Africa, and North America.

King William's War   The implications of this trade and colonial rivalry were already apparent in King William's War, the first of the great wars between England and France. This war began with a grandiose project by Louis XIV to conquer New York. Count Frontenac was sent to Canada as governor with instructions to invade New York from the north while a French fleet attacked Manhattan Island. Neither France nor Canada, however, had the resources for such an ambitious military and naval campaign and Frontenac had to content himself with sending French and Indian raiding parties against settlements in New Hampshire and Maine, as well as the English outpost at Schenectady, New York. New England troops under the command of Governor Phips of Massachusetts retaliated by capturing Port Royal in Acadia in 1690. Furthermore, an expedition of ships carrying two thousand men was led against Quebec by Governor Phips in 1690, but the attempt to strike at the heart of French power was a failure. Hence, when a treaty of peace was signed at Ryswick in 1697, the terms of the treaty regarding North America provided for a return to the pre-war situation.

Queen Anne's War   The War of the Spanish Succession (known as Queen Anne's War in America) was a much more decisive struggle. The conflict was precipitated in 1701 by Louis XIV who was determined to uphold the claim of his grandson, Philip of Anjou, as heir to the Spanish throne following the death of Charles II of Spain. Louis established his grandson at Madrid as King Philip V of Spain and seemed about to accomplish all the objectives that he had sought in the indecisive war with King William and more besides. By means of a family alliance with the Spanish Crown, Louis XIV hoped to dominate the Spanish Netherlands and the vast possessions of Spain in the New World. The English merchants, the English king, and the English people were determined to prevent such fruits of wealth, glory, and power from slipping into the hands of France. King William organized another Grand Alliance against France and a great war was fought over large areas and great distances in Europe and America for 12 long years into the reign of his successor, Queen Anne.

In North America, the governor of Canada launched savage raiding parties of French and Indians at settlements in New England, penetrating, at times, deep down the Connecticut River valley. After much bickering and delay, a British and colonial expedition, organized in 1710, succeeded in capturing Port Royal in Acadia. Subsequently, a large fleet of 70 vessels carrying twelve thousand men was sent against Quebec, but fog and storms created such havoc with the ships that the expedition returned to Boston without striking a blow. During Queen Anne's War, small forces of colonial militia operating with friendly Indians fought against the French in the Lake Champlain region, and against French and Spaniards in Florida and the Carolinas. By and large, however, the Caribbean was the principal theater of war in North America. There, British naval forces and British privateers were able to destroy and capture large numbers of French and Spanish vessels even though they lacked the means to capture French and Spanish possessions. By the end of the war, the grip of the English merchants on the West Indian trade was more secure than ever.

The War of the Spanish Succession was ended by the Peace of Utrecht in 1713. By this treaty, England won some decisive advantages in North America. France ceded to England the Hudson Bay region and Acadia, except for Cape Breton Island. England also obtained full acknowledgement of her title to Newfoundland, although the French retained certain fishing rights. England recognized Philip V as King of Spain but, in return, received a 30-year monopoly of the slave trade of the Spanish Indies. This *asiento,* so-called, granted the privilege of selling 4800 slaves a year to the Spanish colonies and importing directly to England the bullion and commodities taken in exchange for the slaves. Since the *asiento* included the privilege of sending one vessel a year of general merchandise to the Spanish colonial port of Porto Bello, the English merchants were provided with an entering wedge of enormous possibilities into the Spanish trade monopoly in the New World. Fully aware of such possibilities, the English government granted the *asiento* to a large company of merchant capitalists, the South Seas Company. In this way, the fruits of victory in the Treaty of Utrecht were shared by the Crown and the merchants.

After the Peace of Utrecht, the dominant colonial powers in the New World, England, France, and Spain, settled down to a long period of peaceful coexistence. A Hanoverian king had come to the throne of England with the accession of George I, and the Whig oligarchy that controlled the government was anxious to avoid war in order to allow time to establish the legitimacy and stability of the new dynasty. Two internal rebellions, largely of Scottish origin, took place in 1715 and 1745 but neither was successful in restoring a Stuart pretender to the throne. France sympathized with the cause of the Stuarts but, exhausted after the wars of Louis XIV, was equally unwilling to risk the possibility of a major war. Spain, too, joined in the complex diplomatic game of maintaining a wary peace.

A Wary Peace

The 25 years of relative peace after 1713 did not diminish the intense colonial rivalries of England and France in the New World. An aggressive economic and diplomatic competition simply replaced, for a time, the use of armed force to achieve mercantilist objectives. The mercantilists of England—merchants, tradesmen, and pamphleteers—had always regarded warfare as a weapon of last resort in the pursuit of the nation's trade policies. Most of the mercantilist pamphleteers reiterated their hatred of the disruptions of war and the burdensome costs of war preparations. Other things being equal, the merchants always preferred to carry on their trade in a world in which there was no apprehension of violence, no need to fear thieves, pirates, or men-of-war. Thomas Merchant, a leading mercantilist writer in the period of peace after the Treaty of Utrecht, affirmed this deep-seated belief in the interdependence of peace and prosperity in the title of his tract published in 1729, *Peace and Trade, War and Taxes, or the Irreparable Damage of New Trade In Case of War.*

Nevertheless, competitive coexistence proved to be a prelude to a more decisive test of power between England and France. The pressures for such a time of reckoning were built up primarily in the colonial ventures of both powers after 1713. America, more than ever, became attractive to European investors and speculators. The merchant capitalists of both England and France rushed into frenzied financial schemes to exploit the resources of the New World.

In France, the Mississippi Company, organized by John Law in 1717, was given a monopoly of the commerce of Louisiana and the beaver trade of Canada. Law was also able to secure a charter for a national bank; and this huge financial combination of bank and trading company was given charge of the collection of taxes and the issuance of a national currency in addition to its monopoly of French colonial commerce. Since the Mississippi Company promised to pay fabulous dividends, a speculative craze pushed the price of shares far beyond any reasonable possibilities of profit. In 1721 the "Mississippi bubble" burst and the resulting financial panic ruined thousands of investors and drove John Law out of France.

In England, a similar speculative spree took place in the affairs of the South Sea Company. Investors rushed to buy shares in the huge trading company when it was rumored that, in addition to the profits of the *asiento,* the South Sea Company was about to get control of the output of the silver mines of Peru. In 1720 Parliament gave the South Sea Company a more privileged status by authorizing it to manage the national debt. The "South Sea bubble" burst about the same time as the collapse of Law's overambitious operations in France. These financial episodes on both sides of the English Channel revealed the enormous capitalistic energies that were developing in England and France during the years of uneasy peace.

The crash of the "South Sea bubble" brought Sir Robert Walpole to power as chief minister in England, a position which he held for 20 years. Walpole was dedicated to a policy of financial retrenchment as the best means of achieving political stability for the Hanoverian dynasty. Hard-working and efficient, he reorganized the customs system and held the line as much as possible against any increases in taxes or public spending. Such a policy of retrenchment, however, could succeed only by a continued avoidance of war. Hence Walpole temporized and negotiated with great skill in the conduct of foreign policy in order to preserve peace with France and Spain.

Walpole's policies eventually aroused distrust in England and America as the rivalry of England, France, and Spain in the New World created new and more dangerous points of friction. France constructed the most powerful fortress in North America—Fort Louisbourg, on Cape Breton. The fishing merchants of England and New England actually began to lose ground in the face of the aggressive competition of France in the fishery of Newfoundland and New England. Also, it was obvious to anyone that Louisbourg, in time of war, could become a nesting place for French privateers. The situation was all the more dangerous because the loyalty of the French inhabitants in the newly acquired territory of Nova Scotia was doubtful.

In addition, France was pursuing a vigorous diplomacy among the Indian tribes of northern New England and the Great Lakes country. The alliances made by the French with the interior Indian tribes gave them an increasing advantage in the fur trade and posed serious problems of military security for the frontier settlements in the northern colonies of English America. The French were equally active up and down the Mississippi Valley where they and their Indian allies threatened the fur trade and the western land operations of Virginia and the Carolinas.

In the Caribbean, a commercial conflict of great intensity developed between England and Spain as a consequence of the *asiento*. The South Sea Company soon discovered that greater possibilities of profit could be realized from the sale of general merchandise to the Spanish colonies than from the slave trade. Hence, various forms of subterfuge were used to increase the sale of British goods. The annual ship to Porto Bello was stationed offshore where it was restocked at night with additional goods from fast-running trading sloops. The South Sea Company also sent trading vessels to unauthorized ports in Spanish America—Havana, Vera Cruz, Cartagena, and Buenos Aires. Of course, the Spanish struck back against this expanding contraband trade as best they could; they stationed guard ships in the Caribbean to seize unlicensed British vessels and, often in their zeal, the *guarda-costas* seized many innocent vessels.

In the face of increasing friction in the New World, Walpole's policy began to seem inglorious to a new generation of aspiring political leaders in England. Even within Walpole's ministry there were grumblings of discontent; the Duke of Newcastle, one of the younger Secretaries of State, favored a more aggressive policy toward Spain. Among the opposition groups in Parliament there were ambitious young men like William Pitt, the grandson of a buccaneering East Indian merchant, who was thoroughly imbued with the belief that England's greatness depended on seizing and holding a lion's share of the world's trade.

By 1739, Walpole could no longer withstand the growing pressures against his pacific policy. The mercantile interests aroused public and parliamentary sentiment by circulating stories of atrocities committed against British traders by the Spaniards. A certain Captain Jenkins furnished vivid evidence of such atrocities by exhibiting around London one of his ears which he claimed had been cut off by Spanish officials. Walpole wanted to negotiate the Caribbean question with Spain, but the South Sea Company and other merchants combined to defeat his plan. Matters came to a head in May, 1739, when Spain suspended the *asiento* and, in less than six months, the British merchants, Parliament, and his junior ministers forced Walpole to go to war. "It is your war," Walpole said to Newcastle, "and I wish you the joy of it."

The "War of Jenkins Ear" with Spain soon became part of a larger European war when King Fredrick of Prussia attacked the Austrian provinces of Maria Theresa, the new empress of the Hapsburg dominions. France joined with Prussia and then with Spain against an alliance, formed by England in support of Austria, that included Holland, Saxony, and Russia. By means of these complex maneuvers, England and France were at war again in 1744.

King George's War   In America, the most significant event of King George's War was the capture of the powerful French fortress at Louisbourg. This venture was promoted largely by the merchants of Massachusetts who had been greatly alarmed over the French threat to their trade and their fishery. Massachusetts voted £50,000 to support an expedition and troops were contributed by other New England colonies besides Massachusetts. In addition, military supplies and provisions were sent from New York, New Jersey, and Pennsylvania. After a 49 day siege, Louisbourg surrendered to the force of four thousand men and a hundred vessels commanded by Colonel William Pepperell of Maine, one of the richest men in New England with large investments in Maine lands and the New England fishing trade.

The New Englanders, however, were unhappy to discover that their interests in controlling Louisbourg and New England were pawns in a larger imperial game. By the peace treaty signed at Aix-la-Chappelle (1748), Britain returned Louisbourg to France in order to regain for the British East India Company the trading post at Madras, India, captured by the French during the war. Even though England provided large sums of money to New England to help redeem the depreciated currency that had been issued to finance the Louisbourg expedition, the disregard for New England's interests left a legacy of resentment.

In every respect, the Treaty of Aix-la-Chappelle was inconclusive; all conquered territories were returned to their former owners and the main points of friction remained unresolved. Leading Englishmen recognized that a resumption of warfare was only a question of time. In the uneasy peace after Aix-la-Chapelle, the oratory of William Pitt in the Parliament created an enlarged vision of empire in the minds of the English people. Indeed, Pitt was to be called "the Great Commoner" because he seemed to be able to speak so directly to the deeply-felt desires of the people of all classes. Although he filled his speeches with appeals to grandeur and glory, he never forgot the essential interest of the British empire; he fully believed that "when trade is at stake . . . you must defend it or perish."

The opportunity for leadership did not come easily for Pitt. He was hated by George II and regarded as an upstart politician by the Newcastle ministry. But the renewal of conflict with France in the Seven Years' War (1756-1763) gave Pitt the power that he was so eager to use. After the initial reverses of the war, Newcastle was forced to give Pitt a place in the cabinet and the chief direction of the war effort, as well. Pitt's ego was more than equal to the responsibilities of power. "I know that I can save the country," he said, "and that I alone can." It was his driving energy, indeed, which made it possible to organize the great victories against the French in North America, the West Indies, Africa, and India. Although Pitt's task included participation in a European struggle between an alliance of England and Prussia on the one hand and an alliance of France and Austria on the other, the Seven Years' War was truly a war for empire that was fought all around the world.

The French and Indian War

The first skirmishes of the new conflict took place in America a full year before the formal outbreak of hostilities between England and France. As early as 1754, a French force drove a small unit of Virginians led by young George Washington out of Fort Necessity on the headwaters of the Ohio River. The French, thereupon, built Fort Duquesne at the main fork of the upper Ohio River and thereby menaced the fur-trading and land speculative operations of Virginia and other colonies. A force of British troops led by General Braddock and accompanied by colonial militiamen was sent to dislodge the French but was cut to pieces by a combined party of French and Indians. For Virginians, the French and Indian War, as the Seven Years' War was known in America, began a full year before the English government officially declared a state of war with France.

During the Seven Years' War, the main effort of the English in America was directed against the Ohio Valley and Canada. Pitt decided to make America the chief battleground of the entire war against France. Hence, more British ships, troops, and money were sent to North America than in any previous war. Such British forces in combination with colonial troops were able to win striking successes against the French and their Indian allies. In 1758, Louisbourg was conquered, Fort Duquesne was taken and renamed Fort Pitt, and the capture of Fort Frontenac (located on the northeastern side of Lake Ontario) opened a route of invasion down the St. Lawrence River valley. In 1759, a three-pronged attack was launched at the heart of French power in Canada. One force was sent to capture Fort Niagara and separate Canada from the upper Mississippi valley region; a second expedition under Lord Jeffrey Amherst was to proceed toward Montreal over the Lake Champlain route; and a third expedition was to move in a fleet of ships up the St. Lawrence to take Quebec. Lord Amherst was delayed by the winter after seizing Ticonderoga and Crown Point, but Wolfe won a notable victory at Quebec after his daring ascent to the Plains of Abraham. The full conquest of Canada, however, was not completed until 1760 when Lord Amherst was able to move his army and when additional reinforcements reached Quebec from England.

William Pitt, the architect of these great victories in America as elsewhere around the world, was forced to resign because of the opposition of the new king, George III, who had built up considerable influence with members of Parliament. The reorganized ministry, therefore, conducted the prolonged negotiations with France and Spain for peace. Although the Treaty of Paris of 1763 which ended the war was denounced by Pitt because the West Indian islands of Guadalupe and Martinique were returned to France, Great Britain emerged with a lion's share of the spoils of war. By the terms of the Treaty of Paris, Great Britain received Canada as well as French recognition of her territorial claims west to the Mississippi River. Spain ceded Florida to England as the price for the return of Cuba and the Philippines which had been captured by the British during the last years of the war. France compensated Spain for the loss of Florida by ceding the territory of Louisiana west of the Mississippi.

The enlarged vision of a trading empire which had been growing in the English imagination was now a reality. In the words of George Macauley Trevelyan, one of England's foremost historians, "The English race was at the top of golden hours." But the grandeur that was England's was solidly based on the commitment to commerce as the lifeblood of the Empire and the health of the English state. And it was within the framework of such commercial values that the American colonies shaped their aspirations and their destiny in the eighteenth century.

English Mercantilism and Colonial Capitalism

The English people took the highroad to empire in the eighteenth century with a political system that had been significantly altered by the "Glorious Revolution." The problem of sovereign power which had perplexed judges and leaders of Parliament, and which had given focus to the writing of seventeenth-century political theorists, was resolved in favor of the supremacy of Parliament. The Bill of Rights, enacted into law as part of the revolution settlement of 1689, included provisions stating that the king could not suspend laws, nor could he maintain an army or levy taxes without the consent of Parliament. The Bill of Rights also demanded frequent Parliaments and stipulated that the king should not interfere with parliamentary elections or debates.

The Imperial Trading System   Thus, after 1689, the ultimate control of affairs within England and the Empire was in the hands of Parliament but, in actual practice, Parliament, before 1763, did not make full use of its increased authority in the

Young Americans of the early eighteenth century. Two Boys with Pets, c. *1730 by an Anonymous American artist. Philadelphia Museum of Art, Collection of Edgar William and Bernice Chrysler Garbisch, 1967. Photograph by A. J. Wyatt, staff photographer.*

realm of colonial affairs. Many English merchants hoped that Parliament would assume more direct management of the colonies; they were dissatisfied with the Lords of Trade because the latter seemed to represent too much the interests of the landed aristocracy and the royal court. In 1696, a bill actually was considered to create a parliamentary council to manage trade and colonial affairs. King William III, however, was a jealous guardian of what remained of kingly prerogative; he used his influence to head off a final vote on the bill and, at the same time, sought to appease the merchants by creating a new colonial agency—the Lords Commissioners of Trade and Plantations, commonly known as the Board of Trade. Thereafter the Board of Trade became the key agency in shaping colonial policies during the eighteenth century.

The Board of Trade had no power to make or enforce decisions, but it had authority to investigate all matters relating to trade or the colonies and to make recommendations to Parliament and to the administrative departments of the Crown. Although the Board often seemed excessively slow and deliberate, the superior information gathered by the working members enabled them to influence orders of the king's council and acts of Parliament affecting trade or the colonies. Furthermore, in 1752, the Board of Trade was given the authority to nominate for the king's approval the names of all persons to be governors, deputy governors, councillors, and secretaries, as well as the names of inferior officers necessary for the administration of justice. In addition, the Board of

Trade was to prepare all commissions and instructions for such appointees.

During the first half of the eighteenth century, Parliament was content to enact legislation outlining the regulation of trade as well as the particular forms of colonial economic activity that had special significance for the self-sufficiency of the British Empire. Although Parliament abandoned its attempt to set up a Parliamentary council for trade and colonies, a Navigation Act of 1696 satisfied the demands of English merchants by providing for the more efficient enforcement of the acts of trade and navigation. Thereafter, all colonial governors, whether appointed by the king or proprietors, or elected as in Rhode Island and Connecticut, were to serve only if approved by the king and were to be subject to dismissal if they did not take an oath to enforce the navigation laws. In addition, colonial merchants were required to post a bond to assure that any enumerated commodities would not be re-exported to foreign ports; and English customs agents in the colonies were given rights of search as stringent as those possessed by the customs service in England.

The Privy Council added further strength to Parliament's efforts to tighten colonial administration by authorizing colonial governors to establish vice-admiralty courts, which eventually numbered 12. All were subject to a ruling by the king's attorney-general which eliminated the use of juries in cases involving violations of the acts of trade and navigation. Despite the new legislation, English naval units in America were too few to search and seize any large numbers of vessels that were presumed to be violating the navigation laws. Enforcement depended on seizures made in colonial ports; hence, colonial courts continued to claim jurisdiction in such cases originating within the colony and carried on a prolonged struggle with the admiralty courts during the eighteenth century.

Restrictions on Colonial Manufactures

To protect their interests further, the merchants and manufacturers of England were able to secure a series of acts restraining certain forms of colonial economic development. The manufacture of woolens, which had become a major activity in England's industrial development, was in a depressed period at the end of the seventeenth century and members of Parliament were persuaded that one cause was the growth of the colonial cloth industry, particularly in New England. The preamble of a Woolen Act passed by Parliament in 1699 declared that "great quantities . . . of manufactures . . . have of late been made and are daily increasing . . . in the English plantations in America which will inevitably sink the values of lands and tend to the ruin of the trade and woolen manufactures of this realm." The Woolen Act prohibited the exportation of wool or woolen cloth of American production from any colony; thus household manufacturing for the local market of any colony was permitted but the colonial woolen industry was not to be allowed to expand into the common market of the Empire.

In 1732 similar legislation was enacted to restrain the hat industry in the colonies. The Hat Act prohibited the transportation of hats from one colony to another colony or elsewhere, permitting only local manufacture. By the middle of the eighteenth century, also, the iron manufacturers of England were complaining of the growing competition of colonial iron-making. After 1730 numerous forges and furnaces in New England and the middle colonies were turning out bar iron of excellent quality judged by the standards of the eighteenth century. In 1750, therefore, Parliament enacted the Iron Act which prohibited the setting up in America of any new steel furnaces, slitting mills, and plating forges; however, pig iron and bar iron were permitted to enter the English market without any payment of duties. Hence, the Iron Act encouraged the colonial production of crude iron but sought to restrain the further growth of an American iron industry which could produce finished products like steel tools, nails, and sheet iron.

Substantial restraints were also placed on the currency systems in the American colonies. The financial burdens of the wars against the French led many of the colonies to issue bills of credit as a form of currency to help pay the costs of military operations. The issuance of bills of credit on a large scale was particularly necessary in New England where extensive campaigns against the French were supported in each of the wars of the eighteenth century. At the same time, the growth of commerce in the colonies was producing a more sophisticated attitude among American merchants toward the use of various forms of paper credit and currency, especially since specie was always scarce in America. But the rapid depreciation of colonial bills of credit alarmed English merchants who had developed the practice of extending long credits to their buyers in America. It was essential for the security of their exchange and credit operations to have a stable and reliable currency. So, in 1751, Parliament forbade the New England colonies to make any further issues of legal tender bills of credit.

The regulations of colonial economic affairs by Parliament were not always designed to restrain or curtail colonial economic activity. Some measures were intended to encourage colonial productions which were thought to be beneficial to the English mercantilist system. Beginning in 1705, extensive efforts were made to encourage the making of naval stores in the colonies—tar, pitch, turpentine, resin, and hemp. A liberal bounty was provided by acts of Parliament for the delivery of such products at any of the customs houses in England. Similar bounties were offered for indigo after 1748 and, in the 1760's, lumber products of all kinds received generous bounties. Also, by a series of parliamentary statutes, the cutting of white-pine trees, suitable for the use of the Royal Navy, was put under restraint and could not be harvested without a certificate.

To consolidate the imperial trading system further, the English Parliament, from time to time, extended the list of enumerated com-

modities which were to be sent to the English market before reshipment to Europe. By the middle of the eighteenth century naval stores of all kinds—molasses, beaver skins, and copper ore—were added to the original list of commodities enumerated in the Act of 1661. At the same time, the navigation and trade system was used more directly by Parliament as a weapon of economic warfare against France. Thus, the Molasses Act of 1733 was designed to wreck the economy of the French West Indian sugar islands. By this act, high duties were placed on foreign sugar, molasses, and rum imported into the English American colonies; it was hoped that such regulations would give the British West Indies a monopolistic advantage in the American market.

Although the elaborate system of economic controls that was developed for the British Empire between 1660 and 1760 was designed primarily to benefit the mother country, the American colonies waxed rich and strong within the protecting walls of the common market of the

Courtesy of The New-York Historical Society, New York City.

British trading system. Much of this prosperity, however, depended upon evasion of the imperial regulations. Enterprising colonists earned high profits from illegal trade, particularly with the French West Indies.

The shipbuilding industry, already vigorous in seventeenth-century America, flourished to the point of making British North America one of the world's leading shipbuilding centers. Although ships were built everywhere in the colonies, New England remained the main center of the shipbuilding industry. The shipyards of Massachusetts employed highly skilled shipwrights and the forests of New England furnished a plentiful supply of white pine for masts and yardarms, and an almost inexhaustible supply of oak for beams and boards. Early in the eighteenth century as many as 140 ships a year were being launched in Massachusetts shipyards; about a third of these were sold to English merchants and, by 1775, it is estimated that 30 per cent of all ships employed in the commerce of England had been built in America. Indeed, during the first half of the eighteenth century, it was estimated that some Massachusetts shipyards could build a merchant ship for about half the cost of a similar ship built in England. In view of such a comparative advantage, it is not surprising that shipbuilding should have been such an important pacemaker in the growth of the American economy. Shipbuilding stimulated a whole host of subsidiary enterprises in lumbering and in the production of naval stores, sails, and cordage— all of which would probably have flourished even without the added advantage of parliamentary bounties.

The Growth of Colonial Capitalism

Although a large portion of the ships constructed in America was sold to buyers in England, the greater portion was used by colonial merchants. Large numbers were always used in the New England fishery; by 1750 about six hundred fishing vessels were operating in the great cod and mackerel beds off the coasts of Maine and Nova Scotia. In addition, colonial merchants took away from the English merchants the lion's share of the colonial carrying trade outside of the West Indies. In 1753, for example, all but 64 of 496 vessels that cleared from Boston harbor had been constructed in Massachusetts, and only 12 carried a British registration. The American merchants, particularly of the northern colonies, were driving hard and successfully against competing mercantile houses in London and the outports of England.

Such vigorous enterprise on the part of colonial merchants stimulated the rapid growth of all sectors of the American economy. A large distilling industry grew up in New England, New York, and Pennsylvania, where rum was manufactured from the molasses brought from the West Indies. In 1750 the 63 distilleries of Massachusetts alone produced two million gallons of rum for export. Rum was not only the drink of the common people, it was an extremely valuable trading item in the fur trade with the Indians and in the slave trade carried on between Africa and the West Indies.

The enterprise of the colonial merchants lured many and varied types of colonial producers into the profitable markets of the Empire. The farmers, meat-packers, and flour millers of the middle colonies and Virginia began to market large surpluses of wheat, flour, bread, beef, pork, and horses which were carried to the West Indies and elsewhere. These American products were able to compete successfully with English and Irish flour, pork, and beef. Similarly, rice grown in South Carolina was able to compete successfully with Mediterranean rice because of its superior quality; thus rice was added to tobacco as another great staple crop produced for export in the southern colonies. And from the vast interior forests of North America came a great volume of furs and skins acquired by trade with the Indians and shipped to England from the entrepôts of New York, Philadelphia, and Charleston, South Carolina.

Among these impressive evidences of economic vitality, the growth of a flourishing iron industry in eighteenth-century America was startling proof of the strength and sophistication of colonial capitalism. The iron industry was an economic activity of great significance to the economic life of England; iron-making was considered to be one of the sinews of mercantilist self-sufficiency and already exhibited certain characteristics of large-scale organization that would make it an important component of England's industrial revolution. Consequently, Parliament had good reason to be alarmed at the rapid growth of American iron manufacturing. By 1758 there were 14 furnaces and 41 forges in Massachusetts and additional iron works in Connecticut and Rhode Island. Pennsylvania had 37 centers of iron production by 1750 including slitting mills and plating forges as well as the ordinary furnaces and forges; indeed, a few small-capacity steel furnaces had come into operation after 1732. At mid-century, Pennsylvania was clearly the greatest iron producer of all the American colonies.

The Iron Act of 1750, therefore, was a back-handed tribute to the enterprise and technical skills of the American iron-makers. Indeed, the Iron Act could not check the expansion that had already proceeded so rapidly in the first half of the eighteenth century. According to the estimates of a leading authority on the British regulation of the colonial

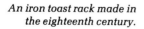

An iron toast rack made in the eighteenth century.

iron industry, the American colonies were producing three times the amount of iron in 1775 that had been produced in 1750; by 1775, there were actually more furnaces and forges in operation in the American colonies than in England and Wales.

The flourishing condition of colonial capitalism was becoming a source of strain and conflict within the mercantile system of the British empire at the turn of the century. The Board of Trade was constantly preoccupied with problems associated with a large amount of illegal trade carried on by colonial merchants. Earlier in the century, this illegal trade sometimes assumed the more virulent form of piracy when colonial privateers took advantage of the war with France and Spain to prey on all forms of commerce. Although piracy was largely suppressed at the end of Queen Anne's War, colonial merchants continued to violate the acts of trade and navigation even in time of war. Indeed, trading with the enemy islands of the French West Indies was flagrant and flourishing during the Seven Years' War. Such activities, however, should not be taken as evidence of any wholesale assault by colonials on the imperial trading system; many merchants carried on a legal trade, still others operated legally or illegally according to particular calculations of advantage.

Cross-Pressures of Class, Ethnicity, and Religion

The economic growth of the colonies within the expanding market of the British Empire enlarged and strengthened the colonial elites. The great family fortunes of eighteenth-century America were derived directly or indirectly from trade; and the peculiar structure of the imperial market increased the natural advantages of those who already possessed large amounts of capital. The evidence is unmistakable that those families that had already achieved high status were able to use their great social advantages to increase their wealth and power.

The preferential position in the English market enjoyed by tobacco, rice, and other southern staples intensified the drive for commercial profits in southern agriculture and widened the distance between large planters and small freeholders. The annual volume of tobacco exports alone increased from 28,000,000 pounds from 1700 to 1710 to 102,000,000 pounds from 1771 to 1775; and as the production of all southern staples became greater, the competitive conditions of the market favored the larger units of production employing larger forces of disciplined laborers. The growth of black slavery became the visible sign of the increasing social power of the aristocratic planters.

The Planter Elite

The importation of slaves in the eighteenth century was enormous. In Virginia, for example, there were 16,000 slaves in a total population of about 70,000; in 1756, Governor Dinwiddie estimated a total population for Virginia of 293,000, of whom 173,000 were white and 120,000 were black. After 1710, indeed, the annual immigration of white indentured servants to Virginia and other southern colonies had dropped sharply. On the other hand, the demand for slaves had become so great that Parliament revoked the monopoly of slave trading which it had granted to the Royal African Company and threw open the traffic to independent merchants and traders within the Empire.

Inexorably, the forces of the market accelerated the development of the slave system in southern agriculture. The planters were continually in debt to the English merchants who extended long-term credit for the purchase of English goods; at the same time, the growing exhaustion of the soil by constant planting of tobacco created an additional economic squeeze. The narrowing margin of profit impelled the planter capitalists to make even greater use of slave labor, thereby increasing the proportion of blacks in the southern colonies. The 120,000 blacks in Virginia in 1756 represented over 40 per cent of the population; in 1751, there were 25,000 white settlers in South Carolina and 40,000 blacks; in 1775 Governor Sharpe of Maryland reported that there were 40,000 blacks there in a total population of 140,000.

Everywhere in the southern colonies, the wealthy planters strengthened their grip on the sources of political power. The political stronghold of the planter elite in each of the colonies was the Governor's Council and the political effectiveness of the leading families was greatly strengthened by a solidarity that was based upon extensive intermarriage. In Virginia for example, during the century from 1680 to 1775, only 57 family names appeared in the list of 91 men who received appointment to the Council; nine of these family names accounted for nearly one-third of the Council seats during that entire period. Similar evidence for the power of planter elites may be found in Maryland and the Carolinas.

In the southern colonies, the councillors who were so closely connected by ties of family and economic interest were able to prevent the development of land or tax policies that were contrary to their interests. Of course, they were greatly outnumbered by the enfranchised freeholders but their wealth and their status gave them enormous advantages in the social climate of the eighteenth century when habits of deference were still fairly strong in the American population.

Whenever the habits of deference could not be counted on, the planter elites were quite willing to use techniques of political manipulation to accomplish their ends. The leading families of the southern colonies were able to influence elections at every level of government. From their group came the principal county officers, the judges, and the colonels of the militia. In Virginia the leading families usually held the majority of the seats in the House of Burgesses as well as in the Governor's Council. Such advantages of power were put to good use by the Virginia gentry who became notorious for their land-grabbing activities in the eighteenth century: Councillor William Bassett and his son-in-law received 15,000 acres in 1720; Councillor John Carter received 20,000 acres in 1728 and 6000 more in the next year; and a group of planter speculators led by

Councillor William Randolph received grants in 1738 totalling 104,000 acres.

The Elite in New York

The elite of New York developed a system of social and political power that was based upon extensive family networks that formed political factions. Between 1691 and 1775, 13 of the 17 families with the largest estates in the province were listed in the rolls of the Governor's Council. Yet it was not a monolithic upper class. By the middle of the eighteenth century much of New York's political history amounted to feuding and conflict among the various factions and family networks, particularly the Livingstons and Delancys. Politics was the mechanism by which these families advanced their interests. And the interests of the family alliances went beyond the landed estates with which they were identified. Each family included relatives who were in the professions and who were New York City businessmen. Indeed, whenever the legality of any of their activities was called into question, representatives of these families generally occupied the judicial posts and sat in judgment on cases materially affecting their relatives.

The Aristocracy of Trade

The rapid expansion of colonial cities was accompanied by visible signs of aristocratic pretension; the social cleavages now became more distinct and the symbols of high social station could be displayed on a grander scale. Carriages and coaches, exceedingly rare in the seventeenth century, became the common mark of gentlemanly status in the eighteenth century. The elite of Boston, New York, or Charlestown rode through the streets in decorated carriages, driven by liveried drivers, and drawn by fine horses—for all to see and for ordinary tradesmen and laborers to envy. Other evidences of riches and display appeared in the cities of America—stately houses, richly carved furniture, gold-framed mirrors, silver plate, and jewels. Everywhere, men of wealth developed a taste for finery; wealthy merchants appeared in brilliantly colored coats and waistcoats fringed with lace and other fashionable materials. By the middle of the century, indeed, London merchants understood very well that Boston and other cities provided them with a ready market for the latest English fashions.

Brocaded silk shoes, probably made in Baltimore, c. 1758. From Index of American Design. National Gallery of Art.

Silver teapot made by John Coney (1655–1722). Boston. Early eighteenth century.

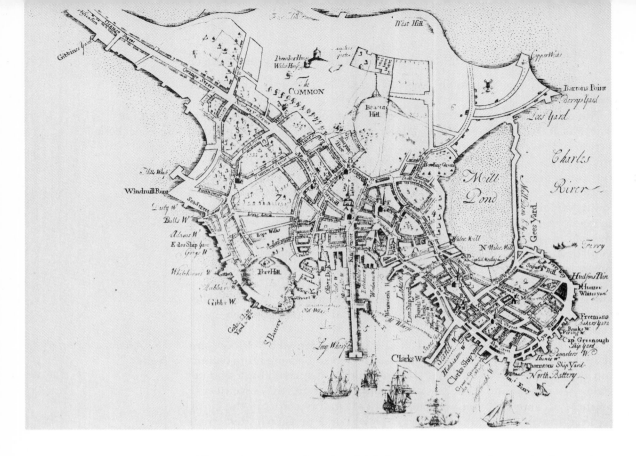

The aristocracy of trade which became so conspicuous in the seaport towns had ready access to the centers of political power. In Pennsylvania, the Council was solidly representative of the Quaker merchant class. Moreover, Quaker merchants frequently served in the Assembly and, until 1756, were able to dominate the law-making body. In addition, the government of Philadelphia was practically a closed corporation controlled by Quaker merchants.

In Massachusetts, also, the merchants of Boston and other eastern towns were able to command political power far out of proportion to their numerical strength. By virtue of the modest property qualifications for voting in the charter of 1691 and the democratic character of the town meetings, Massachusetts had a broadly based political system which has been labelled a middle-class democracy. Yet the key committees in the House of Representatives were often controlled by merchants and lawyers from eastern Massachusetts. The Governor's Council, which was elective in Massachusetts, displayed a pattern of influence similar to that in other colonies; members of prominent merchant families, such as the Cushings, Hutchinsons, Wheelwrights, and Olivers, were elected to the Council more often than any others.

The true character of eighteenth-century American society cannot be defined unless one accepts the historical reality of an elite with aristocratic pretensions—the evidence is unmistakable that the colonial elites envisioned a permanent future for themselves. The high incidence of intermarriage within the relatively small group of ruling families in every province revealed a desire to establish enduring bloodlines of status and power. In addition, the colonial elites had advantages in education and social communication that could not be matched easily by any of the other classes in the social order—their economic operations were wider, they travelled more, they knew more of the larger world of affairs, they shaped and concerted their ideas in their discussion clubs. They were able, indeed, to establish a consciousness of their common class interests across the boundary lines of individual colonies. This was particularly true in the cities where there were constantly widening contacts with the outside world. "Socially and spiritually, as well as in trade and politics," Carl Bridenbaugh observed in his study of eighteenth-century cities, "the gentlefolk of all five cities came to know one another better, to exchange amenities and to sense their common bonds in the leadership of American society."

Although successive generations of dominance nourished hopes of permanence within the colonial elites, the future of such aristocratic pretensions was destined to be precarious. The peculiar conditions of American society created social cross-pressures that undermined the foundations of the American aristocracy while they were being laid. Indeed, the same process of economic growth which benefitted the established families threatened to inundate their exclusive claims to privilege with multiplying claims of wealth and influence. A permanent elite flourishes best in a traditional society or in a society in which new holdings of wealth are not created so rapidly that the newly rich cannot be digested and absorbed by the older gentry. But, in a society where rapid economic development is accompanied by an equally rapid population growth, the claims to higher status cannot be controlled or stabilized so easily.

The Middling Classes

The literature of eighteenth-century America is full of references to the "better sort," the "middle sort," and the "meaner sort"—indicating a widespread acceptance of loosely-defined status. But within this three-fold delineation of status, the most rapidly expanding class in America continued to be the "middling class." America continued to be the place where the ruling passion was to be a freeholder. Cadwallader Colden, the lieutenant-governor of New York, wrote, "The hopes of having land of their own and becoming independent Landlords is what chiefly induces people into America." In the growing towns and cities of eighteenth-century America, the opportunities for economic independence also increased for skilled artisans and craftsmen. As a matter of fact, the worker with special skills—the shipwright, the printer, the tailor, the cabinet-maker—might rise even more rapidly than a freehold farmer to a position of wealth and social position. A Philadelphia newspaper in 1776 took note of the remarkable degree of social mobility in that city with the exaggerated claim, "Is not one half of the property in the city . . . owned by men who wear *Leather Aprons?* Does not the other half belong to men whose fathers or grandfathers wore Leather Aprons?" Although some had a chance of advancing not available in Europe, recent research demonstrates that the number and proportion of poor in Philadelphia and other cities increased over the course of the eighteenth century.

The successful urban middle class developed an ethic of social striving that became firmly implanted in the popular psychology, deflecting attention from the problem of poverty in America and eroding older notions of deference. Character and personal worth were becoming linked with worldly success. The gospel of work expounded by Puritans and Quakers was being detached from its theological base and fashioned into a broader ethic of social and economic achievement.

Benjamin Franklin was an outstanding example of middle-class success in the eighteenth century. He had started in life as a humble printer's apprentice and by careful attention to his trade became a wealthy printer and newspaper publisher in Philadelphia. In addition, he dedicated himself to a program of self-improvement through reading, writing, and reflection, enabling him to advance to a many-sided career as author, scientist, inventor, diplomat, and statesman. He was in every sense a product of the social dynamism of one of America's flourishing cities. In short, he was the living symbol of middle-class success; without the benefit of a great family name, or inherited estates, or a college education, Franklin had surpassed the sons of the gentry anywhere and everywhere in America.

Franklin was an important contributor to the literature of self-improvement which was acquiring a growing popularity in America and in Europe. His *Poor Richard's Almanac* sold thousands of copies in America every year, and the sayings of Poor Richard were translated and reprinted in European countries. Poor Richard extolled all the bourgeois virtues of thrift, industry, diligence, and self-discipline, but always with the saving element of proverbial humor. Every American household became familiar with such maxims as: "Spare and have is better than spend and crave"; "The sleeping fox catches no poultry"; "Early to bed and early to rise, makes a man healthy, wealthy and wise"; "Little strokes fell great oaks." Although Franklin's famous *Autobiography* was not published until after the Revolution, he was already recognized everywhere as a great expounder of middle-class virtues. Abel Jones, the Quaker merchant who urged Franklin to complete and publish his *Autobiography,* told him, "I know of no character living . . . who has so much in his power as thyself to promote a greater spirit of industry and early attention to business, frugality, and temperance with the American youth."

The pervasive influence of middle-class values was not the only element undermining the possibilities for maintaining hereditary forms of privilege in America. A very rapid population growth during the decades before the Revolutionary crisis created a more complex and pluralistic society than had existed in seventeenth-century America. In 1700 the total population of the continental colonies was estimated by various sources to be around 250,000. By 1760 the American population probably exceeded 1,500,000 inhabitants of which 300,000 were blacks. Before 1700, the overwhelming proportion of the population was of English origin (except for significant clusters of Dutch and Swedes in the Hudson and Delaware regions); after 1700, large numbers of non-English immigrants were attracted by the economic opportunities of English America.

The Scotch-Irish were the most numerous among these new ethnic groups which settled in America. Benjamin Franklin estimated that there were as many as 350,000 Scotch-Irish in the colonies by 1750. Most of them had come to America because of economic and religious grievances. The restrictive policies of the British navigation acts and the Woolen Act had a very disastrous effect on the economic life of the Scotch settlers who had emigrated to northern Ireland in the seventeenth century. In addition, these Scotch-Irish Presbyterians cordially hated the established Episcopal Church in Ireland to which they were compelled to pay tithes. And when absentee English landlords began to raise their rents early in the eighteenth century, thousands of Scotch-Irish flocked to America. The Scotch-Irish immigrants moved primarily into the back-country areas of America—New Hampshire, western Pennsylvania, the Great Valley of Virginia, and the piedmont regions of the Carolinas. These new migrants quickly became noted for their ability as frontier Indian fighters and for their contempt for the laws and customs of the older settlements of the coastal regions.

Growing Ethnic Diversity

A massive influx of Germans also moved to new homes in eighteenth-century America. Many of them were fleeing the poverty and destruction caused by Europe's wars in which the German states were so often the favorite battleground. Large numbers of them were peasants who had become radical Protestants or Deists—Mennonites, Moravians, Dunkers, Amish, and others. By the time of the American Revolution there were probably as many as 200,000 Germans in the American colonies; the larger number were settled in Pennsylvania, but other thousands were located in the frontier regions of New York, Maryland, Virginia, and the Carolinas. The Germans were so numerous in Pennsylvania that there were whole districts in which one would hear and see only the German language, German manners, and German religious practices. Benjamin Franklin estimated that the Germans constituted one-third of the population of Pennsylvania in 1751 and expressed his alarm over the possibility that Pennsylvania might "become a colony of aliens, who will shortly be so numerous as to Germanize us, instead of our Anglicizing them."

Other non-English groups also multiplied within the American population. Scottish immigration increased after the failure of the rebellion of '45 when Prince Charles made the last attempt to regain the throne of England for the Stuart family. Large numbers of Irishmen from southern Ireland seeking to escape harsh English landlords and dire poverty came across the Atlantic in a small but steady stream. French Hugenots arrived in considerable numbers in the seaport cities of America after the revocation of the Edict of Nantes and the resumption of a policy of persecution. Swiss immigrants, driven away from their homeland by the specter of poverty, began to come in increasing numbers; many of them, also, were religious radicals.

Using data from the first federal census, scholars have estimated the ethnicity of white Americans in 1790: 60.9 per cent were English; 14.3 per cent were Scotch or Scotch-Irish; 8.7 per cent were Germans; 5.4 per cent were Dutch, French, and Swedish; 3.7 per cent were South Irish; and the remaining 7 per cent fall into a miscellaneous category or were impossible to classify. What stands out in these figures is that two of five Americans were non-English in origin. In addition, about one-fifth of the total population was of African descent. Social diversity had already become a characteristic of American society, and many new groups were already adding new words, cultural styles, and skills.

The Great Awakening

The religious life of Americans had also become more diverse by the end of the colonial period. Much of this stemmed from the immigration of new groups of worshipers, but it was also the product of the Great Awakening, the most important event in eighteenth-century American religious history. The Great Awakening was part of a general religious movement affecting the entire Western world. Although it was a religious event, social developments provide an essential background for it. The avidity with which Americans, especially those in New England, pursued opportunities for wealth made individuals feel guilty; they knew they were abandoning the ways of their fathers and becoming competitive and materialistic. Anxious to have their consciences purged, these people were psychologically ready for sermons stressing their sinfulness. Youths, who may have felt guilty about conflict with their parents, were deeply affected by the Awakening and joined the churches in large numbers.

The origins of the Great Awakening are also rooted in the history of the churches themselves. New England's religious history best illustrates the changes that led to the Great Awakening. In the era of John Winthrop, rules for church membership were difficult to meet. A public expression of faith was required, and this involved giving an account of one's personal experience of conversion. While such emotional experiences were common among the founders of the colony, many of the second generation grew to adulthood without it. This posed a serious practical problem: should the children of these baptized but unconverted adults also be baptized? A solution to this problem was hard to find. If they were not baptized, the church might well wither away; if they were, many unconverted would be brought into a congregation that in Puritan theory included only visible saints. The problem was resolved in 1662 when New England's ministers approved the "Half-Way Covenant."

This established a category of halfway membership that allowed the baptism of the children of church members who had not undergone conversion, but did not extend full communion to them. This distinction, however, was difficult to maintain, and in time it was eroded. The outward and inherited appearance of membership became more important than inward experience. Some ministers began to baptize all children and extend communion to all but blatant sinners. Religion was thus becoming conventional, formal, complacent. Emotional yearnings, as a consequence, went unfulfilled in the churches. Nor was this problem unique to New England. In Virginia, where the established Anglican church had never been strong, the same emotional deadness prevailed, and nonconformist Baptist and Methodist groups were rapidly expanding to fill the religious vacuum.

The leading figures in the Great Awakening were Jonathan Edwards of Northampton, Massachusetts, and George Whitefield, the great English evangelist. Edwards stimulated a religious revival at Northampton in 1734 and 1735. He published an account of the revival in his *Faithful Narrative of the Surprising Work of God* (1737). Other ministers tried to duplicate Edwards' achievement. In a sense, therefore, Edwards prepared the way for George Whitefield. After arriving from England in 1739, Whitefield preached throughout the southern and middle colonies before coming to New England. Everywhere he went, Whitefield drew huge crowds; in fact, they were so large that no church would hold them and he typically spoke in the open air. When he preached his last sermon in Boston, in October of 1740, he drew an audience of over 30,000 to Boston Common—a crowd numbering nearly twice the city's population. After this sermon he went to Northampton to preach in Edwards's own town. His sermon was so moving that Edwards wept through the whole of it.

Soon after Whitefield returned to England, Gilbert Tennent, who had been active in stimulating revivals in New Jersey, made an evangelizing tour through southern New England. Such itinerant preaching was in effect a challenge to established ministers; it was a form of competition. Often this subtle challenge became an explicit attack. Tennent, for example, condemned the intellectual and doctrinal sermons of the "dead ministry" in the established churches and called for the "Ministry of Natural Men." Tennent was frightening to the ministerial establishment. Even worse were the harangues of James Davenport, who went through New England in 1741 and 1742 denouncing the established ministers as unconverted deceivers and "dead husks." In condemning the intellectualism of ministers and appealing to the emotions of ordinary men and women, the revivalists were attacking the ministers for their snobbery. Tennent, for instance, accused the ministry of looking "upon . . . the common people with an Air of Disdain." Stung by such charges and worried about the emotional excesses of the revivalists, the established leaders counterattacked. They outlawed itineracy, and the faculty of Harvard condemned Whitefield's methods in a pamphlet that was endorsed by Yale's faculty as well. This document characterized Whitefield as "an Enthusiast, a censorious, uncharitable Person, and a Deluder of the People." If the ministers were thus defending their own interest, they had a point: the revivalists often fell into a crude anti-intellectualism in the name of "experimental" or deeply felt religion. The extremism of someone like Davenport, who was deported from Connecticut on the grounds that he was a madman, disturbed even friends of the revival. Edwards, for example, worried that such "wild men" too easily dismissed the importance of an educated ministry in their celebration of religion of the heart.

The consequences of the Great Awakening were manifold and largely unanticipated. American Protestantism was divided into two camps; those who supported the revival ("New Lights," or among Presbyterians the "New Side") and those who opposed it ("Old Lights" or "Old Side"). It also eroded the status and authority of the ministry. Indeed, the experience New Lights had challenging traditional authority during the Great Awakening may have made it psychologically easier for them later to challenge imperial authority during the Revolutionary crisis. By challenging the established churches, the evangelicals also advanced the day when church and state would be separated. Finally, the division of churches that accompanied the revival opened an important new area of individual choice in religion. Towns now often had two churches; instead of being born into a church, many Americans assumed the burden of choosing their church.

The Rise of the Assemblies

The Colonial Electorate The legislative assemblies provided the means by which various interest groups and new men of wealth could gain access to the political process. Everywhere in the colonies, the right to vote for members of the elective assemblies was restricted to those who owned property—either a freehold or substantial amounts of personal property. Almost all of the colonies had additional restrictions that kept Jews, Catholics, Indians, and blacks from the polls. On the whole, however, the qualifications for voting were not as restrictive as a mere reading of the laws might suggest. Ownership of real and personal property was so widespread in America that the best estimate based on recent studies of the colonial electorate suggests that 50 to 75 per cent of adult white males were qualified to vote in the eighteenth century.

It would be a mistake, however, to assume that the large proportion of voters in the American population can be taken as evidence of the existence of a democratic political system. Eighteenth-century Americans were still largely in a pre-democratic stage in their political habits and practices. To be sure, the aristocratic leaders were less likely to make the kind of authoritarian statements that were characteristic of John

Winthrop or William Berkeley in the seventeenth century, but they were able to maintain their superiority of political power in a variety of ways. The secret ballot, after all, was rarely used in colonial elections; voice voting or the use of prepared tickets was the common procedure. In the absence of any effective secrecy in voting, the influence of men of wealth could be exercised more easily at the polling places, or in the taverns and ale-houses nearby. One voter wrote a very revealing statement in 1761 for the *New York Gazette* in which he said,

A Squeeze of the Hand of a great man, a few well-timed compliments; . . . an Invitation to his Dining Room . . . a glass of wine well applied, the Civility and good Humor of his Lady, the Drinking a Health, inquiring kindly after the Welfare of a Family, a little facecious chat in the strain of Freedom and Equality, have been sufficient to win the Heart of many a vote. . . .

Furthermore, the voters of eighteenth-century America displayed great political apathy. They often stayed away from elections because of a sheer lack of interest, satisfied to leave the affairs of government to their "betters." The "multitude," said Ezra Stiles, a Connecticut minister who became president of Yale later in the century, "will not leave the plow to have a governor of their taste." Sometimes bad weather or the distance of a few miles to the polling place discouraged voting. In the final analysis, Americans in the eighteenth century behaved much as the people of underdeveloped countries still do; they had little knowledge of the larger world of affairs and tended to be influenced in their voting by personal considerations, family and religious pressures, and ostentatious displays of wealth and influence.

Nevertheless, occasions did arise in the first half of the century when economic or religious issues created hot political controversies. In Massachusetts and Rhode Island, there were bitter conflicts over efforts to expand the currency supply by the creation of "land banks" authorized to issue paper money based on long-term mortgages. Supporters of such schemes were not only farmers but some were also small capitalists and traders looking for new sources of credit to help expand their enterprises. In like fashion, some of the more active religious groups were able to win greater measures of toleration during the years of ferment caused by the great awakening. Thus, in Massachusetts, the most intolerant of all the colonies in matters of religion, the legislature yielded to the pressures of Baptists and Quakers for exemptions from church taxes.

Increasingly, the elective assemblies became schools of political thought and action because of conflicts between colonial interest and the interests of the British Empire. The policy of centralization promoted by James II before the Glorious Revolution was not wholly abandoned by William III and his successors. The wars with France and the further development of England's mercantilist policy required a more elaborate system of colonial administration and more direct means of royal control. Hence, Massachusetts was not allowed to return to its former

The Pressures of Royal Administration

status as a corporate colony; neither was New York returned to its former proprietary control. Both colonies were placed under the direction of royal governors appointed by William III and incorporated in the expanding system of direct royal administration.

The Crown also took steps to eliminate the proprietary arrangements which had been so numerous in the seventeenth century. The proprietary governments were notoriously inefficient and the proprietary provinces were increasingly torn by internal conflicts which threatened the good order of the Empire. Under pressure from the Crown, the proprietors of New Jersey surrendered their proprietary rights and New Jersey became a royal province in 1702. Similar proceedings were begun against the Carolinas during the next decade, but final action was not taken by the Crown until after popular discontent exploded into open rebellion in South Carolina in 1719. North Carolina also became a royal province in 1729. The only reversal in this policy of converting proprietorships into royal colonies came with the founding of Georgia colony in 1732. The Georgia charter placed control of the colony in the hands of a philanthropic board of trustees, led by James Oglethorpe, who were concerned to rescue debtors from the horrors of English jails and settle them as small farmers in Georgia. But the powers of the Georgia trustees were to endure for only 21 years, after which Georgia was to become a royal province. Thus, by the middle of the eighteenth century, all but four colonies had been brought under direct royal control and there was considerable support among the legal advisors of the Crown for the idea of pressing for the surrender of the corporate charters of Connecticut and Rhode Island and the proprietary charters of Pennsylvania and Maryland. All four colonies, however, were successful in staving off such attempts before the American Revolution.

Conflicts Between Royal Governors and Assemblies

The focal point of imperial authority in America was the royal governor. He, more than any other royal official in the colonies, was responsible for carrying out the royal instructions concerning government and trade; it was his responsibility to veto legislation that was contrary to the desires of the Crown or the acts of Parliament. In addition, he commanded the armed forces; he had power to appoint subordinate officials and to supervise financial affairs; often he sat with the Council as the colony's court of last resort. In short, he was the chief symbol of imperial authority, the linchpin of the Empire in the legislative, executive, and judicial affairs of the colony.

The obvious political strategy, then, for political leaders in the colonial assemblies was to work with the governor when it suited their interests and to circumvent his powers when they wished to place their own vital interests above those of the imperial system of trade and administration. A political victory won at the expense of a royal governor was likely to be real and lasting because the Privy Council was always far behind in its work of considering colonial laws for approval or disallowance, or of hearing appeals from colonial courts. Moreover, the procedures for submission and examination of colonial laws was very loose and was usually hampered by factors of distance and delays in-communication. In such a situation, the odds were heavily in favor of any legislation that the assemblies were able to persuade a royal governor to approve. Between 1691 and 1775, approximately 8,500 colonial laws were sent to the Privy Council for approval. Of these, 470 (about 5.5 per cent) were disallowed.

To persuade or to compel the governor's approval for legislation, then, became the primary tactic of the politicians in the assemblies. And in this struggle for power with the governors, the colonial legislatures possessed a very potent weapon: the power of the purse was in colonial hands. This was the natural and inevitable outgrowth of the English practice of granting colonial charters which required the assent of elected representatives to all laws and taxes. But the power of the purse was greater than it might have been because of the failure of the Crown to provide a permanent administrative budget, financed out of the imperial revenues, in any of the colonies; indeed, most royal governors were even dependent on the colonial assemblies for their salaries.

One very important evidence of the growing power of the assemblies was their success in winning legislative privileges akin to those which had been won by the English Parliament. By 1700 the colonial assemblies had already gained two privileges of fundamental importance in the right to assent to laws and taxes and the right to initiate legislation. After 1700 the assemblies grasped for more and more privileges and, before the American Revolution, they had obtained the right of free debate without fear of punitive action by the governor, the right to decide who should be seated in the assembly in case of disputed elections, and the right to establish the rules of legislative procedure. In several colonies, the assemblies struggled hard to win the power to regulate elections and to exclude royal appointees from the elective House, but these efforts were blocked by the royal governors and the Privy Council.

In any case, the assemblies had sufficient strength to encroach steadily on the executive authority of the governors. The governors often had to make important concessions to get the appropriations needed to carry on the affairs of government and to fulfill the demands for men and supplies in time of war. The financial power of the assemblies gave them the leverage by which they designated appointments of colonial treasurers to supervise the expenditure of appropriations; they also encroached on the governors' military powers by stipulating where and how the troops should be used; furthermore, they frequently withheld appropriations until judges were appointed who were sympathetic to colonial interests. In these and other ways, the colonial legislatures were able to control a large share of judicial and executive affairs. Governor Glen of South Carolina, for example, reported in 1748, "Almost all places of profit or of trust are disposed of by the General Assembly . . . The above officers and most of the Commissioners are named by the General Assembly and are responsible to them alone . . . Thus, the people have the whole of the administration in their hands."

De Facto Federalism   Year in and year out, the assemblies were acquiring a degree of legislative sovereignty that made them appear to be miniature Parliaments. The Board of Trade complained as early as 1713 that "most of the assemblies in the plantations claim all the privilege the House of Commons here does, and some of them, others that the House of Commons never pretended to." As a consequence, the American colonies attained a large degree of autonomy in local affairs. Something like a federal division of power was developing in England's colonial system in the New World; indeed, there were inchoate ideas of federalism stirring in the imaginations of Americans by the middle of the eighteenth century.

The most significant effort to formulate an idea of a federal empire came with the Albany Plan of Union suggested by Benjamin Franklin. In 1754, when the possibility of renewed warfare with France seemed very likely, the Board of Trade issued a call for a general colonial congress to meet with leaders of the Indian tribes in order to make preparations for military defence. In June of that year, representatives from the New England colonies, New York, Pennsylvania, and Maryland met in Albany to discuss a common plan of action. After considerable discussion, they adopted a plan of union for all the American colonies which had been prepared by Franklin. By this plan the general government was to be headed by a president-general who was to be appointed by the Crown and by a grand council made up of delegates to be chosen by the elective assemblies of the several colonies. This super-government was to have power to deal with four aspects of British affairs in North America: Indian treaties, war and peace with the Indians, purchase and

Colonials demonstrated some of the proclivities toward union that Franklin called on in the Albany Plan of Union.

settlement of western lands, and the regulation of Indian trade. Representation on the council was to be apportioned according to each colony's contributions to the common treasury, and the council was protected against dissolution or pro-rogation by the president-general. Of course, all enactments of the grand council were subject to disallowance by the king in Privy Council.

No colony, however, was willing to adopt the plan which had been worked out by the imaginative delegates at the Albany Congress; the Board of Trade also refused to approve the idea. Franklin himself made the observation that "the Assemblies did not adopt it, as they all thought there was too much *prerogative* in it; and, in England, it was judged to have too much of the *democratic.*"

Although, the colonial assemblies preferred to cling to the autonomous powers which they had acquired in their struggles with royal governors and other agents of imperial authority their jealous concern for their self-governing powers should not be taken as manifestations of early ideas of independence. The skillful manipulation of local power by the leaders of the colonial assemblies was no more than a normal use of the political process within the Empire. No one imagined that the colonial leaders would wish to exchange the political system which they had manipulated so successfully for the perilous and uncertain conditions of independence. Thomas Pownall, governor of Massachusetts from 1757 to 1760, and a severe critic of colonial politics, had no doubt on this point. He, perhaps, epitomized the best thinking on both sides of the Atlantic at the end of the Seven Years' War when he said, "Some say the colonies will revolt some day. No, their hearts are in England and England is their home, they would not risk losing the rights of Englishmen."

Detail from an engraving by
Peter Maverick, Genius of
Penmanship. *Prints Division.
The New York Public
Library. Astor, Lenox and
Tilden Foundations.*

Crosscurrents of Change in Education

The early and middle decades of the eighteenth century were the springtime of a vigorous American culture. Largely as a consequence of the dynamic forces of diversity and change, Americans were able to escape the drab provincialism and intellectual sterility that has been so characteristic of colonial societies in modern history. The rapid expansion of wealth, the increase in the population, and the growth of cities created the conditions favorable to the quickening of thought and imagination.

A major sign of the thickening texture of American culture was the rapid growth of colonial colleges. Seventeenth-century America had produced only two institutions of higher learning, Harvard (1636) and William and Mary (1693), although one might add Yale (1701) to this list because the leaders of Connecticut had long been interested in founding a college, but were not financially able to support one until the beginning of the new century. In the middle decades of the eighteenth century, however, a notable enthusiasm for the establishment of new colleges developed, stimulated largely by the religious rivalries of the Great Awakening.

The Growth of Colonial Colleges

Thus, Princeton was founded in 1746 by New Side Presbyterians who hoped to develop a ministry that was not dead in spirit. Brown, in 1764, and Queens College (later Rutgers), in 1766, were founded by revivalistic groups—the former by the Baptists of Rhode Island and the latter by the followers of Theodore Frelinghuysen in the Dutch Reformed Church. Dartmouth College (1769) grew out of the reawakened religious spirit of Congregationalists who had organized a missionary school for Indians in New Hampshire. Two other colleges, King's College (1754), later to become Columbia, and the College of Philadelphia (1755), which was to become the University of Pennsylvania after the Revolution, were products of urban conditions rather than of revivalistic influences; but even they were the objects of strenuous battles for control fought between Anglicans and Presbyterians.

To be sure, the multiplication of colleges with private denominational sponsorship could not provide America with centers of learning comparable to Oxford and Cambridge. Indeed, the essentially religious control of seven out of nine colonial colleges kept American higher education close to the brink of a narrow sectarianism that might have made them little more than theological seminaries. This sectarian spirit was clearly articulated by Theodore Frelinghuysen when he said of other denominations, "We have no business with their colleges; they may create as many as they please, and must expect to maintain them too, themselves. Let everyone provide his own house."

Thanks to the peculiar crosscurrents of American life, however, the eighteenth-century colleges were able to achieve a much larger role and a much greater vitality. To obtain students and financial support, it became necessary to soften the original sectarian differences. As a result, the membership of the governing boards of the college began to reflect the growing diversities of American society. At Brown, for example, where the Baptists had been primarily responsible for the founding of the college, Congregationalists, Anglicans, and Quakers were also represented on the governing board. At Dartmouth, a Congregational college, three members of the first board of trustees were Anglican laymen. And, of course, the two most secular of the eighteenth-century colleges, King's College and the College of Philadelphia, had a particularly broad interdenominational representation in their governing boards.

Furthermore an increasing proportion of the members of governing boards were laymen—public officials and other men of wealth and status. In the eighteenth century, four of the colleges (Harvard, Princeton, Brown, and Dartmouth) had governing boards on which clerical and lay trustees were evenly balanced. William and Mary, King's College, and even Queen's College had boards of control that were dominated by laymen, and the board of trustees of the College of Philadelphia consisted entirely of laymen. Thus, the American colleges were laying the foundations of a system of control by nonresident governing boards that was quite different from the European practice of autonomous universities governed by their own faculties. Of course, the clerical members of the boards of trustees were often more assiduous in their attention to the affairs of the colleges, and the presidents, who furnished the real leadership, were usually clergymen. Nevertheless, the mere existence of a pattern of lay membership introduced outside influences that broadened the character of the colleges.

Interestingly, not one of the colonial colleges required students to subscribe to a particular religious creed as a condition of admission. Of course, sectarian considerations did have some influence in the choice of colleges by students and parents, but low fees and geographical proximity were probably more important determinants. Although religious conformity was usually demanded of teachers in the denominational colleges, particularly during the decades when religious feelings were very strong, the schismatic tendencies of the Great Awakening ultimately compelled a large degree of practical toleration.

An Enlightened Curriculum   In general, the most significant characteristic of the eighteenth-century colleges was their growing liberalization, particularly in academic theory and curricular content. This was a very uneven process, and the new educational ideas had to make their way against older conceptions such as that of Yale's President Clap who stated flatly in 1754,

Colleges, are *Religious Societies,* of a Superior Nature to all others. For whereas *Parishes,* are Societies, for training up the *common people;* Colleges, are *Societies* of *Ministers,* for training up Persons for the Work of the *Ministry* . . . Some, indeed, have supposed, that the only Design of Colleges, was to teach the Arts and Sciences . . . But, it is probable, that there is not a College, to be found upon Earth, upon such a Constitution.

Yet, President Clap and others like him could not hold back the new currents of thought that were stirring in American higher education. As early as 1743, Benjamin Franklin had published his *Proposals Relative to the Education of Youth in Pennsylvania* in which he called for the organization of an academy that would prepare young men for a variety of private careers by instructing them in all the more practical arts and sciences. "It would be well," he wrote, "if they could be taught everything that is useful and everything that is ornamental. But art is long and time is short. It is therefore proposed that they learn those things that are likely to be most useful and most ornamental, regard being had for the several professions for which they are intended."

Such an Academy was organized in Philadelphia in 1749, with Franklin as president of the Board of Trustees. Very soon, additional steps were taken to develop the Academy into a college and, in 1755, the corporate name of the institution was changed to the "College, Academy and Charitable School." The first provost of the College of Philadelphia, William Smith, proceeded to develop a curriculum which rivalled in scope the proposals of Franklin. Not only were the usual classical subjects to be pursued, but also logic, mathematics, ethics, history, law and government, commerce and trade, and the whole range of the natural sciences. In this way, the science and philosophy of Europe's enlightenment were given a hospitable home in American education.

A similar interest in a new style of higher education was expressed in the public discussion about the founding of King's College in New York. In 1753 William Livingston, a leading lawyer, published a series of essays in which he affirmed that the goal of education should be "to qualify men for the different employments of life, to which it may please God to call them . . . [and] to render our youth better members of society." The secular spirit of his proposals was underlined further when he declared: "A public academy, is or ought to be a mere civil institution, and cannot with any tolerable propriety be monopolized by any religious sect. The design of such seminaries [is] . . . calculated for the benefit of society, as a society, without any intention to teach religion which is the province of the pulpit."

In view of such considerations, it is not surprising that King's College, under the leadership of its first president, Samuel Johnson, developed a broad curriculum similar to that of the College of Philadelphia. Samuel Johnson was a religious man and was determined that the students in King's College be trained in religion, but he emphasized that they would not be taught the dogmas of any particular sect, but only the common principles of Christianity. Otherwise, the students were to follow a course of instruction that would include logic, mathematics, surveying, navigation, geography, history, husbandry, commerce, government, the several natural sciences, and "everything useful for the comfort, the convenience and elegance of life, in the chief manufactures relating to any of these things."

To be sure, King's College and the College of Philadelphia did not have the importance among American colleges in the eighteenth century that they were to have later. Undoubtedly, also, they suffered in enrollment as much as they did partly because of their pronounced secularism. And, since they had to struggle along with small numbers of students and equally small faculties, their grandiose conceptions of a liberalized and enlightened curriculum were never fully realized in practice.

Nevertheless, the forces of liberalization were able to penetrate other eighteenth-century colleges where religious influences were still strong. Harvard College developed an important curricular reformation during the presidency of Edward Holyoke, 1737 to 1769. John Winthrop IV, who was Hollis professor of mathematics and natural philosophy, helped to prepare the way by basing much of his instruction on Newton's *Principia* and by being the first in America to teach the calculus as used by Newton. In 1742, the faculty of Harvard made a decision to use Locke's *Essay on Human Understanding* as well as textbooks which summarized the teachings of Newtonian science. In like fashion, textbooks and teaching materials that included the new science and philosophy of the enlightenment were used at Princeton almost from the beginning. At William and Mary, a professor of mathematics and natural philosophy was appointed as early as 1711 and, by the middle decades, mathematics and science were being taught excellently by William Small, the Scottish scientist. Even at Yale, Newton's *Principia* and *Optics* were used by Samuel Johnson as early as 1715 when he was a tutor there, although a genuine spirit of innovation did not come into the Yale curriculum until after the American Revolution.

Encyclopedia; *or* A Dictionary of Arts . . . *Philadelphia, 1798. Rare Book Division. The New York Public Library. Astor, Lenox and Tilden Foundations.*

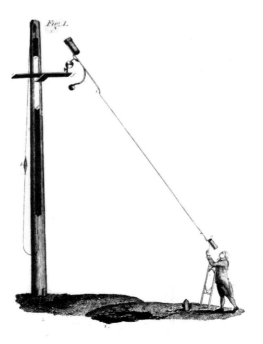

Thus, some of the colleges became focal points for the expanding enlightenment of the eighteenth century. At the same time, the function of higher education in America was broadened as a result of new social conditions; the preparation of students going into the ministry was declining significantly. At the beginning of the century, the proportion of students destined for the ministry at Harvard and Yale was close to 60 per cent; by 1750, it had fallen to approximately 40 per cent. Graduates of the colleges were becoming lawyers, physicians, businessmen, and teachers in increasing numbers.

Notwithstanding the growing vitality of the colleges, the schools in other levels of the colonial educational structure tended to cling to older habits and goals. There was a very considerable growth of parochial schools in the middle colonies, reflecting the great variety of religious denominations that appeared with the population growth in this new century. Elementary education in such schools was religious in purpose and rarely went beyond the barest rudiments. In the southern colonies, education continued to reflect the stratified social system; private tutors taught the children of well-to-do planters, while the children of the lower classes got what education they could from the apprenticeship system or from endowed field schools and charity schools. In New England, the common schools underwent little change in the methods and content of instruction, and public support of them tended to decline as the original Puritan zeal of the seventeenth century was replaced by social purposes more closely associated with the economic and social changes of the subsequent century.

As a consequence, new forms of education were sought after by the expanding and aggressive middle class in America. The high degree of upward social mobility made possible by the economic growth of the colonies engendered special educational needs for the children of successful tradesmen and for those who aspired to become masters in their own trades and professions. Such needs could not be met by the Latin grammar schools and the denominational secondary schools where the dominant methods of instruction emphasized the study of the classical literatures. Latin and Greek might be the proper ornaments of gentlemanly leisure and learning but they had little usefulness in the world of trade. Hence, the middle classes, particularly in the flourishing cities of America, demanded modes of education which were more practical and utilitarian.

New Forms of Schooling

To satisfy these demands, a new kind of secondary school appeared. By the early decades of the century, "private venture" schools began to advertise their educational wares in Boston, New York, Philadelphia, Charleston, and other larger towns. These schools, designed primarily to offer instruction for those who desired a vocational training more suited to the conditions of the business world, generally advertised that instruction would be offered in bookkeeping, accounting, navigation, and surveying as well as practical training in algebra, geometry, and

Nassau Hall at Princeton.
Princeton University Library, Princeton University.

trigonometry. An enthusiastic welcome for such educational ventures was expressed by a writer for the *American Weekly Mercury* of Philadelphia, in 1735, who summed up their main advantages by asking, "Can there be anything more Rediculous than that a Father should waste his own Money and his Sons Time, in setting him to learn the Roman language, when at the same Time he designs for a trade?" And for the daughters of socially ambitious tradesmen, there were private venture schools that taught certain skills and graces that were proper for young ladies of fashion. In Boston, for example, one of these schools offered instruction to young ladies in music and dancing "and also English and French Quilting, Imbroidery, Florishing, Plain Work, Marking in several sorts of Stiches, and several other works."

The rage for self-improvement by means of education also affected those who were still in the lower rungs of the ladder of business·and social success. For those apprentices whose indentures required their masters to furnish them with a certain amount of schooling, a large number of evening schools were available in the larger cities. At least one hundred such schools were organized at various times between 1723 and 1770. In the evening schools an apprentice could learn not only reading and writing, but also the more ambitious could learn geometry, navigation, surveying, and bookkeeping. Some evening schools learned to appeal to such impulses of ambition—one eighteenth-century advertisement, indeed, offered its program of instruction specifically for "emulous sons of industry." Moreover, when Benjamin Franklin organized his

famous discussion club, or "Junto," in 1727, he, in association with printers, scriveners, shoemakers, and joiners, was providing further impetus to such efforts for self-improvement.

Much of the content and method of the private venture schools and the evening schools foreshadowed the growth of the academies and the public high schools in the nineteenth century. But, until such broader educational conceptions received public support, the private venture schools of all types were the only means of satisfying the cravings of the middle class for a more practical type of education. To a certain degree, also, they reflected a vague concern for the newer forms of knowledge that were being stimulated by the expanding forces of enlightenment in the eighteenth century.

Patterns for paper filigree work. The New Ladies Magazine. *London, 1787. The Metropolitan Museum of Art, gift of Mrs. Bella C. Landaur, 1933.*

Trans-Atlantic Intellectual Influences

With each passing decade in the eighteenth century, contacts between North America and Europe multiplied in a variety of ways. The great expansion of commerce, of course, was the main stimulus to the growing trans-Atlantic communication. In order to make business plans and to carry on mercantile operations successfully, American merchants needed to have the latest information of economic and political conditions in Europe such as news about wars and threats of war, commercial regulations, crop failures, new products of manufacture, and the latest fashions in clothes.

Much of this information was relayed back and forth across the Atlantic in business letters carried by captains of merchant vessels. A postal service of sorts had been organized in the northern colonies as early as 1691, but the flow of letters became so heavy by the middle of the eighteenth century that demands increased for improvement in the mail system. The greatest advance in the intercolonial postal system came after 1753 when Benjamin Franklin, of Philadelphia, and William Hunter, of Virginia, were appointed joint deputy-postmasters for the colonies. Franklin had already served as postmaster of Philadelphia for some years and was cognizant of the needs of merchants and tradesmen in the matter of communication. As deputy-postmaster, he employed postriders to ride night and day and managed to cut down the time of delivery between New York and Philadelphia to one day, and to shorten the time between more distant points in America. In 1755, a direct packet line was established between England and New York in order to provide a regular monthly mail service.

Trans-Atlantic Communication

Colonial Newspapers　　　The development of colonial newspapers was closely related to the growth of the postal service in the larger cities. The first successful newspaper, *The News-Letter,* was started in 1704 by the postmaster of Boston, John Campbell. The *Boston Gazette,* founded in 1719 by Campbell's successor, was edited in the following decades by four successive postmasters. Of course, not all colonial newspapers were in the hands of postmasters. Other newspapers appeared rapidly in the larger centers of population as colonial printers became aware of the opportunities for profit in such a regular means of communicating information. Hence, by the middle of the century, newspaper publishing had become an important enterprise. Much of Benjamin Franklin's prosperity as a printer resulted from the success of his *Pennsylvania Gazette.* Some of the printers in Franklin's shop carried his ideas to other colonies—thus the *South Carolina Gazette* was established in Charleston by one of his printers. New York had two newspapers by the 1730's—William Bradford's *New York Gazette,* and John Peter Zenger's provocative *Weekly Journal.* Indeed, competing newspapers existed in Boston, New York, and Philadelphia after the third decade of the century.

The eighteenth-century newspapers functioned primarily as sources of information for the urban mercantile groups. The political and economic news which was reported in these weekly papers was geared to the interests of the merchants and tradesmen, and the early appearance of advertisements improved communication between buyer and seller. Colonial newspapers also contained essays and articles designed to instruct and to entertain their readers. A large part of Benjamin Franklin's early self-education consisted of writing such essays for his brother's newspaper, the *New England Courant,* in imitation of Addison's style. Thus, the better colonial newspapers provided a broad range of informative material which enhanced the general knowledge of their readers. And since the early attempts to start magazines were generally failures, the newspapers were often the only repositories for essays, verses, and other intellectual efforts. By such means, therefore, the newspapers became important channels for the transmission of many of the new ideas of European thinkers to America.

These were important developments because Americans, particularly in the larger centers of population, were becoming much more cosmopolitan in outlook. The wars of the British Empire made all classes of Americans more aware of the larger world of affairs; in the warfare with the French and Indians, colonial militiamen ventured beyond their provincial borders with a frequency that was unheard of in the seventeenth century. The accumulating wealth caused by the growing prosperity of the colonies led to more transatlantic travel; southern planters as well as northern merchants were able to visit England in greater numbers than in the previous century. Consciously and unconsciously, Americans understood that they were part of a larger Atlantic civilization.

And it was an Atlantic civilization that was astir with new ideas. In almost every field of knowledge there was a sense of excitement and discovery. Historians have summed up these intellectual changes in a single word—Enlightenment—to suggest the fundamental changes that were taking place in the thinking of educated men.

The European Enlightenment

The new modes of thought associated with the Enlightenment seemed to establish the primacy of human reason—thus reversing the traditional Christian cosmology which had emphasized that human reason was inferior to the revelations of God. The French philosopher Descartes had declared in his famous *Discourse of Method* (1637) "I think, therefore I am" and proceeded to construct a theory of knowledge which assumed that the thought processes of man's reason can tell him all that he knows. Later in the century, the impressive scientific speculations of Newton and Locke made literate men more willing to give human reason a central place in their conceptions of man and the universe. Moving bodies in the sky and on earth were described by Newton as moving according to an orderly system of mathematical harmonies. And if the universe of Nature was rational and orderly in its organization as Newton's theories indicated, then it followed that human reason, properly used, and not Biblical or patristic writings, offered the best means of understanding man and the universe.

With an equally important effect, John Locke's *Essay on Human Understanding* (1690) articulated a theory of knowledge in common sense language that encouraged men to place their faith in empirical and scientific inquiry. He argued that all knowledge comes from experience. The mind of a small child, he maintained, was *tabula rasa,* a blank page, on which the experience of the senses is recorded. In addition, Locke argued, the mind of man has the ability to organize the sense impressions into more complex and abstract ideas. In this way, he provided an attractive explanation of how men could obtain even the higher forms of knowledge without assuming the necessity of innate ideas or divine revelation.

In short the enlightened men of the eighteenth century had a system of explanation and a faith that pointed to great possibilities of human improvement. Thanks to Newton, gravity, motion, and mass became measurable and predictable events and entities; and they were confident that natural scientists could discover other laws of nature that would explain chemical and biological phenomena with a similar certainty and simplicity. In a like fashion, they believed that human behavior and the characteristics of the social environment could be summed up into a system of social science. Such knowledge would enable men to develop new ways to control their natural environment and to live together peaceably and happily in their social environment. Indeed, by the end of the century, a belief in progress was an essential article of faith for many enlightened men. In France, Condorcet expressed this faith in progress somewhat extravagantly in his *Progrés de l'esprit humain;* in England Jeremy Bentham busied himself with proposals for reform of law and institutions according to his utilitarian formula of "the greatest happiness of the greatest number."

The ideas of the Enlightenment made rapid headway in America. There was, to be sure, no systematic formulation of ideas that could compare with those of European thinkers; indeed, much of what was produced by American writers was often consciously borrowed and full of confusions. Nevertheless, the literate men of America, in the colleges and in the flourishing cities, were eager to gather into their thinking the reflections of European thinkers even though the conceptions of the Enlightenment often threatened traditional forms of intellectual authority.

Jonathan Edward's Theory of Human Understanding

The most ambitious attempt to reconstruct traditional doctrines in relation to the newer conceptions of science was made by Jonathan Edwards, an extraordinary preacher and thinker in Northampton, Massachusetts. Edwards had read Newton and Locke as early as 1717 when he was a student at Yale, and his "Notes on Natural Science" and "Notes on the Mind" reveal some precocious speculations about the manner in which the mind receives the ideas of God through what are apparently sensory impressions. At this very early stage of his development, Edwards came close to expounding a philosophy of immaterialism—suggesting that the only world that we can know is a world of ideas and not of material things which we cannot know except by ideas or impressions that sensations implant in our minds.

As a revivalist preacher associated with the Great Awakening, Edwards was greatly interested in the proper place of emotion and feeling in the life of religion. His *Treatise Concerning Religious Affections,* published in 1746, was not only a significant analysis of the psychology of religion, but also a striking effort to construct a theory of human understanding that would absorb the ideas of Locke into a religious scheme of thought. Edwards argued that there were two natural faculties in the mind of man: the understanding or speculative faculty, and the inclinations, sometimes called the "heart" or the "will." The natural senses of sight, hearing, taste, smell, and touch are the primary servants of the mind and the source of such rational powers as understanding and speculation. The "heart" or "will," on the other hand, is served by an intuitive sense which enables men to perceive the truth and beauty of God's word and will.

Such a theory of religious affections was a remarkable foreshadowing of the transcendentalist philosophy of the nineteenth century. Yet it lacked the popular appeal that such ideas were to have at a later time, because Edwards used the theory as the starting point of a highly intellectual effort to revitalize Puritan doctrines. He dedicated himself to the task of demonstrating that the new ideas of the Enlightenment could not rob God of his glory. Much of his intellectual energy was poured into the task of defending and redefining the doctrines of original sin and predestination in such works as *A Careful and Strict Enquiry into the Modern Prevailing Notions of . . . Freedom of the Will* (1754) and *The Great Christian Doctrine of Original Sin Defended* (1758). These and other works by Edwards are extraordinary achievements; indeed, European scholars consider him to be the only American metaphysician in the eighteenth century worthy of respect. Yet he fought a losing battle; he was expelled from his pulpit in Northampton, and it is doubtful if most of the Americans who were gripped by the religious emotions of the Great Awakening were able to understand his metaphysical dissertations.

Other New England preachers were quite willing to embrace the naturalistic and rationalistic ideas of the Enlightenment without serious qualification. Charles Chauncy and Jonathan Mayhew, the ministers of the two leading churches in Boston, became outstanding exponents of a religion suitable for the Age of Reason. Both men had been educated at Harvard at a time when the college was stirring with excitement over the new scientific and philosophic learning, and both men were convinced that human reason must validate revelation. Chauncy, for example, declared in a sermon delivered in 1744, "Without *Reason* we could never know the *meaning* of a Revelation from God, or prove it to be one." Similarly, Mayhew maintained in his *Seven Sermons* (1749) that, unless there was rational evidence for a purported revelation, "no rational man can receive it as such."

Rational Religion

Both men also rejected the earlier Puritan concept of an arbitrary, self-centered, and punitive God, and with it the concepts of original sin and the depravity of man. Instead, they developed the idea of a reasonable and benevolent God who operates through natural laws for the promotion of human happiness. Thus Mayhew affirmed that there was a natural basis for truth and right—"Truth and moral rectitude are things fixed, stable, and uniform, having their foundation in the nature of things." And Chauncy explicitly repudiated the doctrine of predestination by preaching that man is "an *intelligent moral agent;* having within himself an *ability* and *freedom* to will, as well as to *do,* in opposition to necessity from any extraneous cause whatsoever." To such free moral agents, "The Supreme Being . . . communicates good by *general laws,* whose opposition he does not counter-act, but concurs with in a *regular, uniform* course." In Chauncy's view, evil was largely man-made and the result of man's abuse of his rational faculties; hence man can learn to control evil by means of a reasonable and practical benevolence.

Jonathan Edwards recognized that such doctrines threatened the whole structure of Puritan theology, and much of his preaching and writing was directed against the dangers of the new "Arminianism"—the label applied by orthodox clergymen to the humanistic religion of men like Mayhew and Chauncy. Yet the trend toward a liberalized religion became more and more marked in the churches of eastern

In the mid-eighteenth century Americans emulated the saint who popularized the Bible in an earlier day. Madonna of Saint Jerome *by Matthew Pratt. National Gallery of Art, gift of Clarence Van Dyke Tiers, 1945.*

Massachusetts, and a large number of New England's intellectual leaders moved toward the rationalism of Unitarianism.

A growing rationalist spirit was evident in all the larger cities of America with each passing decade of the eighteenth century. Nevertheless, a radical Deism of the sort that had been developed by such English writers as Tindal, Shaftesbury, and Collins made little headway in America until the Revolutionary period. These radical Deists in England had thrown aside all traditional theologies and reduced the concept of God to that of a supreme architect of the universe who, having created a perfect self-regulating machine, was no longer concerned with his creation.

Benjamin Franklin was one of the more conspicuous Americans who had read and absorbed the ideas of Anthony Collins and Lord Shaftesbury at an early age. He recorded in his *Autobiography* that he became a Deist during his first years as a printer in Philadelphia because he could no longer accept the dogmas of Calvinism. "Revelation," he wrote, "had indeed no weight with me, as such; but I entertained an opinion that, though certain actions might not be bad *because* they were forbidden by it, or good *because* it commanded them, yet probably these actions might be forbidden *because* they were bad for us, or commanded *because* they were beneficial to us, in their own natures, all the circumstances of things considered." Morality to Franklin did not come from attendance at religious services; it was something that could be cultivated by rational men through the daily practice of certain virtues like temperance, frugality, industry, sincerity, moderation, chastity, and humility.

It is very likely that moderate forms of Deism became a mark of sophistication for other upper-class Americans by the middle of the century. Some of the newspapers began to print essays written in support of deistical principles as well as others to refute them. Such articles appeared in the journals of New York and Philadelphia, and a series of essays discussing rationalism and deism ran for a time, during 1739, in the Charleston, *South Carolina Gazette.* John Adams testified on the eve of the Revolution that "the principles of Deism had made considerable progress" even in the interior towns of Massachusetts.

To be sure, there were no *philosophes* in America who produced an *Encyclopedia* to codify the new beliefs of the age. But the tone and style of such *ad hoc* writings as newspaper essays, sermons, and other public addresses revealed a widespread acceptance of the fundamental assumptions of Europe's *philosophes.* It would be a parochial conceit to speak of "the American Enlightenment," but eighteenth-century Americans were clearly the dutiful children of the European Enlightenment.

Eighteenth-Century American Science

An important resonance of the Enlightenment was a new enthusiasm for the pursuit of science. As a result of the rapid economic growth of the colonies, wealth and a degree of leisure time was available to the upper classes in the cities and in the more settled towns of the rural regions. Leading Americans, therefore, were conscious of the growing maturity of their society and gave voice to high aspirations for achievements in the arts and sciences. In 1743 Benjamin Franklin printed a circular letter entitled *Proposals for Promoting Useful Knowledge Among the British Plantations in America* which he sent to various correspondents in the colonies. In this letter Franklin announced that "the first drudgery of settling new colonies which confines the attention of people to mere necessaries is now pretty well over; and there are many in every province in circumstances that set them at ease and afford leisure to cultivate the finer arts and improve the common stock of knowledge." He went on to sketch an ambitious plan for scientific cooperation among men of science and learning in America that would stimulate attainments in natural history, chemistry, mechanical inventions, improvements in agriculture and livestock breeding, the surveying and mapping of the land and coastal waters, and "all philosophical experiments that let light into the nature of things, tend to increase the power of man over matter, and multiply the convenience or pleasures of life."

To a considerable extent, Franklin was simply echoing one of the articles in the faith of the Enlightenment when he expressed the hope that science could be applied to the improvement of the material condition of life. Yet, there was also an upstart quality to his proposal that reflected a deeply felt determination of Americans to emulate the scientific achievements of Europe.

*Americans and
Their Natural History*

At the time that Franklin made his proposal for the cooperative promotion of science on an intercolonial basis, there was an expanding circle of Americans who were interesting themselves in natural history. Indeed, much valuable natural history was written by Americans during these decades of growth for the British Empire. John Bartram, the Quaker botanist of Philadelphia, was contributing papers on various aspects of America's natural history to the *Philosophical Transactions* of the Royal Society by the 1740's. In 1754, Mark Catesby's monumental work, *Natural History of Carolina, Florida, and the Bahama Islands,* containing beautiful line engravings, was published in London and immediately became the most widely read source of information on American plant and animal life.

Gentlemen of learning and leisure throughout the colonies eagerly contributed reports of their observations and knowledge of the flora and fauna of their regions. From Boston, Cotton Mather and Paul Dudley sent specimens and papers regularly to the Royal Society and both were elected to the fellowship of that eminent group. In New York, Cadwallader Colden, physician, merchant, scientist, and eventually lieutenant-governor, supplied Linnaeus, the great Swedish scientist, with descriptions of the flora of New York for publication in the transactions of the Royal Society of Upsala. From Philadelphia, James Logan, a wealthy Quaker merchant and politician, sent important papers to English scientists recording his carefully controlled experiments in the fertilization of plants. In Virginia, William Byrd's *History of the Dividing Line,* written in 1728, contained many keen observations of plant and animal life. By the middle decades of the century, Dr. Alexander Garden of Charleston, South Carolina, was already corresponding with Linnaeus, and his botanical notes and papers won for him election as a member of the Royal Society of Upsala in 1763 and the Royal Society of London in 1773; he is remembered in posterity, however, chiefly for the flower, the *gardenia,* which bears his name.

As a matter of fact, English patrons and promoters had a hand in most of the natural history that was written in eighteenth-century America. The Royal Society took the lead in this effort, but associated natural history clubs also gave encouragement to naturalists in the colonies. Thus Mark Catesby's monumental work was made possible by the financial backing of influential gentlemen in the English natural history circle. Bartram, also, received small subsidies in money and material from Peter Collinson, a Quaker merchant of London who was a devoted student of natural history; in addition, Bartram was assigned a small annual pension by the king in 1763. By the middle of the century, indeed, there was in existence an international circle devoted to the study of natural history. American naturalists, therefore, were participants and correspondents in one of the most dynamic intellectual groups in the European scientific community—a group which included naturalists in England, France, Holland, Sweden, Germany, and Italy.

The academic community, however, made very little contribution to the work of the amateur scientists who composed the growing American natural history circle. The teachers in the eighteenth-century colleges were primarily interested in the study and teaching of mathematics, astronomy, and the physical sciences (natural philosophy). They were not uninterested in natural history—John Winthrop of Harvard, for example, sent botanical specimens and geological specimens to the Royal Society—nevertheless, to them, it appeared to be of secondary importance.

The main contribution to the advancement of science made by the colleges was to train men in mathematics and the physical sciences. At Harvard, Isaac Greenwood, the first occupant of the Hollis chair of mathematics and natural philosophy, published the first arithmetic text in America and a small pamphlet describing his *Experimental Course of Mechanical Philosophy.* After his dismissal for alcoholism in 1738, Greenwood was succeeded by John Winthrop IV, destined to become Harvard's leader in the field of science. During his long career at Harvard, he introduced the calculus to Harvard students and also published six pamphlets, while 11 of his papers were published in the *Philosophical Transactions* of the Royal Society. His most notable papers were studies of the transits of Mercury and Venus observed in the years made favorable by such planetary movements. In addition, Winthrop made important studies of earthquakes which led him to postulate the wave character of earthquakes.

The only other college with a teacher who demonstrated some of Winthrop's capacity was William and Mary. William Small, who became professor of mathematics there in 1758, and professor of philosophy before he left in 1764, was a stimulating and erudite teacher. His short stay in Virginia was a remarkable experience for all who studied with him or who heard his enlightened conversations. Thomas Jefferson recalled, much later, that dinner parties at which William Small was present produced "more good sense, more rational and philosophical conversations than in all my life besides." Such men as Winthrop and Small did much to strengthen the study of mathematics which was woefully weak in the colonies; thereby, they laid the foundations for future scientific work that required a firm grounding in mathematical knowledge.

The colleges never constituted a well-integrated academic community. The diffused pattern of American higher education tended to limit the possibilities of scientific cooperation and the scientific advancement that might result from such cooperation. Dr. Thomas Moffatt of Newport told Franklin in 1764 that each of the seven colleges then in existence was "too narrow and poor at bottom to produce the liberal fruits of art and knowledge." Nevertheless, the function of teaching mathematics and natural philosophy was reasonably well performed in the colleges even if college teachers, themselves, contributed little to the store of scientific knowledge.

Science in the Colonial Colleges

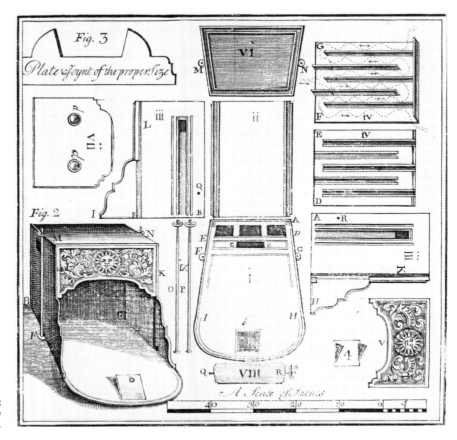

Franklin Stove. Sterling
Memorial Library, Yale
University.

*Franklin's
Scientific Achievements*

The most productive work in science in pre-Revolutionary America
was done by men who were outside the academic community. Indeed,
the greatest achievements in science were made by Benjamin Franklin, a
self-made businessman. Franklin became interested in electrical experiments in the summer of 1743 and, soon afterwards, purchased the
electrical apparatus of an itinerant Scotch lecturer on popular topics of
natural philosophy. Together with some friends in The Library Company
in Philadelphia, he repeated experiments in electrostatics that he had
already seen done with glass tubes, and contrived new ones besides.
Most of his theories about the nature of electricity were the outcome of
several years of experiments with his glass tubes and Leyden jars.
Indeed, his famous *Experiments and Observations on Electricity,* printed
in 1751, was actually written before the kite experiment that was to
become part of the vulgar legend associated with Franklin's scientific
fame.

The *Experiments and Observations on Electricity* was the most famous
book to come out of America in the eighteenth century. Franklin's book
made its way into European scientific circles with the help of Peter
Collinson, the Quaker merchant of London, who had ready access to

most of the important scientific groups in England. Before the century was over, five English editions, three French editions, and one Italian and one German edition were published. The Royal Society of England awarded Franklin its Copley medal and enrolled him in the fellowship of the Society. The king of France sent his personal "Thanks and Compliments" and the French Académie des Sciences elected him a foreign associate. In America, Harvard, Yale, and William and Mary granted him honorary degrees and, in 1762, Oxford University made him an honorary Doctor of Civil Law. Franklin became a world celebrity and the first American to be accepted as an equal by the *philosophes* of Europe.

Franklin's reputation was well-deserved because his *Experiments and Observations on Electricity* revealed a remarkable ability to conceptualize the data of his experiments. His most important accomplishments were in the realm of theory where he was able to show that his single fluid concept fitted the observed conditions of electrical experiments more satisfactorily than the widely held two-fluid theory that had been advanced by Charles Du Fay, the French scientist. Franklin also suggested the terminology by which one electrical charge was called negative and the other positive. Although he incorrectly hypothesized that the flow of current was from positive to negative, his terminology and his conception of a single fluid or current of electricity remained useful for further scientific activity in the generations that followed. I. Bernard Cohen, a leading historian of science, has concluded that "only a scientist of first rank would ever have devised the experiments that Franklin performed, [and] would have drawn from them the theoretical conclusions that Franklin drew."

For his own and later generations, Franklin's dramatic investigations concerning lightning obscured his more basic theorizing. Franklin, as well as French scientists, conducted experiments with pointed bars of iron projected from church spires in order to demonstrate that sparks could be drawn by induction from the electrified rod when low-lying storm clouds passed over. His famous kite experiment was simply another effort to test his hypothesis that lightning was an electrical phenomenon. On the basis of these experiments, he made the suggestion in *Poor Richard's Almanac* in 1753 that lightning rods could be used to preserve houses, churches, and ships from a stroke of lightning. Soon afterwards, lightning rods began to appear in buildings in Philadelphia, and in London and Paris.

Franklin's utilitarian instincts led him to develop other useful inventions and household gadgets besides the lightning rod. He invented bifocal glasses and developed an improved stove which was to be called the "Franklin stove"; he made a stool that opened up into a ladder and a rocking chair that fanned the sitter while he rocked. Yet, it would be wrong to characterize Franklin's scientific endeavors as the work of a man who was essentially a gadgeteer. He spent many more hours in study and speculation concerning a wide range of scientific questions. He theorized that there had been great changes in the climates of the earth in past ages; he was tremendously interested in the great currents of the Atlantic Ocean and kept systematic readings of ocean temperatures; he developed hypotheses about the movement of winds and storms; he speculated about the causes of the common cold; and he suggested improvements in the ventilation of buildings. Franklin went as far as he could with his skimpy mathematical equipment in studies of heat and light; in a letter that was read later to the Royal Society, he expressed discontent with the prevailing corpuscular theory of light and suggested that light consisted of "vibrations" in a subtle elastic fluid filling universal space.

To be sure, many of Franklin's scientific speculations pointed to possibilities for useful application. City dwellers who sought the comforts of life, and who were engaged in trade and ocean travel, welcomed a more precise knowledge of winds, storms, ocean currents, ventilation, and the characteristics of heat and light. Yet this was also the essential character of the faith in science that enlightened men accepted everywhere in the eighteenth century—in Europe as well as in America. When Franklin wrote, "What signifies philosophy that doth not apply to some use," he was echoing the European belief that mechanical inventions were the legitimate fruits of man's rational powers and that improved human technics were human blessings that justified their hopes for the progress of mankind.

The American Philosophical Society

Franklin joined with other perceptive American scientists in seeking to encourage ideas, test each other's hypotheses, and correct each other's mistakes. His *Proposals For Promoting Useful Knowledge* was drafted with the help of John Bartram; moreover, Bartram, Franklin, and Thomas Bond, a Philadelphia physician, were the effective leaders of the American Philosophical Society that was launched in 1743. Cadwallader Colden of New York also gave his full support to the infant society, and letters of invitation were sent to "virtuosi or ingenious men" in other colonies. Unfortunately, this early effort to establish an organized scientific circle in America proved to be premature. Men of learning in America were not ready for such intellectual cooperation and the warfare between England and France in the middle decades of the century drained off much talent and energy into political and military channels.

In 1767, however, the American Philosophical Society was revived by a new and eager group of interested men who republished Franklin's proposal of 1743 as an indication of the Society's aims. This time, the Society had much wider support; in addition to a strong nucleus of Philadelphians, there were members in the middle and southern colonies, and a few in New England and the West Indies. The first paper to be read to the society was prepared by David Rittenhouse, the young prodigy of Pennsylvania, who constructed the first orrery, or mechanical planetarium, in America.

The revived society organized an ambitious effort to gather cooperative

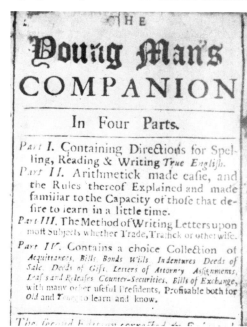

Another secular form of reading instruction for young people. Rare Book Division. The New York Public Library. Astor, Lenox and Tilden Foundations.

observations of the transit of Venus which was expected in 1769. A subsidy was received from the Pennsylvania legislature, while telescopes were assembled in Philadelphia and neighboring areas to make observations. Additional observation points were set up elsewhere in the colonies, many of them stimulated by the enthusiasm of the American Philosophical Society.

The bulk of the transit accounts that were collected by the cooperative effort of the American Philosophical Society were published in its first volume of *Transactions* in 1771. The *Transactions* seemed to betoken a new stage of intellectual maturity for America; American science was becoming something more than the puttering of gentlemen in their gardens or the gadgeteering of homespun inventors. To this extent, therefore, Franklin's vision of scientific progress for America was becoming a reality.

Changing Conceptions of Law and Government

Although their fiercely competitive economic energies and their skillful manipulation of the power of the assemblies indicated that they were restless subjects, colonial Americans took pride and satisfaction in being members of the British Empire. If we assume that Benjamin Franklin was the American who represented best the dominant forces in American life at the time, then his conception of the Empire may be taken as a measure of American expectations concerning the future relationships between England and America. At the time that he proposed his plan of union to the Albany Congress, Franklin wrote, "I should hope . . . that by such a union the people of Great Britain and the people of the colonies could learn to consider themselves as not belonging to a different community with different interests, but to one community with one interest."

In various ways, colonial writers employed symbols of legitimacy that were derived from the usages, rights, and privileges of the English constitutional system. Much of the American political thought in the pre-Revolutionary era is saturated with arguments and precedents taken from English historical experience. This, in itself, is an eloquent testimony of the essential loyalty to the Empire which overshadowed the conflicts of interest that were so apparent in the political and economic affairs of the colonies.

Colonial Conceptions of Natural Law

Yet, with each passing decade, there were significant changes in colonial political thought which opened up possibilities for a crisis of legitimacy. The theories of natural law associated with the intellectual influence of the Enlightenment provided colonial thinkers with ideas and justifications that had far-reaching implications. And, even though many of these new conceptions of law and government were not often employed directly in political arguments with royal governors, or with the Crown or Parliament, their widespread acceptance by enlightened men in America gave them a crucial significance.

John Wise of Massachusetts was the earliest and ablest of eighteenth-century political thinkers who employed theories of law and government associated with the Enlightenment. These ideas were clearly expressed in *A Vindication of the Government of New England Churches,* published in 1717. Wise wrote the book primarily to defend the democratic and autonomous character of the Congregational churches against an attempt led by the Mathers and other orthodox Puritans to bring the churches under a closer system of control by the ministerial associations of Connecticut and Massachusetts. Yet, the arguments that he developed in his work contained a force and a meaning that went far beyond the narrow concerns of the ecclesiastical controversy.

John Wise had studied carefully the works of European philosophical and political writers and he particularly admired the natural-law theories of the German philosopher, Samuel Von Pufendorf. Hence, when he came to write the *Vindication,* he had absorbed much of the philosophy of the natural-law school; he abandoned traditional theological arguments in favor of a rationalistic theory of the nature of man and the origins of the state.

Government, in the opinion of John Wise, was the result of man's use of his rational powers and not of any divine ordinances, although the reason of man, of course, is part of God's creation. "It is certain," he wrote, "[that] civil government in general is a very admirable result of providence, and an incomparable benefit to mankind, yet must needs be acknowledged to be the effect of human pre-compacts and not of divine institution; it is the produce of man's reason, of human and rational combinations, and not from any direct orders of infinite wisdom. . . ." Since all men were endowed with right reason, Wise assumed that they would perceive that "[it] is a fundamental law of nature, that every man as far as in him lies, do maintain a sociableness with others, agreeable with the main end and disposition of human nature in general." Furthermore, he believed that one of the essential qualities of man was "an original liberty, stamped on his rational nature."

Thus, in the theory developed by John Wise, the legitimacy of government must rest on a social compact, and lawful governments exist primarily to cherish and protect the original liberty with which the rational nature of man is endowed. He also affirmed that the best form of government to guarantee the liberty of the individual is one that contains a strong element of "noble democracy." "A democracy in church and state," Wise stated, "is a very honorable and regular government according to the dictates of right reason."

Nevertheless, it would be wrong to assume that Wise had developed a revolutionary theory that rejected the legitimacy of the British Empire or of English institutions. He had no idea whatsoever of throwing off allegiance to England; as a loyal, colonial Englishman, he emphasized to his readers that a "noble democracy" was, in fact, an essential ingredient of the British Empire. In his analysis of the forms of government, Wise had this to say:

Mixed governments . . . are of various and of divers kinds . . . yet probably the fairest in the world is that which has a regular monarchy, settled upon a noble democracy as its basis . . . It is said of the British Empire, that it is such a monarchy as that, by the necessary subordinate concurrence of the lords and commons in the making and repealing all statutes or acts of parliament it hath the main advantages of an aristocracy and of a democracy, and yet free from the disadvantages and evils of either . . . It is a kingdom that, of all the kingdoms of the world, is most like to the kingdom of Jesus Christ, whose yoke is easy and burden light.

By the middle of the eighteenth century the natural rights theory had become commonplace among the rationalist preachers of New England. In this regard, Jonathan Mayhew attracted widespread attention in New England and the mother country with a highly publicized sermon on civil obedience delivered in 1750. This sermon was motivated by a desire to express opposition to the Anglicans and Tories who were seeking to memorialize the anniversary of the death of Charles I and to elevate him to a position of saintly martyrdom.

In his sermon entitled *A Discourse Concerning Unlimited Submission and Non-Resistance to the Higher Powers,* Mayhew fused traditional Calvinist doctrines concerning the right of resistance with the natural-law theories of Locke and other seventeenth-century political philoso-

The Right of Resistance

phers. With regard to the resistance of Parliament to King Charles, he declared in no uncertain terms that this had not been rebellion "but a most righteous and glorious stand, made in defence of the natural and legal rights of the people, against the unnatural and illegal encroachments of arbitrary power." Furthermore, he announced his support of the more universal claim that the people at any time and in any place have the right to resist the commands of any unlawful authority. The people have the right, he affirmed,

to disobey the civil powers . . . in cases of very great and general oppression, when humble remonstrances fail of having any effect; and, when the public welfare cannot be otherwise provided for and secured, to rise unanimously even against the sovereign himself, in order to redress their grievances; to vindicate their natural and legal rights; to break the yoke of tyranny, and free themselves and posterity from inglorious servitude and ruin.

It must be remembered, however, that Mayhew's sermon had no immediate cutting edge. The king of England in 1750 was a Hanoverian, and the Hanoverian dynasty had no desire to have any member of the Stuart family sanctified. The ruling Whig oligarchy in English politics fully sympathized with the view that Parliament had made a rightful and glorious stand against the unlawful uses of power by the Stuart kings. Mayhew was careful to state that resistance to authority was warranted only "in cases of very great and general oppression" or "when the public welfare cannot otherwise by provided for." Nevertheless, the reiteration of the ideas of natural law and natural rights in the election sermons of New England ministers did implant such conceptions more firmly in the minds of Americans.

A Preference for Mixed Government

Furthermore, it must be said that, when Americans reflected about the forms of government in the early decades of the eighteenth century, they continued to display a significant degree of uncertainty about the merits of democracy. John Wise, to be sure, expressed favorable views concerning democracy in church and state and, thereby, rejected the earlier Puritan idea that a "democratie" was the worst of all forms of government. Yet a close reading of his *Vindication* makes it quite apparent that the kind of democracy he had in mind was the democracy of small communities—the church or the town meeting. He did not elaborate any ideas about the institutions of representation that would be necessary and proper for a larger civil society. Indeed, when he did consider the various forms of government, he showed an unmistakable preference for the "mixed government" of the British constitution.

In this regard, William Smith, the first provost of the College of Philadelphia, developed some interesting ideas about the forms of government that would be suitable to the conditions of American society in this century. In his *Brief State of the Province of Pennsylvania* (1753), Smith suggested that the simpler forms of government that were suitable in an infant stage of society were not adequate for the more complex conditions of a rich and populous country. He wrote

Those who have made Politics their Study know very well, that Infant Settlements flourish fastest under a Government leaning to the republican or popular Forms, because such a government immediately interests every Individual in the Common Prosperity, and settles itself at once in a broad and firm Basis. Moreover, the People being but few, and but small Profit in public offices, the Government may also be administer'd without the Faction and Anarchy incident to popular forms. But in proportion as a Country grows rich and populous, more Checks are wanted to the Power of the People; and the Government, by nice Gradations, should verge more and more from the popular to the mixt forms.

Whether Smith had Montesquieu in mind as one of those who had made politics their study is not certain, but his statement certainly echoes the idea stated in the *Spirit of Laws* that the laws and the constitution of a country have a significant relation to natural and social factors like climate, religion, customs, and commerce.

It would be rash, indeed, for a historian to assert that colonial writers in the first half of the eighteenth century were expressing their ideas about the forms of government or about the rights and liberties of the people with any idea of independence in their minds. The British Constitution seemed to be their ideal of a true form of government, as it seemed to be to many enlightened men in Europe. Yet there was a subtle and significant alteration in their ideas of legitimacy. The lawfulness of authority could no longer be adequately justified by references to divine ordinances or to established privileges and usages. To be lawful, the use of authority had to satisfy the "dictates of right reason" and "the common good and safety of society"; the legitimacy of a political system depended on its ability to engender the belief that it was cherishing and protecting the natural liberty and equality of man.

The Pennsylvania Magazine. *Rare Book Division. The New York Public Library Astor, Lenox and Tilden Foundations.*

A New Pattern of Imperial Power

On May 18, 1763, several hundred merchants of London, in an address to King George III, hailed the peace that concluded the Seven Years' War and declared, "We have now the satisfaction to see a war founded in Justice and Necessity, prosecuted with vigor and glory, at length concluded on terms of real and solid advantage." Those who signed the address undoubtedly took great satisfaction in the treaty which added Canada and Florida to the Empire. The acquisition of such vast regions in North America opened up prospects for future markets as the new lands were cleared and settled by men and women who were freed from the fear of foreign enemies and their Indian allies. *The Expanded Empire*

Not all Englishmen, however, were happy over the Treaty of Paris. Pitt and Newcastle, both of whom had been eliminated from their Cabinet posts by the influence of the new king, were opposed to the treaty. They shared the conviction of many Englishmen that the West Indian islands of Guadeloupe and Martinique should not have been returned to France. To them, the West Indian sugar islands were clearly profitable, while Canada and Florida looked like liabilities. Florida seemed to be little more than a wasteland of swamp and sand, while the cost of administering and defending the vast expanse of Canada was certain to become a heavy financial drain.

Despite these disagreements over the Treaty of Paris, it was apparent to all that George III, who had ascended to the throne in 1760, was determined to assert a greater measure of kingly power. He did not, however, make the mistake of trying to rule by prerogative as had the Stuart king in the previous century; he knew that he must accept the sovereignty of Parliament. He attempted, therefore, to work with the existing political machinery of Parliament—using his influence and patronage in Parliament and in elections in order to build up a faction of the king's friends. Thus the ministers who guided bills through Parliament were his ministers; they followed his lead and pulled the strings that would get him the necessary votes in Parliament. *Reorganizing the Empire*

In view of these changes, the ministers who formulated and administered English policies after the resignation of Newcastle in 1762 were disposed to favor measures that would reorganize and strengthen the administration of the Empire. When the Earl of Halifax took the post of Secretary of State for the colonies in the reorganized ministry of 1763, all the colonial agents in England were dismayed because they realized that the general supervision of colonial affairs had come into the hands of a man known to favor a tough policy toward the colonies. Halifax had served as president of the Board of Trade from 1748 to 1761 and, during that time, he had advocated parliamentary taxation of the colonies, stringent measures against colonial commerce with the French West

Indies, the establishment of English bishops in the colonies, and a revision of some colony charters.

It would be wrong to assume, however, that King George and his ministers wished to wield arbitrary or tyrannous power. Some form of imperial reorganization was required no matter who determined the policies of the government. Indeed, Pitt had already led the way toward a stricter enforcement of the acts of trade and navigation during the Seven Years' War. Illicit trade with the French colonies had been a common practice in the years after the passage of the Molasses Act of 1733, and English officials had generally looked the other way. Such trade with the French continued during the early years of the Seven Years' War and became a serious threat to the British war effort in North America. In part, the French fleet in the Caribbean was provisioned with the help of foodstuffs brought in by merchants from the American colonies.

Recognizing the seriousness of the problem, Pitt had sent a circular letter to all the colonial governors in 1760, in which he ordered them, in the name of the king, to "make the strictest and most diligent Enquiry into the State of this dangerous and ignominious Trade . . . and that you do take every Step, authorized by Law, to bring all such heinous offenders to the most exemplary and condign punishment." Pitt's war policy of rigid enforcement of the trade acts effectively reduced the amount of smuggling in the last years of the war. The Royal Navy was used as the chief instrument for breaking up such lawless activities, while English officials in the seaport towns of New England sought to make vigorous use of special writs to search for smuggled goods.

The merchants of Boston, however, seeking to prevent the further issuance of such "writs of assistance," retained James Otis, a leading lawyer, to act in their behalf. In an impassioned plea before the Court, Otis declared that such writs were "against the fundamental principles of law" and that any act of Parliament that authorized such writs was "against natural equity." "Reason and the constitution are both against this writ," he maintained. This appeal to natural law and to constitutional principles in order to limit acts of Parliament was unsuccessful at the time. The Superior Court of Massachusetts, after consulting with English authorities, upheld the legality of the writs. Yet, Otis paved the way for legal and constitutional conceptions that were to be used again by colonial lawyers.

The first measures of a postwar policy that were framed by a new ministry under the leadership of the Earl of Bute merely extended by the decisions and actions of the war years. In February of 1763, both houses of Parliament passed a bill for an enlarged army of 7,500 men to be stationed in America. In October, 1763, the king issued a proclamation regulating settlement and Indian affairs in the territory west of the Allegheny mountains. The proclamation, drafted by the Board of Trade at the urging of Lord Halifax, provided for a line of demarcation, rough-

John R. Freeman & Co.
(Photographers) Ltd.
Harleyson House, London.

ly at the summit of the Alleghenies, to limit further western settlement. Such a policy of restraint on settlement, in effect, confirmed a treaty already made with the Indians at Easton, Pennsylvania, in 1758; by the terms of that treaty, the English had pledged to respect the claims of the Indians west of the Allegheny Mountains and to refrain from disposing of lands or of settling the area without their consent.

The issuance of the Proclamation of 1763 was hastened by news of an Indian uprising in western Pennsylvania and the region south of the Great Lakes, led by Pontiac, the war chief of the Ottawa tribe. Even though the Proclamation of 1763 was designed to be only a temporary measure to stabilize Indian relations in the frontier areas until a more lasting policy was worked out, the demarcation line tended to harden into a permanent policy after Pontiac and his warriors agreed to lay down their arms. As a consequence, an imposing barrier stood in the way of the expansive energies of the American colonists.

Britain's Revenue Problems

The events of 1763 made it clear for all to see that the expanded British Empire in North America, and the enlarged army stationed there to defend it, were going to be costly items in the postwar British budget. Hence, the British ministry faced a serious problem of raising sufficient revenues to support such heavy financial burdens especially because the national debt had swollen to the staggering total of £129,000,000 by 1763, nearly double the amount it had been in 1755. Taxes were so high that it is estimated that any Englishman who had an estate of land that brought in £1000 a year in revenue would have to pay out at least one-third in taxes.

It seemed reasonable, therefore, to many Englishmen that the American colonies should be required to share some of the increased costs of the Empire. Such a policy appeared to be just and equitable particularly because Americans were lightly taxed by comparison with Englishmen. In most colonies the tax burden per head was only one twenty-fifth of the tax burden per head in England.

Moreover, there was much evidence of wealth and extravagance in the colonies. Americans had prospered during the war years; and English army officers and English officials who were entertained in the houses of leading Americans were often astonished at the fine furniture, choice wines, and fashionable clothes that they saw. A London newspaper reported with some envy: "The colonies are in a flourishing condition, increasing every day in riches, people and territory. Britain is exhausted, she is manifestly sinking under oppressive and insupportable burdens."

After the resignation of the Earl of Bute in 1763, a reorganization of the ministry brought George Grenville into the leadership of the English government. Although he had been associated originally with the Whigs, Grenville had attached himself to the king's political friends. As Chancellor of the Exchequer, he had chief responsibility for developing a revenue policy that would enable Great Britain to carry additional governmental costs estimated at £500,000 a year; the annual expense of the 7,500 troops in North America was estimated at more than £220,000.

Grenville first sought to preserve the revenue that was available in the imperial trading system. Smuggling had increased again in the colonies after the treaty of peace, and the Grenville ministry responded by tightening the methods of enforcement for the acts of trade and navigation; new regulations were laid down for certificates, warrants, bonds, etc., so as to bind the colonial merchants in a web of bureaucratic requirements. In addition, Grenville ordered customs officials who had remained away from their posts to take up their duties in America; at the same time, officers of the Royal Navy were commanded to assist in the enforcement of the acts of trade. Such measures brought expressions of dismay almost immediately from the colonial merchants. The *Boston Gazette* reported the complaints of a meeting of merchants who declared, "Men of war, cutters, marines, with their bayonets fixed, judges of the admiralty, collectors, comptrollers, searchers, tide waiters, land waiters, with a whole catalogue of pimps, are sent hither, not to protect our trade but to distress it."

But Grenville was determined to make the customs regulations effective. The powers of the Admiralty courts were enlarged; under new procedures instituted in 1764, a customs officer might make a seizure in any of the colonies and carry the trial to Halifax, where the owner must follow to defend his property. This had the effect of removing such cases from colonial jurisdictions where various devices of delay and obstruction had been so successfully employed by lawyers representing American merchants.

It should be remembered, however, that Grenville was also attempting to improve the collection of a whole series of new taxes that had been imposed on British taxpayers—stamp duties, a window tax, and excises on malt and cider. The cider tax, indeed, was resisted by mobs so violently in many counties of England that Parliament was obliged to repeal the excise in 1765. Thus, Englishmen were giving Americans some valuable lessons in the political techniques by which unpopular measures of Parliament might be overturned.

But a stricter enforcement of existing tax measures could not yield added revenues large enough to meet the needs of the British government. Hence Grenville proposed a new measure which would secure revenue from the importation of foreign molasses into the American colonies. The Sugar Act of 1764, passed by Parliament at his urging, replaced the Molasses Act of 1733, but was quite unlike the earlier measure. The Molasses Act of 1733 had not been designed primarily to raise revenue; the duty on molasses was made prohibitively high in order to destroy the trade with the French West Indies. The Sugar Act of 1764, however, reduced the molasses duty from six to three pence per gallon; and, in view of the stricter measures of enforcement introduced in the customs system, it was clear that Grenville intended to collect the duty. Although the molasses duty was the most important provision, the Sugar Act also placed duties on coffee, pimiento, foreign indigo, and foreign sugar; in addition, a heavy duty was placed on Madeira wine, the most important staple of trade with the Wine Islands.

It was obvious that the Sugar Act was only a prelude to other measures that were equally threatening to the advantages of wealth and power that had been built up in America. Almost immediately after the Sugar Act had been passed, Parliament enacted a measure prohibiting paper money. Such a prohibition had already been applied to New England in the Currency Act of 1751; now it was extended to all of the American colonies. Although most of the colonies favored paper money, the Virginians were particularly aroused by the action of Parliament. The Virginia tobacco planters owed large sums of money to British merchants (estimated later by Thomas Jefferson to be in excess of £2,000,000); hence, they were seeking to lighten their burden of private indebtedness with a depreciated currency.

The Stamp Act

At the same time, Grenville laid the groundwork for the novel policy of taxing the colonies directly by levying a stamp duty as a further means of defraying the expenses of the Empire in America. A bill was prepared by the treasury office in England and presented to Parliament in February of 1765. Opposition to the measure was voiced by a small minority of the members of Parliament, but they were overcome by Grenville's demonstration that the total debts of all the colonies amounted to no more than £900,000, all of which was scheduled to be paid off within four years. He also emphasized the moderation of his measure and pointed out that the Stamp Act was expected to raise about £60,000 a year, only a fraction of the cost of maintaining the British army in America.

The Stamp Act, which received royal assent in March of 1765, required that stamps or stamped paper be used for all such items as newspapers, pamphlets, legal papers, mortgages, bills of lading, parchments, college diplomas, almanacs, calendars, playing cards, dice, tavern licenses, and advertisements. Thus the stamp duties reached into the everyday lives of the colonists—more particularly, they affected the significant activities that had developed in connection with the growth of the colonial economy and the growth of colonial culture. The most dynamic groups in American society, and the most articulate as well, bore the brunt of the new duties.

The Emergence of Revolutionary Politics

The Stamp Act and the other measures implemented between 1763 and 1765 seemed reasonable to Englishmen faced with the problems of administering an expanded Empire. No serious trouble was anticipated by British officials; even the colonial agents representing colonial interests in London failed to predict the swift and vehement colonial resistance. Politicians in London were out of touch with American feelings, and this led them to disastrously misjudge the colonial reaction.

Social Change and Discontent

The frenzied and ultimately revolutionary response of Americans to the proposed changes in the imperial system can be understood only if one recognizes that these innovations coincided with a developing sense of unease within the colonies. America in 1760 was a society in crisis. The very intensity of the revolutionary rhetoric suggests that other sources of social strain were being fed into the controversy with England. A century and a half of development was producing a new kind of society in the colonies. While we might easily recognize in it the roots of nineteenth-century individualism, political democracy, and capitalism, colonial Americans knew only that their increasingly competitive and materialistic society diverged from traditional ideals. At the outset of the imperial conflict, many saw an opportunity for Americans to pull together and restore traditional ways, but precisely the opposite occurred. The revolution accelerated the modernizing process; in fact, one of the triumphs of the revolutionary movement was the articulation of a radical ideology that justified these deviations from the European norm and turned them into a distinctive American ideal.

The atmosphere of crisis in the 1760's also included serious economic fears. Britain proposed to change the rules of economic life at a time when the American economy was in disarray. During the boom years of the 1750's, consumption had increased dramatically. Imports, particularly luxury goods from England, rose more rapidly than exports, and Americans found themselves with an unfavorable balance of trade. In 1760 the colonies had a trade deficit of £2 million; by 1772 it had increased to £4 million. Colonists had moral qualms about the consumption of such luxury items, and they also had to live with the psychological burden known to chronic debtors. A slight quirk of fate—a storm, a shipwreck, or, significantly, a change in trade regulations—could throw a debtor into bankruptcy. The network of debt that developed carried in addition a burdensome sense of dependency that resistance and rebellion might alleviate. The nonimportation program enacted by the Stamp Act Congress, for example, had this effect. If its manifest intent was political and economic, it was also a moral reform that insisted upon frugal living without luxurious imports, and it was an act of individual and social independence.

The extent of the economic crisis went beyond the balance of trade problem. The economies of colonial cities were in a fragile condition; economic decline in Boston, the city most militantly resisting British policy, was precipitous. Such hard times in cities meant grief for artisans as well as merchants. Statistics on poor relief in colonial cities tell an important story: the number of persons requiring assistance increased substantially during this period. But the crisis was not restricted to the cities. Rural communities were faced for the first time in American history with the threat of poverty. Village elders found themselves unable to provide farms for the rising generation. When fathers could no longer perform this role, the traditional pattern of patriarchal authority was threatened. The crisis in colonial family life is also evident in a dramatic rise in premarital pregnancy. Studies of several towns show that about one-third of all brides were pregnant at the time of marriage. Parental permission to marry—and the dowry and land such permission implied—came slowly in hard times. Premarital pregnancy may have been a way of forcing parental decisions. Whatever the motivation of youth, it is clear that traditional patterns of family authority were in crisis.

This erosion of authority affected other major institutions. The Great Awakening, which pitted many Americans against established religious institutions, left them less in awe of traditional patterns of authority and more willing to follow their individual consciences. Rapid population growth, combined with the rapid pace of social change, confused traditional patterns of politics. There was an increase in competition among political elites; one effect of this competition was a new attention to the favor of ordinary voters. While in retrospect we can see that this pointed toward political democracy, at the time people noticed only that it brought a distressing turbulence and uncertainty to politics. American concern about shifts away from traditional ideals of authority—whether in family, church, or government—provides the context for American reactions to British initiatives. This concern helps account for the emotional intensity of revolutionary politics. Paradoxically, however, the revolutionary movement itself was based less upon these older *ideals* and more upon the new social and political patterns Americans had incorporated into their *behavior* and which would become new American ideals only in the course of the revolution.

Colonial Opposition to the New Imperial Policies

Immediately after the passage of the Sugar Act, the merchants fought back in ways that were familiar to mercantile practice in England and America. They boycotted pilots who steered British naval vessels in and out of harbors; they offered experienced seamen higher wages than the Royal Navy was able to pay; and they raised mobs to obstruct any efforts by the Navy to impress seamen in order to fill out their crews. In addition, the American merchants used their market power to bring pressure on English mercantile interests; they warned their business correspondents in England that their American trade would surely decline as a consequence of Grenville's measures. A Philadelphia merchant, for example, told the London merchants with whom he had business dealings that "I would not say much of future Dealings, because I fear that all our Trade with you must come to an End, for nothing can be more certain than its Intirely ceasing if your Legislature will carry into Execution those Resolves. . . ." In letters written to the newspapers of Boston, Newport, and Philadelphia, Americans urged one another to stop buying British manufactures; American ladies, indeed, were encouraged to give up "gaudy, butterfly, vain, fantastick, and expensive Dresses bought from Europe" and to wear "plain dresses made in their own Country."

The passage of the Sugar Act also stimulated the colonial assemblies to adopt resolutions of protest. Most of the assemblies sent petitions to the king or Parliament affirming the inherent right of imposing their own taxes; and while they did not directly challenge the right of Parliament to levy duties as a regulation of trade, they did argue against the Sugar Act on the ground that it would be economically injurious. Some colonial assemblies, like that of Rhode Island, appealed for a return to the older privileges of trade, praying "that our trade may be restored to its former condition and no further limited, restrained and burdened, than becomes necessary for the general good of all your Majesty's subjects."

James Otis, however, published a pamphlet in the spring of 1764 which contained a radical challenge to the authority of Parliament. In his *Rights of the Colonies Asserted and Proved,* Otis argued that a Parliament without American representatives had no right to tax the colonies. He rejected the English argument that duties imposed on the regulation of trade were "external" taxes which had always been a part of the acknowledged authority of Parliament. Otis declared insistently that "there is no foundation for the distinction some make in England between an internal tax and an external tax on the colonies"—Parliament had no lawful authority to levy either one.

The Massachusetts House of Representatives voted to approve Otis's pamphlet and sent it to their agent in London; under pressure from Lieutenant-Governor Thomas Hutchinson, however, they toned down their petition to king and Parliament, asking merely for a continuation of ancient privileges and condemning the Sugar Act on economic grounds. The New York Assembly, on the other hand, refused to follow such an example of restraint. In October of 1764, the New Yorkers sent a resolution to the king and to both houses of Parliament taking the stand against all forms of taxation already advocated by James Otis. The New York Assembly resolved that they should "nobly disdain the thought of claiming that Exemption as a *Privilege.* They found it on a basis more honorable and stable; they challenge it, and glory in it as their Right." To the New Yorkers, ". . . all Impositions, whether they be internal taxes, or Duties paid . . . equally diminish the estates upon which they are charged."

It must be recognized, however, that such resolutions and petitions adopted by the colonial assemblies, even when they challenged the authority of Parliament to tax the colonies, were within the bounds of legitimacy. The colonial assemblies were using the normal channels of petition in the political system of the British Empire; similarly the merchants were using the acceptable devices of market power available to them in the economic system of the British Empire. Understandably, therefore, Grenville was not disheartened by these initial evidences of colonial opposition; he undoubtedly assumed that such opposition merely followed the moves of pressure and counterpressure that any politician should expect in the political game of imperial relations.

Grenville played the game accordingly. One of his secretaries, Thomas Whately, expressed the British ministry's views in a pamphlet which defended the authority of Parliament. Whately acknowledged that the American colonists were not directly represented in Parliament and hence could not directly give their consent to be taxed. But he pointed out that the same was true of most Englishmen who could not vote for members of Parliament because of property qualifications or because they resided in boroughs that sent no member. Such Englishmen, Whately claimed, had virtual representation in Parliament since every member of Parliament was elected to represent the whole English realm and the whole British Empire. By the same reasoning, therefore, one could say that the Americans were *virtually* represented in Parliament. This pamphlet was an unmistakable sign of Grenville's self-assurance.

Photograph of a mezzotint first published in London in 1774. Library of Congress.

Obviously his decision to press ahead with the Stamp Act was based on the assumption that he had nothing more to fear than petitions and pamphlets.

Resistance to the Stamp Act

To Grenville's great surprise, the response of the Americans to the Stamp Act was nothing less than revolutionary in character. From the very first moment that the news of the final passage of the Stamp Act reached the colonies, the tone of American opposition developed notes of defiance that went far beyond the remonstrant forms of address used against the Sugar Act.

The House of Burgesses was in session in Virginia when the news arrived. Almost immediately, Patrick Henry, a new member recently elected to the House, rose to introduce a series of resolutions against the Stamp Act. The speech that he made in support of his resolutions was so strongly worded at one point that the Speaker of the House of Burgesses admonished him for speaking treason. Although the conservatives in the Virginia Assembly were strong enough to rescind the most provocative of the resolutions which Patrick Henry had offered, most of the newspapers of the colonies included the more radical resolution in their accounts as if it had been adopted by the House of Burgesses. Hence, Americans everywhere were stirred by the belief that the Burgesses of Virginia had been bold enough to declare ''that the General Assembly of this Colony, with the Consent of his Majesty, or his Substitute, HAVE the Sole Right and Authority to lay Taxes and Impositions upon It's Inhabitants: And, that every Attempt to vest such Authority in any other Person or Persons whatsoever, has a manifest Tendency to Destroy AMERICAN FREEDOM.''

The exaggerated reports of the Virginia resolves had a striking effect on opinion in all the colonies, particularly in Massachusetts. The House of Representatives, there, had never been satisfied with the restrained petition which they had been persuaded to accept by Lieutenant-Governor Thomas Hutchinson the year before. They were convinced that their moderation had been a serious political error when they learned that members of Parliament had refused to hear any petitions at all at the time the Stamp Act was passed. Hence the House of Representatives adopted a statement which set forth a revolutionary theory concerning parliamentary authority within the Empire. In replying to Governor Bernard's demand for respectful submission to the decrees of Parliament, the Massachusetts House of Representatives stated:

It by no means appertains to us to presume to adjust the boundaries of the power of Parliament; but boundaries there undoubtedly are . . . Your Excellency will acknowledge that there are certain original inherent rights belonging to the peoples, which the Parliament itself cannot divest them of, consistent with their own constitution: among these is the right of representation in the same body which exercises the power of taxation. There is a necessity that the subjects of America should exercise this power within themselves, otherwise they can have no share in that most essential right, for they are not represented in Parliament, and indeed we think it impracticable.

Moreover, the House of Representatives of Massachusetts had already sent a circular letter to the other colonies, inviting them to meet in a Congress at New York to consider ways of making a united representation of their opposition in petitions to be sent to the king and to both houses of Parliament. Nine of the 13 mainland colonies responded to the invitation and 27 delegates assembled in New York in October of 1765—one month before the Stamp Act was to go into effect in America.

The Stamp Act Congress

The delegates at the Stamp Act Congress drew up a statement of the "rights and privileges of the British American colonies." Some of the declarations in this statement recapitulated the traditional rights of Englishmen; conspicuous among these was the principle "that it is essential to the Freedom of the People, and the undoubted Right of *Englishmen,* that no taxes be imposed on them, but with their own Consent, given personally, or by their Representatives." Other declarations repeated previous complaints that the Sugar Act duties were burdensome and that the scarcity of specie made payment of them "absolutely impracticable."

In a separate address to the House of Commons, the delegates to the Stamp Act Congress attempted to indicate more explicitly what they thought the limits of parliamentary authority ought to be. This address raised the question: "Whether there be not a material Distinction in Reason and Sound Policy, at least, between the necessary Exercise of Parliamentary Jurisdiction in General Acts, for the Amendment of the Common Law, and the Regulation of Trade and Commerce through the whole Empire, and the Exercise of that Jurisdiction by imposing Taxes on the Colonies." Apparently "due subordination" to Parliament meant submission to general laws and trade regulations but not to parliamentary taxation.

Such a delimitation of the authority of Parliament left many questions unanswered. Certainly the colonial Americans did not intend to admit that Parliament should legislate concerning their internal affairs; but to admit the legitimacy of "general acts" of legislation could lead to interference in local matters affecting justice, religion, and education. Also it was not entirely clear whether the illegitimacy of taxation included all duties imposed on commerce, or only those which were designed for revenue. Nevertheless, it was clear enough that the main issue as defined by the Stamp Act Congress was taxation, and that it was on this line that the Americans were prepared to fight their battle.

Violent Tactics of the "Sons of Liberty"

And fight they did. First in Boston, and then in other cities and towns, Americans formed themselves into associations which they called the "Sons of Liberty," announcing their determination to resist the Stamp Act by any and every means. Even before any stamps had arrived in America, a Boston mob attacked and pillaged the home of Andrew Oliver, who had been appointed distributor of stamps for New England. Although Oliver promised quite readily that he would resign his commission when it arrived, the mob made further attacks on the homes of Lieutenant-Governor Hutchinson and of the Comptroller of the Customs. Mob violence also occurred in other cities including Newport, New York, and Baltimore. As a consequence of the organized activities of radical elements everywhere in the continental colonies, the designated stamp distributors for the nine districts of America either resigned or pledged not to distribute stamps.

By November 1, the date on which the Stamp Act was to take effect, the radical Sons of Liberty were exercising a *de facto* authority in the colonies. Since there were no stamp distributors to receive the stamps, they were generally held on board ships in the harbors of the seaport cities under the watchful eyes of the Royal Navy. Trade came to a standstill because, under the terms of the Stamp Act, no ship could leave port, no newspapers could be published, and no courts could be held without stamped paper and certificates. Eventually vessels began to leave port in the last weeks of 1765 and the early months of 1766; in addition newspapers began to publish and courts began to hold sessions—but all without stamps. Nevertheless, most trade relations with England continued to be disrupted because American merchants withheld their remittances due to British merchants.

Thus, it was apparent that the Americans had succeeded not only in nullifying the Stamp Act, but also in dealing a crippling blow to British commercial interests. The Americans owed approximately £4,000,000 in private debts to the British merchants, and their refusal to make any payments hit the British economy hard. A British merchant expressed the fears felt by others like him when he reported in August of 1765:

"The present Situation of the Colonies alarms every Person who has any Connection with them. . . . the Avenues of Trade are all shut up. . . . We have no Remittances, and are at our Witt's End for Want of Money to fulfill our Engagement with our Tradesmen."

In December of 1765, a Committee of Merchants of London petitioned Parliament to grant "every Ease and Advantage the North Americans can with propriety desire. . . ." Additional petitions flooded in on Parliament from such leading commercial centers as Bristol, Liverpool, Manchester, Leeds, and Glasgow—all urging the modification or repeal of the measures which were so obnoxious to America. The decisive weapon of colonial American power was plain enough to see. Robert Walpole's son, Horace, perceived it when he wrote: ". . . the weapon with which the Colonies armed themselves to most advantage, was the refusal of paying the debts they owed to our merchants at home, for goods and wares exported to the American provinces. These debts involved the merchants of London, Liverpool, Manchester and other great trading towns, in a common cause with the Americans, who foreswore all traffic with us, unless the obnoxious Stamp Act was repealed."

In short, the Americans had largely abandoned the legitimate techniques of political conflict which had evolved in the preceding century of imperial relations; they turned instead to uses of power that political scientists usually include in a definition of revolutionary politics. The instances of mob violence, of course, were dramatic, but mobbing is not necessarily sufficient evidence of a revolutionary situation. Much more important was the appearance of organized political associations, such as the Sons of Liberty, with sufficient power to establish extra-legal forms of authority. In most colonies, they, and not the lawfully constituted authorities, determined when courts were to open, when ships could leave port, and when newspapers were to resume publication; in New York, indeed, the Lieutenant-Governor was virtually a prisoner in his own house. In addition the Stamp Act Congress was a significant political device for a unified resistance movement. It was an extra-legal body and, in view of the determined opposition of the Americans, such a colonial Congress could very easily become the headquarters of a revolutionary government—a state within the state.

The mob riots, the colonial boycott of British trade, and the radical acts of the Sons of Liberty convinced many Englishmen that a revolution did, in fact, exist in America. The most rancorous of the parliamentary factions called for the use of military force to put down the rebellion; the followers of the Duke of Bedford called for the dispatch of a fleet and army to stuff the stamps down the Americans' throats. It was said that "the Bloomsbury Gang," as Bedford's faction was often referred to in the British press, was ready to "butcher all America" if necessary to obtain obedience to British authority.

The blusterings of the Bedford faction, however, represented a form of political extremism that was unacceptable to the mercantile interests of

Repeal of the Stamp Act

Britain and to the parliamentary majority. Grenville had resigned before the crisis in America had reached its highest pitch, and his successor, the Marquis of Rockingham, was the leader of a Whig faction that was known to favor conciliation. Strongly influenced by mercantile conceptions, the Rockingham ministry preferred to think of the Americans as angry customers rather than as rebellious radicals. The new ministry, therefore, worked hand in hand with the merchants of London and other commercial towns to secure the repeal of the Stamp Act.

The proposal to revoke the Act gained the valuable support of William Pitt who, more than anyone, had won the expanded empire for Great Britain. The "Great Commoner" said to a crowded Parliament, "I rejoice that America has resisted" and proceeded to spell out his recommendations for a solution to the crisis. He urged that "the Stamp Act be repealed absolutely, totally, and immediately . . . at the same time, let the sovereign authority of this country over the colonies, be asserted in as strong terms as can be devised, and be made to extend to every point of legislation whatsoever. That we may bind their trade, confine their manufactures, and exercise every power whatsoever, except that of taking their money out of their pockets without their consent." With such important support inside and outside of Parliament, the Rockingham ministry conducted its strategic retreat. The Stamp Act was repealed early in March of 1766, and the repeal bill simply noted that the continuance of the Act would be attended with "many Inconveniences, and may be productive of Consequences greatly detrimental to the Commercial Interests of these Kingdoms."

On the other hand, the overwhelming majority of Englishmen were unwilling to admit the colonial claim that Parliament did not have the right and the authority to tax the Americans. The Chief Justice of the King's Bench, Lord Mansfield, reaffirmed the essential authority of Parliament in the strongest terms when he said to the House of Lords, ". . . the British legislature, as to the power of making laws, represents the whole British Empire, and has authority to bind every part and every subject without the least distinction, whether such subject have a right to vote or not, or whether the law binds places within the realm or without." Heedful of such influential sentiments, Rockingham presented a resolution which reaffirmed the sovereign authority of Parliament—a resolution which became known as the Declaratory Act. The Parliament repealed the Stamp Act only after it had voted for the Declaratory Act. Thus, the repeal of the Stamp Act was offered to the American colonies yoked to another act which declared that "the King's Majesty, by and with the advice and consent of the Lords spiritual and temporal and Commons of Great Britain in parliament assembled, had, hath, and of right ought to have, full power and authority to make laws and statutes of sufficient force and validity to bind the colonies and people of America . . . in all cases whatsoever."

There was great rejoicing in America when the news of the repeal of the Stamp Act arrived. The Sons of Liberty, everywhere, organized celebrations with many displays of fireworks and much drinking of toasts in their favorite taverns. All classes in America, but particularly the well-to-do, welcomed the return of internal peace. In England the merchants were joyful at the resumption of trade and commerce, while the politicians found what comfort they could in the phrases of the Declaratory Act. Yet, if we view the situation in the light of history, we must accept the judgment of Lawrence Henry Gipson, a leading authority on the British Empire in the eighteenth century, who maintains that "a fatal breach in the constitution of the Empire" occurred when Parliament was obliged to accept a *de facto* limitation of its powers at the time of the Stamp Act crisis.

Certainly the crisis of legitimacy that had been raised by the Stamp Act controversy remained unresolved. The authority of Parliament had been successfully challenged, and the Declaratory Act had no practical effect whatsoever in the colonies. Furthermore there was growing evidence that the older conceptions of the Empire were dead, and that the older ties of loyalty had lost much of their meaning for many Americans; some Americans, indeed, were able to envision an independent destiny.

The Crisis of Legitimacy

If Benjamin Franklin can be used as a representative American of the eighteenth century, it is possible to see how these changes were taking place in the minds of Americans. In 1754, Franklin had fully accepted the sovereign power of Parliament over the colonies inasmuch as he had proposed that his plan of union be established by an act of Parliament. Serving as a colonial agent in 1765, he had accepted the Stamp Act in a mood of pragmatic realism. By the end of 1765, however, he was defending the riots and resistance of his fellow Americans in a series of letters written to leading London newspapers. In an examination before the bar of the House of Commons in 1766, when the repeal measure was being considered, Franklin testified that the colonies had always been willing to accept external taxes in the form of duties on commerce, but that they would never admit the right of Parliament to levy internal taxes. Reflecting about the whole issue of parliamentary power again in 1768, he came to the conclusion that Parliament could not bind the colonies in any way. "Something might be made of either of the extremes," Franklin wrote at that time, "that Parliament has power to make *all laws* for us, or that it has a power to make *no laws* for us; and I think that the arguments for the latter are more numerous and weighty than those for the former."

Such changes in attitude toward the authority of Parliament and the constitution of the Empire caused the Americans to resent imperial restraint that did not suit their interests. After 1766, relations between the colonies and Britain were never basically compatible. The Americans resorted to various forms of agitation, obstruction, and defiance that have become a familiar pattern in the nationalist movements of the twentieth century. Year by year, it became evident that a subordinate position within the Empire was no longer acceptable for the American colonies in view of their growing social maturity. At a much later point in history, the leaders of Great Britain developed sufficient political imagination to devise a commonwealth of nations in order to provide a more dignified political status for colonies that had reached political and social maturity; but such wisdom was lacking in the eighteenth century. Hence, the decade between 1766 and 1776 saw much fumbling and confusion on both sides of the Atlantic; there were occasional moments of calm, but the main drift was always in the direction of conflict and misunderstanding.

Continuing Political Conflicts   Thus, in a few short months after the repeal of the Stamp Act, the members of Parliament were outraged to learn that the province of New York had refused to obey the Quartering Act of 1765. This Act required the colonies to provide for the housing of the British troops stationed in America and the furnishing of certain items of food and furniture for the comfort of the soldiers. The largest contingent of the enlarged British army was stationed in New York where the Assembly made only a limited provision for the troops, and insisted that England should reimburse the province for all such expenses.

This new refusal to acknowledge the binding effect of parliamentary legislation in the colonies angered even the friends in England who had supported the Americans in the Stamp Act controversy. William Pitt, now the Earl of Chatham, and again the leader of the ministry, was determined that the law should be enforced, and that the time had come for the government to take a firm stand. The result was a Parliamentary act of 1767 which suspended all legislative functions in New York until it met the requirements of the American Quartering Act. Despite the protests of many of the more radical leaders in the province, the New York Assembly backed down and passed a bill which met the stipulations laid down by Parliament for the quartering of troops.

The Chancellor of the Exchequer in Chatham's short-lived ministry was Charles Townshend, a clever and witty politician who was characterized by Edmund Burke as the fair-haired boy of the House of Commons. Townshend delighted his supporters in Parliament with a scheme to obtain revenue from the colonies that might get around colonial objections. He, like many other Englishmen, believed that the Americans objected only to internal taxes as Franklin had testified in 1765; this serious political error revealed that Townshend had failed to take note of the much broader language of American pamphlets and petitions at the time of the Stamp Act controversy. At any rate, Parliament, in 1767, enacted a measure which levied duties on glass, lead, paper, paints, and tea; furthermore the enacting clause of the Act made it clear that the money raised by the duties was to be used not only to defray the expenses of the army in America, but also to support the salaries of royal governors and other civil officials. Thus the royal governors would be able to look to Parliament and not to colonial assemblies for their salaries. To top off the new program recommended by Townshend, Parliament also created a Board of Customs Commissioners to be stationed in Boston in order to insure the collection of the new duties.

The Americans responded to the Townshend duties with renewed resistance and defiance. An impressive attack on Townshend's theory of taxation appeared in the famous *Letters From a Farmer in Pennsylvania to the Inhabitants of the British Colonies,* written by John Dickinson and widely circulated in the colonies. Dickinson made plain that there was no distinction between internal and external taxes, and challenged the authority of Parliament to levy either. In February, 1768, the Massachusetts House of Representatives addressed a Circular Letter, drawn up by Samuel Adams, to the other colonial assemblies denouncing the Townshend duties as violating the right of free men to be taxed only with their consent. The Circular Letter also emphasized the dangers to the power of the assemblies that would result if the British government used the revenues collected from the Townshend duties to pay the salaries of royal governors and other civil officers. Within a few months, the Circular Letter had been endorsed by New Hampshire, Virginia, Maryland, Connecticut, Rhode Island, Georgia, and South Carolina.

Resistance to the Townshend Duties

John Dickinson.
Rush Rhees Library. The University of Rochester.

LETTER II.

Beloved Countrymen,

THERE is another late act of parliament, which seems to me to be as destructive to the liberty of these colonies, as that inserted in my last letter; that is, the act for granting the duties on paper, glass, &c. It appears to me to be unconstitutional.

The parliament unquestionably possesses a legal authority to *regulate* the trade of *Great-Britain*, and all its colonies. Such an authority is essential to the relation between a mother country and its colonies; and necessary for the common good of all. He, who considers these provinces as states distinct from the *British Empire*, has very slender notions of *justice* or of *their interests*. We are but parts of *a whole*; and therefore there must exist a power somewhere, to preside, and preserve the connection in due order. This power is lodged in the parliament; and we are as much dependant on *Great-Britain*, as a perfectly free people can be on another.

Equally important was a nonconsumption movement aimed at British manufactured goods that began in Boston in October, 1767, and soon spread to other towns. This was extended into a more general nonimportation by the merchants of Boston and New York, followed somewhat later by the Quaker merchants of Philadelphia. Furthermore, the newly chosen Board of Customs Commissioners found that they were facing an almost hopeless task in enforcing the new revenue acts. The Commissioners experienced open evidences of contempt and reported to the home government in February of 1769 that in the previous two and a half years, only six seizures had been made by English customs officers in all the colonies and only one of these had been prosecuted with success; and, in three of these cases, the customs officials had been resisted by mobs.

Matters reached a critical point in the summer of 1768 when a crew from a British man-of-war seized John Hancock's sloop, *Liberty,* for alleged violation of the trade acts. Three days later, a mob raised by the radical leaders of Boston drove the customs officials to take refuge in a British fortress at Castle William in Boston Harbor. When news of this open defiance of the Customs Commissioners reached England, two regiments of troops were ordered to Boston from the British Isles, and two others were brought in from Halifax. In addition, Parliament adopted resolutions offering their support to the king in his efforts to obtain evidence for all cases of treasonable activity and to bring the offenders to England for trial.

This was bold language, but few in Parliament were really ready to run the risk of further rebellion in the colonies. They were aware of a sensational letter in the *London Public Advertiser* which pointed out that the Townshend duties had produced no more than £3,500 in revenue in the first year and a half, while the business loss to the British economy from the nonimportation and nonconsumption agreements was estimated at the staggering figure of £7,250,000. In addition, the Chatham ministry was obviously falling apart: Townshend had died at the age of 41 several months after his act had been passed; Chatham had resigned in October of 1768 because of ill health; and his successor, the Duke of Grafton, provided a completely ineffectual leadership in the year before he was forced out of office. In January of 1770, Lord North became the leader of a new ministry that took on the responsibility for settling the American crisis. North tried to pursue a pragmatic policy aimed at two seemingly irreconcilable ends: the upholding of the authority of Parliament and the avoidance of any measures that would give the colonial Americans any reasonable ground for continuing their organized acts of defiance.

In line with such conceptions of policy, the first action of the Lord North ministry was to repeal all the Townshend duties except for the duty on tea. The members of his Cabinet Council agreed that the duties had been "contrary to the true principles of commerce"; and the duty on tea was being maintained, Lord North explained, primarily "as a mark of the supremacy of Parliament, and an efficient declaration of their right to govern the colonies."

Ironically, on the very same day that Lord North made his proposal to repeal the Townshend duties, a bloody clash occurred in Boston between the townsmen and the soldiers of the British regiments stationed in Boston. On March 5, 1770, after much abuse from a hostile mob that had gathered near the customs house, members of the guard of British regulars who were on duty there opened fire on the crowd. Five people were killed and others wounded. The people of Boston and surrounding towns were so outraged at this "massacre" that it seemed likely that they might try to use force to drive the British regiments out of town. Their leaders made full use of the threat of a popular uprising to demand that the soldiers who fired on the people be surrendered to the civil authorities of the colony to stand trial, and that all troops should be withdrawn from Boston. Reluctantly, but seeing no alternative, Lieutenant-Governor Hutchinson and the commanding officer of the British regiments submitted to these demands; subsequently the troops were removed to Castle William in Boston Harbor.

The Boston Massacre

When the news of the repeal of the Townshend duties reached America, the more radical leaders did not see any fundamental alteration in the crisis of legitimacy in the Empire; they wished to continue an economic boycott until the duty on tea was repealed. But the merchants of Philadelphia, New York, and Boston decided to resume commercial activities, and the colonial boycott of English trade came to an end in

1771. This abandonment of the nonimportation policy coincided with an upsurge of colonial prosperity, and a fair degree of tranquility existed in the relations between the American colonies and the mother country from 1771 to 1773.

But it must not be assumed that there was any real prospect that the Americans were becoming reconciled to the constitutional view of the authority of Parliament that Lord North sought to uphold with the tea duty. The Americans did not recede in the slightest degree from their belief that Parliament's power over them was limited. Moreover, the spirit of resistance was by no means dead; sporadic outbreaks of violence against the enforcement activities of customs officers continued. The most serious of these occurred in 1772 when the British revenue vessel, the *Gaspee,* which had run aground near Providence, was boarded at night by a party of Rhode Islanders who burned the vessel, after overpowering the crew and wounding the commander.

Inter-Colonial Committees of Correspondence

A more fundamental development during the years of false calm was the movement to organize a more effective intercolonial political unity. In November, 1772, the Boston town meeting created a Committee of Correspondence to report all British violations of colonial rights to similar committees in other towns. In March, 1773, the House of Burgesses set up a Committee of Correspondence for Virginia and invited all other colonies to do the same. Within a few months a network of intercolonial committees was in existence; and, by this means, an intercolonial solidarity was in the making which foreshadowed the creation of a political union that would bind together the "distinct and separate states" of America. The Massachusetts House of Representatives had already conceived of the political device which should consummate such a union when it told Governor Hutchinson, in January, 1773, that the line "between the Supreme Authority of Parliament and the total independence of the colonies" could only be drawn by all the colonies giving "their consent in Congress." A congress of the colonies was a device unknown to the older constitution of the Empire; indeed, the emergence of such a Congress was to be the first and most fundamental revolutionary act of the Americans when a new crisis destroyed the temporary tranquility of 1771 to 1773.

New troubles began in May, 1773, after Parliament enacted a Tea Act which gave to the East India Company an exclusive license to export tea to the colonies. The Act also eliminated all English duties on such tea; this meant that the only duty left on tea would be the Townshend duty which was collected in American ports. Because of the drawback of English duties, the East India Company was in a position to undersell smuggled tea in the American market.

Resistance to the Tea Act of 1773

As soon as American merchants realized that the East India Company intended to get monopoly control of the sale of tea in America, they were ready to work with the Sons of Liberty groups which had never ceased their agitation against the tea duty. Committees of merchants were

ſlaves of this pernicious cuſtom, to exchange it for milk, the moſt eaſy nouriſhment of nature; but it may be expected, whatever they do themſelves, they will entirely deny it to their children, to whom it is a ſlow but dangerous poiſon.

But if we muſt, through cuſtom, have ſome warm tea, once or twice a day, why may we not exchange this ſlow poiſon, which beſides its other evils deſtroys our conſtitution, and drains our country of many thouſand pounds a year, for teas of our own A-merican plants: many of which may be found, pleaſant to the taſte and very ſalutary, according to our various conſtitutions.——— Even drinking warm water, in moderate quantity, like tea, with ſugar and cream, has relieved many hyſterical caſes; and has cured ſome, even when attended by con-ſiderable convulſions, and flatulen-cies, which were the effects of Green and Bohea Teas, in delicate conſtitutions.——Here permit me to propoſe a liſt of ſeveral kinds of teas, with a hint of their uſes; any of which would be more pleaſant than Bohea, &c. provided we had uſed them as long.———

1. Saſſafras root, ſliced thin and dried, with raſpings of lignum-vitæ, makes a tea exceedingly a-greeable, when made weak. * it beautifies and ſmooths the com-plexion, prevents pleuriſies, ſcur-vies and cachexies, &c.

2. Sweet marjorum, and a little mint, relieve the head and nerves, ſtrengthen the ſtomach, help all the digeſtions, are good in catarrhs and aſthmas, give a good colour to the ſkin, and prevent hyſterics

3. Mother of thyme, and a lit-tle hyſſop, revive the ſpirits, pro-mote chearfulneſs, and are good a-gainſt cold diſeaſes, aſthmas, coughs and vapours.

4. Sage and baume leaves, (the firſt dry, the latter green,) are greatly aſtringent, ſtimulating and ſtrengthening; excellent in fevers, when joined to a little lemon juice, good for weak ſtomachs, gouts, vertigoes, and cachexies.

5. Roſemary and lavender, ex-cellent for diſorders of the head, and weakneſs of the nervous ſy-ſtem, occaſioned by India teas, or otherwiſe; they reſolve cold hu-mours, ſtrengthen the ſtomach and elevate the ſpirits.

6. A very few ſmall twigs of white oak, well dried in the ſun, with two leaves and a half of ſweet myrtle—This ſo exactly counter-feits the India teas, that a good connoiſſeur might be miſtaken in them. Theſe are drying, and very ſtrengthening in all waſting diſeaſ-es and fluxes, ſuitable to women with child, and good againſt agues.

7. Clover with a little camomile. This tea is pleaſant, and has done wonders in obſtructions of the ſpleen, liver, &c. See Baron van Swieten.

8. Twigs of black currant buſh-es, greatly relieve aſthmas, and often cure them in children, with a few worm purges.

9. Red roſe-buſh leaves and cin-que-foil, recruit the ſtrength, mi-tigate pain and inflammations, and are beneficial to conſumptive and feveriſh people, healing to wounds, and ſerviceable in ſpitting of blood.

10. Miſletoe and wild valeri-an. This tea is not the moſt plea-

The Pennsylvania Magazine, *February, 1775. Rare Book Division. The New York Public Library. Astor, Lenox and Tilden Foundations.*

organized in the chief ports of America, and they resolved to do all in their power to prevent the East India Company from selling any tea in America. When the first tea ships arrived in Boston Harbor in December, 1773, a band of men disguised as Mohawk Indians boarded the vessels and dumped the tea chests into the harbor. This "Boston Tea Party" encouraged other colonies in their efforts; a month later, a tea ship approaching Philadelphia was turned back to England; and, in April of 1774, a mob destroyed the tea on one vessel in New York, and permitted another to return to England without unloading cargo. By that time, a universal boycott of tea was in effect throughout the colonies.

The English ministry was highly aroused by the new acts of defiance and violence in America. Completely misjudging the political unity of the American colonies, Lord North proposed a policy of coercion that would be aimed at Massachusetts, the chief center of resistance. Four measures, therefore, were passed by Parliament in the spring of 1774 to carry out this formula of coercion. The Boston Port Bill closed that port to all commerce until compensation would be paid to the East India Company for the loss of its tea. A second bill changed the organization of the Massachusetts government: the council was made appointive rather than elective; the royal governor was given power to appoint local judges and local sheriffs; and all town meetings were severely restricted. A third measure altered the administration of justice in Massachusetts by providing that any magistrate, customs official, or soldier who was indicted for capital offense in the performance of his official duties should be carried to Nova Scotia or to England for a trial where he would not have to face a local jury. A fourth act strengthened the Quartering Act by giving the governor power to determine what buildings should be used for British troops.

At the same time that Parliament was adopting these coercive measures, another important bill, the Quebec Act, was debated and passed. This act was not intended to be one of the coercive acts, but the timing of the measure as well as its content made it seem equally threatening and oppressive to America. The Quebec Act extended the boundaries of the province so as to include all the Ohio and Illinois country—that is, the territory that lay west of the Proclamation line of 1763. Within this enlarged province, the language and customs of the French-speaking inhabitants were to be protected and the Roman Catholic church was to retain its official position. On the other hand, the customary English liberties were largely limited; particularly significant was the denial of the privilege of having any elective assembly. Thus, a large expanse of North America was apparently destined to be deprived of the privilege of local self-government that had become so central to the political thinking of Americans.

The Coercive Acts provoked open rebellion in America. They openly challenged the conceptions of autonomy which had been firmly implanted in the minds of Americans; in addition, they represented an effort to force Americans to accept an economic measure that violated the tradition of open and equal competition by all merchants within the imperial market. Thus, vital American interests were at stake, and the British Empire no longer seemed to be the beneficial source of wealth and power; loyalty and lawfulness, after all, are sentiments that can only be sustained by satisfying the expectations of the major groups within a political system.

When news of the Coercive Acts reached America, Sons of Liberty groups everywhere made the cause of Massachusetts their own. County and provincial conventions were called, resolutions of protest were adopted, and declarations of rights were proclaimed in ringing terms. In most of the colonies, Sons of Liberty groups gathered military supplies and prepared themselves to resist by force of arms. On June 17, 1774, the Massachusetts House of Representatives called for a general meeting of all intercolonial committees of correspondence; on September 5, delegates from all the colonies except Georgia met in Philadelphia. A continental Congress was in existence, and the way was open to revolution.

The Ideology of Revolution

The Continental Congress contained delegates who represented a fairly broad spectrum of political views. There were men of conservative views, such as Joseph Galloway of Pennsylvania, and men of radical views like Samuel Adams of Massachusetts and Richard Henry Lee of Virginia; in between these two extremes there were men of moderate views such as James Duane and John Jay of New York. Yet, there were no delegates, not even Joseph Galloway, who wished to restore the old Empire. Indeed, Galloway proposed a plan of union which, if it had been adopted, would have altered fundamentally the political constitution of the Empire that had been in existence before 1767. Hence, while the Galloway plan was offered as a basis for compromise, its conception of a federalized Empire was revolutionary in character.

In brief, the Galloway plan called for the creation of a united American government that would have a legislative council composed of delegates chosen by the assemblies of each of the colonies. This government was to have authority to regulate all commercial, civil, and police affairs that concerned the colonies as a whole. In addition, the legislative council was to have the right to veto all legislation of Parliament affecting the colonies. To balance the division of power within this federalized empire, Galloway proposed that Parliament should have the right to veto any laws passed by the American legislative council.

Although Galloway's proposal was a revolutionary conception with far-reaching implications for the future, it was not radical enough to satisfy the majority of the delegates to the Continental Congress. Instead, they adopted a declaration of rights and resolves, on October 14, 1774, that denied the right of Parliament to legislate for them or to levy taxes, internal or external; only in the case of commercial regulations were the members willing to recognize the legitimacy of Parliament's enactments. At the same time, Congress voted to create a nonimportation, nonexportation, and nonconsumption Association for all the colonies, and warned the king and Parliament that the boycott of all trade relations with Britain would continue in force until all colonial grievances

A Quasi-Revolutionary Government

had been redressed. In this mood of defiance, the Congress adjourned, after recommending that another Congress should meet in the following spring.

Lord North, however, refused to make any substantial concessions to this new show of colonial defiance. He was willing to replace the tea duty with a requisition system by which each colony would tax itself in order to contribute money for the expense of the Empire. But these "conciliatory propositions" ignored the American principle of taxation which claimed the freedom not merely to raise money but to decide how it should be used. Edmund Burke, a friend of America who had opposed the Coercive Acts, urged the House of Commons to adopt a more generous course of conciliation. In a great speech, he reminded his fellow members of Parliament that "magnanimity in politics is not seldom the truest wisdom, and a great empire and little minds go ill together." But the majority of the members of Parliament wanted a tougher policy; accordingly Parliament passed an act to restrain the entire trade and fishery of New England.

On their side the Americans proceeded to enforce their economic boycott in a way that revealed their willingness to use the most extreme measures to accomplish their ends. Local committees of patriots used forceful methods against merchants and other Americans who preferred to maintain a position of loyalty and obedience to the mother country. Such loyalist Americans were forced to submit to high-handed inspections of their houses, and, in some cases, were tarred and feathered and paraded through the streets as a warning to others who refused to subscribe to the rules of the Association. Rivington's *New York Gazetteer,* a newspaper with pronounced loyalist sympathies, accused the committees of the Association of violating the natural rights of those Americans who disagreed with them: "[They] swear and drink," said the Tory-minded writer about the members of the self-constituted committee on enforcement, "and lie and whore and cheat, or rob, and pull down houses, and tar and feather, and play the devil in every shape. . . ." Such complaints fell on deaf ears, however; the enforcement of the Association was regarded by the American patriots as the infallible means of getting concessions from the English ministry because similar methods had produced results in the case of the Stamp Act and the Townshend duties.

Forming a Revolutionary Army   In fact, the American patriots were willing to go even further in their use of violence to attain their ends. Militiamen everywhere conducted their training sessions in a more serious mood; in Massachusetts, special companies of "minute-men" were formed to assemble at a minute's notice against any effort to employ British troops against the people. Proof of their determination came on April 19, 1775, when a British regiment marched from Boston to Concord intending to seize powder and guns stored there by the Americans. A brief skirmish took place at Lexington; at Concord, the British troops were fired upon before they could destroy all the gun powder, and they were ordered to retreat to Boston. On the way back they were subjected to the grueling fire of minute-men who were hidden behind trees, houses, and walls along the way. After the weary British soldiers re-entered the city, the militiamen camped around it, and the seige of Boston began.

Thus, when the members of the Continental Congress assembled in Philadelphia in May, 1775, they found themselves facing a war and the necessity to make further decisions about the use of military force. The Congress quickly voted to raise a "Continental Army," and chose George Washington of Virginia to be the commander. Even before he arrived to take charge of the troops surrounding Boston, a fierce battle was fought at Breed's Hill, adjacent to Bunker Hill in Charlestown, where the militia had established themselves on a high point overlooking Boston. The British took the hill after heavy losses and only after the Americans ran out of ammunition. Despite their loss of the hill, the Americans took heart from the fact that they had been able to hold ranks against a frontal assault made by British regulars.

Although the radicals were clearly in control of the Continental Congress, they agreed to go along with moderates like John Dickinson who wished to make a last petition for reconciliation to the king. Men like Dickinson hoped that the king and Parliament might seize the opportunity to seek conciliation by repealing the Coercive Acts and by withdrawing troops from the American colonies. But such hopes were dashed when the news came that George III had refused to receive the "Olive Branch Petition." On August 23, 1775, King George issued a proclamation which stigmatized the recalcitrant Americans as rebels and ordered all persons to refrain from giving them any assistance. At the same time, he began negotiations to hire mercenary soldiers from the German states in Europe, in order to obtain the additional troops needed to restore imperial authority in America. Parliament gave its support to this policy of coercion by passing an act in December, 1775 prohibiting all trade with the colonies.

The Americans now faced a greatly narrowed choice of alternatives— submission or independence—with almost no prospect of a middle ground. Despite their adamant assertions of colonial autonomy for more than a decade, this was a difficult choice to make, and the will to make it was aroused by the publication in January, 1776, of a pamphlet entitled *Common Sense,* written by Thomas Paine, a recently arrived Englishman with radical views on a variety of subjects. In *Common Sense,* Paine was able to say what Americans were ready to believe; thousands of copies of the pamphlet were sold and helped to crystallize American opinion in favor of independence.

In *Common Sense,* Paine asserted flatly that reconciliation between England and America was impossible: "Reconciliation is *now* a fallacious dream." He rejected the notion that America needed its connection with Great Britain because of its economic advantages. He argued instead that

Ideological
Principles
of the Revolution

a free commerce would secure greater benefits: "Our plan is commerce, and that, well attended to will secure us the peace and friendship of all Europe. . . . Our corn will fetch its price in any market of Europe, and our imported goods must be paid for by them where we will. . . . As Europe is our market for trade, we ought to form no partial connection with any of it."

Furthermore, Paine maintained that the colonies had reached a degree of social maturity that made further dependence on England absurd. "To be always running three or four thousand miles with a tale or petition," he wrote, "waiting four or five months for an answer, which when obtained, requires four or five months for an answer to explain it in, will in a few years be looked upon as folly and childishness. There was a time when it was proper, and there is a proper time for it to cease." In any case, Paine believed that America had a different social system and a different destiny. "There is something absurd," he declared, "in supposing a continent to be perpetually governed by an island. In no instance hath nature made the satellite larger than its primary planet; and as England and America, with respect to each other, reverse the common order of nature, it is evident that they belong to different systems. England to Europe; America to itself."

Paine also attacked the theory of kingship as being contrary to common sense and natural right. "For all men being originally equals, no one by birth could have a right to set up his own family in perpetual preference to all others . . . One of the strongest natural proofs of the folly of heredity right in Kings is that nature disapproves it, otherwise she would not so frequently turn it into ridicule, by giving mankind an *Ass for a Lion.*" This must have been strong medicine for most Americans who read it because they had always emphasized their direct political relationship to the king. Sensing this, Paine defined a concept of sovereign authority which was more acceptable to rational men than a king. He wrote, "But where, say some, is the King of America? I'll tell you, friend, he reigns above and doth not make havoc of mankind like the Royal Brute of Great Britain. Yet that we may no appear to be defective even in earthly honours, let a day be solemnly set apart for proclaiming the Charter; let it be brought forth placed on the Divine Law, the Word of God; let a crown be placed thereon, by which the world may know . . . that in America the law is King. For as in absolute governments the King is law, so in free countries the law ought to be King; and there ought to be no other."

Most politically-minded Americans had already arrived at the ideological position asserted in Paine's *Common Sense.* In 10 years of debate over parliamentary measures, colonial pamphleteers had developed theories of representation and consent which had transformed the familiar concepts of English political thought and practice. Representation, they argued, must be *direct* and not *virtual.* To be direct, the elected representatives must represent the true interests of their constituents; indeed, their constituents had an inherent right to bind them with instructions. Thus the consent of the people was to be made direct through continuous relations between legislators and their constituents, and not simply in those critical moments, as Locke had argued, when the people exercised their right of revolution. Furthermore, legislators would become creatures of their constituents only if their powers were fixed and limited by written constitutions.

Such ideological principles were written into the leading manifesto of the American revolution. A committee of the Congress, headed by Thomas Jefferson, drafted a Declaration of Independence which was debated and approved in the early days of July, 1776. The opening sentence of the Declaration claimed that there were certain truths that were "self-evident" to enlightened men. Foremost among them was "that all Men are created equal, that they are endowed by their Creator with certain inalienable rights, that among them are Life, Liberty and the Pursuit of Happiness." Such rights, moreover, are not granted by kings or governments; they are derived directly from "the Laws of Nature and of Nature's God" and they are written, as Alexander Hamilton had affirmed in the public discussion of American rights, "in the whole volume of human nature" where they may be discerned by the rational faculties of man.

The Declaration of Independence

If life, liberty, and the pursuit of happiness are natural and inalienable rights, then it follows that the only lawful government is that which secures such rights—in Jefferson's phrasing ". . . to secure these Rights, Governments are instituted among Men, deriving their just powers from the Consent of the Governed, [and] whenever any Form of Government becomes destructive of these Ends, it is the Right of the People to alter or abolish it, and to institute new Government, laying its foundation on such Principles and organizing its Powers in such Form, as to them shall seem most likely to effect their Safety and Happiness."

According to the theory of government expressed in the Declaration, governments are instituted to *secure* the rights which are thought of as pre-existing any form of government—that is, as belonging to all men as an inherent quality of their human nature. Hence, to be legitimate, the government not only must secure the rights of the people, but also must derive its powers from the continual consent of the people; otherwise the people have the right to change or abolish it.

It must be remembered, however, that Jefferson and his colleagues did not advocate frequent revolutions; the right of revolution was justified in the Declaration only as an action of last resort. "Prudence, indeed will dictate that governments long established should not be changed for light and transient causes," it was emphasized in the Declaration. The people, therefore, should use restraint in judging the motives and actions of their governments—only when "a long train of Abuses and Usurpa-

tions . . . evinces in Design to reduce them under absolute Despotism"
is it their right and duty "to throw off such Government, and to provide
new Guards for their future Security."

In view of such considerations, the bulk of the Declaration of Independence consisted of a long indictment of the "Injuries and Usurpa-
tions" of "the present King of Great Britain." Specifically, the king was
charged with refusing to give his consent to laws passed by the colonial
assemblies, of repeatedly dissolving colonial representative assemblies,
and of interfering with the administration of justice. The king was also
accused of quartering troops on the colonists, of sending "swarms of
officers" to harass the people and "eat out their substance," and of
imposing taxes on the people without their consent. In addition, the
Declaration charged the king with cutting off the trade of the colonies
with all parts of the world, of waging war against the lives and property
of Americans, and of hiring mercenaries to commit further acts of
"death, desolation, and tyranny." All these acts, the Declaration asserted, had "in direct object the establishment of an absolute tyranny
over these states."

It would be unhistorical to assume that these charges were made
largely for propaganda purposes, and that to single out the king, rather
than Parliament, was an outright manipulation of the facts of history. We
must remember that the king, in British constitutional theory, was the
king in Parliament; moreover, in the reign of George III, this was not a
legal fiction because he actually did manipulate the parliamentary
majorities, and he did control the ministries. Furthermore, if anyone
thinks that "tyrant" was a distorted term to apply to King George, he
should consider that Jefferson was probably using the word in the sense
attributed to it by Locke and Milton. Locke had defined the term in his
Two Treatises of Government by saying, "Tyranny is the exercise of
power beyond right"; Milton had written "A Tyrant . . . is he who
regarding neither Law nor the common good, reigns only for himself and
his faction." Either definition would have given Jefferson a sufficient
justification for charging King George with tyranny.

In any event, the Declaration of Independence was hailed by enlightened men in Europe. Indeed, one might say that the American Revolution fulfilled many of the expectations of the Age of Enlightenment. To
many Europeans, the American Revolution encouraged their hope for a
further improvement of mankind. It seemed to prove that it was possible
to assimilate into the institutions of a society their ideas about natural
rights, liberty, equality, and the sovereignty of the people.

The Winning of Independence

"The bells rang all day and almost all night." So John Adams wrote in
great excitement when the Declaration of Independence was published

and proclaimed. Yet John Adams was a political realist. In the very moment of his high enthusiasm he wrote to his devoted wife, Abigail Adams, "You will think me transported with enthusiasm, but I am not. I am well aware of the toil, and blood, and treasure that it will cost us to maintain this declaration, and support and defend these states."

Looking only at the cold statistics, the Americans had taken on a seemingly hopeless task. Numbering about two and a half million people in a loosely organized confederation, the American states had to face a nation of 10 million people which had become the greatest imperial power in the eighteenth-century world. Besides being mistress of the seas, Great Britain had maintained an enlarged standing army after the Seven Years' War; in 1775, the British land forces numbered 49,000, with about 8,500 stationed in America. In addition, the British government hired almost 30,000 mercenary soldiers during the war: 17,000 from Hesse, 6,000 from Brunswick, and the rest from other German states.

Military and Political Weakness of American States

Against such military forces, the 13 American states had a small continental army which usually numered less than 5,000 men and militia forces of varying size in each of the states. Indeed, most Americans who supported the Revolution preferred the short-term and flexible militia service; in the militia, they could fight a few weeks and then go home to tend their farms and cattle. Even those who joined the Continental Army enlisted for relatively short terms. During the war, there were 395,858 enlistments in all of the American forces, of which 164,087 were for the militia forces. Yet General Washington never had more than 20,000 men under his command; during some of the darkest days of the war, the Continental Army dropped as low as two or three thousand men.

Both the British and the Americans failed to make the best use of their military potential. During the early years of the war, the Americans were prone to rely too heavily on the expectation that, whenever they were needed, a large mass of men with militia training would rally where needed, as had been the case at Bunker Hill, and in the siege which forced the British out of Boston in March, 1776. Washington soon learned that such expectations would not be fulfilled whenever the war went badly for the Americans. After the American defeat on Long Island in August, 1776, he found his militia forces melting away and he complained to Congress that they were quitting his army "almost by whole regiments, by half ones and by companies at a time." For their part, the British operated with the unrealistic belief that the Loyalists in America would rise up in behalf of the king as soon as any British forces appeared. This contributed to costly mistakes in sending forces that were too small to accomplish their missions. In 1781, too late to be useful, one British officer perceived these serious miscalculations in his govern-ment's Loyalist policy when he wrote, "We cannot with reason expect those that are Loyal will declare their sentiments until they find us so strong in any one place as to protect them after having joined. Our taking posts at different places, inviting the Loyalists to join us, and then

Evacuating those posts, and abandoning the people to the fury of their bitterest Enemies, has deterred them from declaring themselves."

It was fortunate that the British failed to exploit the division of opinion that existed among the Americans. Unquestionably, the existence of a large Loyalist party affected the American will for independence. While it is not easy to make simple generalizations about the Tories in terms of status and property—they were of every social station and occupation— we do know that Anglican clergymen, many wealthy merchants in the towns, wealthy landowners, lawyers, and other professional men worked hard to undermine popular support for the war. No one knows how many Americans were Loyalists, or "Tories," as they were called. Many historians have shown a preference for the symmetrical estimate that the American population was equally divided among patriots, Loyalists, and neutrals. More likely, the patriots were more numerous than the Loyalists, if military service is used as an indicator. According to the most competent authorities, an estimated 50,000 Loyalists took up arms for Britain—a number smaller than the total patriot enlistments.

Undoubtedly the British did not make better use of the Loyalists because they were confident of their own superior military power. But they had to transport troops and supplies over 3000 miles of ocean; and, although they never had to storm the beaches to land their troops in America, they had to fight on unfamiliar terrain and over long distances of countryside that were lacking in decent roads and often covered with forests. Hence the British troops were generally used near the coast or near navigable rivers where their naval forces could keep them supplied and, if necessary, move them out of trouble. Whenever the British troops ventured too far into the interior, they courted disaster; with their supply lines extended, the military advantage shifted to the Americans who relied primarily on skirmishes and quick raids to harass the enemy and to force his retreat.

General Washington was not a particularly brilliant or daring military leader, but he made skillful use of the advantages of terrain and of skirmishing tactics. Most of all, he became a symbol of patient and determined resistance. Even in the darkest days of the war, he kept an army in being and doggedly kept alive the hope that one day, somehow, America would prevail. When we remember that the struggle for independence continued for seven long years, the Americans were fortunate, indeed, to have a commander who possessed such simple and unwavering faith in the destiny of the new nation.

The Dark Time
of the Revolution
It should be remembered that, notwithstanding their early success at Boston, the years 1776 and 1777 were a dark time in which the American patriots hung on grimly in the face of great odds and disheartening defeats. The evacuation of Boston had given General Howe a chance to reorganize his forces in Nova Scotia and to choose a more favorable place for a renewed campaign against the Americans. In June, 1776, he moved his fleet and army of 32,000 men against New York in a strategic plan to

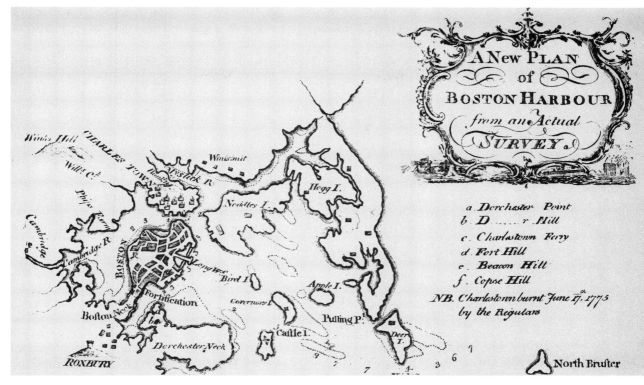

A New PLAN of BOSTON HARBOUR from an Actual SURVEY.

a. Dorchester Point
b. D......r Hill
c. Charlestown Ferry
d. Fort Hill
e. Beacon Hill
f. Copse Hill
N.B. Charlestown burnt June 17, 1775 by the Regulars

North Bruster

The Pennsylvania Magazine, June, 1775. Rare Book Division. The New York Public Library. Astor, Lenox and Tilden Foundations.

split New England and the middle colonies. Seizing Staten Island as a base, the forces under Howe's command crossed over to Long Island and easily shattered Washington's army at Brooklyn Heights, August 27, 1776.

The British occupied New York City and Washington was forced to retreat to New Jersey, after the Americans had spurned General Howe's offers of a generous settlement if they would agree to lay down their arms. Washington's forces were greatly reduced at this point and he failed to get the cooperation of another continental army which Congress had placed under the command of General Charles Lee. Lee was defeated and captured by the British but Washington saved his force by ferrying his men across the Delaware. In December, 1776, when the American cause looked very bleak indeed, Washington revived hope by suddenly recrossing the Delaware and winning two brilliant victories over separated British forces at Trenton (December 25, 1776) and Princeton (January 3, 1777). Throughout the winter months of 1776 to 1777, Washington kept the patriot cause alive by so harassing the British line of communications that Howe decided to return his forces to New York.

Meantime the British military planners in London formulated a master plan of military movement which was designed to crush resistance in the northern states. General John Burgoyne was to lead one army southward from Canada down the Lake Champlain route, a second force under Lieutenant-Colonel Barry St. Leger was to move eastward through the Mohawk River valley, and General Howe was to lead his army up the Hudson River from New York. With the three forces making a juncture near Albany, New England would be cut off from the other states and the English hoped to be able to destroy the American forces piecemeal in the northern theater of the war.

Happily for the Americans the British plan was mismanaged by General Howe. Instead of cooperating with Burgoyne, Howe set sail for Philadelphia. Disembarking at Elkton, Maryland, Howe forced the hard-fighting men of Washington's small army to retreat at the Battle of Brandywine on September 11, 1777; two weeks later, Howe entered Philadelphia. Discovering a weakness in Howe's arrangement of forces around Philadelphia, Washington tried a surprise attack on the main British force near Germantown on October 4, 1777, but the Americans were defeated.

Without the cooperation of Howe, the British campaign in New York state went badly. St. Leger was severely defeated by General Herkimer at Oriskany (August 3, 1777) and withdrew to Canada. Burgoyne, who advanced southward on the Lake Champlain route, taking the strong point at Fort Ticonderoga, reached Fort Edward on the Hudson just about the time St. Leger had been forced to retreat to Canada. Thus Burgoyne's army, far from its base of supplies, had to face the concentrating forces of militiamen from New England and New York. A large British foraging party was decisively defeated at Bennington, Vermont, by American militiamen under Colonel John Stark; and when Burgoyne reached Saratoga, he faced a large patriot army of twenty thousand men who had rallied to complete the entrapment of the outnumbered British army. Two bloody battles near Saratoga, in which the Americans proved their superiority, convinced Burgoyne of the hopelessness of his position. On October 17, 1777, he surrendered his remaining army of about 5000 troops to General Horatio Gates, the commander of the American forces.

The French Alliance   The decisive defeat of Burgoyne's army not only frustrated the master military plan of the British but also enabled the American agents in Europe to bring their diplomatic efforts to a successful fruition. From the very beginning the American revolutionaries had placed almost as much reliance on diplomatic weapons as they had on military action. Leaders such as Benjamin Franklin, John Jay, and John Adams were informed students of European affairs and fully aware of the imperial rivalry between England and other powers, particularly France. Even before independence had been declared, the Continental Congress created a secret committee to negotiate with foreign powers for aid in their struggle with the British. By seeking foreign aid and intervention, the American revolutionists established a pattern that has been followed by other revolting colonials in other areas of the world down to the present day.

France was the most likely country from which to obtain aid. American leaders assumed that France, remembering her defeat in the Seven Years' War and the loss of her American empire, would welcome a chance for revenge against the British. Indeed, political relations with France seemed so important that Silas Deane, Arthur Lee, and Benjamin Franklin were sent, late in 1776, to the French Court to play this crucial game of power politics.

Agents were also active in other European capitals. John Jay was sent to Spain, John Adams to Holland, and others to Vienna, Berlin, and St. Petersburg. Austria, Prussia, and Russia refused to give aid, but France and Spain, whose ruling kings were both of the Bourbon family dynasty, cooperated very readily with the American envoys. American ships were sheltered in their ports and a brisk trade developed in necessary supplies. Consequently, a steady stream of shoes, blankets, tent cloth, medicines, and munitions flowed across the Atlantic from French and Spanish ports to help sustain the revolutionary effort of the Americans.

After a year of warfare, it became clear that the Americans needed more than funds and supplies—they wanted an alliance that would bring armed assistance. At this stage, Benjamin Franklin became the key figure in our French diplomacy. Much admired by the French for his electrical experiments, he was welcomed in the leading salons of Paris as a "philosophe." By means of his skill and gallantry, Franklin endeared himself to the French and did much to win French admiration for the struggle of the American patriots against heavy odds. During these months of 1777, enthusiastic French officers like the young Marquis Lafayette crossed the ocean to fight with the Americans.

The French ministry was cautious, however. French finances were badly disordered and during many months of 1777 the future of the revolutionary cause seemed very uncertain. To give open military aid would mean war with England, and France was not yet ready for war. Then on December 4, 1777, came the startling news that Burgoyne's army had surrendered at Saratoga. This defeat of a large and well-trained British army persuaded the French foreign minister, Vergennes, that the moment had arrived for active French intervention.

In February, 1778, therefore, treaties of alliance and commerce were signed and the French declared war on Great Britain. After some hesitation, Spain entered the war in 1779 on the side of France. In 1780, the war spread further when England declared war on Holland because the Dutch were aiding the Americans with credits and supplies. In that same year, the Russians organized a League of Armed Neutrality among the Baltic powers to prevent British naval forces from searching their ships. This hampered the British considerably in the European war in which they now found themselves.

The treaty of alliance with France changed the character of the war in America. In the years before Saratoga, the Americans had developed considerable effectiveness in fighting a harassing type of war, but they

Winning
the Final Victories

had not demonstrated that they had the means to win independence for themselves. The entrance of France into the war and the widening of the conflict by the inclusion of other continental powers made it possible for the Americans to force a recognition of American independence upon the English government.

Of course, we can see this turning point in the war more clearly than any American in 1778 did. Indeed, only a few months before Saratoga, General Washington at Valley Forge had asked the anguished question: "What is to become of the army this winter?" At one point in the winter of 1777, food was so short that Washington expressed his fear that "three or four days of bad weather[would] prove our destruction." Furthermore, there were increasing signs of war weariness and low morale among civilians and soliders as the war dragged on into its fourth, fifth, and sixth years. Benedict Arnold, who had fought bravely in the patriot cause by leading a daring expedition into Canada in 1776, and by brilliant leadership in the battles with Burgoyne, succumbed to British gold, in 1779, in one of the more dramatic episodes of the Revolution.

Benedict Arnold's treason was not the only sign of war weariness. The states were responding poorly to requisitions for supplies. Soldiers in the underfed and underpaid Continental Army began to desert. There were mutinies in the army in May of 1780 and again in January of 1781.

Yet the will to independence remained constant enough in the patriot party to survive these crises of morale. Somehow, the Americans always managed to counteract British victories with enough military successes of their own. In 1778, George Rogers Clark with a small force of men marched hundreds of miles into the territory north of the Ohio River to defeat Colonel William Hamilton and his Indian allies, thereby establishing a firmer claim to the Ohio and Illinois country for America. On the other hand, large British forces led by General Clinton won striking victories in Georgia in 1778 and Lord Cornwallis swept everything before him in the Carolinas in the next two years, starting with a smashing victory over the Americans under General Horatio Gates at Camden, South Carolina, in August of 1780. The Americans struck back with smaller successes of their own, such as the partisan warfare of the daring "Swamp Fox," Francis Marion, or the victory at King's Mountain in October, 1780, when a thousand Tories were soundly defeated.

Despite his victorious sweep through the Carolinas from 1780 to 1781, Lord Cornwallis was hardly in a favorable military position. General Nathaniel Greene, who had taken over the command of the Continental Army in the South after Gates' defeat at Camden, conducted harassing operations against the extended position of the British forces in the South. By the end of 1781, Greene drove the British out of most of South Carolina and bottled the rest up in Charleston; hence the gains of the British Carolina campaign were largely nullified.

To strengthen his position, Cornwallis took up a position at Yorktown, Virginia, believing that British naval superiority would enable him to evacuate his seven thousand troops from that point if necessary. But he was not aware that a French fleet under the command of Admiral le Grasse was on its way to Chesapeake Bay. De Grasse drove the British fleet out of Chesapeake Bay in the summer of 1781; and Washington moved south to Virginia with his portion of the Continental army to join the small American force led by Lafayette which had been following Cornwallis' movements. In addition, a French army that had recently been sent to America joined forces with General Washington. Pinned down between the French fleet and the combined French-American army of 16,000 men, Cornwallis surrendered on October 19, 1781. On that day, the British troops at Yorktown stacked their arms under the watching eyes of the victorious Americans while their bands played a march called "The World Turned Upside Down."

The surrender of the British army at Yorktown virtually ended the conflict between England and America. Lord North, who had long wanted to retire, resigned in March of 1782, and the new ministry was ready to talk peace with the Americans.

The Congress designated Benjamin Franklin, John Adams, and John Jay as the American peace commissioners with instructions to consult closely with France on matters of diplomacy. But all three American commissioners knew full well that France and Spain had entered the war primarily to serve their own interests. Consequently, the American commissioners ignored their instructions and, without consulting the French, agreed to a preliminary treaty with the British emissaries which recognized the Mississippi River as the western boundary for the independent American states. The French ministers protested to Franklin, but he made full use of his skill and prestige to soothe their feelings, and even managed to extract another sizeable loan for the United States.

The final draft of the Treaty of Paris was signed September 3, 1783. By the terms of the Treaty, Great Britain acknowledged the independence of the United States and her claim to the territory west to the Mississippi, bounded by the Great Lakes to the north, and the Floridas to the south. Great Britain also agreed that Americans should have the right to fish on the banks of Newfoundland and to cure fish in the unsettled bays of Nova Scotia and Labrador. The United States, in turn, agreed to place no "lawful impediments" in the way of British creditors who attempted to collect private debts owed to them, and that Congress should recommend to legislators of the states that they take steps to restore Loyalist property confiscated during the war.

The Peace Treaty

Thus, the Americans had won not only their right to independence, they had acquired a continental empire as well. A new destiny had begun for the New World. The European yoke had been thrown off successfully in one very important area of North America and the time was not far distant when Thomas Jefferson would say "America has a hemisphere to itself. It must have its separate system of interests; which must not be subordinated to Europe."

chapter eight

Building a New Constitutional Order

Justice, *probably from Skillins' Workshop. Boston, c. 1800. Index of American Design. National Gallery of Art. Washington, D.C.*

The Shaping of Republican Institutions

In our own era of nationalist revolutions, we have learned all too clearly that revolutionary politics can be very turbulent and changing. We know that it is not easy for a people to establish a stable government when they have lived for years with the violence and passions of a revolutionary struggle. All too often, the political consequence of such warfare has been the emergence of some form of strong man rule or outright dictatorship.

The American Revolution deserves the continued respect of mankind because the Americans demonstrated to the world that they could fight a revolutionary struggle for seven long years and still create a government that was based upon the libertarian principles proclaimed in the Declaration of Independence. This was possible largely because the leaders of the American revolutionaries were men of political experience. As a matter of fact, two-thirds of the signers of the Declaration of Independence had held office in the colonial governments and roughly the same proportion held political offices in the states during and after the Revolution. Hence the American revolutionaries were led by men who had been trained in the uses of political power and who were highly conscious of their heritage of self-government.

It would be a mistake, however, to think that, in establishing their independent governments, the Americans of the revolutionary generation were merely ratifying their past political experience. The political phase of the Revolution was truly creative even though it revealed a remarkable continuity with colonial experience.

Certainly we must not forget the revolutionary significance, in an age of monarchy and autocracy, of the establishment of republican governments. A revolution always generates certain symbolic requirements; the people who share the sacrifices of a revolutionary struggle develop expectations of fundamental changes in the political arrangements which affect their lives and liberties. For Americans, the explicit consent of the governed became the necessary basis of good government and political happiness. This was a significant symbolic change because, although the American colonies had often behaved like little republics before 1776, most Americans had not been republicans in an ideological sense. They had almost never criticized the monarchy and aristocracy of Great Britain as such; indeed, much of their political theory justified a limited or mixed monarchy as the best form among the governments of the earth.

When the decision to separate from Great Britain came in 1776, the Americans had to become republicans in a practical as well as an ideological sense. In May, 1776, the Continental Congress passed a resolution calling upon the colonies to suppress all forms of royal authority and recommending the adoption of forms of government that would place all powers of government under the authority of the people. Between 1776 and 1780, all the states except two adopted new written

The Republican Ideal

constitutions. In Rhode Island and Connecticut, the old charters were adapted to accord with the circumstances of independence.

Ten of the states gave themselves new constitutions rapidly in 1776 and 1777. In three of these states, the revolutionary assemblies drafted the permanent constitutions without seeking a special mandate from the people, and while carrying on ordinary legislative business. In seven others, special elections were held for conventions to draft constitutions, but these conventions also acted as legislative assemblies. In none of the states which adopted constitutions in 1776 and 1777 did a provincial convention submit a drafted constitution to the people for approval; instead the new charters were merely proclaimed to be in effect.

Each of the states had its particular combination of economic and social interests, so that American politics were very confused and turbulent during the Revolutionary period. Modern studies of socioeconomic groups in the thirteen states demonstrate the difficulty of developing a spectrum of revolutionary politics based on class differences. But on an ideological plane, the pattern of conflict delineates clearly enough a struggle between those who wished to restructure power on a decentralized, popular basis and those who sought to check "democratic despotism" by strengthening executive power and by giving a weighted position to property and status in the upper house of the legislature.

At the start of the Revolution, executive power was virtually annihilated—understandably so, because of the deep distrust of executive authority that had come out of the prolonged and bitter controversies between royal governors and assemblies. In all the earliest state constitutions, with the exception of New York, the governor was elected by the legislature; his authority was closely hedged in matters of appointment and his veto could be overridden by a mere majority of both houses of the legislature. In North Carolina, indeed, it was provided that the Speaker of the House should sign bills before they became law, thus prompting one conservative critic of the North Carolina Constitution to remark that the governor had been given only enough power to sign a receipt for his salary. In New York, the veto power was vested in a separate council of revision composed of the governor and several judges.

Radical Republicanism   In Pennsylvania, however, the revolutionary party in the western counties and in the city of Philadelphia succeeded in creating a frame of government that differed from that of the other states. After a mass meeting in Philadelphia, in May of 1776, delegates were elected to a Constitutional Convention by somewhat irregular methods, in a mood of revolutionary enthusiasm. Meeting in Philadelphia, the Convention proceeded to draft a constitution which became a model of radical politics elsewhere. The Pennsylvania radicals were strongly influenced by the writings of English radicals of the mid-eighteenth century who sought to revive "the old Saxon model of government" by political devices which would bring the entire government—legislative and executive—under the control of the people.

The Pennsylvania Constitution provided that all legislative power should be vested in a single house. To exercise executive power, a council was set up, headed by a president who simply functioned as a chairman. The president and the executive council were severely limited in their executive powers; they had power to appoint some public officials but no power to veto legislation. Every freeman 21 years of age who paid taxes could vote for members of the Assembly and of the executive council. All such freemen were eligible to hold any public office in the state. All officers, except members of the council, were elected for only one year; councillors served for three years. Rotation in office was provided for by limiting the number of times that legislators, councillors, and the president could be re-elected. Finally, every seven years a council of censors was to be elected to see if the constitution had been violated and to call a convention to amend it if necessary.

The Pennsylvania Constitution contained many democratic features that did not appear elsewhere in the 13 states. Most states still had property qualifications for voting similar to those that had prevailed during the colonial period, although a half dozen of them liberalized their property requirements during the revolutionary period. Many states also retained heavy property requirements for legislators and governors. In Maryland, members of the lower house of the assembly had to have £500 in property, senators had to have £1000, and the governor had to have £5000; in North Carolina, the members of the upper and lower houses of the legislature had to have freeholds of 300 and 100 acres respectively, and the governor had to own a freehold worth £1,000. Thus Pennsylvania provided for a popular participation in voting and an access to public office that was broader than that in most of the states.

To some American revolutionaries, the Pennsylvania constitution became the ideal form of government for the enhancement of republican principles. Yet, in actual practice, the Pennsylvania government did not function in a truly democratic fashion. The constitution was never submitted to the people for ratification and the revolutionary party that controlled the legislature conducted the war and the revolution in a dictatorial manner. Many people in Pennsylvania objected to the constitution from the beginning, particularly the upper-class groups that had dominated Pennsylvania politics before the Revolution. One of these, who signed himself "Brutus," demanded, in a letter to the *Pennsylvania Packet,* "Must gentlemen who have ruled society for a century past, be trampled down to the level of common mechanics in an instant and be obliged to consult their humors before they can have the least chance of filling a department of the government?"

It would be incorrect, however, to assume that the political battles over the forms and practices of government in the states was polarized along class lines as so often seemed to be the case in Pennsylvania. There were many upper-class leaders among the American revolutionaries who sought to create republican forms that avoided the twin dangers of aristocratic privilege and democratic despotism. Such men feared the concentration of power in any form; Thomas Jefferson, for example,

Moderate Republicanism

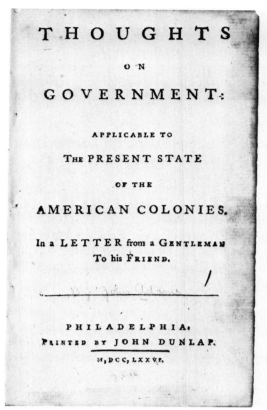

THOUGHTS
on
GOVERNMENT:

APPLICABLE TO

The PRESENT STATE

OF THE

AMERICAN COLONIES.

In a LETTER from a GENTLEMAN
To his FRIEND.

PHILADELPHIA,
PRINTED BY JOHN DUNLAP.
M,DCC,LXXVI.

Title page from John Adams'
Thoughts on Government
*New York Public Library,
Rare Book Division, Astor,
Lenox and Tilden
Foundations.*

criticized the Virginia Constitution of 1776 in his *Notes on Virginia* saying, "All powers of government, legislative, executive, and judiciary, result to the legislative body. The concentration of these in the same hands is precisely the definition of despotic government . . . One hundred and seventy-three despots would surely be as oppressive as one." Similarly, John Adams was horrified by the kind of government that was proposed for Pennsylvania. In his *Thoughts on Government,* written in 1776, he pointed out that the concentration of power in a single legislative assembly would lead to tyranny. In his view, only by a careful separation of powers between the executive, legislative, and judiciary, and by a balance of power between two houses of the legislature, could America avoid the dangers of despotism and usurpation.

For John Adams, the Massachusetts Constitution of 1780 was the proper model for a republican government. In Massachusetts, indeed, the people acted out fully the ritual of making a social compact. The provincial congress of Massachusetts had drafted a constitution in 1777 but, when the document was submitted to the towns for approval, it was rejected because it had been drafted by the legislature and not by a convention called to perform the organic function of drafting a supreme law for the state. In 1779, therefore, delegates to a special constitutional convention were elected by universal male suffrage; and this body drafted a constitution which was submitted to the people in 1780 to be ratified in their town meetings. For the first time, therefore, the whole people of a state had truly acted as the constituent power.

The Massachusetts Constitution of 1780, drafted largely by John Adams, provided for a careful separation of powers. The governor was elected by the people and was given much greater powers than was granted to the executive in any other state at the time. He was given a veto power that could be overridden only by a two-thirds majority of both houses of the legislature. In addition, the two houses of the legislature were carefully differentiated by means of property qualifications; senators had to have a freehold of £300, or a total estate worth £600; the representatives had to have a freehold worth £100, or a total estate worth £200. The members of the judiciary were chosen for life as a means of guaranteeing their independence. The people of Massachusetts proudly proclaimed their theory of government in a section of the Bill of Rights which formed the opening part of the constitution: "In the government of this commonwealth, the legislative department shall never exercise the executive and judicial powers, or either of them: the executive shall never exercise the legislative and judicial powers, or either of them: the judicial shall never exercise the legislative and executive powers, or either of them: to the end that it may be a government of laws and not of men."

With the exception of Massachusetts, to be sure, the idea of the separation of powers was not so fully applied in the practical organization of revolutionary state governments as it was to be in our later political history. In most of the states, power was concentrated in the legislature, and in the hands of the revolutionary factions that controlled the legislative bodies. But the concept was clearly present in the thinking of some of the revolutionary leaders as the writings of John Adams and Thomas Jefferson indicate. Furthermore, the principle of the separation of powers was stated in almost every one of the declarations of rights that were incorporated in the state constitutions of the revolutionary period.

Indeed, during the early years of the revolutionary period, the Americans preferred to rely on constitutional declarations of rights rather than on formal arrangements of power to protect the liberties of the people. Seven of the state constitutions contained separate bills of rights, and the remainder included provisions of this kind at appropriate places in their texts. By these declarations, written into the fundamental laws of the states, the natural rights of all men were proclaimed in language that was not very different from that of the opening sentences of the Declaration of Independence. In addition, such constitutional provisions specifically guaranteed to the people the right of free election of their representatives, protection from arbitrary arrest and seizures, and procedural rights of fair trial in the courts of law.

In these various activities of state politics during the revolutionary generation, a theory of republicanism was slowly emerging in America which demanded that the people should be the actual and not the mythical constituent power, and that the powers of government should be so organized as to prevent the exercise of arbitrary power by any elected officials. Most of the revolutionary leaders in America also believed that republican institutions could best be supported by a citizenry that had a stake in society. They believed that the ownership of some property was a necessary qualification for participation in the political process. Thomas Jefferson, who had written the eloquent phrases of the Declaration of Independence, firmly believed that a man who owned and cultivated his own plot of ground could truly function as an independent and moral citizen. A man without property could easily become a dependent, and "dependence," Jefferson wrote in 1785, "begets subservience and venality, suffocates the germ of virtue, and prepares fit tools for the designs of ambition." However, Jefferson believed that the future of republicanism was secure in America because the abundance of land provided the best hope for the maintenance of a sturdy republican citizenry.

The Revolution and Social Change

Many historians who compare the American Revolution with the French Revolution, the Russian Revolution, or the nationalist revolutions of our own time emphasize the conservative character of the American Revolution. There was, after all, no American equivalent of a Robespierre or a Lenin; and there was no deliberate effort to reconstruct the basic relations of the American social order. While such interpretations have considerable merit, we should not overlook the fact that the revolutionary situation provided Americans with an opportunity to alter certain aspects of their institutional life.

Some of the revolutionary leaders perceived the advantages which were offered by the revolutionary situation. Thomas Jefferson, for example, declared in his *Notes on Virginia* that the "spirit of the times" provided this generation with the opportunity "for fixing every essential right on a legal basis." He warned that, "From the conclusion of the war, we shall be going down hill . . . The shackles, therefore, which shall not be knocked off at the conclusion of this war, will remain on us long. . . ."

Advances in Religious Freedom   One of the shackles that Jefferson had in mind was the requirement to support established churches. And one of the significant social changes that was accomplished was the disestablishment of the Anglican Church which had existed as the state supported church in all of the colonies south of the Mason and Dixon line and in parts of New York and New Jersey. To be sure, the Great Awakening had undermined the position of the Anglican establishments by creating strong dissenting denominations. But the established churches were by no means ready to fade away. They were shorn of their privileges largely because the revolutionary situation gave dissenting religious groups and enlightened political leaders in America the power to make the necessary legal and constitutional changes.

The most spectacular battle to disestablish the Anglican Church took place in Virginia. There, Thomas Jefferson, James Madison, and George Mason played leading roles in the battle for religious freedom. In their efforts they received invaluable aid from strongly organized Presbyterian and Baptist groups. And it was a long struggle because, although the Virginia Bill of Rights adopted as a part of the state constitution of 1776 contained a ringing declaration in favor of the "free exercise of religion" for all men, the Anglican Church continued to have a privileged status in law and in practice. Further measures were necessary before disestablishment could be accomplished—such as the suspension of the payment of tithes, the right of all ministers to perform marriages, and the delimitation of the property rights of the disestablished Episcopal Church. Final victory for the forces favoring religious freedom did not come until 1785 when Jefferson's "Bill for Establishing Religious Freedom" was adopted by the assembly of Virginia.

The Virginia statute of 1785 made Virginia the first state in the modern world with complete religious freedom and complete separation of church and state. The far-reaching character of Jefferson's bill was expressed succinctly in the enacting clause of the measure:

. . . no man shall be compelled to frequent or support any religious worship, place, or ministry whatsoever, nor shall be enforced, restrained, molested, or burthened in his body or goods, nor shall otherwise suffer, on account of his religious opinions or belief; but that all men shall be free to profess and by agreement to maintain their opinions in matters of religion, and that the same shall in no wise diminish, enlarge, or effect their civil capacities.

Although the disestablishment of the Anglican Church in all of the other states where it had a privileged status was accomplished with relative ease by means of religious freedom clauses in the revolutionary state constitutions, certain forms of religious privilege lingered on. In South Carolina, the Constitution of 1778 established "the Protestant religion" in the state without specifying any denomination, but the profession of faith required of all ministers followed the Anglican service of ordination. Not until 1790 did South Carolina provide for the free exercise of religion and worship "without any distinction or preference." In New York, also, the religious freedom clause of the constitution of 1777 was not fully realized in practice until 1784 when the legislature repealed all acts of the colonial period which had granted certain "emoluments and privileges" to the Episcopal Church.

In New England the religious establishment was strong enough to delay the forces of religious freedom for a longer time. In New Hampshire, Massachusetts, and Connecticut, the towns were still required by the state constitutions to support "public Protestant worship" and to require attendance at such religious services; and, because the

Congregationalists were the effective majority in the town meetings, the Congregational Church was the publicly supported place of worship. All three states, however, exempted members of other religious denominations from supporting the Congregational Church provided they could certify that they attended and supported a regularly organized church. Nevertheless, the Congregational Church was still the official church and received many special favors in law and in legislative grants. Complete disestablishment was achieved in New Hampshire in 1817, in Connecticut in 1818, and in Massachusetts in 1833.

Reform of Criminal Laws

The revolutionary ideology, with its emphasis on liberty and equality, also stimulated significant efforts of humanitarian reform. The first successful attempts to reform the harsh criminal codes that had existed in the colonial period were the consequence of a concern for humanity and human rights engendered by the revolutionary struggle. In Pennsylvania, where there was a curious mixture of Quaker and radical influences, a revision of the criminal code was completed in 1794 by which the death penalty was reserved for deliberate homicide. In Virginia, Jefferson, who was familiar with the writings of Beccaria on the improvement of the criminal laws of Europe, led the movement for reform; in 1796 the Virginia legislature finally adopted a criminal code providing that only treason and murder should be capital crimes.

Slavery: Abolition and Manumission

A more significant indication of the power of the revolutionary ideology was the increased opposition to slavery during this era. Many leading Americans acknowledged that slavery was inconsistent with the doctrines of liberty and equality expressed in so many of the public declarations of rights. Patrick Henry and Thomas Jefferson condemned slavery as destructive of liberty and as repugnant to the laws of God and Nature. In addition, antislavery societies headed by men such as Benjamin Franklin carried on a campaign against the slave system; and Quakers, Methodists, and Mennonites were especially active among religious groups in condemning the practice of slaveholding.

Consequently, during the first years of the American Revolution, when "the spirit of the times" was especially strong, all of the states except South Carolina abolished the slave trade—although, by the end of the war, Yankee shipowners and southern planters were eager to replenish the supply of black laborers which had been disrupted during the years of warfare. Significant progress toward ending slavery, however, was made in the northern states. Vermont, though not yet recognized as a state, abolished slavery outright in its constitution of 1777. In Massachusetts, a decision by the Supreme Judicial Court in 1783 declared a slave free because the declaration of rights in the Massachusetts constitution of 1780 stated that "all men are born free and equal." Elsewhere more gradual methods were used. In 1777, Pennsylvania was the first state to enact a law providing for the gradual emancipation of black slaves; and other northern states followed with similar legislation, although in New York and New Jersey the process of emancipation was very gradual indeed.

In the southern states where black slavery represented a heavy capital investment and was deeply entangled in racist attitudes, there was no significant progress toward the abolition of slavery. Virginia eased its manumission laws and some enlightened masters like George Washington provided for the manumission of their slaves in their last wills and testaments. But by the 1790's, there was a general lessening of such private efforts particularly after the Haitian revolution raised fears of a slave insurrection.

The limited success of the effort to eliminate slavery was an indication of the glacial character of the forms of social status that had been established in American life during the several generations of the colonial period. Nevertheless, the American Revolution altered the balance of social relations in a very significant way. In particular, the older aristocratic order gave way to newer conceptions of social distinction. Measured in purely quantitative terms there was a weakening of the older aristocracy of America by the emigration of almost 100,000 Loyalists to Canada and England. All Loyalists, to be sure, were not aristocrats, but those who did come from wealthy landholding and mercantile families were generally the more ardent defenders of the Crown, the Anglican Church, and the aristocratic social order of Eng-

Lady Undressing for a Bath, *American School, first half of eighteenth century. Collection of American Primitive Paintings. National Gallery of Art, gift of Edgar William and Bernice Chrysler Garbisch, 1956.*

land. The confiscation of their estates and their removal by exile from America did not erase the colonial elite—a large and influential elite of wealth, politics, and culture remained in every one of the 13 states—but the symbolic character of the American upper class was fundamentally transformed.

Attacks on Hereditary Privileges

The ardent republicanism in which the Americans had enclosed the natural rights philosophy was as destructive in its import for hereditary forms of artistocratic privilege as it was for hereditary monarchy. The declarations of rights in many of the state constitutions explicitly forbade the creation of any hereditary honors or titles in America. The Massachusetts Constitution of 1780, for example, proclaimed that

no man, nor corporation, or association of men, have any other title to obtain advantage, or particular or exclusive privileges, distinct from those of the community, than what arises from the consideration of service rendered to the public; and this title being in nature neither hereditary, nor transmissible to children, or descendants, or relations by blood, the idea of a man born a magistrate, law-giver, or judge, is absurd and unnatural.

Such considerations also motivated Thomas Jefferson and others in their efforts to change the laws of inheritance. A few months after he wrote the Declaration of Independence, Jefferson introduced a measure in the Virginia legislature for the abolition of entail; a few years later, another law swept away the requirement of primogeniture in the inheritance of estates. Other states enacted similar legislation, and within the 10 years following the Declaration of Independence, every state except two had provided for equality of inheritance among sons and the free alienation of inherited estates. Even though recent historical research indicates that neither primogeniture nor entail had operated to any important degree in Virginia and other states before the Revolution, the fact remains that the laws abolishing these hereditary distinctions disavowed the essential basis of aristocratic privilege that had existed in Europe for more than a thousand years.

The Theory of Natural Aristocracy

It would be a mistake, however, to assume that Americans were ready to disavow all forms of social distinction. Many prominent leaders acknowledged that social distinctions were natural and inevitable. John Adams expressed his views on the questions of class and status more explicitly than any member of the revolutionary generation in his *Defence of the Constitutions of Government of the United States of America,* written in 1786 to 1787. In America, he asserted, there were no "artificial inequalities of condition, such as hereditary dignities, titles, magistracies, or legal distinctions; and no established marks, as stars, garters, crosses, or ribbons"; there was instead "a moral and political equality of rights." But he asked "what are we to understand here by equality? . . . Was there, or will there ever be, a nation whose individuals were all equal, in natural and acquired qualities, in virtues, talents, and riches?" The "answer of all mankind," Adams declared, must be in

Mrs. Isaac Foster, *early eighteenth century by Joseph Badger. Collection of American Primitive Paintings. National Gallery of Art, gift of Edgar William and Bernice Chrysler Garbisch.*

Catharine Hendrickson, *American School,* c. *1770. National Gallery of Art, gift of Edgar William and Bernice Chrysler Garbisch, 1953.*

the negative. "It must then be acknowledged," he wrote, "that in every state, in Massachusetts, for example, there are inequalities which God and Nature have planted there, and which no human legislator can ever eradicate."

There are several natural inequalities which Adams pointed out: that of wealth which results from greater skill or industry, and also from inheritance; that of birth which results from the advantages of social prestige that come from an illustrious family name; and that of merit which results from the superior talents and virtues of individuals. John Adams was more willing to admit the influential role of wealth and birth in American society than many of his contemporaries, but no one who reads his works can deny that he shared his generation's hatred of all forms of hereditary titles and privilege.

Thomas Jefferson, in his *Notes on Virginia,* written as early as 1781, accepted the idea of natural and inevitable distinction between the classes of the rich and the poor. He was more hopeful than Adams that merit could become the chief criterion of a superior status in America; in particular, he hoped that by means of a system of public education, "the best geniuses" could be "raked out" from "the classes of the poor" so that their talents would be available to the higher forms of politics, art, and science in American society.

Such attitudes revealed that the Americans of the revolutionary generation were ready to justify only those social distinctions that had a clear relation to individual achievement. And if individual achievement rather than inheritance becomes the basis of social esteem, the class system not only loses its stable character, but also acquires a different psychological orientation. Dignity and manners count for less and assertiveness and success count for more. Given the abundance of America's material resources, a franker evaluation of success in terms of wealth and power began to compete with the older forms of personal and family distinction.

The New Dynamics of Business Enterprise

A speculative spirit was evident in all forms of business activity during the revolutionary generation. General Washington, frequently beset by problems of supply, complained that "speculation, peculation, and an insatiable thirst for riches seems to have got the better of every other consideration and almost every order of men." The extraordinary wartime conditions offered opportunities for quick gain and stimulated reckless activities that prudent merchants would have hesitated to undertake in time of peace. New trading ventures were developed with France, Spain, Sweden, and other European countries when the Continental Congress overthrew the British navigation laws and opened American commerce to the world. During the war such trading activities were carried on at great risk because of the blockading actions of the British navy, but the profits of a successful voyage were always high enough to tempt the more enterprising merchants. Privateering became another form of business activity in which the risks were great but the possibilities of gain were enormous. Thus, an advertisement promoting a privateering venture in Wethersfield, Connecticut, was addressed to "all Gentlemen *Volunteers* who are desirous of making their fortunes in eight weeks. . . ."

New Forms of Business Enterprise

Merchants and other men of capital in America acquired a greater degree of economic and political sophistication during the seven years of the Revolutionary War than they had in more than a century of experience in the old colonial system. Not only did they develop new trading ventures, but the high risks of wartime trade encouraged them to develop larger and more complex forms of business organization. Many of the privateering ventures were cooperative activities financed by a share system. In Massachusetts, shares in privateering ventures were bought and sold as a part of normal trading activity.

Similarly, the sale of supplies to the Continental Armies encouraged the formation of private business associations of a greater size and complexity than any that had existed in colonial days. Jeremiah Wadsworth of Connecticut, Commissary-General of the Continental Army from 1778 to 1779, became a powerful postwar capitalist largely because of the important financial and business associations he had developed in New York and New England. Robert Morris organized a group of business associates in Philadelphia with extensive connections in Connecticut, New York, Maryland, and Virginia. His position as Financier of the United States from 1781 to 1784 enabled him to develop a contracting system for army supplies that provided close business contacts with leading businessmen in every commercial town of America.

The large networks of commercial and financial relations which men like Morris and Wadsworth had built up during the Revolutionary period were only the more spectacular examples of the growing scale and complexity of economic activity. At the same time, there was a marked expansion of the credit system and a significant development of new investment techniques. The large borrowings by the Continental Congress and by the state governments in order to carry on the war created a huge supply of negotiable securities for the investment activities of men of capital. Loan offices established by the Congress issued enormous amounts of certificates to merchants and contractors in payment for supplies. Such loan office certificates were more desirable than bills of credit—or Continental currency—issued by the Congress because they carried a promise of interest payments amounting to 6 per cent.

Merchants and other men of capital preferred to hold substantial amounts of interest-bearing certificates since they depreciated less rapidly than the Continental currency. And well they might, because, by the end of 1779, Congress had issued slightly more than $240,000,000 in paper currency to secure some of the revenues needed to carry on the war. In addition, several states had issued paper money of their own amounting to about $210,000,000. The states also adopted laws making paper money legal tender in payment of debts, but made no provision for redemption of the currency out of tax revenues. Since Congress had no power to tax, it had to depend on requisitions of money and commodities laid upon the states; this method, however, proved to be inefficient and unsuccessful. Hence, by 1781, $100 of paper money was worth only $1 in silver, and Americans were paying fantastically inflated prices for the necessities of life—$40 for a bushel of corn, $100 for a pair of shoes, $1500 for a barrel of flour. In 1780, therefore, Congress was forced to wipe out the larger portion of the paper money that had been issued during the war; a measure was adopted which provided for the exchange of Continental currency already issued for new interest-bearing notes at a rate of exchange that effectively repudiated 80 per cent of the value of the original notes.

It is not surprising, then, that merchants chose to receive interest-bearing certificates for the supplies which they sold to the government and that they quickly used whatever paper currency they had to purchase additional certificates from the loan offices. About $60,000,000 of such certificates were disposed of by the loan offices during the war and, since they were negotiable, they became important instruments of capital for further business transactions. In addition, the loans made by foreign capitalists offered an additional stimulus to investment. Private Dutch bankers extended large commercial credits to American merchants which effectively replaced the large credits from English merchants that had financed American trading operations before the Revolution.

As a consequence, American businessmen were learning to live in a world of mobile capital that had been virtually unknown to them in

New Forms
of Mobile Capital

colonial times. A new business psychology was developing that encouraged American enterprisers to employ the more flexible instruments of transferable stock certificates as a means of organizing larger business undertakings. Schemes for the organization of banks and joint-stock corporations sprouted up in the principal commercial centers by the end of the war. In 1781 Robert Morris and his associates organized the Bank of North America at Philadelphia. The original subscribers to the stock of the Bank of North America included not only the leading merchants of Philadelphia, but also important capitalists in other states: Jeremiah Wadsworth of Hartford was the largest single stockholder; nearly a dozen large merchants of Boston were also among the subscribers as well as a few men of capital in the port of New York. In addition, the Bank of North America was connected with important national and international interests, since the Confederation government was a large subscriber, and Dutch financiers purchased some $50,000 worth of stock.

The success of the Bank of North America encouraged similar efforts in other leading commercial cities. The Bank of New York began to function in 1784. Like the Bank of North America, the New York institution was controlled by the more enterprising men of wealth; such directors as Nicholas Low and Isaac Roosevelt represented families that had already been prominent among the colonial gentry, while another director, Alexander Hamilton, was a young man who had advanced his personal fortune by serving on General Washington's military staff and by his marriage to a daughter of the powerful Schuyler family. Furthermore, Jeremiah Wadsworth was a large investor in the stock of the bank and served as president in the year 1785 to 1786. The Bank of Massachusetts, organized in the same year as the New York bank, was supported by a combination of men who represented old wealth as well as by new men who had profited from the war. Thus the Cabots, Lowells, Lees, and Higginsons were joined by such newly rich men as Oliver Phelps who had made much of his fortune as a contractor for army supplies during the war.

Nationalist Impulses
of the Investing Elite   Such combinations of wealthy men represented the most dynamic elements in the American economy at the end of the Revolutionary War. The new banks that they created were important institutions for credit and for investment. The businessmen associated with the new banks, more than any others, sparked the drive for other large-scale enterprises. They were the men who pushed for additional chartered banks in the lesser commercial centers; they promoted internal improvement schemes like the Potomack Company of Virginia, the Western Inland Lock Company of New York, and the various projects for the improvement of the Connecticut River; and they furnished much of the capital for turnpike and toll bridge corporations that began to radiate from the principal commercial centers. Some of the earliest ventures in large-scale manufacturing were attempted by many of the same enterprisers. Robert Morris and his associates invested heavily in manufacture in the Dela-

ware River valley; the Boston merchants organized a textile factory at Beverley; in Rhode Island, the wealthy merchant Moses Brown invested in banking and manufacturing schemes; and Jeremiah Wadsworth had a hand in several manufacturing companies in Connecticut.

The expansive business psychology that was displayed in the appearance of banks, internal improvement schemes, and manufacturing companies was also evident in land speculation. Speculative purchases of land, of course, had always been a constant element in colonial economic life, but, at the end of the Revolution, American men of capital began to invest in land on an unprecedented scale. The Revolution had released from imperial regulation the vast area of western land, and the more dynamic businessmen of the commercial cities promoted ambitious schemes for the development of such lands. Robert Morris and several of his wartime associates began a series of land speculations with the Illinois and Wabash Land Companies that were expanded into the over-ambitious North American Land Company in the 1790's. In New York, representatives of the older colonial gentry like Philip Schuyler and Jeremiah Van Rensselaer, and newcomers like the war-trader, John Taylor, bought extensive tracts from confiscated Tory estates in upstate New York. Indeed, throughout the states, the large speculator often

Jedidiah Morse, American Gazetteer. *Boston, 1804. Rush Rhees Library. The University of Rochester.*

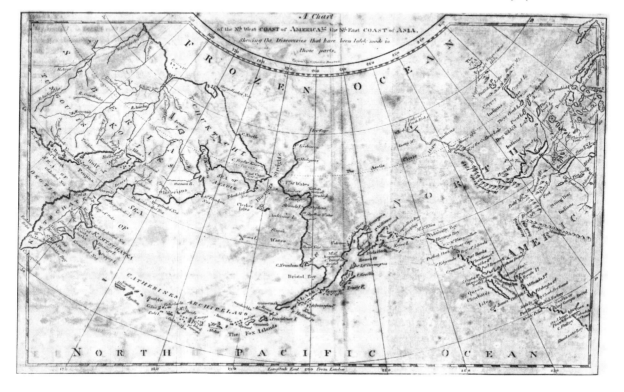

outbid the small farmer for choice tracts of confiscated lands. Thus, by the end of the 1780's, huge joint-stock operations like the Ohio Associates, the Scioto Company, and the Miami Company, with subscribers in almost all of the northeastern states, were pressing Congress to sell them millions of acres of land at bargain prices.

Not all men of capital were as speculative as Robert Morris or Jeremiah Wadsworth; some were suspicious of the "epidemic rage for stocks and bonds" and preferred to do business on the basis of a solid personal reputation rather than through the more impersonal devices of joint-stock companies and corporations. Nevertheless, the pacesetters in the American economy at the end of the Revolutionary War were the businessmen who were spurred on by larger and more daring visions of America's economic destiny. They were men with a highly developed national interest. Their economic interests transcended the particular interests of their own states; their investments flowed across state boundaries; their personal and business associations linked them to the businessmen of other key cities on the Atlantic seaboard; and their sons and daughters sometimes cemented their business alliances with the more intimate ties of marriage. Such men furnished not only the dynamism of an expanding national economy, but also much of the impetus for the centralization of political power once American independence had been achieved.

The Problem of National Power

Although the states had framed new state constitutions rapidly during the Revolution, the task of creating a national constitutional system was a thorny one indeed. When independence was declared in 1776, there was a high tide of nationalist emotion. The delegates of the Continental Congress styled their most famous document, "The Unaminous Declaration of the Thirteen United States of America." And in the celebrations that followed the Declaration of Independence, men like Thomas Paine often spoke of America in the singular sense—as a nation which was separating its destiny from Britain and from Europe. Nevertheless, it was not easy to translate this nationalist feeling into the organized institutions of a central government. After all, it was a central government—the government of the British Empire—which had been the cause of the political difficulties leading to the war for independence.

The Articles of Confederation   At any rate, the revolutionary leaders did not try to avoid the task of establishing a central government. A draft of a plan of union prepared by John Dickinson was presented to the Continental Congress soon after the Declaration of Independence. Dickinson's proposal provided for a central government in which there should be a Congress of delegates from each state—with one vote for each state no matter how many delegates were sent by the state. Important legislation was to require a two-thirds majority of the states. The Congress was to have power to make peace and war, to apportion state quotas of men and money for the common defence and general welfare, to make treaties and alliances, to coin money and regulate its value, to establish post offices, and to regulate Indian affairs. On the other hand, Congress could not levy taxes, or regulate commerce; these powers were reserved to the state. Moreover, the Articles of Confederation, as outlined in the Dickinson draft, could be amended only after Congress and every state legislature had given their assent.

Although the Congress in the proposed plan of union was to have significant powers, it was left without the power of the purse. Only through the power to tax and to regulate commerce could a central government hope to be financially strong. And, as every eighteenth-century statesman knew, a government without economic strength could not be strong in political and military affairs.

John Dickinson had tried to cure the obvious imbalance between the powers of the states and the powers of the Confederation government by including an article which provided that the states should use the rights and powers reserved to them only "in all matters that shall not interfere with the . . . Confederation." What this article would have meant to the relations between the central government and the confederation will never be known. The delegates to the Continental Congress struck out the centralizing language in the Dickinson draft and replaced it with an article which affirmed the "sovereignty, freedom and independence" of each state in the Confederation.

When the Articles of Confederation were sent to the states for ratification in November, 1777, it was clear that the men of the Continental Congress preferred a decentralized system of government. If the drafters of the Articles had expected quick approval, they were disappointed. States without western land claims derived from their colonial charters were afraid that states with western lands would have great political and economic advantages over them. Maryland, indeed, refused to ratify until the seven states in question (Massachusetts, Connecticut, New York, Virginia, the Carolinas, and Georgia) ceded their lands to the Confederation government. Not until March 1, 1781, did Maryland ratify the Articles of Confederation, after the last of the seven states formally ceded its western lands.

For four long and crucial years, therefore, the Continental Congress had to act as a *de facto* government. It was this provisional government that appointed army commanders, raised troops, requisitioned the states for money and supplies, and carried on diplomatic relations with European powers. The Continental Congress was successful enough in keeping alive the revolutionary struggle for independence and in obtaining the crucial treaty of alliance with France, but its lack of success in financial affairs was an augury of the difficulties which any Congress under the Articles of Confederation would experience. The Continental

Financial Difficulties of the Confederation

Congress made four requisitions upon the states for a total of $95,000,000 in paper money between 1777 and 1779; it received a little more than $54,000,000. By the end of the war, the states were becoming more laggard. Between August, 1780, and March, 1781, the Continental Congress made three requisitions for specie, and received a little more than $1,500,000 out of a total of about $10,500,000 requested from the states. Much of the chaos in the currency system resulted from the fact that Congress simply had to resort to paper money in order to carry on its fiscal responsibilities.

Thus, discerning men could already foresee the weaknesses of any government under the Articles of Confederation when they were finally ratified in 1781. Indeed, on the very day that the Articles were ratified, a committee of Congress, headed by James Madison of Virginia, urged that the Articles be amended so as to give the Congress authority to "employ the force of the United States as well as by sea as by land to compel the states to fulfill their federal engagements." In August another committee of Congress noted serious deficiencies in the Articles and recommended a general enlargement of the powers of Congress to include taxation, the regulation of commerce, and the right to distrain the property of states that failed to pay their requisitions to the Confederation government.

Congress took no action on either report—the prospect of using force against any of the states was too frightening, and the states were still too jealous of their economic powers to yield any of them to the Confederation government. The Congress did submit to the states for ratification a proposed amendment to the Articles which would permit the Confederation government to levy an import duty of 5 per cent *ad valorem* as a means of obtaining an independent revenue. Twelve states responded favorably to this modest request, but the Rhode Island legislature, anxious to retain the revenues of the state's impost duties, refused. In 1783 Congress made another effort to secure a revenue amendment based on import duties; again Rhode Island refused, while several other states failed to take any action on the proposal.

Unable to secure an independent revenue, the Congress of the Confederation was continually beset by financial difficulties. The army was unpaid, and the troops were becoming mutinous. In 1782, a small group of officers with General Washington's army, then stationed at Newburgh on the Hudson, proposed a drastic solution for the troubles of the army and the nation—the establishment of a limited monarchy with Washington on the throne. Washington was thoroughly shocked by the proposal and wrote to the leader of the discontented officers, saying: "Let me conjure you . . . if you have any regard for your country . . . to banish these thoughts from your mind." But he warned Congress that the army should be paid and disbanded without delay saying: "[it] is a dangerous instrument to play with."

Congress forestalled further mutinous activity on the part of the army by giving the troops three months back pay before they were sent home, and by promising full compensation for five years to the officers. But the disbanding of the army after the treaty of peace did not diminish the financial troubles of the Confederation. Sales of public land in the west yielded some revenue, a loan from Holland helped for a time, and the Bank of North America loaned large sums to the government which enabled it to meet some of its more pressing obligations. Nevertheless, the government of the Confederation was able to pay only part of the interest on the domestic debt so that government securities were selling on the market at far less than face value.

Although the lack of an independent revenue proved to be a great political as well as economic weakness, it would be a mistake to assume that government under the Articles of Confederation was a completely incompetent affair, carried on by men devoid of ideas. The Congress of the Confederation made an impressive record in framing basic policies for the development of the national domain which was acquired when the states ceded their claims to western lands.

The Confederation and the National Domain

The need for a well-ordered policy for the vast area west of the Alleghanies was pressing. Enormous and conflicting pressures were developing as speculative land companies, army officers, and land-hungry settlers jostled for valuable land sites north and south of the Ohio River after the end of the war in the spring of 1783. Something had to be done to mediate the conflicting claims of speculators and settlers and to prevent lawless squatting from provoking the Indians to take the warpath.

The man chiefly responsible for laying down the guidelines of policy for the development of the public domain was Thomas Jefferson. He envisioned the growth of self-governing republican communities in the west peopled largely by small farmers; and his ideas formed the basis of the Land Ordinance of 1784, prepared by a committee of Congress, of which he was chairman. This act provided that the western territory should be divided into districts which would eventually become states. Whenever the territory of a district had twenty thousand people, they were to hold a convention, adopt a constitution, and elect a delegate to Congress. And when the population of a territory equalled the number of free inhabitants in the smallest of the 13 states, it was to be admitted to the Union as a new state on an equal basis with the original 13 states. An article prohibiting slavery in any of the national territories after 1800 was defeated by a single vote, but the basic principles of self-government and eventual statehood were approved by the Congress.

Jefferson also had a considerable part in preparing the Land Ordinance of 1785, although he left to replace Franklin as minister to France before the Ordinance was completed. By this Ordinance, which laid down certain basic policies for the surveying and settlement of the western territories, the western lands were to be settled only after the Indian titles had been extinguished by treaties, and after the land had been surveyed by the government. All lands were to be surveyed in a regular pattern into townships 36 miles square. Each township was to be subdivided into 36 lots or "sections" of 640 acres each. Four sections in each township were to be reserved for the United States; in addition, one section was to be set aside to support public education. All other sections were to be auctioned off by the loan office commissioners in each state at the minimum price of $1 an acre in specie or its equivalent, with the minimum unit of purchase to be one 640-acre section.

The third great enactment by the Congress of the Confederation, dealing with the development of the national domain, was the Northwest Ordinance of 1787. This measure replaced Jefferson's Ordinance of 1784 and provided for a more complex pattern of political evolution. The territory northwest of the Ohio River was to be divided into not more than five and not less than three districts. During the first phase of settlement, a district was to be administered by a governor, a secretary, and three judges appointed by Congress. Whenever the population of a district reached five thousand free white males, the landholders could choose a legislative assembly and a delegate to the Congress, but the governor was to retain an absolute veto over all laws. When the population of any of these districts reached a total of sixty thousand free inhabitants, it could be admitted to the union as a co-equal state with its own constitution and state government. The Ordinance of 1787 also prohibited slavery in any of the northwest territories.

The ordinances concerning the public domain that were adopted by the Congress of the Confederation contained imaginative and significant policies that remained the fundamental basis for the disposition of public lands and for the growth of self-government as the people of the United States expanded across the continent in the nineteenth century. The regular pattern of survey and sale offered the settler a chance to compete with the speculator in the purchase of desirable lands; and the Northwest Ordinance, in particular, revealed the intention of American political leaders to avoid the dangerous conflicts of power that would arise if the settlers of the west were kept in a state of colonial subjection.

The fruition of such policies lay in the future, however. At the time of the adoption of the Northwest Ordinance, the Congress of the Confederation was clearly unable to make its policies effective. Squatters without lawful claims to their lands continued to pour into the western areas, and even the use of troops by the Confederation government failed to check the lawless activity of the land-hungry settlers. The intrusion of large numbers of squatters also provoked the Indians to warfare. Between 1783 and 1790, bloody battles between white settlers and the Indians were a constant feature of frontier life, and Congress seemed unable to develop any effective control over the situation.

At the same time, Congress succumbed to the lobbying pressures of a powerful group of eastern speculators associated with the Ohio Company and the Scioto Company. In 1787 Congress actually granted a million and a half acres to the Ohio Company at the minimum price of $1 an acre, but payable in land bounty certificates that had been issued to officers and soldiers in the Continental Army. Such certificates were selling for as little as 10 cents on the dollar in the open market at the time, and land speculators were buying large amounts for their speculative ventures. In addition, the promoters of the Scioto Company received an option to take up five million acres on similar terms. Such favoritism, of course, undermined the well-ordered policy of survey and sale that had been written into the Ordinance of 1785.

The Confederation government was unable to deal successfully with the problems of security and commerce in the great heartland of North America. The British continued to occupy their military and fur-trading posts in the Northwest contrary to the terms of the treaty of peace in 1783. Since the Confederation government lacked sufficient military power to eject the British garrisons from American soil, the British were able to retain control of the valuable fur trade of the upper Mississippi valley as well as a significant amount of influence over the Indian tribes of the region. Nor was there much hope that the Confederation government could obtain by negotiation what it was unable to get by any show of force. The states refused to comply with the stipulations of the Treaty of 1783 that the property of Loyalists be restored and that no impediments be placed in the way of British creditors seeking to collect the debts owed to them. Consequently, the British were all the more prone to ignore the repeated efforts of Congress to persuade them to evacuate the posts in the northwest.

Problems of Security and Commerce in the West

Similarly, the Confederation government was unable to resolve important problems in our relations with Spain in the southwest. The Treaty of Paris in 1783 had granted the United States all the territory north of Florida as well as the same rights of navigation on the Mississippi River which had been granted to British and French subjects by the Treaty of 1763. Spain, however, ignored both of these provisions; the Spanish promoted vigorous efforts to keep the Indian tribes of the southwest—Creeks, Choctaws, and Chickasaws—under their influence. Moreover, they used Spanish gold freely with a number of American frontier leaders, hoping to encourage secession movements. Hence, the diplomatic efforts of John Jay were unsuccessful in getting Spain to reopen the Mississippi to navigation. Indeed, Jay seemed more interested in getting favorable commercial rights for northern merchants in Spanish ports than in opening the port of New Orleans to the goods shipped down the Mississippi River by western settlers.

The difficulties experienced in the Mississippi valley region were matched by troubles for American merchants in vital areas of foreign trade. A British Order-in-Council of 1783 required that all commodities from the United States must go to their West Indies in British rather than American vessels. This was a serious disadvantage because the West Indian trade was as crucial as ever to the American economy. To be sure,

Losses in Foreign Trade

many American shipowners resorted to their old art of smuggling, but the British restrictions were an irritating threat to the business calculations of the American mercantile community.

The commercial depression that began in 1784 increased popular antagonism against the British and most of the states passed legislation favoring American shipping over British shipping and American products over those made in England. Such state laws regarding British commerce were reasonably effective, but they were not uniform. American merchants, therefore, sought to obtain the uniformity and stability that only centralized governing power could provide.

In response to such demands, an amendment was proposed in Congress to give to the Confederation government power to forbid the import and export of goods in the vessels of countries not having treaties with the United States. In support of this idea, the amending resolution declared that British restrictions on Americans in the West Indian trade were "growing into a system" and that "unless the United States in Congress assembled shall be vested with powers competent to the protection of commerce, they can never command reciprocal advantages in trade, and without these our foreign commerce must decline and eventually be annihilated." The proposed amendment, however, was never sent to the states. It was defeated in Congress largely because of the opposition of southern delegates who feared that the restriction of foreign competition would benefit only the northern merchants, while southern planters would have to pay high rates for their great cargoes of rice and tobacco that were shipped to European markets.

In the light of these considerations it becomes clear why so many American merchants and business enterprisers supported the efforts to strengthen the Articles of Confederation by granting Congress the power to regulate commerce and to raise an independent revenue. American enterprisers in the 1780's were vigorous and dynamic, but their avid pursuit of larger schemes for private profit made them impatient of the confusion of political sovereignties and the resulting political instability under the Articles of Confederation. For such men, America's economic growth required a reorganization of national power.

The Movement for a New Constitution

A political movement for an invigorated national government began even before the Articles of Confederation were ratified. In August, 1780, a convention of New England states held in Boston called upon the American states to form a "more solid union," and invited New York and other states to meet with them in Hartford later in the year. The Hartford Convention, however, failed to become a general convention of constitutional reform as some political leaders had hoped; it was attended by delegates from only four New England states, although the New York legislature voiced approval of the general purposes of the meeting. At any rate, the delegates in the Hartford convention declared that the lack of coercive power was the greatest defect in "the general government of the continent" and urged that compulsive power should be used against states that were deficient in furnishing money and supplies to the Continental Congress.

Although these early efforts to strengthen the central government failed to win substantial support, they revealed the emergence of a group of political leaders who were fully committed to a nationalist orientation in their political activity. Merrill Jensen, in his careful study of the United States under the Articles of Confederation, has identified nine men as the leading nationalists in America during the 1780's: Robert Morris, John Jay, James Wilson, Alexander Hamilton, Henry Knox, James Duane, George Washington, James Madison, and Gouverneur Morris. These leaders believed that national independence and prestige could be maintained only by a powerful central government; they believed that efficiency and energy in government would come only with a proper organization of executive power; and they were convinced that the prospects for the security of property and of economic growth could be greatly enhanced under a system of strong national sovereignty. In the last analysis, they were the leaders who worked tirelessly to reform the Articles of Confederation, hoping to create a national government that could fulfill the destiny of America in the grand terms in which they conceived of it.

The Nationalist Elite

All their efforts to reform the Articles by direct means in the Congress or through proposed amendments referred to the states met with frustration and failure. And then, by an indirect but significant route, the movement for constitutional reform suddenly gathered momentum in 1786. Aided by a fortunate conjuncture of circumstances, the nationalists were finally able to break through the tangled web of political cross-pressures which had paralyzed all their previous attempts at reform.

The Movement for Constitutional Reform

The fresh political momentum that came from the Annapolis Convention of 1786 actually had its beginnings in a conference between the commissioners of Virginia and Maryland over the regulation of commerce on the Potomac River. George Washington had taken the lead among Virginians in promoting projects for the improvement of navigation on the Potomac. He had extensive investments in western lands and, like most dynamic enterprisers of his day, he had a grand vision of developing the commercial and industrial resources of the vast hinterland between the Potomac and Ohio rivers. Washington's project enlisted the enthusiastic support of other prominent Virginians. Jefferson urged him on, noting that a link between the Potomac and the Ohio would give Virginia "almost a monopoly of the western and Indian trade." James Madison prepared the legislative charters for the companies that would build the canal and toll roads.

To complete the scheme for the improvement of navigation on the upper waters of the Potomac, however, it was necessary to have the consent and cooperation of Maryland. Hence Madison arranged for a conference between commissioners of Maryland and Virginia to discuss the regulation of commerce and navigation on the waterway that was so vital to the economic life of both states. The result of the meeting was an interstate compact by which Virginia and Maryland settled their long-standing disputes over the regulation of commerce on the Potomac River.

The success of the interstate agreement encouraged Madison and others to believe that the idea could be extended to commercial questions that were more general in character. Hence, Madison and his collaborators persuaded the Virginia Assembly to adopt a resolution inviting all other states to send delegates to a convention in Annapolis, Maryland, "to consider how far a uniform system in their commercial regulations may be necessary to their own interest and common harmony." Moreover, Madison's correspondence contains abundant evidence of his hope that the creation of a common market in America would lead to other nationalist reforms.

Indeed, such larger nationalist conceptions prevented the Annapolis Convention from being another political failure. Delegates from only five states were present at the appointed time of meeting in September, 1786. The New England states held back because they doubted the interest of the southern states in commercial questions or suspected that the convention was designed to benefit southern economic interests; the Carolinas and Georgia seemed to be completely indifferent. Nevertheless, the 12 delegates that were present were very much of one mind in their conception of national power. They decided to seize the opportunity to make an even more audacious effort to secure reform, by calling upon the states to send delegates to a general constitutional convention to meet in Philadelphia in May, 1787.

The Political Effect of Shay's Rebellion

In one sense this was a revolutionary act because the Annapolis Convention was an extra-legal body without any authority under the Articles of Confederation to call conventions for the amendment of the Articles. And for several months, indeed, the Congress refused to give its official endorsement to the call for a convention. Hence it is quite likely that the Philadelphia Convention would have been another failure if it had not been for the political effect of Shays' Rebellion in Massachusetts.

Shays' Rebellion was an uprising of farmers who were in dire economic straits because the commercial depression during the years 1784 to 1786 had made it impossible for many of them to pay their debts to private creditors. In addition, they objected to the unfair burden of taxes on land, the harsh foreclosure proceedings against debtors in the courts, and the exorbitant fees charged by lawyers. Consequently, the discontented farmers organized town and county conventions to petition the legislature for laws that would stay the foreclosure proceedings, and for the issuance of paper money to alleviate the shortage of currency and credit. When the legislature failed to meet these demands, the more radical-spirited farmers organized themselves into armed bands. Under the leadership of Daniel Shays, a former Revolutionary War officer, they attacked courthouses in order to force the suspension of foreclosure proceedings, and attempted to seize the federal arsenal at Springfield, Massachusetts. Governor Bowdoin, however, moved swiftly to restore law and order. Late in 1786 a force of four thousand men under the command of Benjamin Lincoln was sent out against the rebels by the government of Massachusetts, and the rebellion was quickly crushed.

In any reasonable perspective of history, Shays' Rebellion was truly "a little rebellion" in the mildest sense of Thomas Jefferson's famous remark. The Shaysites had no intention of overthrowing the legitimate government of Massachusetts or of destroying property rights. They were a group of distressed debtors who had been hurt by the depression of the mid-1780's and by the deflationary fiscal policy of the Massachusetts government which had put into effect a rapid liquidation of the state debt and a high rate of taxation. The Shaysites never rallied the majority of the people, and the rebellion was crushed quickly and completely.

On the other hand, Shays' Rebellion had a greater influence on the course of events that led to the Constitutional Convention at Philadelphia. More important than the rebellion itself was the impression it created outside of Massachusetts. Many Americans feared that the Shaysite uprising presaged a future of disorder and anarchy for America. Everywhere, therefore, large numbers of Americans rallied to the side of constitutional reformers. America's leading military hero, George Washington, was thoroughly aroused by the news from Massachusetts. "Let us look to our national character, and to things beyond the present period," he wrote his fellow Virginian, James Madison. "Thirteen sovereignties pulling against each other . . . will soon bring ruin on the whole, whereas a liberal and energetic Constitution, well guarded and closely watched, to prevent encroachments, might restore us to that degree of respectability and consequence to which we had a fair claim, and the brightest prospect of attaining."

Virginia, indeed, led the way toward the creation of a "liberal and energetic constitution" with a stirring resolution in November, 1786, calling upon the other states to send delegates to Philadelphia. A brilliant delegation to the Convention was chosen, composed of George Washington, Patrick Henry, Governor Edmund Randolph, John Blair, James Madison, George Mason, and George Wythe; Patrick Henry, however, refused to attend because he was suspicious of the nationalizing tendencies of the movement for constitutional reform. By May, 1787, all other states except Rhode Island and New Hampshire had chosen delegates, and New Hampshire later sent two men.

The Philadelphia Convention

Other states had followed the example of Virginia and chosen men of outstanding ability and experience to represent them. Massachusetts sent men like Rufus King, Elbridge Gerry, and Nathaniel Gorham who had served in the Congress of the Confederation; Rufus King, indeed, had married the daughter of one of New York's leading merchants and had developed a close political friendship with Alexander Hamilton. Connecticut sent Roger Sherman, Oliver Ellsworth, and William S. Johnson, three able men who had developed outstanding careers in Connecticut politics and in the Congress of the Confederation. The New York delegation contained one outstanding nationalist in the person of Alexander Hamilton; the other two delegates, John Lansing and Robert Yates, were jealous defenders of state sovereignty.

Pennsylvania was represented by such outstanding leaders as Benjamin Franklin, whose 81 years made him the sage of the Convention; Robert Morris, the financier of the Confederation from 1781 to 1783; and James Wilson and Gouverneur Morris, who were known to be ardent nationalists. From Delaware came John Dickinson, a political veteran, and the New Jersey delegation included William Paterson, an able defender of the interests of the smaller states. Among the southern delegations, the Virginians outshone all others, but John Rutledge and Charles Pinckney of South Carolina were effective men in the Convention, while Luther Martin of Maryland was an able spokesman for decentralist principles.

Of the 74 delegates appointed to the Convention, only 55 attended with any regularity, and only 39 signed the document which resulted from the work of the Convention. As a group, the members of the Philadelphia Convention were part of the political elite of the new nation: 39 had served in Congress at one time or another; 8 had signed the Declaration of Independence; 7 had been governors of their states. They were mostly younger men—their average age was 42—who had made their careers in the years of the Revolution; 21 of them, in fact, had fought in the Revolution.

Although Thomas Jefferson afterwards described the Convention as "an assembly of demi-gods," the delegates can more aptly be described as representatives of America's "natural aristocracy" in the sense in which John Adams used the term. Most of them came from the middle and upper classes of America. Thirty-four of the delegates were lawyers, 30 had money invested in public securities, 15 were engaged in, or associated with, mercantile activity, and at least 12 had significant amounts of money invested in banking or money-lending activities. No delegate was of the small farming class which was the most numerous class in America. On the other hand, 31 members of the Convention owned lands that were being used for farming purposes, and at least 16 carried on large-scale agricultural operations, most of them as slaveholding planters. In addition, 12 members had speculative investments in undeveloped lands. Although not one delegate represented the mechanic or artisan class, men like Benjamin Franklin and Roger Sherman had risen from the artisan class to positions of wealth and influence. The common element in the social and economic backgrounds of the members of the Constitutional Convention was their relationship with the more dynamic elements of economic enterprise: commercial farming, land speculation, commerce, security-holding, banking, and money-lending. In their economic as well as in their political activities they stood for initiative and energy.

The record of the debates in the Philadelphia Convention indicates that the delegates were hard-headed men who were not interested in ringing oratory, but rather in working out solutions for the practical problems with which they had to contend. Nevertheless it would be incorrect to say that there was an absence of political theory in the making of the Constitution. After all, no less than 29 of the delegates were college graduates and were well versed in the history of government and political philosophy as it was taught in the eighteenth century. But the men of the Convention used their theory in direct application to the practical problems of demarcating the boundaries of power within the structure of the national government and between the central and state governments.

In the perspective of history, the work of the Philadelphia Convention is distinguished by a high degree of agreement on fundamental objectives and a genius for compromise on the divisive issues that were inevitable in a republic of such a large geographical extent and of such a plurality of social and economic interests. The decision of the Convention to conduct its deliberations in secrecy relieved the delegates from all outside pressures and put a premium on logical persuasion and the meeting of minds. In addition, the element of secrecy enabled the delegates to try out various ideas without being accountable to the public for everything they said. Such flexibility facilitated the process by which the delegates came to terms with each other. Hence, in just four months of work, the men at Philadelphia hammered out a Constitution that the majority were willing to sign and to defend to the people of the United States.

Framing a New Constitution

The central problem confronting the delegates to the Constitutional Convention was to construct a frame of government that would adjust the opposing claims of liberty and power in an "energetic constitution." A few years after the Constitution was ratified, James Madison wrote, "Every word of [the Constitution] decides a question between power and liberty." Madison's emphasis on the relationship between liberty and power in the making of the Constitution is particularly significant because his journal of the proceedings of the Convention is the most complete record of what the framers of the Constitution said and did at Philadelphia in the summer of 1787.

The Principle
of National Supremacy

The opposing claims of liberty and power had to be adjusted on a national scale because the overwhelming majority of the delegates were committed to some form of nationalist thinking. In the Virginia Plan, which served as a starting point for the deliberations of the delegates, it was proposed that a "National Legislature" of two branches should be empowered to enjoy all the powers already exercised by the Congress of the Confederation and "to legislate in all cases to which the separate States are incompetent." Moreover, the plan offered by Governor Randolph of Virginia provided the national legislature with power "to negative all laws passed by the several states, contravening in the opinion of the National Legislature, the articles of Union; and to call forth the force of the Union against any member of the Union failing to fulfill its duty under the articles thereof."

A month later, a counterproposal known as the New Jersey Plan initiated a major disagreement on the structure of the legislature. Even so, this plan contained features that were as strongly nationalistic as the Virginia Plan. In particular, the New Jersey Plan, offered by William Paterson, contained more specific grants of power to the Congress of the new government concerning the raising of revenue and the regulation of commerce. Paterson's proposal also contained a more detailed plan for the creation of a national judiciary that would have jurisdiction in all cases touching the powers and the officers of the federal government. Furthermore, the New Jersey Plan contained a highly significant section which declared that all laws and treaties of Congress should be "the supreme law" and that "the Judiciary of the several states shall be bound thereby in their decisions, anything in the respective laws of the Individual States to the contrary notwithstanding."

Thus, by the time that the New Jersey Plan came before the Convention for discussion, it was evident that the delegates were in essential agreement about the nature of the power that should be possessed by the central government. They believed that the new government should have the power of the purse and the power to regulate commerce. They envisioned a government that would be truly national in that it would act directly on individuals rather than upon the state, and that it would possess its own police power, exercised by courts, marshals, revenue officers, and the like, to carry out its functions and impose its will. Finally, a conception of the supremacy of national law over that of the states was taking shape in the minds of the delegates.

The Problem of
Representation

The rapidity with which the Convention moved toward essential agreement on the principles of national supremacy has often been obscured in historical writing because of the dramatic character of the battles between the large and small states over the schemes of representation put forth in the Virginia and New Jersey Plans. Such a battle was inevitable and necessary to bring about a meeting of minds on the fundamental adjustments of liberty and power. After all, a central government was being created which would have greater powers than the respective states had been willing to concede to Parliament or the British Empire before the Revolution. Hence the control of such powers became an issue of fundamental importance; it was necessary to construct institutional arrangements that would give all the major groups in American society a reasonably equal share in the process by which political decisions were made concerning the use of such powers.

When Governor Randolph offered the Virginia Plan to the Convention, he proposed that each state's representation in both houses of the national legislature be apportioned to the free population. Members of the lower house would be elected directly by the voters, and the members of the upper house were to be chosen by the lower house. This proposal aroused the opposition of delegates from the smaller states who feared that in a system of proportional representation the largest states would seek to aggrandize themselves at the expense of the smaller. Hence, when William Paterson presented the New Jersey Plan, he included the counter-proposal of a unicameral legislature as existed under the Articles of Confederation, with equal representation for each of the states. In his attack on Randolph's scheme for proportional representation, Paterson declared that, under such a plan, New Jersey "would be swallowed up" and that he would "rather submit to a monarch, or a despot than to such a fate." The debate over the question of representation was so heated that it brought the convention close to a crisis; at one point, threats to dissolve the Confederation were hinted at by some of the delegates.

But the men at Philadelphia were not doctrinaire in temper; their political realism led them to explore the possibilities of compromise. A special committee appointed to study the alternatives proposed a workable solution that had originally been suggested by Roger Sherman. According to this scheme, there would be a bicameral legislature: in the upper house, membership would be equal for all states; in the lower house, membership would be apportioned according to population. This "great compromise" was accepted by the majority of the delegates and removed one of the major obstacles to the harmony of the Convention.

The debate over representation contained much frank talk about the selfish interests of individuals and groups in the large and small states. This brought into the open other issues that reflected clashes of interest in American society. One of these, already apparent at the time of the Annapolis Convention, was the conflict of economic interests between the North and the South. One aspect of this controversy had to do with slavery and the other concerned the regulation of commerce.

Compromising Sectional Differences

Northern delegates wished to count black slaves in the apportionment of taxes since they were a form of property, but did not wish them to be counted as part of the population in apportioning representatives in the lower house. Southern delegates, on the other hand, wished to count slaves in the apportionment of representation, and were opposed to counting slaves equally with free men in the allotment of direct taxes.

In regard to commerce, southern members of the Convention feared that the power to regulate commerce might be used to levy export taxes on southern staples or that commercial treaties would be negotiated that would disadvantage their tobacco and other crops in the competitive world market. Some were also worried that the national legislature might prohibit or restrict the slave trade. Delegates from the commercial states of the North, however, believed that full national power to regulate foreign and interstate commerce was the best guarantee for the rapid growth of American economic enterprise.

The Convention settled these differences between the northern and southern states by several compromise arrangements. In the matter of taxes and representation, the Convention adopted the so-called "three-fifths" formula whereby only three-fifths of the black slaves were counted for the apportionment of both taxes and representation. With respect to commercial matters, the Convention provided that all treaties, including commercial treaties, must have a two-thirds majority in the Senate, that Congress could not levy any taxes on the export of any commodities from the United States, and that for 20 years Congress could not prohibit the importation of black slaves. In addition, it was stipulated that each state should provide for the rendition of fugitive slaves. In return for all these concessions to southern interests, northerners were given the advantage of a constitutional requirement that a simple majority in both houses of Congress would be sufficient for all laws affecting commerce.

The Organization of Executive Power

Although the debates over representation and taxation were more dramatic, the most time-consuming problem during the four months of the Convention was the organization of executive power. There were long discussions and many stalemates before the delegates could agree on the many vexatious questions relating to the executive. Some of the delegates continued to advocate the revolutionary doctrine of legislative ascendancy and a weak executive power. Others, particularly Hamilton,

James Madison. Rush Rhees Library. The University of Rochester.

Madison, James Wilson, and Gouverneur Morris believed in a powerful executive chosen by direct popular election. They were convinced that only with a strong executive could national power become effective. In Wilson's words, they wanted an executive who could act with "energy, dispatch, and responsibility."

The strong-executive delegates attacked Randolph's plan to have the executive elected by the Congress because they believed that with such a mode of election the executive branch would become too dependent on the legislative branch. On the other hand, they were never able to get much support for their idea of a direct popular election because most of the delegates were too distrustful of popular majorities. Not until the end of August, near the close of the Convention, did the delegates arrive at an acceptable compromise. It was voted to have the President chosen by an electoral college composed of electors chosen in each of the states according to the number of representatives in both houses of Congress. Each state could choose its electors in such a manner as its legislature might direct—thus leaving the door open for the popular election of electors.

According to the final arrangements, the electors were to vote by ballot for two persons, and the man receiving the highest number of votes would become President, provided that his vote constituted a majority of all electors. If no candidate received a majority, then the House of Representatives, voting by state, would elect a President from the five highest candidates on the voting list. At the same time, other details, such as the President's tenure of office, were settled. The President was given a four-year term—longer than the terms of most governors in the states, but shorter than some of the advocates of a strong executive would have preferred. On the other hand, the proposal of Governor Randolph to make the executive ineligible for re-election was dropped, and a President might seek re-election as often as he chose at four-year intervals.

The definition of federal judicial power was something of a compromise also. The nationalists in the Convention generally supported the ideas in the Virginia Plan which would have given the national legislature the power to negate all laws of the several states that "in the opinion of the National Legislature" contravened the Constitution. This would have given Congress the power to define the extent of its own authority, and that of the states, within the federal union. Such an extremely nationalistic solution of the problem of federalism was wholly unacceptable to the state's rights men as well as to many moderates in the Convention. Ultimately, the Convention accepted a formulation similar to that of the New Jersey Plan which made the Constitution, laws, and treaties of the United States "the supreme law of the land" and bound the judges of every state thereby, "Any Thing in the Constitution or Laws of any State to the Contrary notwithstanding."

Apparently, the delegates most concerned about the rights of the

The Judiciary and National Power

states believed that this section of the Constitution would give the state courts as much power as the federal courts to determine the extent of state and national authority under the Constitution. In the actual historical development of the federal judiciary, however, the supremacy clause of the Constitution was interpreted to make the Supreme Court— an arm of the national government—the final arbiter of the process of the national and state governments.

National Economic Powers   Aside from the difference between the North and the South concerning the apportionment of taxes and the regulation of commerce, there was very little controversy over economic questions. When it came to detailing economic powers, the members of the Convention exhibited an extraordinary degree of consensus. In the final votes, the clauses granting Congress power to regulate commerce, pay debts, borrow money, and provide for the common defense and general welfare were adopted unanimously. The vote to give the national legislature power to collect taxes and imposts was nearly unanimous. Only one state was opposed to the stipulation that all public debts "should be as valid against the United States under the Constitution as under the Confederation." The clause forbidding the states to issue bills of credit was passed by an overwhelming vote, and another that forbade the states to interfere with the obligation of contracts was adopted without debate.

The evidence is unmistakable that nobody in the Convention would have thought of questioning the idea that the Constitution should defend the rights of property. The delegates were men of property of all kinds—real and personal—and they saw no need to explain or defend such a fundamental right in the widely held natural rights philosophy. It should be noted, however, that most of the economic clauses in the Constitution removed the defects of the Confederation which had been so troublesome to men of enterprise. The power of the national government to regulate interstate and foreign commerce promised to create a stable and protected political environment within which to expand the American market economy. The revenue-raising power of the federal government and the guarantee of the validity of the public debt enhanced the possibilities of using public securities as instruments of investment and credit. The restrictions on the power of the states to issue paper money or to interfere with private interests assured the kind of stable monetary system which creditors and men of capital desired. Furthermore, the power of Congress to raise and to equip an army and navy, and to call forth the militia "to execute the laws of the Union, suppress insurrections, and repel invasions," provided additional guarantees for men of property against such uprisings as Shays' Rebellion.

Thus, because of their successful completion of the task of drafting a new frame of government, the friends of the Constitution, or Federalists as they came to be called, achieved a dramatic advantage in political initiative. They were able to appear before the country with a Constitution that proposed to remedy all the defects of the Confederation that had become so apparent in the decade of the 1780's. Furthermore, they set the terms of ratification in such a way as to dramatize the constituent power of the people. They bypassed the state legislatures (presumed to be strongholds of states' rights thinking), and asked for approval of their work by state conventions elected by the people for the express purpose of ratifying the Constitution. They also proposed that the Constitution should go into effect when it had been ratified by only nine states.

Thus, the Federalists recreated a sense of revolutionary ardor and urgency. They appeared before the American people as men of energy and initiative seeking to fulfill the destiny of the Revolution. Indeed, James Madison specifically invoked the revolutionary symbols of the Declaration of Independence when he defended the irregular procedure of ratification saying, ". . . in all great changes of established governments, forms ought to give way to substance . . . a rigid adherence . . . to the former, would render nominal and nugatory the transcendent and precious right of the people to 'abolish or alter their governments as to them shall seem most likely to effect their safety and happiness.'"

The Ideological Basis of the New Constitutional Order

Compared to the Articles of Confederation, the ratification of the Constitution was accomplished with remarkable speed. By January of 1788, a scant four months after the document had been submitted to the people, five states had ratified the Constitution, three of them (Delaware, New Jersey, and Georgia) by unanimous votes. In Connecticut there was a three to one majority in favor of the new government and, in Pennsylvania two-thirds of the votes cast in the ratifying convention were favorable. By the end of June, 1788, 11 of the 13 states had ratified the Constitution—more than enough to form a new government according to the recommendations of the Convention.

The Debates over Ratification

Of course, one very important reason for the swift political success of the movement for the new Constitution was the shrewd decision by the members of the Philadelphia Convention to abandon the principle of unanimity which had been included in the Articles of Confederation. This time, a single state would not be in a position to use its veto power for bargaining purposes or to obstruct the will of the overwhelming majority. Indeed, two states, North Carolina and Rhode Island, did not ratify the Constitution until after the new government went into operation and they faced the intolerable alternative of being excluded from the American union. North Carolina ratified in November of 1789, and Rhode Island in May of 1790.

Although the first 11 states accepted the new frame of government within nine months after the adjournment of the Philadelphia Convention, ratification did not proceed so smoothly in all of the states as it had in the first five. Opponents of the Constitution had already begun to raise

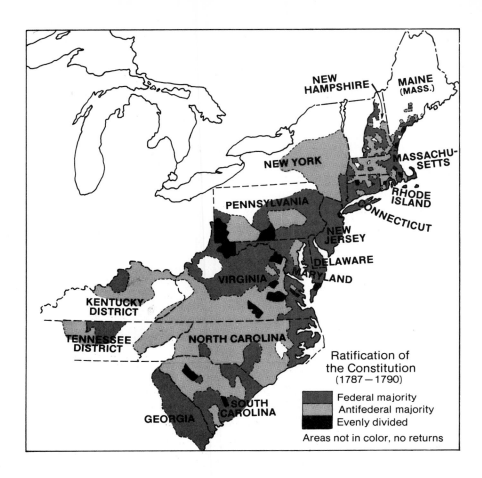

Ratification of
the Constitution
(1787—1790)

- Federal majority
- Antifederal majority
- Evenly divided

Areas not in color, no returns

serious objections in the ratifying conventions of Connecticut and Pennsylvania; and in the winter and spring of 1788, the Anti-Federalists fought some spectacular battles against the Constitution in the key states of Massachusetts, New York, and Virginia. The loss of any one of these large states would have destroyed any chance of success for the new government.

In Massachusetts, the vote was exceedingly close; the Federalists were able to win a majority of 187 to 168 only by placating such influential opponents as Samuel Adams and John Hancock, and by promising to support the addition of amendments that would guarantee the liberties of the people. In Virginia, there was a very high order of debate on all aspects of the new Constitution. Only by promising the addition of a Bill of Rights, and by making good use of the knowledge that George Washington would probably be the first President, were the Federalists able to win by a vote of 89 to 79. In the New York ratifying convention, the Constitution squeaked by with a slim majority of three votes. In New York, also, the Federalists had to promise to work for certain revisions of the Constitution, particularly the addition of a Bill of Rights.

The crucial political contests in such key states stimulated a vigorous public debate over the Constitution. In New York, Governor Clinton began a concerted attack on the Constitution as soon as it was published, in a series of letters signed "Cato" to a leading New York newspaper. The "Cato" letters contained a bitter critique of the consolidated power given to the central government by the new Constitution, and raised fears about the dangers of such a government to the liberties of the people. Fully aware of Clinton's great political influence, Alexander Hamilton persuaded John Jay and James Madison to assist him in writing a series of letters for the New York *Independent Journal* that would explain and defend the new Constitution. These essays, signed "Publius" by all three authors, were effective in meeting the arguments of the "Cato" letters and other Anti-Federalist writings such as Richard Henry Lee's *Letters of a Federal Farmer.*

Collected and published later under the title, *The Federalist,* the 85 essays written by Hamilton, Jay, and Madison not only constitute a most valuable commentary on the Constitution by its contemporary supporters, but they are also the finest expression of American political thought produced in the eighteenth century. In essence, they elaborated more systematically many of the ideas that had been expressed in briefer and more transitory ways during the Convention. Taken together, the *Federalist* essays develop a fairly coherent political theory that has controlled the American political dialogue ever since.

The Federalist Science of Politics

Most of the Federalists shared a distrust of human nature and a fear of any arrangement of political power that could be used in an arbitrary manner. "Men love power," Hamilton had declared in the Convention, ". . . All the passions . . . of avarice, ambition, interest . . . govern most individuals, and all public bodies."

This conception of men as being motivated primarily by self-interest and ambition was the point of departure for Federalist political thought. Thus, Madison argued that the selfish egoism that exists in every man was the source of most of the problems that have existed in popular governments. In the brilliant tenth essay of *The Federalist,* Madison maintained that self-love leads men to join together in groups or factions to pursue their special interests even to the point of doing injury to the rights of other citizens or "to the permanent and aggregate interests of the community."

The Problem of Factions

Drawing upon his knowledge of history, Madison pointed out that the tendency of men to form factions has been exhibited in a variety of ways. Sometimes a zeal for different religions, or attachments to ambitious and popular leaders, or differences concerning the forms of government have "divided mankind into parties" and excited violent political conflicts. "But," he concluded, "the most common and durable source of factions has been the various and unequal distribution of property. Those who hold and those who are without property have ever formed distinct interests in society. Those who are creditors and those who are debtors, fall under a like discrimination. A landed interest, a manufacturing interest, a mercantile interest, a moneyed interest, with many lesser interests, grow up of necessity in civilized nations, and divide them into different classes, actuated by different sentiments and views."

Hence, the regulation of such varying and conflicting interests is the inescapable task of popular governments. The causes of faction cannot be removed without destroying the liberty of men to pursue their individual interests and happiness: ". . . it could not be less folly," Madison affirmed, "to abolish liberty which is essential to political life, because it nourishes faction, than it would be to wish the annihilation of air, which is essential to animal life, because it imparts to fire its destructive agency." The art of government, therefore, consists in arranging political power in such a way as to hold the balance of justice among the various interests which compete with each other in a society wherein men believe that individual liberty is essential to political life.

Social and Political Checks and Balances

Madison believed that the extended sphere of the national government organized at Philadelphia contained the means of controlling the effects of faction. The great geographical extent of the Republic made this possible. "Extend the sphere [of government]," he wrote, "and you take in a greater variety of parties and interests; you make it less probable that a majority of the whole will have a common motive to invade the rights of other citizens." Thus, to Madison, there was a greater safety in a larger number of factions which would provide a system of social checks and balances that would limit the emergence of overbearing majorities.

Furthermore, Madison argued, in a Republic of such large extent, the government would have to be delegated to a small number of citizens chosen by the rest. The effect of this would be "to refine and enlarge the public views, by passing them through the medium of a chosen body of citizens, whose wisdom may best discern the true interest of their country." If the elected representatives had to compete for the approval of a larger number of citizens, the support of the people would be more likely "to center in men who possess the most attractive merit and the most diffusive and established characters."

If Madison could have foreseen the development and influence of mass media of communication in America, he might have been less willing to believe that large constituencies would produce elected representatives of "attractive merit" and "established characters." On the other hand, neither Madison nor other Federalists were willing to rely completely on the expectation that enlightened statesmen would more likely appear in the extended system of national government created by the Constitution. "Enlightened statesmen will not always be at the helm," Madison acknowledged; hence "auxiliary precautions" were necessary. "The constant aim," he said of the Constitution, "is to divide and arrange the several offices in such a way as that each may be a check on the other." Indeed, since all men are motivated by self-love, power should be so constructed as to turn private interest into a guardian of public rights.

"Ambition must be made to counteract ambition." Madison wrote, "The interest of the man must be connected with the constitutional rights of the place."

Thus, the separation of powers in the Constitution was designed to be a scheme by which the lust for power of men in one branch would be counteracted by rival interests in the other branches of the government and, as a consequence, no man or group of men would be able to wield arbitrary power in behalf of any factional interest in the society. No man was to be trusted, not even a popular hero like Washington. "It may be a reflection on human nature," Madison acknowledged, "that such devices should be necessary to control the abuse of government." "But," he pointed out, "what is government itself, but the greatest of all reflections on human nature? If men were angels, no government would be necessary."

Many twentieth-century historians have been led astray by the incisiveness of the fifty-first *Federalist* paper. They have all too easily assumed that the system of checks and balances described by Madison was designed to thwart popular majorities through an organized system of political deadlock—wittily described as a "harmonious system of mutual frustration." Such an explanation simply cannot do justice to the political science of the Federalists as it was expounded in the full range of the essays in *The Federalist.*

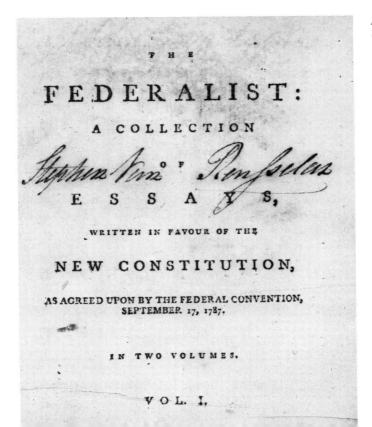

Rush Rhees Library. The University of Rochester.

Madison, himself, was careful to point out that a rigid adherence to the principle of a separation of powers would not be workable. Hence he opposed an absolute veto in the hands of the President, even though such a power would enhance the separation and independence of the executive. Similarly, he defended the appointment of federal judges by the President with the consent of the Senate, rather than an absolutely separate mode of election, because he believed that it was necessary to preserve some degree of dependence and communication among the three branches of the government. Otherwise, "the permanent tenure by which the appointments are held in that (judicial) department, must soon destroy all sense of dependence on the authority conferring them."

Conceptions of Power   It should not be forgotten, either, that the authors of *The Federalist* assumed that the great powers conferred on the central government would actually be used in the pursuit of national goals. They were not the prisoners of a negative conception of power. Hamilton, for example, wrote the essays on the presidency in order to explain and defend the idea of an active and energetic executive. "Energy in the Executive," he wrote, "is a leading character in the definition of good government. . . . A feeble Executive implies a feeble execution of government. A feeble executive is but another phrase for a bad execution; and a government ill executed, whatever it may be in theory, must be, in practice, a bad government." Again and again, Hamilton hammered out the symbols of action in his essays; "decision," "activity," "dispatch" are the key qualities which a vigorous executive can infuse with the operations of government.

Similarly, Hamilton, who feared power less than his colleagues, wrote many of the essays defending the powers of Congress to tax, to regulate commerce, and to provide for the common defense. Yet, it was Madison who wrote the point by point defense of the powers delegated to the general government under the Constitution. And it was he who first developed an elastic conception of that clause in the Constitution which grants to Congress the power "to make all laws which are necessary and proper for carrying into execution the foregoing powers and all other powers vested by this Constitution in the Government of the United States, or in any Department or Office thereof." Madison explicitly defended a doctrine of implied powers in the construing of the Constitution: "No axiom is more clearly established in law, or in reason, than that whenever the end is required, the means are authorized; whenever a general power to do a thing is given, every particular power necessary for doing it is included." He believed that to restrict the Congress only to powers expressly delegated would disarm the general government of any real authority. "Without the substance of this power," he wrote concerning the "necessary and proper" clause, "the whole Constitution would be a dead letter."

In the light of such considerations, Madison's later observation that every word in the Constitution "decides a question between power and liberty" takes on more meaning. The Federalists feared concentrated power wherever it might be—in an overbearing popular majority, or in the hands of men who held office. Yet they needed an active and energetic use of national power to protect national honor and independence, and to promote the rapid growth of American economic enterprise. Hence they created a national government with greater powers than king and Parliament had exercised before the Revolution: they willingly accepted the calculated risk that an overbearing majority might use those powers at some future time to injure the minority in their property or other rights.

And in the minds of the Federalists, this was truly a great risk. Madison's fears of an overbearing majority, expressed inside and outside of the Convention, were genuine. Hamilton often spoke of the "turbulence" of the people and their susceptibility to "the arts of designing men." Of course, they, and their Federalist friends, hoped that the system of checks and balances would save them from the worst errors and oppressions that might be inflicted by factious majorities. Hamilton looked to the federal judiciary to "moderate the immediate mischiefs" of "unjust and partial" laws and, in No. 78 of *The Federalist,* he explicitly defended the idea that the Supreme Court should have the power to declare invalid any statutes that contravened the Constitution. Nevertheless, Madison realized that, in the last analysis, they would have to depend upon the people, "who can by the election of more faithful representatives, annul the acts of the usurpers."

The willingness of the Federalists to accept the risks of majority rule becomes more apparent when their views are compared to those of the Anti-Federalists in the battle over ratification. The Anti-Federalist writers not only shared a distrust of human nature, but they feared power, including the power of popular majorities, when it was remote or distant from the people. Moved by such fears of governmental power, the Anti-Federalists led the drive for the addition of a Bill of Rights to the Constitution. Hence, they, more than the Federalists, must be credited with the initiative for the guarantees of civil liberties which have become an invaluable part of the American constitutional tradition. But their main defense against the lust for power, and the selfishness of its use, was to decentralize power. They believed that republicanism could work only in small states, where the population was small and relatively homogeneous, and where the seats of power were close to the people. In this respect they were closer to the original principles of the revolutionary ideology.

Fifty years ago, Charles A. Beard, in his *An Economic Interpretation of the Constitution of the United States,* tried to show that the Constitution was a document drawn up by a "consolidated economic group whose property interests were immediately at stake," and that the battle over the ratification of the Constitution between Federalists and Anti-Federalists reflected a basic clash of interests between the holders of

The Constitution and Economic Interests

property in the form of *realty* (landed property) and the holders of property in the form of *personalty* (public securities, money loaned at interest, investments in commerce, manufacturing, and land speculation). More recently, Forrest MacDonald's meticulous state by state investigation of the economic interests of Federalists and Anti-Federalists, published under the title *We the People* (1958), has destroyed much of the usefulness of the simple economic categories used by Beard. The economic interests of the framers of the Constitution were more diverse and more mixed than Beard had indicated. Although a large proportion of the framers had investments in forms of property that Beard called "personalty," the most common form held by the delegates to the Philadelphia Convention was agricultural property.

Nevertheless, this new evidence still suggests that an unusually high proportion of the framers were interested in economic enterprise of a more adventurous and speculative character. "Agricultural property," as Forrest MacDonald reminds us, comprised two basic forms of economic behavior at the time of the adoption of the Constitution—"subsistence farming" and "market farming." By and large, the framers of the Constitution were men who were involved in those varieties of farming operations that had to do with raising crops for commercial markets, and that required the investment of larger amounts of capital and the employment of larger amounts of labor—including slave labor in the South. Such forms of agricultural activity were closer in method and spirit to the other forms of American business enterprise represented by commerce, banking, land speculation, and manufacturing.

At any rate, the Anti-Federalists saw it that way and made frequent appeals to class interests during the battle over ratification. In the Massachusetts convention, a delegate from a village of small farmers expressed his analysis of the selfish interests of the Federalists in the following terms: "These lawyers, and men of learning, and moneyed men, that talk so finely, and gloss over matters so smoothly, to make us poor, illiterate people swallow down the pill, expect to get into Congress themselves; they expect to be managers of this Constitution, and get all the power and the money into their own hands, and then they will swallow up all us little folks, like the great leviathan, Mr. President; yes, just as the whale swallowed up Jonah. . . ."

In the New York convention, Melancton Smith made a more sophisticated analysis of the political prospects under the new frame of government. "I am convinced," he said, "that this government is so constituted that its representatives will generally be composed of the first class in the community, which I shall distinguish by the name of the *natural aristocracy* of the country." In using the term, "natural aristocracy," he meant to refer to men of birth, education, talents, and wealth. Smith argued that in the national system of politics which was created by the Constitution, this class of men would be able to command great influence and, by reason of their far-flung personal and business contacts, be able to organize parties on the scale necessary to win control of the government. "The great," he concluded, "easily form associations; the poor and middling class form them with great difficulty."

Such appeals to the great majority of "little folks" and small farmers did not rally the countryside in the battle over ratification. The fragmentary evidence concerning the popular vote for delegates to the state ratifying conventions suggests that not more than 5 per cent of the population or about 160,000 voters exercised the constituent power of the people of the United States from 1787 to 1788. The low percentage of popular participation cannot be ascribed to the disfranchisement of voters by property or other qualifications for suffrage for we know that a much larger number of voters were qualified under existing suffrage laws than took the trouble to vote in the election of delegates to the ratifying conventions.

Historians can only speculate about the meaning of the widespread abstention of voters from the process of creating a fundamental frame of government for America. But in view of what we know about previous patterns of political behavior in eighteenth-century America, it seems reasonable to assume that large numbers of "little folks" and subsistence farmers were apolitical. Subsistence farmers are likely to be limited and parochial in their interests and attitudes. They are less likely than commercial farmers to develop a calculating spirit and the manipulative skills to obtain wide-ranging legal and political advantages. It would take another generation before the spread of the national market economy would draw the mass of America's farmers into the jostling competition of interest groups that was to characterize the political system that grew up under the new Constitution.

Memorial to General
Washington, c. *1815.
Garbisch Collection.
Philadelphia Museum of
Art. Photograph by A. J.
Wyatt, staff photographer.*

Washington's Presidential Leadership

Following the adoption of the Constitution, the political energies of the Federalists were mobilized in a struggle to obtain control of the instruments of power in the new government. They were aware that the character of the new political system would depend as much on the methods and objectives of the men who used the powers of the federal government as it would upon the provisions of the Constitution itself. Hence, the Federalist leaders rallied their followers for the political campaign to choose presidential electors and members of Congress. Washington, himself, believed that "the fate of the Constitution" would be decided by the men who were chosen to implement it and he urged his Federalist friends to continue their efforts, saying, "There will . . . be no room for the advocates of the Constitution to relax in their exertions; for if they should be lulled into security, appointments of Anti-Federal men may probably take place; and the consequences which you so justly dread be realized."

As Washington anticipated, the Anti-Federalists put up congressional candidates in every state except Georgia, and, in some states, the fight was as spirited as that over the ratification of the Constitution. But all the advantages were on the side of the Federalists. They enjoyed the benefit of the political initiative that had been gained with the adoption of the Constitution. Moreover, they had the enormous advantage of Washington's prestige. Washington was already the legendary hero of the American Revolution, and affection for him and trust in his personal character were among the most important unifying sentiments among the mass of the people throughout the country.

Federalist Control of New Government

As a result of these advantages, the first election under the new Constitution was an overwhelming victory for the Federalists. Washington was chosen President by a unanimous vote of the presidential electors. The office of Vice-President went to John Adams of Massachusetts whose writings had articulated many of the basic political ideas that were embodied in the Constitution.

The election also resulted in large Federalist majorities in the House of Representatives and the Senate. Eleven out of 26 senators and 9 out of 55 members of the House had been members of the Philadelphia Convention; indeed, 37 members of both houses of Congress had been supporters of the Constitution in the Constitutional Convention, or in the state ratifying conventions. Only eight Anti-Federalists were elected to the House of Representatives, and it was said at the time that they were "so lukewarm as scarcely to deserve the appellation." Moreover, other staunch Federalists were appointed by Washington to fill administrative and judicial offices, so that more than half of the members of the Constitutional Convention of 1787 were serving the new government in either the legislative, executive, or judicial department.

The inauguration of Washington as President on April 30, 1789, in New York, the first seat of the government, was followed by significant and far-reaching developments in the uses of national power. President Washington shared fully the views of most leading Federalists that a strong executive was indispensable to an energetic and efficient national government. His inaugural address sounded the keynote of *authority* with the firm assertion that the American people must learn "to distinguish between oppression and the necessary exercise of lawful authority . . . to discriminate the spirit of Liberty from that of licentiousness." The legitimate use of authority, he believed, was necessary for the good society; without it, indeed, there could be no real prospect for any meaningful use of liberty.

Under Washington, the office of the Chief Executive acquired an impressive dignity which it has never lost even in the presidential terms of lesser men. In fact, Washington deliberately maintained a posture of majesty and dignity which was sometimes criticized as an imitation of monarchical forms by members of the opposition party. In his own personality, Washington was reserved and aloof; hence his personal style of behavior tended to reenforce his view that the presidency should be an office of great respect and prestige.

When he appeared in public or official occasions, Washington always rode in a coach drawn by four or six horses. In addition, he held weekly levees, noted for their austere formality, at which he always appeared in black velvet dress, with a powdered wig, and knee and belt buckles, and wearing his long sword. One contemporary account reveals how severe this ceremony was:

He stood always in front of the fire-place, with his face towards the door of entrance. . . . He received his visitor with a dignified bow, while his hands were so disposed of as to indicate, that the salutation was not to be accompanied with shaking hands . . . . even with his most near friends. . . . As visitors came in, they formed a circle around the room. At a quarter past three, the door was closed, and the circle was formed for that day. He then began on the right, and spoke to each visitor, calling him by name, and exchanging a few words with him. When he had completed his circuit, he resumed his first position, and the visitors approached him in succession, bowed and retired. By four o'clock this ceremony was over.

During the first weeks after the inauguration of the new government, members of Congress argued noisily over the titles and ceremonies that were to be used to surround the President with appropriate dignity. In the Senate, John Adams, from his vantage point as presiding officer, was most vehement in supporting proposals to address the President as "His Excellency" or "His Elective Highness." Washington, himself, indicated that he would like to be addressed as "His High Mightiness, the President of the United States and Protector of their Liberties."

The Anti-Federalists listened to this debate over titles with dismay and charged that the Federalists were seeking to imitate the forms and

ceremonies of monarchy. Before long, a considerable number of Federalists began to feel uneasy about the question perhaps because they sensed the powerful political weapons that might be used against them by the Anti-Federalists who were already giving Vice-President Adams the derisive title of "His Rotundity" behind his back. Furthermore, Washington, himself, came to regret that the issue of titles had been raised. In the end, common sense republicanism prevailed. The American people have preferred to follow the Constitution which calls the Chief Executive simply "President of the United States."

However, there was more to Washington's presidential leadership than pomp and circumstance. He had to build an administration with very little in the way of bureaucratic experience that he could take over from the expiring Confederation government. When power was transferred from the old government to the new, there was a foreign office with John Jay at the head and a couple of clerks to deal with dispatches from the United States ministers in London and Paris; there was a Treasury Board with a nearly empty treasury; and a "Secretary at War" in charge of an authorized army of 840 men. Indeed, after a decade of existence, the Confederation government was still a shadowy affair even by eighteenth-century standards. The machinery of government that would give the country a vigorous and responsible executive had to be created from scratch.

The achievement of Washington in creating an effective national administration was remarkable. By the end of his first administration, Washington had established a Department of State with an active diplomatic and consular service. A Department of the Treasury had been

*Organizing
Executive Authority*

organized, and regular collections of revenue were flowing into the vaults of the central government. The army was reorganized under a War Department with supervision over military and naval affairs. In addition, an Attorney General's office with the assistance of district attorneys of the United States were giving force and meaning to federal laws in the lower federal courts. Moreover, the Postmaster General was steadily establishing new post offices, and extending the postal routes into every district of the nation. In a variety of ways, governmental authority was acquiring a greater national focus.

In the making of policies, however, Washington did not develop a bold or aggressive style of leadership. The large degree of presidential authority which was established in his administrations was primarily the result of Washington's personal taste for formality in the conduct of his office, and also of the marked deference of the Federalists in Congress to a leader whom they venerated. The main executive impulse often came from Washington's department heads, notably Alexander Hamilton; and it is largely in the measures pushed through Congress by the influence of Hamilton that the full extent of executive power in the Federalist administration can be seen.

The Hamiltonian System

In accordance with his hope that "whatever there be of wisdom, of prudence, and patriotism on the Continent, should be concentrated in the public councils," Washington chose men of recognized ability and reputation to head the departments of administration created by Congress for the new government. Thomas Jefferson was chosen Secretary of State, although John Jay continued to serve temporarily as Secretary for Foreign Affairs until Jefferson returned, in March, 1790, from his post as minister to France. When Robert Morris declined to accept appointment as Secretary of the Treasury, Washington offered the post to one of his wartime military aides, Alexander Hamilton. General Knox, who had been Washington's chief of artillery in the Revolution and "Secretary of War" under the Confederation, continued in the War Department in the first Washington administration. To the post of Attorney General, he appointed Edmund Randolph of Virginia, who had played key roles as a framer of the Constitution at the Philadelphia Convention and as a critic of the constitution in the Virginia ratifying convention.

Although the Constitution made no mention of a President's Cabinet, it was inevitable that Washington should develop the practice of consulting with such able men on larger questions of policy as well as on matters pertaining to the functions of their particular departments. Because of their intellectual brilliance, Hamilton and Jefferson were able to exercise a significant influence on Washington's policies. Hamilton had more influence than other members of the Cabinet because Washington did not always understand the intricacies of finance and, consequently, was inclined to follow Hamilton's lead in such matters. Since President Washington had strong views on foreign policy, he was less dependent on Jefferson's advice. In military matters, he needed little advice from Henry Knox. And Attorney General Randolph soon discovered that his role made him "a sort of mongrel" who had to scavenge for duties in the undefined zone between state and federal judicial activities.

Inevitably Alexander Hamilton would have a large role to play in the new government because financial problems were the most critical of all the exigencies confronting the new federal government. And he was especially fitted to do so. He was a brilliant and extremely ambitious young man who had rapidly made his way up the ladder of social success after coming to the continent, in 1773, from the British West Indies to continue his education at King's College in New York. During and after the Revolution he had played a variety of roles with éclat: he was an outstanding officer on Washington's military staff, he was an able lawyer and a skillful pamphleteer, he was a key figure in the growing network of banking and investment activities in New York, and his contributions to the Federalist papers had already identified him in the public mind as a leading exponent of an energetic use of executive power. To Hamilton "Energy in the executive" was "a leading character in the definition of good government," and he was determined to see that the executive impulse should be employed to the fullest extent in the new administration.

*Hamilton's
Policy-Making Role*

The sheer magnitude of the fiscal problems connected with the management of the foreign and domestic debt caused the members of Congress to look to the Secretary of the Treasury for leadership. Ten days after Hamilton's appointment, Congress directed him to prepare a report on the public credit. Eagerly grasping the initiative which was placed in his hands, he proceeded to develop a comprehensive fiscal policy that would strengthen the power of the national government and invigorate the American economy. Eventually, Hamilton's ideas were elaborated in four great public reports: the first dealing with public credit, the second recommending excise taxes, the third proposing the creation of a national bank, and the fourth urging the stimulation of manufacturing enterprise in America.

Undoubtedly, many of the members of Congress who voted to have the Secretary of the Treasury prepare a report on the ways and means of supporting the credit of the federal government hoped to accomplish this objective as cheaply as possible. They remembered the precedent set by the Continental Congress, in 1780, when promises to pay represented by the Continental currency were scaled down by setting an official value of 40 continental dollars to one specie dollar. For most Congressmen such a wholesale repudiation of the interest-bearing public securities was unthinkable, but many of them were prepared to advocate a policy of paying off the public creditors at less than the face value of their

Collection of j mara gutman.

certificates. They believed that very little injustice or hardship would be inflicted by such a policy since many of the original holders—particularly small holders like soldiers or farmers who had been paid for supplies and service in interest-bearing certificates—had already sold their securities to investors and speculators for considerably less than their face value.

Hamilton, however, had come to the settled conviction that the national debt, if properly managed, could become the chief cornerstone of a new structure of political and economic power in America. In his "Report on Public Credit," delivered to the Congress in January, 1790, he not only repeated the stock arguments that the foreign debt must be paid in full if America was to maintain its credit among the civilized nations of the world, but he was also frank to admit the material advantages that would come to the American economy from a policy of funding the national debt at its full value. His business experience had taught him the usefulness of public securities as a source of investment capital. He reminded Congress that "transfer of stock or public debt are . . . equivalent to payments in specie; or, in other words, stock in the principal transactions of business passes current as specie." To Hamilton, the benefits of such a flexible and transferable source of investment funds seemed enormous. "Trade is extended by it," he declared, "because there is a larger capital to carry it on . . . Agriculture and manufacture are also promoted by it, for the like reason, that more capital can be commanded to be employed in both . . . The interest of money will be lowered by it: for this is always in a ratio to the quantity of money and to the quickness of circulation."

Hamilton's political boldness went far beyond his assertions that the national debt could be "a national blessing." Not only did he urge Congress to fund the national debt at face value, but he also proposed that the federal government assume all the state debts as part of the same funding program. The assumption of the state debts, he believed, would give the national government a stronger claim upon the states in the use of its revenue powers. "These circumstances combined," he said, "will insure to the revenue laws a more ready and satisfactory execution." Furthermore, with unabashed frankness, he argued that the assumption of state debts would bind the political interests of all security holders to the new administration: "If all the public creditors receive their dues from one source distributed with an equal hand, their interest will be the same. And, having the same interests, they will unite in support of the fiscal arrangements of the government—as these, too, can be made with more convenience where there is no competition." Clearly then, Hamilton was prepared to use fiscal policy to organize the men of capital in America into a factional interest that would be firmly bound to the political fortunes of the Federalist administration.

Specifically, Hamilton proposed that Congress authorize three new bond issues: one to refund the foreign debt, another to refund the chaotic collection of interest-bearing certificates that had been issued by the

Continental Congress, and the third to refund unpaid state debts at par. All these government obligations were to be refunded at face value, although the domestic security holders were to receive a reduced rate of interest. Strictly speaking, this was not preserving full faith and public morality in dealing with public creditors, but Hamilton hoped that, in exchange for the advantages offered by the funding system, he could afford to take what he called "a stout slice" from the accrued interest owed by the government to the public creditors. On the average, this reduction provided for an interest rate of 4.5 per cent instead of 6 per cent for the security-holders who were being asked to turn in their old certificates for the new bonds.

It should be recognized, also, that Hamilton had no desire to create any program for the rapid extinguishment of the national debt. His primary objective was to fund the debt in order to restore its value and to uphold the credit of the national government. Therefore, his settled policy was to service the debt by providing for regular payments of interest and not to pay it off. To his way of thinking, the continued existence of the debt was a necessary and valuable stimulus to the expansion of business enterprise.

In preparing his Report on Public Credit, Hamilton included facts and arguments that revealed a shrewd anticipation of the objections that might be raised against his proposals. Nevertheless, while he foresaw the likely arguments of the opposition, he failed to foresee the source from which those arguments would come. The leader of the opposition to his funding and assumption schemes was none other than James Madison, his old friend and collaborator in the writing of the Federalist papers. And the evidence is clear that Madison's opposition did hurt, because Hamilton privately charged Madison with "a perfidious desertion of the principles which he was solemnly pledged to defend."

Opposition to the Funding Program

Although Madison freely admitted that public morality required the government to make full payment of the public debt, he believed that Hamilton's funding program would have the pernicious effect of rewarding speculators with great gains, without redressing the injustice that had been done to public creditors during the years of the Confederation when public securities had often been sold for as little as one-fourth of their face value. He proposed, therefore, to mitigate the inequities of Hamilton's funding scheme by discrimination between original holders and secondary purchasers of government securities.

In a lengthy speech in the House of Representatives, Madison classified security holders into four groups: original holders who had never sold their paper, original holders who had sold their securities, present holders of previously owned securities, and intermediate holders through whose hands securities had passed in the transfers of many and varied private transactions. For the first group, the original holders who had not sold their securities, Madison advocated full payment in recognition of their sustained faith in the promises of the government to pay despite all the lean years of non-fulfillment in the Confederation. As for the last group, the intermediate holders, Madison agreed that it would be impossible to determine just what claims, if any, needed to be compensated—"their pretensions," he acknowledged, "would lead us into a labyrinth, for which it is impossible to find a clue." But, for the two remaining groups of creditors, the original holders who had alienated their securities, and the present holders who had bought for speculative purposes, Madison proposed a policy of more exact justice: "Let [the present holders] have the highest price which has prevailed in the market; and let the residue belong to the original sufferers." Inasmuch as public securities had not risen to anything like their full value—even with the speculative wave of buying that had developed after Hamilton's Report on Public Credit—the original holders who had alienated their securities could hope to get a small portion of the funding loaf to compensate them for any loss they had suffered because of the financial weakness of the government under the Articles of Confederation.

Hamilton used all his influence among members of Congress to combat the resistance to his funding scheme. In a preliminary vote, Madison's proposal to discriminate between original holders and speculative purchasers was defeated in the House of Representatives, 36 votes to 13. Of the 64 members of the House at that time, 29 appeared on the funding books of the government as security holders according to a law passed later in the year. How many of these 29 voted for the measure in the first voting test will never be known because there was no roll call vote.

Sectional Controversy Over the Assumption of State Debts

Hamilton, however, had little time to rejoice over this first victory for his program because it became clear that Madison had only begun to fight. The Virginia leader immediately concentrated his opposition on the second part of Hamilton's funding-assumption bill—the assumption of the state debts. In this phase of the legislative battle, Madison held a position of greater political strength. Maryland, Georgia, and North Carolina had very small debts, and Virginia had already paid off half of its very considerable war debt by paper money issues. The southern representatives, therefore, believed that it was unfair to require the citizens of states with low indebtedness to help pay the debts of the heavily indebted states. Moreover, the assumption of the state debts would mean an increase in the domestic national debt of 50 per cent since the funding of the national securities was estimated to require about $40 million worth of new bonds, and that of the state debts about $21 million.

Meanwhile a noticeable speculative mania in public securities had developed in the principal commercial cities of the United States. Without the knowledge of Hamilton, his Assistant Secretary of the Treasury, William Duer, was leaking inside information about the refunding plans of the Treasury to certain privileged individuals with large amounts of capital who turned such information to profit in their speculative operations. In January, 1790, when the funding scheme was being debated in Congress, several fast ships loaded with speculators and cash sailed from New York and Philadelphia to southern states to buy up what was available before the holders obtained full knowledge of the prospects for the assumption of state debts. It should be said, however, that if northern speculators got rich, it was not because of the ignorance of the southerners, but rather because they were convinced that the assumption scheme would be defeated in Congress. As Hamilton said in another connection, the sellers speculated upon the purchasers and "each made his calculation of chances."

The southerners who unloaded their depreciated securities so gleefully had calculated their chances shrewdly. In five different test votes during the spring of 1790, the assumption proposal was rejected by narrow majorities in the House of Representatives. The debate dragged on into the hot summer and became increasingly bitter as James Jackson of Georgia rallied southern members against the bill. To him, Hamilton's proposal was simply a scheme to tax one section of the community for the benefit of another. He warned that the inhabitants of the southern states could "see through this thin veiled artifice to take a portion of their state power from them, and they will feel that continual drain of specie which must take place to satisfy the appetites of basking speculators at the seat of the government." By the early weeks of July, tempers were worn so thin that members of Congress from the North as well as the South were beginning to talk about disunion; Senator Richard Henry Lee, for example, declared he would prefer dissolution of the Union to "the rule of a fixed insolent northern majority."

But the capacity for political compromise that had already manifested itself in the battle over the Constitution provided a way out of the crisis. Hamilton proposed to Jefferson, his Cabinet colleague, that he use his influence with southern members to get them to change their votes on assumption and, in return, he would use his influence with northern Congressmen to get them to vote for locating the permanent federal capital in the South. The agreement was made and Jefferson always believed (with a considerable show of regret) that he had played a key role in allowing Hamilton's funding scheme to go through. Actually, he overestimated the importance of his bargain with Hamilton. The main bargaining for votes was carried out by House and Senate members and their trade-offs included generous allotments to debtless states to settle their claims for wartime expenses, as well as arrangements linking votes on assumption with those on the location of the capital. In its final version, the funding-assumption bill passed late in July of 1790; meanwhile, Congress had designated Philadelphia as the temporary capital for 10 years and chose a site on the Potomac River as the permanent seat of the national government.

As a result of the funding and assumption legislation, the national debt (including about $20 million owed to foreign countries) had soared to a total of over $80 million. To service this debt, a large portion of the

UNITED STATES.					VALUE of several FOREIGN CURRENCIES in UNITED STATES MONEY.				
	Population in 1790.		Value of a Dollar in Currency.	Number of Representatives in Congress.		D.	d.	c.	m.
	Free.	Slaves.	Total.							
* Maine	96,540	none	96,540	72 pence	See Mafsts.	Pound fterling of G. Britain	4	4	4	0
New Hampfhire	141,728	157	141,885	72	4	Pound fterling of Ireland	4	1	0	0
Vermont	85,573	16	85,589	72	2	Crown Englifh - -	1	1	1	0
Maffachufetts	378,787	none	378,787	72	14	Crown French - -	1	1	0	0
Rhode Ifland	67,877	958	68,825	72	2	Livre Tournois of France	0	1	8	5
Connecticut	235,182	2,764	237,946	72	7	Florin or Guilder of the United Netherlands	0	3	9	0
New York	318,796	21,331	340,120	96	10	
New Jerfey	172,816	11,423	184,239	90	5	Mark Banco of Hamburg	0	3	3	5
Pennfylvania	430,636	3,737	434,373	90	13	Rix Dollar of Denmark	1	0	0	0
North W. Territory	4,280	none	4,280	72	.	Ruble of Ruffia - -	1	0	0	0
Delaware	50,207	8,887	59,094	90	1	Real Plate of Spain -	0	1	0	0
Maryland	116,692	103,036	319,728	90	8	Mexican Dollar - -	1	0	0	0
Virginia	454,983	292,627	747,610	72	19	Milree of Portugal -	1	2	4	0
Kentucky	59,247	12,430	73,677	72	2	Tale of China - -	1	4	8	0
† North Carolina	293,179	100,572	393,751	120	10	Pagoda of India -	1	9	4	0
Tennaffee	32,274	3,417	35,691	96	1	Rupee of Bengal -	0	5	5	5
South Carolina	141,979	107,094	249,073	56	6	Silver coin, by ounce	1	1	1	0
Georgia	53,284	29,264	82,548	56	2	Standard Silver 1,485 pure to 179 alloy				

* Maine is a part of the State of Maffachufetts.   † Dollars were formerly 96 Pence.

national revenue was required. In fact, between 1790 and 1800, over 40 per cent of the national revenues were used to pay the interest alone on the national debt. Yet Hamilton saw no reason for alarm. He was able to see, as many of his contemporaries did not, that there was a connection between national income and the national debt, and that the debt would not be burdensome if the productive forces of the country were rapidly expanded. Americans, he believed, could well afford to pay 5 or 6 per cent for the support of public securities which, invested in the productive enterprises of the country, would stimulate higher returns for agriculture, trade, and manufactures.

Since he believed that funding would stimulate prosperity, Hamilton felt no compunction at all about placing the main burden of taxation on the mass of the taxpayers rather than on the classes in whose hands the bulk of the money and capital was concentrated. He asked Congress to raise the additional revenues needed to support the huge debt structure by increasing the tariffs on articles of common consumption and by levying an internal tax on whiskey. Congress adopted his proposals, although the excise tax on the domestic production of whiskey was not enacted into law until March, 1791, because of the bitter opposition of men like James Jackson of Georgia who charged that the excise tax was "odious, unequal, unpopular, and oppressive."

The adoption of the excise tax was indispensable for the success of Hamilton's program. With the revenue from excises and customs, he was able to meet the charges of the national debt without placing any undue burdens of taxation on the productive enterprise of the country— particularly commerce and manufacturing. The success of his program in attracting additional investment capital to America was immediate. By the end of 1794, the United States had the highest credit rating of any nation in the world. European investors began to divert large amounts of their capital to American securities, particularly after the French Revolution, and the general war which followed. By 1795 foreigners held over $20 million in the domestic debt of the United States; by 1801 their holdings had reached $33 million.

Although the funding program channeled a great deal of capital into the hands of the men, who, in Hamilton's opinion, were most likely to use it for constructive economic purposes, he was not satisfied merely to sustain the face value of the governmental debt. He intended a more active role for the government in the American economy as he made clear in his further reports on economic policy.

In a report submitted to Congress in January, 1791, Hamilton proposed the chartering of a Bank of the United States which would be founded on the combined credit of the government and private citizens. According to this plan, the national bank was to have a capital stock of $10 million; of this stock the government was to own one-fifth, and in addition it was to appoint five members of the Board of Directors; the ownership of the remaining four-fifths of the stock and the choosing of 20 directors was left to private investors.

Hamilton's National Bank Proposal

To persuade Congress of the usefulness of such an institution, Hamilton pointed out that the bank would serve as the principal depository of government funds, as the fiscal agent of the treasury for the transfers of money in domestic and foreign operations, and as a source of short-term loans to keep such operations running smoothly. More important to Hamilton, however, than such assistance to the government in collecting taxes and administering the public finances was his proposal that the Bank of the United States should be authorized to issue bank notes. These notes—payable upon demand in gold or silver—were to be receivable for all payments owing to the United States government. By this means, Hamilton hoped that the bank notes would become the principal circulating medium in the country.

The note-issuing power of the bank, therefore, represented Hamilton's solution for the lack of an adequate money supply in the American economy. He and other Federalists shared a deep distrust of a paper currency that was issued by the government because of the unhappy experiences with such paper money issues in the Revolution and in many of the states during the Confederation period. He believed that in a representative government, men were subject to political pressures that caused them to resort too readily to the devices of inflation, devaluation, and repudiation in the management of a paper currency. "Government," he said, "being administered by men, is naturally, like individuals, subject to particular impulses, passions, prejudices, and vices . . . to inconstancy of views and instability of conduct."

But, if the note-issuing power was placed in the hands of men of capital who had subscribed to the stock of the national bank, the management of the bank notes would come under the control of the competitive system of rewards and penalties that was built into the market economy, thus avoiding all the evils of government-issued paper money. "To attach full confidence to an institution of this nature," Hamilton emphasized, "it appears to be an essential ingredient in its structure, that it shall be under a *private* not a *public* direction—under the guidance of individual interest, not of public policy." The participation of the government in the ownership of stock and on the board of directors, he argued, would keep an element of government control, without the harmful effects of too much governmental interference.

To attract private capital, Hamilton proposed that the stock in the Bank of the United States should be purchased with government bonds up to three-fourths of the value of the stock, and the rest was to be paid for in specie. Thus, the moneyed men of the United States, already the owners of public securities, would be bound together even more closely as stockholders of the national bank. And, in their hands, the note-issuing power could be used to channel credit into the right forms of productive enterprise.

Madison and Jefferson Oppose the National Bank

Hamilton's Report on a National Bank encountered vigorous opposition in Congress. Recognizing that the Secretary of the Treasury's proposal followed the example of the Bank of England, James Jackson of Georgia charged that the corrupting influence of Old World institutions would destroy the free institutions of the New World. "What was it drove our forefathers to this country?" he demanded. "Was it not the ecclesiastical corporations and perpetual monopolies of England and Scotland? Shall we suffer the same evils to exist in this country . . .?" He warned his colleagues in the House of Representatives that the national bank was "calculated to benefit a small part of the United States—the mercantile interest only; the farmers, the yeomanry of the country, will derive no advantage from it." James Madison, for his part, charged that the proposed bank was unconstitutional; Congress could not charter a corporation with power to issue bank notes and conduct commercial banking, because that would stretch the implied powers incidental to the "necessary and proper" clause far beyond the bounds of reasonable construction.

Although the debates in Congress were passionate, the vote in favor of chartering the Bank of the United States was 39 in favor and 20 opposed. Most of the votes in favor—33 out of 39—were from New England, New York, New Jersey, and Pennsylvania; most of the nays—15 out of 20—were from Virginia, the Carolinas, and Georgia. Nevertheless, the constitutional arguments used by Madison succeeded in raising serious doubts about the measure in the mind of Washington. Hence, before signing the bill, President Washington requested opinions from Jefferson, Hamilton, and Edmund Randolph concerning the power of the Congress to create corporations.

Jefferson and Randolph agreed with Madison's view that the bill was unconstitutional. Jefferson, in particular, took great pains to develop a closely reasoned exposition of a strict construction of the Constitution in order to persuade the President that the chartering of corporations was not expressly granted to Congress by the Constitution and that the Bank of the United States was not a "necessary and proper" means of carrying out the taxing and borrowing powers which were granted to Congress. Significantly, Jefferson made use of the Bill of Rights which had been drawn up and submitted to the states for ratification by the Congress immediately after the new government went into operation. His conception of the limited character of the enumerated powers of Congress was based on the premise of the Tenth Amendment that "all powers not delegated to the United States by the Constitution, nor prohibited by it to the states, are reserved to the states respectively, or to the people."

Jefferson's reasoning must have seemed persuasive because Washington informed Hamilton that, unless he could answer Jefferson's arguments, the bill would not be signed into law. Hamilton, therefore, made his answer a major effort. In his written opinion, he argued that a bank was a necessary and proper means of aiding the government in the collection of taxes and in the regulation of trade. He conceded that the federal government was a government of limited, enumerated powers, but he contended that if the ends were legitimate every reasonable means of attaining the ends was also proper. "The national government, like every other," he wrote, "must judge in the first instance the proper exercise of its powers." In short, Hamilton's basic contention was little more than a paraphrase of Madison's explanation of the "necessary and proper" clause in *The Federalist,* No. 44.

His doubts largely removed by Hamilton's arguments, Washington signed the bill into law; and, on July 4, 1791, the stock of the Bank of the United States was put up for sale. Within a few hours, crowds of purchasers had bought up all of the stock. To Jefferson, the rush by men of wealth to purchase bank stock was proof of "the delirium of speculation" which had seized the country. And while the evidence does not support Jefferson's belief that the speculation in bank stocks had gotten wholly out of hand, it is clear that most of the capital stock was bought up by capitalists in the northern states and in Europe. Moreover, Hamilton soon made it clear that the Bank was to serve the needs of businessmen rather than the farmers, for he refused to support the suggestion that the Bank should lend money to southern planters on the security of their tobacco warehouse receipts.

While the chartering of the Bank of the United States accomplished another step in Hamilton's grand design to stimulate the growth of business enterprise in the country, his Report on Manufactures, submitted to Congress in December, 1791, was intended to complete his blueprint for rapid economic growth. Indeed, the Report was a far-reaching plan to transform the American economy by following the example of Great Britain and other powers in fostering industrialization.

Hamilton's Proposal to Foster Manufacturing

If the United States was to survive in a world of competing mercantilist systems, Hamilton believed that it must develop a mixed economy, composed of manufacturing as well as agricultural industries. Otherwise, the producers of the United States would be at the mercy of future mercantilist regulations that might close the markets of other nations to their lumber, wheat, livestock, tobacco, rice, and indigo.

In fact, Hamilton's vision of the productive power of manufacturing was more radical than that of the leading economic theorists of Europe at the time. In the opening section of the Report on Manufactures, he disputed the contention of the French Physiocrats that agriculture alone was productive because nature worked with the farmer to produce an enormous increase of his crops and his livestock; and that manufacturing was sterile because it merely altered the shape of materials taken from the soil, the forests, and the sea. Similarly, he took issue with Adam Smith's cautious assertion in *The Wealth of Nations* that the productivity of manufacturing was not as great as that of agriculture because an equivalent portion of raw materials were consumed in the manufacturing operations. Hamilton maintained that nature could work with man in industry so as to produce a greater degree of productivity than he could achieve by the bounty of nature in agriculture. He pointed out that labor-saving machinery harnessed the forces of nature and made them work with man to produce goods at a fantastically greater rate than the hard-working methods of the household industry or the farm.

Therefore, Hamilton urged Congress to aid the infant industries that had already sprung up in the American economy in the eighteenth century. His Report contained an exhaustive list of the many forms of manufacturing being carried on in the households of America as well as in the few larger enterprises of iron, steel, shipbuilding, distilling, flour-milling, etc. Specifically, the governmental assistance that Hamilton recommended included protective tariffs, bounties for the establishment of new industries, premiums and awards for the encouragement of inventions and of labor-saving machinery. By such means, Hamilton hoped to stimulate a rapid growth of the economy based on a grand division of labor within a great national market—northern ships would carry southern raw materials to northern factories instead of to Europe. And, in the mutual exchanges of goods within this common market, everyone would benefit: farmers, ship owners, merchants, artisans, and manufacturers.

Congress, however, was unwilling to pursue Hamilton's visions of America's economic destiny any further. The representatives from agrarian sections suspected that this was simply another attempt to benefit the business interests of the north at the expense of all other sections and groups. In addition, many merchants in the northern states were not ready to divert capital from their profitable investments in commerce, land speculation, and turnpike and canal companies. Congress did pass a Tariff Act in 1792, but largely for the purposes of revenue; and, except in the case of the fisheries, the system of bounties advocated by Hamilton was not put into effect. The United States had to wait a full generation before internal improvements in transportation and communication would enable private investors to see, at first hand, the possibilities for profits in manufacturing that Hamilton had conceived only in his lively imagination.

The French Revolution and the Rise of Party Conflict

A few weeks after Washington's inauguration, the aroused masses of Paris stormed the Bastille and the French Revolution became a cataclysmic reality in the political affairs of the European world. At first, the American people were united in their enthusiasm for the revolutionary cause, believing that the French people had been inspired by the example of the American Revolution. French songs and French revolutionary slogans became immensely popular in America—so much so that contemporaries commented on the "Bastille fever" and the "love-frenzy for France" that seemed to take hold of the people.

American Attitudes Toward the French Revolution

Shortly after the fall of the Bastille, Lafayette sent President Washington the key to the captured fortress-prison, and Washington graciously acknowledged the token of the common bond of freedom that united the French and American peoples. Yet, in August, 1790, he began to express his personal fears of the dangers that might come to the French people "from too great eagerness in swallowing something so delightful as liberty."

On the other hand, his Secretary of State, Thomas Jefferson, was ready to support the cause of the French Revolution regardless of its excesses. Even when the bloody events of the "reign of terror" were taking place, he could say that "the liberty of the whole earth was depending on the issue of the contest, and . . . rather than it should have failed, I would have seen half the earth devastated."

The difference between the apprehensiveness of Washington and Jefferson's unswerving support marked the deep division that was to destroy the initial unity of American opinion concerning the French Revolution. As the Revolution moved into its more radical phases, many leading Federalists began to express their revulsion. Hamilton no longer saw any resemblance between the two revolutions in the New World and the Old: "Would to heaven, we could discern in the mirror of French affairs the same humanity, the same decorum, the same gravity, the same order, the same dignity, the same solemnity, which distinguished the cause of the American Revolution." John Adams, already well-known for his writings on the American constitution, composed a series of political papers entitled *Discourses on Davila* in which he assailed the form of government and the ideology espoused by the French Revolutionaries. First published in the *United States Gazette* in 1791, the

Discourses rallied conservative opinion in America in much the same way that Edmund Burke's *Reflections on the Revolution* in France had rallied Englishmen the year before.

In the *Discourses on Davila,* Adams upheld the theory of checks and balances which he had previously defended as the essential principle of republicanism. He condemned the concentration of power in the single National Assembly of France as another form of despotism. Furthermore, he ridiculed the claims of the French revolutionary leaders that they had abolished hereditary titles and privileges, and dissolved all forms of social distinction by the use of "citizen" as the democratic form of address for all men. "Are riches, honors, and beauty going out of fashion?" he asked scornfully. "Has the progress of science, arts, and letters yet discovered that there are no passions in human nature? no ambition, avarice, or desire of fame?" As long as such passions exist in the nature of man, Adams maintained, there will be "rivalries and emulations" among mankind, and social distinctions will arise despite any pretensions to the contrary.

The publication of Adams' *Discourses* created a political uproar. Jefferson and other sympathizers with the French revolutionary cause were outraged by the frank defense of the naturalness of social classes and social distinctions. To them, the social theories of the Vice-President seemed to reveal a fondness for aristocratic and monarchic forms, the more so because Adams had played a conspicuous part in the effort to create high-sounding titles at the start of Washington's administration.

Consequently, Jefferson used his personal influence to provide for the publication in America of Thomas Paine's *The Rights of Man,* which contained a fervent defense of the doctrine of the French Revolution. And Federalists everywhere in America were shocked and outraged at Paine's unqualified defense of majority rule, which he developed even to the point of denying the validity of the restraints of constitutions or precedents. "Every age and generation," he declared in *The Rights of Man,* "must be free to act for itself in all cases as the ages and generations which preceded it. The vanity and presumption of governing beyond the grave is the most ridiculous and insolent of all tyrannies. . . . Every generation is, and must be, competent to all the purposes which its occasions require. It is the living, and not the dead, that are to be accommodated."

The French Revolution as a Political Issue

Thus, the French Revolution added the cutting edge of ideological differences to the political conflicts that were developing over Hamilton's economic program. Indeed, the differences between Hamilton and Jefferson widened into open antagonism by the end of Washington's first administration. When Hamilton began to subsidize John Fenno's *Gazette of the United States* with printing contracts and loans, Jefferson sought to establish a newspaper in Philadelphia that would counteract what he called "the pure Toryism" of Fenno's newspaper. With Madison's help Jefferson persuaded Philip Freneau, who enjoyed the reputation of being America's "poet of the Revolution," to use his talents in behalf of the principles of true republicanism. In 1791 Freneau was given a clerkship in the State Department and, with the assistance of a friendly printer in Philadelphia, the *National Gazette* was established. Thereafter, Freneau's formidable literary talent was devoted to attacks on Hamilton and his program.

The Republicans, as the party of opposition called itself, were not as well-organized as the Federalists, who had formed their party earlier, and who enjoyed the prestige of being closer to the men in power during the Washington administration. Moreover, the Federalists had talented writers like John Jay, Rufus King, and Noah Webster to speak for them and, undoubtedly, the larger portion of the intellectual community of America shared their views. In addition, influential newspapers like the New York *Minerva,* the Hartford *Courant,* and *Porcupine's Gazette* shaped public opinion in support of Federalist policies.

In fact, the Republicans did not have a full-fledged political party at the time of the election of 1792. No effort was made to oppose the re-election of Washington, and the Father of His Country received the unanimous vote of the electoral college for a second time. But Vice-President John Adams was a tempting political target. The Republicans were able to garner 50 votes for George Clinton of New York against 77 for Adams in the contest for the vice-presidency. In addition the voting patterns in the House of Representatives indicated that the party division was becoming nearly equal.

Not until Washington's second administration did the Republican party acquire the character of a national party. The *ad hoc* political sniping of the early years of the Washington administration was replaced by an organized and persistent opposition to the policies of the Federalists, notably their foreign policy.

In his first years as Secretary of State, Jefferson had not developed any serious differences with Washington and Hamilton over foreign affairs. When revolutionary France went to war with Great Britain, Jefferson supported the general purposes of Washington's "Neutrality" Proclamation because he was convinced that the national interest could be served better by playing a neutral role. Nevertheless, as twentieth-century Americans know only too well, neutrality is a very slippery concept in international relations, and Jefferson's belief proved to be different from that of either Washington or Hamilton.

Problems of Washington's Neutrality Policy

Mindful of our obligations to France under the Treaty of Alliance of 1778, and concerned for the success of the French Revolution, Jefferson favored a policy of neutrality that would be benevolent toward France, but that would hold Great Britain to a strict accountability for any of her actions affecting American commerce in the West Indies and elsewhere. Hamilton, on the other hand, favored a policy of neutrality that was benevolent toward Great Britain. He hoped that the revolutionary regime in France would be defeated and the French monarchy restored. More particularly, he was unalterably opposed to any actions by the American government that would jeopardize our commercial relations with Great Britain. The entire structure of his elaborate fiscal system rested on the revenues received from excises and customs—two-thirds of the revenue, indeed, came from import duties, and most of them were collected on goods imported from Great Britain. President Washington, who had the final power of decision, hoped to keep out of foreign entanglements completely. He wanted a genuine neutrality that did not favor either France or Great Britain. He was willing to yield to Jefferson's insistence that the word "neutrality" ought not to be used in his Proclamation of April 22, 1793, but he was careful to stress that the United States intended to follow "a conduct friendly and impartial towards the belligerent powers." Furthermore, the President's Proclamation prohibited American citizens from "aiding or abetting hostilities, or otherwise engaging in unneutral acts."

Jefferson spent several uncomfortable months in Washington's Cabinet after the Proclamation. In his own words, he and Hamilton were "daily pitted like two cocks" in their quarrels over questions of further relations with Great Britain and France. Hamilton took the position that the United States no longer had any obligations to France under the Treaty of 1778 since the revolutionary government of France could not be considered securely established. Moreover, he opposed the reception of Citizen Edmund Genêt who was appointed in 1793 minister to the United States by the revolutionary government of France which had proclaimed itself a republic and declared war on Great Britain.

Although Jefferson was successful in persuading Washington that Genêt should be received by the United States as the representative of the duly constitutional government of France, he was embarrassed by the behavior of the French minister when he arrived in America. Citizen Genêt was an ardent young revolutionist who hoped to equip privateers in American ports to harass British shipping, and to make the United States a base of operations against the Spanish and British in Louisiana, Florida, and Canada. He assumed that the American people must be overwhelmingly sympathetic toward the Republic of France and that, as an ally, the United States would give as much aid, clandestine and otherwise, as France had given to the American Revolution before outright intervention in the conflict of 1778.

Genêt was at least partly right about the sentiments of the American people. His journey from Charleston, South Carolina, where he had arrived in America, to Philadelphia was a continuous triumphal procession of parades and dinners. Everywhere, Americans seemed desirous of expressing their admiration of the French people in their struggle for liberty. Mistakenly assuming that the official policy of the United States government would be as partial to France as these signs of popular favor, Genêt purchased the services of George Rogers Clark, a minor hero of the American Revolution, to lead an expedition against Louisiana and

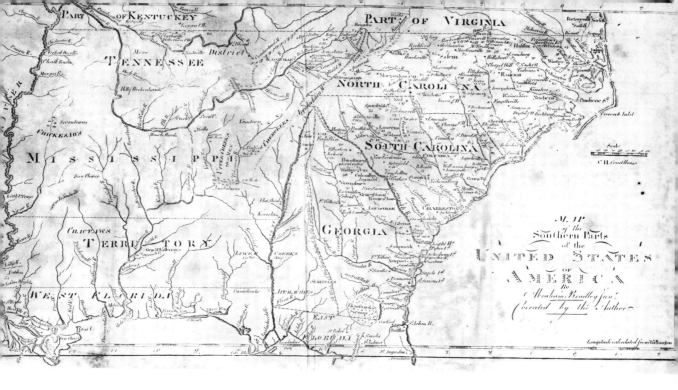

Florida, and lavishly distributed other commissions for the same adventure. When he arrived in Philadelphia, he reminded the Washington administration that French naval vessels were respecting the neutral rights of American shipping, while the British were seizing American ships that were carrying French goods. He insisted that the American government should take steps to defend the principle of "free ships, free goods" which had been written into the Treaty of Alliance with France in 1778.

Genêt even went so far as to commission American privateers on his own to prey on British shipping. Twelve such privateering ships soon captured over 80 British ships. Their prizes were brought into American ports, where Genêt insisted that they should be condemned and sold by special tribunals set up by French consuls in American ports.

President Washington was outraged at these violations of his announced policy of impartiality toward the belligerents. He sought to prevent George Rogers Clark and other westerners from organizing filibustering expeditions in the southwest; meanwhile the Supreme Court declared that the French consular tribunals on American territory were illegal. Furious at these efforts to clip his wings, Genêt threatened to appeal to the American people over the head of Washington. Indeed, he demanded that Washington call a special session of Congress so that the representatives of the people could judge between the President and the minister of the French Republic. This was too much, even for Thomas Jefferson, who characterized Genêt at this time as "hot-headed, all imagination, no judgment, passionate, disrespectful & even indecent

Map of the Southern Parts of the United States of America. Rush Rhees Library. The University of Rochester.

towards the President." He, therefore, supported Washington in his request that Genêt be recalled by the French government. And the French government, which had just come into the control of the radical Jacobins, was only too glad to comply, since Genêt belonged to the discredited faction in France.

The Crisis Over
British Naval Warfare

In December, 1793, Jefferson resigned from the Cabinet, leaving Hamilton in a position of unchallenged dominance among Washington's advisors. Upon retiring as Secretary of State, Jefferson sent a special report to Congress concerning the privileges and restrictions of the commerce of the United States in foreign countries. In this report he pointed out that American ships were allowed to trade freely with the West Indian colonies of France, whereas Great Britain had barred American ships from its colonies in the West Indies. Unknown to Jefferson when he made this report was a new British Order-in-Council of November 6, 1793, which ordered all British naval vessels to seize all neutral ships carrying provisions and other supplies to the enemy's colonies or transporting the products of those colonies. This was obviously aimed at the American trade with the French West Indies, and, before American merchants and shipowners were able to learn of the new Order-in-Council, 250 unsuspecting American merchantmen were captured by British crusiers and privateers.

In support of Jefferson's views James Madison, on January 3, 1794, introduced in the House of Representatives a series of resolutions calling for retaliatory duties on British ships and merchandise. According to Madison, such regulations would foster the growth of American commerce and shipping, encourage American manufacturing, and end the dangerous dependence of the United States on British markets and British credit. In this curious way the leaders of the Republican party had become identified with a concept of American protectionism that went much further than anything that Hamilton had proposed in his Report on Manufactures.

The news of the British depredations under the new Order-in-Council reached the United States just as Madison's resolutions were being debated in the Congress. In the resulting upsurge of popular indignation, Madison's resolutions were pushed aside in favor of more drastic measures. Newspapers and Congressmen reminded Americans of all their accumulated resentments against the British. American anger had already been mounting as a result of the Indian troubles in the Northwest Territory that followed a disastrous defeat in November, 1791, for a small force of Americans led by General St. Clair, the governor of the territory. The British were accused of fomenting the Indian uprisings from their military posts on American soil that they continued to hold in violation of the treaty of 1783.

Congress was ready to vote for a drastic nonintercourse act and other provocative measures that could have led to war with Great Britain in 1794. Understandably, the Federalists viewed with dismay the turn of events that had taken place. Either nonintercourse or war with Great Britain would wipe out the import duties from which the government drew the larger portion of its revenues, and the whole Hamilton fiscal program would be overthrown. Equally disturbing were the signs of the increasing political strength of the Republicans. The debates on Madison's resolutions and other measures of retaliation brought to the Republicans a considerable amount of support from representatives of the Middle States and New England. Convinced that they faced certain defeat in the Congress, Hamilton and a group of Federalist senators persuaded the President, in March, 1794, to send a special envoy to England in the hope that war might be averted by negotiating the crucial questions at issue between the two countries. Washington chose John Jay as minister plenipotentiary, and this use of presidential initiative had the important political effect of heading off the Republican efforts in Congress to pass retaliatory legislation.

Jay's mission to England, however, did not dampen the political crisis for the Federalists. The storm center of political controversy merely shifted temporarily from foreign to domestic issues. In the summer of 1794, the Hamiltonian fiscal program was threatened by an insurrection in western Pennsylvania, caused by discontent over the excise tax on whiskey.

There had been murmurings of discontent, as early as 1792, among farmers of the western regions who depended on the distillation of whiskey as the only feasible way of moving their grain to the eastern markets, especially as long as the Mississippi River remained closed to Americans. During the next two years, remonstrances were sent to Congress from western districts, and every kind of local difficulty was created for federal enforcement officers. By 1794, however, the popular opposition to the Federalist tax program was more effectively organized, sometimes with the help of political clubs known as Democratic Societies.

Political Ramifications of the Whiskey Rebellion

These Democratic Societies grew out of the popular enthusiasm for the French Revolution that had swept the country after France had been declared a Republic in 1793. In fact, Genêt had been one of the founders of the Philadelphia Society in 1793, and 40 others were organized in the United States during the next year. They corresponded with each other much as the committees of correspondence before the American Revolution had done, and many of them consciously sought to revive "the spirit of 1776." Their statement of aims revealed a dedication to the cause of republican liberty in the United States as well as fervent support of the French Revolution. They vowed to rid American life of all aristocratic and monarchical influence which they believed had been given a new lease on life by the Hamiltonian financial system. They did much to organize and bring out voters in elections and, thereby, aided the political fortune of the Republican party.

The Whiskey Rebellion, therefore, provides an interesting example of the manner in which foreign and domestic issues were being blended into party ideologies. Of course, the Federalists regarded the Democratic Societies as tools of French policy in America, charging that Genêt had brought "the eggs of these venomous reptiles to our shores." Others charged that the Democratic Societies were imitations of the French Jacobin clubs, and that they would hatch sedition and terror even as the Jacobins of France had done. President Washington was convinced that the insurrection in western Pennsylvania was "the first formidable fruit of the Democratic Societies" and publicly denounced them in his first message to Congress after the insurrection had been oppressed. Modern historians, however, do not share Washington's rather simple causal explanation. While it is true that some leaders of the two Democratic Societies in western Pennsylvania played a prominent part in the riots, it must be remembered that vehement opposition to the whiskey excise antedated the appearance of the Societies.

Be that as it may, the evidence is clear that armed mobs stopped federal judicial proceedings in August of 1794, and a force of armed men, estimated variously at 1500 to 7000 men, captured a small body of regular troops of the United States who were guarding the house of the federal excise inspector for western Pennsylvania. After a presidential proclamation calling upon the insurgents to disperse had been ignored, President Washington called upon the states to furnish twelve thousand militiamen to uphold the authority of the federal government. In his zeal to see the rebellion stamped out, Hamilton left Oliver Wolcott in charge of the Treasury, and joined the troops in their march across Pennsylvania.

The large-scale show of force by the Washington administration produced a quick collapse of resistance; most of the insurgents disappeared as the federal troops marched across the Alleghanies; though a small number of prisoners was taken, only two were found guilty of levying war against the United States and Washington pardoned them both when he was informed that one was a "simpleton," and the other "insane."

Jefferson was highly critical of the conduct of the Washington administration. He charged that "an insurrection was announced and proclaimed and armed against, but could never be found." The Federalists, however, made a great deal of political capital out of the whole episode—claiming that the vigorous action taken by the federal government was a vindication of the "energy" of the national government.

Nevertheless, Hamilton's political position was no longer secure. Republicans in Congress continued to harass the Secretary of the Treasury with charges of corruption in the administration of his financial program. Weary of "the jealousy of power and the spirit of faction," Hamilton resigned his office in January, 1795—although he continued to exercise an enormous influence on party affairs.

Conflict Over   Because of his persisting influence, Hamilton was able to play an
Jay's Treaty   important role in the new political storm that swept the country after

March, 1795, when the treaty that John Jay had signed in Great Britain reached the United States. Hamilton, indeed, had assisted in drafting Jay's instructions the year before, and advised him to conduct himself in his negotiations with "energy," but "without asperity." The British quickly sensed the softness in the attitude of the American government, particularly after Hamilton, while still in office and without Washington's authorization, told the British minister in Philadelphia that he need have no fear that the United States would associate itself with the League of Armed Neutrality that was being formed by other neutral nations.

Jay's specific instructions from President Washington were to obtain the cession of the western posts, reparation to American citizens for losses suffered as a result of the seizures of American ships, compensation for the slaves carried away by the British army in 1783, and as favorable a commercial treaty as possible. In the treaty which Jay signed, the British agreed to evacuate the posts in the Northwest; they also agreed to submit to arbitration American claims for compensation arising out of ship seizures, if the United States would accept arbitration of claims by British creditors against American citizens. In return, Jay made large concessions to the British. A provision was included in the treaty that upheld the British interpretation of the rules of search and seizure in time of war. A further provision bound both countries to give most-favored-nation treatment in tariff and tonnage duties, thus removing any threat of American economic warfare against the British. Another provision restricted American ships in the West Indian trade—only American vessels of 70 tons or less were to be permitted to go to the British West Indies. No mention was made anywhere in the treaty of compensation for slaves taken by the British army during the Revolution.

When the terms of Jay's treaty became known, the public outcry was so great that there seemed to be no chance that it would be ratified. Charles Pinckney of South Carolina called for the impeachment of John Jay. Hamilton was stoned in New York City at a public meeting in which he attempted to defend the treaty. In Philadelphia, a Republican orator urged the American people to "kick this damned treaty to Hell."

Indeed, President Washington privately remarked that the first outcry against the treaty was "like that against a mad dog." He was determined at first not to approve it. Yet, since he could see no alternative except war with England, he decided to sign Jay's Treaty and send it to the Senate for ratification. When the final vote was taken, the Federalists were strong enough in the Senate to secure a bare two-thirds majority for ratification. On the other hand, the Republicans were able to influence enough votes to suspend the objectionable article referring to West Indian trade. In the bitter partisan battle over the treaty, Washington, himself, did not escape open condemnation in Congress and in the Republican press. Even Jefferson went so far as to say of the President: "Curse on his virtues; they have undone the country."

Jay's treaty did have one unforeseen consequence of great benefit to the United States. The political effect of the treaty in Europe led the Spanish government to seek a similar peaceable adjustment of disputes with the United States. In October, 1795, Thomas Pinckney, the American minister in Madrid, signed a treaty by which the northern boundary of Florida was fixed at the latitude of 31 degrees. Furthermore, Spain agreed to open the Mississippi River to American navigation, and to allow Americans the free use of the port of New Orleans for three years, with the privilege of renewal there or in some equivalent place.

Pinckney's treaty was immensely popular and was ratified unanimously by the Senate, on March 3, 1796. The Republicans were particularly pleased with the opening of the Mississippi River, and the prospect of a lessened Indian danger in the southwest as a result of the relinquishment of Spanish claims north of the latitude of 31 degrees. Indeed, during the long and bitter controversy over Jay's Treaty, many Republicans had finally come to the conclusion that the evacuation of the British from the posts in the Northwest was worth more than all the other issues involved. The United States, for the first time since the treaty of peace in 1783, was fully in control of the great trans-Allegheny territory, and the redemption of the American domain in the West opened up visions of a national destiny that the Republicans could respond to with even greater enthusiasm than many Federalists.

The Crisis of Federalism

At the conclusion of his second term, Washington announced his intention to leave public life. Weary of political strife, and disheartened by the venomous attacks of Republican newspapers, he was anxious to return to the peace and quiet of Mount Vernon. To announce his decision, he prepared a political testament to the people in the form of a Farewell Address which appeared in the newspapers of the country in September, 1796. Although the Farewell Address had been prepared with the help of Hamilton and Jay, the ideas expressed in it constituted a reconstruction of Federalist ideology as it had been refined in the cauldron of partisan politics.

Washington's Farewell Address

Most of the Farewell Address was devoted to comments on the state of the Union and the problems created by the rise of political parties. Washington was particularly moved to warn his countrymen of "the common and continual mischiefs of the spirit of the party." He looked upon the existence of political parties as a standing danger to the Republic. The spirit of party, he maintained, "serves always to distract the Public Councils and enfeeble the Public administration. It agitates the Community with ill-founded jealousies and false alarms, kindles the animosity of one part against another, foments occasionally riot and insurrection."

To Washington, parties were dangerous not only because they threat-

ened to tear apart the community but also because they opened the door
to the "insidious wiles of foreign influence." Hence, he added the further
advice that "the great rule of conduct for us, in regard to foreign nations
is in extending our commercial relations to have with them as little
political connection as possible . . . Europe has a set of primary interests, which to us have none, or a very remote relation." He reminded the
American people of their detached and distant geographical position.
"Why forego the advantages of so peculiar a situation?" he asked. "Why,
by interweaving our destiny with that of any part of Europe, entangle our
peace and prosperity in the toils of European Ambition, Rivalship,
Interest, Humour, or Caprice?" Therefore he urged his countrymen to
follow a policy of disentanglement in foreign affairs as well as a
disinterested patriotism in domestic affairs.

A careful reading of the Farewell Address makes abundantly clear the
fact that Washington and his followers in the Federalist party were
unable to accept the legitimacy of political conflict carried on by
permanently organized parties. In this respect they were still beset by
their fears of an overbearing majority which had been expressed so
frankly by Madison in *The Federalist* at the time of the ratification of the
Constitution. To the Federalists, party warfare could only become
warfare to the death in which one faction annihilated the other. As
Washington put it in the Farewell Address,

The alternate domination of one faction over another, sharpened by the spirit of
revenge natural to party dissension, which in different ages and countries has
perpetrated the most horrid enormities, is itself a frightful despotism . . . The
disorders and miseries, which result, gradually incline the minds of men to seek
security and repose in the absolute power of an Individual: and sooner or later
the chief of some prevailing faction more able or more fortunate than his
competitors, turns this disposition to the purpose of his own elevation, on the
ruins of Public Liberty.

The existence of such imagined terrors in the minds of Federalists
constituted a serious danger to the further development of the American
constitutional system. As long as they were warped by such fears, there
was a real possibility that the Federalists themselves would transform the
party battle in America into a war of annihilation—that they would be
unable to grant that other politically active groups should have a
legitimate access to the seats of power.

In fact, the first all-out party battle under the new Constitution took
place in the election of 1796. The Republicans put forward Thomas
Jefferson as their candidate for the presidency, thus bringing the highest
office in the land within the arena of political conflict. On the Federalist
side, Washington evidently looked upon Vice-President Adams as his
successor; at any rate he went carefully over matters of general policy
with Adams when he announced his decision to retire.

Hamilton, however, was noticeably cool toward the candidacy of
Adams. He knew that he and Adams did not share the same attitude

A Two-Party System

toward the use of power. Hamilton loved power and was always ready to use it to the fullest extent; he was suspicious of Adams' pedantic strictures on the dangers of undivided power in the *Discourses on Davila*.

Hamilton, therefore, conducted a political intrigue to maneuver Thomas Pinckney, the second man on the Federalist ticket, into the presidency in 1796. He sought to persuade enough southern electors to cast their ballots for Pinckney, but to withhold a few votes from Adams. The plan misfired, however, when enough New England electors, having heard of the plot, deliberately wasted their second votes to make sure that Pinckney would not top Adams. As a result, Adams won election to the presidency with 71 votes. But Jefferson, because of the blank second ballots cast by so many Federalists, was second with 68 votes. With only 59 votes Pinckney even failed to obtain the vice-presidency.

In the popular voting for the various federal offices in 1796, however, the political lines were more tightly drawn, and it is possible for historians to identify, with some assurance, the groups which were supporting the two parties. By and large, the wealthy commercial groups in the principal trading centers supported the Federalist party. These were the men who had invested their capital in shipping, shipbuilding, handicraft manufactures, the export and re-export trade, banking, and retail merchandizing. But the commercial and manufacturing interests, even in New England, were not numerous enough to account for the political strength of the Federalists. The evidence is unmistakable that they had considerable strength in agricultural areas. As the voting maps indicate, Federalist strength was located in those farming regions where much of the crop was produced for the market—near the larger seaports, or along navigable rivers, or in places like Connecticut and eastern Pennsylvania where roads and turnpikes were being developed. Hence, we may conclude that commercial farmers of various kinds tended to support the Federalist party, while subsistence farmers, still untouched by the commercial spirit of the growing market economy, tended to favor the Republicans.

But not all commercial farmers were Federalists. In the southern states, a larger number of wealthy agrarians—the planters—supported the Republican party than was the case in other sections of the country. Manning J. Dauer, in his study of the Adams Federalists, suggests that the political alignment of wealthy agrarians was influenced by the proportion of commercial interests in the state. The existence of a strong nucleus of merchants in a leading commercial center usually enhanced the numerical strength of the Federalists elsewhere because the wealthy agrarians of the surrounding region tended to line up with the merchants politically as well as socially. Thus, in South Carolina, the strong commercial element in Charleston led many wealthy planters into the Federalist party—whereas, in Virginia, without any great commercial centers, a large portion of the well-to-do agrarians moved into the Republican party.

Sometimes, religious patterns tended to re-enforce the patterns of voting based on income and economic behavior. Thus, in New England, the dominant Congregationalist groups tended to be Federalist in their sympathies; Quakers in Pennsylvania were generally Federalists; and Episcopalians in the middle and southern states tended toward Federalism. Baptists, Methodists, and Presbyterians, particularly among the back country farmers, furnished many supporters for the Republicans.

Moreover, while the official ideology of the Republicans extolled the virtues of the yeoman farmer, the voting statistics indicate that Republicans were developing considerable strength in the wards of larger towns and cities, where the low property valuations suggest that the inhabitants were primarily of the mechanic and laboring groups. Indeed, in New England, the Republicans often did better in the lower-class wards of the cities than they did in the farming districts—even those inhabited by small farmers.

Despite the close vote in the electoral college in 1796—and the Republicans never let Adams forget that he was "President by three votes"—it seems only reasonable for the historian to assume that the Federalist party still had a viable future. The federalists were able to retain control of the federal government even without the magic of Washington's name. If they could remain united as a party, and if they could retain their large measure of agrarian support, they might continue to be the majority party.

Both opportunities, however, were lost in the Adams administration. As soon as he took office, Adams was swept into a political crisis over foreign affairs. Furthermore, his administration was weakened from the very beginning because he made the mistake of retaining in his Cabinet such holdovers from the Washington administration as Secretary of State Timothy Pickering and Secretary of the Treasury Oliver Wolcott—both of whom were pliant tools of Hamilton's political purposes.

The great problem in foreign affairs that confronted Adams arose from relations with France. In the eyes of the French, the ratification of Jay's Treaty was an unfriendly act, particularly because the United States had conceded the right of Great Britain to establish its own rules of naval warfare. Hence, in retaliation, the French began to seize American ships bound for British ports. By the time of Adams' inauguration in March, 1797, the French had captured three hundred American ships; Charles Pinckney, the American minister to France, was ordered to leave the country, and when he stayed too long, he was actually threatened with arrest.

John Adams and the XYZ Affair

The more vociferous of the anti-French elements in the Federalist party called for warlike measures against France, but Adams decided to resort to the device of an extraordinary mission which had been used by the Federalists when they sent Jay to Great Britain after similar provocation. This time, the mission sent out consisted of three men: Charles C. Pinckney of South Carolina, John Marshall of Virginia, and Elbridge Gerry of Massachusetts. They were instructed to seek compensation for the losses inflicted on American shipping, and to secure a modification of the Franco-American treaties of 1778 that would release the United States from the pledges to defend the French West Indies, and that would readjust the commercial arrangements between the United States and France.

The three American plenipotentiaries encountered a series of humiliations in Paris. Talleyrand, the French Foreign Minister, refused to deal with them directly; instead, three subordinate agents were sent to negotiate with them. These three agents suggested that, before any negotiations could begin, the Americans should pay a bribe of $250,000 to Talleyrand, and that they should bind their government to make a loan of $12,000,000 to the French Directory. The three Americans were not particularly shocked by the demand for a bribe, since such methods were an accepted part of eighteenth-century diplomacy, but they were unwilling to pay without getting anything more than a promise of negotiations in return. Pinckney and Marshall left Paris in disgust, convinced of the futility of further negotiations. Gerry, who had Republican sympathies, stayed on to see if he could soften Talleyrand's attitude.

When the American envoys reported back to their government, and when the entire correspondence with the French agents, anonymously labelled in the President's report as X, Y, and Z, was laid before the Congress in April, 1798, a wave of patriotic fervor swept the country. A newspaper coined the slogan, "Millions for defense but not one cent for tribute"; and the Federalists reached a new peak in popularity in their role as champions of national rights against French aggression.

The Federalist War Faction

The Republicans, who had been harassing the Adams administration with continual attacks on his foreign policy, were thrown into confusion by the XYZ Affair; in the words of Fisher Ames, a staunch Massachusetts Federalist, the Republicans "were confounded, and trimmers dropt off from the party like windfalls from an apple tree in September." Responding to the popular mood, Congress voted large sums of money to complete three frigates already under construction for the navy, and authorized the purchase and construction of 40 additional ships. Hundreds of privateers were commissioned to prey on French commerce, and a separate Department of the Navy was created to administer this greatly increased naval establishment. The regular army was trebled in size, and work was begun to fortify the principal harbors of the country.

As the United States approached the brink of war, Hamilton became the conspicuous leader of the war faction in the Federalist party, and the leading promoter of the idea of a large army. Without waiting for any recommendation from the President, he had called for the creation of a large standing army. Although President Adams was cool toward the

John Quincy Adams, *engraved by J. W. Paradise from a painting by A. B. Durand.*

Alexander Hamilton *by John Trumbull. Brown Brothers, New York.*

idea, believing that a large navy was sufficient for the defense of national interests, the Hamilton Federalists were strong enough in Congress to secure the enlistment of an "Additional Army" of 10,000 men and a "Provisional Army" of 50,000 men. To raise money for these extraordinary measures, direct taxes were imposed on land, houses, and slaves.

The more impetuous men of the Federalist party pushed through Congress a series of measures supposedly designed to curb any seditious activites against the government by those who continued to sympathize with the French Revolution. For several years, the Federalist press had been accusing such American "Jacobins" as being a faction in the control of a foreign power and, in 1798, popular hysteria was whipped up by rumors that French agents, aided by disloyal Americans, were planning to set fire to Philadelphia. The *Gazette of the United States*, the leading Hamiltonian newspaper, stigmatized the opponents of the administration as "democrats, mobocrats, and all other kinds of rats" who were "making a truly diabolical effort to corrupt the minds of the Rising Generation, to make them imbibe, with their very milk as it were, the poison of atheism and disaffection."

The first of these laws to curb dissent, the Naturalization Act, increased the probationary residence requirement for American citizenship from five to fourteen years. (Many of the recently arrived immigrants were assumed to be French Jacobins, or Irishmen fleeing an unsuccessful rebellion in their own country, bringing with them a dangerous revolutionary spirit.) In addition, Congress adopted an Alien Act that gave the President power to imprison or deport aliens in time of peace, and an Alien Enemies Act that gave the President virtually

Federalist Effort to Curb Dissent

unlimited power to jail enemy aliens at his pleasure in case war should be declared. Most repressive of all was an "Act for the Punishment of Certain Crimes," known as the Sedition Act, which prescribed heavy fines and imprisonment for those judged guilty of writing, publishing, or speaking anything of "a false, scandalous and malicious" nature against the government, or specifically against the President or either house of Congress.

The vindictive spirit of the Federalists reached its height in the enforcement of the Sedition Act. Fifteen indictments were brought under the law—and 10 of these resulted in conviction and punishment. Although historians love to dwell on the details of the trial and imprisonment of the colorful Republican editor, Matthew Lyon ("the Spitting Lyon" of Vermont), it is much more important to note that the editors of four leading newspapers in the country— *The General Advertiser* (Philadelphia), the New York *Argus*, the Richmond *Examiner*, and the Boston *Independent Chronicle*—were prosecuted, and three prominent Republican editors, Thomas Cooper, James Callender, and William Duane were convicted of violating the law. The Federalist judges who heard the cases under the Sedition Act were notoriously partisan in their conduct, the worst offender being Justice Samuel Chase of the United States Supreme Court, who presided over the trials of Cooper and Callender while on circuit court duty.

Needless to say, the Republicans were aghast at what they called "the Federalist reign of terror." By the end of 1798, some Virginia Republicans were calling the Adams administration "an enemy infinitely more formidable and infinitely more to be guarded against than the French Directory." Jefferson and Madison combined their talents to organize an effective political opposition to the dangerous use of power by the federal government; both believed that the Sedition law violated the Bill of Rights.

The result of Jefferson's and Madison's collaboration was the Virginia and Kentucky Resolutions. Jefferson wrote the Kentucky Resolutions and Madison those adopted by the Virginia legislature. Both argued that the Constitution was a compact between sovereign states that had granted certain powers to the national government, reserving all other powers to the states and to the people; thus, the states were to be judges of when the federal government had usurped powers not granted to it. In the Kentucky Resolutions, Jefferson maintained that each state had "an equal right to judge for itself, as well as of infractions, as of the mode or manner of redress." But in the Virginia Resolutions, Madison declared that the states together might interpose and take the necessary and proper measures of correction. Although Jefferson came closer to a theory of nullification than Madison, he used his influence within the Republican party against any proposals or threats of secession.

John Adams' Search for Peace

The Federalists characterized the Virginia and Kentucky Resolutions as "mad and rebellious," but President Adams was deeply troubled by the direction that his party was taking. He disliked the growing war spirit in his party, and he resented the growing influence of Hamilton. When the "Additional Army" was created, Washington was called out of retirement to assume the role of commanding general, but he made it clear that he would take active command only if the situation became critical. Hence the question of who was to be second in command became a matter of great importance. Adams wanted General Henry Knox of Massachusetts to have the post, but Washington, by threatening to resign, forced him to appoint Alexander Hamilton, Major-General, and second in command.

Hamilton was eager for a break with France and seriously planned to use the occasion of open war to lead the "Additional Army" in a campaign of conquest against Louisiana and Florida, and even, to use his own words, "to squint at South America." His henchman in the cabinet, Secretary of State Pickering, went so far as to propose the possibility of an alliance with Great Britain to support such a project.

Early in 1799, however, Adams became convinced that the French Directory really wanted peace. Elbridge Gerry had returned from France bringing peace overtures from Talleyrand. Moreover, the Directory ordered a halt to the wholesale condemnation of American ships. Under these circumstances, Adams saw no reason to continue the undeclared naval war against France. "The end of war is peace," he declared, "and peace was offered me." On February 18, 1799, he sent to the Senate the nomination of William Vans Murray as envoy to France.

Adams' proposal created a deep split in the Federalist party. The Hamiltonian wing fought against any negotiations with France, but they succeeded only in securing the addition of two more envoys to the special mission—Oliver Ellsworth of Connecticut and William Davie of North Carolina. Arriving in France, the three American envoys found Napoleon Bonaparte in control of affairs as First Consul. After several months of difficult negotiations, a Convention was signed in September, 1800, by which Napoleon agreed to abrogate the Franco-American treaties of 1778, if the United States would forget all claims against France for the seizures of ships and cargoes. Thus at one stroke, peace returned, and the United States was disentangled from the commitments to France made in the critical years of the American Revolution.

Division and Defeat of the Federalists

The Hamiltonians, however, could not forgive Adams for negotiating with their hated enemy. The rift within the party became even greater when Adams removed two leading Hamiltonians from his cabinet— Secretary of State Pickering and Secretary of War McHenry. As the election of 1800 approached, Hamilton worked covertly within party circles to organize opposition to Adams' re-election. Learning of these efforts, Adams denounced Hamilton as "the bastard brat of a Scotch pedlar." In return, Hamilton demanded an explanation of these references to the peculiar circumstances of his birth, and when none was forthcoming, he began to attack Adams publicly.

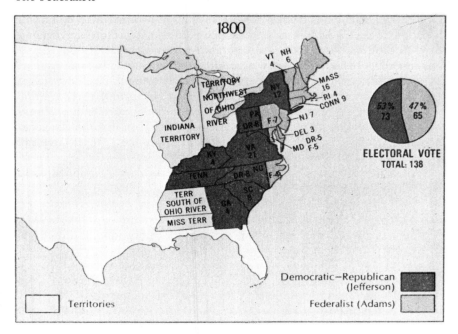

From The National Atlas of
the United States of
America. *United States
Department of Interior
Geological Survey.*

With his party so divided, Adams had little hope of victory. Since the states voted for electors at various times between October and December, it was clear that the Republican candidates, Jefferson and Burr, would have a substantial lead. The voting statistics indicate that the Federalists lost substantial strength in the middle and southern states where the direct tax on land and slaves alienated agrarian elements that had previously voted for the Federalists.

In the final tally, Jefferson and Burr each had 73 electoral votes, Adams had 65, and Pinckney had 64. Adams received all the electoral votes of the New England states, and of New Jersey and Delaware; in addition, he picked up half of the electoral votes of Maryland and North Carolina, and nearly half in Pennsylvania. Except for the split votes in Maryland and North Carolina, Jefferson swept the electoral votes of all of the southern states, and of the two frontier states of Kentucky and Tennessee; he received all the electoral votes of New York and the larger half of Pennsylvania's 15 votes. Furthermore, in the House of Representatives, the Republicans elected 65 members to 41 for the Federalists, indicating that public sentiment for the Republicans was stronger than the electoral college vote seemed to show.

After 12 years of power, therefore, the Federalist party went down to a decisive defeat. Unquestionably, John Adams' decision to send a mission to France brought about the division and disarray that weakened the once powerful party. To most Federalists, the mission to France was a traumatic experience—most of them would have supped more willingly with the Devil than with Napoleon. So much of the Federalist ideology had been built upon a hatred of the French Revolution and all that it stood for that any possibility of peaceful coexistence with France seemed unthinkable.

Nevertheless, John Adams believed that he had acted in accordance with the highest principle of executive behavior. In his *Defense of the American Constitutions*, he emphasized the importance of a disinterested executive, who rose above the conflicts of passions and parties in the legislature, and who led the people in the paths of unity, consistency, and righteousness. In his later years he wrote, "I will defend my missions to France, as long as I have an eye to direct my hand, or a finger to hold my pen. They were the most disinterested and meritorious actions of my life. I reflect upon them with so much satisfaction, that I desire no other inscription over my gravestone than: 'Here lies John Adams, who took upon himself the responsibility of peace with France in the year 1800.'"

Liberty. *1431 (former title:
Columbia) by an unknown
artist. Gift of Edgar William
and Bernice Chrysler
Garbisch. National Gallery
of Art, Washington, D.C.*

The Transfer Of Power

Although the election results of 1800 revealed that John Adams had been defeated, it was not certain that Jefferson would be allowed to become President of the United States. Republican party discipline was so effective that both Jefferson and Burr received 73 electoral votes. In view of the tie in the presidential balloting, the election devolved upon the House of Representatives; and, since the Constitution prescribed that the balloting in the House of Representatives must be decided by a majority of states, the Federalist members were numerous enough to decide the result. Consequently, the more astute Federalist leaders were quick to see an opportunity to manipulate the transfer of power to the advantage of their party's interests.

The Electoral Crisis of 1800

The campaign of 1800 had been unusually virulent. The voters had been told by Federalist newspapers that, if Jefferson were elected to the presidency, the people of the United States must expect "dwellings in flames, hoary hairs bathed in blood, female chastity violated . . . children writhing on the pike and halberd." Jefferson himself had been attacked as a "Jacobin," a "howling atheist," and an "intellectual voluptuary" who had begotten a brood of mulatto children. President Timothy Dwight of Yale predicted that religious worship would be replaced by "a dance of Jacobian phrenzy" if Jefferson were elected. "Shall our sons become the disciples of Voltaire," . . . he exclaimed, "or our daughters the concubines of the Illuminati?"

To be sure, most Federalist leaders were probably not convinced by their party propaganda any more than the masses of the voters. Most of them were educated gentlemen who had read the works of many of the enlightened philosophers of Europe and were as free of vulgar fears and superstition as any of their Republican counterparts. But they did take seriously the question of Jefferson's attitude toward the Hamiltonian fiscal system. During the campaign, many Federalist newspapers had charged that Jefferson would do everything in his power to overthrow the funding system. Indeed, one writer for the *Columbian Centinel* of Boston had warned:

Tremble, then in case of Jefferson's election, all ye holders of public funds, for your ruin is at hand. Old men who have retired to spend the evening of life upon the fruits of industry of their youth. Widows and orphans with their scanty pittances. Public banks, insurance companies, literary and charitable institutions, who confiding in the admirable principles laid down by Hamilton and adopted by Congress, and in the solemn pledges of the national honor and prosperity, have invested their moneys in the public debt, will be involved in one common, certain, and not very distant ruin. . . .

Some Federalist leaders, therefore, wished to elevate Aaron Burr to the presidency in order to keep out Jefferson. Theodore Sedgewick of

Massachusetts, an influential Federalist in the House of Representatives, urged the members of his party to support the shrewd New York politician as the best means of preserving the proper fiscal policies. "He (Burr) holds no pernicious theories," Sedgewick reasoned, "but is a mere matter-of-fact man. . . . The situation in which he lives has enabled him to discern and justly appreciate the benefits resulting from our commercial and national systems; and the same will afford some security that he will not only patronize their support but their invigoration. . . ."

Not all Federalist leaders were willing to play such a Machiavellian game. Hamilton, in particular, distrusted Burr. He had seen Burr's political methods at close hand in the politics of New York and was convinced that Burr was a wily and dangerous politican who would employ "the rogues of all parties to overrule the good men of all parties." In a letter circulated among Federalist leaders, Hamilton warned his party with the words: "Adieu to the Federal Troy . . . if they once introduce this Grecian horse into their citadel."

Nevertheless, when the balloting began in the unfinished capitol building in the new federal city on the Potomac, most of the Federalists stood firm for Burr. On the first ballot, Jefferson carried the votes of eight states, Burr had six, and two were divided. And so it continued for 35 ballots during the early weeks of February, 1801. It was rumored that some Federalists were willing to continue the deadlock past the date of inauguration with the hope that the Federalist Senate might then appoint a Federalist as President, to serve until another election might be held. Jefferson took such rumors seriously enough to warn that the day such an action was taken "the Middle States would arm" and that "no such usurpation would be tolerated even for a single day."

Moreover, Burr, himself, refused to give any encouragement to the Federalists either publicly or privately. Undoubtedly he knew that, by negotiating with them, he would lose all hope of support from the Republicans—and it was only with some Republican votes that he could nose out Jefferson. Accordingly, he played a silent, waiting game, carefully avoiding the one action that would have put an end to the deadlock—an announcement that he would not serve as President if elected.

Burr's behavior aroused the suspicions of Congressman Bayard, the Federalist representative from Delaware. He had preferred Burr to Jefferson, but Burr's refusal to negotiate led him to suspect that the New York political leader was too slippery a character to serve the Federalists' purposes. And since he was the sole representative of the state of Delaware, Bayard had it in his power to shift the vote of his state from Burr to Jefferson, thereby giving Jefferson the nine states required for election.

The Election of Jefferson   Accordingly, Bayard negotiated with men who were close to Jefferson in order to obtain assurances that Jefferson would uphold the fiscal

James Barton Longacre,
Thomas Jefferson. *Prints
Division. The New York
Public Library. Astor, Lenox
and Tilden Foundations.*

system established by the Federalists, maintain the army and navy, make no removals from office of subordinate officers, and continue the policy of neutrality laid down by Washington and Adams. Apparently, Bayard believed that he had received such assurances from Senator Smith of Maryland, an intimate friend of Jefferson's, but Jefferson later denied that he had given any specific promises.

When Bayard informed his Federalist colleagues in February that he intended to vote for Jefferson, "The clamor," he wrote later, "was prodigious, the reproaches vehement." Indeed, some Federalist diehards vowed that "they would go without a constitution and take the risk of civil war" rather than vote for "such a wretch as Jefferson." Finally, however, an arrangement was worked out by which enough Federalists abstained from balloting to insure the election of Jefferson.

The Federalists took one further action before they yielded the reins of power. Fully aware of the fact that the Republicans would control both houses of Congress as well as the presidency in the new administration, they proceeded to convert the judiciary into a last line of defence against the victorious Republicans. The Judiciary Act of 1801, passed almost simultaneously with the final balloting for the presidency, completely reorganized the federal judicial system. In addition to providing for new district courts, the act created six circuit courts, requiring the appointment of 16 new circuit judges; the Supreme Court justices, thereby, were to be relieved of the necessity of riding the length and breadth of the United States over poor roads in order to serve as circuit judges.

Furthermore, the number of Supreme Court justices was reduced from six to five, in a deliberate attempt to forestall an opportunity for an appointment to the Court by the new President.

President Adams had barely enough time to sign the commission of the newly created judicial officers before the expiration of his term. Indeed, the new judges were popularly known as the "midnight judges" because Adams is reputed to have stayed up all night on his last day in office signing judicial commissions. And, among the important appointments made at the end of his administration was that of John Marshall as Chief Justice of the Supreme Court.

Republicans denounced the act and the appointments as another barefaced attempt to frustrate the popular will as it was declared in the election of 1800. "They have retired into the judiciary as a stronghold," Jefferson wrote, ". . . and from that battery all the works of Republicanism are to be beaten down and destroyed."

Many of Jefferson's more militant followers would have welcomed a policy of full-scale reprisals against the Federalists, but Jefferson had no desire to fan the fires of party extremism. He apparently understood, as many of his followers did not, that the successful transfer of power demanded a considerable degree of magnaminity from the victorious party, even as it had required a just acceptance of the popular will from the defeated party.

In his inaugural address, therefore, Jefferson sounded the keynote of harmony and reconciliation. Warning his countrymen of the dangers of the politics of reprisal and annihilation, he said, "And let us reflect that having banished from our land that religious intolerance under which mankind so long bled and suffered, we have yet gained little if we countenance a political intolerance as wicked, and capable of as bitter and bloody persecutions." In fact, the new President went so far as to suggest a distinction between the revolutionary principle of political action engendered by the French Revolution, and the republican principle which formed the basis of American politics:

During the throes and convulsions of the ancient world, during the agonizing spasm of infuriated man, seeking through blood and slaughter his long-lost liberty, it was not wonderful that the agitation of the billows should reach even this distant and peaceful shore; . . . that this should divide opinions as to measures of safety. But every difference of opinion is not a difference of principle. We have called by different names brethren of the same principle. We are all republicans—we are all federalists.

Jefferson and the Federalist Judiciary

In one regard, however, Jefferson showed great willingness to carry out a policy of political reprisal. He was determined from the outset to destroy the bastion which the Federalists had created for themselves in the judiciary system. The original draft of his first message to Congress contained a statement of his belief that the three powers of government—executive, legislative, and judicial—had been distributed by the Constitution among three equal authorities, each constituting a check on one or both of the others. In this draft, Jefferson also asserted that each of the three branches of government had a right "to decide on the validity of an act according to its own judgment and uncontrolled by the opinions of any other department." At the last moment, however, the paragraph was withdrawn from the message as being too provocative; instead, Jefferson inserted the cryptic statement that "the judiciary system . . . and especially that portion of it recently enacted, will of course present itself to the contemplation of Congress."

The Republicans in Congress did not waste much time in contemplation. Early in January, 1802, a bill was introduced to repeal the Judiciary Act of 1801 and, thereby, to sweep into the dust heap of history the "midnight judges" appointed under the Act. Federalist spokesmen in the Congress heatedly opposed the measure, and declared that the repeal of the Judiciary Act would violate the provision of the Constitution that guaranteed tenure during good behavior to all federal judges. The Republicans, in return, argued that since the Constitution had given Congress power to create and abolish inferior courts, they were removing judgeships rather than judges. Furthermore, the Jeffersonians had the votes and, on March 31, 1802, the repeal bill became law.

This drastic action set the stage for a prolonged political conflict between the judiciary and the other two branches of government during the first Jefferson administration. Chief Justice John Marshall realized the necessity for a bold defense of Federalist constitutionalism, especially because some leading Republicans in Congress had openly stated Jefferson's doctrine that the three departments of government were equal and coordinate, each having exclusive authority on matters committed to it by the Constitution. John Randolph of Virginia had denied the need for any judicial check on Congress with the rhetorical question: "Are we not as deeply interested in the true exposition of the Constitution as the judges can be? Is not Congress capable of self-government?"

Marshall's Theory of Judicial Supremacy

Marshall found his opportunity for a counterattack in the case of *Marbury* v. *Madison*, (1803). This case resulted when James Madison, the Secretary of State, refused to deliver a commission of office to William Marbury, who was one of President Adams "midnight" appointees to the office of justice of the peace for the District of Columbia. His commission had been signed and sealed but not delivered before Jefferson took office; but Madison withheld the commission on the basis of specific orders from the new President. Thereupon, Marbury applied for a writ of mandamus, under Section 13 of the Judiciary Act of 1789, to direct the Secretary of State to perform his duty by delivering the commission.

In February, 1803, Marshall delivered the decision of the Supreme Court on Marbury's application for a mandamus. In his closely argued opinion, Marshall contended that, when a commission had been signed and sealed, the appointment was legally completed. Therefore, he was able to admonish Madison (and Jefferson) with his severe judgment that,

"To withhold his [Marbury's] commission, . . . is an act deemed by the court not warranted by law, but violative of a vested legal right."

It was only after he delivered this stinging rebuke to the Jefferson administration that Marshall took up the crucial question of whether the Supreme Court could issue a writ of mandamus in the case before it. Marbury's application had been made under Section 13 of the Judiciary Act of 1789, but Marshall argued that the language of the Constitution that prescribed the original jurisdiction of the Supreme Court did not specify the issuance of writs of mandamus to federal officials. Therefore, the grant of such authority in the Judiciary Act of 1789 "appears not to be warranted by the Constitution."

Marshall's opinion was a shrewd political attack on the Jefferson administration. By disclaiming authority to issue a writ of mandamus, he avoided giving the Jeffersonians any opportunity to defy the Court. He knew that, if the writ of mandamus had been issued, Madison would have refused to comply, and a precedent would have been established which might seriously damage the prestige and authority of the Supreme Court. Furthermore, in refusing to issue the writ on the ground that Section 13 of the Judiciary Act of 1789 was unconstitutional, the Chief Justice gave himself an opportunity to restate the Federalist doctrine of judicial review.

Closely following the reasoning of Hamilton, developed earlier in *The Federalist*, Marshall argued that the Constitution was a "superior, paramount law, unchangeable by ordinary means." The justices of the Supreme Court, he went on to say, are sworn not only to uphold "the Constitution and the laws of the United States," but their special duty is "to say what the law is" in cases that come before them. And, if the law which applies to a particular case should be in conflict with the Constitution, "the court must determine which of these conflicting rules governs the case." To Marshall, only one determination was possible in a legal system based on a written constitution: "If, then, the courts are to regard the constitution, and the constitution is superior to any ordinary act of the legislature, the constitution, and not such ordinary act, must govern the case to which they both apply."

Despite Marshall's bold use of a technical issue to set forth his claim for judicial supremacy, the doctrine of judicial review was to have little importance during the first half of the nineteenth century when Jeffersonian ideas of limited government held sway. It should be remembered that in his first inaugural address, Jefferson had defined the sum and substance of good government as "a wise and frugal government which shall restrain men from injuring one another, which shall leave them otherwise free to regulate their own pursuits of industry and improvement." As long as the executive and legislative branches were guided by such a concept of limited government, there was little likelihood that there would be any federal laws that the Supreme Court could invalidate.

Even so, Marshall's doctrine of judicial review was extremely irritating to the Jeffersonians since it challenged their views on the coordinate authority of the three branches of government. Consequently, they sought to strike back at the Supreme Court with a weapon that the Constitution made available—the impeachment process.

Under the Constitution, the House of Representatives was authorized to impeach "all civil officers of the United States" for "Treason, Bribery, or other high Crimes and Misdemeanors," and the trial of such impeachments was to be held before the Senate. Jefferson's supporters took an extremely broad view of the impeachment power, so that any form of misconduct on the bench—even excessive political partisanship—might be construed as falling within the proper meaning of "high Crimes and Misdemeanors." And when the Federalists argued that this would drag the judiciary through all the confusions and conflicts of politics, the Jeffersonians replied that the Supreme Court had already entered the political arena and that it must accept the consequences.

The Failure of Jefferson's War on the Judiciary

The Republicans first tried the impeachment method against Judge John Pickering of the Federal District Court of New Hampshire. In February, 1803, Jefferson sent documents to the House of Representatives which revealed that Pickering had been intoxicated and profane on the bench. Accordingly, the House voted to impeach Pickering, and he was adjudged guilty by a 19 to 7 vote in the Senate. The vote followed party lines, although many Republican Senators were persuaded by the evidence that Pickering was insane and, therefore, could not properly be convicted on any of the charges in the articles of impeachment. Apparently, they voted with the majority only as a means of removing Pickering from office.

Immediately following Pickering's trial in the Senate, the Republican leaders of the House of Representatives prepared to go after bigger game in their war with the judiciary. At Jefferson's suggestion, the House appointed a committee to inquire into the conduct of Justice Samuel Chase of the Supreme Court. Chase had been notoriously partisan in his handling of cases under the Sedition Act and, in 1803, he had included, in a charge to a Baltimore grand jury, a long political harangue, during which he attacked Congress for repealing the Judiciary Act and predicted that under the Jefferson Administration "our republican Constitution will sink into a mobocracy."

In a strictly partisan vote, the House of Representatives voted to impeach Justice Chase on eight counts, most of them covering his conduct as the presiding judge in criminal trials under the Sedition Act, but also including the charge that he had delivered an "intemperate and inflammatory political harangue . . . with intent to excite the fears and resentment of the good people of Maryland . . . against the government of the United States. John Randolph, a kinsman of the President, was chosen to conduct the trial before the Senate.

Chase's trial began in February, 1805, when the Jeffersonians were riding high after the great victory they had won in the election of 1804.

Everyone understood that the trial was one of great significance for the future development of the American political system. The Senate was elaborately decorated for the occasion, with special places reserved for heads of departments, foreign ministers, members of the House, and the general public. Further dramatic interest was added to the scene by the fact that Vice-President Burr, who was presiding over the trial, had just returned to Washington, fresh from the duel on the heights of Weehawken where he had fatally wounded Alexander Hamilton.

For a month, all other Senate business was practically suspended while John Randolph, speaking for the administration, and Luther Martin, representing Chase, engaged in a spectacular battle of eloquence and logic. The defense counsel did not try to claim that Chase's conduct was above reproach; but Martin hammered home the principle of due process—that for an offense to be impeachable it must be indictable in law. Randolph, and other spokesmen for the House of Representatives, merely argued logically that since impeachment was the only constitutionally prescribed method of removing judicial officers, the words "high Crimes and Misdemeanors" must necessarily include all forms of misconduct in office whether indictable or not.

Enough Republican senators, particularly from the northern states, were unwilling to accept the broad interpretation of the impeachment power with its unlimited and dangerous political possibilities. The administration forces were able to get a majority vote on three counts, but they failed to secure the necessary two-thirds majority for conviction.

Bitterly disappointed at the failure of the Chase impeachment, the Republican leaders in both houses of Congress introduced resolutions to amend the Constitution so as to provide for the removal of judges "by the President on joint address of both Houses of Congress," but no one really believed that enough states would ratify such an amendment. Jefferson, himself, was heartily sick of the whole business and pronounced the impeachment method "a farce which will not be tried again."

Significance of the First Transfer of Power   Thus, the transfer of power from the Federalists to the Jeffersonians was accomplished without any serious disruption in the constitutional system of the nation. This is particularly remarkable when we remember that no other republic which emerged from the democratic revolutions of the eighteenth and nineteenth centuries was able to achieve a similar stability in so short a time. In the French Republic, the transfer of power was invariably accompanied by the imprisonment, execution or exile of opposition leaders. In the new republics of Latin America that came into being in the early decades of the nineteenth century, civil conflicts and military dictatorship were the usual consequence of any political situation that required the transfer of governing power.

The United States managed to escape the political convulsions that were the unhappy fate of so many other republican societies because American political leaders had learned the habits of restraint and tolerance. The Federalists yielded power grudgingly, to be sure, but they never challenged the legitimacy of the transfer. The Jeffersonians, on their part, exhibited an understandable urge to inflict reprisals in their war against the judiciary, but they stopped short (albeit grudgingly) of the step that would have seriously compromised the independence of the judiciary in the further development of democratic institutions in America.

Our civics textbooks often emphasize that the lesson learned from the transfer of power after the election of 1800 was the need to eliminate the possibility of a tie vote for the presidency. Thus, during the first session of Congress in the new administration, the Twelfth Amendment to the Constitution was sent to the states, which ratified it by September of 1804. This amendment provided that, thereafter, the presidential electors should "name in their ballots the person voted for as President, and in distinct ballots, the person voted for as Vice-President."

This was a useful and necessary amendment—one that eliminated a standing temptation to politicians to manipulate the results of future elections. But even more important than this formal constitutional change were the habits and attitudes of political restraint that were being built into the American political system during the critical transference of power from Federalists to Jeffersonians. Jefferson, in particular, had dramatized this important lesson of democratic politics when he called for a political toleration that would match the degree of religious toleration already attained in American society.

Jefferson, who achieved the presidency at the head of an opposition party, accepted the legitimacy of party conflict to a degree that Washington did not. But he never really grasped the modern idea of permanently competing parties. In his first inaugural address, Jefferson did, it is true, welcome "the contest of opinion." Such freedom, he said, marked republican government because "error of opinion may be tolerated where reason is left to combat it." He explained further that "though the will of the majority is in all cases to prevail . . . the minority possesses their equal rights, which equal laws must protect, and to violate would be oppression." Yet Jefferson is here speaking as the defender of individual liberties, particularly freedom of speech, not as a theorist of a system of perpetual party competition. Jefferson assumed that the victory of his party in 1800 would end the necessity of an opposition party.

The Jeffersonian Program

In his more exuberant moments, Jefferson liked to think of his election to the presidency as "the revolution of 1800—as real a revolution in the principles of government as that of 1776 was in its form." Consequently, Jefferson took great pains to develop a tone of "republican simplicity" in his administration. He did away with the formal levées established by

Jefferson's Presidential Style

Washington and all other "mimicry . . . of royal forms and ceremonies." He wore simple clothes and even received the British minister, as one observer noted, "wearing yarn stockings, and slippers down at the heels."

Despite his informality, Jefferson was more lavish in his hospitality than Washington or Adams had been. He had guests for dinner every day and the excellence of his food and wines became legendary. Moreover, the new President deliberately ignored questions of precedence and protocol at state dinners much to the consternation of several of the foreign ministers. He even went so far as to draw up rules of etiquette for his official family in which he stated his famous principle of "pêle mêle"—"To maintain the principle of equality, or pêle mêle, and prevent the growth of precedence out of courtesy, the members of the Executive will practice at their own houses, and recommend an adherence to the ancient usage of the country, of gentlemen in mass giving precedence to ladies in mass, in passing from one apartment where they are assembled into another."

Although Jefferson made a great show of changing the tone and style of the presidency, his use of executive power maintained the Federalist conception of a strong executive power. His methods, however, were different because the Republican theory of executive power, developed during the years of opposition to the Federalist administrations, was based on a fear of executive encroachments. Republican rhetoric was full of professions of faith in the people and their representatives; the party spokesmen, therefore, emphasized that policy and financial proposals should originate in Congress. Even Jefferson himself had once described the conflict between Republicans and Federalists as being based on the difference between those who would give a little more weight to the legislature and those who would magnify executive power.

Jefferson's Methods
of Leadership
Jefferson was shrewd enough to make no heavy-handed attempt to impose a formal executive direction of policy. Instead, he developed new techniques of executive influence that made him a stronger President than either of his predecessors. With the help of Albert Gallatin, his Secretary of the Treasury who had served as floor leader of the Republicans in the House during the previous administration, Jefferson made effective use of informal caucuses as a means of keeping close relations between the executive and legislative branches. More often than not, members of Congress met at Gallatin's house, and party leaders found it easy and natural to gather there for frequent informal meetings with their one-time Congressional associate. Such informal meetings undoubtedly influenced the boarding house groups of the Washington community in which Congressional representatives discussed measures and voting strategies on a day to day basis.

In short, Jefferson built up an effective system of executive influence, operating by the use of consultation and conference, rather than by relying on formal deference or ceremonial dignity. To be sure, the effectiveness of the system depended heavily on Jefferson's force of character and intellect. Under his less forceful successors, the House leaders were able to get control of the speakership and the machinery of caucus, both formal and informal, and, thereby, to control a great deal of policy-making and administration.

Jefferson was determined to use his large degree of executive influence to bring about "the revolution in the principles of government" which he believed had been made possible by the election of 1800. Part of this change of direction came almost without effort when Jefferson pardoned those who had been imprisoned under the Alien and Sedition Acts (both of which had expired) and, Congress repealed the Naturalization Law. Indeed, John Adams had paved the way for the destruction of these repressive measures by his decision to make peace with France.

Other goals of "the revolution of 1800" which he and other Republican leaders had in mind were suggested in the definition of a "wise and frugal" government that he had proposed in his inaugural address. His conception of limited government obviously called for a reconstruction of the Hamiltonian fiscal system.

Since the Hamiltonian system became the focal point of reform for the Republican administration, much of the responsibility for the details of fiscal reconstruction were worked out by Albert Gallatin, Jefferson's Secretary of the Treasury and financial expert of the Republican party. Consequently, a knowledge of Gallatin's fiscal model is essential for an understanding of many of the key policies of Jefferson's administration.

Jeffersonian Fiscal Policies

Gallatin's fiscal theory started with the proposition that the existence of a national debt was "an evil of the first magnitude." Unlike Hamilton, he did not regard the national debt as a "national felicity" which would stimulate the productive energies of the country. In an elaborate attack on the Hamiltonian system—*A Sketch of the Finances of the United States*—written in 1796, Gallatin had contended that all expenditures of government, and especially those based upon borrowing, constituted "a destruction of the capital employed to defray them." In the later elaboration of his economic ideas, Gallatin was ready to admit that government expenditures devoted to internal improvements such as roads and canals were productive, but he steadfastly maintained that ordinary civil expenditures were unproductive, and that all expenditures for war were totally destructive of national capital.

In Gallatin's view, government borrowing simply decreased, by a like amount, the capital that could be productively employed by the private sector of the economy. "The labor of men employed in the public service," he wrote, "had it been applied to the pursuits of private industry, would not only have supported them, but probably afforded them some reward beyond mere sustenance, and therefore would have produced an excess beyond their consumption, an addition to the national wealth, an increase of the capital of the community."

Gallatin's economic theory was also entangled in a great deal of moralizing against the *principle* of indebtedness. He believed that a public debt was as much of a curse as a private debt—that it encouraged waste and extravagance. He feared that borrowing would become a national habit, laying the foundation for national demoralization. In this the Secretary of the Treasury had the wholehearted support of Jefferson who expressed the belief that "government has no right to perpetuate a debt beyond one generation because one generation has no right to bind the next. Perpetuating a debt has drenched the earth with blood and crushed its inhabitants under burdens ever accumulating."

Accordingly, Jefferson's fiscal policy was dedicated to extinguishing the national debt—in Jefferson's words, to "the emancipation of our posterity from that moral canker." And Gallatin's method of public budgeting was as simple and direct as that of any private family: "I know but one way that a nation has of paying her debts; and this is precisely the same which individuals practice. 'Spend less than you receive'; and you may then apply the surplus of your receipts to the discharge of your debt."

At the same time, the Jeffersonians were opposed to all internal taxes. In the political memory of the Republicans, the excise taxes imposed by Hamilton were particularly odious. To Jefferson, indeed, the internal taxes of the Federalists were hostile to the genius of a free people because they had already begun the process of "domicilary vexation . . . covering our land with officers and opening our doors to their intrusions." Accordingly, the Republican majority in both houses of Congress complied eagerly with the President's recommendation that all such taxes be repealed; and, on April 6, 1802, Jefferson signed the bill repealing the entire internal tax system.

Of course, the elimination of the internal taxes deprived the government of one important source of revenue. Nevertheless, Gallatin did not propose to substitute new or additional revenues in place of the internal taxes. He accepted the existing revenues from customs duties and land sales as given, and proposed to accomplish the reduction of the national debt by drastic economies in the level of government expenditures.

In 1801, Gallatin estimated that he could count on permanent revenues of about $10 million a year—$9.5 million from customs duties, and the rest from public land sales. By the last year of the Federalist administration, the net ordinary expenditures of the government, exclusive of interest on the debt, had reached $7 million a year. Gallatin succeeded in bringing down these expenditures to less than $5 million for the year 1801, and to an average of $4 million a year for the next three years. This meant drastic reductions in the enlarged army and navy created by the Federalists, and the cutting of the civil list to the barest minimum. By such means, Gallatin hoped to be able to apply half of the annual revenues of the federal government to the extinguishing of the national debt.

In line with this fiscal policy, the Republicans were able to achieve a remarkable reduction of the national debt during the peacetime years of the Jefferson and Madison administrations. Gallatin had hoped to reduce the $80 million debt that had been inherited from the Federalists to only $47 million by 1810. At the end of 1808, the unredeemed portion of the debt totalled $57 million; and by 1812, it stood at $45.2 million. Indeed, by the end of Jefferson's second administration, the Treasury had succeeded in retiring all the federal debt that was callable, and nearly all the foreign debt.

This achievement is all the more impressive when it is noted that in 1803, $11,250,000 was added to the national debt as a result of the financial operations associated with the Louisiana Purchase. Furthermore, by October 1, 1808, Gallatin had succeeded in building up a Treasury balance of almost $14 million. There was more truth than poetry, therefore, in Jefferson's exultant claim that "it may be the pleasure and pride of an American to ask, what farmer, what mechanic, what laborer has ever seen a tax-gatherer of the United States?"

This golden age of Jeffersonian finance resulted from circumstances that had not been foreseen even by the most optimistic Republican policy-makers. The beginning of Gallatin's debt reduction program had coincided with a temporary peace settlement in Europe, and the Federalists predicted that the policy would fail because with peace there would be a sharp decline in the volume of domestic exports and, therefore, in the means with which to pay for imports. Actually, the predicted decline in imports and custom duties failed to materialize. The peace in Europe lasted only one year, and was followed by a prolonged war to the finish between England and France and their respective allies.

American ships continued to sail the seas in greater numbers, and the tremendous growth of the export trade provided the balance to pay for an even greater volume of imports. Customs revenue soared far above the prudent estimates that Gallatin had made in 1801: in 1808, $16 million was collected from this source alone by the federal government. All together, between 1801 and 1808, actual revenues exceeded Gallatin's total estimate for the period by more than $20 million.

The Jeffersonian ideology has so frequently been called "agrarian" by modern historians that we are tempted to overlook the deep-seated ambiguities in the economic policies of the Jeffersonian administration. To be sure, in his earlier years, Jefferson had expressed a rhapsodic view of the self-reliant farmer in America. "Those who labor the earth," he had declared in his *Notes on Virginia*, "are the chosen people of God, if ever He had a chosen people, whose breasts He has made His peculiar deposit for substantial and genuine virtue."

In the same statement, Jefferson had expressed hostility toward the idea of the political economists of Europe who maintained that every nation should endeavor to manufacture for itself. "While we have land to labor . . .," he wrote, "let us never wish to see our citizens occupied at a work-bench, or twirling a distaff . . . for the general operations of

Jefferson's Ideas of Political Economy

manufacture, let our workshops remain in Europe. It is better to carry provisions and materials to workmen there, than bring them to the provisions and materials, and with them their manners and principles . . . The mobs of great cities add just so much to the support of pure government, as sores do to the strength of the human body."

Yet, when he was President, Jefferson acquired a more complex view of the proper political economy for America. When it became apparent that the Treasury balance would continue to grow, Jefferson and Gallatin concerned themselves with the question of what to do with the growing surplus. The reduction of import duties was one possibility that was considered; but Jefferson rejected the idea in his annual message to Congress in December of 1806, with the rhetorical question, "Shall we suppress the impost and give that advantage to foreign manufactures?"

Instead, Jefferson envisioned other desirable possibilities to which the growing surplus might be applied. He proposed that it should be used "for the great purposes of public education, roads, rivers, canals, and such other objects of public improvement as it may be thought proper to add to the constitutional enumeration of federal powers." Moreover, he pointed out that, since imports were levied on luxury items, the wealthier classes would supply the greater part of the revenue.

While one might see in this an abandonment of Jefferson's agrarian ideals, it was not. Improved transportation and national market integration were, it is true, vital elements in the creation of an urban-industrial society later in the century, but Jefferson did not perceive this possibility. Better market access would, he thought, bolster the self-reliant yeoman farmer, not destroy him. If Jefferson realistically accepted the necessity of supporting "agriculture, manufactures, commerce and navigation" as the "four pillars of our prosperity," he did not imagine that in so doing he was repudiating his agrarian ideals. He accepted manufacturing and commerce as elements of an advanced agricultural economy, not as the beginnings of a new urban, industrial society.

Internal improvement programs depended on maps such as these. Coller, Survey . . . New York, 1789. Rare Book Division. The New York Public Library. Astor, Lenox and Tilden Foundations.

Fully in accord with Jefferson on the wisdom of internal improvements, Gallatin prepared an elaborate plan in 1808 that called for a

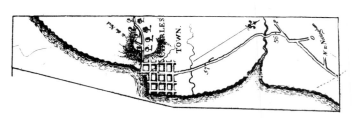
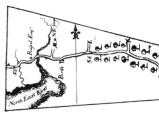

10-year cost of $20 million, to be spent at the rate of $2 million a year. His proposals included a turnpike from Maine to Georgia; canals across the four main coastal impediments (Cape Cod, New Jersey, Delaware, and the Dismal Swamp in Virginia and North Carolina); a road system across the mountains through New York, Pennsylvania, and Virginia, into Kentucky and Tennessee; and a road and canal system into the Great Lakes region.

It was a magnificent plan and, if adopted, would have created a veritable transportation revolution in the United States, and certainly would have accelerated the pace of industrial and commercial growth that was to take place in the nineteenth century. In 1810, furthermore, Gallatin issued a report that stressed the vital importance of manufactures for America's economic independence, and proposed a program of government subsidies to accelerate their development. Unfortunately for Gallatin, the difficulties leading to the War of 1812 wiped out much of the surplus and, thereby, destroyed any prospect of carrying forward his ambitious plans for developing transportation and manufactures in the United States.

It should be noted, also, that in all these discussions concerning the government surplus, there was no more than a cautious effort to reduce the price of land for settlers in the western territories, even though few small farmers were satisfied with the public land policy of the federal government. In 1796 the Federalist Congress had modified the original Land Ordinance of 1785 by permitting a year's credit to any purchaser; but the minimum price was raised to $2 an acre, and the minimum purchasable unit remained at 640 acres. Under pressure from those desiring to settle in the West, the Harrison Land Act of 1800 eased the requirements of purchase considerably. Thereafter, a settler could purchase his lands in a unit of not less than 320 acres; the price remained at $2 an acre but the settler could pay for it in installment payments over a four-year period. In 1804, the Jeffersonian Congress reduced the minimum purchasable unit to 160 acres (a "quarter section"), fixed the minimum price at about $1.64 an acre, and retained the four-year credit system.

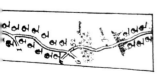

When the Treasury surplus became a matter of concern to the Jefferson administration, no one came forward with any suggestions to reduce the price of public lands further, or even to make western lands available free of charge to actual settlers. As a matter of fact, the loss of revenue from public land sales resulting from a policy of free homesteading would not have been greater than that which had been lost by the abolition of all internal taxes. The evidence is unmistakable that such a policy was never even considered as a practical alternative by the Jeffersonians. Indeed, the liveliest question of land policy in Jefferson's second administration arose from an attempt by the leaders of the administration to award a large area of land near the Yazoo River to a group of influential land speculators.

The Yazoo
Lands Question

The Yazoo land issue had been a thorn in the side of the federal government for more than a dozen years. These lands were located in an area falling within the boundaries of present day Alabama and Mississippi, where the federal government claimed jurisdiction under the Treaty of Paris of 1783 and the Pinckney Treaty of 1795. The state of Georgia, however, continued to claim the area in question, despite the cession of all western land claims made by the original states at the time of the ratification of the Articles of Confederation.

To complicate matters even further, in 1795 the Georgia legislature sold about 35,000,000 acres of Yazoo lands to several speculative land companies at the price of 1.5 cents an acre. When it was revealed that all but one of the Georgia legislators had a financial interest in this extraordinarily favorable land grant, the indignant voters of Georgia elected a new legislature which rescinded the sale. In the meantime, however, large amounts of stock had been sold to outside speculators in the Middle States and New England; and they demanded delivery of their lands since they had purchased their stock certificates in good faith.

By 1798 the national government had entered the picture by organizing the Territory of Mississippi and, in 1802, Georgia finally ceded the disputed area to the United States. At the same time, the Yazoo stock-holders carried their claims to the Jefferson administration. To investigate their claims, as well as to fix Georgia's new boundary, President Jefferson appointed a special commission composed of the Secretary of the Treasury, Albert Gallatin, the Secretary of State, James Madison, and Attorney General Levi Lincoln. In 1803, the three cabinet members recommended that the Yazoo claimants be reimbursed by the sale of five million acres of Yazoo lands.

Jefferson urged Congress to approve the recommended settlement, but he encountered an aroused opposition in the House, led by John Randolph of Virginia. Despite persistent efforts by Jefferson and his successor to secure Congressional approval, Randolph fought a successful battle for 10 years to prevent any reimbursement of the Yazoo speculators. He charged that the Jefferson administration had connived with northern speculators, and the bitterness of his attacks led to an open break with the administration in 1805. Thereafter, Randolph led a small group of anti-administration Republicans known as the "Tertium Quids."

Only after the Supreme Court had added the weight of its judicial decision to the controversy did the proposed settlement of the Yazoo claims gather sufficient support for Congressional approval. In the case of *Fletcher* v. *Peck* (1810), Chief Justice John Marshall declared that the Georgia sale of 1795 was a legal and binding contract, and that the rescinding law of the next Georgia legislature was an impairment of the obligation of contract that was specifically forbidden to the states by the Constitution. Accordingly, in 1814, Congress awarded the Yazoo claimants a settlement amounting to $4,282,151.125.

Jefferson's willingness to temporize with the more inexorable economic forces of his time can also be seen in his uncertain policy toward the Bank of the United States. As a member of Washington's cabinet, he had opposed the chartering of the Bank on constitutional grounds. As President, he proposed two ideas for reform to Gallatin. One was to parcel out government deposits among favored state banks; the other was to set up some kind of independent treasury system by which the federal government might hold its own deposits and use its own treasury notes, free of any dependence on private banks.

Jefferson's Bank Policy

Gallatin, however, had little sympathy for such proposals. While a member of the Pennsylvania legislature in 1793, he had played a leading part in establishing the Bank of Pennsylvania, organized on the model of Hamilton's Bank of the United States. Hence, he used all his considerable influence to persuade Jefferson, in 1805, to sign a bill authorizing the Bank of the United States to establish a branch in New Orleans. Indeed, Gallatin was fully convinced of the great usefulness of the Bank to the federal government because of "the instantaneous transmission of [public moneys] from one part of the continent to another," and "the great facility which an increased circulation and discounts give to the collection of the revenues." Accordingly, in March, 1809, a few days before Jefferson left office, he issued a report urging Congress to renew the charter which was due to expire in 1811.

Not until January, 1811, was the renewal of the charter of the Bank taken up and debated actively in both houses of Congress. In the House of Representatives, renewal was postponed indefinitely by a vote of 65 to 64; in the Senate, it was defeated by a vote of 18 to 17 when the Vice-President, George Clinton of New York, cast the deciding vote. An analysis of the vote reveals that the alignment against the Bank was composed of two groups: southern Republicans who clung to the original economic and constitutional principles of the party; and northern and western Republicans who were closely associated with state banks, and who reflected the desire of the business interests associated with such banks to be free of the competing and controlling influence of the Bank of the United States. Thus, even though Hamilton's bank was allowed to die, state banking interests were infiltrating the Jeffersonian Republican establishment, raising political and economic issues that were left unresolved.

The Perilous Diplomacy of Disentanglement

Those Federalists who professed to believe that Jefferson would be a willing tool of French interests if he became President had mistaken their man. The new President was as fully committed to an independent foreign policy for America as Washington and Adams had been. His intended foreign policy was summed up in the simple prose of his inaugural address: "Peace, commerce, and honest friendship with all nations—entangling alliances with none."

Jefferson's Conceptions of World Politics

Jefferson was passionately devoted to peace, believing that America was destined "by nature" and "a wide ocean" to enjoy a peaceful existence "free from the exterminating havoc of one quarter of the globe." Shortly after becoming President, Jefferson stated to Thomas Paine that he was determined "to avoid, if possible, wasting the energies of our people in war and destruction." In fact, he believed that America could lead the world toward a new code of international conduct. In a letter to Dr. John Mitchell, the Virginia botanist, in which he compared the natural phenomena of the Old World and the New, Jefferson reached this conclusion: "Nor is it in physics alone that we shall be found to differ from the other hemisphere. I strongly suspect that our geographical peculiarities may call up a different code of natural law to govern relations with other nations from that which the conditions of Europe have given rise to there."

Although not unaware of the difficulties of pursuing a policy of disentanglement from the conflicts of the European state system, Jefferson hoped that he could defend America's interests without resorting to war. When Dr. George Logan suggested, at the start of the new administration, that the United States ought to join in a league of armed neutrality to defend its commerce, Jefferson replied:

It ought to be the very first object of our pursuits to have nothing to do with the European interests and politics. Let them be free or slaves at will, navigators or agricultural, swallowed into one government or divided into a thousand, we have nothing to fear from them in any form . . . Our commerce is so valuable to them that they will be glad to purchase it when the only price we ask is to do us justice. I believe we have in our hands the means of peaceable coercion.

For a brief and fearsome interval at the beginning of Jefferson's administration, this benign concept of disentanglement was threatened with utter annihilation by the news that Spain had retroceded Louisiana to France, which had been forced to give up the vast territory at the end of the Seven Years' War in 1763. The seriousness of this transaction was felt almost immediately in America when the Spanish Intendant at New Orleans suspended the right of deposit there, in October, 1802, without designating another place as promised in Pinckney's Treaty. Western farmers who shipped their products down the Mississippi River were alarmed, and the legislature of Kentucky sent a memorial to the President demanding action to defend American interests. Furthermore, with the hope of recouping their declining political fortunes, the Federalists seized upon this issue and demanded war with France and Spain.

Jefferson was disturbed by this turn of events, not only because the Republican political coalition was heavily dependent on southern and western support, but also because the transfer of Louisiana to France threatened to revive the power rivalries of European states in the American hemisphere. Once Louisiana and the Mississippi River fell into the hands of Napoleonic France—the greatest military power in Europe—the United States could not hope to escape the broils of Europe. Indeed, he declared to Robert Livingston, the American minister to France, that

There is on the globe one single spot, the possession of which is our natural and habitual enemy. It is New Orleans, through which the produce of three-eighths of our territory must pass to market . . . The day that France takes possession of New Orleans, fixes the sentence which is to restrain [the United States] forever within her low watermark . . . From that moment we must marry ourselves to the British fleet and nation. We must turn all our attentions to a maritime force . . . and having formed and cemented together a power which may render reinforcement of her settlement here impossible to France, make the first cannon, which shall be fired in Europe, the signal for tearing up any settlement she may have made, and for holding the two continents of America in sequestration for the common purposes of the United British and American nations.

The Louisiana Purchase

Before taking the measures that would have destroyed his most cherished hopes for America's destiny, Jefferson decided to send James Monroe to France as a special envoy to assist Robert Livingston in negotiations with Napoleon. This was a shrewd political move because Monroe was popular in the West where he had large investments in land, and he was regarded by the French as a friend of France—indeed, he had been recalled from his post as minister to France by President Washington some years earlier because he was thought to be too friendly to France.

Jefferson's instructions to Monroe and Livingston contained three alternatives which revealed his hope of finding a solution without resorting to the wastefulness of war. The American envoys were to ask France to sell New Orleans and the Floridas to the United States; in return, they were to offer to France not more than $10 million, plus the right of deposit at New Orleans, and, if necessary, a guarantee to support forever the claim of France to the territory on the left bank of the Mississippi. If the French declined to sell New Orleans, an attempt was to be made to get some other place with the right of deposit near the mouth of the Mississippi River. If, however, the French seemed determined to force a showdown by closing the Mississippi, the American envoys were to go to London to seek an alliance with Great Britain.

The negotiations with France were started by Livingston at a very opportune moment. Napoleon had decided to reopen war with England and to pursue his ambitions for further power and glory on the European continent. He realized, therefore, that it would be impossible for France to hold Louisiana in a war with England; he would either lose it to the English or to the Americans, or to combined action by both nations. On the other hand, by selling Louisiana to the United States, he would not only enrich his war chest, but he would also destroy any likelihood of an alliance between England and the United States.

Accordingly, even before Monroe had reached Paris, Talleyrand, the French foreign minister, asked Livingston what the United States might be willing to pay for all of Louisiana. The American minister was not immediately prepared to deal with such an astonishing proposition, but when Monroe arrived with the President's reasonably flexible instructions, the two American envoys quickly decided to arrange for the purchase of the whole territory of Louisiana for $15 million. On April 30, 1803, a treaty of purchase was signed for a territory vaguely described as "Louisiana with the Same extent it now has in the hands of Spain, and that it had when France possessed it; and Such as it Should be after the Treaties subsequently entered into between Spain and other states."

Vague as these provisions were, Monroe and Livingston knew they had purchased a great continental empire. When he signed the treaty, Livingston declared: "We have lived long, but this is the noblest work of our whole lives. . . . From this day, the United States take their place among the powers of the first rank. . . . The instruments which we have just signed will . . . prepare ages of happiness for innumerable generations of human creatures."

Livingston could not foresee all the consequences of the Louisiana Purchase, but he did understand that it ended the long struggle for the possession of the Mississippi valley and prepared for the ascendancy of the United States in the New World. Indeed, the further expansion of the United States into Florida, Texas, and California was a logical outcome of this decisive stride into the heartland of North America. And from that strategic base, the United States was in a position to control the destiny of the entire Western Hemisphere.

The Louisiana Purchase nearly doubled the territory of the United States; the additional territory, in fact, was equal to the entire area of Great Britain, Germany, France, Spain, Portugal, and Italy—all among the significant countries in the European state system that had first opened up the New World. The sheer immensity of the area enlarged the American imagination and encouraged Americans to measure their achievements by the scale of the prairies and the Rocky Mountains. Not

The dream of America as an Edenic land where the lion and the lamb might lie down together persisted into the nineteenth century. Folk artists repeated this theme of a peaceable kingdom again and again. Did they believe that America could escape the sins and failings of world history? Was America a chance to start over? Many dreamed this utopian dream . . .

Adam and Eve *by an unknown artist, c. 1830, oil on cardboard. Collection of the Whitney Museum of American Art, New York. Gift of Edgar William and Bernice Chrysler Garbisch.*

*. . . others, however, tried to suppress a frightening nightmare about
the American landscape. What if America was not a garden but
rather a treacherous swamp? What if Americans had already lost
their way in the New World landscape?*

Merced River, Yosemite Valley *by Albert Bierstadt (1857). The Metropolitan Museum of Art. Gift of the sons of William Paton, 1909.*

Both of these images are, of course, extremes. For most Americans, nature had more complex and ambiguous meanings. Natural scenery had deeply religious meaning, but it was not quite Edenic. It was comforting while it was challenging. Nature expressed force, the power of God, and it was often awesome, even a bit frightening, but it was usually beneficent.

Fur Traders Descending the Missouri *by George Caleb Bingham. The Metropolitan Museum of Art, Morris K. Jessup Fund, 1933.*

Static images of nature, however, miss the transforming effects a rapidly growing society can have upon nature and popular perceptions of nature. Americans found untouched wilderness inspiring, but it was the cultivated agricultural landscape that seemed to symbolize the popular meaning of American nationality. Americans strove to "improve" nature—or was it to "conquer" and "exploit" it? Fur traders penetrated the West . . .

. . . and they were followed by settlers. Forests became fields and trees became houses. These illustrations, from a history published in 1850 chronicling the progress of a farming area in western New York, begin with a rude log cabin in a small clearing hacked out of the forest.

*With constant work, farm families cleared enough land to give shape
to the farm to come. The struggle against the forest was gradually
being won, and before long the rude cabin had become a respectable
farm house. The first three illustrations portray the expansion of
cultivated fields, while the wilderness has receded in favor of a quiet
rural scene.*

*Eventually, the development of a prosperous village marks the social
maturation of an area only recently settled.*

Illustrations from O. Turner,
Pioneer History of the Holland Land Purchase of Western New York *(1850).*

Cities grew up in the forests. At first cities in the East and the West were essentially pastoral in appearance. Surrounded by nature, they were hardly a denial of nature.

Baltimore c. *1752. I. N. Phelps Stokes Collection of the Prints Division. The New York Public Library. Astor, Lenox and Tilden Foundations.*

St. Paul, Minnesota, *in 1856. Minnesota Historical Society.*

But it was not long before cities became larger and more densely built. Nature disappeared in the cities that were spreading across the continent. Could this apparent triumph of civilization over nature pose a problem for nineteenth-century Americans? Since they were not primitivists, they embraced the progress of civilization. Yet because they located moral value in nature they worried about its eclipse.

Broadway, New York, 1836. In the I. N. Phelps Stokes Collection of American Historical Prints. Prints Division. The New York Public Library. Astor, Lenox and Tilden Foundations.

The Course of Empire 1,
The Savage State. *Courtesy
of the New-York Historical
Society, New York City.*

*What would happen if Americans lost touch with nature? It was this
theme that occupied Thomas Cole in a five panel painting titled
"The Course of Empire" (1836). Writing to the New York merchant who commissioned the work, Cole explained that he proposed
to show "the history of a natural scene . . . showing the natural
changes of landscape, and those effected by man in his progress
from barbarism to civilization." The first picture, therefore, presents
the wilderness state.*

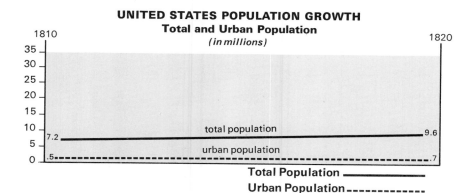

Cole called the next picture the "Arcadian or Pastoral" stage. This picture is, perhaps, an idealized portrait of America in the 1830's, but . . .

The Course of Empire 2, The Arcadian or Pastoral. *Courtesy of the New-York Historical Society, New York City.*

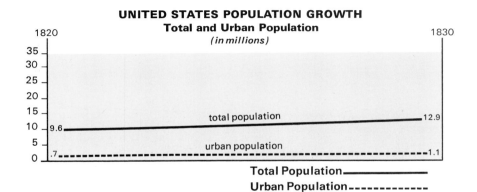

UNITED STATES POPULATION GROWTH
Total and Urban Population
(in millions)

1820   1830

total population   12.9

urban population   1.1

9.6   .7

Total Population⎯⎯⎯⎯
Urban Population------------

The Course of Empire 3, The Consummation of Empire. 1836. *Courtesy of the New-York Historical Society, New York City.*

. . . the third panel points directly to the future of prosperity and cities toward which the United States seemed to be rushing. Note that nature, which had dominated the first two panels, is nearly obliterated in the third.

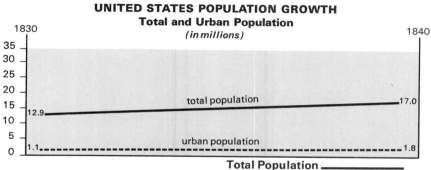

UNITED STATES POPULATION GROWTH
Total and Urban Population
(in millions)

Total Population ———
Urban Population - - - - - - -

With nature thus overwhelmed by artificiality, the fourth picture is inevitable within the context of the American philosophy of nature. The corruption, luxury, and war that was formerly known to Europe but not America destroys the republic.

The Course of Empire 4, Destruction. 1836. *Courtesy of the New-York Historical Society, New York City.*

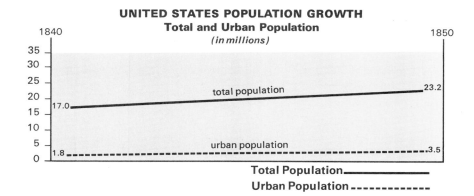

UNITED STATES POPULATION GROWTH
Total and Urban Population
(in millions)

Total Population —————
Urban Population - - - - - - -

The Course of Empire 5,
Desolation. 1836. *Courtesy
of the New-York Historical
Society, New York City.*

*The final picture, Cole explained, portrayed "the funeral knell of
departed greatness, and may be called the state of desolation."
These massive canvases drew large and enthusiastic crowds when
they were shown in museums, and James Fenimore Cooper, whose
Leatherstocking novels considered the same American dilemma,
called Cole's painting "the work of the highest genius this country
has ever produced." But no one could have missed Cole's frightening message.*

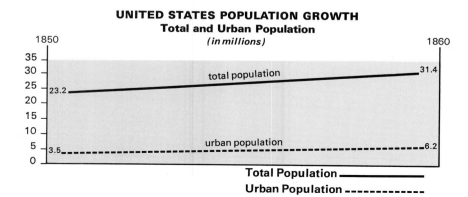

UNITED STATES POPULATION GROWTH
Total and Urban Population
(in millions)

1850   1860

total population — 31.4 (from 23.2)

urban population — 6.2 (from 3.5)

Total Population ————
Urban Population - - - - - - -

Must the progress of America bring on its own destruction? Were there any solutions to this paradoxical philosophy of nature and progress? Was there a way of preserving the moral value of nature in an urban civilization such as the United States clearly was going to become? Perhaps natural sanctuaries could be preserved. Central Park, an enormous rural park in the center of Manhattan, was established in 1857, and in 1872 Congress undertook to preserve Yellowstone Park in its natural condition. Perhaps Americans, even city people, could still keep in touch with nature.

John Bachman, Central Park, 1863. Courtesy of the New-York Historical Society, New York City.

CENTRAL PARK.

Andrew Jackson Downing, an architectural critic and landscape architect, thought that rural or suburban homes might counter the tension, disorder, and moral corruption of the growing cities. The naturalistic and romantic landscaping that Central Park brought to the city could be provided in a more private way in suburbs for those who could afford it. The rural home, with elaborately landscaped grounds, became an upper-class ideal in the 1840's and 1850's. Here America's most prosperous families could find domestic repose, safely removed from the disorder, poverty, and environmental degradation of the cities where the heads of suburban families earned the money that made suburban living possible. In numerous magazine articles and books, Downing extolled this suburban ideal; at his home in Newburgh, on the Hudson River, he exemplified it.

Residence of Andrew Jackson Downing, Newburgh, N.Y. From Rural Essays *by A. J. Downing, © 1853 by George P. Putnam & Co.*

long after he had left the presidency, Jefferson prophesied to his European friend, Baron Alexander Von Humboldt: "In fifty years more, the United States alone will contain fifty millions of inhabitants, and fifty years are soon gone over . . . And you will live to see the period ahead of us; and the numbers which will then be spread over the other parts of the American hemisphere, catching long before that the principles of our portion of it, and concurring with us in the maintenance of the same system."

More than any other act, the purchase of Louisiana insured the fulfillment of Jefferson's hope that the United States and the entire American hemisphere might have a separate destiny from that of Europe. As soon as the news of the extraordinary bargain arrived from Paris, Jefferson knew that the United States had been saved from the entanglements in Europe's wars that he so greatly dreaded. He wrote, ". . . giving us the sole dominion of the Mississippi, it excludes those bickerings with foreign powers which we know of a certainty would have put us at war with France immediately: and it secures us the course of a peaceable nation."

To be sure, the Louisiana Treaty caused Jefferson some anguish of spirit because the acquisition of territory by the executive department or the appropriation of money for the purchase of the territory was not explicitly authorized by the Constituion. He had been one of the chief architects of the principle of strict construction that became a sacred dogma of the Republican party, restated most recently in the Virginia and Kentucky Resolutions. Privately, Jefferson admitted that to carry out the terms of the treaty would make a "blank paper" of the Constitution, and he would have preferred a constitutional amendment to validate the action. But he realized that any delay might cause Napoleon to change his mind, and deprive the United States of an historic opportunity. Hence he urged the Senate to ratify the treaty, and Congress to appropriate the money of purchase, hoping "that the good sense of our country will correct the evil of loose construction when it shall produce ill effects."

The Louisiana purchase strengthened Jefferson's determination to pursue a policy of pragmatic pacifism. Like most Republicans he was eager to dismantle the large Federalist military establishment created after the XYZ Affair and thus reduce the burden of military expense for the American people. Even the newly-built naval force of seven frigates inherited from the Federalists was "laid up dry" in the navy yard on the Potomac to save expense of maintenance and repair. Instead the Jefferson administration constructed small gunboats for the defense of coastal waters.

Jefferson's
Pragmatic Pacifism

Jefferson's gunboat policy became a subject of considerable ridicule among the Federalists, particularly after one gunboat was washed ashore several miles inland by a coastal storm. To anyone who knew anything about ships and naval warfare, it was obvious that the "mosquito fleet" of gunboats would never be effective against any naval vessels that might be sent to the waters of the New World to protect the commerce of European nations. But Jefferson refused to abandon his gunboat policy even in the face of great provocation by the belligerent nations of Europe. He even begrudged the expense of using a few frigates against the Barbary corsairs—even though the use of American naval power in the Mediterranean was successful in reducing the tribute demanded by the pirate states of North Africa.

Instead, Jefferson pursued methods based on his conviction that the United States would create a new code of international conduct through the use of "peaceable coercion." And his theory was put to the severest test because the desperate character of the renewed war between England and France made wholesale interference with American commerce inevitable.

The Defense of America's Neutral Commerce

Alarmed at Napoleon's success in bringing the greater part of the continent of Europe under his domination, and convinced that it was impossible to defeat him on land, the British were determined to use their naval supremacy to bring him to his knees. In 1805 British prize courts began to enforce stricter rules against the thriving neutral commerce between the French West Indies and European ports under French control. American merchants were making enormous profits out of their successful evasions of the British blockade policy in the Caribbean. They had developed a fictitious "re-export" trade in French West Indian goods, by carrying goods to an American port, paying duties, and then reloading the cargo, sometimes on the same ship, and receiving back most of the duties paid, before carrying the cargo to Napoleon's Europe. In the *Essex* case, which involved a captured American merchantman, the British court ruled that French colonial goods could be carried to an enemy port only if the American vessel went to a home port and paid a bona fide duty on them. Otherwise, the vessel and cargo would be conceived of as engaging in a direct trade between the French colonies and France, in violation of the British rules of blockade.

In their zeal to enforce the *Essex* decision, British frigates began to patrol the waters of American ports in such numbers as to constitute a virtual blockade. Large numbers of American vessels were being interrupted immediately after they left port, and protests from American merchants began to pour into Washington. At the same time, British naval commanders began to use the harsh policy of impressment in American waters as a means of keeping up the crews on their ships. Since many American merchantmen carried seamen of all nationalities, it was an easy matter for British boarding parties to find sailors on American ships who looked and talked like Englishmen. Knowing that many sailors carried false naturalization papers, British naval officers tended to ignore all such claims of American citizenship. Consequently, several thousand bona fide American citizens were impressed into the

British navy during the final decade of warfare with Napoleonic France.

Merchants and shippers of the leading commercial centers of America sent memorials to Congress demanding protection for their ships and cargoes, but their troubles were just beginning. Napoleon responded to the tightening of the British blockade with his famous Berlin decree of November, 1806, proclaiming a blockade of the British Isles, to be enforced by his ruling that any neutral vessel that stopped at an English port would not be admitted to a European port under his control. The British retaliated with new Orders-in-Council that extended their blockade of continental ports under French control, and required all neutral ships bound for the blockaded zone of Europe to stop at a British port to secure a license and to pay special transit duties. Napoleon countered with the Milan decree of December, 1807, which declared that any neutral ship that submitted to search by a British naval vessel, or entered a British port to secure clearance, would be confiscated by the French.

The net effect of these orders of blockade and counterblockade was to put all American commerce in European waters in jeopardy. If an American vessel sailed directly to the continent of Europe it was liable to capture by the British; if it put into a British port to secure a license to proceed to Europe, it might be confiscated by the French when it arrived in a European port under French control.

Jefferson responded to these blows against American neutral rights with a variety of measures. In view of the large number of British naval vessels in American waters, steps were taken to increase the numbers of gunboats, to provide the main seaports with heavy cannon for harbor fortifications, and to place the militia in a state of readiness. Believing that Great Britain was the main offender, he also resorted to the favorite American device of a special mission that would seek to adjust all matters in dispute with England. William Pinckney, a distinguished Maryland lawyer, was sent to London to assist James Monroe, the American minister there, in the effort to persuade the British to relax their rules of blockade, to renounce the right to impress sailors on American vessels, and to pay damages for recent seizures of American ships. Monroe and Pinckney were able to get a treaty that granted some concessions in the West Indian trade, but Jefferson refused to accept it because it did not contain a renunciation of the right of impressment.

Relations between the United States and England reached the breaking point in June, 1807, when an American naval vessel, the *Chesapeake,* was raked with three broadsides from the guns of the British frigate, the *Leopard,* and then boarded by a searching party which proceeded to take off four seamen alleged to be deserters from the British navy; three of them actually were Americans who had escaped from the British frigate after having been impressed. When the battered *Chesapeake* sailed into port with its dead and wounded, a wave of indignation and patriotic fervor swept the country. "Never since the battle of Lexington," Pres-

The Failure
of "Peaceable Coercion"

ident Jefferson observed, "have I seen the country in such a state of exasperation as at present, and even that did not produce such unanimity."

A special session of Congress, called in October, 1807, immediately appropriated large sums to strengthen the navy. But Jefferson refused to take advantage of aroused public sentiment to lead the country into a war. Instead, he ordered all British warships out of American waters, and instructed the American minister in England to demand reparation and a complete renunciation of the impressment of American ships. At the same time, he asked Congress to employ a drastic form of "peaceable coercion" against the warring powers of Europe. Since both England and France were depending heavily on American foodstuffs, Jefferson believed that they could be forced to respect America's neutral rights if they were deprived of American goods. Accordingly, he asked Congress to enact a sweeping embargo on all trade with Europe. And despite vehement Federalist opposition, Republican majorities in both houses of Congress passed an embargo act embodying Jefferson's proposals, in December, 1807.

The Embargo Act proved to be disastrous for the American economy, especially that of commercial areas like New England. The American export and re-export trade had doubled in value in the four years between 1803 and 1807—rising to a high point of $108 million. In 1808, exports dwindled to $22 million and signs of economic stagnation were evident in all of the seaports of the country: ships rotting at their wharves,

William Charles, The Ghost of a Dollar. Prints Division. The New York Public Library. Astor, Lenox and Tilden Foundations.

THE GHOST of a DOLLAR or the BANKERS SURPRIZE

shipbuilding at a standstill, mercantile bankruptcies increasing from month to month, and declining farm prices in those sections of the country that depended on foreign markets.

The British, on the other hand, suffered very little. The British Isles were blessed with bumper crops in 1808, and British shippers gladly took over much of the trade in West Indian goods formerly carried by their American rivals. As for Napoleon, he welcomed the American embargo as an additional weapon in his economic warfare against the British.

The increasing economic distress soon produced explosive reactions in the United States. The Federalist party gained renewed popularity in New England for its opposition to Jefferson's "Dambargo." New England merchants began to resort to smuggling on a large scale across the Canadian border and, even in Jefferson's own southland, a vigorous smuggling trade developed along the Florida border.

Angered by the resistance to his experiment in "peaceable coercion," Jefferson asked Congress for more drastic powers of enforcement. The Force Act of January, 1809, marked the high point of Jefferson's grim determination to make the embargo work; federal customs officials were given powers of search and seizure that were more arbitrary than the writs of assistance that the British had used against colonial merchants before the American Revolution.

Such use of arbitrary power merely strengthened the will to resist in New England and elsewhere. The Federalist governor of Connecticut refused to obey a request by the Jefferson administration to use the militia to help enforce the embargo. Dr. George Logan, the President's Quaker friend in Philadelphia, went so far as to denounce the administration for "dastardly attacking the humble cottages" of American citizens instead of "meeting in open and armed conflict the armed battalions of our enemy."

It was apparent that the disastrous effect of the embargo on the national economy and the galling experience of using arbitrary measures against individual liberties was becoming too much for the Republican party to bear. On March 1, 1809, Congress repealed the embargo, replacing it with a Nonintercourse Act that prohibited trade with England and France only, and provided that, if either of the two nations would cancel its blockade decrees against American shipping, then nonintercourse would be continued only against the other. Jefferson signed both measures with a heavy heart, although, privately, he confessed that the embargo experiment had been three times more costly than war.

Under this cloud of failure, Thomas Jefferson retired from the presidency and returned to the tranquillity of private life at Monticello. He chose not to avail himself of the opportunity to advise his countrymen in a farewell address; but, in a little speech to his neighbors in Albemarle County, he simply said, "I gladly lay down the distressing burthen of power, and seek, with my fellow citizens, repose and safety, under the watchful cares, the labors and perplexities of younger and abler minds."

Republican Nationalism

There was little repose and safety for Americans, however, in the administration of Jefferson's successor. James Madison was an estimable man who had served his country well in the making of the Constitution, in the preparation of the Bill of Rights, and as Jefferson's Secretary of State for eight years. His intellectual gifts were outstanding: he read widely, he conversed knowledgeably on many subjects, and he wrote brilliantly on political and constitutional questions. Nevertheless, he lacked the force and driving power that was needed in a good executive; he lacked the particular skills of influence that Jefferson had used in dealing with Congress.

The new President was unable to lead Congress or to exert his influence against the growing factional intrigues within the Republican party. He suffered a humiliating defeat at the very outset of his administration when Senate Republicans refused to support his nomination of Gallatin to the post of Secretary of State. Madison nearly lost Gallatin from his cabinet when he failed to assist him in his effort to persuade Congress to recharter the United States Bank. Gallatin attempted to resign shortly after the bill was defeated in both houses of Congress and it was only by a great personal effort that Madison was able to persuade him to remain at his post.

The Failures of Madison's Diplomacy

Like Jefferson, Madison hoped to protect America's neutral rights by a combination of diplomacy and "peaceable coercion." The new British minister to Washington, David Erskine, seemed more friendly to America and offered to withdraw the British Orders-in-Council if the United States would give up her policy of nonintercourse with Great Britain and retain it against France. Madison agreed to an arrangement on these terms, and even put aside the question of impressment in order to facilitate a diplomatic detente.

The smoothness of his negotiations with Erskine led Madison to make a disastrous blunder. Taking it for granted that the Erskine agreement would be accepted by the British government, he proclaimed the end of nonintercourse with Great Britain on June 10, 1809. Accordingly, hundreds of American vessels put to sea loaded with foodstuffs and other commodities for the British market, and carrying with them the high hopes of American merchants for large profits that would wipe out the memory of their hard times under the embargo.

Then came the startling news that George Canning, the British Foreign Minister, had repudiated the Erskine agreement and recalled Erskine for having exceeded his instructions. Since nonintercourse against England was hastily restored, the American ships already at sea found themselves at the mercy of the blockade decrees of England and France. Madison was condemned by his political opponents as the dupe of Canning, and the American people lost further confidence in the diplomacy of "peaceable coercion."

Anxious to retrieve his position, Madison blundered in the opposite direction. On May 10, 1810, Congress sought to break out of the diplomatic stalemate by replacing nonintercourse with a more Machiavellian measure known as Macon's Bill No. 2. This bill restored trade with England and France, but held out a tempting lure to the belligerent powers by stipulating that if either country repealed its blockade decrees against American shipping, then the United States would resume a policy of nonintercourse toward the other.

Napoleon was more than equal to the mischievous opportunities presented by Macon's Bill No. 2. His Foreign Minister persuaded Madison that the French were willing to revoke their decrees if the United States would restore nonintercourse against Great Britain. Madison again acted precipitately by announcing that nonintercourse would be restored against Great Britain before he had any proof that the French had actually revoked their decrees. In fact, Napoleon continued to issue secret orders for the seizure of American ships and, quite naturally, the English government refused to revoke the Orders-in-Council until it was clear that Napoleon had abandoned his blockade. Congress, nevertheless, passed the measure which restored nonintercourse against England in March of 1811.

The War Hawks

Madison's ineffective presidency enabled a group of young Republicans to seize the reins of leadership at the opening of the twelfth Congress in 1811. They captured the machinery of control in the House of Representatives by electing Henry Clay, the energetic and magnetic Kentuckian, as Speaker of the House in his first term of office—an unprecedented event in the history of Congress. This striking victory for the young Republicans was a manifestation of the aroused nationalist spirit that had infected the rising generation of Republicans as a result of the humiliating episodes of the *Chesapeake-Leopard* affair, the embargo, and the blunders of Madison. Many of them were truly new men in national politics; in the Congressional elections of 1810, 63 of the 142 members of the previous House of Representatives had been swept out of office—most of them Republicans who were replaced by aggressive and ambitious young men in their late twenties and early thirties.

Besides Clay, these new men, including John C. Calhoun of South Carolina, Felix Grundy of Tennessee, Peter B. Porter of western New York, and John A. Harper of New Hampshire, were so strident in demanding war against Great Britain that John Randolph, the leader of the "Old Republicans," called them the "War Hawks"—a name that has been appropriated by historians as the most apt description of their political views and style. Many of the War Hawks were from the lower South and the West—from the new states or from the frontier regions of the older ones. These western and southern regions were more concerned about the effects of the British blockade than the commercial centers of New England and the Middle States. In fact, Eastern merchants were quite willing to put up with the blockade rules of England

and France; profits were so great that if one cargo out of three got through a merchant could still make money.

The western and southern farmers who depended on the export market had experienced a decline in prices and an economic depression in the years after 1802. They, more than the merchants of eastern seaports, became the ardent champions of American neutral rights on the high seas. Many westerners felt that the patriotism of the East had been subverted by the desire to make money—Clay called it the "low, groveling parsimony of the counting-room." Other westerners, however, were frank to admit their own economic motives. Felix Grundy, for one, said in Congress: "It is not the carrying trade, properly so-called about which this nation and Great Britain are at present contending. . . . The true question in controversy, is of a very different character; it involves the interest of the whole nation. It is the right of exporting the productions of our own soil and industry to foreign markets."

Westerners also blamed the Indian troubles of their region on the British. Tecumseh, a great Shawnee chief, was attempting to form a grand confederacy of the Indian tribes from the Great Lakes to the Gulf of Mexico, and he warned Governor William Henry Harrison of Indiana Territory that, henceforth, no Indian tribe would be permitted to cede any land to the Americans. In the autumn of 1811 General Harrison decided to lead an attack on the main base of Tecumseh on the Tippecanoe River, while the Indian leader was on a journey among the southern tribes seeking to organize a consolidated force of southern warriors. In a sharp engagement on the banks of the Tippecanoe, the Indians were repulsed and their village burned, but Harrison's small army suffered heavy losses. Angered at the destruction of his headquarters village, Tecumseh rallied his Indian allies for a general war against the Americans. By the spring of 1812, the whole frontier area lived under the threat of the Indian scalping knife.

Since British weapons were found on the field of battle after the Indians had been repulsed at Tippecanoe, frontiersmen everywhere believed that the British in Canada were supplying Tecumseh with arms and urging him on against the Americans. The Lexington (Kentucky) *Reporter* voiced the conviction of many westerners when it declared: "The War on the Wabash is purely British. The British scalping knife has filled many habitations both in this state as well as in the Indian territory with widows and orphans."

The War Hawks in Congress took up the cry of the frontiersmen and called upon the United States to wipe out the British base in Canada. Felix Grundy of Tennessee made the angry threat: "We shall drive the British from our continent—they will no longer have an opportunity of intriguing with our Indian neighbors, and settling on the ruthless savage to tomahawk our women and children." Henry Clay assured the members of the House: "The conquest of Canada is in your power. I trust I shall not be presumptuous when I state that I verily believe that the militia of Kentucky are alone competent to place Montreal and upper Canada at your feet.''

Not to be outdone by their northern colleagues, southern War Hawks began to raise a similar clamor for Florida. At the very least, they believed, the United States was entitled to have West Florida. After all, Monroe and Livingston had asserted that West Florida was included in the Louisiana Purchase, and President Madison had issued a proclamation in 1810 declaring that, by the terms of the Louisiana Purchase, the United States territory extended into West Florida as far as the Perdido River.

By the spring of 1812, the pressures for war were becoming irresistable. Bitterness against England increased when the Madison administration published the so-called Henry letters, purchased from John Henry, a British agent, which seemed to indicate that the British were collaborating with Federalist leaders in New England to promote disunion. The evidence in the Henry letters was quite unsubstantial, but, in the prevailing popular mood, there were many who were prepared to assume the worst about the British.

On June 1, 1812, Madison asked Congress to declare war on Great Britain. In his war message, Madison stressed the problems of impressment and maritime rights, but the War Hawks already had their own reasons for going to war. In the House, they rushed through a war resolution on June 4, by a vote of 79 to 49; in the Senate, the debate was more prolonged and the resolution passed by the narrower margin of 19 to 13 on June 17. Unknown to the Congress, the British government had announced the repeal of the Orders-in-Council just a day before the vote in the American Senate—but it is doubtful if even this news could have stemmed the drive toward war by the aggressive wing of the Republican party.

The War of 1812

An analysis of the vote on the war resolution shows that the decision to go to war was largely sectional in character. Generally speaking, the representatives from western and southern states were strongly in favor of war with Great Britain, as were the frontier sections of eastern states like New Hampshire, Vermont, New York, and Pennsylvania. Most of the votes in opposition came from the maritime centers of New England and the Middle States.

Indeed, the Federalists of New England were never willing to abide by the decision to go to war. To them it was "Mr. Madison's War," and it was being fought against the wrong enemy. They believed that Napoleonic France had committed as many wrongs against American maritime rights as England. In fact, in the five years before 1812, Napoleon had confiscated 558 American vessels, while Britain had seized 389. Federalist members in Congress, therefore, issued an address to the American people after the war resolution was adopted in which they declared: "If honor demands war with England, what opiate lulls that honor to sleep over the wrongs done us by France?"

While many Republican members of Congress were willing to admit that the French had violated our neutral rights, and that Napoleon had been treacherous and double-dealing in his diplomacy, they were not moved emotionally by the French offenses to the same degree as they were by Britain's actions. The humiliating impressment of American sailors, and the actual killing of American citizens as in the *Chesapeake* incident, inflicted deeper psychological wounds than the more impersonal statistics of ship confiscations. Nothing less than a war could satisfy their need to restore a sense of national pride and self-respect. Andrew Jackson, a rising young political leader in Tennessee, manifested this impulse to war very simply when he said: "We are going to fight for the reestablishment of our national character . . ."

The Confusions of an Unpopular War

Be that as it may, the War of 1812 produced very few psychic satisfactions for the American people. The United States, indeed, had little chance of achieving the objectives that the War Hawks had in mind. After the lean years of Jeffersonian parsimony, America's navy could not possibly be enlarged rapidly enough to challenge Britain's naval supremacy even in the waters of the New World. America simply lacked the kind of power that could have forced any concessions from the British regarding impressment as long as she was involved in a war to the death with Napoleon. Furthermore, the American army and the militia of the several states were wholly inadequate for the ambitious tasks of conquering Canada and Florida. It was fortunate for the United States that Great Britain was preoccupied with the great military campaigns on the continent of Europe that were to achieve the defeat of Napoleon, because the American war effort was marked by an extraordinary amount of confusion, blundering, and disunity.

Secretary of the Treasury, Albert Gallatin, seriously hampered by the loss of the Bank of the United States as a fiscal agency of the government, sought to finance the war by new taxes and heavy borrowings. It was not an easy matter for him to ask Republicans to impose internal taxes, but there was no other alternative in view of the sharp decline in customs revenues that resulted from war with Great Britain. In fact, Gallatin found it necessary to propose a greater number of internal taxes than the Hamiltonian Federalists had ever imposed; he told Congress that they must do so in order to bring in an annual revenue of $5 million to make up for the losses in the imposts. Aghast, Congress delayed its decision as long as it could, and finally accepted the bitter necessity of reimposing internal taxes in 1813. However, evasion of the new taxes was widespread, and in 1814, collections totalled only $3,890,000.

Consequently, Gallatin was forced to resort to large loans as a means of financing the war. But the new bond issues ran into strong opposition from mercantile and financial circles in New England. Many of the Federalist banking interests were opposed to the war anyway, and Republican bankers soon became so disillusioned with the war effort that they were unwilling to risk any capital in government bonds. By 1814, a particularly inglorious year in the war, the war loan policy came to an almost complete breakdown. In that year, the Treasury attempted to float $25 million in long-term bonds, in three separate installments. The Treasury was unable to raise the first installment of $10 million; the second installment of $6 million failed by a wider margin; the third failed almost completely.

Similar confusion marked the efforts of the Madison administration to create an army for the war. To increase the regular army, the President was authorized to accept 50,000 volunteers for a year's service. But the brave talk of the War Hawks was apparently forgotten, for there were barely 5,000 such volunteers in service in the first six months after the declaration of war. In addition, the President was authorized to call up 100,000 state militiamen. Yet many militiamen refused to serve outside their own states, and in one of the early campaigns against Canada, the militiamen under General Dearborn's command at Plattsburg refused to fight on foreign soil. Furthermore, in September, 1814, the Federalist governors of Massachusetts and Connecticut actually withdrew their militia from the federal service. Indeed, most New England Federalists probably agreed with the Boston *Gazette* when it exclaimed: "Is there a Federalist, a patriot, in America, who conceives it his duty to shed his blood for Bonaparte, for Madison or Jefferson, or that Host of Ruffians in Congress who have set their faces against the United States for years?" Thus, New England Federalists withheld troops from service, refused to lend money to the war effort, and even sold large quantities of provisions to the British in Canada.

The war itself went from bad to worse. The campaigns against Canada launched from American bases in Detroit, Fort Niagara, and at various points on Lake Ontario were not able to make any deep penetrations of Canadian territory, although by the end of 1813, the Americans had substantial control of the waters of Lake Erie and Lake Ontario. On the sea, American warships—the *Constitution, United States, Essex,* and *Hornet*—won some notable victories in single ship engagements. In addition, American privateers captured more than 1300 English vessels. But the superior weight of British naval strength eventually smothered American sea power. By 1814, most of the American men-of-war were bottled up in port, and the American merchant marine was either destroyed or effectively blockaded.

In April, 1814, moreover, Napoleon abdicated, and the British were able to divert additional military strength to the New World. In August of the same year, a British naval force entered Chesapeake Bay and landed a force of regulars which marched on Washington. Easily routing the force of Americans mobilized to defend the city, the British entered Washington and set fire to the Capitol and the White House. While this raid in Washington was of little military importance, it was a devastating blow to American morale and to the prestige of the Madison administration.

Meanwhile the British were preparing three major assaults against the

United States, using veteran troops of the campaigns against Napoleon in Europe. One force was directed at Fort Niagara, another was to move down the Lake Champlain route, and the third was to strike at New Orleans and the mouth of the Mississippi River. In the face of these threats, the Madison administration seemed to be increasingly demoralized. Envoys were sent to Europe in the spring of 1814 to talk peace with the British, and when the American negotiators, Albert Gallatin, Henry Clay, John Quincy Adams, James Bayard, and Jonathan Russell first arrived in Ghent, it seemed likely that the United States might have to accept the loss of territory in Maine and the Northwest as the price of any peace treaty.

In September, 1814, however, Captain Thomas MacDonough brought a ray of hope to America's prospects when he destroyed the British flotilla on Lake Champlain and effectively checked the movement of an army of 10,000 British veterans under Sir George Prevost down the Champlain route. In the Southwest, however, the American force under General Andrew Jackson was still awaiting the arrival of a British invading army of 8,000 veteran troops and no one dared predict the outcome of the battle that was certain to take place.

The Hartford Convention

To New Englanders, the Madison administration seemed to be on the brink of further military and economic disasters. The tightened English blockade had ended the profits of wartime commerce and British raiding parties were actually being landed on the Maine coast. Massachusetts Federalists, led by Noah Webster, drafted a circular letter calling for a convention of northern states to urge amendments to the Constitution that would reduce the disproportionate influence of the southern states and protect the commercial rights of the northern states. A flood of petitions moved Governor Caleb Strong to summon the Massachusetts General Court into special session in October, 1814. The General Court quickly adopted a report prepared by Harrison Gray Otis calling for a convention of Eastern states "to lay the foundation for a radical reform in the national compact." Three states—Massachusetts, Rhode Island, and Connecticut—responded by sending official delegates to a convention that met in Hartford in December; the Connecticut River counties of two other states, Vermont and New Hampshire, also sent representatives.

There had been rumblings of secessionist talk among extremist Federalists in Massachusetts and Connecticut in the Jefferson administration, especially at the time of the embargo, and such sentiments were heard again in the weeks before the Hartford Convention met. But when the convention assembled, the more moderate Federalists, led by Harrison Gray Otis of Massachusetts, won control. They contented themselves with proposing a series of state-rights amendments designed to protect the minority position of New England. One amendment would have eliminated the three-fifths clause in the Constitution, and thus reduced the voting power of southern states in the Congress and in presidential elections. Another would have limited the presidency to a single term, and prohibited the election of a President from the same state in two successive terms. Other amendments would have required a two-thirds vote of Congress for the imposition of an embargo or for the declaration of war. The delegates also agreed to reconvene the Hartford Convention if Congress did not accept their proposals.

If the war had dragged on much longer, it is possible that proposals to secede and make a separate peace with England might have had some chance of success in New England. Shortly after the Hartford Convention adjourned, however, came the electrifying news of the Treaty of Ghent ending the war, and of a great victory for the Americans at New Orleans where General Jackson inflicted a decisive defeat on the British expeditionary force led by Sir Edward Pakenham. These happy events made the Hartford Convention look absurd, and in the mood of nationalist exuberation which followed, the Federalist party went into a total collapse under the weight of its reputation as a party of secession and disloyalty.

While the War of 1812 had made a state-rights party out of the Federalists, the opposite was true of the Republicans. All the blunders and failures of the war were forgotten overnight in the mood of exhilaration that followed. To be sure, the Treaty of Ghent settled none of the issues that had taken the country into war with Great Britain. The British and American negotiators simply agreed to a settlement on the basis of the formula of *status quo ante bellum*—with the return of prisoners and the restoration of territorial conquests by each side; nothing was said about impressment, maritime rights, or Indian affairs. But the news of the great victory at New Orleans provided the American

John Bull Before New Orleans by William Charles, 1815. Neims and Weitenkampf's Century of Political Cartoons. *The New York Public Library.*

people with a psychological lift that made it easy to dismiss any dismal reflections about a costly war that had apparently settled nothing.

A Program of Economic Nationalism

The nationalist mood of the Republicans was soon expressed in a series of domestic measures that "out-Federalized the Federalists" as one of their opponents remarked. In 1816 the Republican majority pushed through Congress a series of measures that would have delighted Alexander Hamilton, although they rested upon a rationale that had been shaped by the experiences of "peaceful coercion" and war.

One of the key measures of this program of Republican nationalism was the protective tariff law of 1816—designed to protect the domestic manufactures that had grown up in the country during the embargo and the wartime British blockade. Indeed, cotton mills had multiplied so rapidly, especially in New England, that the number of spindles in the United States increased from 8,000 in 1807 to 500,000 in 1815. Advances were also made in iron manufacturing and other industries. These infant industries were clamoring for protection against the postwar influx of British goods, but the Republicans in Congress needed no prodding.

The floor manager of the Tariff of 1816 in the House was John C. Calhoun, a leading War Hawk in 1812 and now the chief architect of the nationalist program in Congress. The bill which he helped to prepare levied protective duties on cotton and woolen cloth, bar iron, and other commodities. In support of the measure, Calhoun argued: "It is the duty of the country, as a means of defense, to encourage its domestic industry, more especially that part of it which provides the necessary materials for clothing, and defense. . . ."

Although New England commercial interests opposed the Tariff of 1816 on the ground that it would diminish the carrying trade, Calhoun had the support of most of the representatives of other sections of the country, and of the older leaders of the Republican party. Madison had recommended such protection in his annual message to Congress and Jefferson, in retirement, reiterated his conviction that "experience . . . has taught me that manufactures are now as necessary to our independence as to our comfort." Indeed, Jefferson had paved the way for the national security argument which was being used to justify the Tariff of 1816. Shortly after leaving the presidency in 1809, he had expressed the view that "an equilibrium of agriculture, manufactures, and commerce is certainly become essential to our independence."

A second leading measure of the nationalist program of the Republican party was a bill to charter the second Bank of the United States. The charter of the new national Bank was similar to Hamilton's measure in all essential respects. One-fifth of the capital of $35 million was to be subscribed by the government, and 5 of the 25 directors were to be appointed by the President of the United States. The Bank was authorized to issue bank notes, and all notes and deposits were to be payable on demand in specie. All government receipts were to be deposited in the Bank and its branches, unless the Secretary of the Treasury should order otherwise. In return for its exclusive 20-year charter, the Bank was to pay into the federal treasury a sum of $1.5 million. Again, Calhoun led the debate on the measure, arguing that the 260 state banks that had grown up in the previous decade were vitiating the constitutional power to regulate currency that was given exclusively to Congress.

The nationalist Republicans also pushed through a major internal improvements bill near the end of Madison's administration. This measure—called the "Bonus Bill"—embodied Calhoun's proposal that the $1.5 million paid by the Bank for its charter, plus the dividends received by the government in its bank stock, should be set aside as a fund for the building of roads and canals. In support of this bill, Calhoun said: "What can add more to the wealth, strength, and political prosperity of our country than the cheapness of intercourse? It gives to the interior the advantages of the seaboard. It makes the country price, whether in the sale of the raw product or in the purchase of the article to be consumed, come near to the price of the commercial town, and it benefits the seaboard by enlarging the sphere of demand. . . ."

The Bonus Bill passed the House by the narrowest of margins, however. The middle and western states were in favor; New England, fearing the growth of the West, was strongly opposed; and the South was divided. This evidence of sectional hostility may have influenced Madison's attitude toward the measure. Expressing his doubts about the constitutionality of federal expenditures for such internal improvement schemes, he vetoed the bill. But Madison spoke for an older generation of Republicans. The clamor for internal improvements among Republican nationalists continued to grow with each passing year.

"America Has a Hemisphere to Itself"

The crowning achievements of Republican nationalism in foreign affairs came during the administration of James Monroe, the last of the Presidents to come from the "Virginia Dynasty" that held the reins of leadership for nearly a quarter of a century. In shaping his policies, Monroe depended heavily on a talented New Englander, John Quincy Adams, who served as a Secretary of State in his two administrations. Adams had left the party of his father shortly before the war of 1812 when he became disgusted with the narrow-minded particularism of New England Federalists. He brought into the Republican party a thoroughgoing devotion to expansive conceptions of American destiny.

Among the first successes of the Monroe administration were the agreements which settled some of the issues which continued to plague America's relations with England. The first of these was the Rush-Bagot Agreement of 1817, negotiated by Charles Bagot, the British minister in Washington, and Richard Rush, the Acting Secretary of State. This Agreement, which provided that both countries should reduce their *Detente with England* armed forces on the Great Lakes, was ratified by the Senate so that it acquired the status of a treaty; in later years it became the basis for further actions that made the Canadian-American border the longest demilitarized frontier in the world.

Other issues were removed by the Convention of 1818 which settled the dispute over the boundary between Canada and the United States from the Great Lakes to the Rocky Mountains; the convention also provided for the joint occupation of the Oregon country around the Columbia River basin. Satisfactory adjustments were also made in an older dispute over the right of Americans to catch and dry fish within Canadian coastal waters; and both countries put tariff and navigation regulations in their home ports on a "most favored nation" basis. For the first time since independence, American relations with England were on a reasonably peaceful basis—and with the end of the Napoleonic Wars, the troublesome questions of impressment and maritime rights just faded away.

At the same time, Adams used the utmost diplomatic pressure to persuade Spain to part with East Florida and the remainder of West Florida. The Spanish government had lost effective control in much of East Florida which had become a hideaway for pirates, runaway slaves, and raiding parties of Seminole Indians. Late in 1817, General Jackson, the commanding general in the southern military department, was authorized to use troops against the Seminoles and to pursue them across the East Florida boundary if necessary. Jackson carried out his task with greater gusto than the Monroe administration had expected. He not only chased the Seminoles into East Florida, but he proceeded to seize Spanish towns there, and even went so far as to set up an American as governor of East Florida.

Besides punishing Indians, Jackson also tried by court martial and executed two British subjects on charges of having incited the Indians to warfare. This incident created an uproar in the British press, but the British ministry refused to support English demands for redress because the two renegades were believed to have placed themselves by their actions beyond the protection of any civilized government. Monroe, of course, had to disavow the actions of Jackson that had exceeded his instructions. The captured towns were returned to Spain, and the government that Jackson had set up in East Florida was dismantled.

The Transcontinental Treaty with Spain

Adams, nevertheless, took full advantage of the whole incident. He told the Spanish minister that Jackson was fully justified in his invasion of East Florida because of the continual Seminole raids and hinted that American forces might go into Florida again. The Spanish government, already facing revolts in its American colonies, decided it would be wise to cede Florida to the United States rather than to risk losing it without compensation. Hence Adams was able to work out a Treaty in 1819 that settled the Florida question as well as other boundary disputes with Spain.

The Treaty of 1819 gave the United States title to both Floridas, and the United States, in return, agreed to pay the claims of its own citizens against Spain, amounting to $5 million, which Spain owed them for depredations against American commerce. In addition, Spain recognized the title of the United States to the territory north of a line from the Sabine River in east Texas to the 42nd parallel, and thence to the Pacific. In return the United States abandoned its claim to Texas based on the Louisiana Purchase. The Spanish government also asked Adams to give a promise of nonrecognition regarding the revolutionary republics in Spanish-America, but Adams steadily refused. Reluctantly, Spain gave in, and the treaty was ratified early in 1821.

Thus, by treaties with two European powers, England and Spain, the United States was recognized as a continental power with the right to expand to the Pacific. A structure of national security and expansion was being erected which would make the United States the dominant power in the Western Hemisphere. And the moment had arrived for the United States to proclaim to the world what Jefferson had already asserted privately: "America has a hemisphere to itself. It must have its separate system of interests, which must not be subordinated to those of Europe.

The opportunity for such a declaration was created by the successful revolt of the Spanish colonies in the New World, and the response of the European state system to the revolutionary movements in Spanish America. Following the defeat of Napoleon, a remarkable degree of unity was developed among the Old World powers in an attempt to preserve the established institutions of monarchy, nobility, and religion. The Quadruple Alliance joined the four victorious powers—England, Austria, Prussia, and Russia—in a guarantee of the peace settlement drawn up by the Congress of Vienna. Restored to the rule of the Bourbon dynasty, France was soon welcomed into the alliance, while Alexander I of Russia promoted a "Holy Alliance" that united most of the rulers of Europe against any revolutionary attempts to overthrow monarchical institutions.

When a rash of revolutions broke out in Spain, Portugal, Naples, and Greece, the concert of European powers hastily authorized Austria to send troops to crush the Neapolitan revolution in 1821; and France was given the dubious honor of invading Spain in 1823 to restore Ferdinand VII to his throne. The Holy Alliance considered the possibility of calling a Congress for the purpose of authorizing a joint French and Spanish expedition to America to restore Spanish control over her revolting colonies.

The British, however, viewed all these proceedings with distrust. In particular, the British government was disturbed by the French intervention in Spain and the prospect of a shift in the balance of power that might result from French influence in Spain. Furthermore, British merchants were anxious to exploit the lucrative Spanish-American markets; hence, the British ministry, always sensitive to the needs of its powerful commercial interests, was not willing to see any attempt to restore Spanish despotism in America.

Americans watched these developments with increasing anxiety. American public opinion was completely sympathetic toward the Spanish-American revolutions, and the United States was the first to recognize the independence of the new republics in 1822. Hence the prospect of European intervention appeared to be a threat to the security of republican principles in the New World. Moreover, the Monroe administration was alarmed at the news of a Russian edict of 1821 which extended the southern boundary of the Russian province of Alaska southward to the 51st parallel—well within the Oregon country. In view of these developments, Adams and Monroe agreed that the United States must take action to repel all Old World interference anywhere in the American hemisphere.

Monroe and Adams were encouraged in their decision by the knowledge that England was also opposed to any intervention by the Holy Alliance in America. In fact, George Canning, the British Foreign Secretary, actually proposed to Richard Rush, the United States minister in London, that the two countries make a joint declaration to head off any action by the European powers. Monroe was inclined to accept the offer, particularly after asking the advice of Jefferson who replied favorably. Adams, however, wished to reject Canning's offer. He saw that the United States could have all the advantages of British support without getting involved in any entangling agreement. Besides, he did not, as he said, want the United States to appear to "come in as a cock-boat in the wake of a British man-of-war."

The Monroe Doctrine   Adams' arguments convinced the President and his Cabinet, and Monroe decided to announce the policy of the United States in a unilateral declaration in his message to Congress in December, 1823. The Monroe Doctrine, as the policy came to be called, contained three important principles. The first of these stated to the Holy Alliance (and to Britain) the principle of noncolonization: " . . . the American continents, by the free and independent condition which they have assumed and maintain, are henceforth not to be considered as subjects of future colonization by any European powers." The second warned against any European intervention in the affairs of the New World: "The political system of the allied powers is essentially different . . . from that of America. . . . We owe it, therefore, to candor and to the amicable relations existing between the United States and those powers to declare that we should consider any attempt on their part to extend their system to any portion of this hemisphere as dangerous to our peace and safety." The third principle reiterated the American intention to remain separate from the internal affairs of Europe: "Our policy in regard to Europe, which was adopted at an early stage of the wars which have so long agitated that quarter of the globe, nevertheless remains the same, which is, not to interfere in the internal concerns of any of its powers, to consider the government *de facto* as the legitimate government for us."

To be sure, the continental powers of Europe were contemptuous of Monroe's declaration. They knew full well that the United States lacked the military power to support the large pretensions of the Monroe Doctrine. It was Great Britain's diplomatic pressure on France, and not the Monroe Doctrine, that forestalled any intervention in the Spanish-American republics. Even the Spanish American leaders were inclined to believe that Britain, rather than the United States, had saved them from the Holy Alliance. Nevertheless, the Monroe Doctrine was the capstone of Republican nationalism in the United States. It expressed the national mood of confidence in the ability of Americans to create their own destiny separated from the despotism and degradations of Europe. The principles of the Monroe Doctrine became an essential part of the American value system, as sacrosanct as the political principles embodied in the Constitution.

Detail from a copy after the original, Portrait of John Adams *by John Singleton Copley. Museum of Fine Arts. Boston, Massachusetts.*

The Democratic Aristoi

Despite the cherished belief that their party had saved American society from the pernicious influence of the "monocrats" and "aristocrats" in the party founded by Hamilton and Washington, the Jeffersonian Republicans were not ready to accept a society without some form of gentility. The leaders of the "Virginia dynasty," after all, were products of a social system in which the gentry held an effective monopoly of political power, and set the standards of esteem in manners, education, taste, and culture.

In the Virginia political system, the pathway to power was controlled in the first instance by the county courts. The first upward step in a political career was admission to the office of justice of the peace, and thereby to a seat on the bench of the county court. As a member of the county court, an aspiring young politician received the broadest possible education in the practical affairs of government. The county court, it should be remembered, was an administrative as well as a judicial body; it heard civil and criminal cases, it fixed local taxes, and it administered the affairs of local government.

The Jeffersonian Gentry

Normally, it was only after such training in a county court that a young man with political ambitions could get into the House of Burgesses, and into higher political offices in the government of Virginia, or of the United States. Washington, Jefferson, Madison, Monroe, as well as a large majority of Virginians who went to the Constitutional Convention, or who held seats in the Congress of the United States, served in the county courts of Virginia at the beginning of their careers.

As Charles Sydnor makes clear in his *Gentlemen Freeholders*, no one entered this first gate in the pathway to political power without being a member of the gentry, or closely associated with it. Only rarely in Virginia politics was a candidate not a member of the gentry, and it was also most difficult for anyone of radical or unpredictable behavior to begin a political career. This screening process by the Virginia gentry was particularly effective since the members of the county courts held office for life, and commissions were issued by the governor for new justices only on the recommendation of those already in the county court.

Although the influence of the gentry was indispensable to make a start in politics, the rising young politician needed to cultivate other forms of influence that would advance him further toward political success. To become a member of the House of Burgesses, he had to win the approval of the voters in county elections; and to seek other offices, such as the governorship or a seat in Congress, he had to win the approval of the voters of an even larger constituency. Consequently, the approval of ordinary freeholders was as necessary to the further development of a political career as the influence of the gentry was to the first upward step. Thus, a successful political leader had to develop the qualities and skills that would make him attractive to the freeholders. He had to cultivate agreeable and friendly relations with voters of lesser social status—he had to be ready to offer treats, shake a hand, answer questions, and show concern for local needs. The top leadership of the Republican party—"the Virginia dynasty"—was formed by this double winnowing of the Virginia political system, first by the aristocracy and then by the freeholders. This provided them with an enlarged sensitivity that made them more effective as political leaders. They had great respect, on the one hand, for the talent, refinement, and social responsibility of the gentry; on the other hand, their dependence on the good will of the freeholders made them more aware of the aspirations of the whole political community.

Jefferson's Theory of Natural Aristocracy

By training and experience, therefore, Jefferson was well-fitted for the task of reconciling the values of gentility with those of democracy. Despite his continued emphasis on equal rights and majority rule, Jefferson always looked hopefully to the emergence of a natural aristocracy that could furnish leadership for America in government, and in the arts and sciences: "I agree with you," he wrote to John Adams soon after he had retired from the presidency, "that there is a natural aristocracy among men . . . The natural aristocracy, I consider as the most precious gift of nature, for the instruction, the trusts, and the government of society."

Hence, Jefferson's theory of democracy required the continued existence of an *aristoi*—a class of men who rose above the rest—as had been the case for centuries past in previous social systems, as far back as Periclean Athens. But, for Jefferson, the only acceptable grounds for such a natural aristocracy in the United States were "virtue and talents." No other basis of aristocracy had any legitimacy in a democratic, equal rights society. "There is also," he wrote, "an artificial aristocracy, founded on wealth and birth, without either virtue or talents. . . . "such an artificial aristocracy, he maintained, was "a mischievous ingredient in society, and provision should be made to prevent its ascendancy." The leaders of the American Revolution had already shown the way to do this by abolishing hereditary titles and distinctions. "I dislike and detest hereditary honors, offices, emoluments established by law . . . I am for excluding legal, hereditary distinctions from the United States as long as possible."

In his friendly discussions of the nature of gentility with John Adams, Jefferson strove mightily to build his conception of a democratic *aristoi* on merit alone. He not only refused to yield anything to Adams' claims for the inevitable influence of wealth and birth in a republican society, but, in order to score points in his argument, he even went so far as to say that personal attainments such as beauty, good humor, politeness, and other accomplishments had "become but an auxiliary ground of distinction." Nevertheless, there is abundant evidence in Jefferson's letters to indicate that he valued good manners almost as much as virtue

The Westwood Children, c. 1810 by Joshua Johnston. National Gallery of Art, gift of Edgar William and Bernice Chrysler Garbisch.

and talent, and that he preferred to think of all these qualities as being combined in his gentlemanly ideal. The essential characteristics of a gentleman were summed up beautifully in a letter to his grandson, Francis Eppes:

But while you endeavor, by a good store of learning, to prepare yourself to become a useful and distinguished member of your country, you must remember that this never can be without uniting merit with your learning. Honesty, disinterestedness, and good nature are indispensable to procure the esteem and confidence of those with whom we live, and on whose esteem our happiness depends. . . . Above all things and at all times, practice yourself in good humor; this of all human qualities, is the most amicable and endearing to society.

Such natural gentlemen should not be given any special privileges by law, nor should places of trust be reserved for them by property and other qualifications for office. Jefferson believed that such a natural aristocracy would rise to the top in American society without factitious aid; the free citizens of a republican society would inevitably recognize true virtue and talent in the choice of their leaders: "I think the best remedy is exactly that provided by all our constitutions, to leave to the citizens the free election and separation of the *aristoi* from the *pseudo-*

aristoi, of the wheat from the chaff. In general they will elect the really good and wise. In some instances, wealth may corrupt, and birth blind them; but not in sufficient degree to endanger the society."

Jefferson and his followers frequently invoked the slogan of "equal rights for all and special privileges for none." Likewise they were generally warm supporters of the movement for universal manhood suffrage that was underway in the various states of the union in the opening years of the nineteenth century. Nevertheless, a system of gentry politics prevailed throughout the quarter of a century during which the Jeffersonians controlled the White House and most of the states houses in the Republic. Democratic politics in the modern sense had hardly developed at all. The enfranchised voters were largely apathetic and the caucus system flourished in this period as a device by which gentlemen nominated each other for high public office. Moreover, the widespread use of party ballots and oral voting provided the gentry with a final weight of influence in the electoral process. In short, the natural aristocracy that led the nation in the Jeffersonian era was closer to John Adams' rather than Jefferson's conception.

The Education of Worth and Genius

In the decades after independence was achieved, the leaders of the new American nation recognized the importance of education as a socializing device for a republican system of government. President Washington expressed a widespread sentiment in his first annual message to Congress when he declared: "Knowledge is in every country the surest basis of public happiness. In one, in which the measures of government receive their impression so immediately from the sense of the community, as in ours, it is proportionately essential." Indeed, the entire intellectual community of the United States was alive with ideas and projects for promoting general literacy and enlightenment in the new nation. Between 1786 and 1800, such outstanding intellectual leaders as Benjamin Rush, Noah Webster, and DuPont de Nemours published essays setting forth their ideas for educational improvement. In 1796 the American Philosophical Society offered a prize for a plan for "the best system of liberal Education and Literacy instruction adapted to the genius of the Government of the United States." The two winning essays stressed the importance of a universal system of education for the American people because of the close relationship between enlightenment and self-government.

Jefferson's
Educational
Ideas

Of all the leaders of the nation, however, no one was more conspicuous in his support of educational reform than Thomas Jefferson. As early as 1779, he had introduced *A Bill for the More General Diffusion of Knowledge* in the Virginia Assembly. This was a proposal for the public support of elementary and secondary schools in the state of Virginia on the grounds that education was the only reliable means of protecting the citizens of a popular government from the inevitable tendency of those entrusted with power to convert their power into tyranny.

Specifically, Jefferson proposed that each county of the state be divided into wards in each of which an elementary school should be established at public expense. All children were to be entitled to free tuition in these schools for at least three years, and as much longer at private expense if their parents wished. In addition there was to be a system of grammar, or secondary schools, to be established under the supervision of a public board of visitors who were to acquire land and buildings at public expense, and to appoint teachers and examine students. The instructional expenses of these secondary schools, however, were to be paid by private tuition; but scholarship students, whose parents were too poor to give them further education, were to be selected from the elementary schools and sent to the grammar schools at public expense. These "public foundationers" were to be examined at the end of the first year at which time the lower third would be dropped; after two years, all public foundationers were to be discontinued except for the one "best in genius and disposition" who was to be allowed to continue longer at public expense. Finally, the public visitors, after "diligent enquiry and examination," were to choose each year one member of the senior class in each of the grammar schools, who was "of the best learning and most hopeful genius and disposition," to be sent to William and Mary College "there to be educated, boarded, and clothed, for three years," at public expense.

The established class and religious interests in Virginia, however, were opposed to the adoption of such a scheme of public education. Jefferson's bill was not passed by the legislature, although he continued to work for such reforms in his native state throughout his lifetime.

At no time did Jefferson ever advocate a wholesale system of popular education. While he saw the necessity of creating a comprehensive system of public education under public control, his scheme was designed to maintain social distinctions based on education. In a later elaboration of his plan prepared in 1814, Jefferson stated explicitly: "The mass of our citizens may be divided into two classes—the laboring and the learned. The laboring will need the first grade of education to qualify them for their pursuits and duties: the learned will need it as a foundation for further acquirements." Indeed, Jefferson believed that the critical separation of the two classes should occur at the end of three years of elementary instruction: "At the discharging of the pupils from the elementary schools, the two classes separate—those destined for labor will engage in the business of agriculture, or enter into apprenticeships to such handicraft art as may be their choice; their companions, destined to the pursuits of science, will proceed to the college, which will consist, 1st of general schools; and, 2nd, of professional schools. The general schools will constitute the second grade of education."

Educational Changes in
the Jeffersonian Era

Thus Jefferson's educational schemes were closely related to his conception of a democratic *aristoi*. The educational system was to be the means of recruiting and maintaining a natural aristocracy for America. In his own words: "Worth and genius would thus have been sought out from every condition of life, and completely prepared by education for defeating the competition of wealth and birth for public trusts."

Small wonder, then, that there was so little progress in the development of public education in the first generation after the American Revolution. Jefferson's scheme for separating "the laboring and the learned" in the educational system was not likely to rally a mass movement for educational reform in America. Indeed there was surprisingly little progress in the development of free public schools during the 25 years that the Jeffersonians had political control of the federal and state governments. To be sure, they extended the policy, already established by the Land Ordinance of 1785, of "reserving" a section of land in each township of the West for the support of education; beginning in 1802, Congress gave to each new state admitted to the Union the sixteenth section in every township for the maintenance of schools. But land grants do not make a school; the energy, enthusiasm, and financial support of local citizens were needed before free public schools could exist. And the fact is that the people in most of the western states were laggard in creating such public schools in the first half of the nineteenth century.

Among the older states, also, the idea of universal and free education remained in the field of theory rather than of fact. The main accomplishment in most of them was the creation of permanent school funds, the income of which was designed to aid localities in maintaining schools. To build up these funds, many states used proceeds from the sale of unoccupied lands, conducted public lotteries, and reserved revenues from other sources such as fines, licenses, and special taxes. During the first quarter of the century, however, the income from such funds was insignificant in relation to the total child population in all states except Connecticut and New York. In many states, moreover, the money was used primarily to support the education of pauper children.

Even in New England, where a considerable degree of public support had taken root in the colonial period, the common schools languished in the decades after the Revolution. An increasing number of towns in Massachusetts failed to maintain the Latin grammar schools required by state law. Throughout New England, the elementary schools were generally of poor quality and maintained at the lowest possible cost. In 1827, one of the early advocates of educational reform in Massachusetts described the situation with brutal frankness: "The country schools are every where degraded. They stand low even in the estimation of their warmest friends. It is thought a mean thing for a man of competent estate, or for any but the mechanic, the artisan, or the laborer, to send their children to them for their education."

New England Village,
*American School early
nineteenth century.
Collection of American
Primitive Paintings.
National Gallery of Art, gift
of Edgar William and
Bernice Chrysler Garbisch,
1955.*

Men of means in New England and elsewhere sent their children to private academies. Such privately managed, tuition schools had already appeared in the larger towns in the eighteenth century to serve the needs of the rising middle class by offering instruction in surveying, navigation, modern languages, mathematics, as well as in the classical languages. Academies of this type grew so rapidly in number that by 1820 they were to be found throughout the entire nation. Wherever settlement had progressed far enough to develop a more complex economic life and a growing middle class, an academy was almost certain to be started.

Many of the state legislatures responded to the growing middle-class pressures by granting such schools favorable rights and immunities in their charters. The properties of such academies were made exempt from taxation; they were often allowed the privilege of raising money by lottery or subscription; sometimes they were given land or money grants by the states.

A considerable number of academies were founded by churches and religious organizations whose leading laymen were often conspicuous members of the growing middle class in the trading centers that mushroomed everywhere with the economic growth of the country. In fact, the greatest output of energy in the educational field during the first decades of the nineteenth century came from philanthropic efforts that were religiously motivated. The Sunday School movement was a notable effort of this kind to provide instruction for the children of the poor. Religious instruction for children on the Sabbath was, of course, a very old practice in America and Europe, but an Englishman, Robert Raikes, expanded the idea to include instruction in reading and writing for the children of operatives in the factory towns of England. The idea was brought to America shortly after the Revolution, and such Sunday schools began to appear in Boston, New York, Philadelphia, Charleston, Pittsburgh, and other larger towns. In 1820 Boston reported 22 schools with four hundred teachers. Makeshift as many of these schools were, they educated more children than some of the pauper schools supported by many of the states.

Equally significant were some of the charitable schools supported by public subscription societies, and designed "to give the poor the power to read." The most famous of these school societies was the Free School Society of the City of New York, first organized in 1805, and reorganized as the Public School Society in 1826. Many prominent New Yorkers served on the Board of Trustees: the first president was DeWitt Clinton, and among the trustees were two Van Rensselaers, Peter Jay, James Roosevelt, and Hamilton Fish. The leading Protestant denominations were particularly influential in the Public School Society, and by 1826, nine schools had been founded with an attendance of approximately four thousand pupils. The schools of the society were so successful that both the city and state granted financial aid in the form of a reserved portion of the property tax.

The Jeffersonian Struggle for Public Universities

In comparison with the philanthropic efforts of religious groups, the accomplishment of the Jeffersonains in the improvement of education were meager indeed. Only in the field of higher education did they exhibit an equivalent energy. Jefferson and his friends were convinced that higher education was rightfully a function of the state, and that the proper development of learning, particularly in the field of science, could not take place unless higher educational institutions were freed from the control of the vested interests of religious organizations.

As early as 1779, Jefferson had led an unsuccessful effort to amend the charter of William and Mary College to bring the institution under closer public control. A similar effort was made in Connecticut to bring Yale under state control; but the reorganization effected in 1792 simply made the governor, lieutenant governor, and six state officials ex-officio members of the corporation. Hence, under President Timothy Dwight, Yale continued to exhibit a strong religious orthodoxy. In 1810 the Massachusetts legislature attempted to change the status of ex-officio members on the Harvard Board of Overseers to one that was largely elective and, hence, more responsive to the public will; but Harvard was able to escape any curtailment of its chartered privileges.

The Jeffersonians came very close to success, however, in their efforts to alter the status of Dartmouth College. The charter of Dartmouth College, established in 1769 under Congregationalist auspices, provided for public representation on the Board of Trustees only to the extent of making the governor an ex-officio member. With the growth of the

Jeffersonian party in New Hampshire, a movement for reorganization gained strength among the people and in the legislature. When President Wheelock associated himself in 1815 with these efforts of the Jeffersonian Republicans, the Federalist Board of Trustees removed him. After winning control of the legislature in the following year, the Jeffersonian Republicans passed an act that sought to change the college into a state university, to be called Dartmouth University, and to be controlled by a board of overseers composed of certain state officials and appointees of the governor.

The Board of Trustees maintained that the act was unconstitutional. For a while, two rival administrative groups were in being—one operating an institution called Dartmouth College and the other an institution called Dartmouth University. The original trustees, therefore, sought relief in the courts of New Hampshire, but the New Hampshire Superior Court upheld the act of the legislature on the ground that the college was essentially a public corporation whose powers and franchises were exercised for public purposes and therefore subject to public control.

The Jeffersonians applauded this decision of the New Hampshire court, but their feeling of triumph was short-lived. The trustees of the college retained Daniel Webster and Joseph Hopkinson, two of the ablest lawyers of the day, and an appeal was taken to the Supreme Court of the United States which handed down its decision in the case of *Dartmouth College* v. *Woodward* (1819). The ruling of the New Hampshire court was reversed, and the act of the New Hampshire legislature was declared unconstitutional on the ground that it violated the obligation of contract.

Chief Justice John Marshall, in giving the opinion of the Court, admitted the constitutional argument of the Jeffersonians that the framers of the Constitution did not intend to restrain the states in the regulation of their public institutions, when they included the section that prohibits a state from impairing the obligation of contract. But he argued at great length that Dartmouth College was not a public institution but rather a "private eleemosynary institution." Hence the charter granted to this private charitable corporation was a contract within the meaning of the Constitution and could not be repealed or altered by the legislature.

The Dartmouth College decision was a stunning defeat for the Jeffersonians because it foreclosed any hope of reorganizing other colonial colleges as state universities under full public control. Indeed, Donald G. Tewksbury, a leading authority on the founding of American colleges and universities before the Civil War, has argued that the decision significantly retarded the development of state universities for half a century. Furthermore, it may also be said that Marshall's judicial opinion marked a double defeat for the Jeffersonians since it also strengthened the line of precedent that favored the immunity of all corporate charters—including those in the fields of finance, transportation, and industry—from retroactive interference by state legislatures.

Jefferson, however, could find solace in the development of a new state university for his native state. If the Dartmouth College decision put an end to hopes for the reorganization of some of the leading colonial colleges, it was still possible to develop new publicly supported institutions, free from inherited private and religious prejudices. Jefferson's University of Virginia was clearly the best of the eight or ten state universities established in America in the decades before the Civil War.

The University of Virginia was a model institution in many ways. The architecture of the buildings and the arrangement of the campus expressed Jefferson's love of classicism as well as of utility. Dominating the terraced quadrangle of his "academical village" was a rotunda inspired by the Roman Pantheon, while on either side were two-storied, porticoed buildings each with its lodgings above for the professors and its classrooms below for the students. Within these porticoes of learning, Jefferson proposed to create an aristocracy of virtue and talent.

Consequently a curriculum was designed for the new university that would prepare leaders in politics and in all the higher branches of the arts and sciences. In the report of the committee to fix a site and develop a program for a university which Jefferson chaired in 1818, the following were among the educational objectives listed: "To form the statesmen, legislators, and judges, on whom public prosperity and individual happiness are so much to depend . . . to develop the reasoning faculties of our youth, enlarge their minds, cultivate their morals, and instill in them the precepts of virtue and order . . . to enlighten them with mathematical and physical sciences, which advance the arts, and administer to the health, the subsistence, and comforts of human life."

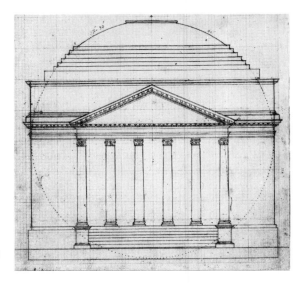

The University of Virginia Library.

Specifically, Jefferson's committee proposed that the University of Virginia should be organized into 10 separate branches covering such areas of learning as ancient languages, modern languages, mathematics, physics, natural philosophy, botany, medicine, government, law, and "ideology" (Ethics, Rhetoric, Belles Lettres). Furthermore, a student would be "free to attend the schools of his choice, and no other than he chooses," rather than being forced into required classical and religious studies.

Ironically, however, Jefferson's main concept of a democratic leadership based on talent and learning was already an anachronism when the University of Virginia opened its doors in 1825. The new champions of democracy in the United States looked with suspicion on book learning and the claims of social superiority for college-educated men; they emphasized instead the sufficiency of common sense, natural virtue, and intuitive wisdom. Jefferson did not live to see the full development of the new democratic ideology, but it seems safe to assume that he would have regarded a reliance on intuition without knowledge as a form of democratic heresy. In 1810, when he had encountered such ideas in the disparagement of legal learning, he had written sarcastically: "Now men are born scholars, lawyers, doctors; in our day this was confined to poets." By 1825, however, the day of the Virginia dynasty was dying, and new heroes and ideals were stirring the imagination of the American people.

The Makers of Taste and Opinion

One of the significant consequences of the American Revolution was a remarkable upsurge in the number of newspapers in the United States. By 1801, there were already two hundred newspapers being published in the country and, by 1830, the number had increased to about 1200. Most of these were weekly newspapers, but daily newspapers were making their appearance in the larger commercial centers: 20 daily newspapers were being published in 1800, and three times that many by 1830.

The Multiplication of American Newspapers

Obviously, there were forces at work in American society that demanded the forms of social communication which newspapers had to offer. In the larger cities, much of the impulse to read newspapers came from the rapidly growing mercantile class. The merchants and tradesmen needed up-to-the-minute information on the arrival of sailing vessels and the prices of imported goods. At the same time, the newspapers served as a means of advertising local wares and services. Indeed, the names of many leading newspapers conveyed this important journalistic function in a most literal way: one of the leading newspapers in Philadelphia at the end of the eighteenth century was called the *Pennsylvania Packet and Daily Advertiser*; the leading daily in New York was called the *Daily Advertiser*.

Furthermore, the development of party politics after the adoption of the Constitution provided added incentive to the establishment of newspapers. In view of the large geographical expanse of the Republic, the ethnic and religious diversity of the population, and the strength of local traditions and prejudices, newspapers became an indispensable means by which political leaders could educate their party followers and rally them in united forms of action. Moreover, the technology of printing was still relatively simple and inexpensive, so that even the smaller towns could afford to have two or more newspapers which carried on vigorous debates in the party battles of Federalists and Republicans.

In terms of sheer numbers and boldness of expression, nothing like the American press existed anywhere in Europe. In England, newspapers were still crippled by special taxes, and there was little freedom of the press especially for reformers. On the continent, censorship and other repressive measures were even harsher than in England. Only in the United States was there a wide freedom of comment on political topics.

Undoubtedly, the strong republican spirit generated by the Revolution helped to create the conditions favorable to the exercise of so much freedom by American newspapers. Jefferson, for example, firmly believed that the liberty of the press was an indispensable requirement for the existence of a free government. He wrote in 1787: "The basis of our government being the opinion of the people, the first object should be to keep that right; and were it left to me to decide whether we should have a government without newspapers, or newspapers without a government, I should not hesitate a moment to prefer the latter." While others might not have been willing to accept Jefferson's exaggerated alternatives, there was a universal demand for special constitutional guarantees for the freedom of speech and press that was incorporated in the Bill of Rights. Hence, the first amendment to the Constitution included the following provision: "Congress shall make no law . . . abridging the freedom of speech, or of the press. . . . "

Encouraged by such evidence of popular support, the American press developed a raucous sense of freedom in the early decades of the Republic. The intensely partisan spirit that developed in American politics by the time of Washington's second administration produced a great amount of personal abuse in the newspapers. Abusive attacks on such leaders as Adams, Hamilton, and Jefferson became commonplace. The scurrilous attacks made by newspaper editors on each other displayed a similar lack of restraint: the Philadelphia *Aurora* called Noah Webster "an impious, disorganizing wretch," and a Federalist newspaper of Boston hailed the death of Benjamin Franklin Bache of the *Aurora* with the words, "The Jacobins are all whining at the exit of the vile Benjamin Franklin Bache; so they would do if one of their own gang was hung for stealing."

To be sure, one way to curb such licentious use of the freedom of the press was to sue for damages suffered from a personal libel. But such libel suits were not commonly used until the early decades of the nineteenth century. The preferred method was to administer a beating to an opposing editor in some public place. Indeed, Benjamin Franklin, in the year before he died, recommended this method as the best way to regulate the freedom of the press in America: "My proposal then is, to leave the liberty of the press untouched, to be exercised in its full extent, force and vigor; but to permit the *liberty of the cudgel* to go with it *pari passu.*"

Many Federalists, however, were not amused by Franklin's witty comment. They resented the abusive attacks on their leaders in public office, and the growing criticism of Washington in his second administration was regarded by them as a form of sacrilege. The political controversy carried on in newspapers over Jay's Treaty was particularly defamatory. "There is a liberty of the press," declared the *Columbian Centinel* of Boston at the time, "which is very little short of the liberty of burning our houses."

Hence the Sedition Act of 1798 was a product of Federalist resentments that had built up over several years, as well as a response to the crisis with France after the XYZ Affair. But the Sedition Act proved to be a costly political error and the Republicans undoubtedly gained additional votes because of it in their march to triumph in the campaign of 1800. Yet the price of this victory for the liberty of the press was much higher than Jefferson had ever expected to pay; he became one of the chief victims of the abusiveness of an opposition press. Nevertheless he endured the abuse by opposition newspapers with remarkable patience and self-control because he knew that the preponderance of the press was in Federalist hands. In 1804, he told a friend, " . . . tho' not 1/25 (of the) nation, they command 3/4 of its papers."

Jefferson was not wholly averse to the use of libel laws against the press for he stated in his second inaugural: "No inference is here intended, that the laws, provided by the State against false and defamatory publications, should not be enforced: he who has time, renders a service to public morals and public tranquillity, in reforming these abuses by the salutary coercions of the law. . . ." But he made clear that he preferred not to use his time in such methods; he chose to rely on the hope that "the public judgment will correct false reasonings and opinions, on a full hearing of all parties."

Throughout his presidency, Jefferson sought to encourage the development of more Republican newspapers in order to counteract the preponderance of the Federalist press. His most successful action in aid of Republican journalism was the encouragement of the *National Intelligencer,* a triweekly newspaper established in Washington to act as the authoritative spokesman of the Jefferson administration. The editor of the *National Intelligencer,* Samuel Harrison Smith, was a man of

Jefferson and the Liberty of the Press

recognized literary ability who wrote with the calm rationality that Jefferson believed should be the proper style of a democratic press. Moreover, Jefferson lived to see Republican newspapers overcome the Federalist dominance which had existed during most of his presidency. As the waves of settlement rolled into the western districts, and as the growing Republican majorities in the larger eastern towns began to assert themselves, the proportion of Republican newspapers increased, so that by the time of the War of 1812, there was already a slight majority of newspapers with Republican sympathies.

Joseph Dennie's   But despite these gains in the number of Republican newspapers,
Port Folio   Jefferson's opponents still commanded great positions of influence in the making of public taste and opinion. This was particularly true in the development of the general magazines that were devoted to a miscellany of essays on political and literary subjects as well as some fiction and poetry reprinted from English sources or written by aspiring American authors. These included the *Port Folio* of Philadelphia, the *Portico* of Baltimore, the *American Review* and *Literary Journal* of New York, and the *New England Galaxy* of Boston. Among these, undisputed pre-eminence was held by Joseph Dennie's *Port Folio*.

There were strong political motives in the founding of the *Port Folio*. Dennie was determined to carry on an unrelenting political warfare against the new order of things which the Jeffersonians wished to introduce. He announced proudly in an early issue of the magazine that he would make it a torch in "this dark night of jacobinism" that had beclouded the destiny of America. But the *Port Folio* was always much more than a political journal; Dennie also wished to make it the leading literary periodical in the United States. He characterized his brain child as "not quite a Gazette, nor wholly a Magazine, with something of politics to interest Quidnuncs, and something of Literature to engage Students."

Many of the writers for the *Port Folio* were recruited by Dennie from the Tuesday Club, a circle of young gentlemen in Philadelphia, most of them Federalist in politics and imbued with a desire to gain literary fame. But Dennie, himself, was the most important contributor to the literary reputation of the *Port Folio*. Under the pseudonym "Oliver Oldschool," he turned out a constant stream of reviews and essays on classical authors, English writers, and American manners. The readers of Dennie's recurrent "Author's Evenings" were made acquainted with such English writers as Wordsworth, Coleridge, Thomas Moore, and Walter Scott, for Dennie was a fervent admirer of English literature.

Dennie was particularly concerned to uphold English standards against the deteriorating influences of American conditions. Manners occupied a great deal of space in the issue of the magazine. Thus, American men were rebuked for their habit of keeping their hands in their pockets and for their vulgar habits of pronunciation. Indeed, the editor of the *Port Folio* fought a continuing battle with Noah Webster

THE PORT FOLIO.

CRITICISM——FOR THE PORT FOLIO.

" To mark how wide extends the mighty waste
" O'er the fair realms of Science, Learning, Taste,
" To drive and scatter all the brood of lies,
" And chase the varying falsehood as it flies,
" The long arrears of Ridicule to pay,
" And drag reluctant Dulness back to day."

The COLUMBIAD, a Poem, by JOEL BARLOW,—Philadelphia, C. &
A. Conrad & Co. Quarto, pp. 470. Printed by Fry & Kammerer.

A quarto epic poem—polished by twenty years labour—issuing in all the pomp of typographical elegance from an American press—the author an American—the theme, the history of
our own country ! What an era in our literature ! What an epoch
in the history of our arts ! what a subject for the reviewer !

From The Port Folio, *1809.*
Rush Rhees Library. The
University of Rochester.

because of the great lexicographer's preferences for Americanisms in
American speech. Even though Webster was as thoroughgoing a Federalist as he was, Dennie criticized him again and again for using such
American terms of speech as "dicker," "snack," "bran new," "hellnifer-
ous," and "neat as plush." Such debasement of the older, English
standards of speech was regarded by Dennie as further evidence of the
decline of the graces in the United States.

But even Dennie could not hold back the rising tide of American
literary pretensions. Before his death in 1812, such American writers as
Joel Barlow, Robert Treat Paine, Royall Tyler, William Dunlap, and
Charles Brockden Brown had received favorable reviews in the pages of
the *Port Folio*. After his death, American writers were given more
favorable attention. Under Nicholas Biddle, Dennie's immediate successor as editor, the *Port Folio* was saying: "Americans are the only people
on earth who uniformly undervalue the efforts of literary genius in their
own country and hold in undue estimation much feebler efforts when
received from abroad." In 1816 the magazine was purchased by Harrison
Hall, the head of one of the leading literary families in Philadelphia. The
new editor, John Ewing Hall, declared that it would be his principal
object "to vindicate the character of American literature and manners
from the aspersions of ignorant and illiterate foreigners."

It was evident that the War of 1812 had aroused a national spirit that foreshadowed the end of the cultural dependence on England which had been encouraged by the sophisticated gentlemen of the fashionable literary clubs in larger cities like Boston, New York, Philadelphia, and Baltimore. It would take another generation, however, before this cultural assertiveness in America would produce a genuine literary renaissance.

Quest for Cultural Independence

*The Call
for Literary
Independence*

The impulse toward cultural independence had already manifested itself before the War of 1812: demands for an authentic American literature were heard as soon as the Revolution was successfully terminated. "America," Noah Webster declared, "must be as independent in *literature* as she is in *politics*." In the first edition of his *Grammatical Institute*, published in 1783, Webster asserted further that "for America in her infancy to adopt the present maxims of the Old World, would be to stamp the wrinkles of decrepid age upon the bloom of youth. . . . " Joel Barlow, who had been Webster's classmate at Yale but who had followed a deviant path into the party of the Jeffersonian Republicans, shared the same desire to create an authentic American culture. He called for the creation of an epic that would celebrate America's achievements and express the American genius of liberty. Americans, he believed, should seize the opportunity to direct poetry and the arts to the end "that true and useful ideas of glory may be implanted in the minds of men here, to take [the] place of the false and destructive ones that have degraded the species in other countries." Barlow actually undertook to write an epic poem that would be a direct expression of American ideas and sentiments. Published in final form in 1807, *The Columbiad* was received with great public fanfare, but Barlow's effort now seems to be an astonishing example of poetic flatulence.

*Washington Irving's
Literary Success*

Nevertheless, the public acclaim that greeted *The Columbiad* revealed that a growing reading audience was waiting for the appearance of an American writer who could be truly accepted as the equal of English writers. And such expectations were quickly gratified as Washington Irving achieved the most dazzling literary reputation in America during the first quarter of the nineteenth century. His career is a remarkable example of the convergence of individual talent with the favorable growth of those instruments of culture—colleges, magazines, literary and theatrical circles—that were necessary to support the appearance of a national literature.

Washington Irving grew up in a New York that was rapidly acquiring a sophisticated social and literary life. He prepared for a career in the law, but he was fascinated by the exciting intellectual life offered by the clubs, periodicals, and theaters of Manhattan. In a short time, Washington

Irving became the leader of a talented group of young men wth a taste for literature and bacchanalian supper parties. The activities of this youthful circle prepared Irving for his first literary success in the publication of the booklets of the *Salmagundi; or the Whim-Whams and Opinions of Launcelot Longstaff, & Others* (1807). Written largely by Washington Irving in collaboration with his brother William and James R. Paulding, *Salmagundi* was a collection of satiric and gossipy essays dealing with national and local politics, confidential notes on theaters and other literary matters, and, above all, the society and manners of New York.

Within two years, Irving won even greater acclaim with *Diederick Knickerbocker's History of New York*. His burlesque of the city's early history was a skillfully constructed satire. Many of his readers were fully aware that much of the wit was aimed at the foibles and pretensions of their present social leaders under the guise of a mock history. For this and other reasons, *Diederick Knickerbocker's History* appealed to readers outside of New York as much as it did to those who were daily participants in the life and legends of the city. The work was reviewed in several English journals, and no less a person than Sir Walter Scott took great delight in reading it even though he could not catch all the satirical allusions to American society and politics.

Having tasted the honeyed fruits of a larger literary fame, Irving yearned for further approval by the literary men of England as well as

The Return of Rip Van Winkle, c. *1845 by John Quidor. National Gallery of Art, Andrew Mellon Collection, 1942.*

the fashionable literary societies of America. Hence, he cultivated a felicity of style that imitated English literary fashions. In fact, when his famous *Sketch Book* was published, there were some English reviewers who even doubted that the author was an American.

By that time, Irving may have had some doubts himself. He had sailed for England in 1815 and remained there for several years completely enraptured by "the accumulated treasures of age" that he found there. Both *The Sketch Book* (1819) and *Bracebridge Hall* (1822) were written in England, and each reflected his growing love for old times and old places—the one in the tales of Rip Van Winkle or Ichabod Crane in his native Hudson River region, and the other in the castles, customs, and classes of Old England.

For 17 years Irving remained abroad—as a traveller, as Secretary to the American Legation in London, and as an attaché in the American Legation at Madrid. Much of his energy was poured into works that developed European rather than American themes: *Tales of a Traveller* (1824); *The Life and Voyages of Columbus* (1828); the *Conquest of Granada* (1829); *The Companions of Columbus* (1831); and *The Alhambra* (1832). Nevertheless, when he returned to the United States, he was still accepted as an arbiter of American letters, although by that time a new generation of writers was appearing, many of whom were no longer dazzled by Irving's literary success.

By and large, however, Irving had clung to those modes of writing for which Americans had shown a preference in the previous century. His favorite forms were the essay, the short tale, the travel sketch, and works of history. While there is abundant evidence of a fictive imagination in all his writings, he never attempted to write fiction on a larger scale. Indeed, America did not seem to offer a favorable soil for the development of novels before the second quarter of the nineteenth century.

Charles Brockden Brown's Literary Experiments

It was Charles Brockden Brown who made the most notable effort to make the novel an appropriate vehicle for American literature. Although his effort was a distinct failure, especially when compared to the golden success of Washington Irving, his failure proved to be instructive to those American critics who were concerned with the question of an authentic American literature.

Brown strove to make the novel a vehicle for exhibiting "the man of soaring passions and intellectual energy" in the native scenes of American life. "To the story-telling moralist," he wrote in a prefatory statement for his first work, "the United States is a new and untrodden field. He who shall examine objects with his own eyes, who shall employ the European models merely for the improvement of his taste, and adapt his fiction to all that is genuine and peculiar in the scene before him, will be entitled at least to the praise of originality."

In an extraordinary burst of creative energy, Brockden Brown wrote six major novels in Philadelphia between 1798 and 1801—*Wieland, Ormond, Arthur Mervyn, Edgar Huntley, Clara Howard,* and *Jane Talbot*—in addition to a considerable number of shorter pieces of fiction. His novels displayed a thorough familiarity with all the literary devices used by European writers of novels and romances; furthermore, many of his ideas concerning religion, marriage, women's rights, and humanitarianism showed the influence of William Godwin's *Political Justice.* Nevertheless, his novels have a truly original character—there was no other writer quite like him among his contemporaries in Europe or America.

In fact, Brown was too original for his American readers. He was particularly fascinated with certain psychological and moral problems that were deeply rooted in human behavior, and his favorite subject, he once told a French correspondent, was "the great energies employed in the promotion of vicious purposes." Thus his plots were built around such problems as religious fanaticism in *Wieland,* criminology in *Edgar Huntley,* philosophical anarchism in *Ormond,* humanitarian reform in *Arthur Mervyn,* and marriage in *Jane Talbot* and *Clara Howard.* But somehow his uncanny incidents and philosophical probings failed to win the literary success that Irving enjoyed.

In a perceptive essay written for the *North American Review* in 1819, Edward Tyrell Channing observed that the real failure of Brown's novels lay in their lack of essentiall relevance to the American experience as it was sensed by most Americans. "Our cities are large," he wrote, "but new, and they constantly suggest to us gainful habits and the secure houses of a recent and flourishing population; the laboring and happy are seen every where and not a corner or recess is secret. The deserted street at midnight produces no awful sense of solitude or danger, and the throng that passes us by day would scarcely suggest the thought that any one was alone in the crowd, buried in contemplation, and perhaps brooding over mischief in darkness." A people living in such a social state could not identify with the scenes and persons that Brown had set before them in his novels. The actions that Americans were prepared to "witness and encourage," Channing argued, "are the useful rather than the heroic, such as tend to make society happier, not such as to disturb or darken it."

Although Channing undoubtedly underestimated the American appetite for depictions of the deeper and darker purposes of human nature, it is true that much literary effort in the early decades of the Republic was being directed toward the celebration of the useful virtues. A host of writers, eager to explore the meaning of the nation's independence, gave their energies to the writing of national and state histories. Noah Webster published a full-length *History of the United States* (1787) in which he traced the idea of self-government back to the first settlements. Mercy Otis Warren, a sister of James Otis, and the wife of a Massachusetts patriot, wrote a three-volume *History of the Revolution* (1805) which contained interesting characterizations of leaders like John Hancock and Sam Adams. Jeremy Belknap's three-volume *History of*

*The Search
for Authentic Fables
and Heroes*

New Hampshire (1784–1792) and his two-volume *American Biography* (1794–1798) added greatly to the growing store of biographical and historical information attractively packaged in patriotic sentiments.

In various ways, these writers were creating a gallery of American heroes—most of them associated with the revolutionary effort against Great Britain. But it was the cult of Washington as the revered father of his country that shaped the symbols that were becoming commonplace in the American imagination.

Although Washington had faced fierce partisan attacks by the end of his second administration, all Americans joined together to pay homage to his memory after his death. In the first year after his death in 1799, some 350 eulogistic sermons rolled off the printing presses in towns and villages throughout the broad expanse of the Republic. In succeeding years, Washington's Birthday orations became a regular ritual in American life. The apotheosis of Washington was carried forward rapidly as scores of biographies were written about him. In addition, reproductions of Gilbert Stuart's famous portrait helped to fix the image of a dignified and virtuous statesman in the popular memory.

Parson Weems and the Cult of Washington

No one was more active in furthering the cult of Washington than Mason Locke Weems, an Anglican clergyman who became a writer and book-peddler. He decided to expand a eulogistic sketch that he had written immediately after Washington's death into a biography that would "capture the taste of the American people." In a letter to Matthew Carey, the Philadelphia publisher, he wrote: "It is in our power to make this thing profitable and beneficial—Everybody will read about Washington—and let us hold up his Virtues—Some, may go and do likewise." In particular, Weems was determined to show his readers that Wash-

Another tribute to Washington. Rush Rhees Library. The University of Rochester.

General George Washington,

Who died at Mount Vernon, December 14th, 1799, in the 68th

year of his age.

――――――

WRITTEN

At the request of the citizens of Newburyport, and delivered at

the first Presbyterian Meeting-House in that town,

January 2nd. 1800.

ington's rise was due to such virtues as: "1. His Veneration for the Diety [sic], or Religious Principles. 2. His Patriotism. 3. his Magnimity [sic]. 4. his Industry. 5. his Temperance and Sobriety. 6. his Justice. . . ." The expanded edition, issued in 1806, entitled *Life of Washington, With Curious Anecdotes Equally Honorable to Himself and Exemplary to His Young Countrymen,* contained many illustrative anecdotes, including the famous cherry tree story.

Modern Americans know that the cherry tree story was pure invention, but Weems was more interested in creating an acceptable panolpy of virtues for the American people than in pursuing historical reality. At any rate, American readers liked Weems' book. In its time, it was the most popular book written by an American writer, running to 40 editions by the time of Weems' death in 1825. During those years, it even exceeded in sales the nation's best-selling work of fiction—Mrs. Susanna Rawson's *Charlotte, A Tale of Truth,* or *Charlotte Temple.*

The tremendous popularity of Weems' book provides the social historian with unmistakable evidence that the American people were eager to embrace a mythology that would combine the older virtues of religious piety with the middle-class virtues of industry, self-reliance, temperance, and sobriety. In the case of Washington, his true character as a formal and aloof Federalist gentleman had to be covered over by the homespun cloak of Parson Weems' folklore. To a significant degree, therefore, the popularity of Weems' book foreshadowed the end of the aristocratic Republic. The American people would soon seek living heroes who would act out the virtues held up as exemplary by the book-selling parson.

By THOMAS PAINE, A. M.

" Oh ! for a mufe of fire, that would afcend

" The brighteft heaven of invention !

" An empire for a ftage, heroes to act,

" And angels to behold the fwelling fcene !

" Then fhould the MIGHTY SHADE again affume

" His local habitation, and his name,

" Mantling our fphere with his fupernal glory !

" Virtue and Fame fhould pioneer his way

" Thro' planets wonder-ftruck ; while at his heels

" Valor and Victory (leafht in like hounds)

" Crouch for employment !"

Ship's figurehead c. 1850.
Designed and made by Isaac
Fowle of Boston. Original
owned by the Bostonian
Society, Old State House,
Boston, Massachusetts.
Index of American Design.
National Gallery of Art,
Washington, D.C.

The Fluctuations of Economic Growth, 1815–1860

The end of the War of 1812 was followed by an era of tremendous expansion in the national economy that had far-reaching effects on every aspect of American life. Not only was the pace of economic growth greater than it had been in previous generations, but there was also a fundamental shift away from dependence on Europe toward a reliance on the internal economy of the United States as the mainspring of expansion. Thus the basic configuration of the American economy was drastically altered in comparison to what it had been in the first generation of national independence.

The main stimulants of economic expansion before the War of 1812 had been the export and carrying trades. Between 1790 and 1807, the value of exports rose fivefold from $20.2 million to $108.3 million. A major portion of this impressive expansion of exports came from the rapid development of the re-export trade, consisting largely of West Indian goods carried to the markets of Europe in American vessels. While the value of domestic exports doubled between 1790 and 1807, re-exports increased from $0.3 million to $59.6 million in the same period; in 1807 indeed, the value of re-exports actually exceeded by $11 million the value of domestic exports.

Precarious Prosperity During Napoleonic Wars

Nevertheless, the unequalled American prosperity that resulted from the tremendous growth of the re-export trade was a precarious one; it was highly dependent on the national policies of the warring powers of Europe. Consequently, much of the economic expansion was halted when England and France began to tighten their blockade policies, and particularly when the Jefferson administration adopted a policy of economic retaliation. The Embargo Act not only caused an economic collapse in the United States, but also foreshadowed new directions of economic development. Never again did the export and carrying trade return to its former position of primacy in the national economy. To be sure, there was a notable recovery of export trade after the War of 1812, but it was no longer an expansive force in the structure of the economy; it functioned chiefly as a factor in America's balance of payments.

The failure of the export and carrying trades to achieve anything more than a partial recovery had a depressing effect for a time on the economic growth of the nation. Even the domestic manufactures that had multiplied so rapidly after the Embargo did not seem to offer much hope for an alternative use of capital and resources because English manufactured goods, which had been kept out of the American market during the war years, were dumped on the American market in huge quantities after 1815. The newly developed American manufacturing industries simply could not compete successfully with the superior technological and marketing skills of their English competitors. Hence the years immediately after the War of 1812 were years of painful readjustment for many merchants and manufacturers in New England and the middle states.

Only the cotton trade showed signs of vigorous profitability; and it was in the South that signs of prosperity and expansion were most striking. The demand of the English textile industry for raw cotton was in excess of supply; as a result, the price of cotton rose from 20 cents to 29 cents a pound in the year after the Treaty of Ghent, and remained at slightly higher levels until 1818. Such attractive prices caused a notable shift toward cotton production in older southern states such as Georgia and South Carolina, while speculative capital was drawn into land sales and cotton production in the new lands of Alabama, Mississippi, and Louisiana. At the same time, foreign buyers, especially the British, began to purchase large quantities of wheat, flour, and tobacco, at attractive prices, so that agriculture and commerce in the North and the West began to enjoy their most prosperous years since the Embargo and the wartime blockade had disrupted the export and carrying trades.

Other factors also contributed to the growing speculative boom in the South and the West. The number of state banks had grown tremendously in the interval between the expiration of the charter of the First Bank of the United States of 1811 and the chartering of the Second Bank in 1816. By 1816 there were 246 state banks in existence, eager to extend liberal credit to the multitude of enterprises associated with the expansion of agriculture and commerce, and the purchase of new lands in the South and West. The note issues of these state banks rose by more than 50 per cent from 1815 to 1816. Moreover, the newly created Bank of the United States refrained from exercising any pressure against excessive note issues by the state banks; in fact, by 1818, the Bank of the United States had added to the inflationary pressures in the national economy by placing $8 million of its own notes in circulation, and making loans of over $41 million.

The inevitable break in the speculative bubble began in the autumn of 1818. With the return of good harvests in England and Europe, the market for American foodstuffs collapsed and grain prices tumbled rapidly downward. At the same time, a severe readjustment of the general price level set in as the expansion of output in the whole European economy that had taken place after the Napoleonic Wars began to exceed demand. The rapid deflation of prices caused a financial and industrial crisis in England; hence English creditors ceased to extend their loans to American exporters and producers, and pressed payment on those already due. In the face of such pressures, prices for American cotton, which had been the most glamorous commodity in the economic boom, dropped in a spectacular fashion.

As a consequence, the greatly overextended credit system in the United States was badly strained. Loans extended on the basis of 20 or 30 cent cotton in the South could not be collected on nine cent cotton. Other farming regions were equally hard pressed as the American economy plummeted into its most severe financial panic since the winning of independence. Many of the state banks failed, and the Bank of the United States avoided bankruptcy only by sharply contracting its loans—a policy that necessarily served to aggravate the deflationary debacle.

The agricultural sector of the economy was particularly hard hit. Sharply collapsing prices wiped out farm purchasing power, and the bank notes that were circulating became greatly depreciated as many of the state banks teetered on the brink of bankruptcy. Unable to make payments on their loans contracted during good times, distressed farmers sought help from their state legislatures. In the South and West several state legislatures enacted relief laws designed to extend the time of mortgage payments; Kentucky created a state-owned Bank of the Commonwealth authorized to issue paper money without specie backing in a desperate effort to create an adequate money supply for hard-pressed debtors.

But the farmers of the West and South were not the only victims of the panic of 1819; the resulting economic depression soon affected every sector of the national economy. Mathew Carey, a prominent spokesman for industrial and banking interests in Philadelphia, pictured the situation in that eastern city in darkest terms: ". . . the enlivening sound of the spindle, the loom, and the hammers has in many places almost ceased to be heard . . . our merchants and traders are daily swept away by bankruptcy one after another . . . our banks are drained of specie . . . our cities exhibit an unvarying scene of gloom and despair. . . ."

Although by 1821 there was a gradual recovery from the severe depression that followed the panic of 1819, all the available economic indexes indicate that the rate of growth in the national economy was relatively slow in the twenties. The following decade, on the other hand, was one of rising prices with sharp but brief downward fluctuations in 1834, 1837, and 1839. Moreover, the general pattern of economic advance was based on a genuine productive expansion, despite the fact that the economic boom of the thirties was jolted by financial panics in 1837 and 1839.

The Economic Boom of the 1830's

Cotton played a leading role in this movement of economic advance. After a full decade of low prices and low profits, the price of raw cotton soared; in the Charleston market, cotton rose from a level of 6.5 cents to 20.5 cents between 1831 and 1836. During those same years, the value of cotton exports rose from $25 to $71 million. The increased profitability of cotton production led to a new surge of government land sales in such new southern states as Alabama, Mississippi, Louisiana, Arkansas, and Florida. Consequently, a notable shift of planters and slaves from the old South to these new states took place. Net emigration from South Carolina during the decade of the thirties has been estimated at 65,031 whites and 56,683 blacks. The movement of black slaves from Virginia to the new cotton lands of the lower South was even greater; the *Virginia*

Times estimated the export of slaves from that state at 40,000 in the single year of 1836.

The spectacular boom in the cotton lands of the South was an impetus to expansion in other sectors of the economy. The steadily increasing demand for foodstuffs for the expanding plantation population of the lower South stimulated the movement of settlers into the entire Mississippi valley region. The annual income from farmers near the Ohio and other tributary rivers found a profitable market for their foodstuffs shipped down the Mississippi River to New Orleans and other river ports. The value of products shipped down the Mississippi in the late twenties averaged a little over $20 million a year; by 1837 it had increased to a total of $45.6 million. In the Northeast, the financial, transport, and marketing services associated with the cotton trade also prospered; northern manufacturers discovered a growing demand in the South for their cotton goods, shoes, and farm implements. Thus, the boom in cotton exports played a strategic role in the quickening of economic activity; if there ever was a time when cotton was king in the American economy, the decade of the thirties was it.

While the era of expansion between 1831 and 1839 was notable for the multitude of enterprises in every field—in the raising of cash crops by farmers and planters, in the manufacture of cottons, woolens, shoes and leather products, iron and machinery, in the construction of canals, turnpikes, and bridges, and in the building of houses, stores, churches, schools, and courthouses for the rapidly growing communities of the eastern and western states—the growth of financial and investment functions was particularly striking. State banks grew at a phenomenal

The I. N. Phelps Stokes Collection of American Historical Prints. Prints Division. The New York Public Library.

rate. From 1820 to 1830, the number of state banks had increased only slightly, from 307 to 330, and their issue of bank notes had expanded from $44.9 million to $61.3 million. In the next seven years, however, the number of state banks more than doubled reaching the high total of 778 in 1837, with a bank note circulation of $149 million.

Many of these state banks were wildcat enterprises, with insufficient specie reserves to back their overextended note issues. Consequently, the country was flooded with a bewildering variety of state bank notes, many of them circulating at large discounts. The Bank of the United States tried for a time to restrain state bank note issues by continually presenting such notes to the bank of issue for redemption in specie. But after 1834, when President Jackson's war on the Bank had drastically impaired its credit control functions, the Bank of the United States joined in the unrestrained competition to furnish credit for the rising volume of land sales in the West and the increased business activity everywhere.

Other techniques for the raising and investment of capital were multiplying at the same time. The corporation, which had become a favorite device of business organization for banking, insurance, turnpike, and bridge companies before 1815, became increasingly popular in manufacturing, particularly as the scale of operations expanded in the cotton and woolen factories. In the New England states alone, 591 corporation charters were granted to manufacturing and mining companies in the period from 1800 to 1830, 803 from 1831 to 1843, and 1,853 in the years from 1844 to 1862. This rapid increase clearly foretold the coming of the corporate age in American business, even though most American manufacturing before 1860 was still carried on by small units organized as individual proprietorships, family enterprises, or partnerships.

The corporate form of business organization made it possible to secure capital from a larger number of persons than could be brought together in a family enterprise or partnership. The corporation also provided a flexibility of ownership and control that resulted from its transferable shares of stock. And when the states began to grant the privilege of limited liability, an even greater number of people were willing to risk their capital in such ventures. In 1830 a Massachusetts statute granted limited liability for corporate stockholders and, subsequently, other states adopted the same legal principle.

The multiplication of stock issues that resulted from the rapid growth of corporations led to the appearance of private banks and brokerage houses that began to specialize in the marketing of such securities. One of the leading brokerage houses in the 1830's was Astor and Sons, founded by John Jacob Astor, who had become one of the wealthiest men in America through his land speculations and the activities of the American Fur Company. A New York Stock Exchange was organized as early as 1817, but extensive daily transactions in shares did not characterize its operations until the 1830's. By that time, also, the Boston Stock

Exchange was establishing its undisputed leadership in the sale of industrial securities, a position that was maintained until the Civil War.

Thus American business enterprise after 1830 was moving more rapidly than ever before toward new techniques of management and toward patterns of ownership in the form of paper securities. The quick infusion of transferable shares into the investment and credit structure undoubtedly added to the speculative zest of Americans in the economic boom of the 1830's. Furthermore, a tremendous volume of securities, mostly state bonds issued to finance public improvements, flooded the American market in 1836. English investors, including many English joint-stock banks, were attracted by such speculative opportunities, and a significant portion of the Bank of England's specie reserve was drained away to the capital markets of the United States.

The Panic of 1837   Alarmed by the declining specie reserve, the Bank of England began to raise its discount rates late in 1836, and in the early months of the following year it refused to rediscount the bills of some leading British mercantile firms that had greatly overextended their credits against the shipments of the cotton crop of 1836. This sudden curtailment of credit resulted in a chain of contractions that affected banking and commercial houses on the other side of the Atlantic. Cotton prices fell precipitously; by the middle of March, leading cotton brokers in New Orleans and New York were bankrupt; on May 10, the New York banks suspended specie payments and the banks of Boston and Philadelphia soon followed suit. President Jackson's Specie Circular of July 16, 1836, requiring that all payments for public lands be made in gold or silver, further aggravated the deflationary crisis. In the spring and summer of 1837, a large number of commercial failures and a general stagnation of business brought the prosperous boom to a crashing halt.

The Panic of 1837, however, was an interruption and not an end to the forces of economic expansion; the chief sufferers were banking and commercial houses that were most vulnerable to the contraction of credit that resulted from the Bank of England's deflationary policy. The sharp drop in cotton prices, moreover, reflected a readjustment in American price levels that had gone too far out of line in comparison with foreign prices, rather than a large increase in cotton production. The prices of western grains held up well throughout 1837 and 1838 and, by the spring of 1838, cotton prices were rising again. The improving profitability of cotton and western staples encouraged a new flow of British capital and credit to the United States, with the result that large issues of state bonds for internal improvements were selling as briskly in 1838 as they had two years earlier.

Economic Depression,   In the summer of 1839, a second crisis, more severe and more
1839–1843   fundamental than that of 1837, struck the American economy. The Bank of the United States, deeply involved in disastrous speculations in cotton, suspended specie payments in October, and other banks soon

followed. Prices of all commodities plunged downward; the depression which followed was one of several years duration. This time, economic recovery was not mainly a matter of readjusting unrealistic credit policies and price levels because the sharp rise in the output of cotton and western staples from 1838 to 1839 had created a fundamental imbalance between productivity and effective demand.

The depression of 1839 to 1843, therefore, was one of the most severe in the history of the United States. Prices continued their downward course for four years: between 1839 and 1843, wholesale prices declined about 25 per cent at Philadelphia, 40 per cent at New York, and more than 50 per cent at New Orleans. The total amount of public lands sold by the government shrank to less than 6 per cent of the acreage sold in the peak year of 1836.

Farmers were particularly hard hit since agricultural prices declined more drastically than those for manufactured products. Nevertheless, actual suffering was not as great as in later American depressions because most farmers, even those who were heavily involved in the market economy, were more or less self-sufficient; in the South, indeed, many cotton planters shifted some of their arable acreage to the production of corn and hogs in order to feed their families and field hands.

By 1843, the depression had run its course and the American economy moved into a long cycle of growth that continued without serious setbacks for 14 years. Developing slowly at first, the new surge of expansion quickened tremendously in the last years of the 1840's and continued into the 1850's.

Several fundamental factors contributed to this sustained economic advance. The enormous land acquisitions by the United States whetted the economic appetites of American investors—by adding Texas in 1845, Oregon in 1846, California and the Southwest in 1848, and the Gadsden Purchase in 1854, the continental boundaries of the United States were rounded out, and a vast area of rich resources was added to the natural abundance already available for exploitation by the American people. The California gold rush was a showy symbol of the new opportunities that were beckoning men and capital toward the underdeveloped areas of the national domain. As the economy rode forward on its tremendous wave of expansion, immigration and the natural fertility of the native population helped to fill up the Mississippi valley and to establish the first settlements in the Far West.

The Economic Boom of the 1850's

One of the most recent studies of American commodity output suggests that the decade, 1844 to 1854, was one of remarkable growth compared to the decennial rate of increase for the rest of the nineteenth century. According to Robert E. Gallman, there was a general rate of increase of 69 per cent (based on 1879 prices) for the years from 1844 to 1854. This remarkable rate of growth was not to be exceeded again (and then only slightly) until 1874 to 1884. Gallman's figures show that the rate of manufacturing output increased most rapidly between 1844 and 1849, while agriculture, mining, and construction had their highest rate of increase in the next five years. Specifically, the value added to American commodities of manufacturing, from 1844 to 1849, increased nearly 70 per cent, while the quinquennial rates of increase for agriculture, mining, and construction, for the years 1849 to 1854, were approximately 33, 50, and 75 per cent respectively. The steady growth of agriculture during this period indicates that cotton was still an important influence in the American economy as it had been in previous decades; but it was clear that cotton was no longer king—other economic activities had become the strategic carriers of economic growth.

It was the new capital investment in factories, ships, telegraph lines, and railroads that stimulated economic expansion during the long cycle of growth after 1843. The role of railroad investment was particularly significant though it had been a minor factor in the American economy before 1840. By 1850, railroad construction had commanded a capital outlay of $372 million; in the next seven years an additional $600 million was invested in railroad construction, making the total investment in American railroads approximately one billion dollars. The accelerating impact of these totals can be imagined when we remember that five times as much capital was invested in railroads between 1850 and 1857 as there was in transportation improvements represented by canal construction during the whole period from 1816 to 1840.

A severe financial panic in 1857 brought a temporary halt to a long continued wave of new investment in railroad building and other productive activities. Sources of capital in Europe were drying up and new investments by American enterprises were discouraged by increasing evidence of declining profitability in the new productive equipment that had been built so rapidly in the 1850's. In the summer of 1857, a number of leading New England textile mills closed down because of lack of demand for their product. By the end of August, the decline in business confidence had become a panic; a significant number of banks, railroads, and commercial firms failed and, by October 14, most banks throughout the country had suspended their specie payments.

For a time, it seemed that the panic of 1857 might lead to consequences as severe and as prolonged as those associated with the crisis of 1839. This time, however, the monetary effects were less severe; gold flowed into the banks promptly from California and abroad, and specie payments were resumed by most of the banks in the country early in 1858. By 1859 to 1860, conditions were considerably improved, particularly in the manufacturing activities of the Northeast. Thus the American economy was achieving a position of great resiliency, its role as a manufacturing nation was assured, and the rapid development of its agricultural domain continued to be sustained by the growing demand for American food and fibers in the markets of Europe and the Far East.

The Transportation Revolution

The spectacular growth of the American economy from 1815 to 1860 was based upon revolutionary changes in economic behavior that brought the major portion of American productive activities into an intricately interdependent market economy. Before the War of 1812, less than half of the American population was significantly involved in the web of transactions, motives, and expectations that are associated with a market economy. In fact, as the population flowed into the backcountry regions of the seaboard states and into the more remote interior of the country after the Revolution, an increasing number of farmers were added to the more backward sector of the economy that was based upon self-sufficient activities. The farmer and his family, like their colonial forebears, raised a variety of grains, fruits, vegetables, and livestock, and kept up a busy round of household manufacturing activities by which they made their furniture, clothing, utensils, and farm equipment. The lack of roads and other means of transportation kept them out of the profitable activities associated with urban and overseas trade, and separated them from the commercial spirit of those who were linked to the market economy.

The Need for Improved Transportation

Only those farmers who were near the seaport cities, or whose lands lay along navigable rivers, were able to produce tobacco, cotton, timber, grain, and other products for overseas markets. Such farmers were part of the staple-exporting sector of the American economy and their economic destinies were closely tied to the carrying trade which was organized so successfully by the enterprising merchants in the leading commercial centers of the Atlantic seaboard.

As late as the War of 1812, the transportation of bulky goods over appreciable distances by land was prohibitively expensive. In 1816 a ton of goods could be brought three thousand miles from Europe to America for almost nine dollars, but for the same sum it could be moved only 30 miles over the wretched roads that were available. The merchants of Northampton, Massachusetts, found that it was cheaper to ship their grain to Boston over a circuitous water route of three hundred miles down the Connecticut River and around Cape Cod, even though the direct overland distance was only one hundred miles. In the year that the Erie Canal was authorized, 1817, a committee of the New York legislature reported that the cost of transporting wheat from Buffalo to New York City was three times the market price, for corn it was six times, and for oats it was twelve times the market price. It is little wonder then that the national market economy remained only a thin shell enclosing an underdeveloped, self-sufficing agrarian heartland.

Such economic constraints presented a challenge to the merchant capitalists who were already enjoying the profits of the market economy. Their restless pursuit of wealth made them anxious to extend the range of their marketing activities to include the large numbers of Americans who were moving into the interior of the country, particularly into the trans-Appalachian West; indeed, the population of the country beyond the Applachians doubled between 1810 and 1820, and doubled again in the following decade. Thus the dynamic energies that had developed earlier in the staple-exporting and carrying trade sectors of the economy were ready to furnish much of the impetus for the revolutionary improvements in transportation that brought most of American economic activity within the enveloping web of a national market system before 1850.

Turnpike Builders

The first efforts to extend internal commerce were made in the construction of improved roads which were typically built by private joint-stock companies or chartered corporations. In 1794, such a company chartered by the Pennsylvania legislature built a graded and paved road on which tolls were charged from Lancaster to Philadelphia. The excellence of the Lancaster Turnpike and its financial success stimulated the building of similar toll roads. By the War of 1812 most of the major cities in the Northeast were connected by turnpikes and, after the war, the turnpike craze began to spread into the West. Most of these turnpikes were financed by the private capital of merchants, manufacturers, and farmers, particularly in those regions that would benefit most directly. In Pennsylvania, Virginia, and Ohio, the state governments invested public money in the stocks of turnpike companies as a way of granting a partial subsidy. In South Carolina before 1830, and in Indiana, turnpikes were built and completely financed by the state.

The most spectacular of all of the turnpikes was a project of the federal

Conestoga Wagon, 14 feet in length, c. 1800. Chicago Historical Society.

government—the National Road. This road was started in 1815 at Cumberland, Maryland, and was extended gradually westward during the first half of the nineteenth century; by 1818, the road had reached Wheeling, by 1833, Columbus, Ohio, and by about 1850, further construction was abandoned when Vandalia, Illinois, had been reached. The National Road project was hampered by political problems throughout its history—constitutional objections were raised in Congress, the possibility of presidential vetoes threatened every step of its development, and sectional jealousies continually raised further barriers.

Wherever they were well built and properly maintained, the turnpikes were a great improvement. When traveling by either carriage or stage coach, the relatively smooth roads provided added comfort and convenience; for the thousands of migrants pushing westward, the new roads reduced the hardships which had to be borne. In addition, the costs of wagon hauling were reduced wherever the toll-roads were kept in good repair. But it was soon apparent that the turnpikes could not solve the problems of cheap transportation. Their economic benefits were limited to short hauls; for long freight hauls, their costs were still prohibitive.

Much more important, particularly in the great distances of the West, was the introduction of the steamboat. The early settlers in the Ohio Valley had floated their goods in flatboats down the tributary rivers and the Mississippi to New Orleans. Journeys of a thousand or two thousand miles were not unusual and the down river trip alone might take a month or six weeks. To return upriver took four times as long; keelboats and barges had to be poled, rowed, and towed in a slow backbreaking fashion. The expense of such upriver transportation was so great as to limit the possibility of any extensive return flow of commerce in exchange for the goods floated down the river.

Steamboats and Internal Commerce

The solution to this problem came with the development of the steamboat by Robert Fulton and John Stevens: Fulton's successful demonstration took place on the Hudson River in 1807, and that of John Stevens occurred two years later on the Delaware. Within a few years, successful steamboat companies were organized and financed by eastern capitalists and, by 1820, there were already 60 steamboats on the Mississippi and its larger tributary rivers. A decade later, the steamboat was the dominant means of transportation on the western rivers; by 1860, there were more than a thousand steamboats operating in the Mississippi River system alone. By 1860, also, steamboats were moving freight approximately five times as fast as they could be moved by wagon, and it is estimated that downstream freight rates had declined to about 25 or 30 per cent of what they had been in 1815, while upstream rates were averaging only 5 to 10 per cent of their levels in 1815 to 1819.

As the steamboat was vastly extending the effective range of the market economy in the West, other forms of water transportation were being constructed to link the East and the West. In 1817 the New York

Canal Building

TRAVELLING ON THE ERIE CANAL.

legislature, urged on by Governor DeWitt Clinton, authorized the
construction of the Erie Canal along a route from Albany on the Hudson
River to Buffalo on Lake Erie. The completion of the 364-mile canal by
1825 was an epic undertaking that had an immediate and far-reaching
influence on the development of a national marketing system. Traffic on
the new canal was so heavy that the tolls paid for the cost of construction
in nine years. More important, the Erie Canal became a major stimulant
to the developing market revolution as a flood of western grains and
foodstuffs flowed eastward in exchange for the eastern and European
manufactured goods that poured westward to satisfy the insatiable
desires of a rapidly growing population seeking to acquire the comforts
and conveniences of civilization.

The success of the Erie Canal set off a nationwide craze for canal
building. Pennsylvania built a competing canal system, with a spectacular portage railroad over the highest ridge of the Alleghanies, linking
Philadelphia with Pittsburg. Elsewhere in the eastern states, canals were
built primarily to improve transportation between the upcountry and the
coastal ports; while in the West, they were built primarily to connect the
Ohio-Mississippi River system with the Great Lakes.

Whereas the capital that was needed for the largest turnpike companies rarely exceeded a few hundred thousand dollars, a canal of any
appreciable size required capital expenditures of several millions of
dollars. The Pennsylvania "main line" canal system to Pittsburg cost
over $10 million to build. The initial investment in the Erie Canal was
about $7 million, and in the 1840's and 1850's, an additional $44,500,000
was invested to enlarge and rebuild the Erie Canal system. Between 1816
and 1840, about $125 million was spent for the construction of canals in
the United States totalling 3,326 miles; by 1860, an additional $75 million
was invested to improve and extend the existing canal systems.

These huge capital needs could not be satisfied by the resources of private investors in the national economy. Consequently, the canals were financed to a great extent through public aid. Indeed, the great contribution of New York to the canal building era was not limited to the engineering accomplishments of the Erie Canal; the example of New York also demonstrated that large amounts of public capital could easily be raised for public works through the sale of state bonds. Thus, a virtual revolution took place in the management and use of public credit in the second quarter of the nineteenth century: the amount of state bonds issued from 1820 to 1824 had been only $13 million, by 1835 to 1837 it had risen to $180 million; and it is estimated that over $60 million of the latter sum had been raised for canal construction. Almost every state in the union had pledged a substantial amount of public credit to canal building, either in state-owned and operated canals, or through the purchase of shares in privately owned canals. Moreover, although Congress had earlier refused to aid New York in the building of the Erie Canal, it later made substantial contributions toward the construction of other canals. By 1860 the federal government had granted about four million acres of the public domain to western canal projects, and had subscribed over $3 million to the stock of canal companies, primarily the Chesapeake and Ohio Canal. Likewise, countless local governmental units, counties, towns, and cities purchased stock in private canal ventures.

Thus the canal building era was a critical stage in the market revolution. Not only did the canals provide an interim solution to the problem of hauling bulky goods over long distances, but the financing of the canals also stimulated the more rapid development of sophisticated techniques of capital formation, and greatly extended the fruitful rela-

Collection of Regional History. University Archives. Cornell University.

NEW-YORK
CANAL LANDS
ON SALE.

THE unsold part of that extensive tract bounded on the *East end of Lake Ontario,* extending North from the mouth of *Salmon River,* to the Towns of *Henderson* and *Adams,* watered by the *Big Sandy* and *Little Sandy* Creeks, and their innumerable tributary streams; every part of the tract being within one day's easy drive of the *Erie Canal,* at the Village of Rome, and at Salt Point or Salina, and will be accessible to it by water, (from the outlets on the Lake) as soon as it shall be united to the Lake at *Oswego,* which it is supposed it will be in two years.

That part of the tract more particularly recommended to the notice of Settlers of industrious and steady habits, includes the Town of *Ellisburgh,* and number one of *Lorraine,* forming the south-west part of the *County of Jefferson;* and the Township No. 10, of *Richland,* north of Salmon River, and *Nos. 6, 7, and 11, of Orwell,* making the north part of the *County of Oswego.*

It contains about two hundred thousand acres, more than one half of which is now under actual improvement, and a great portion of it paid for and deeded; and having been from 10 to 15 years regularly advancing in settlement, has a numerous population, and possesses most of the advantages of old countries, as to schools, public worship, mills, distilleries, mechanics, manufactures, &c

Betterments, or partially cleared farms, may be had reasonably. The price of wild lands has always been held very moderate, and will be continued so until the whole are settled. A reasonable chance as to pay will be afforded, and the same fair and liberal treatment toward settlers, as has been heretofore practised, will be continued, of which information can be best obtained on the spot.

The present price (the choice as to quality allowed to the pu-

tionship between private and public credit. To be sure, some of the canals, both public and private, suffered from poor business management, others were based upon unrealistic calculations, and speculation in canal stocks tended to increase the difficulty of having a fair return. Nevertheless, the financing of the canals broke down many traditional psychological barriers to the use of public and private credit on such a large scale, and prepared the way for the enormous capital requirements of the railroads.

The Development of Railroads

It was the steam railroad, rather than the steamboat or the canal, that provided the most successful means of conquering the vast distances in the great interior market of the United States. There were great areas of virgin forest, grassy plains, and high mountains, where water transportation was not available or feasible; only some method of transportation by land—cheap, fast, and reasonably ubiquitous—could bring such areas into the enveloping net of the market revolution. The timely invention of a method of steam locomotion on iron rails provided Americans with the effective means to transform the structure of their economy.

First developed in England where its commercial feasibility was demonstrated in 1829, railroads grew rapidly in the United States. A few short lines were already being developed in the early 1830's by such important commercial cities as Baltimore, Charleston, and Boston where there was little hope of developing any inland waterway connections. By the end of the decade, other coastal and interior cities were enthusiastically building railroad lines to develop nearby market areas.

In 1840 there were already about 3,300 miles of railroad in operation in the United States compared to 1,800 miles in all of Europe. A few of the larger Atlantic states had appreciable mileages, but in most states railroads still lagged behind canals. In the next two decades, however, railroad construction drew ahead of canal building by leaps and bounds: in 1850 there were 8,879 miles of railroads compared to 3,698 miles of canals; by 1860 railway mileage in the United States exceeded 30,000 miles, whereas canal mileage was actually declining.

In addition to the fourfold increase in railway mileage, the 1850's were also notable for a marked tendency on the part of railroad promoters to combine short lines into larger systems. By 1860, all the major market cities of the North had been linked together by railroad lines, and the first trunk lines connecting the East and the West were already completed. The Erie Railroad had connected New York City with Lake Erie, seven smaller lines were combined to connect Albany and Buffalo in what was to become the nucleus of the New York Central system, the Pennsylvania Railroad had already become a unified system between Philadelphia and Pittsburg, and the Baltimore and Ohio had reached the Ohio Valley. Although no unified system linked any of the key eastern cities with Chicago or St. Louis, connecting railroad lines for those western trading centers were available for the goods and passengers moving over the four trunk lines that had penetrated the Appalachian barrier.

The building of such an impressive railway net in a little more than two decades was made possible by generous grants of public aid. This is not to say that private enterprise was laggard or unimaginative. On the contrary, no other form of economic activity received such enthusiastic support from private investors as the railroads. Furthermore, Americans of every sort and condition understood that the investment of capital in a railroad would have a great multiplier effect on the productivity and the prosperity of an area served by railroad transportation. Farmers, manufacturers, and mine owners expected better prices and a larger volume of sales; landowners and land speculators expected real estate values to rise; merchants, middlemen, and bankers expected to augment their profits; and even the consumers expected to get more for their money in the variety and quality of goods available. Nevertheless, despite such rising expectations, there was simply not enough private capital that could be mobilized to build 30,000 miles of railroads in a single generation. Hence, the Americans who were most directly affected by the spirit of enterprise demanded that their federal, state, and local governments ally themselves with private enterprise to quicken the tempo of economic progress.

The state governments contributed their aid to the rapid development of the railroad in several ways. In the first place they granted to the railroad companies charters that contained sweeping privileges. In addition to the privilege of limited liability that was available to corporations in other fields of economic activity, the railroad charters usually granted special privileges of eminent domain; many charters also exempted railroads from taxation for long periods of time—sometimes, the railroads were given lottery and banking privileges to help raise the capital needed. To be sure, many of the railroad charters imposed limitations on the freight rates to be charged, but these were so loosely drawn as to impose no burden at all.

But much more important than special charter privileges was the tremendous amount of direct financial aid given to private railroad companies by state and local governments. A study of the debt structure of the American states reveals that, in the 15 years before the Civil War, state governments had borrowed more than $90 million mainly to finance railroad construction. In addition, it has been estimated that local and municipal contributions equalled about one-fifth of the construction costs of the railroads before 1870.

No section of the country exhibited more enthusiasm than the West for this new form of transportation. The men who controlled the state legislatures and the local governments in the West firmly believed that the railroad was the key to prosperity and the growth of civilization in the newly settled areas. Up to 1857, Missouri authorized loans of nearly $25 million to railroads, and in the very first year of statehood, Minnesota loaned $5 million to four railroads in the state. By 1860 Texas had made loans of $2 million and had given about five million acres of lands to encourage railroad building within the state.

Western political pressure was also influential in the development of the first federal land grants to subsidize railroad construction. In 1850, the first significant federal land grant was made to the Illinois Central Railroad, which was planned as a great north-south trunk line that would extend from northern Illinois to Mobile, Alabama. The land grants to this project totalled 3,736,005 acres and, before the decade was over, Congress had granted another 18 million acres to 10 states, to be used for the aid of 45 railroads.

By the 1850's the railroad had definitely triumphed over other forms of transportation. Furthermore, steam railroads were moving freight five times as fast as was usual by wagon or by canal boat. In 1817, goods could be shipped most expeditiously from Cincinnati to New York first by keelboat to Pittsburg, then by wagon to Philadelphia, and finally by wagon or river to New York; generally, such shipments required more than 50 days to reach their destination. By the early 1850's, the same shipment could be moved from Cincinnati to New York over the Ohio Canal, the Erie Canal, and the Hudson River in 18 days; by steam railroad it took only 6 to 8 days. In 1815, the lowest freight rates by wagon averaged about 30 cents per ton mile; by the 1850's, the freight rates for railroads averaged 2 to 9 cents per ton mile, and on canals they averaged about 1 to 3 cents per ton mile.

Sectional Economic Patterns

Such remarkable changes in the speed and cost of transporting bulky goods transformed the structure of the American economy. The most immediate consequence of the transportation revolution was the spectacular expansion of commercial agriculture in all sections of the country. With each passing decade, the self-sufficing agrarian sector of the economy shrank in relative size and importance, as farmers shifted their production to those staples that they could produce most efficiently in order to maximize their chances for profit in the national market economy. Increasingly, therefore, the American economy began to develop along the lines of regional specialization which can be most conveniently analyzed in terms of three reasonably distinct, yet interdependent, sections—the South, the West, and the Northeast.

The Economic Structure of the South   The South had already been a staple-exporting region even in the colonial period of American development when tobacco, rice, and indigo production had been profitable forms of activity in the plantation economy of the tidewater regions from Maryland to Georgia. After the American Revolution, cotton became the most profitable staple crop largely because England, and then New England, developed the machinery for the rapid manufacture of cheap cotton cloth. Furthermore, the invention of the cotton gin by Eli Whitney in 1797 solved the problem of separating cotton fibers from the seeds, and opened the way for the spread of cotton production into the interior of Georgia and South Carolina, and then into the rich southwestern lands extending from Alabama to Texas. Cotton production rose from 3,135 bales in 1790 to a staggering total of 3,847,402 bales in 1860.

Although cotton was clearly the dominant crop in the South, there were other important staples in the expanding sector of southern commercial agriculture. Rice culture continued to be profitable in the coastal region of South Carolina and Georgia; tobacco production flourished in new areas of North Carolina, Kentucky, Tennessee, and Missouri; hemp, used for baling cotton, became a profitable crop in Kentucky and Missouri; while a booming sugar plantation economy developed in Louisiana after the War of 1812.

In the production of these staple commodities, other salient features of the southern economy were developed or strengthened. In general, large-scale organization, reflecting important economies of scale, had a clear advantage over smaller units of production. In cotton, sugar, and rice production, particularly, large amounts of labor and land provided the lowest unit cost of production. In the expanding market economy, the large plantation owner using a considerable number of black slaves had an important advantage over small farmers using few or no slaves. According to a recent analysis of the economies of slavery, the crop value per slave rose from $14.68 in 1802 to $101.09 in 1860; thus the continued rise in the price of slaves in the same period may be taken to represent a rational calculation of the profitability of the slave labor system.

The spread of cotton production into the more fertile lands of the Southwest, from Alabama to Texas, tended to increase the advantages of large-scale production, particularly in cotton. In addition there were other differences between the plantations in the new South and those in the old South; not only were production costs lower in the new states, but plantation operations were generally more specialized than in the old South. The relative cheapness of western foodstuffs shipped down the rivers of the Mississippi valley enabled the planter in the Southwest to keep all his best land in cotton. Because of the high transportation costs of western foodstuffs across the mountains planters in the seaboard South kept a greater portion of their lands in corn to supply food for the slave labor force. As a result there was a gradual shift toward a greater diversification of agricultural operations in the seaboard South during the years of depressed prices in the 1840's. Northern Virginia became an area of general farming; in North Carolina, there was a visible increase in wheat and corn production, although tobacco continued to be a major cash crop; in South Carolina, farmers began to raise greater amounts of livestock.

While the cleavage between the commercial and the self-sufficing sectors of agriculture was rapidly diminishing elsewhere, the economic advantages of large-scale organization in the production of southern staples tended to keep a large part of the remaining segment of southern farming in the more primitive state that characterized the majority of American farmers at the end of the eighteenth century. Only a small minority of the southern white population owned substantial numbers of slaves; in 1860, probably not more than 400,000 out of 8,000,000 southern whites were slaveholders and, of these, 277,000 held fewer than 10 slaves apiece. The great majority of southern farmers owned no slaves at all, and a large percentage of this group made very little cash income; in short, there seemed to be very little tendency for them to be pulled into the market economy, even on a local scale. The large planters either raised their own foodstuffs, or bought the cheap and plentiful western foodstuffs.

The economic situation of the South that was shaped in response to the market revolution was backward in other respects also. There was a notable lag in urbanization over the entire area. Only the few ports that were significant in the cotton trade (Charleston, Savannah, Mobile, and New Orleans) seemed to follow the pattern of urban growth elsewhere in the country, particularly after 1830. At the same time, industrialization was conspicuously lower in the South than elsewhere. Even the retail trade, the most rudimentary of the services associated with a market economy, was significantly laggard. In the enumeration of retail stores that was included in the census of 1840, all southern states except Louisiana were listed at the bottom of the tabulation of retail stores per thousand of population.

These deficiencies in the structure of the southern economy were often obscured by the dazzling profitability of cotton production and the cotton trade; some southern leaders even imagined that the farmers of the Northwest would become the willing satellites of the southern economy. Actually, however, the regional economy of the Northwest was built on a more solid foundation of growth and diversification in the period between 1815 and 1860. The turnpike, the steamboat, the canal, and the railroad had a much greater impact on the economic development of the new states north of the Ohio River, and such border states as Kentucky and Missouri, than similar improvements in the South. Not only was the growth of population more rapid in this region than in the South or Southwest, but a much larger portion of the farmers shifted rapidly out of self-sufficiency into the market economy.

With each successive surge of transportation developments associated with roads, canals, and railroads, commercial wheat production expanded steadily westward from the Susquehanna valley in Pennsylvania, to the Mohawk and Genesee valleys in New York, and then to the fertile lands of Ohio, Indiana, and Illinois. After 1840, a steadily increasing stream of wheat, flour, corn, pork, beef, and livestock was flowing from the farms of the Old Northwest to the markets of the East and the South.

Furthermore, an ever growing portion of this trade in western food-stuffs was being redirected toward eastern markets, and toward European markets via the seaboard cities of the East. The southward shipments of western commodities continued throughout the decades before 1860; but after 1840, the economic destiny of the Northwest became less and less dependent on the down river trade.

The natural advantages of the West made possible a great variety of products for export. In addition to the favorable conditions of soil and climate that gave the region an obvious comparative advantage in the production of wheat, corn, and livestock, westerners began to develop lead mining in Missouri, copper mining in Michigan, and iron mining first near Pittsburg, and then in the Lake Superior area. Throughout the pre-Civil War decades, lumber and other timber products represented another production activity that had profitable export possibilities.

Furthermore, wheat, corn, and livestock could be most efficiently produced in family size farms, given the possibilities of early nineteenth-century agricultural technology. Even such striking improvements as John Deere's steel plow and the McCormick reaper, which were put into factory production in the 1840's and 1850's, did not threaten the position of the family size farm. Such new devices of agricultural technology were still horse-drawn, and fitted easily and naturally into the rhythms of family farm operations. In consequence, large numbers of farmers with relatively small amounts of capital were drawn out of the static relations of self-sufficiency and into the restless pursuit of profit in a market economy.

The increasing specialization of western farmers in cash crops resulted in the appearance of a great variety of subsidiary industries. In view of the primitive methods for food preservation and storage available in the first half of the nineteenth century, there were obvious advantages to processing wheat and corn into flour and corn meal, or whiskey, or preparing ham, bacon, salt beef, and salt pork. Cincinnati became the leading meat packing center of the country—"the Porkopolis of the West"—with Chicago and St. Louis not far behind. In addition, soap and candle making developed as by-products of the meat-packing industry in Cincinnati and elsewhere. In like fashion, promoters in the agricultural machinery and implement industry found it advantageous to locate their manufacturing establishments in the West. John Deere's steel plow was produced in a small factory at Moline, Illinois, and Cyrus McCormick chose Chicago as the location for his reaper plant.

Moreover, the growing amount of cash income received from the market economy affected a large portion of the western population and led to a growing consumer demand for finished products and special services. As soon as a farm family escaped from the primitive economic constraints of self-sufficiency, both the farmer and his wife were less willing to continue the drudgery of the many tasks associated with household manufacturing; manufactured cloth replaced homespun, and woodenware gave way to metal ware. As a result, an impressive number of small industries began to flourish in the towns of the West: blacksmith shops, small machine and tool shops, leather goods shops, printing and publishing shops, retail stores, barber shops, taverns, and the like.

Thus, in contrast to the South, the growing income from the staple-exporting activities and associated processing enterprises was spread widely among the inhabitants of the West and hastened the diversification of the economy. In this respect, the economic structure of the Northwest began to resemble that of the Northeast.

The Mixed Economy of the Northeast

The New England and Middle Atlantic states, to be sure, had developed a considerable diversification of agricultural, commercial, and manufacturing activities even before the market revolution in the nineteenth century. But the revolutionary changes in transportation that linked the Northeast with the Northwest after 1815 forced the farmers, merchants, and artisans to develop new forms of specialization and new methods of production.

Farmers in the less productive soils of the northeastern states found it almost impossible to compete with the more cheaply produced grain and meat products of the Northwest. Hence they turned to producing perishable commodities for which they had a distinct local advantage—fruits, vegetables, poultry, and dairy products. Furthermore, the dense population in eastern towns and cities associated with the development of manufacturing made these local markets for perishables all the more profitable. Many eastern farmers developed improved breeds of wool-bearing sheep to meet the increased demand from an expanding woolen industry in the factory towns of the Northeast; at least until the Civil War, eastern wool raisers were able to hold their own in competition with western wool production.

But the most significant response of the Northeast to the market revolution came in the field of manufacturing. Between 1815 and 1860, the dynamics for the region as a whole shifted from commerce and trade to manufacturing. The tremendous reduction in transportation costs and the extension of the size of the national market economy encouraged the promotion of larger manufacturing plants, with a heavier capital investment in machinery, and the production of large amounts of goods of standardized quality for a mass market. New England led the way in the development of cotton and woolen manufacturing, but cotton and woolen mills began to spring up in the Middle Atlantic States and in the Ohio valley also. Similarly, the boot and shoe industry began to concentrate in New England, particularly Massachusetts, but the primitive conditions of manufacturing enabled small shoemakers serving a localized market to survive in large numbers in the decades prior to the Civil War.

Iron production tended to concentrate in Pennsylvania because of superior natural resources of iron, wool, and coal—by 1860, more than half of the pig iron in the United States was being produced in that state. On the other hand, the various products that were derived from it were more scattered. Bar, sheet, and railroad iron were concentrated in Pennsylvania, while Massachusetts led in iron wire and iron forgings; New York, Pennsylvania, and Massachusetts were the leading states in the production of iron castings.

By the 1840's, manufacturing in the United States began to spurt ahead in a spectacular fashion. In the 1850's a decade of unusually rapid economic growth, cotton textile output increased by 77 per cent; woolens by 42 per cent; carpets by 45 per cent; boots and shoes by 70 per cent; pig iron by 54 per cent; bar, sheet, and railroad iron by 100 per cent; and steam engines and machinery by 66 per cent. New England led the way in this tremendous acceleration of industrial output: between 1850 and 1860, the value of output in New England mills increased 62 per cent, compared to 7 per cent in the Middle Atlantic states, and 10 per cent in the West.

All these regional changes in the structure of the American economy were to have a profound effect on thought and behavior. Political issues tended to become sectional issues, and foreign travellers were quick to discern differences in regional traits of character. Viewed in larger social terms, however, the American society was being transformed by the driving engines of industrial progress; and every region felt the powerful pull of the new forces of industrialization.

The Coming of the Factory System

Behind the cold statistics of industrial progress lay a remarkable transformation in American behavior and American values in the first half of the nineteenth century. Foreign visitors often commented on the "go aheadism" and the eager responsiveness of Americans to shifting economic opportunities. In his classic commentary, *Democracy in America,* Alexis de Tocqueville went so far as to characterize "the pursuit of industrial callings" as the psychic drive that motivated the overwhelming majority of Americans. The high focus on personal advancement was being channeled increasingly toward initiative, originality, and boldness in the use of new manufacturing techniques.

At the end of the War of 1812, most American manufacturing was still in the handicraft stage or in the even more primitive stage of household manufactures. Indeed, much of the increased output of manufactured goods occasioned by the severe restrictions on English imports resulting from the Embargo and the wartime blockade represented an expansion of household production. Especially in the making of textiles and clothing, the farmer's family functioned as an important unit of manufacturing activity. "Plain homespun" clothing became the badge of Ameri-

Household Manufactures and Handicraft Workers

can patriotism; according to estimates made as late as 1820, about two-thirds of the clothing worn in the United States was the product of household manufacture..

In the more densely settled areas of the East, household manufacturing.declined rapidly after 1820; it remained as a practical necessity in the frontier states of the West, but there, too, the decline was quite general following improvements in transportation. By 1860, except for various forms of food preservation, household manufactures had already disappeared in most parts of the country.

Even when household manufacturing was at its peak, a considerable amount of manufacturing was carried on by craftsmen specializing in particular fields of economic activity. Wherever there were villages or towns of sufficient size there were likely to be cobblers, blacksmiths, coopers, tailors, weavers, and others. In 1815 the town of Mount Pleasant, Ohio, with a population of 500, was described by the *Niles Register* as possessing the following manufacturing interests: ". . . 3 saddler's, 3 hatter's, 4 blacksmith's, 4 weaver's, 6 boot and shoemaker's, 8 carpenter's, three tailor's, 3 cabinet maker's, 1 baker's, 1 apothecary's, and 2 wagon maker's shops—2 tanneries; 1 shop for making wool carding machines; 1 with a machine for spinning wool; 1 manufactory for spinning thread from flax; 1 nail factory; 2 wool carding machines." In addition, there were "within a distance of six miles from town—9 merchant mills; 2 grist mills, 12 saw mills, 1 paper mill, with two vats; 1 woolen factory with four looms, and 2 fulling mills." Such enclaves of manufacturing activity carried on in small neighborhood establishments must have been a familiar sight everywhere in the East and the West as soon as the density of population and favorable means of transportation created the first possibilities for market production.

The Growth of Factory Production

In fact, market-oriented production was a prime requisite of the development of a factory system. Many enterprising merchant capitalists, seeking to meet the demands of an expanding market, began to furnish raw materials to men and women who worked in their own homes to produce products which the merchant collected, assembled, and finished if necessary in a central shop. By such methods, merchant capitalists organized the hat-making industry in Danbury, Connecticut, and the boot- and shoe-making industry in eastern Massachusetts. Similarly, the merchant weavers of Philadelphia employed many craftsmen to do home weaving of fine ginghams which were then sold widely in other regions of the country. A putting-out system in ready-made clothing flourished even after the invention of the sewing machine by Elias Howe in 1846, for it was found that most sewing machine work could be done effectively and at low cost by women in their own homes.

Generally speaking, however, new inventions paved the way for the establishment of a factory system in which larger aggregations of workers were assembled in buildings that contained power-driven machines, and where the machines and not the craftsmen controlled the standard and rhythms of work. In such a system, the trend was toward heavy capital investment, the integration of industrial processes, the standardization of production, and the use of unskilled and semi-skilled wage laborers.

Some of these factory characteristics had already appeared in some sections of the iron industry in the later decades of the eighteenth century, but the most dramatic developments of the factory came in the textile industry—a change that was all the more poignant since cloth-making was still strongly associated with the family household for many Americans in the early decades of the nineteenth century.

The technological innovations that enabled the factory to triumph so decisively in the manufacture of cloth had already been developed to a considerable degree in England during the second half of the eighteenth century. American merchant capitalists were eager to borrow the jealously guarded secrets of English textile manufacturing and there were several abortive attempts to establish textile mills shortly after the American Revolution. The first successful introduction of the Cartwright water frame for spinning cotton came when the mercantile partnership of Almy and Brown in Providence, Rhode Island, obtained the services of Samuel Slater, an English emigrant, in setting up a small mill in 1791. By 1815, a considerable number of spinning mills of this type had sprung up in southeastern New England, and were successfully spinning yarn. All of them were small; generally they employed children as well as their parents, and their yarn was put out to weavers in their own homes to be made into cloth.

The factory in its most innovative form, however, appeared in a bold *The Waltham System* new venture, organized at Waltham, Massachusetts, in 1813 under the name of the Boston Manufacturing Company. In that year, Francis Cabot Lowell and a group of wealthy merchants financed the project that involved far-reaching and far-sighted innovations in the techniques of production and of business organization. Indeed, only men of considerable wealth could have financed such a venture inasmuch as $600,000 was poured into the new company in the first six years.

Lowell and his associates built the first fully integrated cotton factory in the United States. In the Waltham plan of factory organization, all the principal processes of cotton cloth production, such as spinning, weaving, bleaching, dyeing, and printing, were carried on in a single plant and under unified management. Such full-scale integration was made possible because Francis Lowell was fortunate enough to secure the services of a talented mechanic, Paul Moody, who perfected a power loom that was superior to English machines for weaving. Such superior technical devices enabled the Boston associates to produce standardized cloth in large quantities for the mass market, and, despite the difficult times following the War of 1812, the Waltham Company was spectacularly successful. The leaders of the Boston Manufacturing Company also developed new techniques of salesmanship by establishing their own marketing agency instead of selling through a large number of local jobbers and commission agents.

Between 1820 and 1850, various members of this group of Boston businessmen and their kinfolk established other factories on the Waltham plan along the swift-moving rivers of New England, notably at Lowell, Lawrence, Manchester, N. H., and other towns on the Merrimack River. The success of these companies stimulated further technological innovations in textile manufacturing. In 1824 Samuel Batchelder perfected a loom that wove pattern fabrics in cotton. In 1828 John Thorp of Providence developed the "ring spinner," improved soon after by William Mason of Taunton, which permitted spindle speeds three times as fast as those in the Arkwright machines developed in England. In 1826 John Goulding invented a cording machine that greatly facilitated the growth of woolen factories; and in 1840 a tremendous advance in woolen manufacturing was made with the development of the Crompton loom at the Middlesex Mills in Lowell. The Crompton loom made possible for the first time the weaving of figures and patterns in woolen cloth, and the new machines came into rapid use both in the United States and England. In a similar fashion, carpet-making which had been almost completely a hand industry was thoroughly revolutionized after 1845 largely because of the power looms invented by Erastus H. Bigelow and developed by the Lowell Manufacturing Company.

The innovative spirit of the Boston associates was apparent in other ways as well. A unique scheme was devised for attracting a large labor force. To tend the machines in their relatively large-scale operations, factories of the Waltham type recruited young women from New England farms and housed them in dormitories and boarding houses erected in the factory towns. These boarding houses were designed not only to provide economical food and shelter for the girls, but also to insure an environment that would overcome the prejudices of rural New Englanders against industrial employment in the new factory towns. Women of highest respectability were placed in charge of the boarding houses, and the standards of behavior required of the operatives were as high as those at the best female seminaries of learning. The factory girls were required to be in their rooms at 10 P.M., to attend church services regularly, and to be exemplary in their moral conduct.

View of Lowell, Massachusetts. The I. N. Phelps Stokes Collection of American Historical Prints. Prints Division. The New York Public Library.

For several decades, the factory town of Lowell with its boarding house for "female operatives" enjoyed the reputation of a model industrial community. High government officials, including President Andrew Jackson, and distinguished foreign travellers such as Charles Dickens, Harriet Martineau, Alexis de Tocqueville, and Michael Chevalier, made Lowell a stopping place on their visits to New England. By the 1840's, however, Lowell was changing. At its center was a depressing slum, and labor in the city was exploited through ruthless cuts in wages. At the same time, moreover, the era of the Waltham-Lowell type of industrialism was passing. Because of the influx of poor Irish immigrants, the geography of industrialism changed as factory owners turned to this source of cheap labor in the slums of Boston and other coastal cities.

Thus, the factory became a familiar part of the New England landscape in the second quarter of the nineteenth century. By 1830 many of the best water power sites in New England were harnessed to move the spindles and looms of the rapidly growing cotton and woolen factories. The success of the Waltham system hastened the wide adoption of the factory form of organization in other areas as well. Textile mills spread into New York, New Jersey, and Pennsylvania, many of them using steam engines for driving mill machinery when water power could not easily be obtained. Encouraged by the growing national market economy, Americans developed a peculiar genius for technical inventions that extended the possibilities of mass production. Largely as a result of the efforts of Eli Whitney and Simeon North, the principle of interchangeable parts was introduced into the manufacture of firearms and extended to the manufacturing of clocks and certain kinds of machinery.

Growth of Technical Inventions

One of the great inventions of this era was the electric telegraph, which was patented by Samuel F. B. Morse in 1840, although Joseph Henry, one of America's ablest scientists, had already demonstrated the practical possibilities of transmitting electrical impulses over a wire nine years earlier. The electric telegraph was perfected for commercial use in 1844 when Morse arranged a dramatic demonstration of the new technical device by sending his famous message "What hath God wrought?" from the Supreme Court Chambers in Washington to Baltimore where his partner, Albert Vail, sent the same message back to Washington to the amazement and delight of the spectators. Many companies began to bid for the right to use the new communications device, and by 1860 there were already 50,000 miles of telegraph wire in use in the United States.

The commercial development of the electric telegraph coincided with other technological changes in the newspaper field. A "penny press," catering to the mass of people in the rapidly growing cities of the nation, had made its appearance in the 1830's. With the further improvement of the steam engine, it became possible to develop rotary presses that could print 1,000 newspapers an hour; in 1847 Richard Marsh Hoe perfected a rotary press that could turn out 10,000 newspapers an hour. The development of telegraphic communication and the improvements in printing enabled the newspapers to supply the public with news within a few hours after it had been received.

When the great "Crystal Palace" Exposition took place in London in 1851, several American inventions won prizes in the international competitions, and thanks to the work of men like Eli Whitney, American machine tools surpassed those of Europe in originality, variety, and efficiency. By that time, the school children of America were being taught to envision a future in which the factory as well as the farm would be a primary force in the national economy—one of the widely-used schoolbooks of the 1850's, Rensselaer Bentley's *Pictorial Reader,* contains an emblematic frontispiece which depicts the Goddess of Liberty pointing to a banner on which is inscribed: "Agriculture, Mechanics *and Manufactures:* on these Depend the Prosperity of the Nation."

The need for such new images of social reality was recorded in the Census of 1860. By that time 1.3 million men and women were working in 140,000 manufacturing establishments in the entire country: nearly 400,000 of these were employed in over 20,000 establishments in New England, and over half a million in more than 53,000 establishments in the Middle Atlantic states. Furthermore, less than 60 per cent of the total labor force in 1860 was still engaged in agricultural pursuits, the rest was in manufacturing, trade and other nonagricultural pursuits.

The Troubled World of the American Workingman

When Jefferson wrote his *Notes on Virginia* at the end of the American Revolution, he expressed the hope that America would remain an agrarian society as long as possible. "While we have land to labor . . .," he wrote, "let us never wish to see our citizens occupied at a workbench or twirling a distaff." In those years, also, he often expressed the hope that the vast extent of unoccupied land in the Republic would enable Americans to avoid for a longer time the creation of large cities. "When we get piled upon one another in large cities as in Europe," he declared, "we shall become corrupt as in Europe."

The Independent Craftsman as a Symbol

Although Jefferson retained his antipathy toward cities to the end of his life, he revised his views concerning the appropriateness of the manufacturing arts in American society. Near the end of his first term as President when a new edition of the *Notes on Virginia* was being prepared, he indicated that he had come to accept American handicraftsmen as the equal of the cultivators of the earth in morality and independence. "As yet our manufacturers are as much at their ease, as independent and moral as our agricultural inhabitants," he wrote, "and they will continue so as long as there are vacant lands for them to resort to; because whenever it shall be attempted by the other classes to reduce them to a minimum of subsistence, they will quit their trade and go to

In the same way that Longfellow idealized the blacksmith American artists idealized the town. Twenty-two Houses and a Church, *mid-nineteenth century. Collection of American Primitive Paintings. National Gallery of Art, gift of Edgar William and Bernice Chrysler Garbisch, 1958.*

laboring the earth." The abundance of land, so greatly increased by the Louisiana Purchase, seemed to provide a natural safety valve that would prevent the American artisan from falling into the subservience and degeneracy that characterized the laborers of Europe.

This conception of the independent handicraftsmen retained a powerful hold on the imaginations of Americans during the first half of the nineteenth century. Henry Wadsworth Longfellow reinforced the image in the verses of *The Village Blacksmith:*

> His hair is crisp, and black and long
> His face is like the tan;
> His brow is wet with honest sweat,
> He earns what e'er he can
> And looks the whole world in the face
> For he owes not any man.

As long as new communities continued to enter the stage of economic development represented by Hezekiah Niles' description of Mount Pleasant, Ohio, there were carpenters, tailors, cobblers, and weavers who corresponded to the social type depicted in Longfellow's *The Village Blacksmith.* On the other hand, the rise of the factory and the spreading net of the market revolution with each passing decade from 1820 to 1860 foretold a future in which the skilled artisan who aspired to be an independent master craftsman would be replaced as a prevailing social type by the workingman who was permanently caught in his wage earner status.

The Growth of Cities   Furthermore, an increasing proportion of the wage-earning class did not resort to the vacant lands of the West. To be sure, a westward movement of population was a major characteristic of internal migration in the United States before 1860, but we must not overlook the fact that a significant process of urbanization was taking place in the same period. In 1820, the proportion of the total population living in cities (in places of 2,500 or more, by the Bureau of Census definition) was only 6.1 per cent. In 1860, nearly 20 per cent of the people of the United States were classed as urban dwellers. Between 1820 and 1860, the total population of the nation increased 226 per cent, but the proportion living in cities increased nearly eightfold. In 1820, furthermore, there had been only 12 cities in the United States with a population exceeding 10,000, and only two of these exceeded 100,000. In 1860, there were 101 cities with a population exceeding 10,000; eight of these had more than 100,000, and New York exceeded 1,000,000.

Much of the rapid increase in the total population after 1820 came chiefly as a result of the natural fertility of the American population. Large families were the rule and children were welcomed as an economic asset on the farm and in the factory. Yet it seems reasonable to assume that the growth of the cities would not have been so rapid, if there had not been a notable increase in immigration.

The Tide of Immigration   For 50 years after the American Revolution only a few thousand immigrants a year were reaching American shores. The Napoleonic wars and the political and economic readjustments of the postwar years had blocked many of the old channels of migration. But in the 1830's, the flow of immigrants rose to an average of 60,000 a year, and increased to over 200,000 a year in the late 1840's, reaching a peak of over 427,000 arrivals in the single year, 1854. In all, some six million newcomers landed in the United States between 1820 and 1860; and the proportion of foreign born in the population reached its highest point in American history in 1860—15 per cent.

A steady stream of these immigrants continued to come from Great Britain, but about 1.5 million were Irishmen who were driven to the United States by desperate conditions of poverty, particularly after the potato famines in the 1840's. A million more were Germans who sought to escape the political repressions after the failure of the revolutions of 1848 and the economic pressures caused by the advancing industrial revolution in western Europe. Large numbers of Scandinavians also began to come in the forties and fifties, while the rest of Europe contributed smaller groups.

Many of the new immigrants were able to move to farms in the West where they formed clusters of English, German, and Norwegian settlements. But larger numbers of them remained in the cities and towns of the Northeast. Considerable numbers of the English and German

THE EMIGRANT'S BRIDE.

Ballad.
The Words by J. F. SMITH ESQ.RE
Author of ROBIN GOODFELLOW,
The Music Composed by
W. WILSON.

LONDON, PUBLISHED BY J. DUNCOMBE & C.° 17, HOLBORN HILL, OPPOSITE FURNIVAL'S INN

Collection of j mara gutman.

migrants were artisans whose skills were still in demand in the rapidly growing American economy. The great majority of Irish immigrants, however, had known nothing but the impoverished conditions of tenant farmers or landless agricultural laborers. Most of them settled in the cities of the Northeast where they formed a large supply of cheap and unskilled labor eagerly sought after by mill owners and builders of canals and railroads. In the New England textile mills, Irish women replaced the daughters of Yankee farmers; everywhere in the cities, Irish girls soon displaced native-born help as domestic servants.

It is not surprising, therefore, that pauperism and other manifestations of urban poverty became a persistent problem in this period. In 1846, for example, the number of paupers in New York City was declared by a labor newspaper to be 50,000, or one person out of every seven. Living conditions among the poor in the cities were so shockingly bad that they began to attract the attention of leading American writers and editors. Mathew Carey, a writer on economic affairs, reported that living conditions of the poor in Philadelphia were revoltingly bad even in the prosperous years of the 1830's. In one part of the city 55 families amounting to 253 persons were crowded into 30 small tenements without toilet facilities of any kind.

In Boston in 1849, Dr. Henry Clark investigated a tenement house with a triple cellar in the notorious slum area known as the "Half Moon

*Urban Poverty
and Social Unrest*

Place." His report to the Committee on Internal Health of the City of Boston included the following description:

. . . One cellar was reported by the police to be occupied nightly as a sleeping-apartment for thirty-nine persons. In another, the tide [of water] had risen so high that it was necessary to approach the bedside of a patient by means of a plank which was laid from one stool to another; while the dead body of an infant was actually sailing about the room in its coffin.

The average length of life for the Irish living in Boston at that time was reported as being not over 14 years.

From Graham's Magazine.
Collection of j mara gutman.

Horace Greeley's *New York Tribune* reported the findings of similar investigations of the cellar population of that city under the lurid title "Dens of Death." One in 20 of the population of New York City was said to be living in cellars. In some of these there were three classes of boarders. The first class paid 37.5 cents a week for the privilege of sleeping on straw thrown loose over the floor and of eating at what was called the "first table." The second class paid half as much to sleep on the bare floor and to eat at the "second table." The lowest class paid nine cents a week, and slept on the floor only when there was room, being turned out into the streets when second-class lodgers were available; they also had the dubious privilege of eating at "the third table," that is, to eat what was left over after the first- and second-class lodgers had taken their picks.

Thus, the great cities of the United States were housing increasing thousands of workers who were completely divorced from the land and the resources of self-help available in rural towns and villages. Large numbers of unskilled wage earners lived in a state of economic insecurity that was relatively new in the American experience. This insecurity arose not only from the seasonal character of many occupations, but also from the recurrent crises that temporarily paralyzed business activity as the market economy began to develop its characteristic cycles of boom and depression. The low wages of the many workers left them without any margin of savings to carry them through periods of unemployment.

In the major economic crises of the period, Americans living in the great cities of the nation began to witness conditions of mass unemployment and social unrest. In the depression year of 1837, mass meetings were held in New York City to protest unemployment and mobs broke up warehouses in the "flour riots" of that year. Horace Greeley declared in January, 1838, that about one-third of the 200,000 wage earners in New York were unemployed, and that 10,000 of these were in "utter and hopeless distress." Similar conditions prevailed two decades later, after the panic of 1857. Major labor riots took place in New York in 1835, in Philadelphia in 1843, and in Baltimore in 1857. Unrest and violence were common occurrences among the unskilled laborers who dug the canals and laid the tracks for the railroads. Sometimes, to relieve the strain of grueling labor and the misery of living in shanty towns, the men fought among themselves; Irishmen were often involved in pitched battles fought with clubs and guns. At other times, the resentment of such workers turned against their employers and they struck out blindly and savagely in rioting and destruction. In 1834 federal troops were called out to quell a large-scale riot of Chesapeake and Ohio canal workers.

The social strains created by technological changes and the shift from household to factory production were also evident in the organized labor movements from 1820 to 1860. The number and variety of labor organizations has given rise to considerable disagreement among historians concerning the nature and the objectives of such workingmen's movements. Yet it should not surprise us to find variety and diversity in the aims and tactics of organized groups of working men at a time when American society was moving rapidly through the stages of transition toward a national market economy. Sometimes their objectives seemed to be aimed at preserving the dignity and status of the Jeffersonian handicraftsman; at other times, they seemed to be groping toward methods of collective bargaining concerning such practical matters as better wages, shorter hours, and better working conditions. But throughout the period, articulate labor leaders and editors seemed determined to resist the idea that the American worker must settle for the status of a permanent wage earner in a factory system of production. Again and again, the resolutions of labor groups expressed a rudimentary ideology that looked toward cooperative or communal social arrangements.

In the late twenties and the early thirties, the leaders of the workingmen's movement were preoccupied with political methods that would secure the establishment of equal rights and equal opportunities for workers and their children. The first workingmen's party was organized in Philadelphia in 1828 as an outgrowth of a Mechanics Union of Trade Associations. For a few years it nominated candidates in city and county elections, but only in 1829 did it exert any significant influence in the election of a candidate. The Workingmen's party of New York, organized in 1829, was somewhat more successful. Several victories were won in the local elections of that year, and one of its candidates was elected to the state assembly. Similar organizations appeared in Boston and other eastern cities, and workingmen's candidates met with some success in New England, New Jersey, and Delaware.

The Formation of Workingman's Parties

The platforms of the Philadelphia and New York parties advocated universal free education, the abolition of chartered monopolies, the abolition of imprisonment for debt, equal taxation, and the revision or abolition of the militia system. The original platform of the New York Workingmen's party clearly reveals that its leaders hoped that the new political movement might be able to prevent the drift toward an "unnatural and unequal organization of society . . . that places over us task masters with power to require unreasonable toil, with power to withhold adequate recompense, with power to deny employment altogether."

Ship in dry dock, Boston Navy Yard. Photograph by Southworth & Hawes about 1852. George Eastman House Collection.

Many of the leaders of these workingmen's parties were skilled artisans who hoped to restore the dignity and status of the handicraftsman. Consequently, they tended to stress such objectives as the abolition of monopolies, especially banking monopolies, that seemed to give special privileges to bankers, factory masters, and merchant capitalists. In addition, they gave great emphasis to their demands for free, universal education so that their children should have an equal chance in the race of life with the children of the rich. Indeed, the New York Workingmen's party proclaimed that "next to life and liberty, we consider education to be the greatest blessing bestowed upon mankind."

As a matter of fact, these workingmen's parties conceived of the "workingman" in the broadest sense. To them, the term included not only urban laborers and artisans, it also included all real "producers": farmers, active tradesmen, and even honest merchants. Only unproductive individuals like bankers and speculators were excluded. This broad concept of the "productive" or "laboring" class is suggested by the name of the leading labor organization in New England in the early thirties, "The New England Association of Farmers, Mechanics and Other Workingmen."

Such workingmen's organizations attracted the interest of social reformers with schemes for the reconstruction of American society that were designed to forestall the appearance of a miserable and degraded proletatian class such as existed in Europe. Social visionaries like Robert Dale Own and Frances Wright, who had been associated with utopian community experiments in the West, came to New York and tried to lead the workingmen's party toward the advocacy of public boarding schools in which children would be taught the true principles of equality and social cooperation away from the pernicious influences of the family and neighborhood. Other radical reformers like Thomas Skidmore sought to lead the organized workingmen toward schemes of collective ownership and property redistribution. Middle-class reformers, like Theodore Sedgewick and William Gouge, urged workingmen to give their political support to the Jacksonian war against the bank and the paper money system. In New York, such diverse aims led to bitter factional quarrels, and the Workingmen's party soon became hopelessly split into three factions each with its newspaper and party candidates. Before long, the followers of the New York party as well as other workingmen's parties were lured into the support of one or the other of the major parties by politicians who were seeking to attract the labor vote in the party battles of the Jacksonian decade.

Meanwhile, a more significant form of organized labor activity in the 1830's was developing through the rapid growth of trade unions in the leading industrial cities. Between 1834 and 1837, about 150 trade unions and local labor socieities were established in Boston, New York, Philadelphia, and Baltimore. Eleven cities formed central trade unions to concert the efforts of these local labor organizations. In 1834, delegates representing six industrial cities—Boston, Philadelphia, Newark, Brooklyn, Poughkeepsie, and New York—assembled in New York where they organized the first National Trades Union. Further conventions were held in 1835 and 1836, and in the latter year delegates came from as far away as Washington, Pittsburg, and Cincinnati. The total trade union membership in the cities represented at the 1836 convention is estimated to be 300,000. The National Trade Union conventions demanded a system of free, universal education and the abolition of chartered privileges for the "favored few" as had the workingmen's parties before them; but they also advocated a 10-hour day for all workers, and urged that public lands, which were being acquired by speculators, be made available to actual settlers only. In 1836, a special committee of the National Trades Union convention urged local trade unions to organize cooperative workshops instead of exhausting their funds by supporting strikes.

Many of the trade unions that had appeared so rapidly organized strikes to secure better working conditions. At least 173 strikes were called in the United States between 1833 and 1837; more than a hundred of these were for higher wages and the rest were for a 10-hour day. Most of these strikes were conducted by skilled artisans—tailors, carpenters, printers, shoemakers, and the like—but a few were organized by factory

Early Trade Unions

workers who had been much slower to join the trade union movement. Carpet weavers at Thompsonville, Connecticut, struck for higher wages in 1833, and the factory girls at Lowell, Massachusetts, organized a brief strike against a threatened wage reduction in the following year. In 1835 an extensive strike of cotton textile workers took place in Paterson, New Jersey, involving 20 mills and 2000 workers.

Efforts to organize the bargaining power of workingmen against employers were doubly difficult because strikes were illegal according to the law of the land at the time. Between 1805 and 1815, workers' societies had been hauled into state courts by employers when they conducted strikes, and the courts in a half a dozen cases had condemned such strikes on the ground that they were unlawful conspiracies.

A notable legal victory was won for the trade unions, however, in the Massachusetts case of *Commonwealth* v. *Hunt* (1842). Hunt and other members of the Boston Bootmaker's Society had been tried and convicted in a Boston court for conspiring to compel master bootmakers to employ only union men. The case was promptly appealed to the state Supreme Court by the bootmakers who had the aid of Robert Rantoul, a brilliant, Harvard-trained lawyer with reformist sympathies. In the decision read by Chief Justice Shaw, a distinction was made between the legality of a labor combination and the legality of its methods. "We think, therefore," Chief Justice Shaw declared, ". . . that the legality of such an association will therefore depend upon the means to be used for its accomplishments. . . ." A combination which sought to attain its objectives by peacefully refusing to work for an employer was lawful, but one which sought to obtain its objectives by "criminal means" may be stamped with the character of conspiracy.

Justice Shaw's decision was a highly controversial one at the time and it was only the first step in a long struggle to legitimize the existence of labor unions in the United States. Moreover, this legal victory came at a time when the promising trade union movement of the 1830's had been virtually wiped out by the depression that followed the Panic of 1837.

Utopian Yearnings

Disappointed in their hope for reforms from political action and trade unionism during the thirties, many workingmen seemed willing to embrace some of the utopian schemes of humanitarian reform that were prevalent during the hard times following the economic crises of 1837 and 1839. Some of these schemes were nourished by peculiar American conditions; others were influenced by ideas which came from the humanitarian and utopian impulses that grew out of the industrial revolution in Europe.

The large public domain in the United States inspired idealistic hopes based on land reform. George Henry Evans, who had been active in the Workingman's party in the 1830's, proposed to solve the problem of the industrial worker by means of a relatively equal distribution of land in the public domain. He envisioned the establishment of "rural republican townships" in the West, where farmer-craftsmen would produce and exchange their products in a simple harmony. Evans' dream was a new version of Jefferson's society of sturdy yeomen and independent handicraftsmen; but the speculative urges in the settlement of the West had already taken America far beyond the possibilities of such a rural arcadia. To be sure, the National Reform Association which Evans organized made a minor contribution to the movement for free homesteads in the West, but the Homestead Act of 1862 contained none of the limitations on the ownership and resale of property that were contained in Evans' original proposals.

Another scheme of social reconstruction that attracted the attention of workingmen in the 1840's was associationism. Associationism was based on the teachings of the Frenchman, Charles Fourier, who encouraged the creation of cooperative communities, or phalansteries, in which production was to be so organized that each person would but realize the fullest degree of passional harmony and avoid monotony by moving from task to task. Remuneration was to be assigned to capital, labor, and managerial skill according to predetermined ratios.

The associationist movement developed rapidly in the United States largely because of the effective propaganda efforts of Albert Brisbane, a wealthy young American who had been converted to Fourierism during his travels in Europe, and Horace Greeley, the energetic editor of the *New York Tribune*. Brisbane had the social and intellectual attainments that gave him immediate entrée into circles of middle-class humanitarian reformers, and Greeley's weekly edition of the *Tribune* circulated widely in almost every county of the northern states. About 30 or 40 phalanxes of the Fourierist type were actually started during the decade of the 1840's, but most were short-lived.

Although few workingmen actually became members of these Fourierist communities, associationist leaders like Brisbane and Greeley were able to secure much favorable attention from labor groups, with the result that cooperative schemes of a more limited sort were attempted. Thus, working-class associationism became a matter of organizing cooperative societies—both producers' and consumers' cooperatives. A number of producers' cooperatives had sprung up during the 1830's with the active encouragement of the National Trades Union, but they had been wiped out after the Panic of 1837. In the late 1840's, a much more vigorous producers' cooperative movement arose. Lynn shoemakers organized a cooperative workshop as early as 1845 and, in 1848, the iron molders of Cincinnati set up a successful cooperative shop that inspired imitation by molders in other iron-making towns such as Wheeling and Pittsburg. The movement spread very rapidly in New York City and, by 1851, producers' cooperatives had been formed among tailors, seamstresses, bakers, shoemakers, carpenters, and others.

Numbering many more people than the producers' cooperatives was the movement for consumers' cooperation which became a major reform activity in the New England area. Getting started in 1845, and reaching a peak from 1852 to 1853, more than 800 consumers' cooperatives societies, or protective unions as they were called, were formed. Most of these cooperative societies were members of the New England Protective Union which through its Central Agency did much of the wholesale buying. It is estimated that at least thirty or forty thousand persons were members of these societies.

But neither the producers' nor consumers' cooperatives were able to strike deep roots in American society. They were usually starved for capital; moreover, they had great difficulty in developing able and responsible managerial talent. Like many of the Fourierist communities they were often torn by internal dissension and personal rivalries for power.

The Ten-Hour Movement

More significant for the future position of the American laborer was the organized movement for a shorter working day. In the 1830's workingmen commonly worked 12 hours a day or longer, and the trade union organizations of that decade had begun to agitate for a 10-hour day as the standard working day. Some gains were made in this direction by the more skilled craftsmen, and there was general rejoicing among laborers when President Martin Van Buren decreed a 10-hour day for federal employees in 1840. But the greater number of industrial workers, particularly the factory workers who were largely unorganized, continued to work longer hours.

During the forties, however, the 10-hour movement began to grow very rapidly in New England and elsewhere. The factory girls of Lowell and the mechanics of Fall River were leaders in a large-scale petition campaign designed to galvanize the Massachusetts legislature into action. The movement reached its peak in the years 1845 to 1848 when a series of conventions representing workers from many parts of New England were held in Boston to arouse additional public support for a 10-hour day. Agitation for a shorter working day also became a favorite cause with factory workers elsewhere.

As a result of such organized campaigns of petition and public agitation, a number of states began to pass 10-hour legislation: New Hampshire in 1847, and Pennsylvania, Maine, New Jersey, Ohio, and Rhode Island in the next half dozen years. Most of these laws were full of loopholes which made it possible for employers to negotiate "agreements" with their operatives for a longer working day. It would take another decade and more before effective 10-hour laws were adopted, but factory workers were beginning to take their first fumbling efforts toward large-scale organization, political agitation, and collective bargaining.

These first efforts toward a self-conscious labor movement among factory operatives, however, crumbled before the flood tide of immigrant workers who poured into the factories during the 1850's, especially in the New England area. Irish men and women were hired in large numbers by New England factory masters to take the place of native-born workers, and there was little chance to preserve any effective labor solidarity in the midst of the ethnic and religious tensions caused by the rapid influx of immigrants. Attempts to organize national trade unions along craft lines even among skilled workers were not notably successful either. Eight or nine national unions along craft lines were established in the 1850's, but only a few were able to survive the fluctuations of the business cycle—the National Typographical Union (1852), the Hat Finishers National Association (1854), and the Journeymen Stone Cutters Association (1855).

The emerging wage-earning class in America was not yet ready for job-conscious trade unions devoted mainly to strikes and collective bargaining. American workingmen focused their hopes on broader programs of political and social reform. Against the entrepreneurial ideals fostered by the market revolution, they developed a rudimentary working class ideology that envisioned a cooperative commonwealth in which there would be a relatively equal distribution of landed property, craftsmanship would continue to be honored, and the producing classes would live together in simple harmony.

chapter thirteen

The Emergence of
Democratic Politics

The Morning Glory, *1832.*
Rush Rhees Library. The
University of Rochester.

The Twilight of Gentry Politics

In 1816, James Monroe, Madison's Secretary of State, and the third Virginian in succession, was selected by the Republicans as their party's candidate for the presidency. Deprived of their ideological identity when the Republicans took over much of the Hamiltonian program, the Federalists were unable to offer any effective opposition. When the electoral results were tallied, Monroe received 183 votes, while Rufus King with 34 votes was supported only by Massachusetts, Connecticut, and Delaware. Four years later, in the election of 1820, the Federalists did not even bother to nominate a candidate; all but one of the electoral votes were cast for Monroe.

At the time of his first inauguration as President, Monroe was 61 years old. Tall and dignified in bearing, he seemed all the more venerable because he still wore the knee breeches and buckled boots of an earlier day. Everything about him suggested that he belonged to the generation of the founding fathers who had fought in the Revolution and had created the governing institutions of the new nation.

The Drift Toward One-Party Politics

The new President obviously wished to make his office the symbol of national unity. Soon after his election, he made a good will tour through the country, including a visit to New England where Federalist opposition to his predecessors had been most rabid. After a notably warm reception in Boston, the *Columbian Centinel,* a leading Federalist newspaper of that city, observed that "an era of good feelings" had arrived in American politics.

The nation appeared to be ready to accept a system of one-party politics. There no longer seemed to be any significant cleavages of party principle that could sustain a two-party system. Political conflict took another form as the drift toward one-party politics gave rise to an increased development of personal factions within the Republican party. Everywhere in the states, well-to-do leaders and socially superior men formed shifting alliances to win the advantages of political power. Like his predecessor, Monroe had to tread warily among important factions within the party such as the Clintonians in New York, the Duane-Leib clique in Pennsylvania, the Smith clique in Maryland, or the Tertium Quid followers of John Randolph in his own state of Virginia.

In a two-party system, the threat of an electoral victory by the opposing party has a disciplining effect upon such alliances of personal cliques, but in the absence of a strong opposition, a one-party system tends to dissolve into numberless factions. Hence the Era of Good Feelings was really a confused period of political transition. Despite Monroe's efforts to maintain an appearance of political unity in the nation, there was considerable disarray in state and national politics, as shifting alliances of personal factions were formed and reformed for almost every electoral contest.

The disintegrative consequences of one-party politics were fully revealed in the struggle over the question of the presidential succession. During the years when the Virginia dynasty held sway, the office of Secretary of State had been the stepping-stone to the presidency. In 1808, and again in 1816, the congressional caucus of the Republican party had decided the crucial question of succession in this fashion. And hoping for the same result in 1824 was John Quincy Adams, Monroe's talented Secretary of State.

Factionalism in the Election of 1824

The old mechanism of presidential choice failed to work in 1824, however. Five candidates became actively involved in the campaign to succeed Monroe: besides John Quincy Adams, William H. Crawford, John C. Calhoun, Henry Clay, and Andrew Jackson aspired to the highest office in the nation.

All five candidates were Republicans. All but one might be called members of the Republican establishment in Washington; the exception was General Jackson, a military hero, who had had only limited experience in national politics as a member of the Senate for two brief periods. In the eyes of the established leaders of the party, Jackson was an outsider: "I feel much alarmed," Jefferson remarked in private conversation with a congressional leader at Monticello, "at the prospect of seeing General Jackson President. He is one of the most unfit men I know of for such a place."

In the confused and somewhat murky campaign for the presidency in 1824, the question of the presidential caucus became a leading issue. Among the five candidates, William H. Crawford appeared to have built up a larger number of supporters within the established machinery of the congressional caucus and among the elder statesmen of the Virginia dynasty. After all, he had been born in Virginia and had carefully cultivated his public image as a man who was devoted to the original principles of Jeffersonian Republicanism. Consequently he seemed to be the logical heir-apparent to the long line of Virginia Presidents. With good reason, therefore, his four opponents supported the growing opposition to the caucus system. When only 66 members of Congress (about one-third) turned out for the meeting of the congressional caucus and cast their votes for Crawford, it appeared that the legitimacy of "King Caucus" had been effectively challenged. The other candidates were put into nomination either by state legislatures or by irregular mass meetings summoned by their political managers. The day of the national party convention had not yet arrived, but in 1824, almost any method other than the congressional caucus appeared to be more democratic.

Even though Calhoun withdrew at a late stage in the campaign, the voters were unable to register any clear cut choice among so many candidates. In those states where presidential electors were chosen by popular vote, Jackson led in the popular voting, but not with a majority: Jackson had 153,544 votes compared to 108,740 for Adams, 47,136 for Clay, and 46,618 for Crawford. In the electoral college count, Jackson received 99 votes to Adams's 84, Crawford's 41, and Clay's 37. Jackson's main strength was in the South and Southwest, where he captured the electoral votes of all states except Virginia and Crawford's Georgia. In addition, he received the electoral votes of Indiana and Illinois in the Northwest, and Pennsylvania, New Jersey, and Maryland in the Northeast. Adams carried all of New England and New York, and Clay took the electoral vote of his own state of Kentucky plus Ohio and Missouri. Outside of his own state, Georgia, Crawford received the votes of Virginia and Delaware.

Since no candidate had received a majority of electoral votes, the final decision, according to the Twelfth Amendment to the Constitution, was left to the House of Representatives which was to choose among the candidates with the three highest electoral vote tallies. As the candidate with the lowest total, Clay was out of the running, but as Speaker he had enormous power and prestige in the House of Representatives.

The friends of Adams, Jackson, and Crawford all courted Clay's support in such a manner as to earn the disgust of even that seasoned politician. Crawford's prospects were not very good since he had suffered a paralytic stroke in the summer of 1824. As between Jackson and Adams, the logic of politics made Adams the obvious man for Clay to support. Jackson, after all, was Clay's most dangerous rival for the political support of the West. Furthermore, Jackson's position on domestic issues was obscure, whereas Adams was known to be a firm supporter of the policies of Republican nationalism that Clay had furthered in his long career in the Congress.

A few weeks before the voting took place in the House of Representatives, Clay met privately with Adams and the two men arrived at a mutual understanding. There is no adequate evidence that Adams actually offered Clay any political office in return for his support, but such would have been the normal expectation according to the pattern of personal political alliances that prevailed in American politics at the time. In any case, Clay gave his support to Adams, and the House of Representatives elevated Monroe's Secretary of State to the presidency.

The friends of Jackson were naturally indignant. They believed that the electoral results had clearly demonstrated more popular support for Jackson than for any other candidate. When the new President announced that he would appoint Clay as his Secretary of State—the likely stepping-stone to the presidency—their anger was unrestrained. "The Judas of the West has closed the contract and will receive the thirty pieces of silver," Andrew Jackson exclaimed when he heard the news. Jackson men everywhere raised the charge of a "corrupt bargain" to make it appear that the popular will had been betrayed by the manipulations of a group of political insiders.

Although there was nothing improper about the appointment of Henry Clay as Secretary of State, the "corrupt bargain" charge struck a responsive chord. "King Caucus," seemingly overthrown the year before, had suddenly been re-enthroned. The choice of the President, in

*Political Changes in
Western and Eastern
States*

the end, had really been made by a group of political insiders in Congress just as it had always been during the long reign of the Virginia dynasty.

Notwithstanding the outcome of the election of 1824, the dominance of gentlemen and "natural aristocrats" in American politics was waning. Everywhere, there were unmistakable evidences of the growth of democracy in American life. The process of change was perhaps most evident on the western frontier, to which large numbers of Americans began to migrate in the opening decades of the nineteenth century. The trans-Appalachian population of more than one million in 1810 increased to 2.2 million in 1820, and 3.7 million in 1830. By 1840, more than six million Americans, or slightly more than a third of the total population, lived in the new western states of the Union.

The great landed domain of the West lay open to individual exploitation, beckoning every man with initiative and courage to make a place for himself regardless of his previous social condition. By 1820 a new land law had been passed in Congress which reduced the price of land to $1.25 an acre, and the minimum unit of purchase to 80 acres. Hence farmers could now obtain 80 acres of fertile land for a modest cash outlay of $100; and the result was an extraordinary enhancement of equal opportunity for men to win fortune and success through their own skill and industry.

In such a fluid social situation, older class distinctions and aristocratic pretensions were difficult to maintain. Alexis de Tocqueville, the aristocratic Frenchman, whose *Democracy in America* is a classic commentary on American society in this period, observed, ". . . in the Western settlements we may behold democracy arrived at its utmost limits. . . . In this part of the American continent . . . the population has escaped the influence not only of great names and great wealth, but even of the national aristocracy of wealth and virtue."

Consequently many of the state constitutions of the new western states were very democratic in character, particularly in regard to the broadening of suffrage and the reduction of religious and property qualifications for officeholding. In several of his famous essays, therefore, the American historian, Frederick Jackson Turner, developed the theory that the growth of American democracy was due primarily to the influence of the frontier. "The wind of Democracy," he wrote, "blew so strongly from the West, that in the older states of New York, Massachusetts, Connecticut, and Virginia, conventions were called which liberalized the constitutions by strengthening the democratic basis of the state." Turner implied that the major motive for suffrage reform in the East was to prevent the drain of population to the West. The work of other historians demonstrates, however, that the activities of suffrage reform in the seaboard states do not support this thesis; that although western examples were occasionally cited in eastern constitutional conventions, they never achieved the status of major arguments.

After all, the social situation in the East was also dynamic. The rapid growth of the market economy, and the steady expansion of industry and commerce, created new opportunities for ambitious, strong-willed, and energetic men to push ahead and to seize new opportunities to win fame and fortune. The established systems of class and privilege that had developed in the seaboard states in the previous century tended to disintegrate before the rapid upsurge of self-made men. Tocqueville noted the rapidity of these social changes in the seaboard states in the same chapter in which he commented on the democratic conditions in the western states: "And, now, after a lapse of little more than sixty years, the aspect of society is totally altered; the families of the great landed proprietors are almost all commingled with the general mass. In the state of New York, which formerly contained many of these, there are but two who keep their heads above the stream; and they must shortly disappear. . . ."

Some of the effects of these powerful democratic forces can be seen in the widespread movement for constitutional reforms in the eastern states. Not since the days of the American Revolution had there been such an intense preoccupation with constitution-making, and the popularly chosen constitutional convention became the favorite method for achieving such reforms. Between 1815 and 1850, most of the states, new as well as old, held conventions to adopt their first constitutions or to make important amendments to older frames of government.

Most of the constitutions of this period provided for the popular election of nearly all state and county administrative officials, whereas formerly most of their offices had been filled by appointment. Furthermore some state constitutions stipulated that the judges of inferior courts should be popularly elected. At the same time, there was a general movement throughout the states to democratize the machinery for electing a president. In 1800 nearly two-thirds of the electors were chosen by the state legislatures; by 1828 only South Carolina had not given a direct choice of presidential electors to the people.

The Growth of Politically Conscious Electorate

From T. G. Bradford's Illustrated Atlas of the U.S. and Adjacent Countries. *Philadelphia, 1838. Rush Rhees Library. The University of Rochester.*

As a result of all these changes, voter participation in elections, particularly national elections, began to increase far more rapidly than the growth of the population as a whole. Despite the large number of candidates, only about 26.5 per cent of the adult white males in the country voted in the presidential election of 1824. By 1828 the proportion of voter participation more than doubled as 56.3 per cent of adult white males flocked to the polls. The percentage of voter participation hovered around the 55 per cent level in the presidential elections of 1832 and 1836, and then rose to the highest level of the pre-Civil War period in 1840, when 78 per cent of the adult white males turned out for the election. An era of mass politics had clearly arrived!

These great increases of voter participation were caused only in part by the trend toward universal suffrage. Important also was the strengthening of party organization and the emergence of a new style of democratic politics. The irresistible demand for making all officials elective opened the doors to new men in politics and made it increasingly difficult for the voters to learn the qualifications of so many candidates. Political parties

Victor Prevost photograph of American painting. Photography Division. Smithsonian Institution.

became all the more important as a means of bringing together large numbers of voters with diverse interests, and also as a means of bringing some kind of central direction to the choosing of officials who had to achieve office on the basis of individually conducted election campaigns.

Thus, as the constitutional machinery of election became more democratic, political parties became more tightly organized. Moreover a new kind of political leadership came to the fore. The new-style democratic politician had to be skillful in manipulating and combining a motley mass of voters. The new politics was the creation of professional politicians—men who made careers out of organizing political power. Often coming from ordinary backgrounds, they sought to achieve through party organization what wealth and status conferred on the previous generation of political leaders.

The New Politics

When Davy Crockett entered politics in the 1820's, he quickly learned that "telling good-humored stories" gained him more votes than the "fine speechmaking" of his opponents. The gentlemen of "knowledge and virtue," central to the idea of a natural aristocracy, were uncomfortable and ineffective in this new political world. They were not "stump-speakers" by nature or by training. Furthermore, many of them abhorred the crasser motives associated with the spoils system. Increasingly, therefore, the successful political leader tended to be a self-made man, a political entrepreneur who got ahead by developing the skills of electioneering and political horse-trading.

The new-style politicians who aspired to high office learned to make use of the cheap daily newspapers to establish a network of communication to the party faithful in every town and county. In addition, these politicians made increasing use of the spoils system as a necessary weapon of party discipline. Every form of patronage—appointive offices, bank charters, subscriptions to the stock of transportation companies, printing contracts—became a means of binding together the diverse and jostling groups that composed the parties of this era.

Such men as Martin Van Buren and Thurlow Weed exemplified the new men who were making their way to positions and influence and leadership in the new game of politics. They understood the value of organization, and they relished party conflict because they knew it was not personal. After years of competition, Van Buren and Weed remained cordial. The son of a tavern-keeper, Van Buren entered politics at an early age, and his talents for organization and intrigue brought him rapid advance. Known to contemporaries as "the little magician," he became the leader of the Democratic political machine in New York known as the "Albany Regency." Weed, a newspaper editor, rose to power on the opposite side of the fence. He became the most formidable opponent of the "Regency"; he ultimately forged a powerful Whig party organization which united old National Republican followers of Adams and Clay with supporters of a grass roots movement known as the Anti-Masonic Party.

The sudden appearance of the Anti-Masonic party provided visible evidence of the new popular currents that were rushing into the mainstream of the American political system. The party mushroomed into a powerful political movement almost overnight, after the disappearance and presumed murder of a stone mason named William Morgan in upstate New York. Since Morgan had published a book revealing the secrets of the Masonic order, it was widely believed that he had been abducted and murdered by a conspirational group of Masons. The Morgan mystery touched off an astonishing political uprising among the rural voters of western New York whose resentment against rapidly changing social conditions found an outlet in their almost fanatical conviction that the Masonic order was a secret, oath-bound conspiracy that had put the control of government and business in the hands of an undesirable and snobbish class of people. Anti-Masonry put a great deal of emphasis on moral conduct, and its appeal was strongest to those who wished to preserve older and simpler ways of piety in American life. As a moral and democratic movement of obvious power, it furnished Thurlow Weed with a mass base for his political machine.

The new style of politics required new institutional devices of influence and control. The outcry against "King Caucus," and the political supremacy wielded by the older elite groups in the nation and the states, had led to the increasing use of delegate conventions as a means of selecting candidates for office. Party conventions were an essential counterpart of the accelerating democratic revolution because they appeared to be a democratic device whereby the delegates chosen by the rank and file nominated the candidates who would run for public office. Established at first in a more or less sporadic fashion, a network of district, county, and state conventions soon covered the country and, by 1831, national party conventions had made their appearance as key institutions in the American political system.

Significantly, in 1831, the first national convention was organized by the Anti-Masonic party in Baltimore to rally the followers of the movement that had spread like a forest fire in New England, the Middle States, and Ohio, and to nominate candidates for the presidency and vice-presidency. The example of the Anti-Masons was soon followed by the supporters of Henry Clay and Andrew Jackson. A national convention of delegates of the National Republican party met in Baltimore later in 1831 and nominated Clay for the presidency. In the spring of 1832, the Democratic Republicans met in a convention which endorsed Andrew Jackson for the presidency and nominated Martin Van Buren for the vice-presidency.

Party conventions were made to order for the new-style politicans. There they could practice all the demagogic arts of rabble-rousing and wire-pulling to great advantage. The spoils system gave them a powerful nucleus of disciplined party workers who were usually able to sway a majority of delegates in favor of nominees selected by the master organizers of the new party machinery. Hence the network of party conventions at every level provided a ladder of ascent for political entrepreneurs who were ambitious for place and power. One of the primary purposes, indeed, for the holding of the first Democratic national convention in 1832 was to create the appearance of a spontaneous popular demand for the nomination of Van Buren for the vice-presidency.

The nominating convention is a unique American institution. From the very beginning, party conventions at all levels were noisy and raucus affairs that reflected the more vulgar appetites of men in an era of mass politics. Demagogic oratory, parades, songs, banners, and demonstrations furnished the populace with political entertainment that had a circus-like character. At the same time, an atmosphere of intrigue and behind-the-scenes connivance became a regular feature of such proceedings. It should be remembered, however, that with the advent of mass politics, such conventions became the only available means of focusing the popular will in support of a party's candidates and a party's principles. Because of it, there sprang up a vigorous national party system which could act as a major stabilizing force in America's onrushing democratic revolution.

Sectional Cross Currents of Politics

The new politics was not simply a matter of formal changes in suffrage and the electoral machinery. It was also an intricate pattern of informal relationships between politicians and voting groups who were impelled by the rapid forces of social change to seek to advance and defend their interests in the political arena. In the days when America was largely a society of self-sufficient farmers men could afford to remain apolitical; as the market revolution proceeded, politics became a universal necessity. Most Americans realized that the decisions of courts and legislatures could have a profound effect on their lives and livelihood.

The panic of 1819 was not only the first severe crisis to affect the developing national market economy, it was an event that had far-reaching political consequences. The crisis of 1819 shook the confidence of many Americans, and the continuing depression of the economy for nearly a half dozen years sharpened feelings of class and sectional antagonism as impoverished farmers and speculators in the West and South sought to fix the blame for the disaster that had fallen upon the country.

Impelled by strong popular pressures, especially in the hard-hit states of the West and South, legislatures began to pass "relief" legislation in the form of "stay laws" designed to prevent foreclosures of debtors' property. In addition such "relief" parties established state banks or loan offices to issue paper money for loans to desperate debtors—mostly

"Relief Wars" in the West and South

farmers. In Kentucky, a particularly radical "relief law" was enacted in 1820. This measure prohibited the sale of any property in foreclosure proceedings for less than three-quarters of its value as appraised by a jury of neighbors, unless the creditor would consent to receive paper notes of the state bank in discharge of the debt. If a creditor did not consent to receive the new paper money, execution against the debtor's property was to be postponed for two years. Inasmuch as the notes of the "Bank of the Commonwealth" rapidly depreciated to approximately 50 cents on the dollar, creditor groups in Kentucky were violently opposed to the new legislation.

The creditor groups in Kentucky, however, were determined not to be placed in one of those nightmarish situations, as imagined by a noted American conservative, where "creditors were seen running away from their debtors, and debtors pursuing them in triumph, and paying them without mercy." The new law was challenged in the courts and, in 1823, the Kentucky Court of Appeals declared the relief law unconstitutional. The decision of the Kentucky judges was based upon doctrines that had been set forth by Chief Justice John Marshall of the United States Supreme Court in *Sturgis* v. *Crowinshield* (1819). This case had involved the constitutionality of a New York law for the relief of insolvent debtors whose debt had been contracted before the law was enacted. In his decision, Marshall had ruled that bankruptcy laws were invalid when they impaired the obligation of contracts.

A similar relief system was attempted in Tennessee, where Andrew

Jackson, a large landholder and speculator, joined the opposition to the paper money system. Yet it must be noted that the basis of his opposition was not quite the same as that of other propertied men in the West. Jackson was suspicious of all forms of paper money—whether issued by private banks or state-owned institutions set up for the relief of desperate debtors. He believed that only specie—gold and silver—should be the legitimate basis of payment in all contractual obligations.

In the bitter struggles over relief legislation in the states, two major institutions were stigmatized with villainous roles in the popular demonology of the discontented groups—the Bank of the United States and the Supreme Court. The Bank was blamed for the Panic of 1819 because it had instituted the contraction of credit that had precipitated the collapse of overextended state banks and the accompanying decline of commodity prices. This was somewhat unfair since the Bank had not created the chaos of speculation; it had merely participated in the boom of psychology and the general expansion of credit until the pressures of the balance of payments in foreign trade forced American bankers and businessmen to pull in their horns. Despite the bad judgment of its directors during the speculative boom, the Bank was a much sounder institution than the state banks—many of them wildcat operations, especially in the South and the West.

Attacks on the "Monster Bank"

But the agrarian debtor was in no mood to be so discriminating in his analysis of the economic crisis; indeed, he understood very little of the mysteries of banking and foreign exchange. To him the Bank had clearly started the panic by calling in loans and by forcing state banks to do the same when it presented their notes for redemption in specie. Throughout the country, the Bank became familiarly known as "The Monster," and western representatives in particular were relentless in their attacks upon the institution. "All the flourishing cities of the West," said Senator Thomas Hart Benton of Missouri, "are mortgaged to this money power. They may be devoured by it at any moment."

In the midst of this rising tide of popular anger against the Bank of the United States, the Supreme Court handed down a momentous decision in the case of *McCulloch* v. *Maryland* (1819) which challenged the existence of the Second Bank of the United States in a very fundamental way. In an act passed in 1818, the legislature of Maryland had required all banks doing business within her borders, and holding charters which she had not granted, to pay an annual tax of $15,000 and to issue notes of only certain denominations. Such a law, if upheld, would have given to the states the power of life and death over branch banks of the United States operating within their jurisdictions.

Bank Politics and the Supreme Court

Naturally, the Baltimore branch of the Bank of the United States refused to pay the tax or to abide by the limitations on the issuance of the bank notes. Whereupon, the officials of the state of Maryland sued the cashier of the Baltimore branch, James McCulloch, for the payment of fines and penalties prescribed by the law. When the state courts upheld the Maryland statute, the Baltimore bank appealed the case to the Supreme Court of the United States.

The case before the Supreme Court was elaborately argued by some of the greatest lawyers in the country, including Daniel Webster for the Bank, and Luther Martin for the state of Maryland. Great public interest was aroused because the case raised some crucial constitutional questions that had been in dispute since Hamilton's first bank had been chartered in the 1790's: did Congress have power to incorporate a bank? And if it had such power, did a state have the constitutional right to tax a branch of the national bank?

Chief Justice Marshall handed down the unanimous judgment of the court in a decision that constituted the most comprehensive exposition of the American constitutional system since its adoption in 1788. Marshall admitted that sovereignty was divided between the states and the national government. But the national government, he argued, "though limited in its powers, is supreme within its sphere of action." To be sure, Marshall recognized that the right to establish a bank was not one of the specifically enumerated powers of Congress, but he took the position that the national government also possessed *implied* powers. He justified the doctrine of implied powers by a broad interpretation of the "necessary and proper" clause as Hamilton had done in 1791. "Necessary and proper," he declared, did not mean absolute necessity because there were always varying degrees of necessity. Hence the test for determining the constitutionality of an implied power should be a broad one: "Let the end be legitimate, let it be within the scope of the Constitution, and all means which are appropriate, which are plainly adapted to that end, which are not prohibited, but consist with the letter and spirit of the Constitution, are constitutional."

As to the question of whether or not the state of Maryland could constitutionally tax a branch of the national bank, Marshall invoked the principle of national supremacy. Relying on the clause making the Constitution, treaties, and acts of Congress the supreme law of the land, he argued that when a state law conflicted with national law, the state law must give way. Since the bank was a necessary and proper instrument of federal authority, the act of Congress must prevail against any state attempt to control the bank's functions. Maryland's attempt to tax the bank was therefore illegal, for "the power to tax involves the power to destroy."

The decision of the Supreme Court aroused a storm of public controversy. Conservative men in the Northeast supported Marshall's judgment because they approved of a broad construction of the powers of the Constitution and a general nationalist orientation of public policy. On the other hand, the decision was bitterly denounced in many of the western and southern states. Newspapers, public meetings, and state legislatures protested that the decision threatened to destroy the rights reserved to the states by the Constitution. Five state legislatures formally approved a proposal for a constitutional amendment that would have granted to the states the power to exclude the national bank from their jurisdictions, but the proposal failed to rally sufficient support in other states.

A more defiant action was taken by the state of Ohio where feeling against the national bank was particularly bitter. In 1819 the Ohio Legislature had levied a heavy tax of $50,000 on each branch of the Bank within that state, and had granted to the state auditor sweeping powers of search and seizure in collecting the tax. In order to prevent collection of the punitive tax, the Bank of the United States obtained an injunction from the federal Circuit Court against Ralph Osborn, the state auditor. Osborn, however, defied the federal injunction, and his aides proceeded to invade the premises of the Chillicothe branch of the Bank where they forcibly seized bank notes and specie. The Bank replied with a suit for damages against the state officials involved, whereupon the state legislature attempted to ban the Bank from Ohio completely.

The controversy finally reached the Supreme Court in the case of *Osborn* v. *The Bank of the United States* (1824). Chief Justice Marshall's decision in the Osborn case reaffirmed the doctrines of the McCulloch decision, and strengthened the power of federal law even further by ruling that the agent of a state (i.e., Osborn), acting under the authority of an unconstitutional state statute, was personally responsible for any injury or damage inflicted in his attempt to execute the act.

The McCulloch decision and its aftermath served to develop new ideological cleavages in American politics. A significant group of Republican leaders regarded the Court's decision as the culmination of a centralizing trend in law and public policy that threatened to betray all of the original principles of Jeffersonian Republicanism. Such men as John Randolph, John Taylor of Carolina, and Judge Spencer Roane of the Virginia Court of Appeals sought to redefine the true principles of Republicanism in the face of the powerful nationalistic impulses at work in American society.

The Ideology of "Old Republicanism

These "Old Republicans," as they were styled, bewailed their party's surrender to Hamiltonian principles in chartering a second national bank and enacting a protective tariff law. In addition, Spencer Roane carried on a persistent campaign in his judicial opinions and in newspaper articles against the appellate jurisdiction of the Supreme Court. Judge Roane took the position that state courts should have the right to pass with finality upon the validity of legislation enacted in their own states. He maintained that the constitution contained no provision which authorized the central government to be the final judge of the extent of its own powers. Although he recognized that judges in every state were sworn to uphold the Constitution, and that laws and treaties made under its authority are the "supreme law of the land," he insisted that they were bound as state judges only and, therefore, their decisions were not subject to review by the courts of another jurisdiction, viz. the Supreme Court of the United States.

The leading theoretician of the Old Republicans, however, was John Taylor, a well-to-do Virginia planter who had turned his back on a promising political career to devote himself to agricultural improvements and the writing of books at his plantation in Caroline county. In his first great political tract, *An Inquiry Into the Principles and Policy of the Government of the United States* (1814), Taylor warned his countrymen of the appearance of an insidious "aristocracy of paper and patronage," based upon banks, bank stocks, land speculation, and stock-jobbing of all forms. The root of the spreading evil of special privilege in American society was the "irrepealable law charter," by which he meant the conception of a public grant as a contract as developed by John Marshall in his decision in the case of *Fletcher* v. *Peck* (1810). Even before the more explicit definition of the meaning of the obligation of contracts clause that was developed by Marshall in the Dartmouth College case (1819), Taylor foresaw the possibility of a vast expansion of corporate privileges in American life under the protective shield of such legal definitions.

Taylor watched with dismay as his own party granted charter privileges to the Second Bank of the United States, and protective privileges to manufacturers in the tariff of 1816. But the decisions of the Supreme Court in the McCulloch and Dartmouth College cases in 1819 sent him into a frenzy of writing activity. Three more polemical books came from his pen in quick succession: *Construction Construed, and Constitution Vindicated* (1820) in which he attacked Marshall's reasoning in the McCulloch decision; *Tyranny Unmasked* (1822) in which he castigated protective tariff legislation as "a transfer of property by law to feed an oppressive government and foster exclusive privilege"; and *New Views of the Constitution* (1823) which proposed a way to prevent the creeping growth of the aristocracy of paper and patronage. The latter was a fully developed theory of decentralism and states rights.

Taylor argued that, with great precision, the Constitution had established a final arbiter of any conflicts of power that might arise between the federal and state governments. He denied that the Supreme Court of the United States could be the final arbiter, because the Supreme Court is a mere agency of the federal government and, consequently, cannot be a disinterested judge of such conflicts of power. The supreme constitutional arbiter is to be found in the amending process: it consists of a two-thirds majority of each house of Congress, and three-fourths of the states speaking through their legislatures or conventions.

Hence, according to Taylor, any state that wished to stop the encroaching tyranny of "the aristocracy of paper and patronage" had the legitimate right to invoke this system of ultimate appeal. A state could refuse to accept any federal law that appeared to be invading its sovereign rights reserved to it by the Constitution, and it would become a law only if two-thirds of each house of Congress and three-fourths of the states upheld it. If the federal government was upheld, then, a true constitutional majority would have decided the issue. As a practical matter, of course, Taylor's theory really set up the machinery for an effective minority veto. If as many as one-fourth of the states, plus one, developed common economic and political interests, they could challenge any significant law that depended upon implied powers to any degree, no matter how reasonable or logical such a construction of the enumerated powers of Congress might be.

Taylor's books never attracted a mass audience, but they were read and widely discussed by influential men in politics. In the hands of reasonable men, his books supplied an incisive critique of the dangers of monopoly and privilege in the new economic policies of the federal and state governments. In the hands of extremists, his doctrines could be used to destroy the unity of the Republic. In either case, his principles became ideological weapons of great import.

Such ideological weapons had an extremely explosive potential due to another issue that aroused a serious form of sectional rivalry. Soon after the bitter antagonisms created by the Panic of 1819 and the McCulloch decision of the Supreme Court came a passionate controversy over the question of the admission of Missouri to the Union. The rapid migration of settlers to the western territories had brought a procession of new states into the Union in quick succession: Louisiana in 1812, Indiana in 1816, Mississippi in 1817, Illinois in 1818, and Alabama in 1819. In the latter year, also, the settlers of the Louisiana territory in the region where the Missouri joins the Mississippi were seeking admission to the Union under the name of Missouri. Many of the settlers of Missouri were southerners who had brought their black slaves with them; it is estimated that there were nearly 10,000 slaves in the territory when it reached the total population that would qualify it for statehood.

The Missouri Controversy

No one expected any problem over the admission of Missouri—such questions had become routine. But the situation changed significantly in February, 1819, when Representative James Tallmadge of New York offered an amendment to the Missouri bill to prohibit the introduction of additional slaves into the new state. Furthermore, his amendment proposed that all children born of slaves in Missouri be freed when they reached the age of 25.

Tallmadge's action shocked the southern representatives, but the amendment passed the House of Representatives by a narrow margin in a strictly sectional vote. "You have kindled a fire," shouted Congressman Cobb of Georgia at Tallmadge and his supporters, "which all the waters of the ocean cannot put out, which seas of blood can only extinguish!" The Senate, however, dampened the fire very quickly by defeating the Tallmadge amendment near the end of the session of Congress in March, 1819.

In the intervening months before the next session of Congress, the country had a chance to debate the issue. Although there were religious and philanthropic groups in the northern and border states like the Quakers and the American Colonization Society which were working for the eventual extinction of slavery, it became clear to politicians, in both the North and the South, that the Tallmadge amendment raised questions of political power that were more interesting than the moral and humanitarian issues. When Congress reconvened in December, 1819, Alabama was admitted to the Union as a slave state without any controversy; but the admission of Alabama established an even balance between the slave and free states with 11 each. Hence the admission of Missouri, without conditions, would make it the twelfth slave state, thus giving southern senators a virtual-veto over any legislation unfavorable to their interests that might be enacted by the House of Representatives, where the more populous northern states had a majority.

Consequently, the Missouri controversy quickly became a struggle in which considerations of power were more important than the moral issue. Northerners like Senator Rufus King of New York saw a chance to create a northern party that would break the southern control of the federal government that had prevailed for so long under the "Virginia dynasty." King had been an important Federalist leader, and he was the political favorite of many Federalist-minded northerners who never tired

Hall of Representatives. Growth of the place of the House of Representatives in the political system. The I. N. Phelps Stokes Collection of American Historical Prints. Prints Division. The New York Public Library.

of denouncing the three-fifths clause of the Constitution (counting three-fifths of the slaves in determining a state's representation in Congress) because they claimed that it gave an unfair advantage to southern states in national politics.

A spectacular debate took place in both houses of Congress in the early months of 1820, during which hard things were said on both sides. But a solution was found by skillful politicians like Henry Clay, the Speaker of the House, when the northeastern district of Massachusetts applied for admission to the Union as the independent state of Maine. After much parliamentary maneuvering, an omnibus measure known as the "Missouri Compromise" was passed by both houses of Congress. Maine was admitted as a free state, and Missouri as a slave state. But the most significant provision in the compromise bill was a section that prohibited slavery "forever . . . in all territory ceded by France to the United States . . . which lies north of 36° 30′ . . . not included within the territory of [Missouri]."

The compromise bill nearly failed when President Monroe hesitated to sign it. The President was not certain that Congress had the constitutional power to exclude slavery from a territory, especially if the word "forever" was meant to extend to the territory after it became a state. But, he finally consented to give the measure his signature when the members of his Cabinet unanimously agreed that the Missouri bill was "consistent with" the Constitution.

The Missouri debate alarmed many of the leading statesmen of the Republic. Thomas Jefferson told a friend that "this momentous question . . . like a fire-bell in the night awakened and filled me with terror." His anxiety stemmed from a belief that "a geographical line, coinciding with a marked principle, moral and political, once conceived and held up to the angry passions of men, will never be obliterated: and every new irritation will mark it sharper and deeper."

Nevertheless, the danger was not nearly as great as Jefferson imagined it to be, for a second phase of the Missouri debate demonstrated that the moral and political rift between the North and the South did not yet go very deep. When the Missouri state constitution was completed, it contained a clause forbidding free blacks or mulattoes to enter the state. This was clearly a defiant gesture, because it violated the clause of the federal Constitution which provided that "the citizens of each state shall be entitled to all the privileges and immunities of citizens of the several states." Congress, however, contented itself with the adoption of a pious amendment affirming the privileges of citizenship guaranteed by the Constitution as part of the resolution which formally admitted Missouri to the Union. Of great significance is the fact that, in the discussion of this resolution, northern congressmen acquiesced in the assumption that the black race was inferior to the white race. Indeed, many of their states also had constitutional and legislative discriminations against free blacks.

Thus it appears that while the Missouri question aroused significant sectional rivalries, no deep fractures appeared in the racial attitudes of American society. The northern leaders who participated in the Missouri debates showed little disposition to take any absolutist stands about the moral or intellectual equality of the black. Questions of power and morality were not yet lined up along one geographical axis of controversy.

The "American System" as a Focus of Conflict

The Growth of Protectionist Sentiment

While the Missouri question flared up and faded away within the short space of two years, divisions over the tariff question drew a growing number of interest groups into the political arena in the 1820's. The depression that followed the Panic of 1819 aroused considerable protectionist sentiment not only among the hard-hit American manufacturers, but among other classes in the North as well. Grain farmers saw little hope for any enlargement of European demand for their products, particularly with the revival of European agriculture after the Napoleonic wars. Hence the farmers of the Middle States and the Ohio Valley were easily persuaded that their main hope lay in enlarging the home market by stimulating the growth of domestic manufacturing. In addition, other farmers like the hemp growers of Kentucky and the sheep raisers of Vermont, Pennsylvania, and Ohio began to blame their depression hardships on imports of hemp and wool, and to see a remedy in tariff protection. Furthermore, many of the unemployed workers in the leading manufacturing cities blamed their plight on foreign competition

An early machine for making barrels. Collection of j mara gutman.

and clamored for increased tariff duties to protect the infant industries of the United States.

The defeat of a bill in 1820 to increase tariff rates on manufactured goods revealed the growing rivalry of interest groups in the struggle to obtain political advantages. Southern representatives voted overwhelmingly against the measure because the economy of the South had become so dependent on the export of cotton to England that they were unwilling to jeopardize their profitable relationship with their English customers. Furthermore, they had no wish to pay higher prices for the manufactured goods that they purchased for their families. At the same time, nearly half of the New England representatives were against the measure, because they spoke for commercial and shipping interests who feared that high tariffs would diminish the carrying trade.

Despite their defeat in 1820, manufacturers and their protectionist allies among farmers and handicraftsmen continued to press for a higher tariff. Henry Clay became their most conspicuous spokesman in Congress by expounding a new rationale for a policy of economic nationalism that came to be known as the "American System." Clay recognized that the national security arguments which had rallied widespread support for the tariff of 1816 no longer had any force or meaning; no one feared a renewal of war with England any more. Instead, he held forth a glittering vision of rapid economic growth that would be stimulated through the development of American manufactures and the American home market. He proposed a program of high tariffs linked to a nationally subsidized system of internal improvements that would facilitate the marketing of farm surpluses in the growing factory towns of the national

Clay's
"American System"

Making barrels in a factory late in the eighteenth century. Collection of j mara gutman.

market economy. "We must then change our course . . . ," he declared in the tariff debates of 1824. "We must give a new direction to . . . our industry. We must speedily adopt a genuine American policy . . . let us create also a home market to give further scope to the consumption of the products of American industry."

The supporters of the American System were strong enough to push through a new law in 1824 that provided increased tariff rates for cotton and woolen manufactures and gave protection also to the producers of wool, iron, hemp, lead, and glass. The vote in the House of Representatives reveals the extent to which the "home market" argument had won the allegiance of the farming and manufacturing interests in the Northeast and Northwest: 60 Middle State representatives voted for the measure, and 15 were opposed; 31 representatives from the West voted in favor, and only 5 were opposed. New England continued to be divided because of the heavy investment of merchants in the carrying trade: 15 votes from that section were cast in favor, and 23 were opposed. The South was almost unanimous in opposition to the measure: only a single vote from that section was cast in favor, while 57 votes were opposed.

Clay and the supporters of the American System were also anxious to initiate a federal program of internal improvements. They knew full well that the development of an effective home market required a transportation system on a national scale that would transcend the localized barter and exchange system that prevailed in the self-sufficing agrarian sector of the economy. Accordingly, they pushed through both houses of Congress a General Survey Act which was designed to pave the way for federal expenditures in a large program of internal improvements, and for federal subscriptions to the stock of private companies engaged in such enterprises.

The Supreme Court and Interstate Commerce

Such visions of a growing national economy were given much aid and comfort by a significant decision of the Supreme Court in the case of *Gibbons* v. *Ogden* (1824). This case arose out of an exclusive privilege to operate steamboats in the waters of the state which the legislature of New York had given to Robert Fulton and Robert Livingston, pioneers in the development of steamboat navigation. On the basis of this monopoly grant, Fulton and Livingston had assigned to Aaron Ogden the exclusive privilege to operate steamboats across the Hudson River between New York and New Jersey. Thomas Gibbons, however, proceeded to compete with Ogden in steamboat navigation in the same waters on the basis of a federal license granted under the Coasting Act. The New York courts upheld Ogden's suit to restrain Gibbons from invading his monopoly grant. Gibbons' appeal to the Supreme Court raised significant questions involving the interpretation of the power of Congress to regulate interstate commerce. Moreover, the Court's decision was bound to have a profound effect upon the future growth of the American economy, because the rapid growth of steamboat traffic on the navigable rivers of the United States had demonstrated the enormous possibilities for the growth of interstate commerce more dramatically than any other development in transportation up to that time.

Speaking for the Court, Chief Justice John Marshall declared that the monopoly grant to Ogden was illegal saying that the power of Congress to regulate interstate commerce "is complete in itself, may be exercised to its utmost extent, and acknowledges no limitations other than those that are prescribed in the Constitution." He rejected the argument that the word "commerce" should be narrowly defined to include the mere buying and selling of goods, but not the transportation of goods. Commerce, he maintained, includes "every species of commercial inter-course"—thus it encompasses navigation and transportation, as well as the commercial relations of buying and selling. While he granted that the regulation of the internal commerce of a state was reserved to the state, he also declared that interstate commerce cannot stop at the external boundary line of every state—"it comprehends navigation within the limits of state in the Union." Hence, Marshall's broad definition of the interstate commerce power of Congress, and his conception of the flow of interstate commerce within the states themselves, provided the indispensable legal framework for the growth of a national market economy.

But for the support of Clay's American System, a favorable legal framework for a national market economy was not, by itself, sufficient. Positive legislation to encourage national economic growth was need-ed—particularly new measures of tariff protection. This protectionist effort came to a climax near the end of John Quincy Adams' administra-tion when a convention of manufacturing interests assembled in Harris-burg at the call of the Pennsylvania Society For the Promotion of Manufactures and the Mechanic Arts. A hundred delegates—representing all but nine states, most of the latter being in the South—adopted a petition to Congress calling for increased tariff rates on a variety of commodities.

The "Tariff of Abominations"

The supporters of Andrew Jackson attacked the Harrisburg Conven-tion as a political stratagem employed by the Adams administration to win the support of Pennsylvania and other protectionist states in the forthcoming presidential elections. But Jacksonian leaders knew full well that protectionist sentiment was strong among wool growers and hemp growers in the Middle States and the Ohio Valley. Consequently, they were determined to construct a pattern of tariff schedules that would do the most good for their party's political fortunes in the key states of this region.

A majority of northern and western Jacksonians controlled the House Committee on Manufactures which was charged with the responsibility of framing a suitable bill in 1828. The most important man on the committee was Silas Wright of New York, a member of the Albany Regency and Van Buren's trusted henchman. The Committee majority prepared a bill for presentation to the House that was skillfully arranged to embarrass Adams and the supporters of the American System and, at the same time, to retain the loyalty of protectionist groups in the Jacksonian political coalition.

The result was a lopsided bill that was particularly advantageous for farmers   but wholly inadequate for manufacturers. High duties were proposed for raw wool, flax, hemp, and pig iron, but the increased schedules on manufactured goods were not enough to offset the price increases in raw materials. The bill was particularly offensive to New England interests where woolen manufacturers and shipbuilders would feel the pinch of rising costs for raw materials. By 1828, also, more and more New England merchants were diverting investments of capital from the carrying trade to the rapidly growing manufacturing establishments of the region.

The followers of Adams and Clay were outraged by this calculated effort to force New England representatives to join with southerners in voting against the bill. They were convinced that the bill was designed to be defeated in such a way that the blame for the defeat could be laid to the supporters of the Adams administration. Even John Randolph, one of the bitterest opponents of the Adams administration, accepted this view of the political motives of the majority of the House committee on manufactures when he sarcastically described the bill as referring to "manufactures of no sort or kind, but the manufacture of a President of the United States."

The letters of Silas Wright to the Albany Regency, however, reveal

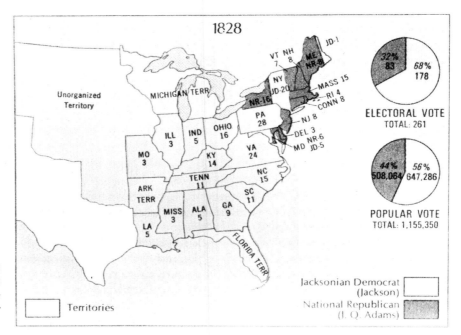

From The National Atlas of the United States of America. *United States Department of the Interior Geological Survey.*

that the purpose of the committee majority was to frame a bill that would really be advantageous to the friends of Jackson among the iron producers, wool growers, and hemp and flax raisers of New York, Pennsylvania, Ohio, and Kentucky. In the complicated parliamentary maneuvering that followed, particularly in the Senate, it was the southerners who consistently pursued the strategy of trying to keep the bill as odious as possible for New England interests; but when the Senate added amendments increasing the rates for New England woolen manufacturers, Jackson men such as Van Buren of New York, Eaton of Tennessee, and Benton of Missouri voted with the majority to pass the bill.

The result was a tariff act that contained greatly increased duties on both raw materials and manufactured goods. Southern representatives were astonished and enraged that such a bill should have been passed, and the new law was quickly dubbed the "Tariff of Abominations." Furthermore, even John C. Calhoun, once an ardent nationalist, was now ready to join in the violent reaction against the measure. When Congress adjourned, he returned to his home in South Carolina where he set about writing his *Exposition and Protest* in which he enunciated a theory of nullification that resembled the arguments in John Taylor's *New Views of the Constitution.*

By the end of the 1820's, therefore, the tariff issue was emerging as the most volatile element in the boiling cauldron of political conflict. For some politicians, the conflict of interest groups offered new opportunities to use the manipulative strategies of the new politics. But it was a dangerous political game to play because the tariff question had aroused southern economic interests, and behind the economics of cotton production lay the explosive question of slavery, defused for a time by the Missouri Compromise. Because its political ramifications were so extensive, the tariff issue was destined to provide one of the crucial tests of the new political system that was being shaped by the onrushing democratic revolution.

*From the title page of
Sartain's Union Magazine,
1849. Rush Rhees Library.
The University of Rochester.*

The Election of a Democratic Hero

The theories of John Taylor and the principles of Henry Clay's American System marked the opposite poles of the ideological debates in the 1820's. There was, to be sure, no polarization of parties around these two extremes of opinion—the realities of democratic politics in a highly mobile society would compel political leaders to rally their coalitions somewhere between the two extremes—but one thing was certain: the peculiar one-party system of the Virginia Dynasty could not survive in the new social environment. A new party system was required, and it would need to be a two-party or multi-party system to give voice to the great variety of social needs being created by the rapid process of social change.

The reappearance of a contest for the presidency in 1824 provided a stimulus for the formation of a new party system. The peculiar outcome of the confused election produced even more bitter feelings than the political campaigning of the candidates and their friends. Jackson's followers in Congress were determined to fight what they believed was a corrupt bargain between Adams and Clay, and the policies of John Quincy Adams soon provided them with new allies.

The Jacksonian Coalition

Adams was an ardent Republican nationalist and he hoped to use his presidency to promote a bold program of national improvements that apotheosized the principles of the American System. His inaugural address called for the bold use of national powers for "laws promoting the improvement of agriculture, commerce, and manufactures, the cultivation and the encouragement of the mechanic and . . . elegant arts . . . and the progress of the 'sciences.'" The President insisted that "to refrain from exercising them (national powers) for the benefit of the people themselves would be to hide in the earth the talent committed to our charge." He even went so far as to urge Congress not to shrink from the formidable legislative tasks required or to be "palsied by the will of our constituents."

The overweening economic nationalism and elitism of John Quincy Adams' proposals had the immediate effect of uniting his most powerful opponents against him. When the new President took his oath of office, his opposition had been divided into three factions: the Jacksonians, the Crawford men, and the followers of Calhoun. Calhoun had accepted the vice-presidency in 1824 with the hope that he might be next in line in the presidential succession. Immediately after Adams had announced his choice of Henry Clay as Secretary of State, the Calhoun men had rushed into the Jackson camp; since that position had been the traditional stepping stone to the presidency, the Adams-Clay combination threatened to block Calhoun's road to the presidency. On the other hand, the Crawford men in Congress, led by such men as Martin Van Buren of New York, had accepted the nomination of Clay calmly and had even voted for confirmation. After all, seasoned politicians like Van Buren understood the system of political rewards and would have been surprised if Adams had acted differently.

But, after hearing the President's Annual Message, the Crawford men were ready to join forces with the Jacksonians. More than any other group in Congress, Crawford's followers had been strongly influenced by the constitutional views of men like Spencer Roane and John Taylor. Because of their strict adherence to a states rights philosophy and a narrow interpretation of the Constitution, the "Radicals," as Crawford's followers were called, were stunned by Adams' sweeping interpretation of the powers of the national government. William Crawford characterized the message as being "replete with doctrines which I hold to be unconstitutional." Thomas Jefferson, now in the last year of his life, charged that the ideas expressed in the new President's annual message would lead to "a single and splendid government of an aristocracy, founded on banking institutions, and money incorporations under the guise and cloak of their favorite branches of manufactures, commerce and navigation, riding and ruling over the plundered ploughman and beggared yeomanry."

At the same time, Martin Van Buren was shrewdly calculating the possibility of an alliance with the Jackson men. "If General Jackson and his friends will put his election on old party grounds . . . ," he wrote, "we can by adding his personal popularity to the yet remaining force of old party feeling, not only succeed in electing him but our success when achieved will be worth something." Thereafter, the Radicals in Congress joined forces with the Jacksonians in harassing the Adams administration at every turn.

Jackson's Presidential Campaign

This loose coalition of congressional leaders was forged into a new national party organization by such men as Calhoun and Van Buren in a series of personal negotiations with influential politicians in some of the key states of the South, West, and Northeast. By 1827 a Central Committee was formed in Washington to act as a clearinghouse of political information and to keep state organizations well stocked with pamphlets and printed copies of congressional speeches. The chairman of this committee, General John P. Van Ness, was a New Yorker closely associated with Van Buren's political machine.

Such efforts were aided immeasureably by a vast nationwide newspaper network. A chain of "newspaper posts" from New England to Louisiana and in the new western states was created by the Jacksonians in 1827 and 1828. Nine new Jackson papers were started in North Carolina in 1827, 18 more appeared in Ohio, and others sprang up in such strategic states as Massachusetts, New Jersey, Pennsylvania, Indiana, and Illinois. By 1828 the network included well-established newspapers that influenced key areas of public opinion. These included Duff Green's *United States Telegraph* in Washington, Thomas Ritchie's *Enquirer* in Richmond, Edwin Croswell's Albany *Argus*, Isaac Hill's New Hampshire *Patriot*, Nathaniel Green's Boston *Statesman*, the New York

Evening Post, the Philadelphia *Palladium*, the Charleston *Mercury*, the Nashville *Republican*, and Amos Kendall's *Argus of the West* (Kentucky). The columns of this mushrooming Jackson press were filled with constant attacks on the Adams administration and a steady supply of articles favorable to the General.

Since Jackson was precluded by tradition (adhered to by Federalists and Jeffersonians alike) from actively campaigning for the presidency, the network of newspapers became the primary means of shaping the new party's ideology. This was not an easy matter because there were many differences of interest and outlook among the supporters of Jackson inside and outside of Congress. The new party, indeed, was a patchwork of interest groups, classes, and parties: included in the combination were old Republicans, new-style Democrats, and disgruntled Federalists. In addition, the party embraced a wide variety of social types in every region of the country, ranging from farmers and mechanics to planters, bankers, and businessmen. Hostile newspaper editors repeatedly charged that the Jacksonians were an "unnatural alliance" of irresponsible opportunists held together by little else than the desire to oust Adams.

The politically astute General avoided clear-cut statements about issues and policies that might create strains within this broad political coalition. Late in 1827, he outlined some of his ideas for Amos Kendall's *Argus of the West*. He told the Kentucky editor that he planned to "reform the government" by removing all officeholders who had been appointed to their positions "against the will of the people," and all others "who are incompetent." As for the tariff, Jackson told Kendall that he favored a "middle and just course," a comment that seemed equally pleasing to protectionists in the Northeast as well as anti-tariff men in the South. Radicals were happy to read of his opposition to federally sponsored internal improvements, but the General was careful to hold out some hope to enterprising farmers and businessmen in the Northwest by proposing to distribute surplus federal revenue to the states to help them develop their own roads and lands. Furthermore, Jackson was already popular throughout the South and the West because of his advocacy of a policy of total removal for the Indian tribes toward lands located west of the Mississippi.

But above all, Jackson became the symbol of the hopes and aspirations that had been aroused by the developing democratic revolution. The theme that was repeated again and again in the network of Jackson newspapers was: "Andrew Jackson is *the candidate of the people*." Campaign orators made the most of the fact that Jackson was an orphan boy who had made his way in life by his own merit and force of character. The *Ohio State Journal* declared that the old hero deserved the confidence of the people because he was "not raised in the lap of luxury or wealth." To the vast number of farmers and mechanics of the country, Jackson was described as a man of the soil who had left his plough like

Cincinnatus of Rome to respond to his country's call in the War of 1812.

Of course, Jackson's greatest asset was his reputation as "the Hero" of the Battle of New Orleans. The managers of his party organized a monster celebration on January 8, 1828, the anniversary date of the victory at New Orleans. There Jackson was toasted again and again with the theme, "Andrew Jackson. His Titles are his Services. His Party the American People!" Fourth of July celebrations everywhere in the states were turned into Jackson rallies by supporters who waved flags and hickory sticks and shouted for "Old Hickory."

Furthermore, every effort was made to contrast the republican simplicity of Jackson with the aristocratic tastes and intellectual snobbery of the ex-Harvard professor in the White House. A great storm over the "royal extravagances" of President Adams was whipped up when the Jackson press charged inaccurately that public funds had been used to purchase a billiard table and an expensive set of chessmen for the East Room of the White House. And when an Adams campaign pamphlet sneered at Jackson's lack of education, claiming that the backwoods general could not spell correctly "more than about one word in four," the Jacksonians portrayed their candidate as a man whose natural wisdom and common sense were superior to the effete book learning of John Quincy Adams. "Plain simple common sense" marked the general's style according to one Jacksonian newspaper editor who proudly told his readers that they would encounter in Jackson's statements "no Greek quotations, no toilsome or painful struggles after eloquence" of the sort that came from the pen of the "learned man" in the White House.

Some of Adams' backers sought to discredit Jackson's hero image by assailing him as a border ruffian who fought duels, and a hard military commander who had unjustly executed six militiamen. Others went so far as to brand Mrs. Jackson an adultress because Andrew Jackson had married her under the mistaken impression that her divorce from her previous husband had been granted, necessitating a second marriage to make their conjugal relationship legal. Mrs. Jackson, a pious and sensitive woman, suffered terribly from these attacks on her moral character; her death from a heart ailment shortly after the election was undoubtedly hastened by her personal torment.

The Election of 1828   The slanders had little effect in damaging the general's public image, however, for the voters who went to the polls in 1828 gave him an impressive victory. The old hero's popular vote was 647,276 (56 per cent) compared to Adams' 508,064 (44 per cent). In the electoral college count, the margin was more overwhelming, for Jackson secured 178 votes to Adams' 83. His sweep included the entire South and West, together with Pennsylvania, more than half of the electoral votes of New York, and a portion of those in Maryland.

Jackson's victory was all the more impressive because of the tremendous increase in the voter turnout. The 1,155,340 voters who flocked to the polls in 1828 represented an increase of more than 800,000 actual

voters over the previous presidential election in 1824, and they constituted more than 56 per cent of the adult white male population.

The size of the popular vote convinced Jackson's supporters that there
had been a stupendous outpouring of voters for the old hero. And,
although it can be shown that similar proportions had turned out in
exciting state elections previous to 1828, they were right; this was the
first time that such large numbers had turned out on a national scale.
What is also worth noting is that the National Republicans accepted the
same version of the meaning of Jackson's victory. "Well," wrote one of
them, "a great revolution has taken place . . . This is what I all along
feared but to a much greater extent." And this pervasive sense of a
democratic revolution at work in American society was to shape the tone
and substance of the battles in the new party system.

The inauguration of Andrew Jackson provided visible evidence of the
rise of the common man in American life. One of Adams' supporters
who watched the proceedings wrote, "to us, who had witnessed the quiet
and orderly period of the Adams administration, it seemed as if half the
nation had rushed at once into the Capital. It was like the inundation of
the . . . barbarians into Rome. . . ." When the ceremony of the inauguration was over, most of the immense crowd which had gathered to hear
the President's address followed him to the White House, where
confusion and disorder quickly ensued. Those who belonged to the older
natural aristocracy of the Republic were scandalized by such scenes of
tumult in "the President's House." Justice Story of the Supreme Court,
an old Federalist who left the President's reception in disgust, declared:
"The reign of King Mob seemed triumphant."

*The People's
President*

Indian Removal

Between Jefferson's presidency and Jackson's, a series of wars broke
Indian resistance and opened the way for white settlement to the
Mississippi River. The battles of Tippecanoe and Detroit in 1811 and 1813
broke the pan-Indian cultural movement and resistance effort in the Old
Northwest that had been organized by the Shawnee chief Tecumseh and
his brother, the Prophet. About the same time Andrew Jackson's victory
in the Battle of Horseshoe Bend (1814) opened the Old Southwest. By
1832, with the conclusion of the Black Hawk war, Indian resistance in the
North east of the Mississippi was at an end. Pacification in the South
took slightly longer; the uprising of the Seminoles in 1833, under Chief
Osceola, was not finally put down until 1842.

While these victories opened the way for massive western migration,
the administration of Andrew Jackson was confronted with a different
kind of Indian land problem. Many Indian tribes possessed lands, now
quite valuable, within the borders of existing states. During the 1820's
many tribes decided that they had relinquished enough land and would

*Indian Land
and White
Expansion*

sell no more to the United States government. At Jackson's urging, Congress responded to this problem in 1830 by authorizing the President to exchange the public domain west of the Mississippi River for Indian lands in the East that were increasingly coveted by American farmers. Although this policy met with some political opposition, primarily from religious leaders supporting Indian missions, the broad support Jackson had for the policy is more significant.

The removal of Indians was a central issue of the period. Never before, in fact, had Indian-white relations been so central to the experience of both whites and Indians. Divisions and conflict within tribes had formerly been related to internal issues or to inter-tribal issues. Now divisions were increasingly related to the question of whether particular leaders were willing to collaborate with whites or were militantly opposed to them. Similarly, Indians mattered more to whites than at any time since settlement. The aggressive expansion of the period was accomplished by dispossessing the Indians of their lands.

The policy of Indian removal was especially important in the Southeast, the home of the so-called Five Civilized tribes (Creeks, Cherokees, Choctaws, Seminoles, and Chickasaws), and the nature of the problem is most clearly illustrated in the controversy over the removal of the Cherokee Indians from their Georgia lands. The Cherokees had negotiated many treaties over the years with the English and American governments securing their land and giving them internal self-government. But when it became clear that the Cherokees would give up no more land, Georgia authorities began to harass them. The Georgia legislature, with encouragement from President Jackson, passed a series of laws in effect nullifying tribal authority and rendering Indian land titles worthless.

The Indians appealed to Andrew Jackson for the protection of their treaty rights against the actions of Georgia. Jackson replied that "the President of the United States has no power to protect them against the laws of Georgia." The Indians then turned to the Supreme Court. In *Worcester* v. *Georgia* (1832), Chief Justice John Marshall held that only the federal government had authority in Indian affairs. "The Cherokee Nation," he wrote, "is a distinct community . . . in which the laws of Georgia have no force." Jackson, who as President was responsible for the enforcement of federal law, reportedly exclaimed: "John Marshall has made his decision, now let him enforce it." Of course, the Chief Justice had no way to enforce the Court's ruling. The Cherokees, thus confronted with the inevitable, accepted removal. Their government-sponsored migration, known as the "trail of tears," was filled with grief. Perhaps one-third of the Indians who began the trek died enroute. Remarkably, the survivors prevailed and even prospered in the drastically different ecological setting of the trans-Mississippi West.

Ideological Justification   The justifications Congress and Jackson used for removal illuminate deeply held cultural beliefs. Congress based its policy on the "natural superiority . . . [of] the claims of civilized communites over those of savage tribes." Indians must either civilize themselves, that is adopt white man's ways and take up agriculture, or they must remove themselves so that they do not obstruct progress. Andrew Jackson drew upon this deeply embedded American prejudice when he asked Congress for the authority to remove Indians to the West: "What good man would prefer a country covered with forests and ranged by a few thousand savages to our extensive Republic, studded with cities, towns, and prosperous farms . . . and filled with all the blessings of liberty, civilization, and religion." Although Indians had taught settlers at both Jamestown and Plymouth how to grow corn, nineteenth-century Americans consistently argued that Indians were inferior (and could be deprived of their land) because they were hunters rather than farmers. In fact, prior to European contact, the Woodland Indians, including the Cherokees, had lived in stable agricultural communities. These patterns of life had been disrupted by contact with Europeans. Expansionist pressure, combined with the opportunities presented by fur-trading with Europeans, encouraged Indians to make hunting a major rather than a peripheral economic activity. The Cherokees stopped selling land partly because they wanted to re-stabilize their agricultural way of life.

The ideology of dispossession was thus at odds with the actual conditions of Indian life, particularly in respect to the Cherokees. Under the influence of Protestant missionaries and whites who had married into the tribe, they had adopted many visible elements of white "civilization." They followed advanced practices of agriculture and most had adopted "American dress." They were also literate, published a newspaper, and were governed by a written constitution. The irony or even hypocrisy of removal may have escaped some, but James Madison, the former president, quietly noted it.

Yet for all their outward resemblance to the yeoman farmer, the Cherokees and other southern tribes retained key tribal values relating to landholding and religion. They continued to hold land as a community rather than as individuals, and land was not an economic commodity for them. The Creeks, for example, declared: "We would not receive money for land in which our father and friends are buried. . . . We love our land; it is our mother." This organic and sacred attachment to the land as the foundation of community was the focus of the cultural conflict between the Indians and the dominant white culture, in which land was increasingly treated as a commodity.

The white society refused to take tribal cultures seriously as legitimate ways of living. Instead Jacksonian leaders sought to pry Indians from their communal bonds and from their historic and mystical ties to the land. Government officials acted to deprive tribal cultures of their autonomy and to make them dependent upon the United States government. This quest for paternalistic dominance is reflected in the language whites used in Indian-white relations. Whites insisted that Indians assume the role of children in relations with the "Great White Father." Those Indians who sought to preserve their tribal cultures rejected this language. When William Henry Harrison, for instance, attempted to place himself, rhetorically, in a fatherly relationship to Tecumseh, the militant Shawnee chief replied: "My father! The sun is my father, and the earth is my mother." Tecumseh was speaking the language of Indian cultural autonomy, but other Indians, either because they profited from the bribes offered by whites or because they saw no other alternative, accepted removal and the paternalism that led ultimately to the reservation system.

War Against the "Money Power"

The Bank Issue The major economic issue of Jackson's administration was the Bank of the United States and the machinery of credit associated with banking. Agrarian debtors in the West and Southwest had long been opposed to the policies of the Bank, but they were now joined by diverse allies elsewhere. The appearance of workingmen's parties in Philadelphia and New York revealed that eastern laborers also had a strong antipathy toward chartered monopolies—especially banks. An "Address of the Philadelphia Workingmen" issued in 1830 attacked bank notes as "an unequal, fluctuating, and easily imitated currency" that did great injury to the people. The workingmen's suspicion of bank notes resulted from the unscrupulous practice of employers who often paid off their workers in depreciated bank notes—contemptuously referred to as "rag money" by labor newspapers. The opponents of the Bank also included many of the new entrepreneurs who were engaged in the restless pursuit of economic opportunities opened up by the market revolution. Easy credit was indispensable for the enterprises of these men on the make, and they found that state banks were more responsive to their needs. They looked upon the Bank of the United States as an institution which represented the interests of men of established wealth who used their economic power to restrict the entry of newcomers in the scramble for control of the rich resources of an expanding economy.

Nicholas Biddle's Banking Policies To a certain extent, the policies of the Bank of the United States justified the suspicions of these new entrepreneurs, but not necessarily for the reasons that were asserted in their public criticisms. Under the leadership of Nicholas Biddle, who had become president in 1823, the Bank had initiated some rudimentary practices of central banking in the American economy. Although the functions of central banking were little understood at that time, Biddle, with the peculiar means at his disposal, made the Bank of the United States a self-appointed regulator of the country's credit system between 1823 and 1832.

The precocious son of a prominent Philadelphia merchant, Biddle had learned by the age of 13 all that the University of Pennsylvania could offer him, and then went to Princeton where he graduated at the head of his class two years later. At the age of 18, he was already a contributor to Dennie's *Port Folio,* and served briefly as secretary to James Monroe when he was minister to England in 1806. He was elected to the state legislature of Pennsylvania in 1810 and, at the time of his election to the state Senate in 1814, he attracted the favorable notice of Thomas Jefferson and other important Republican leaders. When Monroe became President, Biddle was appointed one of the five government directors of the Bank of the United States. In 1823, at the age of 37, he was chosen to be president of the largest corporation in America.

Under Biddle's leadership the Bank of the United States became a major influence in the expanding American economy. He was determined to secure a uniform currency as the best means of preventing such violent fluctuations in the business cycle as had occurred in 1819. This meant that the Bank and its branches (25 in number by 1830) controlled the note issues of state banks by continually presenting them for redemption in specie. Thus the Bank was able to aggressively expand its own lending business in competition with the state banks. The lack of complete reports on state banking activities makes any exact comparison difficult, but when Jackson became President in 1829, the loans of the Bank of the United States totalled $40.6 million, while those of the 329 state banks were $137 million—$13 million less than the total in 1815. It was apparent then that the rate of growth in the lending business of the national Bank under Biddle's leadership greatly exceeded that of the state banks.

During these same years, the Bank of the United States acquired the lion's share of the business of discounting promissory notes and bills of exchange. The economic specialization of regions that accompanied the market revolution increased the demand for short-term borrowing by commercial farmers, merchants, and manufacturers to finance the great inter-regional movements of farm commodities and manufactured goods. Since most of the buyers of these goods made their purchases with drafts or bills of exchange, the sellers were anxious to turn these drafts into cash by selling them to banks at discounted rates of interest amounting to 6 or 7 per cent. And, inasmuch as the Bank of the United States had branches located in all the important commercial centers of the country, it was able to get the largest share of the business of discounting such domestic bills.

The opponents of the Bank charged that it wielded a dangerous amount of political power because it made sizeable loans to Congressmen and newspaper editors. The Bank's records, however, show that many of its borrowers were Jacksonian Democrats, including members of Jackson's "Kitchen Cabinet"; hence the extent of its political influence is debatable. But no historian who makes a careful assessment of the financial history of this period can deny the great degree of economic power which the Bank possessed. Although the Bank's power over the currency and credit system of the country was not absolute, it clearly had more power than the national government in regulating currency and credit. Indeed it had become the main nerve center of the complex web of credit transactions associated with the growth of the national market economy.

Biddle's arrogant manner tended to increase public fears about the power of the Bank. Although he had started out as a government director, he did everything possible to keep the Bank's affairs free from public control once he had gained the presidency. Government directors were rarely consulted about basic policies; in Biddle's view, the Bank was an independent, private corporation. In the very first year of his presidency he demanded that all subordinate officers of the Bank should be "prepared to execute the orders of the board (of directors), in direct opposition, if need be, to the personal interests and wishes of the President and every officer of the Government." In testifying before a congressional committee in 1832 he denied quite truthfully that the Bank of the United States had ever oppressed any of the state banks, yet he could not pass up a chance to flaunt his sense of power by adding his opinion that "there are very few banks which might not have been destroyed" by the Bank of the United States if it had chosen to exert its powers.

It is not surprising, therefore, that Biddle approved the scheme of Henry Clay and Daniel Webster to introduce a bill for rechartering the Bank in 1832. The Bank's original charter was not due to expire until 1836, but Clay and Webster believed that the bank issue would be useful to the National Republicans in the presidential election of 1832. They were confident that a majority of both houses of Congress would support such a bill, and they assumed that congressional sentiment reflected the popular will.

Accordingly, a bill for recharter was pushed through both houses of Congress with comfortable majorities and sent to the President early in July for his signature. Jackson had displayed a willingness to temporize with the bank issue during most of his first term, but the obvious attempt to embarrass him politically put him in a fighting mood. To Martin Van Buren who had just returned from England, he declared: "The bank, Mr. Van Buren, is trying to kill me, *but I will kill it!*"

Jackson's Veto of the Bank Recharter Bill

Jackson promptly returned the recharter bill to Congress with a ringing veto message. Placing his own views in opposition to those of the Supreme Court, he declared that the Bank of the United States was unconstitutional, and that the monopolistic privileges of the Bank had served to enrich private stockholders, including foreign stockholders, at the expense of the labors and earnings of the American people. The most eloquent portion of the veto message, however, was that which expressed Jackson's social philosophy:

It is to be regretted that the rich and the powerful too often bend the acts of government to their selfish purposes. Distinctions in society will always exist under every just government. Equality of talents, of education, or of wealth can not be produced by human institutions. In the full enjoyment of the gifts of Heaven and the fruits of superior industry, economy, and virtue, every man is equally entitled to protection by law, but when the laws undertake to add to these natural and just advantages artificial distinctions, to grant titles, gratuities, and exclusive privileges, to make the rich richer and the potent more powerful, the humble members of society—the farmers, mechanics, and laborers—who have neither the time nor the means of securing like favors to themselves, have a right to complain of the injustice of their Government. There are no necessary evils in government. Its evils exists only in its abuses. If it would confine itself to equal protection, and, as Heaven does its rains, shower its favors alike on the high and the low, the rich and the poor, it would be an unqualified blessing. . . .

These concluding comments of the veto message set forth the first principles of the evolving Jacksonian ideology. Jackson granted that natural inequalities existed in every society, but the only social distinctions that were "natural" and "just" were those which were based upon "superior industry, virtue, and economy." Hence the overriding goal of a democratic government must be to provide all citizens with equal protection of the laws. The first duty of government is to stand against any and all legislation which grants special privileges or advantages that would increase the wealth and power of individuals or groups beyond what they could attain through their own industry and virtue.

Jackson's social philosophy was stated broadly enough to win a responsive resonance from the diverse groups with grievances against the Bank of the United States. The proponents of the recharter bill were unable to muster enough votes in Congress to override the veto, so they pinned their hope on the forthcoming presidential election. The choice before the people was reasonably clear; the candidates themselves personified the opposing forces in the war on the Bank because Henry Clay was nominated by the National Republicans to oppose Jackson. In the outcome, Jackson won easily with 219 electoral votes to 49 for Clay. But his margin in the popular vote was less than what he received four years before due to the appearance of the Anti-Masonic party in the presidential contest: Jackson, 55 per cent; Clay 42.4 per cent; and Wirt, 2.6 per cent.

Convinced that Biddle had used loans to Congressmen and subsidies to newspapers to defeat him for re-election, Jackson was determined to press the offensive against the Bank. "Until I can strangle this hydra of corruption, the Bank," he declared, "I will not shrink from my duty . . . ." Shortly after his re-election, therefore, the President decided to curtail Biddle's power by removing all government deposits which had been placed in the Bank according to the provisions of the Act of 1816 establishing that institution.

Action on the removal of deposits was delayed some months because

Jackson's Removal of Bank Deposits

of a crisis created by South Carolina's attempt to nullify the tariff laws. Furthermore, the Cabinet was seriously divided over the advisability of such a policy. According to provisions of the Bank's charter, the Secretary of the Treasury's assent was necessary for any removal of deposits, but William Duane, who had been appointed to that post in Jackson's second administration, refused to agree and at least two other members of the Cabinet supported him.

Failing to obtain Duane's cooperation, Jackson dismissed him from his office and appointed Roger Taney to the position. As Attorney-General, Taney had helped to write Jackson's veto message against the recharter bill, and he was more than ready to carry out the President's wishes. On September 26, 1833, the new Secretary of the Treasury announced that government deposits would no longer be made in the Bank of the United States, but rather in seven selected state banks—all but one of them controlled by Jacksonian Democrats. Indeed, Taney was a stockholder of a Baltimore bank that was included in the favored group.

Biddle responded to the removal of large government deposits by contracting the lending and discounting operations of the Bank—so much so, that a severe credit stringency, known as "Biddle's panic," developed in the leading commercial centers of the country. Because of the removal of governmental deposits, some curtailment of the Bank's credit operations was necessary, but it is also clear from Biddle's correspondence that he pushed the contraction policy further than necessary in order to create so much distress that public pressures would force the Jackson administration to retreat. "I have no doubt," he wrote, "that such a course will ultimately lead to a restoration of the currency and the recharter of the Bank."

But it was Biddle and not President Jackson who was forced to retreat. The Jackson administration and the Democratic majority in the House of Representatives held firm, and by the summer of 1834 business and financial groups brought pressure on Biddle to abandon his curtailment of loans, and to enlarge his discounting activities according to the needs of the business community. The defeat of Biddle in this instance was far-reaching in its consequences. Shorn of the government deposits and the claims against the state banks which they often provided, the Bank of the United States ceased to have any significant regulatory powers over the currency and credit systems. The Bank, thereafter, joined in the unrestrained competition of private banks that fed the speculative boom of the mid-1830's.

Jackson's
"Hard Money"
Program

But Jackson was not content to push a policy that was merely punitive and negative. To replace the regulatory functions exercised by the Bank of the United States, Jackson and his advisers resolved to institute a "hard-money" policy. Much of the theory that lay behind this policy had been developed by William Gouge in his *A Short History of Paper Money and Banking in the United States.*

According to Gouge, paper money in the form of bank notes was the cause of the treacherous cycles of boom and bust that were afflicting the American economy and causing a serious derangement in the natural distribution of economic rewards to the productive and industrious members of society. Banks, he argued, tend to overissue their notes; prices then begin to rise and a general wave of inflation sweeps over the country. People tend to spend too freely, and businessmen begin to take risks in the pursuit of profits that are no longer prudent or sound. Finally the note issues that support the inflated volume of loans and discounted bills begin to depreciate, and foreign banking and mercantile houses begin to demand specie in payment for the balances owed them on goods and loans. Banks start to call in loans, a general panic sets in, and the speculative boom quickly turns into an economic collapse. Businessmen become bankrupt, laborers are unemployed, farmers suffer from depressed prices, while a few speculators and bankers manage to manipulate the situation to get possession of the lands and businesses of those who cannot meet their credit obligations. The remedy, therefore, lay in a policy that would reduce bank paper and encourage the use of a truly stable form of currency—in short, hard money in the form of gold and silver.

The hard money program of the Jackson administration included two basic policies—one was to restore gold to circulation and the other was to suppress the use of small bank notes as a form of currency. The restoration of gold to circulation was to be accomplished by a revaluation of the coinage ratio between gold and silver. Gold had become undervalued by the official ratio set at 15 to 1 when Alexander Hamilton was Secretary of the Treasury. As a result, since 1805 no gold had been sold to the Treasury to be minted and most gold had left the country. In June, 1834, a bill to revise the valuation of 16 to 1 passed Congress, and within two years the Secretary of the Treasury reported a substantial increase in the minting of gold coins. In addition, the total supply of specie in the country had increased impressively largely because of favorable trade balances—in October, 1833, there had been only $30 million of specie in the country, of which $26 million was in banks; in December, 1836, the totals had risen to $73 million and $45 million, respectively.

But the revival of gold coins would not be enough without measures to suppress bank notes. The Jacksonians were determined to push a policy that would encourage the use of hard money in the ordinary purposes of life, and thereby discourage the overissue of bank notes which created such tremendous fluctuations in the business cycle. Accordingly, a Treasury circular of April, 1835, banned all notes under $5 in receipt of tax payments, and banks holding government deposits were forbidden to issue such notes. In February, 1836, another Treasury order extended the ban to notes under $10, and a congressional act of April, 1836, prohibited notes under $20 after March 3, 1837.

Such measures, however, proved to be a poor substitute for the regulatory functions of a central bank. The Treasury's restrictions on small notes could be effective only with those state banks which had government deposits. And, although the Jackson administration increased its leverage with state banks by expanding the number of "pet banks" receiving deposits to 33 in 1835, and 89 in 1836, they never represented more than a small minority of such institutions. The tremendous speculative pressures that became so strong after 1834 led to a rapid increase in the number of state banks. By 1836, there were 713 state banks in the United States, compared to 506 in 1834, and 329 in 1829. State bank note circulation had grown from $48.2 million in 1829 to $94.8 million in 1834, and $140.3 million in 1836.

The Jacksonian leaders watched the speculative boom with profound dismay. In 1836, Secretary of the Treasury, Levi Woodbury, predicted "much distress, embarrassment, and ruin, before . . . the excesses of paper [can be] sufficiently curtailed, and the exorbitant discounts gradually lessened." And Senator Benton, the leading defender of the hard money policy in the Senate, said emphatically: "I did not join in putting down the Bank of the United States, to put up a wilderness of local banks. I did not join in putting down the paper currency of a national bank, to put up a national currency of a thousand local banks."

For quite different reasons, the hard money policy was also viewed with dismay by western interests in the Jacksonian party. State banking interests and land speculators in that region favored looser bank practices and an inflationary credit policy that would keep pace with the speculative urges of their region; indeed, one of the basic causes of the economic boom after 1835 was land speculation in the West. Therefore, the state banking interests, the land speculators, and a large portion of the profit-hungry farmers in the West had little enthusiasm for the hard money policies of the Jackson administration; and they found willing allies among state bankers and their commercial associates in the East.

Locofoco Democrats   But, in many states of the Northeast, there emerged a radical group of Democrats, composed of intellectuals, small business and professional men, and workingmen who were not only enthusiastic supporters of the Jackson administration's hard money program, but who were also determined to push for a more vigorous antimonopoly program. The editor of the New York *Evening Post,* William Leggett, declared in 1835 that his newspaper would support only those candidates who were committed unequivocally against bank notes under $5. Leggett and other radical democrats also advocated the enactment of general laws of incorporation that would permit groups of "co-partners," no matter how small their capital, to obtain charters of incorporation without applying to the legislature for special acts of incorporation. In October, 1835, a group of radical Democrats in New York City organized a revolt against the conservative Tammany leaders of the party. When the Tammany regulars tried to quell their opponents at a party meeting by turning off the gas lights, the insurgents carried on the meeting by the light of

friction matches—newly invented and popularly-known as "locofocos."
Henceforward, the radical Democrats became known as Locofocos, and
"Locofocoism" began to infest other Democratic party conventions in
key states of the Northeast.

These rifts in the Democratic party deepened when President Jackson
decided to take drastic measures to halt the wild speculation in western
lands which was clearly associated with the mushrooming growth of
state banks and state bank notes. On July 11, 1836, he issued an
executive order, known as the "Specie Circular," which required that
public land offices should take payment only in specie, and no longer in
notes issued by banks. By this action, Jackson punctured the bubble of
land speculation and set in motion a deflationary plunge of land prices
which contributed to the Panic of 1837.

Jackson's
Specie Circular

Perhaps if the Specie Circular had been made part of the Administration's hard money policy earlier, the speculative land boom might have
been slowed down before it got out of control. One wonders why Jackson
moved so slowly in this matter, particularly because the Washington
Globe, as early as the spring of 1835, was issuing dire warnings about the
obvious signs of inflation. Very likely, the President felt a natural
reluctance to take such a drastic step to limit land sales, since he had been
making a vigorous effort to encourage western settlement by his Indian
removal policy. At any rate, the outcry of westerners against the measure
was immediate, and a combination of Whigs and conservative Democrats passed a bill which would have repealed the Specie Circular by
authorizing land offices to receive bank notes. Jackson had to overrule
Congress with a veto in order to sustain his belated measure to halt the
speculative boom.

The effect of all this on the political fortunes of the Democratic party
was apparent in the election of 1836. Martin Van Buren, Jackson's
designated successor to the presidency, was elected by a narrow margin
of 30,000 votes in a total of 1,500,000. The Whigs made serious inroads
into former areas of Democratic strength in the West—capturing the
electoral votes of such states as Ohio, Indiana, Kentucky, and Jackson's
home state of Tennessee. Two years later, the Whigs captured control of
the state government in Van Buren's home state, thus ending the long
reign of the Albany Regency.

The Jacksonians blamed their troubles on the state banks and their
wildcat bank notes, but it seems clear in retrospect that the hard money
policy was a failure. Even if the Jacksonians had been able to persuade a
majority of the state legislatures to suppress small notes, it is doubtful if
the inflationary pressures of the 1830's could have been halted. Bankers
and businessmen were developing a vast array of paper devices—bills of
exchange, promissory notes, bank drafts, discounting procedures—that
were beyond the reach of any of the crude contrivances of the hard
money program. Indeed, it is doubtful whether Nicholas Biddle could

have or would have controlled the speculative boom, even if he had been able to retain his regulatory power over the state banks.

The Jacksonian generation simply did not understand the intricacies of the currency and credit system which was developing in association with the market revolution. They knew full well that the national economy was becoming prey to wild binges of speculation followed by severe periods of depression, but they knew too little about the factors that contributed to the business cycle to be able to control it. They were particularly deficient in their understanding of the effect of foreign trade balances on the flow of specie into the American economy. They sensed correctly enough, however, that all of the multiplying mechanisms of credit and capital—banks, paper money, privileged corporations—contributed to the inflationist mentality that provided the driving purposes of the market revolution.

The Jacksonian Ideology

In their warfare against the "Monster Bank" and the note-issuing state banks, the Jacksonians evolved an ideology that validated the social discontents of those groups in the electorate whose fears had been aroused by the dislocations of rapid economic growth. The social philosophy that was first set forth in Jackson's veto of the Bank Bill in 1832 extolled the entrepreneurial ideal: every man ought to be allowed to get ahead in the race of life on the basis of his own merit and ability, but no man ought to be able to get a head start because of any favors that the government might give him. Jackson's idealization of the self-made man had a broad popular appeal that could embrace the crassest men as well as the most innocent victims of the reckless processes of the market

Cincinnati, 1848

revolution. But as the battle against banks and bank notes reached new heights of political tension in Jackson's second administration, the ideological tenets of the Jacksonian Democrats became sharper and more divisive.

More and more, the Jacksonians emphasized the claims of "the honest capitalist," "the honest laborer," and "the honest producer" against those who have made commerce "a game of haphazard." The only increase of wealth beyond what was necessary to gratify the physical needs of men that can be justified was one that comes from "vigorous industry and watchful economy." According to William Gouge, a leading ideologist of the Jacksonian party, the passion for quick riches that infected so many Americans was destructive of self and society. The reckless pursuit of wealth not only produced a society in which "institutions operate to the advantage of the few, and to the disadvantage of the many," but also gives the pursuer "less gratification from the actual possession of a large [fortune], than from the constant increase of a small one."

The final version of the Jacksonian ideology, therefore, sought to rally the "real producers" in American society against the nonproductive monopolists and speculators whose wealth and power came from factitious advantages. The Jacksonians idealized a vision of society in which economic activities could be carried on by the palpable efforts of "hard-working" men and women and in which the social landscape would be free of the large-scale machinery of capital and credit. In the

Rare Book Room. Cincinnati Public Library.

words of Jackson's Farewell Address it would be a society in which "the planter, the farmer, the mechanic, and the laborer, all know that their success depends on their own industry and economy—they are the bone and sinew of the country. . . ."

The Nullification Crisis

The South Carolina Nullifiers

When the "tariff of abominations" had been passed in 1828, the legislature of South Carolina had formally protested against the constitutionality of the measure. James Hamilton, a rice planter and Charleston capitalist, who represented the tidewater districts of South Carolina in Congress, warned his constituents that moderate remedies would not avail against the "tyranny" of the northern majority which had imposed the tariff: "we must come back to [the] . . . practical and downright principle, as our 'rightful remedy'—a nullification by the 'State'. . . ." The public pressures created by Hamilton and other South Carolina militants brought John Calhoun, once an ardent nationalist, to an open endorsement of the doctrine of states rights; Calhoun became a principal drafter of the *Exposition and Protest* in which the South Carolina legislature denounced the Tariff of 1828.

Following the theory of John Taylor, Calhoun argued that the Constitution was a compact entered into by the sovereign states of the Union; the Constitution granted a limited number of enumerated powers to the

federal government and reserved the rest to the states and the people. Each state also modified "its original right as sovereign" by placing the definition or amendment of the boundaries of power between the federal government and the states in the amending process—specifically in the hands of three-fourths of the states—"in whom the highest power known to the Constitution actually resides." Hence, South Carolina has the sovereign right to invoke this process by nullifying a federal law which, in its judgment, has exceeded the powers granted by the Constitution.

No extreme action was taken by the South Carolina legislature in 1828 because John Calhoun had allied himself with the Jacksonian coalition in his campaign for re-election as Vice-President. When Jackson won the presidency, the followers of Calhoun looked hopefully to the new administration for a redress of their grievances. By 1832, however, it was apparent that these had been vain hopes; Calhoun had broken with the administration over personal and political matters, and the tariff of 1832, passed with the President's approval, made only minor changes in the duties on manufactured goods.

In the fall elections of 1832, a nullifier party won a sweeping victory that gave them control of three-fourths of the South Carolina Senate and almost four-fifths of the House of Representatives. James Hamilton was elected governor and immediately called for a special session of the newly-elected legislature to summon the voters to elect a convention to prepare a nullification ordinance. A duly-elected Convention met in

Rare Book Room. Cincinnati Public Library.

Columbia, South Carolina, in November and promptly adopted an Ordinance of Nullification which proclaimed the tariffs of 1828 and 1832 null and void in South Carolina and forbade any effort to collect tariff duties within the state. The Convention also warned that the passage of any act by Congress that authorized the use of military and naval forces against South Carolina would be "inconsistent with the longer continuance of South Carolina in the Union."

The rebellious mood of the majority of South Carolinians reflected two problems that had become acute during the preceding decade. Many South Carolina planters were feeling the economic squeeze of competition with the new plantations of the Gulf states and they blamed the tariff for their economic troubles. At the same time, they feared that the same doctrines of consolidated national power which northern majorities had used in behalf of protective tariffs would be used to interfere with the institution of slavery. "The same doctrines," Governor James Hamilton declared, "which enable the general government to tax our industry for the benefit of the industries of other sectors of this Union . . . would authorize the federal government to erect the *peaceful* standard of servile revolt . . . [and] to give the bounties for emancipation here. . . ."

Hamilton, indeed, had been one of the leaders charged with special authority to suppress the slave conspiracy organized by a free black, Denmark Vesey, 10 years earlier. Betrayed by informers, the conspirators were rounded up by the state militia: 35 blacks were hanged, and 37 others were banished from the state. The swift suppression of the

Vesey conspiracy did not allay the fears that were aroused by it. South Carolinians experienced a series of insurrection alarms throughout the 1820's. Undoubtedly the bloody Nat Turner insurrection in Virginia in 1831 helped to make these fears an important aspect of the emotional intensity associated with the nullification movement in 1832.

When he heard the news from South Carolina, Jackson was determined to uphold the authority of the federal government. He issued a proclamation to the people of South Carolina informing them that they had been deceived by their leaders in assuming that nullification could be a peaceable remedy. He warned them that he intended to execute the laws of the United States with every power at his command.

The President reminded the people of South Carolina that there were only two appeals from an unconstitutional act passed by Congress—one to the judiciary and the other to the people and the states by means of a constitutional amendment. "I consider, then," he said, "the power to annul a law of the United States assumed by one State, *incompatible with the existence of the Union, contradicted expressly by the letter of the Constitution, unauthorized by its spirit, inconsistent with every principle on which it was founded, and destructive of the great object for which it was formed.*"

Even while he was making clear his intention to enforce federal laws, Jackson urged Congress to lower the tariff schedules in the acts of 1829 and 1832. But this gesture of reasonableness had little effect on the more militant nullifiers. Congressman George McDuffie spoke scornfully of

Jackson and the Nullifiers

Rare Book Room. Cincinnati Public Library.

THE UNION,
It Shall be Preserved.

A MEETING will be held at the Buffalo House on Friday Evening, at 7 o'clock, for volunteers to organize a Battalion or Regiment of patriotick Young Men, who will arm and equip themselves and be ready if necessary, to march in five days from the date of this meeting, to aid the Government in preserving the Union, and their services to be at the disposal of the President, when, where, and in such manner as he may order.

Thomas C. Love,	David Welty,
Wm. Wilkeson,	A. Q. Stebbins,
Geo. A. H. Patterson,	O. H. Marshall,
A. E. Mather,	R. S. Brown,
M. Long,	P. Hodge,
D. L. Hempsted,	W. H. Hubbard,
Geo. P. Barker,	Wm. K. Dana,
T. A. Jerome,	Wm. A. Whiting,
Lucius H. Pratt,	J. T. Hudson.

Buffalo, Dec. 21, 1832.

Buffalo and Erie County Historical Society.

the President's proclamation as "the mad ravings of a drivelling dotard." The South Carolina legislature responded by calling for the equipping and training of an army of volunteers to defend the state if necessary. Over 25,000 men volunteered, and Carolina uniforms and blue cockades were soon visible everywhere in the leading towns of South Carolina.

Angered by these signs of defiance, Jackson asked Congress in January of 1833 to enact a "Force Bill" that would give him full power to use the armed forces of the United States to collect revenue duties in South Carolina. Privately, he is supposed to have declared that he was ready to hang every leader of the nullifiers, "irrespective of his name, political or social position." Publicly, he moved cautiously to avoid any actions that might have required the large-scale use of force.

Meanwhile, South Carolina leaders began to feel increasingly isolated as other southern states adopted unfavorable resolutions concerning the Ordinances of Nullification. Although other state legislatures were willing to express opposition to the tariff, they abhorred the means that the nullifiers had chosen to remedy the situation. The Alabama legislature called the nullification scheme "unsound in theory and dangerous in practice;" Georgia lawmakers denounced it as "rash and revolutionary;" the legislature of Mississippi charged that South Carolina had acted with "reckless precipitancy." Calhoun, therefore, urged a strategic retreat toward some of the compromise proposals being developed in Congress.

The Compromise of 1833

The result was a Compromise Tariff of 1833, passed with bipartisan support, which provided for a gradual reduction of duties over a nine-year period until they reached the average level of 20 per cent *ad valorem* in 1842. The Force Bill and the Compromise Tariff were both passed by Congress on March 1, 1833. Ten days later, South Carolina repealed the Ordinance of Nullification, but added one final gesture of defiance by passing a new ordinace to nullify the Force Bill. However, it was an action which had only an abstract significance since there was no longer any practical need to use the powers of the Force Bill.

The Compromise of 1833 took the tariff issue out of politics for the rest of the decade. There was, however, another largely covert issue involved in the nullification crisis that made it a prelude to the Civil War. South Carolina took a strong stand on constitutional grounds in respect to the tariff because its pro-slavery leaders wanted to establish states' rights principles on the issue of the tariff before attention focused on federal powers regarding slavery in the states. If the federal government had broad powers to establish high tariffs, promote internal improvements and the like, it might also have the power to regulate the inter-state slave trade and perhaps even outlaw slavery itself. Northern abolitionists were beginning to raise this possibility, and the deep fear of such a prospect gave intensity to the dry economic and constitutional arguments over the tariff.

American Whiggery

The acidifying character of Jacksonian ideological appeals was an essential ingredient in the political chemistry that completed the formation of a new two-party system. In its first stage of composition, a new party of opposition was brought together by complementary resentments against Jackson's use of executive power. John Calhoun, nursing the political wounds inflicted on him during the nullification crisis, hoped to lead his southern states' rights followers out of the Jacksonian Democratic party into a new party. At the same time Republican nationalists led by Clay and Webster were fighting a bitter but futile battle against Jackson's removal of deposits. Charging that Jackson had violated the law which made the Secretary of the Treasury an agent of Congress in regard to the deposit of public money in the Bank of the United States, Clay sponsored a Senate resolution of censure with an impassioned speech in which he concluded: "We are in the midst of a revolution, hitherto bloodless but rapidly tending toward a total change of the pure republican character of the government and to the concentration of all power in the hands of one man."

Jackson's belligerent response to the resolution of censure adopted by the Senate contained a vigorous statement of his conception of presidential power. He reminded the Senate that the President alone was "the direct representative of the people"—of the constituency of the whole, so

The Whig Coalition

to speak—and dared them to impeach him. Galling as the language of Jackson's famous "Protest" was to his senatorial opponents, they knew they lacked the votes to impeach the President. Hence they organized a political combination to recapture the presidency through the electoral process.

"Executive usurpation" became the first rallying cry of the new political combination. The *National Gazette* of Philadelphia expressed the common sentiment of those who were anxious to create a new party with these words: "Presidential power—as claimed and exercised, nullifies laws and charters—is limited only by personal desire and will—and reduces the first functionaries in the departments to a subserviency as degrading and complete as any which ever existed at the footstool of Asiatic despots." The name that was attached to the new political combination by the summer of 1834 underscored this alarm over the power of the President. The name "Whig" revived memories of the earlier struggle of Americans in the Revolution against the tyranny of the British king, and Whig journalists soon developed the habit of referring to Andrew Jackson as "King Andrew I."

The Whigs Overthrow the Albany Regency

The Whig label had a powerful appeal at the grass roots level. It was used with conspicuous success in New York City where the Whigs won control of the Council in 1834. In other parts of New York State the large popular following of the Anti-Masonic party poured into the ranks of the new party; in fact, every one of the top six leaders of the Whig party of New York—Thurlow Weed, William Seward, Horace Greeley, Francis Granger, Millard Fillmore, and Luther Bradish—had been Anti-Masons. And it is also not without significance that the Anti-Masons had already developed much of the political rhetoric that became an essential part of the Whig ideology. As early as 1832, Anti-Masonic campaign documents had charged that Jackson had "issued arbitrary Veto's upon wholesome and constitutional laws thus endeavoring to imitate the Ancient Monarchs of France, who used the *Veto* and the Bastille for the most arbitrary and tyrannical purposes. . . ."

The rapid influx of new blood and new leaders enabled the New York Whigs to achieve a remarkable degree of success within a few years after the formation of their party. Under the skillful leadership of Thurlow Weed, the master organizer of the party, the Whigs were able to produce an attractive young candidate for the governership, and to develop issues that had as much popular appeal as the Bank issue had had for the Democrats earlier in the decade. By giving their support to a free banking law, they were able to appear as champions of the people against "monied monopolies."

The banking system of New York had been controlled by the Albany Regency ever since the Safety Fund system had been instituted during Van Buren's governorship in 1829. Under the provisions of the Safety Fund law, banks would contribute to a state-controlled reserve fund, and this fund would be used to redeem the notes of any bank that failed. This was a significant banking innovation that foreshadowed one of the features of our modern Federal Reserve system, but it should be remembered also that the new law made banking in New York an even more tightly controlled legal monopoly. The law created a board of three bank commissioners—one to be chosen by the governor and two by the banks—to inspect all banks to determine their solvency, and, by court action if necessary, to close a bank. Furthermore, by a "restraining" provision, all unincorporated associations were prohibited from issuing notes or lending money. Thus, the legislature alone had power to incorporate a bank, to decide where it should be located, and by whom it should be operated. And by controlling the legislature and the Board of Bank Commissioners, the Albany Regency was able to manipulate the Safety Fund system to the advantage of the state bankers who were allied with the Democratic party.

The disastrous Panic of 1837 forced the New York banks to suspend specie payments, and it was clear that the Regency's Safety Fund system could not cope with the crisis. In the elections for the legislature in the fall of 1837, the Whigs won a sweeping victory—electing 100 out of 128 assemblymen, and six out of the eight senators who were up for election in the staggered system used for senatorial elections in New York at that time. In the following year, William H. Seward ousted William Marcy from the governorship in another Whig sweep.

When the new legislature met, the Whigs assumed that they had a mandate to reform the banking system of New York. Many of them had become committed to free banking ideas when they had played coalition politics with the Locofocos in order to undermine the Regency-controlled banking system. But, the banking bill of 1838 which was introduced and passed by the Whigs was different in several fundamental ways from the kind of free banking that the Locofocos favored. And these differences provided significant clues to the ideological orientation of the new Whig leadership.

The Whig
Free Banking Law

The free banking law of 1838 authorized indivduals or associations to engage in banking without any special charter from the legislature— provided, however, that they raised a capital of at least $100,000. Furthermore, the law provided that stockholders' liability for bank losses should be limited to their capital invested. On the other hand, the law set forth strict rules for banking operations and established a bank board with broad supervisory powers. Thus the free banking law of 1838 was contrary to Locofoco ideas at several key points: the capital requirement of at least $100,000 was not at all consonant with Locofoco doctrines, and neither was the limited liability for stockholders.

In the emerging Whig conception of political economy, therefore, it was important to liberate capitalism from the burden of securing special legislative charters but only if stability and strength were kept in the monetary and credit system. A Whig Address prepared after the passage of the free banking law declared:

The great objects to be accomplished were in our judgments, to put an end to all political influence over our monied institutions—to do away with everything like monopoly or special privilege in the hands of any favored class, and to give free scope to the employment of capital and credit, wherever and by whomsoever they could be beneficially employed. On the other hand, we looked upon it to be a duty of the highest obligation to protect every individual in the community from being imposed upon by a worthless currency—whether rendered worthless by speculation, imprudence, or by fraud.

Thus the Whigs were willing to give entrepreneurs considerable freedom in organizing the machinery of capital and credit. But they were not prepared to accept the anarchic system of free banking advocated by the Locofocos; they believed that strength and stability in a market economy required sufficient capitalization for "trade in money"; in addition they were willing to use the authority of the state to set the standards that should govern the flow of credit in the economy.

The Election of 1836   Whig doctrines took additional shape in the struggle against a further extension of the hard money policy by the national government. In the election of 1836, the newly formed Whig coalition was still too weak to defeat Martin Van Buren, Jackson's chosen successor in a direct two-party contest. Instead, the party leaders decided to run three presidential candidates with strong sectional backing: Daniel Webster to appeal to New England voters, General William Henry Harrison to woo the West, and Hugh Lawson White of Tennessee to attract southern votes. It was hoped that with so many candidates in the field the election might be thrown into the House of Representatives where the Whigs hoped to be able to manipulate the situation in favor of one of their candidates. The plan failed, however, when Martin Van Buren won by a narrow margin of 27,000 votes—762,000 to a total of 735,000 for all of his opponents combined. Yet William Henry Harrison demonstrated unexpected strength as a vote-getter, taking more than 549,000 of the 735,000 votes cast for Whig candidates. Thus, the election of 1836 revealed that the new party was developing a broader popular base and that the voters apparently preferred new leaders like William Henry Harrison to older leaders like Webster.

Despite their defeat in the presidential contest, the Whigs were able to exploit the growing divisions within the Democratic party over Martin Van Buren's efforts to extend the hard money program. When the new President took office he faced a critical situation that resulted from the Panic of 1837. Banks were suspending specie payment and many were forced to close their doors. The shutting down of factories caused widespread unemployment and the miseries of workingmen were made all the worse because food prices remained high or went higher as credit stringencies brought commerce to a virtual standstill in many areas. Flour riots in New York City which involved thousands of unemployed workers underscored the gravity of the situation for the new administration.

One problem required immediate attention by President Van Buren. The suspension of specie payments by state banks holding government deposits meant that they could no longer qualify as depositories for federal funds. Conservative Democrats favored the repeal of the Specie Circular as a way of easing the pressure on state banks, but the new President was more disposed to favor the advice of the radical, Locofoco wing of the party which blamed the inflationary note-issuing policies of state banks for the suspension of specie payments. Leaders of the radical wing of the party, like Senator Benton, were calling for a complete divorce between the government and the private banking system.

Van Buren, therefore, called upon Congress to meet in a special session in September, 1837, and urged the legislators to enact a bill that would create an independent treasury system. According to his plan, government funds would be removed from all state banks and placed in subtreasuries in various key cities around the country. Thus government funds could no longer become the basis for overissue of bank notes or the overexpansion of credit. Furthermore, the Independent Treasury bill required that all government dues be paid in specie; thus no bank notes of any description were to be receivable by the federal government for taxes, customs duties, land sales, etc. In short, the Independent Treasury bill proposed to cure the depression with the most drastic deflationary techniques that the federal government could employ.

Van Buren's Independent Treasury Bill

It should not surprise us, in view of what we have already discovered about the growing divisions within the Jacksonian party, that Van Buren's independent treasury scheme was opposed by members of his own party as well as by the Whigs. The bill passed the Senate in 1837, and again in 1838, but both times it was defeated in the more popular branch of the Congress. Not until the summer of 1840 did the Independent Treasury bill pass both houses of Congress, but the specie clause was not scheduled to go into effect until 1843.

The Independent Treasury Act was a great victory for Locofoco radicalism in the Democratic party, but the political price that the Jacksonian party had to pay was staggering. As the presidential election of 1840 approached, the country was still in the depths of economic depression. The delegates at the Democratic national convention renominated Van Buren; yet they knew full well that popular discontent with the party in power had greatly reduced their prospects of political success.

The Whigs, on the other hand, scented the promise of victory. The younger "new-school" Whig leaders successfully combined their efforts to sidetrack older leaders like Webster and Clay in favor of William Henry Harrison, who had demonstrated his appeal to the masses of the voters in 1836. Thurlow Weed personally conducted a vigorous campaign against Henry Clay in the Whig convention in favor of the candidate who could be presented to the people as a plain man who "leaves the plough to save his country."

The 1840 Whig Triumph

Successful in obtaining the nomination of Harrison, the Whigs cam-

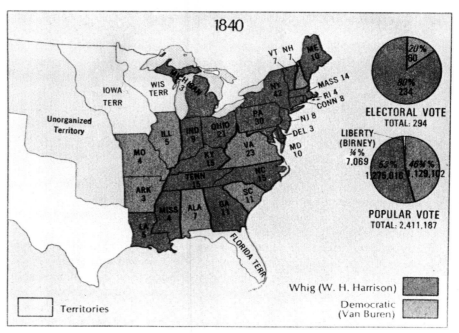

From The National Atlas of the United States of America. *United States Department of the Interior Geological Survey.*

paigned with energy and enthusiasm. Almost immediately, a Democratic newspaper in Baltimore played into their hands by sneeringly characterizing Harrison as a minor backwoods military hero who would be content to live out the rest of his life with a pension, a log cabin, and a barrel of hard cider. With enormous gusto, the Whigs turned this political taunt to their advantage and log cabins and barrels of hard cider became their chief party symbols overnight. Nothing could possibly have served better to make Harrison appear to be the exemplar of simple, homespun virtues, while Van Buren was open to attack as the effete easterner who drank expensive wines, or as the Sly Fox of Kinderhook who had made a career out of political trickery.

Harrison's campaign utterances were as effective in their vagueness as General Jackson's had been in 1828. He was content for the most part to ride on his reputation of being the victor at the Battle of Tippecanoe. The old soldier conducted himself with a kind of simple dignity; he said earnestly to one of the crowds which gathered to hear him: "I believe and I say it is true democratic feeling, that all the measures of the government are directed to the purpose of making the rich richer and the poor poorer." Proposals to remedy this situation were never clearly developed in any of his speeches, but a significant clue to his thinking was apparent when he remarked in a speech in Dayton, Ohio: "Methinks, I hear a soft voice asking, Are you in favor of paper money? I am."

The result of the demagogic log cabin and hard cider campaign was a smashing victory for the Whigs. Harrison defeated Van Buren with a popular majority of nearly 140,000 votes or nearly 53 per cent of the total vote; and his electoral college margin, 234 to 60, was equally impressive. Moreover, voters turned out in much larger numbers than ever before in the elections of the Jacksonian era. Nearly one million more voters flocked to the polls in 1840 than in 1836, and the total percentage of eligible voters who participated in the election reached 78 per cent, well above the highest levels achieved in both of Jackson's campaigns for the presidency. It was obvious that the Whigs had mastered the skills of mass politics and the *Democratic Review* admitted as much when it made the rueful comment: "We have taught them how to conquer us!"

The Whigs, however, were unable to translate their astonishing electoral victory into an effective legislative program. As leader of the Whig party in the Senate, Clay hoped to play a dominant role in shaping the policies of the new administration and, indeed, Harrison awarded most of the places in his Cabinet to friends of Clay. But the new President, who was 68 years old at the time of his inauguration, died a month after taking the oath of office. Very likely, Harrison would have supported Clay's efforts to revive the principles and policies of the American System, but Vice-President John Tyler was a southern state-rights Whig who had always opposed high tariffs and internal improvements. Like Calhoun, Tyler had started out as a supporter of Jackson and then moved into the Whig camp after the nullification crisis.

The Whig Schism

Clay believed quite correctly that he represented the views of the majority in the Whig party—especially of the Whig majorities in both houses of Congress. But Tyler refused to give him any assurance of support. "Go you now . . . Mr. Clay," he is reported to have said after a stormy interview, "to your end of the avenue, where stands the Capitol and there perform your duty to the country as you shall think proper. So help me, God, I shall do mine at this end of it as I shall think proper." Clay arrogantly accepted the challenge, and is reported to have said to his friends, "Tyler dares not resist me. . . . I will drive him before me."

Subsequent events proved, however, that Clay had underestimated Tyler's ability to frustrate his program. Perhaps if he had played the game more skillfully he might have been able to build up a position of overwhelming strength that Tyler would not have dared to challenge. But Clay chose to ram through Congress a measure which would have restored the Bank of the United States, reviving an issue that Thurlow Weed had characterized as a millstone around Whig necks.

The first step was to clear the way by repealing the Independent Treasury Act. This was done in August, 1841, in the midst of the special session of Congress called by Tyler, and Tyler was quite willing to sign the bill which overthrew a policy that had been repeatedly attacked by Whig orators during the campaign of 1840. But when the followers of Clay pressed their advantage by passing a bill creating a "fiscal bank" of the United States, Tyler promptly vetoed the measure on constitutional grounds. To overcome his constitutional objections, the Whig majority in Congress quickly pushed through another measure creating a "Fiscal Corporation" with limitations on its power to create branches within the states. This, too, was vetoed by the President.

In a mood of disappointment and rage, a special caucus of Whig Congressmen, mostly followers of Clay, adopted a manifesto prepared by John Pendleton Kennedy, a novelist who was associated with the Whig elite of Baltimore. In this manifesto, Tyler was in effect read out of the Whig party and all the members of Harrison's Cabinet (retained as a gesture of party unity by Tyler) resigned except for Daniel Webster, the Secretary of State. He remained in his post for another two years in order to complete his difficult negotiations with the British concerning the Maine boundary and other issues.

With this serious rupture in the party, other aspects of the Whig program were impaired by the factional fighting of sectional groups in Congress. One of Clay's pet ideas was the re-enactment of a distribution bill by which the proceeds of western land sales could be distributed to the states to be used for the support of schools and internal improvements. Such a measure had actually been passed in 1836 when the Jackson administration was faced with a mounting treasury surplus, but the law had been quickly repealed at the start of Van Buren's administration when the Panic of 1837 diminished the revenues of the government to the vanishing point.

When Clay reintroduced the distribution proposal in 1841, western representatives led by Senator Thomas Hart Benton countered with a proposal for a pre-emption law. The principle of pre-emption had tremendous popular appeal in the West where many settlers were squatters and wanted a chance to buy their land with such improvements as they had made at the minimum price of $1.25 an acre before the government put them up at public auction. Many eastern representatives were opposed to pre-emption legislation, not only because it would reduce their chances of getting federal grants out of a distribution bill, but because they believed that the pre-emption principle encouraged a lawless and reckless process of settlement.

To complicate matters even further, the tariff issue became intertwined with the controversy over land policy. Low tariff men, including President Tyler, believed that the distribution bill was really a stalking horse for a high tariff law; they felt that the distribution of the proceeds of public land sales would create such a "vacuum" in the Treasury that Congress would be obliged to raise duties above the levels of the Compromise Tariff of 1833 in order to provide more revenue.

The outcome of this complicated legislative jockeying was a compromise public land law in 1841 which provided for both pre-emption and distribution. The law allowed squatters on the public domain to pre-empt 160 acres of public land for the minimum price of $1.25 an acre when the

FOR SALE.

INDIAN LANDS

IN THE STATE OF

NEW-YORK.

For Sale by *Public Auction*, in the *City of Buffalo*, on the 15th day of June next, about **16,000** acres of Land, in the County of Erie, being part of the Tract called the *Buffalo Creek Reservation*, the north line of which is bounded on the Corporation line of the City of Buffalo.

And on Monday, the 19th of June, at *Batavia, in Genesee County*, about **8000** acres of Land, in that County, being part of the Tract called the *Tonnewanda Reservation*, lying on the Tonnewanda Creek, near the Town of Batavia.

The possessory right in these Tracts, hitherto reserved by the Seneca Indians for their own occupation, has been lately sold by them to the pre-emptive owners. They are now surveyed and subdivided into convenient farms, amounting in number to about **320**, containing generally from **50** to **140** acres each.

Collection of j mara gutman.

lands were put up for public sale by the government. At the same time, revenues obtained from the sale of western lands were to be distributed among the states in proportion to their representatives in Congress. To satisfy the demands of low tariff men, however, an amendment was added to the Pre-emption-Distribution bill which stipulated that distribution was to cease if it should become necessary to levy tariff duties in excess of 20 per cent *ad valorem.* Thus Clay had to make a choice between distribution and protection and, in 1842, he chose to push through Congress a tariff law which returned duties to about the level of the Tariff Act of 1832. Tyler grudgingly signed the bill only because the continuing depression made it necessary for the government to find more revenue.

Frustrated by his inability to develop a coordinated legislative program that would reestablish the American System, Clay resigned from the Senate at the end of the legislative session in 1842 to campaign actively for the presidency against Tyler who had been anathematized as a party traitor. By that time, over two hundred Whig newspapers had declared in favor of "Harry of the West," and in the following year so many Whig state conventions had endorsed him that it seemed certain that he would be given the chance to lead the party into a battle for "the true principles" of American Whiggery in the election of 1844.

Ten years of party conflict had often blurred the issues between the Whigs and the Democrats but underlying the humbuggery of election campaigns and the broker tactics of legislative leaders was a significant ideological debate about America's future. We have already noted the

The Whig Ideology

difference between the Jacksonian Democrats and the Jeffersonian Republicans. Obviously the Whig party was not a reincarnation of the Federalist party. Although the Whig party contained old-time Federalists like Daniel Webster, the old political vocabulary of Federalism had no place in the Whig party; no one, not even Daniel Webster, dared to say any more, as he once had, that "political power, naturally and necessarily goes into the hands which hold the property." Calvin Colton, a leading intellectual spokesman for the Whigs, wrote in 1839 that the word "democracy" had become "a word of deep meaning and potency in America. No political party can dispense with it. . . . Whatever their principles, radical or conservative, their best passport is democracy." The Whigs, like the Jacksonian Democrats, were shaped by the irresistible democratic tendencies of the day.

Moreover, the Whig conception of democratic politics tended to be more hopeful than that of the Jacksonians whose vocabulary was filled with metaphors of conflict. To the Jacksonians American society seemed to be torn by irreconcilable conflicts caused by the market revolution: country versus city, rich versus poor, virtuous farmers and mechanics versus greedy speculators, frugality versus extravagance, equality versus privilege. The Whigs, on the other hand, evolved an ideology which called for a new equilibrium of interests in an economy of rapid growth.

The speeches of Daniel Webster provide a useful barometer of the new ideological orientation of American Whiggery. In the Massachusetts Constitutional Convention of 1820, Webster had declared that "there is not a more dangerous experiment than to place property in the hands of one class, and political power in those of another." By 1836 he was warning a Boston audience against the fallacy of applying "European maxims" respecting classes to American conditions:

In Europe . . . the laborer is always a laborer. He is destined to no better condition on earth, ordinarily he rises no higher. We see proofs, melancholy proofs, of this truth often in the multitudes who come to our own shores from foreign countries for employment. It is not so with the people of New England. Capital and labor are much less distinctly divided with us. Few are they, on the one hand, who have need to perform no labor; few are they, on the other, who have no property or capital of their own. Or if there be those of the latter class among the industrious and the sober, they are young men who, though they are laborers today, will be capitalists tomorrow.

It is tempting to dismiss Webster's new views as a form of political hypocrisy, but the same theme appears again and again in the utterances of other Whigs, who did not have a Federalist past.

Furthermore, it must be remembered that such ideas found their way into higher forms of theorizing. Henry Carey, one of the leading economic writers in America at midcentury whose writings attracted favorable notice in Europe, incorporated the idea of rapid economic growth without class conflict into some of his major works on political economy. The persisting depression after 1837 led him to declare his independence of English economic thought and to assail free trade as a doctrine fostered by England to preserve her initial advantage in manufacturing and to keep other countries in the raw materials stage of economic development. America, he argued, had enormous possibilities of economic growth, and protective tariffs were needed to stimulate these latent productive capacities. These views achieved summation in his work entitled, significantly, *The Harmony of Interests; Agricultural, Manufacturing, and Commercial* (1851) in which he stressed the mutual dependence of all classes and interest groups in American society. All were interdependent and all would benefit from a protective tariff law because a protected home market would bring not only high profits to manufacturers, but larger markets for farm products, and more jobs for laborers. Under the forced draft of protectionism, agriculture and business would prosper, laborers would have steady employment, morality and education would benefit, and political freedom would advance.

Thus, in the Whig ideology, enterprise and growth became key metaphors. Calvin Colton, a Yale graduate who left to become a Whig editor and pamphleteer, developed the most complete and forceful statement of the theories of American Whiggery in a series of political tracts written in 1843 to 1844 under the name of "Junius." To Colton, the entrepreneurial energy of Americans was the country's most favorable asset. "Enterprise," he wrote, "is capital. With slender means, it has evoked unbounded wealth from the long repose of a continent, and erected thereupon a vast national estate. No other species of capital has contributed so largely to this stupendous result. As the collective power of national enterprise is composed of individual enterprise, we find, accordingly, the same character in isolated conditions, chequering the whole surface of society with great achievements effected by single persons." Furthermore the corporation is the great social invention which will make possible still further miracles of enterprise. "The object of corporations," Colton declared "is to combine the surplus or spare capital of numerous individuals, for enterprises which are usually beyond the reach of single persons. Properly organized by the statute of incorporation, by a division of capital into small shares, they are well adapted to a democratic state of society, by bringing down the powers of government, distributing them among the people, and vesting them in the hands of all persons who can raise twenty, or fifty, or a hundred dollars according to the price of shares."

The culture hero of the Jacksonian generation—for Whigs and Democrats alike—was the self-made man. "This is a country of self-made men, than which nothing better can be said of any state of society," Colton wrote proudly. But more and more for the Whigs, the self-made man assumed the shape and character of a corporate entrepreneur rather than a village capitalist. To be sure, Locofoco Democrats espoused general laws of incorporation, but they hoped that such laws would encourage the formation of "co-partnerships" which would unite the efforts of men of small means—a conception that was not too different from the workingmen's ideal of producer's cooperatives.

The Whigs were not dismayed by the multiplication of corporations. Neither did they fear the legal doctrine announced by Chief Justice Taney in the *Charles River Bridge* case (1837) which rejected the older Federalist doctrine of implied contracts and asserted that no rights were granted in any act of incorporation except those that were explicitly conferred by the working of the charter. As long as the principle of limited liability was included in such efforts to "democratize" the corporation, the Whigs knew that the mobilization of capital through shares of stock would engender the growth of enterprises which were usually beyond the reach of individual entrepreneurs. And to speed the processes of corporate capitalism, the Whigs looked to the government to boldly and liberally aid the great works of internal improvement— canals and railroads—which were beyond the means of unassisted corporate enterprise.

In short, the Whigs, unlike the Jacksonians, eagerly embraced the market revolution and the industrial revolution and sought to create a legal environment that would accelerate the processes of economic growth. They were able to validate, more explicitly than the Democrats, an ideological fusion of democracy and industrial capitalism.

Nevertheless, the history of the Whig party is a record of frustration and failure. Part of the reason for this was already clear in the Harrison-Tyler administration. Its vigorous espousal of corporate capitalism doomed the Whig party to have an insecure political base. Southern leaders were already beginning to differentiate between southern culture and the capitalist culture of the northern states in the defense of their peculiar social system. Indeed, there is considerable uncertainty about the political base of the Whigs in the North and Northwest where they continued to compete with the Democrats on virtually equal terms in the 1840's. So far, historians have failed to determine whether Whigs and Democrats appealed to different or similar constituencies. Some rather crude empirical studies of the socioeconomic status of Whig leaders and voters in selected states have produced contradictory results. It is very tempting, therefore, to conclude that both parties appealed to roughly similar constituencies and that the outcome of elections was largely dependent on whether Americans were voting their hopes or their fears.

There is a considerable degree of arrogance, however, in any attempt to reduce the politics of this period to a psychological problem. An acceptable historical explanation must begin with the assumption that the Jacksonian generation took its ideological quarrels seriously. At the very least one must recognize that Jacksonian political behavior was not the reflex of a single entrepreneurial ideal. There were two variants of the entrepreneurial ideal and each expressed a passionate response to the advent of industrialization in a society that had been largely agrarian. Only when historians have developed a more precise analysis of socio-economic groups located along a political spectrum will it be possible to determine how deeply the ideological differences between Whigs and Democrats penetrated the minds and hearts of the electorate in the Jacksonian generation.

From the title page of
Sartain's Union Magazine,
1849. Rush Rhees Library.
The University of Rochester.

Revivalism as a Source of Social Order and Reform

Protestant Christianity attained an overwhelming dominance in the shaping of American culture during the decades preceding the Civil War. This tremendous resurgence was a result of the popular fervor associated with revivalism. Revivalistic preachers had already appeared with the Great Awakening in the eighteenth century, but in the early years of the nineteenth century a national movement of evangelical churches sustained revivals for several decades. Those denominations most receptive to revivalistic methods—Methodists, Baptists, and Presbyterians—grew more rapidly than other churches in this period of general Protestant expansion. Although the influx of Irish and German Catholics during the 1830's and 1840's offered a growing challenge to Protestant hegemony, the census of 1860 reported that almost 80 per cent of the seating capacity of America's 38,113 church buildings belonged to Protestant denominations. An aggressive Protestantism achieved hegemony.

The Resurgence of Protestant Christianity

Although it is often assumed that revivals were characteristic of the frontier where they helped relieve the harshness and drabness of life in the backcountry districts, they were important in urban areas as well. The revival offered an experience of community in the rapidly growing, disorderly, and increasingly anonymous cities. Evangelical religion, moreover, had an important social impact that was at once reactionary and progressive. This militant Protestantism had a censorious and bigoted dimension that took the form of hostility toward immigrants and their religion and tried to impose a particular Protestant morality on all Americans. But this quest for social control represents only part of the evangelical legacy. Men and women touched by the spirit of religion during revivals often assumed greater responsibility for their fellow human beings. Many movements for urban reform—whether to aid children, prostitutes, the deaf and blind, widows, the poor—had their roots in revivalistic religion. Protestant women were particularly active in these humanitarian efforts in behalf of the weak and dependent members of society. The greatest moral crusade of the antebellum years, the antislavery movement, drew much of its strength from the revivalistic religion of the period. Evangelical religion and the revivals contributed two things to these movements. Men and women absorbed a very optimistic view of human character that insisted that perfection, not mere gradual improvement, was possible and that this moral reformation could be achieved immediately through an act of will. This assumption, so alien to the strict Calvinism of earlier revivals in the eighteenth century, gave great force to the reform impulse in diverse areas of American society. Secondly, the organizational experience and techniques acquired in church activities, especially by women, were transferred to other areas of reform.

The Second Great Awakening also brought a proliferation of small sectarian groups. The emotionalism associated with revivals tended to increase the fragmentation of Protestantism into a bewildering number of sects, especially as ill-trained leaders under some inspiration of the moment chose to sanctify some word or phrase in the Bible. The schisms among the Baptists brought into existence a variety of seceding groups who distinguished themselves from the regular Baptists with such names as Seventh-Day Baptists, Free Baptists, Free-Will Baptists, General Six Principle Baptists, or Seed-in-the-Spirit Baptists. Yet sectarian divisions should not be taken as evidence of any serious weakness in Protestant Christianity; the regular Baptist, Methodist, and Presbyterian organizations, for example, retained the support of the overwhelming majority of the church members. And many of the newer sects never had more than small followings.

Of far greater significance than its sectarian character was the growing unity of theology and practice in the inner life of American Protestantism. As Protestant Christianity approached the high tide of its power and influence in the second quarter of the nineteenth century, the major segments of all denominations had embraced the general approach of revivalism. The only significant deviation from the prevailing pattern was the emergence of Unitarianism Congregationalists. The Unitarians were led by able ministers, like William Ellery Channing, whose sophisticated and rationalistic style appealed to the wealthy and well-educated in the larger towns of eastern New England. They preferred a theology which rejected the concept of the Trinity, and which emphasized that Jesus Christ had been a mortal man who had taught the great moral truth that God was a merciful and loving father. They also believed that man was naturally good, and not depraved by the taint of original sin. Hence goodness and love were made the essence of religion by such preachers as Channing. Yet the Unitarians were always a minority movement in American Protestantism—the greater number of New England Congregationalists were kept in the fold by the influence of energetic clergymen like Lyman Beecher who successfully used a restrained form of revivalism to combat the twin heresies of Deism and Unitarianism in the old stronghold of Calvinism.

A Theology of Disinterested Benevolence

The old Calvinism was dying out, nevertheless. Everywhere, the inner structure of American Protestantism was cemented by a common commitment to an increasingly benevolent theology which toned down the harsher doctrines of Calvinism. When Lyman Beecher went to Boston to lead the orthodox forces of Congregationalism against the threat of Unitarianism, he brought with him the "New Haven theology" of Professor Nathaniel Taylor, who asserted that man's salvation depended upon his free agency to accept or reject God's love. Elsewhere, revivalistic preachers discovered that they had most success when they emphasized that God was ready to save all sinners, if only they would come forward to accept His love and forgiveness.

Thus the major segments of Protestant Christianity developed a theology that was acceptable to a restless, self-reliant, and individualistic people. It accorded with the democratic spirit of the times to think of God as offering his love freely and equally to all who would accept it. The doctrine of predestination belonged to an earlier, aristocratic age—the new age demanded a theology that would allow men a free choice of salvation even as universal suffrage allowed them the right of free election in politics.

Furthermore, the New Haven theology of Nathaniel W. Taylor was also influenced by the theological concept of "disinterested benevolence" which had been developed by Samuel Hopkins, a pupil of Jonathan Edwards. Hopkins taught that moral depravity consisted of self-love, while holiness was the opposite of self-love and sought to express itself in disinterested benevolence. Self-love, he argued, places one's own happiness above the happiness of all other human beings; disinterested benevolence, on the other hand, is primarily concerned with the happiness of others or the greater good of the whole. The disinterested benevolent person, Hopkins taught, "will be willing to suffer positive evil, to save others from greater evil, or when necessary to promote and procure a greater overbalancing good for the whole." These new theological concepts were planted in the minds of young men preparing for the ministry at Yale, Amherst, Williams, and Oberlin, and at such theological seminaries as Andover in Massachusetts and Lane in Cincinnati, Ohio. Through them, the new religious and moral ideas were carried into the continuing revivals of Protestant Christianity during the second quarter of the nineteenth century.

One of the most effective revivalistic preachers of the Jacksonian generation was Charles Grandison Finney, a successful lawyer in western New York who turned to the ministry after an experience of religious conversion. Finney had an abiding scorn for the old Calvinistic clergy who split theological hairs and tangled "election, predestination, free agency, inability, and duty in one promiscuous jumble." He was determined to talk in the pulpit "as a lawyer does when he wants to make a jury understand him . . . the language of common life." Finney used such language with an eloquence and emotional fervor that attracted enormous audiences and tens of thousands of converts.

What made Finney outstanding in his day was not simply his eloquence as a revivalistic preacher. He was rightly seen by one of his contemporaries among Protestant clergymen as the one preacher above all others "who adequately attempted to employ the theology of New Haven in its practical relations." To Finney, it was not enough that a sinner should come forward to announce his conversion; the sinner must acquire a "new heart"; instead of a "preference for self-interest," he must begin to exercise a "preference for disinterested benevolence."

By 1830 Finney and his "Holy Band" of co-workers were sweeping into large eastern cities like Philadelphia, New York, and Boston where the

"The Benevolent Empire"

One of the largest buildings in New York. From Francis' New Guide to New York and Brooklyn. *New York: C. S. Francis & Co., 1856. Collection of j mara gutman.*

"The Benevolent Empire"

more conservative clergy were soon forced to adapt their preaching to the "new measures" of the greatest of all the early nineteenth-century revivals. Furthermore, the evangelical and moral objectives of Finney's Holy Band were given wider currency by the rise of powerful interdenominational societies. Among these were the American Bible Society organized in 1816, the American Sunday School Union (1824), the American Tract Society (1825), and the American Home Missionary Society (1826). The most important of these was the American Home Missionary Society which included representatives of Presbyterian, Congregationalist, Dutch Reformed, and Associate Reformed churches. In 1837, there were 606 missionaries working for the society in eight hundred congregations and missionary districts, and by 1850 the society was employing over a thousand missionaries throughout the North and West. The American Tract Society was an indispensable ally in these efforts; it published an Evangelical Family Library of 15 volumes, and a periodical called the *Christian Messenger* which had a nationwide circulation. In the single year 1855, the 659 agents of the Tract Society visited nearly 650,000 families. Indeed, these great interdenominational societies furnished a permanent organizational structure for the powerful forces of revivalism. Furthermore, they were able to deflect much of the energy of revivalism into channels of social control.

Leaders of the benevolent empire of interdenominational societies persistently worked for legislative sanctions to support their system of social and religious values. In 1828, they established the general Union for Promoting the Observance of the Christian Sabbath whose president, Stephen Van Rensselaer, was also president of the Home Missionary Society. The new society proposed to get people to stop all work and travel on Sundays, and this effort was given a strategic focus by a massive campaign to stop delivery of mail on Sunday. Success or failure on the Sunday mails issue was depicted as crucial to the achievement of the primary aim of the new society: "So long as one steamboat, or one stage, can plead a United States' contract and legislative injunction for Sabbath-breaking . . . we are parties to a flagrant violation of the divine law, and to a wide source of temporal and spiritual calamity."

A huge petition campaign was organized in 1829 to 1830 and hundreds of memorials poured in on Congressmen who must have been impressed with the array of social respectability represented by the petitioners. At any rate, the question was considered important enough to be referred to a special committee in the Senate where Richard M. Johnson, a leading Jacksonian, vigorously opposed the idea of stopping the Sunday mails. Johnson boldly assailed the primary assumption of the petitioners that the United States should be a Christian—especially a Protestant Christian—nation. He declared that the Constitution forbade Congress to recognize one religion as superior to another; a Christian Sunday Sabbath should have no more government recognition than a Jewish Saturday Sabbath. The logical outcome of such a step would be the creation of a form of established church—a "religious despotism."

The close identification of the Sabbatarians with anti-Jackson politicians led to the defeat of their petition campaign. Nevertheless, the leaders of the benevolent empire launched other efforts to win legislative support for their efforts to control the explosive energies of a democratic social order. The American Sunday School Union began a campaign to sell books especially prepared for children in the common schools of the nation. Their efforts encountered strong resistance from educational reformers who were actively engaged in the battle to create free, tax-supported, public schools. Horace Mann, the Secretary of the newly-created Massachusetts Board of Education, flatly refused to recommend the Sunday School Union's books because he believed that the public schools must remain free of any form of religious sectarianism.

The failure to win the support of the Massachusetts Board of Education was a severe blow to the Sunday School Union. Because of this failure, the whole effort collapsed and the Sunday School Union found itself in severe financial straits as it was left with thousands of copies of unsold books on its hands. But in a larger sense, the leaders of the benevolent empire had no reason to be fearful for they were influential in the educational institutes and in the publishing houses. The graded reading texts that poured forth to supply the expanding public schools contained a nonsectarian version of Christian morality that could not have been disappointing to those who were most concerned to harness the energies of revivalism for the purposes of social control.

The American Bible Society was more successful than the Sunday School Union in its efforts to use school facilities to promote general religious and moral values. However, its campaign to persuade state and

Anti-Catholicism

local bodies to make the Bible an instruction book in all the public schools took an ugly turn that was to have lasting consequences for the future development of ethnic and religious relationships in American society. The Bible that the Society wanted to be read and used in the schools was the Protestant version and hence unacceptable to Catholics, who were becoming more numerous because of the great increases in immigration after 1830. The Tract Society and the Home Missionary Society express-ed alarm over the competition of "papist" efforts in the Mississippi valley region and the leading publication of the Home Missionary Society warned that "there the great battle is to be fought between truth and error, between law and anarchy—between Christianity, with her Sab-baths, her ministry and her schools, on the one hand, and the combined forces of Infidelity and Popery on the other."

The most violent battles, however, were fought in the East, where the Catholics were more numerous, and most of the conflicts centered over the questions of education. The clash between Catholics and Protestants over the use of the Bible in public shcools took its most intense form in New York City where the schools were still under the control of the Public School Society, an interdenominational benevolent association that had a virtual monopoly of the disbursement of funds provided by the state of New York.

From the very beginning of its activities, the Public School Society had given a prominent place to Bible reading in the curriculum of its school. Inevitably, the growing number of Catholics in New York City found good cause to complain agianst this monopoly of public educational funds by a Protestant-controlled benevolent society. The King James version of the Bible was read daily in all the schools of the Public School Society and the prayers, singing, and religious instruction were not in accord with Catholic belief. Led by an energetic and outspoken Bishop, John Hughes, the Catholics of New York City refused in 1840 to enroll their children in the schools and asked for a fair share of state funds for their own parochial schools. They won the sympathy of Governor William Seward whose liberal Whig views included the belief that the children of the poorer immigrants must be properly educated if they were to make good citizens.

Governor Seward asked for new legislation that would recognize the just claims of the Catholics. In January of 1842, the legislature responded with an act which extended the state school system to New York City and provided for elective school commissioners in each ward to supervise the ward's schools and to serve collectively as a board of education for the entire municipal system. The latter provision enabled the Catholics to establish control of 31 of the common schools in the wards where they lived, but it also forbade religious instruction in the schools. Since Catholics believed that religious instruction was inseparable from educa-tion, this solution was ultimately unsatisfactory and the Catholic church began to develop a system of parochial schools.

The controversy over religion and education in New York took place within the legitimate channels of political action. Elsewhere, anti-Catholic prejudices were expressed in acts of disorder and rioting. Particularly serious were the riots that disrupted the city of Philadelphia in July, 1844. Whole blocks of houses in the Irish wards were burned out, 13 persons were killed, and 50 wounded. The spark that set off the rioting and killing in Philadelphia was a dispute over Bible reading and religious instruction in the schools. Encouraged by the success of his coreligionists in New York, the Catholic bishop of Philadelphia had requested that Catholic children be allowed to use their own version of the Bible. The school board had granted their request but Protestant citizens, stirred up by their religious press, condemned the action. Mass meetings were organized to bring pressure on the school board to rescind its decision and an attempt to hold such meetings in the Irish wards led to sporadic street fighting that finally exploded into the bloody riots of July.

The memory of the Philadelphia riots served as an emotional stimulus to the rise of organized political nativism in the next decade. In the several states where nativist parties obtained clear majorities in the legislatures, influential Protestant leaders played an active role in the attempt to obtain legislation that would discriminate against foreigners and Catholics. Their efforts, together with those of local societies in New York, led to the creation of the Order of the Star Spangled Banner—a secret society which began to carry on political activity in behalf of "American party" candidates who came to be known as Know-Nothings because they claimed to know nothing when asked about their clandestine organization. The so-called American party made remarkable political gains in 1854 to 1855 in state and local elections.

The Know-Nothings

In Massachusetts, a Know-Nothing legislature launched an investigation of all theological seminaries, nunneries, and convents, in the hope of discovering evidences of dreadful Popish practices. This committee's conduct was so outrageous that the legislature felt compelled to recall the committee and to expel its chairman from the House of Representatives. Massachusetts, however, did adopt a literacy test for suffrage as a way of limiting the voting rights of naturalized citizens. A similar law was adopted in Connecticut, but, elsewhere, no nativist legislation was written into law. Indeed, the rapid decline of the Know-Nothing movement signaled the failure of such attempts by overzealous Protestants to enact discriminatory legislation.

Revivalistic preachers believed that the shockingly high consumption of alcoholic beverages was an obstacle to moral reform and a primary cause of vice, crime, and pauperism. In 1825 Lyman Beecher initiated a campaign for total abstinence; by 1830 a thousand temperance societies had exacted three hundred thousand pledges of abstinence. When the American Temperance Union held its first national convention in 1836, there were over 5000 local temperance societies. While clergymen active in the great interdenominational societies were the initial organizers of

Temperance and Prostitution

Temperance crusade. From Index of American Design. National Gallery of Art.

the temperance movement, leadership gradually devolved into lay hands. In 1840 a group of reformed drunkards who called themselves Washingtonians formed the first Washington Temperance Society in a Baltimore tavern. During the 1840's they attracted thousands to their meetings where confessional techniques were used. Parades, banners, flags, songs, and outdoor meetings also became standard forms of persuasion. Organized temperance even developed a children's division known as the cold water army.

Membership in a temperance organization became the mark of a man who was bent on improving his income and status; the man of sobriety was held up as a model character. Abstinence also became a symbol that was used to further widen the gap between respectability and the lowly Irish and German immigrants who drank whiskey and beer as part of their way of life. Ultimately moral suasion was replaced by political action, and Neal Dow, a leader in the Maine Temperance Union, became a hero of the movement by leading a spectacular struggle to obtain a stringent prohibition law, first passed in 1846 and revised in 1851. By 1855, twelve states had passed prohibition legislation similar to the Maine law of 1851.

If the temperance movement achieved respectability by attaching itself to middle-class aspirations, the attack on prostitution faced more complicated problems. Sexual activity was not a proper topic for public discussion. Yet middle-class evangelical Christian women, with their millenial dreams of personal and social perfection, felt compelled to attack even the unmentionable sin of illicit sex. "The sin of licentiousness," they warned, "has made a fearful havoc . . . drowning souls and exposing us to the vengeance of a holy God." Driven by this Christian impulse, a small group of women met at the revivalistic Third Presbyterian Church in New York in 1834 to found the New York Female Moral Reform Society. Their goals were to end prostitution in the city and to provide leadership for a national movement to reform sexual morality. They proposed to convert New York's estimated 10,000 prostitutes to evangelical Christianity and, through their newspaper, wage a national campaign against the double standard and the male sexual license it condoned.

Within the city they visited—or rather swooped down upon—brothels to pray with and try to convert prostitutes and their customers. They often stood outside known brothels to observe entering and leaving customers, and they were pleased with the effectiveness of this strategy. They also established a House of Reception on the assumption that if a prostitute were convinced of her sin, offered a place of retreat, and given an economic alternative, reform was certain. Their attack on the double standard was less dramatic but perhaps more militant. Accepting the sexual premises of their time, they argued that since women felt little sexual desire, it was clearly men who, using guile to manipulate women's affections, were the "destroyers" of female virtue. While sexual transgressions "ruined" women, men were not condemned at all. Indeed, the double standard by "common consent allows the male to habituate himself to this vice." The women proposed that all men suspected of sexual immorality be shunned and ostracized from female society, and to be helpful they printed names in their newspaper. They also promoted legislation that would make seduction a crime and urged mothers to assume responsibility for the proper sexual education of their sons.

This movement had much in common with other religiously based humanitarian reform, but it was different in one important respect: the partially masked resentment of male social dominance is unmistakable. While not specifically a feminist organization, the New York Female Moral Reform Society was confronting, if in a covert way, central issues of feminism—sexuality, female solidarity, the public roles of men and women.

Before 1830, antislavery sentiment was a sedate form of moral disapproval which enabled the gentry politicians to maintain their system of political cohesion. Such sentiments were channeled by the American Colonization Society, organized by influential political leaders in 1817, to encourage the manumission of slaves by promoting the emigration of freed blacks to Africa or to the West Indies. This approach endangered no one's property rights; it did not even diminish public or private purses because neither Congress, nor the state legislatures, nor private philanthropy provided the sums necessary for the colonization of freed blacks.

The Antislavery Movement

But the revivalist spirit caused many Americans to confront the moral issue of slavery more starkly and, thus, to challenge the sanctions of existing institutional arrangements. Inspired by the example of their evangelical counterparts in England whose agitation and petitions had forced Parliament to debate the question of immediate emancipation of slaves in the British West Indies, Theodore Weld, the merchant philanthropist Lewis Tappan, and others associated with Finney's Holy Band met in New York to formulate plans for an American antislavery society based on the British model. At the same time, William Lloyd Garrison launched a new antislavery newspaper in Boston entitled *The Liberator*—a title that symbolized its radical intent. Garrison denounced all forms of gradualism including the colonization scheme and called for a militant crusade dedicated to the immediate and unconditional abolition of slavery. He told his readers: "I *will be* as harsh as truth, and as uncompromising as justice. On this subject, I do not wish to think to speak or write, with moderation . . . I am in earnest . . . I will not equivocate—I will not excuse—I will not retreat a single inch—and I will be heard." Shortly afterward, Garrison organized the New England Antislavery Society based on his radical doctrine of immediate abolition, but the membership of this society as well as the subscriptions to *The Liberator* remained small by the standards of the time for reform associations. Nevertheless Garrison's influence as an agitator went far beyond the members of his society. For a whole generation, he incarnated an unflinching moral challenge to the contradiction of human slavery in a democratic society.

The New York and New England groups came together in 1833 to form the American Antislavery Society, but the New York group insisted on a formula for action that would tone down the extremism of Garrison's position. The new national society embraced the doctrine of "immediate emancipation, gradually achieved"—a doctrine that closely approximated the revivalist formula of immediate conversion to be followed by a course of conduct that was inspired by disinterested benevolence.

A broader base of popular support for the new antislavery movement of the 1830's was achieved largely through the efforts of one of the ablest members of Finney's Holy Band—Theodore Dwight Weld. Weld employed the same evangelizing techniques to rally thousands of antislavery converts in those areas of New York already "burned over" by the fires of religious revivalism. In 1833, he entered Lane Theological Seminary in Cincinnati, Ohio, where he converted almost the entire student body to the antislavery cause, and led them in a general withdrawal from the school when the Board of Trustees tried to curb their activities. Shifting to a new base at Oberlin College, Weld organized most of the "Lane rebels" into his famous "band of Seventy" to lead the battle in the West, especially in Ohio, Indiana, and Illinois. By 1837, the American Antislavery Society presided over a network of more than a thousand local societies and more than a hundred thousand members.

Antislavery Politics   In addition to the techniques of mass persuasion borrowed from the revivalists, the leaders of the American Antislavery Society employed all the new methods of manipulating public opinion that had appeared in American politics during the Jacksonian generation. Antislavery newspapers sprang up in the areas where Weld and his followers had done their work: James Birney founded the *Philanthropist* in Cincinnati, a group of Weld's co-workers established the *Christian Witness* in Pittsburg, and in Illinois, Elijah Lovejoy made the *Alton Observer* an important outpost in the network of abolitionist influence established by the Seventy. Furthermore, large-scale petition campaigns were organized to influence Congress to abolish slavery in the District of Columbia. Petitions were placed in stores, taverns, barber shops, and passed out at church fairs and camp meetings; but most of them were carried to homes and farmhouses by devoted men and women volunteers.

The tone of Garrison's editorials alarmed many in the North as well as the South. In 1835, Amos Kendall, the Postmaster General, authorized local southern postmasters to refuse to deliver any incendiary antislavery literature and President Jackson urged Congress to prohibit the use of the mails for the circulation of inflammatory publications. The large-scale petition campaigns aroused the hostility of southern Congressmen and, with the help of northern conservatives, the House of Representatives adopted a "gag rule," which prevented the consideration of any petitions relating to slavery. John Quincy Adams, who had been elected to the House of Representatives after leaving the presidency, won the admiration of antislavery supporters and civil libertarians for his eloquent opposition to this infringement on the constitutional right of petition. Even in the North abolitionism was controversial. Prominent antislavery leaders faced hostile mobs, often made up of "gentlemen of property and standing," which sought to destroy abolitionist presses and to break up abolitionist meetings; such a mob murdered Elijah Lovejoy for his antislavery views. At the same time, both Whigs and Democrats in their national conventions made every effort to evade the slavery issue and keep it out of the political arena. For quite different reasons Garrison also opposed making antislavery a political issue. He had publicly repudiated the Constitution as a "covenant with death" because it compromised with slavery, and he feared that political participation, with its characteristic pragmatism, would result in a weakening of the absolutist abolitionist goal of freedom, justice, and equality for blacks.

But the bulk of the antislavery movement, with James G. Birney as its spokesman, proposed to use every sort of political pressure available within the American political system. They felt that agitation had succeeded in making the political climate in the North favorable to antislavery politics. They formed the Liberty party in 1840 and nominated Birney for President in that year and again in 1844. By 1848 dissident factions in both of the major parties were ready to join with Liberty party men in the Free Soil party. Six years later the time was ripe for an even broader coalition, and the Republican party was formed. The growing political power of the antislavery movement did not mean, however, that Garrison's fears had been unfounded. The Republican party did not challenge slavery where it already existed; its program was gradualist and proposed only to limit the extension of slavery in the territories. And the party's stance on racial justice fell far short of Garrison's ideal. Yet politics is the mechanism of social change in a democratic society; when antislavery became an issue of power as well as an issue of morality, the American political system was forced to grapple with slavery and, ultimately, race.

Feminism   Women had been active in the antislavery movement as well as a variety of other humanitarian causes, and this provides the background for feminism. Working with the underprivileged of the cities and agitating for the slaves may well have sensitized women to their own oppression in American society. Surely the sharp criticism they received for their antislavery activism impressed many women with the dilemmas of their position.

In 1837, for example, the General Association of the Massachusetts Congregational Clergy published a pastoral letter condemning the public antislavery speeches Sarah and Angelina Grimké had delivered to mixed audiences of men and women. Women, the letter said, should not assume the place and tone of man as a "public reformer." They should work upon their husbands within the sphere of the domestic circle. "When the mild, dependent, softening influence of women . . . is fully exercised [on men], society feels the effects of it in a thousand forms." Sarah Grimké's response was immediate and direct: "The rights of women, like the rights of slaves, need only be examined to be understood and asserted. Men and women were CREATED EQUAL: They are both moral and accountable beings, and whatever is right for man to do, is right for women to do." The concept of separate spheres, she insisted, degrades relations between the sexes.

Man has adorned the creature, whom God gave him as a companion, with baubles and gewgaws, turned her attention to personal attractions, offered incense to her vanity, and made her the instrument of his selfish gratification, a plaything to please his eye, and amuse his hours of leisure. . . . Nothing . . . has tended more to destroy the true dignity of woman. The idea that she is sought as an intelligent and heaven-born creature, whose society will cheer, refine and elevate her companion . . . is rarely held up to her view.

Organized feminism, which dates from the Seneca Falls convention called by Lucretia Mott and Elizabeth Cady Stanton in 1848, was linked to this broad question of autonomy and equality. The convention's "Declaration of Sentiments and Resolutions," modeled on the Declaration of Independence, declared that "all men and women are created equal." Besides demanding women's suffrage, it protested against laws that deprived married women of legal standing independent of their husbands, that prevented wives from owning property in their own names and from controlling the wages they earned. It complained of unfair divorce laws, employment discrimination, and the subordinate position of women in the churches. Informing the whole document, however, was a rejection of the idea of separate spheres for men and women. Man, it exclaimed at one point, "has usurped the prerogative of Jehovah himself, claiming it as his right to assign for her a sphere of action, when that belongs to her conscience and to her God."

Utopian Patterns

The radicalism of the Garrison abolitionists had an apolitical character that not only restricted its capacity for effective social action but also limited its social thought. Aside from the eradication of the evil of slavery, ther was nothing in their social vision that suggested any radical reconstruction of society. Indeed, abolitionist orators often emphasized the productive superiority of the free labor system and thus emdorsed the existing social organiztion of the North.

Religious Millenialism

More radical visions of social reconstruction, however, emerged with the Utopian movements that were generated in the Jacksonian era. For some, these utopian expectations took the form of religious millenialism—a phenomenon that had often been associated with periods of social strain in the historical experience of European nations. An optimistic form of millenialist preaching was one of the characteristics of Finney's revivalistic method; the success of religious revivals, he believed, would transform social institutions by means of a general acceptance of disinterested benevolence. A more compulsive form of millenialism, however, flared up in a spectacular movement in the troubled years after the Panic of 1837. This movement developed in response to the pessimistic doctrines of the Reverend William Miller who preached that the world was getting worse instead of better, that the millenium would not come until after the Day of Judgment.

Miller was particularly fascinated by the prophecy of the second coming of Christ in the Scriptures, and he developed elaborate and intricate calculations which led him to predict that Christ would return to judge the world in the year 1844. Thousands flocked to hear Miller on his speaking tours throughout the revivalistic strongholds in the northern states, particularly as the dread Last Year approached. Countless hundreds purchased white ascension robes, and assembled on hilltops outside of their towns and villages to await the coming of the Lord on the night of October 21, 1844. Nearly all secular business was suspended in many areas of the country, and the excitement among believers and nonbelievers became so intense that rioting broke out in many places. The failure of Miller's prophecy was a serious blow to the Millerite movement, but his millenial faith was institutionalized in the Adventist Churches that were formed by the most devoted remnants of his following.

The Millerite movement was a crude form of social protest that expressed vague discontent with the sinfulness of society and appealed largely to the poor and uneducated. It was equivalent to the chiliasm of despair that had developed among Methodist "ranters" in the north and west country of England as a form of primitive protest against the process of industrialization in that country. Like the Methodist ranters, the Millerites developed no clear sense of social alternatives other than the conviction that the coming of the Lord would "deliver his own dear peculiar people."

More frequently in the Jacksonian generation, utopian impulses of a religious character were expressed in the organization of community experiments that offered members a chance to develop a social system completely separated from the imperfect institutions of the dominant social order in America. There had already been a few experiments in religious communitarianism established in America by European pietists at the turn of the century—notably the Shakers, and the German-speaking Rappites and Zoarites. But the most truly American of the religiously-oriented communities were the Mormons and the Oneida "perfectionists."

The Mormons   The Mormon church was founded in 1830 in upstate New York when Joseph Smith claimed that an angel had directed him to a cave in which he had discovered some golden plates containing new revelations from God. Smith's claim of direct revelation attracted several thousand converts in areas where the fervor of revivalism had prepared many for new forms of religious experience. For a time, Mormonism seemed about to become another form of millenialism, but a growing emphasis on the communal practices of primitive christianity soon led to the organization of a separate social order. Within a half dozen years the Mormons had moved westward to Illinois where they established a flourishing community at Nauvoo based upon a highly centralized control of all economic activities. It was there that Joseph Smith made known his revelation giving divine authorization for the practice of polygamy. Rumors of such polygamous practices aroused the non-Mormon population of nearby settlements and, in 1844, an Illinois mob aided by the local militia invaded Nauvoo and murdered Joseph Smith after he surrendered himself for trial. Two years later his successor, Brigham Young, led the main body of Mormons on the long trek to their permanent Zion in the region of the great Salt Lake outside of the boundaries of the United States. Even though the Mexican War was to bring them back under the government they tried to escape, their physical isolation was so complete that they were able to develop their separate social system in comparative peace. Their numbers grew to 200,000 in the next generation, and the system of polygamous marriage had continued viability within the patriarchal organization of their peculiar social system.

The Oneida Perfectionists   The "Perfectionist" followers of John Humphrey Noyes also found their opportunity in comparative isolation. Noyes, a Vermont lawyer, was converted to the ministry during one of Finney's revivals. But his conversion led him to some unusual beliefs; he became convinced that the existing social order must be perfected, particularly after he witnessed the hardships of the people in the period of depression following the

Panic of 1837. He believed that a system of common ownership should replace the system of private property, and that a system of "complex marriage" should replace the ordinary family relationship which he believed was full of injustice, jealousy, and dissension. After angry neighbors drove his small following to leave Putney, Vermont, he developed a flourishing community in the more isolated district of Oneida, New York, in the late 1840's. At Oneida, the "Perfectionists" carried on a communal form of economic activity, and within the community each woman was the conjugal partner of every man and *vice versa*. However, no sexual intercourse was permitted without the complete willingness of both parties, and the propagation of children was carefully regulated by the group.

The Oneida community never amounted to more than a few hundred persons, but it proved to be a highly successful and durable social experiment. Noyes was convinced that the success of the community would depend upon industry, and he encouraged the use of machinery to develop other lines of activity besides farming. Factories for the manufacture of sewing silk and silverware were established; indeed, Oneida silverware became a highly prized item in the markets of the United States.

Because of their deviancy in sexual and marital relationships, the Mormon and Oneida experiments were kept largely insulated from the mainstream of American life. There were other ways, however, in which the utopian impulses of the Jacksonian generation were able to achieve legitimacy at least in an equivocal sense. The two major movements of this type were inspired by the proposals of two European reformers —Robert Owen and Charles Fourier.

Robert Owen was a successful English industrialist who had developed a model factory town in association with his cotton mills at New Lanark in Scotland. He was so shocked by the exploitation of wage laborers by other English industrialists that he turned his thoughts to ideas of social reform. After futile efforts to persuade Parliament to enact laws that would improve the wages and living conditions of factory workers, he concluded that the existing societies based on individual competition and greed should be replaced by a more enlightened social system based on cooperation and social benevolence. He envisioned the creation of "Villages of Cooperation" for the poor where, after an initial grant of capital out of taxes, they would pay their own way and become "useful," "industrious," "rational," and "self-disciplined." Unable to get Parliamentary support, Owen decided to demonstrate the workability of his plan in the New World where there seemed to be a greater hope for new beginnings in all aspects of life.

The Owenite Communities

In 1825, therefore, Owen purchased a settlement on the banks of the Wabash river in Indiana, already started by some Rappites. The British industrialist's lofty ideals attracted widespread attention—he was even invited to address Congress—and a considerable number of eager reformers flocked to the new community experiment that was named New Harmony. About a dozen other Owenites communities were established by other groups elsewhere. But the community movement failed when the New Harmony experiment broke up as a result of bitter dissensions within the community.

In America and in England, Owen was never able to overcome an excessively paternalistic attitude toward his followers; it has been said that next to "benevolent" the words most commonly encountered in his writings were "provided for them." This paternalistic attitude was not only ill-adapted to the frontier environment of the Wabash country, it also proved to be a permanent barrier between Owen and the British working class, even though British trade unions adopted and modified many of his ideas. Furthermore, Owen and his leading disciples in America had a strong anti-religious bias. This limited the appeal of Owenism at a time when the religious excitement of revivalism was gripping the very classes of people that Owen wished to "provide for." There was no room at New Harmony for the complex emotional reactions associated with the "religion of the heart"; the emphasis was strongly utilitarian, rationalistic, with much energy directed toward the excellent Pestalozzian school of the community.

The influence of Owenism, however, did not end with the failure of the communities. Owen's son, Robert Dale Owen, and the brilliant young Scotswoman, Fanny Wright, transferred their activities to the workingmen's movement in New York where they campaigned for a radical reform of the educational system in the early 1830's. Moreover, in the 1840's, most of the independent non-Fourierist communities tended to combine Owenism and Garrisonite abolitionism. This combination of reformist principles had already been prefigured by Fanny Wright's abortive community experiment at Nashoba, Tennessee, in the late 1820's where she made an interesting effort to use the cooperative labor system as a means of emancipating black slaves. Her public defense of racial equality and miscegenation attracted public notice even before Garrison launched the *Liberator*.

The American Fourierists

By the 1840's, Owenism was greatly overshadowed by Fourierism. As modified by Fourier's chief American disciple, Albert Brisbane, this new form of utopian socialism was better adapted to the American spirit of reform. Unlike Robert Owen, Charles Fourier had never visited the United States and it was perhaps fortunate for his followers that he had not because his more radical ideas would have caused them considerable difficulty. In 1840, Albert Brisbane published a modified version of Fourier's theories in a book entitled *Social Destiny of Man*, in which he left out most of Fourier's notions suggesting any irregularities in marriage or morals. Brisbane's Fourierism emphasized economic principles that were already acceptable to the Jacksonian generation—that labor is the ultimate source of all wealth and that every man has the right to share in the productivity of his labor. Like the Jacksonians, the

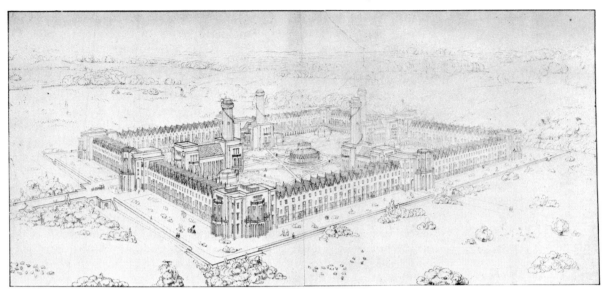

American Fourierists attacked the evils of monopoly and speculation, but they believed that the only remedy was to reorganize industry on the basis of "associationism"—a cooperative order of small communities or "phalanxes," each composed of about sixteen hundred persons. The Associationists (as the American Fourierists preferred to be known) specifically recommended that the communities should take the form of a joint-stock company in which the distribution of income among capital, labor, and skill should be in the ratio of 4:5:3. Such a cooperative order, it was believed, would promote abundance and social harmony.

Brisbane had great success in reaching the reform-minded American public because he was able to convert Horace Greeley to many of his ideas. Greeley's *Tribune* carried a column for nearly two years in which Associationist theories were explained to a large American audience. Many transcendentalist intellectuals in New England were attracted by associationist principles; for a time the leading transcendentalist periodical, the *Harbinger* (1845-1849), was published at the Brook Farm community in West Roxbury, Massachusetts. About 40 phalanxes were organized in the decade of the 1840's—many in the eastern states as well as in the frontier areas of the West where land was always more readily available for such social experiments. Most were short-lived, and the few that were successful were sold off to private enterprisers.

The available evidence seems to indicate that the larger number of Associationists were moderate in their political attitudes. Brisbane was opposed to any theories of class conflict; he even opposed the radical

Architectural vision of New Harmony, Indiana. Library of Congress.

rhetoric of the Locofoco Democrats. "He who proposes a fundamental change in society," Brisbane maintained, "should propose a plan for accomplishing it, which would conflict with the interests and prejudices of no part of the community." And, although Brisbane was somewhat of a rationalist and a skeptic in matters of religion, the Associationists made no effort to combat the religious interests and prejudices of those who entered their phalanxes. Particularly in New York and the West, the phalanxes attracted a heterogeneous group of Baptists, Methodists, Disciples, and others who had been touched by revivalism. Consequently, there was a more comfortable relationship between associationism and revivalism than there had been in the Owenism of the 1820's.

With the failure of the cooperative communities, some of the Associationists drifted into partial ventures in cooperation, like the cooperative stores developed by New England workingmen, but the larger number were diverted to the free-soil movement and the rising intensity of the antislavery issue. It is reasonable to assume that the latter eventually found their way into the Republican coalition of radicals and northern businessmen which was to control the federal government during the Civil War. The southern plantation system proved to be easier to destroy than the dynamic capitalism of the North.

The Popularization of Learning

A significant aspect of the reforming spirit in the Jacksonian period was the battle for the extension of educational opportunities for the children of common men. It was in the decades between 1820 and 1850 that the free public school won the kind of support that would put it on the road to becoming a major institution in American life.

The Struggle for Free Public Schools

The urban workingmen of the Jacksonian generation were among the first to develop an organized campaign for free public schools. They and their children felt most keenly the stigma of inferiority that was frequently attached to the publicly-supported schools of the early Republic. Even in New England where the common schools were grounded in the Puritan heritage, the children of well-to-do families went to private academies, while the common schools suffered from the crippling defects of poor teachers, low salaries, and decrepit buildings. In rapidly growing cities like New York, thousands of the children of the poor wandered the streets without any hope of schooling. From their first moments of organization, the workingmen's parties of New York and Philadelphia regularly adopted ringing resolutions calling for adequately supported public schools that would furnish equal educational opportunities for the children of all classes.

But urban workingmen lacked the strength to win such a battle alone. Success for their efforts came to depend upon the influential support of other significant groups—businessmen, political leaders, and educational reformers. By and large, the greatest gains were won in those states where there was enough urban growth to create sufficient popular support for literacy and culture. Farmers in the more backward rural areas were less likely to give their aid to significant educational reforms.

Massachusetts led the way in providing for a public school system that was based upon democratic conceptions of universal and equal educational opportunity and not on the uncertain mixture of private and public schools—"aristocratic" and "pauper" education—which had characterized the educational institutions of the early decades of the Republic. State after state followed the example of the Massachusetts legislature which created a board of education in 1837 with authority to enforce school laws, to raise the standards of teaching, and to improve the physical equipment of the common schools. Educational reformers like John Carter and Horace Mann in Massachusetts, Henry Barnard in Connecticut, Calvin Stowe in Ohio, Caleb Mills in Indiana, and Calvin Wiley in North Carolina played a decisive role in creating public sentiment for better public schools. Many of them displayed the same crusading spirit that was characteristic of the humanitarian reformers. Horace Mann, indeed, gave up a profitable law practice and a promising political career to take the poorly paid post of Secretary of the Board of Education in 1837. Henry Barnard's zeal for educational reform led him into a spectacular career which included service as Secretary of the Connecticut State Board of Education, State Superintendent of Schools in Rhode Island and Connecticut, principal of the state normal school in New Britain, Connecticut, and chancellor of the University of Wisconsin. Eventually, he became the editor of the *American Journal of Education*, and in 1867 he was appointed first United States Commissioner of Education.

Such men did much to bring the beginnings of a professional attitude into American education. John Carter was one of the leaders in organizing the American Institute of Instruction in 1830 to press for the establishment of training schools for teachers. The first state normal school in the United States was opened in Lexington, Massachusetts, in 1839, and, by 1860, 12 state-supported normal schools had been founded in nine states. At the same time, professional gatherings of teachers became more frequent. During the 12 years that Horace Mann served as Secretary of the Board of Education in Massachusetts, he secured public funds to subsidize teachers' institutes in every county with the hope that these meetings would generate new ideas for the improvement of instruction. Something like a national association of teachers came into existence with the organization of the Western Literary Institute and College of Professional Teachers in 1832 through the efforts of such educational reformers as Calvin Stowe, Lyman Beecher, and Samuel Lewis in Ohio. By 1840 auxiliary societies of the Western Literary Institute had been formed in nearly every state of the Union outside of the Northeast.

New Educational
Methods

Such teachers' institutes, together with influential journals like the *American Journal of Education* and the *Common School Journal*, became the media for the discussion and promotion of new methods of instruction. Carter, Mann, Barnard, and Stowe, in particular, used these agencies to encourage the adoption of new educational methods that had been developed by the Swiss educational reformer, Pestalozzi, and applied in the Prussian school system by German reformers like Herbart and Froebel. These new educational doctrines stressed a more natural development of the child's mind and personality; the tiresome system of rote learning was replaced by imaginative lessons based on sense experience that were designed to cultivate a fuller understanding of the world of nature and human institutions.

But reforms in the content and method of education did not come without opposition. Many conservative-minded men were reluctant to abandon the sterner style of education that had prevailed in American education since colonial days. One critic, writing in the *North American Review* in 1840, described the new learning theories with obvious sarcasm:

Mathematics are taught by toys, geography and history must be mixed up with equal portions of Peter Parley's mythology; the mysterious difference between active, passive, and neuter verbs, instead of being beaten into children's brains, as of old, by hard blows, are more kindly, yet not more wisely, illustrated by the picture of a whipping; while all the mooted points in moral philosophy, which have baffled the wisdom of ages, are despatched in a thin [booklet] which treats but of tops, whistles, broken glass, and stolen sweatmeats.

Such criticism, nevertheless, simply acknowledged the rapid growth of educational innovations in the schools of the Jacksonian generation.

The Schools
as Socializing
Agencies

In any case, there was very little reason to fear that these innovations threatened the stability of the American social order. All the leading educational reformers of the time tended to think in terms of character-building and social control at the same time that they approved of methods of instruction that were pedagogically liberal.

Horace Mann, for example, emphasized that the democratization of American society required a system of universal public schooling of the highest quality. In one of his public lectures prepared shortly after he became secretary of the Massachusetts Board of Education, he warned that "through the right—almost universal—of suffrage, we have established a community of power; and no proposition is more plain and self-evident, than that nothing but mere popular inclination lies between a community of power, and a community of everything else. . . . The arithmetic of numbers is more and more excluding all estimate of moral forces in the administration of the government."

Mann noted, also, that the free institutions of a democratic society tend to multiply human energies, whether for good or evil, and in America they have produced two dangerous tendencies:

perfection

Early nineteenth-century Americans hoped to create a perfect society in which each person would achieve ultimate individual expression. They assumed that they could bring this society into being, that they could control the ultimate course of events. Much as this figure of "Manhood" that Thomas Cole painted as one part of a four-part mural he called "The Voyage of Life," they imagined that they would steer themselves through darkness to emerge in light. If they had not yet arrived in the Garden of Eden, they would eventually.

"Manhood" part of the Voyage of Life *series that Thomas Cole painted. The Munson-Williams-Proctor Institute, Utica, New York.*

Liberty, *1431 (former title: Columbia) by an unknown artist. Gift of Edgar William and Bernice Chrysler Garbisch. National Gallery of Art, Washington, D.C.*

There was to be no conflict between individual and social progress. The free development of particular lives would fall into the grand design of society. Hence the abstract ideal of America is given human form in the artist's conception of "Liberty." In the quest for republican perfection, the individual human being was the starting point and the end point.

Was not the human being the most marvellous of God's creations? Study of the human body's perfection suggested the perfection toward which Americans strove in their society and politics.

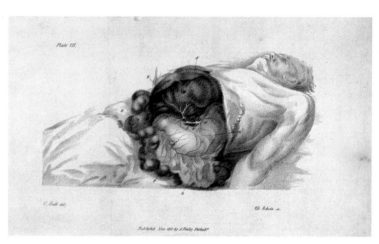

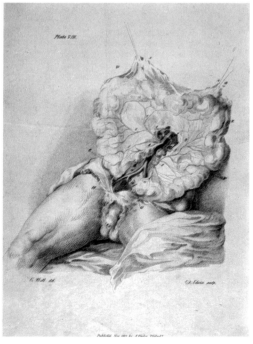

From David Edwin's Scheme of the Arterial System. *Prints Division. The New York Public Library. Astor, Lenox and Tilden Foundations.*

ISRAEL ADAMS.
Dec.r 11. 1819.

ISRAEL ADAMS.
March 1. 1820.

Engravings of Israel Adams
in John Watts' Medical and
Social Register. *American
Antiquarian Society.*

*Of course, even the human body, in all its perfection, was
vulnerable to diseases. Cancers and other diseases could attack and
deform the body . . .*

*. . . yet Americans believed that a cancer could be "extirpated."
Perhaps social evils too could be quickly and totally removed, thus
restoring the social body to its inherent perfection.*

Leadership in a democratic society asserting the value—the virtual perfection—of all persons is problematical. How should leaders be portrayed? Surely imperial pomp was inappropriate. What unique character might be revealed in their portraits? How could their special character be linked with more common qualities? Here Andrew Jackson's portrait suggests a special inner force mixed with a hint of compassion that linked him to the rest of society.

Portrait of Andrew Jackson *by James Barton Longacre. Prints Division. The New York Public Library. Astor, Lenox and Tilden Foundations.*

Although the quest for perfection brought a high seriousness to the business of living, the images created by early nineteenth-century Americans suggest a puckish quality that assures us of their appreciation of the comedy of life. An unknown painter was able to present the usually staid George Washington in deliberately human terms. He appears here almost clumsy enough to fall off his horse. And Mrs. Gilpin, a character in many children's stories, actually fell out of her carriage in an illustration published in 1815.

"George Washington Is My Name" by an unknown artist. B-25, 134. Gift of Edgar William and Bernice Chrysler Garbisch. National Gallery of Art, Washington, D.C.

Illustration from the Humorous Story of Mrs. Gilpin's Return from Edmonton by Henry Lemoine, published in Philadelphia in 1815. Brown University Library.

Eel Spearing at Setauket *by William S. Mount. New York State Historical Association, Cooperstown.*

Was the real promise of perfection in the more ordinary dimensions of life? Surely there was an appealing beauty and goodness in the lives of ordinary people going about their business of living that was captured in many of William Sidney Mount's paintings.

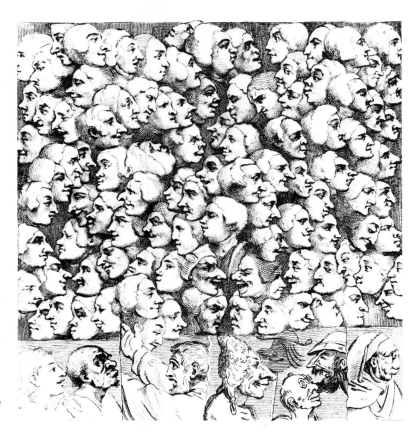

Characters and Caricatures
*by Hogarth. Collection of j
mara gutman.*

Heads Drawn from Hogarth
*by William S. Mount.
Melville Collection, Suffolk
Museum and Carriage
House at Stony Brook, Long
Island.*

The good-humored and engaging sort of perfection envisioned in America is captured as well in the human faces sketched by William Sidney Mount. In contrast to the caricatures of English faces harshly drawn by William Hogarth in the eighteenth century, Mount's faces are mellowed with softer and kinder lines.

Always, however, the American quest for perfection was threatened by a spiral of imperfections. The very forms America had used to express the goodness of their society shaded easily into ugliness . . .

AN EYESORE
What are you goping at Stupid? did you never see a bunged eye afore?

Caricature by D. C. Johnston. From Scraps, a folio of caricatures. Prints Division. The New York Public Library. Astor, Lenox and Tilden Foundations.

(2 /)
ORGAN OF SIZE
One of the knowing faculties Instrumental in smelling a rat

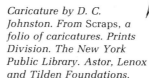

Organ of Size accompanied with Tune

Caricature by D. C. Johnston. From Scraps, a folio of caricatures. Prints Division. The New York Public Library. Astor, Lenox and Tilden Foundations.

Illustration for a story called "The Physiology of Dandyism" in Graham's, *a magazine of commentary and the arts, in 1852. Collection of j mara gutman.*

. . . or a dandified evilness.

Illustration in following month's installment of story on "Dandyism" in Graham's.

Illustration in Sartain's Magazine, *a magazine of literature and art, in 1849. Rush Rhees Library. The University of Rochester.*

Was the natural human being in fact far from perfection? Must the expression of individual particularity be restrained within the limits of fashion? Was Victorian dress a refinement of inner character or a capitulation to falseness and superficiality in social life?

Illustration in The Lady's Book *by Godey, in 1832. Rush Rhees Library. The University of Rochester.*

If they looked about their society, as the artist D. C. Johnson did here, Americans could hardly fail to notice that the natural order they assumed did not always find reflection in reality. Could a people who believed in equality and social perfection define adequate structures of authority at once effective and democratic? How much disorder was tolerable?

Caricature by D. C. Johnston. From Scraps, a folio of caricatures. Prints Division. The New York Public Library. Astor, Lenox and Tilden Foundations.

Americans had to wonder whether the attempt to free the individual from artificial restraint and political oppression had produced social perfection—or chaos. What was the character of authority in ante-bellum America? Were Americans unable to achieve the order they sometimes thought would flow so naturally?

Street scene from Brother Jonathan, *a popular magazine, in 1842. Rush Rhees Library. The University of Rochester.*

Caricature by D. C. Johnston from Scraps. *Prints Division. The New York Public Library. Astor, Lenox and Tilden Foundations.*

What meaning did authority have? Was the political system unable to create order or perfection? Was political wisdom to be replaced by mobs at the polls? What happened to the ideal of the natural aristocrat? Many feared that those who offered themselves for election fell far short of human perfection; they saw self-seeking men acting selfishly and greedily. Would mobs compete to place rogues in office?

Was society breaking down? Was the dream of a religiously-inspired and perfect society lost? Could a secular society discover Divine purpose? Reverend Burchard warned in Laurel Wreath, *a Christian gift book, that since man had to use pride and glory to think he could take over God's work, secular man would only transgress the mightiest of religious principles and fall, as at Balthazar's feast, into the bottomless pit of destruction.*

Balthazar's Feast *in* Laurel Wreath, *a popular Christian gift book in 1845. Rush Rhees Library. The University of Rochester.*

View of Ruined Buildings through porch of Circular Church in Charleston, 1865. From the Brady Collection. Library of Congress.

Was the destruction wreaked by the Civil War perhaps the collapse many feared? Or did the war and the abolition of slavery that it meant cleanse the nation of its worst imperfection and restore perfectionist hopes again?

Whatever inspiration the war offered, was there not a deep and unsettling fear of failure persisting into the 1870's? Did Americans share the fear of Erastus Salisbury Field that rivers of blood and clouds of destruction threatened the republic? Had the Edenic dream been lost at the onset of the age of industrialism?

"He Turned Their Waters Into Blood" by Erastus Salisbury Field, 1935. Gift of Edgar William and Bernice Chrysler Garbisch. National Gallery of Art, Washington, D.C.

Mark how the excitements which our institutions supply have wrought upon the love of gain and the love of place. Vast speculations—such as in other countries would require not only royal sanctions and charters but the equipment of fleets, and princely outfits of gold and arms,—are here rushed into, on flash paper by clerks and apprentices . . . : What party can affirm that it is exempt from members who prize office, rather than the excellence that deserves it? *Where* can I be,—not *what* can I be,—is the question suggested to aspirants for fame.

Whatever is done to control these powerful impulses in American life, Mann concluded, "must be mainly done during the docile and teachable years of childhood."

In similar fashion, the Western Literary Institute was led by men who wished to preserve the moral authority of Protestant Christianity as greater numbers of children came to be educated in public rather than in private schools under denominational control. Lyman Beecher and Calvin Stowe, after all, were emigrant New England ministers who sponsored educational reform as a means of combatting the demagoguery and moral laxity which seemed to be the inevitable consequence of the powerful democratic forces which had been unleashed in American society. It should not surprise anyone, therefore, that the chief contribution of the Western Literary Institute to American education was the famous *McGuffey Readers*. These graded reading texts were first published under the auspices of the Western Literary Institute in 1836, and

Family Magazine, *1832.*
Rush Rhees Library. The
University of Rochester.

hundreds of thousands of school children were absorbing McGuffey's secularized version of Protestant morality.

As a result, the movement for free public schools attracted the support of businessmen and factory owners who could see that the public schools provided an effective socializing force in the new democratic social order. By 1850, nearly three and a half million children were internalizing the common values taught in the public schools. By that time also, the proportion of school children enrolled in publicly supported schools exceeded 90 per cent. To be sure, the typical periods of attendance at such schools was still very short by modern standards, but one may say that, as an agency of social control, the public school system was becoming as formidable as that of the churches and the organized ministry.

The effort to establish public high schools was a logical extension of the public school movement. While many of the private academies that flourished everywhere in America between 1820 and 1860 received some measure of state and local subsidies, they could not meet the growing demands for further education that inevitably followed after the improvement of instruction in the elementary schools. Massachusetts led the way in 1827 with the enactment of a law that required the establishment of a high school in all cities, towns, or districts of five hundred or more families. Other New England states soon followed the example of Massachusetts, and publicly supported high schools appeared elsewhere in such cities as New York, Philadelphia, Baltimore, Louisville, and Chicago; by 1860 the Census Bureau reported that there were three hundred public high schools in the United States. Although the great era of public secondary school education still lay in the future, the high school had taken form in the democratic ferment of the Jacksonian era.

No institution created during the Jacksonian generation was more typical of the popular impulse for knowledge and self-improvement than the American Lyceum. The first lyceum was organized in 1826 by Josiah Holbrook, a Massachusetts farmer who had attended Yale, where he had acquired an enthusiastic interest in natural science. Within a short time, the idea of organizing such popular forums for the discussion of scientific and literary questions had spread throughout his home state, and Holbrook was devoting full time to the promotion of lyceums in other regions of the country. By 1831 delegates representing a thousand local lyceums in New England and New York organized the National American Lyceum in New York City. The movement spread to at least 15 states, mostly in the northern section of the country and, before 1860, approximately three thousand lyceums were functioning from Maine to Minnesota.

In the beginning, the lyceums used local talent for lectures, but as the lyceum movement grew there was a demand for more eminent lecturers. In fact, the lyceum movement became a profitable source of income for teachers, scholars, and writers of all types. Scientists like Benjamin

This mercantile library, founded in 1820, served workers; men and ladies were given equal membership. Collection of j mara gutman.

Silliman of Yale and Louis Agassiz of Harvard became well-known figures on the lyceum circuit; Horace Mann used the platform of local lyceums to spread his educational ideas; and emerging writers like James Russel Lowell, Oliver Wendell Holmes, and Ralph Waldo Emerson found an opportunity to advertise their talents and to express their ideas to a large public. Emerson, who charged a sizeable fee of $50, was especially popular, and many of his favorite themes like "Self-Reliance" and "Reform" were developed as lyceum lectures before they became the published essays now familiar to all students of American literature.

To be sure, the popularization of knowledge was bound to have some costly consequences. This is particularly evident in the development of American colleges. The explosive energies of a democratic culture led to a chaotic multiplication of the institutions of higher learning. The statistics of college growth reveal the situation with stark simplicity. In 1800, there were only 25 colleges in the United States; by 1830 the number had reached 49; in the next three decades 137 additional collegiate institutions proved strong enough to survive. Amazing as these figures are they are modest when compared to the extraordinary number of colleges that failed to survive. An authoritative study of the founding of American colleges in 16 states of the Union before the Civil War recorded the starting of 516 colleges of which only 104, or 19 per cent, managed to survive.

Only 17 of the 186 permanent colleges in existence in the United States in 1860 were state universities; the bulk of the rest were denominational or church-related institutions. Consequently, they reflected many of the

Revivalism and the Growth of Colleges

powerful impulses of evangelical Protestantism, rather than the ideals of enlightenment and excellence that had been embodied in Jefferson's University of Virginia. Indeed, many of the denominational colleges of the South and West were inferior in the quality of their instruction to the grammar schools and academies that had been established in the older states.

But, even in the better endowed colleges of the East there was little opportunity to develop higher standards of learning. Everywhere, the standard college curriculum was the program of studies inherited from the colonial period—especially Latin, Greek, and mathematics. In such leading institutions as Harvard, Brown, Yale, Columbia, and Princeton, political economy, history, the new sciences, and modern languages gradually found their way into the list of courses. Nevertheless, the prescribed classical curriculum remained the core of the college curriculum throughout the decades before the Civil War.

Such a curriculum, to be sure, could cultivate the mind, but its potentialities were often stultified by the widespread use of the recitation method—described by one Harvard professor of the day as "the humble and simple, old-school, tedious business of recitation." In this system of instruction the daily task of the student was to read a text, memorize or translate it, and reproduce it in a classroom presided over by an instructor who spent the greater part of his time ascertaining whether the student had done his work, rather than encouraging the students to explore ideas and knowledge beyond the pages of the text.

Some notable teachers rose above the monotony of the prevailing system of instruction and devoted their energies to the improvement of teaching and scholarship. George Ticknor came back from his studies at a German university determined to elevate the standards at Harvard,

South View of the Several Halls of Harvard College. The I. N. Phelps Stokes Collection of American Historical Prints. Prints Division. The New York Public Library.

where he labored to expand the teaching of modern languages and to enrich the library. Benjamin Silliman of Yale gained a national reputation for his enthusiastic work in geology and chemistry. By the middle of the nineteenth century, Louis Agassiz was vitalizing the teaching of science at Harvard through an expanded use of the laboratory method. At the University of South Carolina, and later at Columbia University, Francis Lieber did distinguished work in political science and law. And Francis Wayland, the president of Brown University, not only encouraged innovations in the college curriculum, but also stimulated the teaching of political economy with his widely used book, *The Elements of Political Economy*. While the efforts of such distinguished teachers were noteworthy, it would take another two generations before the United States began to produce professional standards of scholarship that could be compared to those of Europe.

But, if the colleges in the age of the common man did not produce distinguished professional scholars, they were able to cultivate the minds and characters of large numbers of Americans. The prescribed classical curriculum exposed them to great writers and great ideas. And if the college classrooms were not always the most inspiring places for the discussion of these ideas, the student literary clubs and debating societies gave young men and women a more vital contact with the life of the mind, leading many to discover that philosophic and literary ideas were proper subjects for civilized conversation—more proper than the price of cotton, or the speculative value of railroad stocks. In short, the colleges served to refine the raw energies of a bustling democratic culture and furnished an eager and literate audience for aspiring writers who were seeking to create an authentic American literature.

The Literature of a Democratic Culture

Enterprising editors were quick to sense that the democratic tendencies in American education had influenced a taste for literature in the rapidly growing middle class of the Jacksonian generation. In the three decades before the Civil War, the first great monthly magazines offering a literary miscellany to a mass reading public made their appearance. These popular magazines became a significant proving ground for most of the aspiring writers of the time.

The first successful magazine of this type was the *Knickerbocker*, *Literary Magazines* published in New York (1833-1865) under the editorship of Lewis Gaylord Clark for much of that period. Clark was an editor with excellent literary taste who published the work of the best writers in New York and Boston. The chief rival of the *Knickerbocker* after 1841 was *Graham's Magazine* of Philadelphia, which achieved a circulation of 40,000 by the end of its second year of operations. Edgar Allan Poe served as literary editor of *Graham's* (1841-1842), and among the contributors to the pages

Title page from The Lady's Book, *published by L. A. Godey & Co., Philadelphia, 1832. Rush Rhees Library. The University of Rochester.*

of the magazine were such writers as Cooper, Bryant, Longfellow, and Lowell. Lavish use of copper and steel engravings for illustrations as well as literary content had much to do with the popularity of the magazine. The use of charming, hand-colored engravings also accounted for the phenomenal growth of such women's magazines as *Godey's Lady's Book* which reached a circulation of 150,000 in the 1850's. Mrs. Sarah Josepha Hale, author of "Mary Had a Little Lamb," was co-editor of *Godey's* and, during her long years in that post, sentimental stories and poems were contributed to the magazine by practically every American writer of any distinction.

Other magazines offered further opportunities to American writers to develop their literary reputations. *The United States Magazine and Democratic Review* (1831-1859) encouraged contributions from literary men as well as Democratic journalists and politicians. Indeed, the introductory editorial of the first issue of the *Democratic Review* called for a "national literature" that would be "truly democratic and American." The *American Whig Review* (1845-1862), though it had less literary distinction than its political rival, included contributions from such

writers as Poe and Lowell, as well as from the Whig publicists of the period. The *Southern Literary Messenger* was the best literary magazine in the South throughout most of its life (1834-1864) and served to encourage literary activity in that region of the country.

To be sure, American writers had to make their way against the continued popularity of English writers. The most successful magazine of the pre-Civil War era, after all, was *Harper's Monthly* of New York, begun in 1850 by a firm of book publishers that had made great profits out of reprinting the works of English authors. In the absence of any international copyright agreements, *Harpers Monthly* was able to publish in serial form and at low cost the works of immensely popular English novelists like Charles Dickens, Charles Reade, Wilkie Collins, and others. These popular English novels, together with an abundant use of woodcut illustrations, made *Harpers* an instant success, and brought it to a circulation of 200,000—far more than any other magazine before the Civil War.

Yet the continued popularity of English writers could no longer smother American talent. The Jacksonian generation, more than any before it, displayed a willingness to read American books which provided the encouragement that native American writers needed. Even Tocqueville recognized that a flourishing trade in democratic literature was developing in the United States—where "a writer may flatter himself that he will obtain at cheap rate a moderate reputation and a large fortune."

Not many American writers made large fortunes in this period, but a very large number of literary repuations were nourished by the growing eagerness of Americans to read American works. In the years between 1830 and 1860, there was an extraordinary outburst of literary activity in a variety of forms—poetry, essays, histories, tales, and romances. A single generation produced such writers as James Fenimore Cooper, Henry Wadsworth Longfellow, John Greenleaf Whittier, James Russell Lowell, Nathanial Hawthorne, Herman Melville, Ralph Waldo Emerson, Henry David Thoreau, Edgar Allan Poe, Walt Whitman, George Bancroft, Francis Parkman, and William Hickling Prescott.

The Flowering of an American Literature

Yet it was not only the trading spirit of which Tocqueville spoke that produced such a flowering of American literature. This new generation of writers used American themes and American imagery more successfully than previous American writers had done. They explored and interpreted some of the deepest feelings and attitudes in the emotional experience of the American people. And more often than not, they chose to express themselves by means of allegorical and symbolic suggestion rather than by a realistic description or dissection of the society of their time.

James Fenimore Cooper, the most widely read of the American writers of this generation, exemplifies many of these characteristics of the American imagination. He became a novelist almost inadvertently, yet

Cooper's Cultural Ideals

he created a series of romances that mythologized some of the deeply felt cultural ideals of the Jacksonian generation. The son of a wealthy landowner, Cooper was unwilling to settle for a comfortable life as a member of New York's gentry; he developed a restless urge to write about his countrymen.

In 1820, at the age of 31, he wrote and published his first novel in a burst of irritation over an English novel of manners that he thought he could improve. But this and other early efforts as a writer produced no literary successes. Not until he wrote *The Pioneers* (1823) did Cooper find the methods and materials that were to reveal his true genius as a writer. *The Pioneers* was the story of a frontier settlement in central New York state, and most of its substance was drawn from Cooper's childhood memories since his father had founded such a community and reared his family there in the dignity and comfort that befitted America's natural aristocracy.

The Pioneers was an instant success with the American reading public; on the day of publication the entire first edition was sold out. Undoubtedly many readers were attracted by such melodramatic incidents as the shooting of a panther which is about to attack the heroine, but it seems likely that they were also responding to the qualities of Natty Bumppo, one of the chief characters that Cooper had created. However that may be, Cooper returned to the same character four more times in as many novels, and the great Leatherstocking series became an ineradicable part of the symbolic experience of countless Americans.

The evolution of Natty Bumppo's character is the crowning achievement of Cooper's literary work, even though he was to write more thoughtful novels about American society as well as some essays of social criticism. In *The Pioneers*, Natty Bumppo wins our respect as the tale unfolds and we begin to see him as a self-reliant individualist who is carrying on a rational and moral rebellion against society with its inflexible rules and its wasteful encroachment upon a beautiful and bountiful natural environment. The later books in the Leatherstocking series add still more depth and meaning to Natty's image. In *The Last of the Mohicans* (1826), Natty is depicted at an earlier period of his life when he is feared and respected by hostile Indians as Hawkeye, the experienced scout and warrior. In *The Prairie* (1827), Leatherstocking is far out on the Great Plains in the closing years of his life. At this stage, he exhibits the reflective wisdom of old age, and philosophizes a great deal about the virtues of the "natural" life. *The Pathfinder* (1840) unfolds a story of the rescue of a girl in the Indian-infested forests of the Lake Ontario region when Natty was at the height of his fame as a scout and hunter. The self-sacrificing love affair which is the center of dramatic interest in this story reveals that Leatherstocking stands outside of civilization even in respect to the ties that might come from the love of a woman. In the last of the Leatherstocking books, *The Deerslayer* (1841), Cooper presents Natty as the young Hawkeye, on his first warpath in the company of his faithful Indian friend, Chingachgook. Amidst the idyllic setting of "Lake Glimmerglass," the youthful Hawkeye has already acquired the "natural gifts" which make him a virtuous as well as a resourceful hero; he understands and respects the difference between white men and red men, and he will kill only in necessity.

The enormous popularity of the Leatherstocking tales suggests that Cooper had succeeded in creating a hero myth which expressed yearnings that were deeply rooted in the American consciousness. A generation which revered Andrew Jackson as "The Hero" was ready to embrace a fictional hero who exemplified natural goodness and self-reliant individualism. To this extent, the Leatherstocking tales reveal some of the most widely shared cultural ideals of the age of the common man.

Nevertheless, the tales contain enough ambiguity of meaning to suggest that the pattern of mythology that was developed by Cooper reflected hidden disquietudes in America's democratic culture. In *The Prairie,* for example, Natty's natural goodness is set off against the more sinister character of Ishmael Bush, the squatter who is fleeing with his family from the world of law and title deeds. Ishmael Bush is also a "natural man" who seizes the land that he needs and defends it with his rifle, and whose actions follow a primitive and cruel pattern of retaliatory violence and murder. Cooper is suggesting that it is because of the social and moral disorder that results from the actions of natural men like Ishmael Bush that laws and judges are necessary even in an open society like America.

In much of his other writing, indeed, Cooper is preoccupied with the problem of preserving order and restraint in a society where a rampant individualism was producing rapid changes. In such novels as *Homeward Bound* and *Home as Found*, he satirized the ill-mannered, egotistical, self-made men who were becoming the most characteristic Americans in Jacksonian America. The most fully drawn character of this type is Aristabulous Bragg in *Home as Found*. Bragg is a hard-driving man who firmly believes in equality and progress, who measures achievement in terms of money, and who believes that every man ought to have an opportunity to get ahead on the basis of his own efforts. The vulgar prejudices of Bragg are set against the higher values of the Effinghams who represent a class of civilized gentlemen.

Cooper presents Bragg to his readers as "an epitome of all that is good and all that is bad in a very large class of his fellow citizens." Thus he typifies the countless Americans of the Jacksonian generation who were scrambling after wealth, status, and achievement without any thought of excellence. In the eyes of one of the Effinghams, Aristabolous Bragg is "a compound of shrewdness, impudence, common sense, pretension, humility, cleverness, vulgarity, kind-heartedness, duplicity, selfishness, law-honesty, moral fraud, and mother wit, mixed up with a smattering of learning and much penetration in practical things. . . . " By contrast, the Effinghams exemplify gentility, elevated principles, refinement, and a gracious use of their wealth and attainments. In short, they resemble a natural aristocracy as it was conceived by Thomas Jefferson.

Cooper was not content to develop these ideas through fictional presentation alone. In the same year (1838) that he published *Homeward Bound* and *Home as Found*, he elaborated his ideas in a political essay entitled *The American Democrat*, written to instruct his countrymen in the true principles of democracy. The fundamental issue that he raises in *The American Democrat* is how to control the levelling tendencies of a democracy so as to insure the protection of an intelligent class of gentlemen who are needed to give leadership and direction to the society.

American Romanticism

The popularity of the Leatherstocking tales reminds us that the age of the common man was a romantic one. Most of the literary tendencies of the time were formed by the ideas and sensibilities to which historians have attached the label, Romanticism. By the 1830's an increasing number of educated Americans were coming under the influence of European writers who were reacting against the excessive reliance on science and rationalism which characterized the Enlightenment. Writers like Wordsworth, Coleridge, and Carlyle in England emphasized the emotional and instinctual aspects of the human personality, and asserted that man should trust his intuition more than his intellect. Unwilling to accept the eighteenth-century conception of the universe as a vast machine, they preferred to regard the natural world as "the garment of a divine Spirit"—to borrow Carlyle's metaphor. Consequently, they sought to liberate literature from the constraints and contrivances of a narrow rationalism and to make it more spontaneous and imaginative.

European Romanticism developed two somewhat contradictory tendencies. For some, Romanticism was a highly individualistic movement with revolutionary aspirations. To a considerable degree, this group was influenced by the French writer, Rousseau, who had argued that civilization was corrupt, and that man could achieve happiness only by living close to nature and by following the spontaneous promptings of his natural feelings. Other Romanticists, however, felt that human happiness could best be achieved in an organic social order where every man had a clearly defined role and where there was a maximum interplay of such human values as dignity, honor, charity, cooperation, and service. Many of these writers ended by glorifying the feudal and Catholic social order of the Middle Ages.

In the democratic environment of the United States, however, the individualistic tendencies of Romanticism tended to overshadow all others. To be sure, some American writers found it possible to merge a romantic conception of individualism with the collective consciousness of the people *en masse*. George Bancroft, a leading Jacksonian intellectual, and one of the great historians of his time, felt that there was an organic relationship between the intuitional elements in individual personality and the common sentiments of all men.

Like any good European Romanticist, Bancroft valued intuition more than intellect. "Reason exists in every human breast," he wrote in 1835. "I mean not that faculty which deduces inferences from the experience of the senses, but that higher faculty, which from the infinite treasures of its own consciousness, originates truth, and assents to it by the force of intuitive evidence." As a true democrat, however, Bancroft believed that such intuitive affections are found everywhere; it is "a spirit in man; not in a privileged few." "There is not," he continued, "the difference between one mind and another, which the pride of philosophers might conceive. To them, no faculty is conceded which does not belong to the meanest of their countrymen. . . . If it be true that the gifts of mind are universally diffused, if the sentiment of truth, justice, love, and beauty exist in everyone, then it follows, as a necessary consequence, that the common judgment in taste, politics, and religion is the highest authority on earth, and the nearest possible approach to an infallible decision."

Bancroft's attempt to fashion a democratic transcendentalism appealed only to a particular circle of intellectuals who were associated with the *United States Democratic Review*. Most intellectual leaders in his native state of Massachusetts were less interested in such efforts to merge the individual in the democratic mass. Indeed, American Romanticism developed its most sophisticated character in the transcendentalist writings of a gifted group of intellectuals who were located primarily in New England.

New England transcendentalism was derived in part from German Romantic philosophy (from Kant, Hegel, Fichte, and especially Schelling) and in part from the interpretations of such philosophic ideas as were developed by English writers like Coleridge and Carlyle. In the theory of knowledge expounded by the German philosophers, the human mind was not limited to the phenomena of sense experience as Locke had maintained; man also possessed an intuitive capacity for grasping deeper forms of truth that were beyond the reach of the senses. Hence, some of Kant's followers emphasized a distinction between Reason and Understanding. To them "Reason" was the intuitive faculty of knowing which "transcended" empirical knowledge based upon sensory experience; "understanding" was the term they used to describe the inferior type of empirical thought on which natural science is based.

This transcendentalist philosophy was readily embraced by New England intellectuals because their cultural tradition had already predisposed them to accept such ideas. New England Puritanism had emphasized man's capacity for direct spiritual insight in the conversion experience. Jonathan Edwards, it must be remembered, had argued that there was a supernatural sense in man that led to an immediate and intuitive grasp of ultimate truth. But Jonathan Edwards and most of his Puritan forebears had maintained that the supernatural sense comes only by God's grace to a few, "the elect." On the other hand, the transcendentalists had already passed through the liberalizing experience of Unitarianism and Universalism; to them, all men are created spiritually equal in their ability to communicate directly with the Universal Being.

More than any other single individual, Ralph Waldo Emerson created much of the philosophical framework of New England transcendentalism. He had accepted a Unitarian pulpit shortly after his graduation from Harvard Divinity School, but he had resigned from the ministry three years later because his thinking no longer coincided with the tenets of Unitarianism. After a journey to England and Europe, he returned to the United States in 1835 eager to share with his countrymen the ideas that he had been forming. Within a few years, his essays and public lectures established him as the leading spokesman of New England transcendentalism.

The essential strategy of a transcendentalist way of life, as Emerson conceived it, was set forth in his first little book—an essay entitled "Nature," published in 1836. In this work he expressed his belief that a transcendent reality could be perceived more fully and deeply among the "essences" of Nature: "space, the air, the river, the leaf." "In the woods," he wrote, "we return to reason and faith. Here I feel that nothing can befall me in life,—no disgrace, no calamity, (leaving me my eyes) which nature cannot repair. Standing on the bare ground,—my head bathed by the blithe air, and uplifted into infinite space,—all mean egotism vanishes. I become a transparent eye-ball; I am nothing; I see all; the currents of the Universal Being circulate through me; I am part and particle of God."

Emerson's transcendentalism was closely associated with a belief that it was America's destiny to create new possibilities for life. "Why should we not enjoy an original relation to the Universe?" he asked in the opening sentences of *Nature*. "There are new lands, new men, new thoughts. Let us demand our own works and laws and worship." In his Phi Beta Kappa address delivered at Harvard in 1837, he urged American writers to free themselves from a sterile dependence on Europe and the past: "Let us have done with Europe and dead cultures, let us explore the possibilities of our own new world."

These possibilities, he believed, must have their beginning in a self-reliant individualism. In his famous essay entitled "Self-Reliance," Emerson declared, "Whoso would be a man must be a nonconformist. . . . Nothing is at last sacred but the integrity of your own mind." In his frequently repeated lecture on "Politics," he asserted that the growth of private character in men "makes the State unnecessary."

Emerson's fervent individualism undoubtedly appealed to a great many Americans of his generation because it seemed to sanction their feverish pursuit of private gain, but it must always be remembered that "the sage of Concord" did not intend to endorse a vulgar gospel of individual success. To him, genuine self-reliance came only with the growth of wisdom and private character, and not from the accumulation of material wealth. "The reliance on Property," he declared, "including the reliance on governments which protect it, is the want of self-reliance."

Unquestionably, there was some contempt for institutions in Emerson's thinking. "Society," he wrote, "everywhere is in a conspiracy against the manhood of its members. Society is a joint-stock company in which the members agree, for the better securing of his bread to each shareholder, to surrender the liberty and culture of the eater." Yet in his well-known essay on "New England Reformers," Emerson not only praised the "scrutiny and dissent" that was manifested in the great number of variety of reform movements that attacked churches, marriage, education, and the laws of property, but he also asked, "Can we not play the game of life with these counters as well as those; in the institution of property as well as out of it?" Indeed, he refused to join any of the reform associations—not even the attempt of his friends to create a model community at Brook Farm.

The temporizing tone that is present so frequently in Emerson's writings cannot be discerned in the thinking of his friend and disciple, Henry David Thoreau. The most uncompromising of the transcendentalists, Thoreau transformed the theory of the self-reliant individual into a total rejection of society. The demands of organized society, he believed, even a democratic society such as that which existed in America, forced men to "lead lives of quiet desperation." Hence he deliberately tested the possibilities of self-realization by living a hermit-like existence for two years in a hut which he built for himself on the shore of Walden Pond near Concord. By reducing his physical needs for food, clothing, and shelter to the barest essentials, he hoped to free himself from the burdens and corruptions of society in order to live a fuller and richer life devoted to reading, contemplation, and communion with nature.

Thoreau's Moral Egotism

Thoreau's account of his experiment in his first published book, *Walden*, is a masterpiece of transcendentalist writing. Presented in autobiographical form, *Walden* is a moral essay written to demonstrate that the elaborate structure of institutions in American society had no real moral status—that false assumptions of necessity led men to live their lives of quiet desperation. In the opening pages of his book, he told his readers:

It is very evident what mean and sneaking lives many of you live . . . lying, flattering, voting, contracting yourselves into a nutshell of civility, or dilating into an atmosphere of thin and vaporous generosity, that you may persuade your neighbor to let you make his shoes, or his hat, or his coat, or his carriage, or import his groceries for him; making yourselves sick that you may lay up something against a sick day, something to be tucked away in an old chest, or in a stocking behind the plastring, or more safely, in the brick bank. . . . A stereotyped but unconscious despair is concealed even under what are called the games and amusements of mankind. There is no play in them, for this comes after work.

In the summer of 1846, Thoreau spent a day in the Concord jail for refusing to pay his poll tax as a protest against a government that supported slavery. His essay *On the Duty of Civil Disobedience* is an uncompromising statement of his transcendental anarchism: "I heartily accept the motto—'That government is best which governs least'; and I should like to see it acted up to more rapidly and systematically. Carried out, it finally amounts to this, which I also believe—'That government is best which governs not at all,' and when men are prepared for it, that will be the kind of government which they will have." Unlike most Americans of the Jacksonian generation, Thoreau was unwilling to grant any superior status to the principle of majority rule. "A government in which the majority rule in all cases," he asserted, "cannot be based on justice, even as far as men understand it. Can there not be a government in which majorities do not virtually decide right and wrong, but conscience?—in which majorities decide only those questions to which the rule of expediency is applicable? Must the citizen ever for a moment, or in the least degree, resign his conscience to the legislator?"

Neither was Thoreau willing to resign his conscience to the organized efforts of reformers. He shunned all the institutions of the democratic process—reform associations as well as the machinery of governmental authority. "It is not a man's duty," he declared, "as a matter of course, to devote himself to the eradication of any, even the most enormous wrong; he may still properly have other concerns to engage him; but it is his duty, at least, to wash his hands of it, and, if he gives it no thought longer, not to give it practically his support."

In the last analysis, Thoreau contemplated no social reconstruction; indeed he was incapable of any imagination in that direction. Yet, even though his civil disobedience was not very severely tested by the gentle authority of the village of Concord, he did succeed in making his entire life "a counterfriction" to all the petty expediencies which American society required of its citizens.

Thoreau's *Civil Disobedience* developed conclusions that followed logically from transcendentalist assumptions about individual intuition and individual liberty; and in varying degrees other transcendentalists shared such anti-institutional attitudes. Emerson had already expressed them in his essays and lectures, and similar strains of thinking are evident in the sermons of such transcendentalist ministers as William Ellery Channing and Theodore Parker. Even the transcendentalists who associated themselves in the "Fourierite" community called Brook Farm, near Roxbury, Massachusetts, thought of themselves not so much as an organized society, but as "united individuals" gathered together to make self-perfection easier.

Transcendental Dilemmas

It would be wrong to assume that such moral egotism was the only logical outcome of the Romantic concern for individualism and the individual personality. Other writers, like Hawthorne, Melville, and Poe, who shared the Romantic preoccupation with the contradiction between man's aspirations and the claims of the social structure within which he must live, explored the moral dangers rather than the opportunities of individualism. That such writers should have appeared as important manifestations of American Romanticism is not surprising when we remember that the inherited Protestant culture contained a rich store of ideas and insights which taught that the inevitable outcome of unchecked individualism is a narrow and destructive egotism.

Nathaniel Hawthorne had an excellent opportunity to observe transcendentalists at close hand and to discuss with them their metaphysical speculations. He spent one year at Brook Farm and his marriage to Sophia Peabody in 1842 was followed by three years of residence in Concord where he lived in daily association with the reformers and intellectuals who had stimulated a remarkable renaissance of thought and letters in New England.

Hawthorne found it impossible to accept Emerson's optimistic faith in self-reliant individualism. He distrusted the transcendentalist belief that the voice of God was buried in the intuitive faculty of man. Nor could he accept the belief that the essence of human virtue is reliance on oneself. Hawthorne was continually aware of the contradiction between the individual quest for meaning and the laws and conventions of society, but he was less troubled than Emerson and Thoreau by the dangers of conformity, dependence, and compromise. He was far more troubled by the evil wrought in a man's nature by the deadly tendency to develop an aloof and superior posture toward his fellow man. To Hawthorne, the essence of evil is egotism because it separated the individual from "the whole sympathetic chain of human nature" and led to estrangement and isolation.

Hawthorne and the Problem of Moral Egotism

Most of Hawthorne's works reveal this preoccupation with the evil of human estrangement. In *The Scarlet Letter* (1850), Hawthorne probed the meaning of sin in society—not simply the meaning of adultery in a Puritan village—but the universally destructive character of human definitions of sin for both the judged and the judging. In *The House of the Seven Gables* (1851), he depicted the consequences of guilt and estrangement in an old Salem family whose seventeenth-century ancestor had hanged witches and brought down upon his family the curse of one of his victims. Hawthorne drew upon his Brook Farm experience in *The Blithedale Romance* (1852) in order to portray the destructive impact that a zealous social reformer can have upon those who are associated with him. In all these works, guilt , pride, and moral self-righteousness are revealed as destructive forces in human life. The title of one of his short stories—*Egotism, the Bosom Serpent*—therefore, can be taken as the central allegorical figure in Hawthorne's picture of the human condition.

One of Hawthorne's admiring contemporaries was an aspiring young writer named Herman Melville. In a review of *The House of the Seven Gables*, Melville expressed particular approval of a "certain tragic phase of humanity" which was embodied in Hawthorne's works. To Melville, the duty of a writer was to search for "usable truth," by which he meant

Melville's Search for a "Usable Truth"

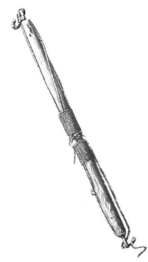

Spreader for schooner rigging. From Index of American Design. National Gallery of Art.

"the apprehension of the absolute condition of present things as they strike the eye of the man who fears them not, though they do their worst to him."

Born in New York in a family with an aristocratic background but little wealth, Melville had worked as a sailor on several sailing ships, including one that had gone on a whaling expedition in the Pacific. When he left the sea and decided to write, his first books were tales of adventure based on his own experiences: *Typee* (1846) and *Omoo* (1847) were narratives of adventures in the Pacific, *White-Jacket* (1850) portrayed the conditions of life for a sailor on a man-of-war, and *Redburn* (1849) told the story of a voyage to England. One of these earlier works, *Mardi* (1848), revealed, by its strange mixture of allegory and fantasy, that Melville was seeking to express deeper and more "usable" truths about life. But not until he published *Moby Dick* in 1851 did Melville achieve the height of his powers as an artist.

In *Moby Dick*, Melville constructed a strange fable of a Yankee whaling captain, with a monomaniacal will, who pursued a white whale. In symbolic terms, the pursuit of Moby Dick by Ahab may be taken to represent the problem of human destiny as Melville saw it. The relentless voyage of Ahab seems to stand for life itself conceived as a search for the deeper meanings that lie behind the outward appearances of life. In the transcendentalist faith of Emerson, the effort to penetrate these appearances should lead to a self-reliant unity of spirit which embodies Justice, Truth, Love, Freedom. But the voyage of Ahab, conducted with the fiercest kind of self-reliance, ends in self-annihilation. Just before the final and fatal encounter with the white whale, Ahab remarks, "the dead, blind wall butts all inquiring heads at last." Thus, the transcendentalist seeker for usable truths cannot fathom the ambiguities of life; good and evil remain impenetrable to the end.

Poe and the Discipline of Horror

Melville was not alone in his fascination for dark and destructive motives of human nature. Another gifted writer of his generation, Edgar Allen Poe, displayed an even greater pleasure in the creation of tales of terror and horror that deliberately destroyed the rational and common sense categories of perception. To Poe, sadness and horror became disciplines that could lead one to discover new meanings in life.

Poe's fascination for horror undoubtedly sprang from his own wretchedly unhappy life. The son of travelling actors, his dypsomaniac father disappeared when he was a mere child, and his mother died in poverty in Richmond, Virginia, soon afterwards. A tobacco merchant raised him as a foster son, but Edgar developed an unstable personality. Gambling debts forced him to leave the University of Virginia and a court martial ended a short experience at West Point. The rest of his short, sad life was spent publishing poems and short stories and writing critical reviews for magazines. He was never able to earn much from his writings, and he wandered from one magazine venture to another in Philadelphia, New York, and Baltimore, torn by the agony of unrelieved poverty and cursing "the horrible intervals of sanity" that made him aware of his condition.

Although death came to Poe when he was hardly 40, he had made his mark as a creative and original writer. One of his best volumes of poems was printed just after his dismissal from West Point in 1831. Included in this collection were such poems as "The Sleeper" and "Lenore," which reveal a preoccupation with fair ladies lying in death, or "City in the Sea" which exploits a favorite romantic theme of the city of the dead. Equally significant, however, was his definition of poetry which was included in the preface to this volume. "A poem," he wrote, "in my opinion, is opposed to a work of science by having, for its *immediate* object, pleasure, and truth." The poet, he believed, should rely on "music" and "indefiniteness" for poetic effect.

And generations of Americans who have recited his most familiar work, "The Raven," will agree that there is much melancholy music in Poe's poetry. He believed that the poetic moods of sadness and horror were essential in the struggles of man to apprehend "a portion of that Loveliness whose very elements . . . appertain to eternity alone." "When by poetry," he wrote in an essay on *The Poetic Principle,* "we find ourselves melted into tears—we weep then, not . . . through excess of pleasure, but through a certain, petulant, impatient sorrow at our inability to grasp *now*, wholly, here on earth, at once and forever, those divine and rapturous joys, of which *through* the poem . . . we attain to brief and indeterminate glimpses."

Hence, like Emerson, Poe affirmed the romantic belief that it was possible to transcend those forms of knowledge and experience that were based on intellect and scientific reasoning alone. Unlike Emerson, however, the route of transcendence for Poe was through the moods of sadness and horror created by the physical power of words in a poem, rather than through the rapturous mood of response to the beauty and glory of nature.

Mythopoetic Vistas of American Democracy

The poet who was able to synthetize the raw vitality and the passionate idealism of the Jacksonian generation better than any other was Walt Whitman. Born the son of a carpenter-farmer on Long Island, Whitman left school early and embarked upon a process of self-education, going from job to job as a carpenter, rural school teacher, journalist, and newspaper editor. His skills as a writer were formed in newspaper work, and his ideas were picked up from the stimulating life of the city, from walks in the Long Island countryside, and from desultory reading.

Democracy's Poet

Whitman was a devoted supporter of the Jacksonian Democratic party and most of his newspaper jobs were with Democratic journals like the *Long Island Democrat, the Democratic Review,* and the *Brooklyn Eagle,* and by 1846 he had become editor of the *Eagle.* Most of his editorials supported Democratic policies, including "manifest destiny" and the Mexican War, although he moved toward a free-soil position regarding the expansion of slavery into the territories acquired from Mexico. In his continued reading and self-education, he developed a strong interest in the essays of Emerson; indeed, Whitman himself was to admit later that his reading of Emerson had brought his simmering ideas to a boil. And when *Leaves of Grass* appeared in 1855, Emerson was the first among established writers to recognize Whitman's genius.

The Self and the En-Masse   The main poem in *Leaves of Grass* is "Song of Myself," which contains in essence nearly all the moral and philosophic ideas that Whitman was trying to express. The self which is the protagonist of the poem is one that moves through many roles; it is a self that expresses the diversity of American life and its open possibilities:

> Of every hue and caste am I, of every rank and religion
> A farmer, mechanic, artist, gentelman, sailor, quaker,
> Prisoner, fancy man, rowdy, lawyer, physician, priest.

Throughout the long poem, there is a restless and searching individualism with repeated images of constant motion and incessant travellings:

> I tramp a perpetual journey (come listen all!)
> My signs are a rain-proof coat, good shoes, and a
> staff cut from the woods.

In the poetic language of "Song of Myself," Whitman provides us with a magnificent expression of the paradox of American democracy already noted by Alexis de Tocqueville in his commentary on American society. Man in a democratic society has two kinds of moral and political identity. On the one hand he is unique, separate, self-reliant; on the other hand, he is equal to, and no more than, everybody else. The opening sentences of *Leaves of Grass* state this paradox in general terms:

> Of one's self I sing, a simple separate person
> Yet utter the word Democratic, the word En-Masse.

Whitman's triumph as a poet consists in merging these opposing ideas of individualism and equality so successfully in the spontaneously flowing verses of "Song of Myself" that one hardly realizes that they are in dialectical opposition to each other. It may be said therefore that Whitman was able to mythicize the key abstractions of democratic idealism. For him, liberty and equality—together—constitute the essential moral nexus of a democratic society.

But the poetic trick of merging the self with the "democratic en-masse" also reveals the limits of Whitman's moral imagination. The "self" in "Song of Myself" is too self-assured in attitude. There are no serious efforts to wrestle with the contradictions of life such as one finds in Hawthorne or Melville. Hence modern critics find the moral dilemmas of Melville and Hawthorne artistically and intellectually more satisfying.

Yet the likelihood is that the majority of Americans in Whitman's time shared his optimistic illusions—the idea of the perfect freedom of the individual who possesses at the same time the ability to "merge" and "identify" with everything else: the democratic masses, the nation, or even the brotherhood of man.

Bancroft and the Moral Meaning of American History

Certainly this was true of George Bancroft, the leading historian of the Jacksonian generation. Like Whitman, Bancroft was an ardent Jacksonian Democrat. Moreover, his democratic sentiments were strongly tinged with romanticism, because after graduating from Harvard he had gone to Germany to study under such outstanding thinkers as Hegel in Berlin and Heeren in Göttingen. His enthusiasm for the new ideas stirring in Europe contributed to his decision to reject the Whiggish prejudices of his family background and to take an active part in radical Jacksonian politics in Massachusetts. At about the same time (1834) he published the first volume of his 10-volume *History of the United States from the Discovery of the American Continent*—the last volume of which was completed in 1874. During these years of research and writing, Bancroft also threw himself into politics with the same gusto that characterized so much of his historical writing. He was an enthusiastic leader of the radical wing of the Jacksonian party in Massachusetts in the 1830's; he wrote a eulogistic campaign biography of Martin Van Buren and was rewarded with the post of collector of the port of Boston; he served as Secretary of the Navy for one year under Polk, and then as minister to England. Indeed, his conception of history was to a large extent an expression of the movement and vitality which were so much a part of American life in his day.

For Bancroft, history offered the key to an understanding of the realities that lay behind the flux of motion and change which seemed to be the very essence of life in the New World. To him, the discipline of the historical method was the primary means by which Americans could discover order and meaning in a society where the dissolution and disappearance of inherited institutions, forms of thought, and habits of mind created a sense of endless mutability and unsettledness. Only the poet comes close to the historian in this function because he often catches "the first beam of light that flows from its uncreated source." But the poet "repeats the message of the Infinite, without always being able to analyze it, and often without knowing how he received it, or why he selected it for its utterance."

Bancroft's analysis of the motion of historical events led him to the conclusion that the law of progress was the governing law of human history. Furthermore, in the progression of events, the New World represented a grand stage in a universal historical process. "The irresistible tendency of the human race is therefore to advancement," he wrote in 1835. "Dynasties perish; cities are buried; nations have been victims to error, or martyrs for right. Humanity has always been on the advance; gaining maturity, universality, and power."

The volumes of Bancroft's history of the United States demonstrate abundantly that America was fulfilling the duty imposed by the law of progress. In these volumes, the growth of liberty provides the major conceptual framework. To Bancroft the history of mankind is fundamentally a struggle between liberty and tyranny, and the American Revolution becomes the ultimate clue to the meaning of human history. Indeed, the American Revolution marked the fourth and most significant stage of history in his conception of the progress of universal history. The first stage comprised the history of mankind from the beginning of the world to the age of Socrates; the second went from the decline of Athens to the coming of Christ; and "the third extends from the promulgation of the glad tidings of the gospel by the Saviour to the American Revolution, which events may be deemed the two most important in the history of mankind; with the latter commences a new and most glorious era. . . ." And the moral meaning of the American Revolution contains the highest possibilities for attainment of liberty and human brotherhood:

The authors of the American Revolution avowed for their object the welfare of mankind and believed that they were in the service of their own and of all future generations. Their faith was just; for the world of mankind does not exist in fragments, nor can a country have an insulated existence. All men are brothers; and all are bondsmen for one another. . . . New principles of government could not assert themselves in one hemisphere without affecting the other. . . .

It would be quite wrong, however, to assume, as some literary historians have, that history for Bancroft was made subservient to a myth which made America the consummation of all moral and political progress. Although every volume of his history of the United States reminds us continually that America is destined to lead mankind to one of the grandest stages in human history, it is not necessarily the final stage.

Bancroft's Theory of Historical Progress

Bancroft recognized that even in the United States, progress was the result of a complicated historical process. In an oration which he delivered to the New York Historical Society in 1854, he pointed out that there is always an antagonism between "the actual state of the world" and "the ideal state toward which it should tend." He likened the process of history to "a rope of three strands" which are most clearly visible in the political conditions that ever have been and ever can be formed in any society:

One party may found itself on things as they are, and strive for their unaltered perpetuity; this is conservatism, always appearing wherever established interests exist, and never capable of unmingled success, because finite things are ceaselessly in motion. Another may be based on theoretic principles, and struggle unrelentingly to conform society to the absolute law of Truth and Justice; and this, though it kindle the purest enthusiasm, can likewise never perfectly succeed, because the materials of which society is composed partake of imperfection, and to extirpate all that is imperfect would lead to the destruction of society itself. And there may be a third, which seeks to reconcile the two, but which yet can never thrive by itself, since it depends for its activity on the clashing between the fact and the higher law.

In Bancroft's view of historical change and motion, all these forces are necessary—the static, the dynamic, and the reconciling. The discipline of history, therefore, became corrective for Bancroft's transcendentalism. The absolutist and perfectionist tendencies of transcendentalist thought are checked by the study of historical change. Bancroft willingly accepted the mediating influence of historical reality—"the actual state of the world," because all societies are imperfect, and "to extirpate all that is imperfect would lead to the destruction of society itself."

By different routes, Whitman the poet and Bancroft the historian arrived at a common destination in their quest for meaning in America's democratic experience. Although both had participated in Jacksonian political warfare and experienced the resulting anxieties and disappointments, they shared a final optimism about America's democratic possibilities. For Whitman, the egalitarian urges of the common man could shape a society in which men can remain healthy, self-reliant selves. For Bancroft, the imperfections of the actual state of the world would be redeemed by history—a history in which a democratic America will lead mankind to the highest attainment of liberty and human brotherhood.

The Magnolia, 1843. Rush Rhees Library. The University of Rochester.

Manifest Destiny

The explosive energies which were released by the politics in the Jacksonian generation led to a new surge of expansionism on the part of the American people. The Jacksonians had broken some of the bonds of privilege in the market economy, and the new Whigs proposed to accelerate the unfettered energies of the American people by employing various techniques of public aid to expand the benefits of the market revolution for all groups—merchants, manufacturers, farmers, and mechanics. In the Whig administration of John Tyler, the stated aim was to promote the vigorous expansion of these liberated energies in the world market. Tyler not only shared the common belief that the destiny of America was to move overland to the shores of the Pacific, but he also talked extravagantly about the duty of Americans to move onward across the Pacific: ". . . walking on the waves of the mighty deep . . . overturning the strong places of despotism, and returning to man his long-lost rights." He was convinced that the future greatness of the United States lay in its ability to penetrate the markets of the world. Caleb Cushing, sent by Tyler as the first American commissioner to China, successfully negotiated a treaty there which extended commercial privileges to the United States on a most-favored nation basis. At the same time, Tyler extended the Monroe Doctrine to the Hawaiian Islands, recognizing that they were steppingstones to the markets of East Asia.

Throughout his administration, Tyler encouraged the State Department to pursue an activist diplomacy that looked toward the acquisition of Texas, California, and Oregon. Indeed, the issue of expansion moved onto the center of the stage of American politics. As the election of 1844 approached, a new ideology of expansionism with a new name made its appearance—"manifest destiny." Though the concept was not wholly novel, the precise combination of words was. Furthermore, it worked so well as a political slogan that it became part of the common language of the day.

It is also significant that the man who coined the phrase in 1845 was John L. O'Sullivan, a leading symbol-maker of the Jacksonian party. Many younger Democratic politicians, still smarting from their defeat in the "log cabin and hard cider campaign" of 1840, sensed the powerful expansionist impulses that were stirring in various segments of the American population. O'Sullivan's famous editorial absorbed the ideology of expansion into Jacksonian democratic doctrine with the claim that it was "the right of our manifest destiny to overspread and to possess the whole of the continent which Providence has given us for the development of the great experiment of liberty and federative self-government entrusted to us. It is a right such as that of the tree to the space of air and earth suitable to the full expansion of its principle and destiny of growth—such as that of the stream to the channel required for the still accumulating volume of its flow. It is in our future far more than in our past, or in past history of Spanish exploration or French colonial rights, that our true title is to be found."

The Texas Question

The concrete issue that led O'Sullivan to coin the popular slogan of manifest destiny was the annexation of Texas. Many westerners had denounced the Florida purchase treaty with Spain in 1819 which had defined the Sabine River as the southwestern boundary of Louisiana, thus giving up the rather shadowy claims of the United States to Texas. Stung by such criticisms of his diplomacy, John Quincy Adams, upon becoming President in 1825, attempted unsuccessfully to begin negotiations with the Republic of Mexico for the purchase of the region beyond the Sabine River. At the beginning of his administration, President Jackson attempted to succeed where John Quincy Adams had failed, but no government in Mexico would have dared to dismember its national domain, which had only recently been won in the war of independence against Spain.

Furthermore, such diplomatic pressures from the United States led the Mexican government to institute new policies for the protection of its territory beyond the Rio Grande. Beginning in 1821, the Mexican Government had encouraged American emigration to Texas by granting to Moses Austin, an enterprising American with large business ventures in upper Louisiana, a huge tract of land with the understanding that he would settle three hundred families on it. Actual colonization was begun by a group of Americans led by his son, Stephen Austin, in the following year. This was the start of a series of favorable land grants to other American settlers who rushed to take advantage of the fertile lands of east Texas favored by easy access to the Gulf of Mexico. By 1830, there were twenty thousand American settlers in Texas, most of them from the slave states and many of them engaged in a flourishing cotton production. By that time, the Mexican government sought to limit the inordinate influx of settlers from the United States, first by abolishing slavery in Texas, and then by direct prohibitions on further immigration. The Texans were so aroused by these new policies that they held two conventions in 1832 and 1833 which demanded the repeal of the objectionable measures. They also demanded that Texas be separated from Coahuila and made a separate state within the Mexican federal system. Any hope for such reforms was shattered, however, by a change in the Mexican national government that brought General Antonio Lopez de Santa Anna to power. The Mexican legislature drew up a "revolutionary" constitution which greatly increased the power of the new President by converting the states of the Mexican federal republic into departments whose governors were mere agents of the President.

As a consequence, the Texans rose up in revolt against the centralized government of Santa Anna and, on March 2, 1836, they declared their independence. Determined to crush the rebels, Santa Anna moved into

Texas with an army of six thousand men, and his superior forces were able to win a few opening skirmishes. But his ruthless extermination of a small garrison of Texans at the Alamo mission in San Antonio, and the cold-blooded execution of 350 prisoners at Goliad, merely strengthened the will of the Texans to resist. On April 21, 1836, the main army of the Texans, commanded by General Sam Houston, decisively defeated the larger Mexican force and took Santa Anna prisoner.

Before being allowed to return to Mexico, Santa Anna was forced to sign two treaties—one agreeing to withdraw all Mexican forces from Texas, and the other stipulating that he was to use his influence to persuade the Mexican government to recognize the independence of Texas with a boundary "not to extend beyond the Rio Grande." The Mexican government refused to recognize these arrangements made under duress but, unwilling to continue the war, withdrew all Mexican troops to positions south of the Rio Grande. Having achieved de facto independence, the people elected Sam Houston president of the new "Lone Star Republic."

The Texan's fight for independence evoked widespread sympathy in the United States. Even before Houston's victory at San Jacinto both houses of Congress adopted resolutions declaring that the independence of Texas ought to be recognized whenever information was received that a stable government was in operation. Jackson, however, delayed extending diplomatic recognition because of the rising antislavery sentiment in the North. Abolitionist editors charged that southern slaveholders had conspired to settle Texas with slaveholders and had organized a revolution against Mexico as a prelude to annexation by the United States so that enough territory would be acquired to provide for the eventual organization of several new slave states. Fearing that the Texas issue might impair Van Buren's chances of winning the election, Jackson did not extend formal diplomatic recognition to the Republic of Texas until the day before his retirement from office.

Although the question of annexation to the United States had been submitted in the form of a plebiscite to the voters of Texas who approved it almost unanimously, President Van Buren refused to take any initiative in that direction. Southern leaders in Congress strongly advocated annexation, but the American Antislavery Society flooded Congress with anti-annexation petitions for which it was claimed six hundred thousand signatures had been secured. Already burdened with serious problems brought on by the Panic of 1837, the Van Buren administration was not willing to risk a divisive quarrel over the Texas question.

Subsequently Texas sought and obtained diplomatic recognition from Great Britain whose government was anxious to develop a market for British manufactures in exchange for Texas cotton and, at the same time, to create a buffer against the expansionist aims of the United States. The British government, having abolished slavery in its own colonies, was also encouraging the government of Texas to consider the possibility of joining the other nations of the civilized world in abolishing the institution of human slavery.

Alarmed by these developments, President Tyler reopened negotiations with Texas on the question of annexation and, by 1844, his new Secretary of State, John C. Calhoun, had obtained the assent of the government of Texas to a treaty of annexation. In submitting the treaty to the Senate for ratification, Calhoun included his correspondence with the British minister on the Texas question in which he made a vigorous defense of slavery. By injecting the slavery issue into the debate over ratification in this fashion, Calhoun threatened the carefully constructed arrangements within both major parties to keep the slavery issue out of politics. Only 16 Senators voted in favor of the treaty, while 35 voted against it—29 of the latter were Whigs.

The leading contenders for the presidential nomination in 1844, Martin Van Buren for the Democrats and Henry Clay for the Whigs (apparently by agreement), took positive action to remove the Texas question as a campaign issue. On April 27, the Washington *Globe* and the *National Intelligencer* published letters from Van Buren and Clay respectively in which the two party leaders opposed any immediate annexation of Texas, although both left the door open for such a future possibility.

Oregon and California   But popular pressures for expansion were too strong to be controlled even by skillful and experienced politicans like Van Buren and Clay. It was also becoming apparent that the expansionist impulse was not limited to one section. Northern interests as well as southern interests were identifying concrete expansionist goals that looked farther west to Oregon and California.

For many years, Americans had shown little interest in Oregon. Small parties of "Mountain Men" hunted beaver skins for the Rocky Mountain Fur Company and John Jacob Astor's American Fur Company, but British fur traders operating for the Hudson's Bay Company held a clear advantage in the fur trade and in relations with the Indians. In the 1830's, however, Methodist and Presbyterian missionaries fired with the zeal of evangelical Protestantism went to the Oregon region to convert the Indians to the Christian faith. Their enthusiastic reports in religious periodicals about the fertile lands and salubrious climate of Oregon attracted large numbers of settlers from the Mississippi valley. Organized bands of pioneer farmers crossed prairies, mountains, and forests in the long trek to the Oregon region. By 1845, there were nearly five thousand Americans in Oregon, and their political desires were made known in the adoption of an Organic Act which set up a provisional government and which stated that its provisions were to apply only "until such time as the United States of America extend their jurisdiction over us."

At the same time, a "California fever" was infecting diverse groups of Americans almost as much as the "Oregon fever." Some emigrants

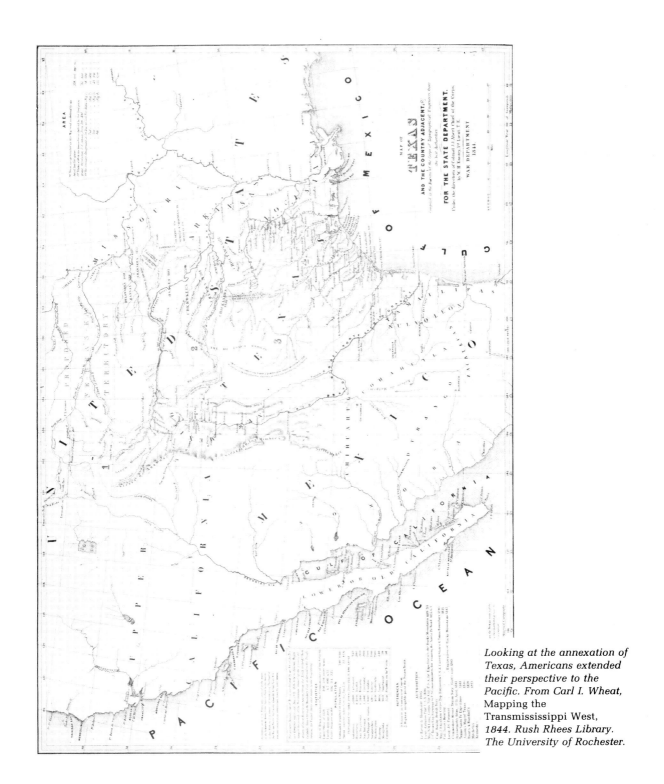

Looking at the annexation of Texas, Americans extended their perspective to the Pacific. From Carl I. Wheat, Mapping the Transmississippi West, *1844. Rush Rhees Library. The University of Rochester.*

began to turn south from the Oregon trail near the Snake River, lured by extravagant descriptions of the land and climate of California. Eastern business interests became increasingly interested in expanding their commercial opportunities in California after Lieutenant Charles Wilkes, who led a naval exploring expedition along the Pacific Coast, published a report in 1845 in which he praised San Diego harbor as one of the finest in the world. Thomas Larkin, a New Englander who had gone to Monterey in 1832 and built up a prosperous trade, aroused further interest among eastern businessmen with enthusiastic articles about California written for newspapers in New York and Boston. In 1843, he was appointed first United States consul in Monterey, and three years later he reported that there were already nine hundred Americans in California and that half of these had come in the previous year.

*Victory of the
Expansionists in 1844*
Thus Oregon and California stirred expansionist hopes among religious groups, farmers, and businessmen in the North, and they proved to be politically stronger than old party leaders who had used their influence very effectively to prevent the annexation of Texas for nearly a decade. In the Democratic national convention of 1844, Van Buren could not muster a two-thirds majority in support of his nomination and after a brief deadlock, James K. Polk of Tennessee won the nomination. Often referred to by historians as the first "dark horse" nominee in American presidential politics, Polk had been a key figure in Jacksonian politics. He had served as Speaker of the House of Representatives and was closely associated with Andrew Jackson in the political affairs of his home state of Tennessee. Jackson, indeed, had publicly declared in favor of the annexation of Texas and privately had suggested that Polk, an ardent expansionist, would make a more suitable candidate for the party in 1844 than Martin Van Buren. In addition to nominating Polk for the presidency, the Democratic party called for "the reoccupation of Oregon and the reannexation of Texas at the earliest practicable period."

The campaign of 1844 followed the pattern of mass politics already established in 1840 with much stress on parades, mass meetings, and popular slogans. Throughout the campaign the expansionist slogans of the Democrats aroused great popular enthusiasm, so much so that Clay began to hedge on his opposition to the annexation of Texas. But Clay's ambiguous position on the Texas issue could not neutralize the more popular appeal of Democratic slogans and it undoubtedly caused him to lose antislavery votes to the Liberty party, especially in New York. In the final count, Polk won the popular vote with a narrow plurality of 38,000 votes over Clay in a vote of nearly 2.7 million. His electoral vote margin of 170 to 105 seems less impressive when we remember that it depended upon New York with 36 electoral votes.

Was the election of 1844, then, a popular endorsement of manifest destiny? To a considerable extent it was. The expansionist issue was the most prominent one in the campaign, and it is hard to believe that anyone who voted for Polk did not expect him to move aggressively with respect to Oregon and Texas. Some historians have argued that Clay would have won the New York electoral vote and the election of 1844 if he had not alienated so many antislavery voters by his double talk about Texas. It seems logical, however, to assume that he would have lost enough southern electoral votes to offset any gains in New York that might have resulted if he had maintained a consistent position on the Texas issue. Furthermore, the congressional contests gave the Democrats a clear majority of 60 in the House and 6 in the Senate.

Polk's Expansionist Policies

Following their electoral triumph, the new leaders of the Democratic party were fully prepared to use expansionism as the way to override quarrelsome sectional issues. Polk's presidential messages stressed the benefits that would come to a broad spectrum of interest groups—pioneer farmers, southern planters, land speculators, naval leaders, traders, shippers, and manufacturers looking for new profits in an expanded national market. This conception of economic growth based on territorial expansion was coupled with older Jacksonian prescriptions for economic freedom. Polk was determined to repeal the Whig tariff law of 1842, to reestablish the Independent Treasury system, and to restrict expenditures for internal improvements. True to the Jacksonian heritage, he believed that there would be greater economic opportunities for all classes if the government avoided all forms of protection and subsidy for banking, manufacturing, and transportation interests. All interest groups were to have equal rights in the competitive scramble for the benefits of expansion.

The Annexation of Texas

The first of Polk's objectives was attained even before he took office because Congress had virtually accomplished the annexation of Texas shortly before his inauguration. In his final message to Congress, Tyler asserted that the election results demonstrated that "a controlling majority" of the people had declared in favor of immediate annexation, and he urged Congress to annex Texas by joint resolution. Such a resolution would avoid the necessity of obtaining a two-thirds majority in the Senate for the ratification of a treaty. Although the joint resolution provoked angry attacks from antislavery Congressmen, it was passed by narrow margins in both the House and the Senate and signed by Tyler a few days before the end of his term of office. Polk approved the action and, by December, 1845, after suitable terms of annexation had been worked out, Texas was admitted as a state.

The Oregon Treaty

The problem of Oregon was not so quickly settled largely because Democratic campaign slogans like "All of Oregon or none" and "Fifty-four forty or fight" had taken the belligerent and inflexible position of demanding the whole territory of Oregon. But the British were too strong a power to yield to such extravagant claims. Polk, however, realized that he could not afford a border war with Great Britain while he was facing a serious crisis with Mexico as a result of our annexation of Texas. Consequently he proposed to Richard Pakenham, the British minister in Washington, a compromise settlement that would have divided Oregon at the 49th parallel. Without consulting his government, Pakenham rejected the offer, insisting instead on an earlier British demand for a boundary line at the Columbia River. Whereupon Polk decided that "the only way to treat John Bull was to look him straight in the eye." He invoked the Monroe Doctrine and gave Great Britain a year's notice of our intention to end the joint occupation agreed to in 1818.

It was a calculated risk that turned out well, because in the eye to eye confrontation John Bull blinked first. The British were not prepared to fight for the Columbia River line, particularly after the Hudson Bay Company, alarmed by the growing influx of American settlers, had moved its main base of operations from the Columbia River to Vancouver Island. In June of 1846, therefore, Pakenham was instructed to accept a compromise treaty that would locate the boundary at the 49th parallel, and Polk submitted the proposal to the Senate. After two days of debate, the Senate advised acceptance, although 14 "fifty-four forty" Democrats, mostly from the upper Mississippi valley, voted with the opposition convinced that Polk had betrayed their interests. But the country was already at war with Mexico and neither Polk nor the Senate was willing to be bound by campaign slogans. Besides, the war with Mexico offered territorial prizes on the Pacific coast that would more than compensate for the loss of a part of the Oregon country.

Polk's Pressure on Mexico   Indeed, it can be argued that one of the primary causes of the Mexican War was the determination of Polk and the expansionists in the Democratic party to obtain California and New Mexico by purchase if possible but by force of arms if necessary. To be sure, Mexico helped to bring on the war by pursuing a negative and inflexible diplomacy, and no historian can ignore the fact that the Mexican press clamored for war and the Mexican government welcomed it when it came. Yet it seems likely that Polk could have avoided war if he had been willing to seek the limited objective of obtaining an agreement to recognize the annexation of Texas and to settle a southern boundary for the new state.

Negotiation over such limited objectives would have been difficult because Mexico had broken off diplomatic relations as soon as the United States had annexed Texas. Even so, the prospect for a diplomatic settlement was not hopeless. Polk himself recognized this when he sent a special envoy, John Slidell, to Mexico with full powers to negotiate a broad agreement that would include other questions besides the Texas boundary. The Mexican government indicated its willingness to receive an envoy but was not prepared to discuss anything more than the Texas boundary. Polk, however, was pursuing a much more adventurous course. He instructed Slidell to propose that the United States should

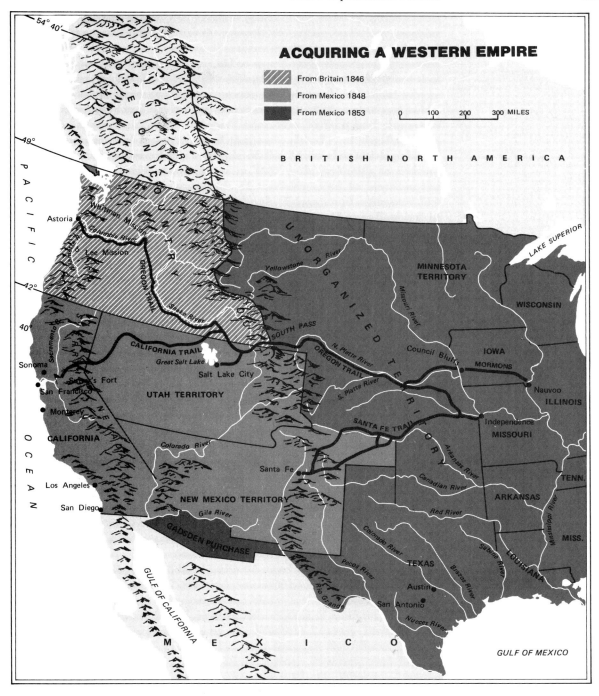

ACQUIRING A WESTERN EMPIRE

- From Britain 1846
- From Mexico 1848
- From Mexico 1853

0   100   200   300 MILES

assume the claims of all United States citizens resulting from Mexico's internal political conflicts (amounting to $2 million) if Mexico would accept the Rio Grande as the southern boundary of Texas. In addition, Slidell was to offer $5 million for the purchase of New Mexico and an additional $25 million for California.

Somehow, news of these instructions leaked out before Slidell had completed his long journey to Mexico City, and the resulting roar of indignation in the Mexican press made it impossible for any Mexican government to attempt negotiations. Slidell was not even given a chance to present his proposals and, in May of 1846, he returned to Washington to report the failure of his diplomatic mission.

War with Mexico   Before that time, Polk had ordered General Zachary Taylor, who had been stationed in Texas with a small force to protect the newly-annexed state, to move his troops to a position on the north bank of the Rio Grande River, across from the Mexican town of Matamoros. On April 25, a force of Mexicans crossed the river and attacked a small American patrol, killing some and wounding others. Polk seized upon the incident as a sufficient cause for full-scale war. In his message to Congress on May 11, 1846, asking for a declaration of war, Polk declared: "Mexico . . . has invaded our territory and shed American blood on American soil . . . War . . . not withstanding all our efforts to avoid it, exists by act of Mexico itself." Two days later, by a vote of 40 to 2 in the Senate and 174 to 14 in the House, Congress declared war and appropriated $10 million to raise and supply an army of fifty thousand volunteers.

President Polk took over personal direction of the war, pursuing a grand strategy designed to secure the disputed Rio Grande region and to take possession of New Mexico and California. These objectives were accomplished speedily in the first year of the war. After defeating a large Mexican force at Palo Alto, north of the Rio Grande, General Taylor crossed that river with his greatly reenforced troops and moved south toward the Mexican city of Monterrey. Late in September, Taylor routed a much larger Mexican force in a battle near Monterrey and at the battle of Buena Vista in February, 1847, he defeated an army of fifteen thousand that General Santa Anna (who had returned to power in Mexican politics) brought northward to drive the Americans out of Mexico.

Meanwhile a force of 1700 men, led by Colonel Stephen W. Kearney, marched overland from Fort Leavenworth, Kansas, to New Mexico, where the important trading center of Santa Fe was taken without firing a shot. Leaving a small garrison in Santa Fe, Kearney marched westward to California where he found that the American settlers had already organized a rebellion and raised the "Bear Flag" of the Republic of California. Among their leaders was an American army captain, John C. Fremont, who happened to be in the region with a small exploring party when war broke out. During these events, an American naval squadron had captured Monterey and San Francisco, so that, when Kearney

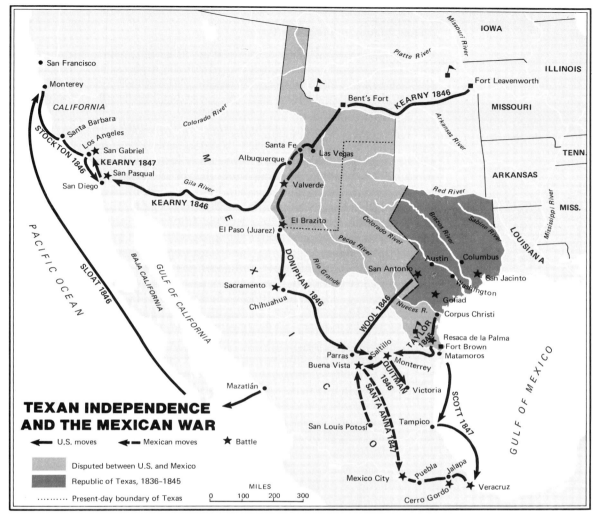

TEXAN INDEPENDENCE AND THE MEXICAN WAR

← U.S. moves ← Mexican moves ★ Battle

Disputed between U.S. and Mexico
Republic of Texas, 1836–1845
.... Present-day boundary of Texas

MILES
0   100   200   300

arrived, all that remained for him to do was to move against scattered
Mexican forces in southern California. By February, 1847, after less than
nine months of warfare, the United States had full control over the vast
region of New Mexico and California.

A third military campaign was necessary to force Mexico to accept
these conquests in a treaty of peace. Polk placed General Winfield Scott
in command of an expedition of ten thousand men sent to take Vera Cruz
and advance over the difficult terrain between that coastal city and the
high plateaus where the Mexican capital was located. Vera Cruz was
taken late in March, 1847, and Scott began the hazardous invasion into
the heart of enemy territory. Although outnumbered in every engagement, he won a decisive victory in April at Cerro Gordo at a point that
controlled the most favorable route into the mountains. By August, Scott
was in the central plateau close to Mexico City and, on September 14,
American troops had forced their way into the city.

After Scott captured Vera Cruz, Polk sent Nicholas P. Trist, a chief clerk in the State Department, to accompany Scott's army with authority to negotiate with the Mexicans whenever they were ready to accept the reality of their military defeat. Trist was empowered to offer terms similar to those that Slidell had been instructed to propose. Because of the confused political situation in Mexico after the capture of Mexico City, Trist was unable to begin negotiations until January, 1848. Impatient at the delay, Polk ordered his envoy back to Washington, but Trist decided to ignore the order because the Mexican peace commissioners were ready to negotiate.

Treaty of Guadelupe   Early in February of 1848, the Treaty of Guadelupe was signed, by which Mexico recognized the Rio Grande boundary and ceded New Mexico and California to the United States; the United States in turn agreed to pay $15 million and to assume the claims of United States citizens against Mexico. At first, Polk was furious with Trist for disobeying his order but he decided to submit the treaty to the Senate for ratification because further demands on Mexico might provoke a prolonged and costly guerrilla war. There was no other rational course that the expansionist President could have taken, because, by 1848, political discord in the American political system had reached a dangerous point.

The Poisonous Fruits of Victory

Polk's presidency marks a significant turning point in the history of the American political system. During the four years of his administration we can see the beginning of the end for the party dialogue which had been formed in the Jacksonian decade and the emergence of new issues which disrupted both major parties. These years provide a remarkable opportunity to see how the pressures of expansionist politics threatened to fracture the national consensus that had preserved a reasonably effective equilibrium in the American Republic since the adoption of the Constitution.

Polk's Presidential Style   In the beginning, it seemed likely that Polk would effectively reestablish the Jacksonian conception of the presidency. Like Jackson, he believed that the President was the direct representative of the will of the people, and that his constituency of the whole people was superior to that of the legislative branch of the government whose representatives were responsible only to the people of particular states or districts. Like Jackson, he was determined to be the chief of his party and to shape public opinion through control of the party press.

Because he was so industrious and thorough in his attention to legislative and administrative details, Polk was more effective in exercising leadership within the executive and legislative branches than outside of the governmental structure. He was much less successful than Jackson in controlling local elements of his party outside of Congress or in attracting a large personal following among the masses of voters. He lacked the personal magnetism that could establish a strong intuitive bond between himself and the people.

These weaknesses, however, made Polk's presidency more vulnerable in the long run than in the short run. At the start of his administration, he seemed to be able to move everything in the direction that he wanted to go. When Polk asked for a declaration of war against Mexico, the House of Representatives, in a half hour's time, with only 14 votes recorded in opposition, passed a bill stating that such a war existed and authorizing the necessary troops and supplies. The measure including some minor amendments was passed by the Senate on the following day with only two dissenting votes. Polk was also successful in obtaining two key measures of economic reform that he had advocated during the election campaign—a general tariff revision and the reestablishment of an independent treasury system. Although the Walker Tariff bill, as it was called, ran into an enormous amount of log-rolling in behalf of special economic interests, Polk used his personal influence to line up doubtful supporters and the bill was passed by the House by a vote of 114 to 95, and squeaked by in the Senate with a vote of 28 to 27. Polk signed the bill into law on July 31 and for the next decade the tariff rates on manufactured goods averaged 25 per cent. An Independent Treasury Bill passed both houses of Congress with more comfortable majorities and was signed by the President on August 8, 1846.

This successful legislative record in the first 18 months of the Polk administration, however, did not create a new consensus based on the application of old Jacksonian economic formulas to a roomier Republic. The very success of the military campaigns in the early months of the war stimulated the competition of sectional interest groups for positions of advantage in relation to the opportunities that a victorious war would bring. Victorious wars do not always enable a people to resolve or to transcend the troublesome realities of their social circumstances. More often than not, a victorious war intensifies the tensions and conflicts that are already present in a society. Ralph Waldo Emerson prophesied at the outset of the Mexican War: "The United States will conquer Mexico, but it will be as the man who swallows the arsenic which will bring him down in turn. Mexico will poison us."

The Wilmot Proviso

On the same day that Polk signed the bill reestablishing an independent treasury system, he had his first bitter taste of political disharmony. The House of Representatives was considering a bill to appropriate two million dollars which the President had requested to facilitate "the adjustment of a boundary between the two Republics" when Mexico was ready to negotiate a peace treaty. Although, on the surface, the appropriation measure appeared to be a routine matter, many members of the House of Representatives understood very well that it would be the first step toward the acquisition of far more territory than was involved in the original dispute with Mexico over the boundary of Texas. With this possibility in mind, David Wilmot, a Pennsylvania Democrat, moved to amend the bill so as to make it "an express and fundamental condition" that "neither slavery nor involuntary servitude shall ever exist in any part of said territory."

Historians have often debated about Wilmot's personal motives—whether Wilmot was influenced by a genuine sensitivity to antislavery sentiments in the North or by the many Democrats who were disgruntled with Polk's relentless vetoes of internal improvements bills. But the question of Wilmot's personal motives is less important than the fact that his Proviso won substantial support within the Democratic party as well as from the Whig opposition. The House passed the appropriation bill with Wilmot's amendment attached, but the bill failed to pass because the Senate adjourned without action. Sidetracked by parliamentary maneuvering in the Senate, the Proviso became a burning issue that was to throw the American political system out of its center of gravity.

In the fall elections of 1846, it was already apparent that the Democratic party in important northern states like New York was being torn apart by factional fights between those who wanted to prohibit slavery in any territories acquired from Mexico and those, like Polk, who believed that the Wilmot Proviso was "mischievous and foolish." Furthermore, influential religious organizations like the Quakers, the Congregationalists, and the Unitarians were attacking the war on moral grounds; William Henry Channing went so far as to declare that if he enlisted in "this damnable war" it would be to fight under the Mexican flag. Moreover, the Whigs made significant gains in the elections of 1846, so much so that the Democrats lost control of the House of Representatives.

Encouraged by their political gains, the Whigs became more outspoken in their criticism of the war. Daniel Webster charged that Polk's decision to go to war had been based on an insufficient pretext. A newly-elected Whig congressman from Illinois, Abraham Lincoln, introduced his famous "spot resolution" which challenged the Polk administration to designate the exact spot of American ground where the Mexicans had supposedly begun the war. The Whig *National Intelligencer* went so far as to praise the Mexicans for their valor while Horace Greeley's New York *Tribune* painted a dismal picture of the moral degeneration that American soldiers were experiencing as they moved deeper into Mexico.

Conflicts Over War Aims   More troublesome for the Polk administration, however, was the willingness of dissident Democrats to cooperate with the Whigs in delaying further measures for the support of the war. In 1847, also, many Democrats supported a second unsuccessful attempt to pass the Wilmot Proviso. The gap between the northern and southern Congressmen in the Democratic party opened wider when Calhoun introduced a series of resolutions in the Senate in 1847 which asserted that the territories were the common property of the states; that Congress had no power to deprive any citizens of the United States of their property rights in the territories, including their property in slaves; and that only when a territory had achieved statehood could it prohibit the institution of slavery. The bitter tone of the debates in Congress made it apparent that the Proviso would be a leading issue in the presidential campaign the following year.

The capture of Mexico City and the prospect of negotiations for a peace treaty could not moderate the passions which had been aroused. Indeed the political disorganization in Mexico after the capture of Mexico City led many Americans to consider the acquisition of more territory than New Mexico and California. In the following months the annexation or absorption by some means of all Mexico became a topic of general interest in Congress and the press, giving rise to new and peculiar forms of political factionalism.

Many Democratic leaders endorsed the idea of annexing all Mexico. New York Democrats, who invited Sam Houston of Texas to address a mass meeting at Tammany Hall, applauded his vigorous assertions that Americans were destined "to pervade the whole Southern extremity of this vast continent." Houston urged his listeners to go to Mexico if that country should be acquired to "look . . . for the beautiful senoritas, or pretty girls, and if you choose to annex them, no doubt the result of this annexation will be a most powerful and delightful evidence of civilization."

Such possibilities of amalgamation, however attractive they may have been to New Yorkers, aroused great misgivings among the southern followers of Calhoun. The South Carolina leader was determined to prevent such an outcome. In a major speech delivered to the Senate in January, 1848, Calhoun reminded his listeners that more than half of the population of Mexico was composed of Indians or persons of mixed blood. "I protest against the incorporation of such a people," he continued. "Ours is a government of the white man. The great misfortune of what was formerly Spanish America, is to be traced to the fatal error of placing the colored race on equality with the white . . . Are we to associate with ourselves as equals, companions and fellow citizens, the Indians and mixed races of Mexico? I would consider such association as degrading to ourselves, and fatal to our institutions."

Conservative northern Democrats also displayed considerable public nervousness over the prospect of racial amalgamation. Lewis Cass, in a Senate speech favoring the annexation of more Mexican territory, was careful to point out that he did not want any "deplorable amalgamation" with the Mexicans. "All we want," he said, "is a portion of territory . . . generally uninhabited, or where inhabited at all, sparsely so, and with a population that would soon recede, or identify itself with ours." Nevertheless, most of the leading Democratic newspapers in the North and West joined the drive for all Mexico.

The expansionists who were clamoring for all Mexico had the support of some very strange allies. A considerable number of antislavery men who had opposed the Mexican War favored the idea of incorporating all Mexico. The *National Era*, founded to support the principles and measures of the Liberty party, had charged throughout 1847 that the Mexican War had been brought about by a slaveholder's conspiracy to expand the institution of slavery. But when Calhoun began to oppose the annexation of all Mexico, the editor of the *National Era* speculated hopefully about the possibility that Mexico would come into the Union as a free territory already populated with a people hostile to slavery. "With such views," he concluded, "we must be pardoned for dwelling with pleasure upon the extension of our territory and the expansion of our population."

To be sure, most antislavery Whigs like Joshua Gidding of Ohio and Charles Sumner of Massachusetts were more consistent—they opposed annexation as they had also opposed the war itself. Yet the ensuing clamor for all Mexico added more fuel to the flames of political factionalism. Northern and western Democrats were divided from slaveholding Democrats on the issue, while antislavery Whigs were thrown into disarray by a confusing-set of alternatives. Thus, Polk's pragmatic decision to accept the treaty of Guadelupe Hidalgo not only brought peace with Mexico on the basis of territorial gains that were "sparsely inhabited," but it probably prevented the disintegration of the party system from proceeding further than it actually did.

The Free Soilers of 1848

From The National Atlas of the United States of America. *United States Department of the Interior Geological Survey.*

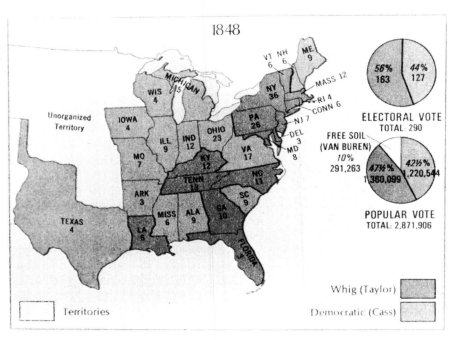

Although the clamor for all Mexico was stifled by the acceptance of the peace treaty, the continuing quarrel over the Wilmot Proviso was bitter enough to threaten party unity. In state after state, in New England, in Pennsylvania, in Ohio, the feuding between conservative and antislavery Democrats was seriously weakening the party organization. In New York, the Democratic party had virtually ceased to exist, so deep was the division between the two factions. When the New York Democrats gathered for their state convention in the spring of 1848, the conservatives with a bare majority voted down all resolutions against the extension of slavery. Whereupon the antislavery faction, largely followers of Van Buren, walked out of the convention and issued a call for one of their own. These radical followers of Van Buren were called "Barnburners" (because they were willing to burn down the barn in order to get rid of the rats), while their conservative opponents within the party were labelled "Hunkers" (because they were men without principle who simply "hunkered" for office).

When Lewis Cass, an outspoken opponent of the Proviso, was nominated by the national convention of the Democratic party for the presidency, free-soil Democrats in several northern states called for an open revolt against the party. The Whig party experienced similar difficulties when the Whig national convention chose a military hero, General Zachary Taylor, as the party's standard bearer, hoping that he would arouse as much popular enthusiasm as General Harrison had done in 1840. But the fact that Taylor was a southerner and a slaveholder made him distasteful to antislavery Whigs. And when the Whig convention sidestepped the issue of the Proviso by deciding not to adopt any platform at all, Conscience Whigs were as ready as the free-soil Democrats to bolt their party.

The Free Soilers of 1848

Within a short time, disgruntled free-soil Democrats, Conscience Whigs, and old Liberty party men agreed to respond to a call issued by a convention of Barnburner Democrats in New York to attend a national convention of antislavery men at Buffalo. In August, 1848, a heterogeneous group of ten thousand reformers of all sorts descended on Buffalo: free-soil Democrats, Liberty party men, Conscience Whigs, land reformers calling for free land, labor leaders from New York, internal improvements advocates, and advocates of cheap postage. In a revivalistic atmosphere, the 465 delegates to the convention proceeded to nominate Martin Van Buren for the presidency and Charles Francis Adams (son of John Quincy Adams and a Conscience Whig) as the vice-presidential candidate. A reformist platform was written which advocated an end to the further extension of slavery, a homestead law, cheap postage, internal improvements, a tariff for revenue, and calling upon all Americans to join a crusade for "free soil, free speech, free labor, and free men."

The new Free-Soil party aroused a great deal of enthusiasm among reform-minded men in the North—indeed, the Buffalo convention bridged the gap between the radicals of both major parties and the humanitarian and utopian reformers of the Jacksonian generation who had worked outside of the party system in the previous two decades. Now they were working together in a spirit of high moral enthusiasm. But such high spirits were largely absent in the two major parties; in contrast to the new third party, the difference between Democrats and Whigs seemed to be little more than the difference between Tweedledum and Tweedledee.

Consequently, the popular turnout in the election of 1848 was not as heavy as it had been in the two preceding presidential elections in the 1840's. Taylor had a comfortable electoral college majority of 163 votes to 127 for Cass, but he won with only 47.4 per cent of the popular vote. Although Martin Van Buren received only 10 per cent of the popular vote and no electoral votes, the Free-Soil party held the balance of power in several key northern states, and a dozen Free Soilers were elected to Congress, including Ohio's new Senator Salmon P. Chase. The Whigs had won the presidential election but no one knew who would control the House of Representatives and there was good reason to doubt that the new national administration would be able to deal with the crucial problems of organizing the new territories which had been acquired from Mexico.

A Patchwork Consensus

Sectionalism and the Party System   The sectional issues raised by the Mexican War had placed a tremendous strain on the two-party system that had emerged with the mass politics of the Jacksonian era. Despite the hubbub of mass politics—the stump oratory, the torchlight parades, the barbecues—the American party system had reached a surprising degree of maturity and stability by the 1840's. Both parties were well organized: underneath all the public noise and confusion there was a network of party committees, topped by the national convention, where the key decisions were made by skillful politicians in smoke-filled rooms.

While the party organizations were manipulative and often corrupt, they were indispensable in the task of broadening the base of popular participation in politics. Universal suffrage and the principle of direct election were not enough in themselves to accomplish this result; party politicians played a central role in enticing the masses of voters to the polls. But above all, the American polity had become more democratic because politics had become competitive. A sharp and close rivalry marked the battles for the presidency and for Congress, and despite all of the claptrap and shibboleths, voters could make choices that combined their more explicit pragmatic interests with their more generalized values and expectations. Each party had a general ideological orientation as well as a set of policies and promises, and each had the machinery to carry them out.

For more than a decade, the brisk competition of the two parties had created a state of balance. To be successful on a national scale, politicians in both parties had to organize broad coalitions of interest groups that reflected the broad sectional, religious, and ethnic diversities of the Republic. Consequently the competition of parties was always moderated by the necessities of broker politics; quarrels over banks, paper money, corporation charters, tariffs, and internal improvements were often carried on with a harsh-sounding political rhetoric, but the policies that were adopted by the party in power were generally half-way measures. This pattern of compromise preserved a workable consensus even when political tensions ran high.

But in 1848, the dissident minorities in both parties scorned the old formulas of compromise. And the same political tensions which drove them to form a third party also drove the major parties to choose candidates that lacked the capacity and the will to deal with new issues. In the ensuing decade, whenever the major parties were closely divided by a burning issue, they moved almost instinctively to an uncommitted, neutral figure rather than to bold and energetic leaders.

Such were the conditions that brought Zachary Taylor, a political nonentity, into the presidency. Before the Mexican War gave him a public image, he had spent 40 years as an Indian fighter and garrison commander at small frontier posts. He had considerable determination and integrity, but he possessed little knowledge of the political world. Horace Greeley, the noted Whig editor, summed him up with the statement: "Old Zack is a good old soul but doesn't know himself from a side of sole leather in the way of statesmanship." Instead of suggesting any lines of executive policy, the new President looked to Congress for guidance in dealing with the problems before the country. "I shall look with confidence to the enlightened patriotism of that body," he said, "to adopt such measures of conciliation as may harmonize conflicting interests and tend to perpetuate the Union which should be the paramount object of our hopes and affections."

But the Congress had to find a way of harmonizing itself before it could play the role that Zachary Taylor was so anxious to assign to it. When the House of Representatives assembled in December of 1849, the members answering the roll call included 108 Democrats, 103 Whigs, and 9 Free Soilers. Consequently, it took 63 ballots over a three-week period before the House was able to elect a Speaker and to transact the business that was to come before it. In the Senate, where the Democrats outnumbered the Whigs, 33 to 25, there was, on the surface at least, no problem about the control of parliamentary machinery. But, overshadowing party labels, there were four principal political groupings: (1) Whigs from the North like William Henry Seward (joined by Free Soilers such as Salmon Chase and John Hale) who wanted slavery specifically

The Sectional Crisis of 1849–1850

excluded from the territories of the United States; (2) Democrats, mostly from the South, who insisted on the right to extend slavery into the newly acquired territories and whose spokesmen were men like John Calhoun and Jefferson Davis; (3) nearly all northern Democrats, plus a few from southern states, who favored some kind of compromise that would leave decisions about slavery to the people of the territories; (4) nearly all southern Whigs, and one or two northerners like Daniel Webster, who were willing to accept the popular sovereignty principle of the northern Democrats.

There was no way to play for time and to avoid a showdown on the territorial question. The discovery of gold in the Sacramento River valley in 1848 caused a tremendous rush of emigrants to the California mountains. During the next year, approximately eighty thousand "forty-niners" came to California from the Mississippi Valley, the eastern states, and even from far away places in Europe, Asia, and Australia. When Taylor was inaugurated, California had already outgrown the system of military rule that had been established as a temporary measure during the Mexican War. Since it was apparent that the military authorities could not cope with the problems of civil government caused by the rapid and disorderly process of population growth, President Taylor decided to encourage the people of both California and New Mexico to form constitutions and apply for immediate admission to the Union.

Californians moved quickly to take advantage of this opportunity and by November, 1849, they had ratified a free-soil constitution. Shortly afterward, state officials were elected, including two Senators ready to take their seats in the United States Senate as soon as the new state was admitted to the Union. New Mexico proceeded more slowly, but by May 7, 1850, the inhabitants of the territory had completed the draft of a free state constitution.

Taylor apparently believed that his pragmatic policy was the simplest and most direct way to deal with the problem of organizing the new territories acquired from Mexico, but southern leaders were aghast at this turn of events. The South, they said, had contributed twice as many volunteers to the armies in the Mexican War as the North, but Taylor's policy threatened to deprive them of any share of the new territories for the expansion of slavery. Calhoun's followers talked recklessly about the dissolution of the Union if southern rights were not respected. Throughout the South mass meetings and legislatures adopted resolutions voicing all the accumulated greivances of the South about territorial questions, inflammatory abolitionist literature, and the laws of northern states which obstructed the return of fugitive slaves. By the time that California was ready to ratify her free state constitution, the southern states were organizing for concerted action. Urged on by Calhoun, Mississippi issued a call for a convention of southern states to meet in Nashville in June of 1850. It was widely assumed that the followers of Calhoun would try to use the Nashville convention to force concessions from the federal government even if it meant taking the southern states to the brink of secession.

Moderate leaders of both parties were convinced that the time had come for Congress to confront issues relating directly to slavery and to work toward some kind of settlement that could reestablish a national consensus. Realizing that Taylor's policy in regard to California and New Mexico had simply aggravated southern resentment, moderate Whigs turned to elder statesmen in Congress like Clay and Webster for leadership in finding a way out of the political crisis. Accordingly, on January 29, 1850, Henry Clay introduced a series of resolutions which offered a comprehensive compromise that would include the following eight steps: (1) California should be admitted with its free constitution; (2) territorial governments should be set up for New Mexico and Utah without any condition or restriction in respect to slavery; (3) Texas should abandon its claims to the eastern portion of New Mexico; (4) the federal government should assume the public debt of Texas contracted before annexation; (5) the District of Columbia should no longer be used as a major depot in the interstate slave trade; (6) slavery in the District of Columbia should be abolished only with the consent of the people of the District and of Maryland, and with just compensation to the owners; (7) a more stringent fugitive slave law should be passed; and (8) Congress should formally declare that it had no power to interfere with the interstate slave trade.

The Compromise of 1850

Clay's plan was the work of a seasoned politician who knew how to play the game of broker politics with consummate skill. The compensatory features of his omnibus compromise were designed to marshal the support of an irresistible combination of major groups in both parties. By admitting California as a free state, it was hoped that his plan would win the support of the President. The recommendations concerning the organization of a territorial government for New Mexico and Utah without mention of slavery would appeal to a large number of "popular sovereignty" Democrats. The limitation on the expansionist claims of Texas would allay the suspicions of antislavery men who feared that a giant-size Texas might be subdivided into several slave states, while Texas bondholders would be pleased to have the value of their securities underwritten by the federal government. Abolitionists presumably would be satisfied to see limitations imposed on the slave trade in the nation's capital, while pro-slavery extremists would presumably be conciliated by a stronger fugitive slave law.

But it was not an easy matter to play the game of broker politics in the political crisis of 1850. In the first place, it was soon apparent that Taylor would not support the new plan. The President resented Clay's rejection of his own proposals concerning New Mexico and, within a few weeks, there were rumors that a presidential veto might be forthcoming. Consequently, the elder statesmen of the Whig party were put in the awkward position of using their oratorical talents to rally moderate men in all sections behind their plan rather than behind the policy of the Whig president. In the great debate that took place over a period of several months, Daniel Webster made one of the most memorable speeches in defense of Clay's compromise proposals. Much of Webster's argument centered on the needlessness of the sectional crisis and the impossibility of peaceable secession. He insisted that slavery would be unprofitable and impracticable in all the territory taken from Mexico and, since the laws of nature dictated that the territory would remain free, why "reenact the will of God" with the Wilmot Proviso? Such unnecessary stipulations simply wounded the pride of southerners and made them more willing to listen to the false prophets of secession. As for the idea of "peaceable secession," Webster demanded, "Who is so foolish . . . as to expect to see any such thing?" Too many common ties—social, economic, and cultural—bound the two sections together. "Can anyone suppose that this population can be severed by a line that divides them . . . , down somewhere, the Lord knows where, upon the lower banks of the Mississippi?"

Webster's speech helped to rally the forces of compromise inside and outside of Congress, but it earned him the denunciation of antislavery men throughout the North, even among New Englanders who had once idolized him. The antislavery Whigs, however, found an able spokesman in Senator William Henry Seward of New York. In reply to those who argued that the Constitution protected the rights of slaveholders in the common territories of the United States, Seward maintained that there was "a higher law than the Constitution which regulates our authority over the demain, and devotes it to [the] . . . noble purposes [of justice and liberty]." He denounced Clay's compromise proposals as "radically wrong and essentially vicious." There was only one practicable policy for moral men to follow and that was one which moved toward the ultimate extinction of slavery "under the steady, peaceful action of moral, social and political causes . . . by gradual, voluntary effort, and with compensation."

As the spokesman for southern states rights, Calhoun was equally vehement in his opposition to Clay's compromise proposals, though for very different reasons. Calhoun's address to the Senate (read by a colleague, because the veteran South Carolina political leader was ill) was a demand for legal guarantees that would protect the minority rights of the South. Calhoun argued that the sectional equilibrium that had existed at the time of the formation of the Constitution had been violated by the growth of the centralized power at the expense of the federal government. This aggrandizement of national power at the expense of states rights had been promoted by the North as a means of carrying out continued aggressions against southern rights by protective tariff laws, by excluding the south from the common territories of the United States, and by public agitations designed to destroy the system of slavery which was the vital center of the southern social fabric. The South, Calhoun said, had no compromise to offer; any compromise would simply be a form of submission and surrender. The only way to save the Union was for the North to guarantee equal rights to southerners in the common territories of the United States, to assist in the faithful execution of the constitutional provisions affecting fugitive slaves, and to suppress the agitation of the slavery question. In addition, the North must concur in a constitutional amendment restoring "the original equilibrium between the two sections"—although he did not specify the exact nature of such a constitutional change.

Thus both Seward and Calhoun took the position that the compromise of 1850 evaded the central issue but each had drastically different solutions to offer. Seward looked to a series of steps that would lead to the ultimate extinction of slavery. Calhoun asked for a guarantee of permanent protection for the South's peculiar institution. Hence Clay's omnibus compromise was threatened with defeat by a combination of Free Soilers, antislavery Whigs, and southern fire-eaters. Not until Stephen A. Douglas, the leader of the moderate Democrats in the Senate, took over parliamentary leadership of the compromise effort was a way found to break the legislative stalemate. Clay's omnibus bill was broken up into separate measures, each of which would be passed by a solid core of moderates allied with the sectional extremists who favored the particular measure. Furthermore, President Taylor's sudden death following an attack of bilious cholera in the summer of 1850 removed the threat of a presidential veto. By September, the basic measures of the Compromise of 1850 passed both houses of Congress and were signed by President Fillmore who had previously announced his support for Clay's compromise efforts: New Mexico and Utah were organized as territories with no restrictions on slavery; the boundary of Texas was fixed at its present western limit, and Texas was compensated by a payment of $10 million from the federal treasury; slave trading in all its forms was prohibited in the District of Columbia; and a new fugitive slave act provided for federal enforcing machinery and severe penalties for all who obstructed the rendition of fugitive slaves.

The popularity of the Compromise was demonstrated in the immediate public response. Cities all over the country held meetings of celebration and support. In New York City, ten thousand merchants endorsed the mass meeting held there and created a Union Safety Committee of a hundred prominent merchants to foster a spirit of national unity. Leading Whigs and Democrats joined in support of similar public celebrations in the Middle West, and New Orleans had one of the largest mass meetings in the South. Many political leaders acquiesced in Stephen A. Douglas' characterization of the Compromise as a "final settlement." "I wish to state," Douglas informed the Senate, "that I am determined never to make another speech on the slavery question—Let us cease agitating, stop the debate, and drop the subject. If we do this, the Compromise will be recognized as a final settlement."

But there were organized groups in both sections that were not ready to drop the subject. Antislavery men throughout the North were announcing their determination to defy the fugitive slave act. This measure of the Compromise struck directly at the legal and social fabric of several northern states which had enacted "personal liberty" laws that prohibited their courts and police officers from assisting in any way the rendition of fugitive slaves, and which guaranteed a jury trial to alleged fugitives. In the case of *Prigg* v. *Pennsylvania* (1842), the United States Supreme Court had ruled that while Pennsylvania could not ban the forcible seizure and removal of fugitive slaves, it was within its rights in prohibiting its magistrates from enforcing a federal law. Encouraged by this decision, several other northern states had adopted such "personal liberty" laws.

The Fugitive Slave Act of 1850 was designed to destroy the effectiveness of the "personal liberty" laws. Full responsibility for the enforcement of the act was given to United States marshals. With their help, owners of slaves were permitted to "pursue and reclaim" their slaves, and to obtain recovery upon affidavit before federal commissioners. The alleged fugitive was not allowed to testify in his own behalf, and his rendition could not be delayed or prevented by any court, judge, or magistrate in the state in which he was recovered. Anyone who attempted to aid a fugitive slave or to obstruct his return would be subject to a fine of $1,000 maximum and six months imprisonment. Furthermore, the act required all citizens to assist United States marshals in the performance of their duties "whenever their services may be required." Finally, a federal commissioner who heard such cases was to receive a ten dollar fee if he ruled that the alleged fugitive was a runaway slave, but only five dollars if he ruled that the black was free.

The harsh provisions of the Fugitive Slave Act were a flagrant deviation from the spirit of compromise. The denial of all rights to the alleged fugitives violated conceptions of justice that were deeply-rooted in the American legal tradition. But even worse was the prospect of southern slaveholders, armed with federal coercive power, invading the towns and villages of the North to hunt their runaway slaves; and the affront was aggravated even more by the command to all good northern citizens to give their assistance when it was required. It does not require very much historical imagination to understand why Free Soilers and Conscience Whigs could not celebrate a compromise which included such flagrant contempt for the concepts of legitimacy and morality in their section of the country. Ralph Waldo Emerson, who had until then held himself aloof from antislavery politics, expressed his revulsion in biting words: "This filthy enactment was made in the nineteenth century by people who could read and write. I will not obey it, by God!"

Throughout the North antislavery men perfected an underground organization to aid fugitive slaves to reach Canada safely. Furthermore, several northern states came close to outright defiance of the law by empowering state courts to issue writs of habeas corpus against any person detaining a fugitive in order to get a judicial hearing on the fugitive's status. Thus the Fugitive Slave Act probably won more popular sympathy for the antislavery cause in the North than 20 years of abolitionist agitation. Indeed, Harriet Beecher Stowe was so outraged by the Fugitive Slave law that she was moved to write her most famous novel, *Uncle Tom's Cabin,* which appeared in book form in 1852. Within one year, 300,000 copies had been sold and throughout the decade of the 1850's hundreds of thousands more wept over the tragic experiences of Uncle Tom and the other characters both black and white who were trapped in the South's peculiar social system.

The fragile nature of the consensus apparently reestablished by the compromise can also be seen in the opposition of southern "fire-eaters." Robert Barnwell Rhett of South Carolina and William Yancey of Alabama denounced the compromise as a betrayal of southern rights. The Nashville convention, meeting before the final passage of the compromise measures, had adopted resolutions calling for more explicit protection of slave property in the territories of New Mexico and Utah. And many southern leaders, after the passage of the compromise measures, endorsed the "Georgia Platform" adopted by a special convention in that state in December of 1850. The "Georgia Platform" endorsed the Compromise in a backhanded way by warning that Georgia in the future would resist any federal acts that would abolish slavery in the District of Columbia, refuse to admit any state to the Union because of the existence of slavery therein, suppress the slave trade between slaveholding states, prohibit the introduction of slaves into New Mexico or Utah, or seek to repeal or modify the fugitive slave law.

The Georgia Platform

Consequently, if the Compromise of 1850 had dissipated the political crisis that had threatened to disrupt the Union, it was also apparent, after the first flurry of public celebration, that the restored national consensus was a shaky one at best in both sections of the country. Political leaders like Douglas were confident that a period of peace and prosperity would inoculate the great majority of Americans against the virus of extremism in both sections. But the problem lay deeper than they imagined. The future success of the Compromise depended not only on whether it could neutralize the extremists of both sections, but whether it could establish a new equilibrium of political and economic forces in a rapidly expanding democratic society.

Triggering an Irrepressible Conflict

The presidential election of 1852 seemed to justify the hope that the Compromise of 1850 would be "a final settlement." The Democratic national convention adopted a platform that pledged the party to "adhere

Consensus Politics

to a faithful execution" of all the compromise measures, including the fugitive slave law, and promised to resist "agitation of the slavery question, under whatever shape or color the attempt may be made." The younger element in the Democratic party favored Stephen A. Douglas who had proved to be an energetic leader in the Senate. These younger Democrats who called themselves the "Young America" group wanted the United States to develop a forward-moving set of policies. Specifically they wanted to push forward the economic development of the West, to avoid quarrels over slavery as an obstacle to national economic development, to encourage liberals and democrats in Europe, and to adopt a bold expansionist policy in the Caribbean. Douglas and his collaborators hoped to rally the support of northern merchants, railroad-builders, and land speculators, and those southern cotton planters who were moved by adventurous entrepreneurial urges; in addition they hoped to win the support of German and Irish immigrants who shared a sentimental attachment to the progressive spirit of Europe which had expressed itself in the liberal revolutions of 1848.

But Douglas was still too young to possess a powerful organization within the party. Older leaders like Lewis Cass, James Buchanan, and William Marcy were strong enough to deadlock the convention, so that the Democratic party turned again to a "dark horse," Franklin Pierce of New Hampshire. But Pierce, unlike Polk, was not a strong-willed and seasoned party leader—he was a pleasant man whose political neutralism made him acceptable to all factions in the party. Even Martin Van Buren found it possible to give the nominee his public endorsement. The Free-Soil party, to be sure, refused to go out of existence, but most of the Barnburners preferred to follow Van Buren back into the Democratic fold.

The Whig party, on the other hand, was hopelessly divided. Their platform also endorsed the Compromise of 1850 but such harsh things were said by antislavery Whigs on the floor of the convention that it could hardly be taken as an expression of genuine agreement within the party. Antislavery Whigs got a measure of revenge against the compromise by rejecting Fillmore and giving their support to the nomination of another military hero, General Winfield Scott. But Scott was too vain and pompous to win a broad popular following, and southern Whigs deserted the party in droves when he failed to endorse the Compromise explicitly.

Pierce's victory over Scott, therefore, was decisive. For the first time since 1840, a presidential candidate was elected with a true popular majority (50.9 per cent of the popular vote). In the electoral college, Pierce's victory was even more impressive (254 votes to 42). Scott carried only four out of 31 states and no states at all in the lower South where the Whigs had done particularly well in 1848. Furthermore the Whig's share of the popular vote had fallen to 44 per cent, the lowest proportion in the party's history. John Hall's 156,000 votes (5 per cent) indicated that there was a strong residue of Free-Soil sentiment in the North despite the defection of the Barnburners.

In his inaugural address, Pierce expressed the fervent hope that the election had put the slavery question at rest and "that no sectional . . . or fanatical excitement may again threaten the durability of our institutions or obscure the light of our prosperity." Seeking to conciliate all factions and to create party harmony, Pierce went so far as to appoint Jefferson Davis to his cabinet as Secretary of War. Davis was one of the chief southern enemies of the Compromise and the spearhead of southern expansionist ambitions. Many northern political observers feared, quite rightly, that the energetic Secretary of War would quickly achieve ascendancy within the administration. And, indeed, several key diplomatic posts went to southerners who were ardent expansionists: James Gadsden of South Carolina went to Mexico, Pierce Soulé of Louisiana went to Spain, and James Y. Mason of Virginia went to France. Secretary of State Marcy often complained that Jefferson Davis was attempting to exercise a controlling hand in foreign relations.

It is significant also that Pierce's inaugural address announced a vigorous policy of expansion. The acquisition of California and Oregon had made the United States a Pacific power, and Pierce was anxious to extend the diplomatic footholds which had been won in the Far East during previous administrations. His Attorney General, Caleb Cushing, had already played a leading role during the Tyler administration in opening China to American trade and missionary activity. A naval expedition to Japan under the command of Commodore Perry led to the successful negotiation of a treaty in March, 1854—Japan's first with any Western state. This treaty opened two small ports to American trade, promised favorable treatment to shipwrecked American sailors, and guaranteed most-favored-nation treatment with respect to any commercial concessions that might be made to other nations. Pierce appointed Townsend Harris, a New York businessman, as first American consul at Shimoda, and his skillful efforts in the next few years pushed open the door to American trade on a broader basis.

Pierce's Expansionist Policies

The policies of the Pierce administration in the Pacific and Far East undoubtedly won approval from northern merchants and railroad promoters who were developing grandiose schemes for transcontinental railroads over which would flow "the vast commerce" of India, Japan, and China. It should be remembered that Asa Whitney, one of the pioneer promoters of such a transcontinental railroad, was a New York merchant who had made his fortune in the China trade. Yet the fruition of such dreams lay in a very distant future; the greatest short run gains seemed more likely to come from expansionist efforts closer to home that favored the explicit goals of southern expansionists.

Importer's sign; carved and painted teakwood; nineteenth century. From Index of American Design. National Gallery of Art.

Cuba offered the more immediate attraction to the expansionists in the

Pierce administration. Beginning with Madison presidents had used their diplomatic influence to prevent the transfer of Cuba by Spain to some stronger European power like France or England because of the strategic position of that island athwart the sea lanes into the Caribbean and the Gulf of Mexico. John Quincy Adams liked to think of Cuba as a ripening apple that could "gravitate only towards the North American Union." And when the manifest destiny fever was running particularly high in the United States during the Polk administration, Secretary of State James Buchanan offered $100 million to Spain for Cuba only to be told by the Spanish foreign minister that his government would prefer to see the island "sunk in the ocean" rather than to transfer it to any other power."

The Whig administration of Taylor and Fillmore showed little interest in any attempts to acquire Cuba by diplomacy, but many southerners had dreams of increasing their political and economic power by annexing this land with a similar social system based on plantations and slavery. Indeed, they were ready to furnish arms and volunteers for several filibustering expeditions organized in New Orleans by General Narciso Lopez, a Venezuelan adventurer. Such schemes probably did not seem particularly reckless or improbable to a generation which had seen New Mexico and California won by a force of a few hundred Americans.

Even after Lopez together with 50 companions was finally captured and executed by the Spanish authorities in Cuba in 1851, southern interest in Cuba remained high—particularly when it became clear that the Pierce administration was ready to make the acquisition of Cuba one of its expansionist goals. John B. Quitman, a former governor of Mississippi, began organizing a new filibustering expedition to bring Cuba into the union as a slave state. Southern senators were ready to give Quitman a measure of official support and, in May of 1854, John Slidell of Louisiana introduced a resolution into the Senate calling for the suspension of the neutrality laws of the United States for 12 months—a proposal deviously designed to remove any legal obstacles to Quitman's operations. Unwilling to be drawn into such crude forms of adventurism, Pierce used his influence to block the resolution and Quitman's expedition, but he promised to use energetic diplomatic means to acquire Cuba.

Secretary of State Marcy had already authorized Pierre Soulé, the American minister in Madrid, to offer $130 million for Cuba, and as southern pressure mounted, he instructed the American ministers to England and France, James Buchanan and James Mason respectively, to confer with Soulé about the best method of acquiring Cuba and of forestalling possible British and French opposition.

The three American envoys gathered together in October for a series of meetings in Ostend and Aix-la-Chapelle after which they dispatched their recommendations to Marcy in a confidential recommendation that was to become notorious as the "Ostend Manifesto." The memorandum recommended that another effort be made to purchase Cuba, and if Spain refused to sell, then the Pierce administration would have to consider very seriously the question of whether the continued possession of Cuba by Spain was a threat to the internal peace and security of the United States. And if such a decision should be affirmative, "then, by every law, human and divine, we shall be justified in wresting it from Spain . . . upon the very same principle that would justify an individual tearing down the burning house of his neighbor if there were no other means of preventing the flame from destroying his own home."

The so-called Ostend Manifesto delighted southern expansionists but aroused the angry opposition of northern representatives in Congress who insisted that the memorandum be made public. The uproar that followed in European capitals as well as in the North moved Marcy to repudiate the memorandum, and Pierce made no further diplomatic efforts regarding Cuba.

Success for southern expansionist aims, therefore, was limited to the purchase of additional Mexican territory south of the Gila River. In the first months of the Pierce administration, the War Department completed a survey of five possible routes for a transcontinental railroad that would connect the Pacific coast with the interior cities of the Mississippi valley. Jefferson Davis, the Secretary of War, was particularly anxious to sponsor a route for such a railroad that would make some southern city like New Orleans its eastern terminus. But the survey indicated that the territory on the American side of the Gila River boundary presented serious engineering difficulties for the construction of a railroad. Hence James Gadsden, a southern railroad promoter, became the chosen agent of the Pierce administration to negotiate a new treaty of purchase with the Mexican Republic which had hardly recovered from the territorial amputations of the treaty of Guadeloupe Hidalgo. Nevertheless, the Mexican government was in need of money and it quickly acquiesced in the sale of the desert area south of the Gila River for $10 million. The treaty of purchase was signed in December, 1853, and ratified by the Senate in April, 1854.

The Pacific Railroad Question

The Gadsden Purchase, therefore, was a significant victory for southern expansionists and a direct response to the dynamic pressures of southern promoters to expand the economic influence of their region to the Pacific. They were by no means ready to accept Webster's dictum that God and Nature had put the new territories acquired in the Mexican War beyond the reach of southern power and southern institutions. California had been admitted as a free state, but southern sympathizers had a strong voice in California politics. William Gwin, one of California's two Senators who served from 1851 to 1860, was a southerner with strong southern sympathies, and a majority of the California members who served in the national House of Representatives in the same period were Democrats with a pro-southern orientation. Furthermore, New

From Sacramento,
California to Lawrence,
Kansas there was a great
"swelling power."
Sacramento, California. The
I. N. Phelps Stokes
Collection of American
Historical Prints. Prints
Division. The New York
Public Library.

Mexico offered interesting possibilities of accomodation to the southern social system. Although there were no significant numbers of black slaves in New Mexico, peonage was widespread and there were probably between 1500 and 3000 Indian slaves in the territory.

The key to the economic development of the new territories of the nation seemed to be the building of railroads that would link the Pacific coast with the rest of the country, and everyone knew that Congress would soon act on the railroad question. Senator Gwin had already had a proposal before Congress to provide land grants for a Pacific railroad that would have its western terminus in San Francisco with several eastern branches in the Mississippi valley—although he was known to prefer a terminus in the South—possibly Memphis.

By and large, railroad promoters in the upper Mississippi valley looked to Stephen A. Douglas as their spokesman. He had played a major role in getting a large federal land grant for the Illinois Central Railroad and for making Chicago rather than St. Louis the northern terminus of the federally subsidized line that would run from the Great Lakes to the Gulf of Mexico. "If ever a man passed a bill," Douglas reminisced later, "I did that one." And after the land grant was voted, Douglas continued to perform many favors for the group of capitalists associated with the Illinois Central.

Furthermore, Douglas had identified himself as the champion of the West in the debate over the Compromise of 1850. He looked to the valley of the Mississippi as the great balance wheel of the Republic:

There is a power in this nation greater than either the North or the South—a growing, increasing, swelling power, that will be able to speak the law to this nation . . . that power is the country known as the great West—the Valley of the Mississippi, one and indivisible from the Gulf to the Great Lakes, and stretching, on the one side and the other, to the extreme sources of the Ohio and the Missouri—from the Alleghanies to the Rocky Mountains. There, Sir, is the hope of the nation, the resting place of that power that is not only to control, but to save, the Union . . . We indulge in no ultraisms—no sectional strifes—no crusades against the North or the South. Our aim will be to do justice to all, to all men, to every section . . .

Douglas firmly believed that practical issues associated with the economic development of the great West should absorb the interest and energies of the American people, rather than abstract issues concerning slavery.

As chairman of the Senate Committee on Territories, Douglas was in a strategic position to influence the choice of railroad routes through the territory of the area west of Missouri and Iowa which was still part of the vast undeveloped region reserved for Indian tribes under the removal policy established in the Jacksonian decade. Moreover, the Illinois Senator had a direct personal interest in his grandiose vision of the future of the West; he had large investments in real estate in the Chicago area, and he had organized a syndicate for large-scale land speculations in the Lake Superior region. Yet he was fully aware of the sectional rivalries that were attached to various Pacific railroad schemes and knew full well that the success of a bill to organize the Nebraska territory would require the highest skills of broker politics.

The Kansas-Nebraska Bill

The bill for the territorial organization of Nebraska that Douglas introduced in January of 1854 was designed to attract southern as well as northern votes. Nebraska was to be organized without any statement for or against slavery, except a clause which read: "And when admitted as a State or States, the said territory, or any portion of the same, shall be received into the Union, with or without slavery, as their constitution may prescribe at the time of their admission." This language was identical to that in the Utah and New Mexico acts which had formed part of the Compromise of 1850 and it was consistent with Douglas' belief that "the principle of popular sovereignty" was the essential principle which would dissolve sectional strife and create a new equilibrium of forces in the Republic anchored in the future economic development of the "great West."

Pro-slavery Senators, however, were not satisifed with language that would simply affirm the principle of popular sovereignty. They wanted an explicit repeal of the Missouri Compromise restriction on slavery north of the line 36°30', so that the chance to share in the economic development of the West would really be open "to all men, to every section" as Douglas had so often emphasized in his public utterances. Needing southern votes, Douglas agreed to amend the bill as proposed although he recognized that it would raise "a hell of a storm." A further amendment divided the Nebraska area into two separate territories, the larger and northern part to keep the name Nebraska, and the southern and smaller part to be called Kansas. By this time the maneuvering in the Senate was exceedingly complex, but the division into two territories seemed to mark out one for slavery and the other for free soil.

Renewed
Sectional Controversy

As Douglas had anticipated, the Kansas-Nebraska bill in its final form produced a storm in Congress and in the northern press. An impassioned statement, entitled "Appeal to the Independent Democrats in Congress to the People of the United States," was prepared for publication by Salmon Chase and Joshua Giddings and signed by other antislavery leaders in Congress like Charles Sumner of Massachusetts and Gerrit Smith of New York. This document, widely published in northern newspapers, charged that the slaveholders of the South were engaged in a "monstrous plot" to convert all the territories of the United States into "a dreary region of despotism inhabited by masters and slaves." Douglas was accused of using the territorial bill to further his political ambitions in language that characterized him as a "servile demogogue" who was willing to make the people of the North his pawns in "the hazards of the presidential game." But the greatest emotional intensity was directed at the repeal of the Missouri Compromise—"a gross violation of a sacred pledge . . . a criminal betrayal of precious rights."

Douglas apparently believed that he could ride out the storm. The Democrats had large majorities in both houses of Congress and party discipline was powerful. He was confident that public opinion in the North would recognize the virtues in the pragmatic principle of popular sovereignty. Consequently his speeches in the Senate were delivered in a forceful and aggressive tone. He extolled the principle of popular sovereignty as the grand principle of the Compromise of 1850 which superseded all previous compromises. He derided the fears that Kansas and Nebraska would become slave states. "In that climate, with its productions, it is worse than folly to think of its being a slaveholding country. I do not believe that there is a man in Congress who thinks it could permanently be a slaveholding country." He poured his contempt on signers of the Appeal like Chase and Sumner, calling them "the pure, unadulterated representatives of abolitionism, Free Soilism, Niggerism in the Congress of the United States."

Douglas lived up to his nickname of the "Little Giant" in the battle over the Kansas-Nebraska bill. His efforts and the influence of the Pierce administration kept most of the Democrats in line so that the measure was passed by a vote of 37 to 14 in the Senate and by a narrower margin of 113 to 100 in the House.

But the victory of the supporters of the Kansas-Nebraska act was a Pyrrhic one. Never had an experienced politican so miscalculated the probable political consequences of his action as Douglas did with the Kansas-Nebraska Act. The political storm that swept the North after the passage of the Act did not blow itself out; indeed it seemed to gather new force every week and its strength came from men who had formerly deplored antislavery agitation. Mass meetings were held in city after city often sponsored by respectable businessmen who were angered at the reckless manner in which the sectional controversy had been reopened by Douglas. Douglas himself remarked that he could have travelled all the way from Boston to Chicago by the light of his burning effigies. Indeed, when he returned to Chicago after the end of the congressional session, a hostile crowd refused to let him finish a speech at a mass meeting organized by his friends and supporters to give him an opportunity to explain his position.

More ominous than the public protests was the shattering impact of the Kansas-Nebraska bill on the party system. All hope of reuniting the Whig party after the disastrous divisions of the campaign of 1852 was destroyed as the Nebraska issue drove the northern and southern wings further apart. Many Whigs were ready to respond to Senator Chase's call for northern Whigs and independent Democrats to unite in a powerful new party based on free-soil principles. Fusionist conventions were organized throughout the northern states; such a meeting in Ripon, Wisconsin, adopted the name "Republican" for the coalition of anti-Nebraska Whigs and Democrats, and the name was taken up by similar conventions in Jackson, Michigan, and Worcester, Massachusetts.

Disintegration of the Jacksonian Party System

In many urban centers of the East, large numbers of Whigs drifted into the Know-Nothing party. For many Whig families this seemed to be the natural political road to take since they were so closely associated with the benevolent empire of the leading Protestant denominations. But Know-Nothingism was a symptom rather than a cause of the disintegration of parties. Nevertheless, it added the emotionalism of nativism to the emotions already generated by the Nebraska question. It was not the kind of political climate in which broker politicians could thrive. Consequently, the Democratic party—the party of neutralism and compromise—experienced a disastrous defeat in the congressional elections of 1854. The new House of Representatives would contain 108 Republicans, 83 Democrats, and 43 Know-Nothings. The Jacksonian party system was shattered, and no one would be able to put it back together again.

The Democratic Schism

By stipulating that settlers in the newly-organized territories could decide for themselves whether or not to legislate slavery, the Kansas-Nebraska Act set the stage for a naked struggle for power between highly-aroused sectional interests. Kansas became the battleground for such a struggle because it adjoined Missouri, and many ardent southern expansionists believed that the slave system could be established in the southern half of the territories organized by the Kansas-Nebraska Act.

Bleeding Kansas

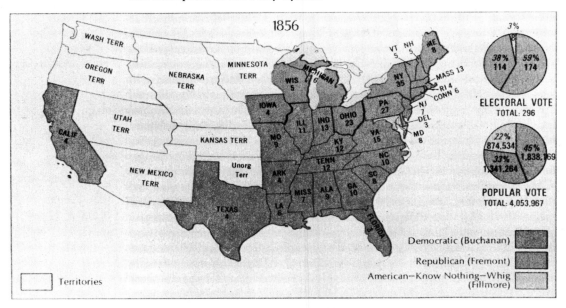

From The National Atlas of
the United States of
America. *United States
Department of the Interior
Geological Survey.*

This was not necessarily an illusory hope, because profitable hemp-growing operations using large numbers of slaves had been developed in the 1850's in those districts of Missouri close to the border of Kansas.

But even those southern leaders who were less sanguine about the economic viability of the slave system in Kansas sought to secure political control of the new territory as a means of obtaining stronger federal guarantees for slave property in all of the territories. In the debate over the Compromise of 1850, Senator Clemens of Alabama had stressed the necessity of a favorable legal environment for slavery in the territories: "The slaveholder would not carry his property there with a threat hanging over him that it was to be taken away from him by operation of law, the moment he landed."

Senator Stephen Douglas failed to anticipate an organized struggle for political control in Kansas. He assumed that the usual process of voluntary migration would take place and that climate and geography would insure the triumph of free-soil principles. The practical logic of events would, therefore, expose the "abstract" and "unreal" character of the debate over the question of slavery in the territories. In both the North and the South, however, organized efforts were made to encourage and finance emigration to Kansas as a means of winning political control of the territorial legislature. The New England Emigrant Aid Company sent more than a thousand antislavery settlers to Kansas in 1854 to 1855; in a like fashion, southern promoters sponsored proslavery settlers, mostly from Missouri but some from as far away as Alabama, Georgia, and South Carolina.

Consequently, Andrew Reeder, the first territorial governor appointed by President Pierce, found that several thousand settlers had already preceded him to Kansas: a census of territorial inhabitants taken by the governor's office indicated a population of about 8500 (including 242 slaves), more than enough to justify elections for a legislature. At this point, pro-slavery groups in Missouri, led by Senator Atchison who remained absent from his seat in the Senate, organized a secret society of Missourians—called variously the "Sons of the South" or the "Blue Lodge." On the eve of the election, no fewer than five thousand Missourians, wearing badges of hemp and many of them armed, rode across the border into Kansas, "enough," as Atchison boasted, to kill every God-damned abolitionist in the territory." By means of force and intimidation, the intruders were able to see to it that all of their candidates save one were elected. The pro-slavery vote totaled 5,427, and the free-soil vote 791; subsequent investigations showed that 4,908 of the votes cast were illegal.

When Governor Reeder tried to disqualify a number of fraudulently elected delegates, President Pierce, responding to pro-slavery pressures, removed him from office. At this juncture, the free-soil settlers took matters into their own hands. They organized a "free state convention," named Andrew Reeder as their territorial delegate to Congress and, in the fall of 1855, drew up a free-soil constitution. In January, 1856, they elected a legislature and a governor, so that the Pierce administration faced two governments—both of questionable legitimacy.

Instead of taking swift action to call for new elections for a territorial government that would have clear legitimacy, Pierce let matters drift. This was a fateful mistake because extremists on both sides were ready to use violence. Many of the Missourians who crossed into the territory were already well-armed. Free-soil settlers were receiving shipments of rifles sent to them by antislavery groups in the North. The junior class at Yale presented the leader of a group of Connecticut emigrants bound for Kansas with a rifle inscribed with the words: *Ultima Ratio Liberarum*; and when the noted preacher, Henry Ward Beecher, blessed a shipment of bibles and rifles sent to Kansas by his congregation, the rifles came to be known as "Beecher's Bibles."

Full-scale violence was not long in coming. In May, 1856, an armed band of pro-slavery men led by a United States marshall rode into the town of Lawrence in search of free-soil officials who had been indicted for "constructive treason." They sacked the town and made a particular point of destroying the presses of an antislavery newspaper whose editorials had been particularly infuriating to them. A short time later, a fanatical abolitionist named John Brown led a retaliating raid on a small pro-slavery settlement at Pottawattomie Creek where five settlers were murdered and their bodies mutilated.

These savage and bloody events in Kansas inflamed the passions of men everywhere in the country. Charles Sumner of Massachusetts, an eloquent antislavery Senator, delivered a bitter speech in the Senate, entitled "The Crime Against Kansas," which included an unrestrained personal attack on some of his pro-slavery colleagues, among them Andrew Pickens Butler of South Carolina. Two days later, Butler's nephew, Congressman Preston Brooks of South Carolina, entered the Senate chamber and beat Sumner over the head with a cane as he sat at his desk. Brooks' assault was so brutal that Sumner remained a semi-invalid for the next three years. The spirit of violence that had broken out on the plains of Kansas was already infecting the American political system at its very center.

The Election of 1856

Indeed, the dominating issue of the presidential campaign of 1856 was furnished by the conflict raging in Kansas. The newly-formed Republican party met in a national convention at Philadelphia that was notable for its spirit of crusading enthusiasm. It was evident that a new alignment of forces was emerging out of the confusion of parties and factions that followed the break-up of the Whig party and the uproar over the Kansas-Nebraska Act. The alliance of Conscience Whigs and free-soil Democrats had become fused into a strong and comprehensive party. A party platform, prepared by a committee headed by David Wilmot, called for the exclusion of slavery from the territories, and demanded the immediate admission of Kansas to the Union with a free-soil constitution. Other platform planks denounced the "Ostend manifesto" and called upon the federal government to give "immediate and efficient aid" to the construction of a railroad to the Pacific "by the most central and practical route."

Although the Republican party contained many experienced leaders like William Seward of New York, Henry Wilson of Massachusetts, Joshua Giddings of Ohio, and Francis P. Blair of Missouri, the overwhelming majority of delegates preferred to nominate a presidential candidate who would symbolize the youth and energy of the new party. They nominated John C. Fremont, famous for his exploring expeditions in the West and politically attractive because he had become identified with free-soil ideas in California politics; furthermore, his marriage to the daughter of Thomas Hart Benton gave him powerful political connections in the Mississippi valley and the East. The combination of "Fremont and Free Soil" sent Republicans into the campaign with an enthusiasm that had not been seen in American politics since 1840.

The Democrats chose to meet this threat with a strategy of compromise that would hold the Democratic party together and transfer the slavery question from the political arena into the courts of law. Pierce's ineptness in dealing with the Kansas issue made him unacceptable to the Democratic party except among southerners who had good reason to feel grateful for his policies. Although Stephen A. Douglas was a better spokesman for young America than Fremont, he was passed over by the

Democratic convention because his political reputation had become too controversial. The Democratic convention nominated James Buchanan of Pennsylvania, who had been out of the country during the controversy over the Kansas-Nebraska Act. He was a cautious and conservative politician and, although he was a northerner, his role in the preparation of the "Ostend manifesto" made him acceptable to the South.

Buchanan won the election with a substantial majority in the electoral college: 174 to Fremont's 114, and 8 votes for Milland Fillmore, the Know-Nothing candidate. Yet, in the popular vote, Buchanan had only 45 per cent of the total. Fremont with only 33 per cent of the popular vote carried all but five of the northern states and could have won the election if he had been able to capture the electoral votes of Pennsylvania and Illinois. Republican political strategists, therefore, had good reason to feel continued confidence in the future of the new party.

Such a possibility was regarded as a perversion of the American political system by President Buchanan. In his inaugural address, the new President denounced "geographical parties" to which the long agitation of the slavery question had given birth and expressed the hope that the agitations which had "exasperated the public mind" would "speedily become extinct." This hope was nourished by the conviction that the question of when and how the people of a territory should decide for slavery was a question which legitimately belonged to the Supreme Court of the United States. Indeed, President Buchanan held out the hope in his address that the question would be "speedily" and "finally" settled, because of a case which was pending before the Supreme Court. He had good reason for such confidence in a speedy decision because his private correspondence with one of the justices of the Supreme Court had given him foreknowledge of what such a decision would be.

The Supreme Court Intervenes

Two days after Buchanan's inauguration, the rest of the country shared that knowledge when the Supreme Court announced its decision in the case of *Dred Scott* v. *Sanford* (1857). The Dred Scott case immediately became one of the most controversial cases in the annals of the federal judiciary, largely because the Supreme Court went out of its way to enter the political controversy raised by the Kansas issue.

Dred Scott was a black slave, formerly the property of an army doctor who had taken Dred to the free state of Illinois and then to Fort Snelling, the free territory of Minnesota. In 1846, Scott had brought suit for his freedom in the Missouri courts, but the Missouri Supreme Court finally rejected his plea on the grounds that his residence in free territory had no effect upon the laws of Missouri which defined his status as that of a slave. In the 1850's, ownership of Scott passed into the hands of a New York citizen named Sandford. Scott, therefore, was able to bring a new suit for his freedom in a federal court on the contention that he was a citizen of Missouri, and that the case involved a suit between citizens of two states. The Supreme Court accepted the case and the main argument before the Court took place in February of 1856 when events in Kansas were moving toward a bloody climax.

At first, most of the justices of the Supreme Court were unwilling to make a sweeping decision about the status of slavery in the territories. It would have been a simple matter to dismiss Scott's case for lack of jurisdiction. A clear precedent for such action was available in the recent case of *Strader* v. *Graham* (1850) in which the Court refused to accept the contention that a slave automatically became free by residence in a free state, and held that the decisions of state courts should be final in determining the status of a black. Hence the Court could have ruled that, since the courts of Missouri had ruled that Scott was a slave, he was not a citizen entitled to sue Sandford in the federal courts on the basis of the diversity of citizenship clause in the Constitution.

But the political pressures inside and outside of the Court were too great to permit such a constricted use of precedent. Two antislavery justices, John McLean and Benjamin Curtis, indicated their intention to prepare dissenting opinions which would discuss the status of slavery in the territories. Several pro-slavery justices were under heavy pressure from southern leaders to develop a comprehensive decision on the issues raised by the Dred Scott case. Above all, most of the leading Democratic newspapers in the North were urging such a course of action because they believed that only the Supreme Court could rescue the Democratic administration from the perils of the Kansas question.

During the final stages of argument before the Court in December, 1856, Chief Justice Taney framed two main questions to be argued by counsel: (1) whether a black in Dred Scott's position could be a citizen of the United States and entitled to sue, and (2) whether Congress had constitutional authority to exclude slavery in the territories. And in his opinion, delivered on March 6, 1857, Taney confronted all the issues raised by these questions. He argued that Scott could not sue because he was not a citizen within the meaning of the Constitution, since, at the time of the framing of the Constitution, the states had excluded blacks from citizenship. Furthermore, inasmuch as Scott had returned to Missouri, his status was determined by the laws of that state. The Chief Justice also dismissed the claim that Scott's residence in a free territory had made him a free man by virtue of the provisions of the Missouri Compromise. The Missouri Compromise, he maintained, was unconstitutional because Congress could only organize territories so as to prepare them for statehood, but not in such a way as to infringe upon the rights of person or property guaranteed by the Bill of Rights. The Fifth Amendment, he pointed out, forbade Congress to deprive any person of his liberty or property, including slave property, without due process of law.

The five other justices who concurred with Taney in declaring the Missouri Compromise unconstitutional wrote separate opinions in which they used somewhat different processes of reasoning. The two dissenting opinions, written by Curtis and McLean, concentrated on the main questions which had been posed in the argument of the case before the Court. They rejected the contention that Dred Scott could not be a citizen, by citing evidence that free blacks had actually been citizens at the time of the Constitution. Similarly, the two dissenting justices attacked the contention that the Missouri Compromise was unconstitutional by citing numerous instances since 1789 in which Congress had legislated concerning slavery in the territories.

If Buchanan had really believed that a Supreme Court decision could splice the severed cords of the national consensus, the Dred Scott case made such an outcome utterly impossible. How could the people of the nation be expected to reestablish a consensus when the justices themselves were unable to agree on the main issues of legitimacy? Each of the nine justices wrote a separate opinion. In no two opinions was the reasoning precisely alike, although there was partial agreement constituting a majority on some points. The Dred Scott decision simply fed the flames of controversy with new and endless debates over the varying legal points raised in the separate opinions of the justices.

Political Response to the Dred Scott Decision

For a brief moment, however, the friends of the Buchanan administration exulted over the decision. They believed that Taney's dictum had destroyed the political future of the Republican party because it made the free-soil principle—the *raison d'etre* of the new party—legally untenable. But Republican leaders found it comparatively easy to escape from the dilemmas posed by the Court's decision. They argued that the majority opinion on slavery in the territories was mere *obiter dictum* and therefore not binding as constitutional law. They also invoked the theory of coordinate powers developed by Jefferson and Jackson and maintained that the Court's opinion was not necessarily binding on the other two branches of the government. Finally, they expressed the hope that the decision could be reversed, especially if the Republicans should win control of the presidency.

While the Dred Scott decision did not seriously discomfit the Republicans, it proved to be a major catastrophe to the Democratic party. Southern leaders of the party, like Jefferson Davis, Howell Cobb, and W. L. Yancey, hailed Taney's opinion and called upon all northern Democrats to make the new constitutional doctrine concerning slavery a cardinal principle of the party. But large numbers of northern Democrats, mostly followers of Stephen A. Douglas, were unwilling to abandon their cherished principle of popular sovereignty.

This conflict between Taney's dictum and the principle of popular sovereignty undermined Buchanan's efforts to settle the Kansas question. Determined to end the disorder in Kansas as quickly as possible, Buchanan appointed Robert J. Walker of Mississippi, a leading southern Democrat who had served in Polk's cabinet, as the new territorial governor of Kansas. Although Walker was an ardent southern expan-

The Failure of Buchanan's Kansas Policy

sionist, he accepted the office only on the understanding that the Buchanan administration would support him in an effort to lead the people of Kansas to adopt a state constitution "by a fair and regular vote, unaffected by fraud and violence." Walker recognized that only by a faithful adherence to the principle of popular sovereignty could a solution be found in Kansas that would maintain a strong link between the northern and southern wings of the Democratic party—a party that he had helped to create in the days of Jackson and Polk.

When he arrived in Kansas in the spring of 1857, Walker issued a call for a constitutional convention, but he soon discovered that the pro-slavery leaders of Kansas were not willing to risk the certain loss of their power in a free and fair election. "You come here with ears erect," one of them said defiantly to Walker at his inaugural banquet, "but you will leave with your tail between your legs. . . . We have unmade governors before, and by God, I tell you, sir, we can unmake them again." The pro-slavery legislature, thereupon, rigged the elections in such a way as to disqualify large numbers of free-soil immigrants who were arriving in the spring and early summer, and to gerrymander the districts inhabited by qualified free-soil voters. Most of the free soilers, therefore, boycotted the election on the ground that it could not be a fair expression of popular sentiment.

Consequently, the convention that began its deliberations at the temporary capital in Lecompton in September was chosen by a scant 2200 voters and the overwhelming majority of the delegates were pro-slavery men. Furthermore, the unrepresentative character of the Lecompton convention was fully revealed to the nation in early October when elections were held to choose a new legislature. Walker had convinced the free soilers that he would really enforce a fair election and they turned out en masse. When the votes were counted, the free-soil

Lawrence, Kansas. The I. N. Phelps Stokes Collection of American Historical Prints. Prints Division. The New York Public Library.

delegates to Congress had won by a majority exceeding four thousand votes, but the pro-slavery forces seemed to have won a majority of seats in the legislature. Subsequent inspection of the balloting, however, revealed flagrant cases of fraud in pro-slavery districts—one settlement with six houses close to the Missouri border reported 1,628 votes. True to his promise, Governor Walker threw out the returns in those districts where there was clear evidence of fraud, opening the way to a clear free-soil majority in the legislature.

The legitimacy of the Lecompton convention, therefore, was clearly in doubt after Walker had revealed the new election frauds. Yet the pro-slavery delegates, knowing that they faced a hostile majority and a resolute governor, were determined to contrive a constitution that would make Kansas a slave state. Although some extremists in the convention wanted to send a pro-slavery constitution to Congress without submitting it to the voters of Kansas, the majority of delegates knew that their best chance of making Kansas a slave state lay in devising an adroit strategy that would offer the voters only a limited and partial choice. The constitution that was drawn up by the Lecompton convention guaranteed the right of property in all its forms, including slave property, enforcement of the Fugitive Slave law was required, and any amendment of the Constitution before 1864 was forbidden. After drafting these and other clauses of the constitution, the convention stipulated that a special referendum was to be held in December, in which the voters could vote to accept "the constitution with slavery" or "the constitution without slavery."

The trick was immediately apparent to all free soilers. If they voted for the constitution without slavery, they could do no more than to prevent future importations of slaves. All slave property already in the territory would be protected by the firm guarantee of the right of property in all forms written into the constitution, and nothing could be done to revise the property clause before 1864. The Republican press throughout the North denounced "the great swindle." Even more significantly, Democratic newspapers which had championed popular sovereignty condemned this perversion of their cherished principle. In the South, however, Democratic leaders and editors were virtually unanimous in defending the work of the Lecompton convention as entirely consistent with the Dred Scott decision.

Buchanan, therefore, faced a difficult choice. He recognized that the northern and southern wings of his own party were openly at odds over the Lecompton constitution. But the southern wing had more influence in his cabinet and Buchanan was also intimidated by the fierce tone of the southern press. He had never really had strong convictions about popular sovereignty, and the Dred Scott decision must have increased his doubts on that score. Hence, the President's annual message to Congress in December, 1857, asserted that the special referendum in Kansas would give the voters "a fair opportunity" to decide the slavery issue. Prompt acceptance by Congress of the Lecompton constitution, however the voters decided about the future admission of slaves, would lead to "the peace and quiet of the whole country" which, Buchanan insisted, was of greater importance than "the mere temporary triumph of either of the political parties in Kansas."

The day after Buchanan's message was read to the Congress, Douglas rose in the Senate to deliver one of the most impassioned speeches of his career. He attacked the tricky Lecompton referendum and declared that popular sovereignty would be meaningless unless the people of Kansas had a chance to vote on the entire constitution. Moreover, he challenged the wisdom of the President's policy saying: "The President of the United States . . . on this point has committed a fundamental error—an error that lies at the foundation of his whole argument in the matter." The angry debate that followed revealed how deeply the Lecompton issue had split the Democratic party.

Furthermore, the debate in the Senate stiffened the resolve of the free soilers in Kansas. They decided to boycott the special referendum set for December, 1857, and pledged resistance to the Lecompton constitution by force of arms if necessary. Kansas was close to civil war and the situation was especially dangerous because Governor Walker was absent from the territory, having gone to Washington to explain and defend his policies. The acting governor, Frederick Stanton, however, gave the free soilers a legal way to express their opposition by summoning the newly elected legislature in special session. Whereupon the legislature proceeded to provide for a full referendum on January 4, 1858, in which the voters were given *three* choices: to vote for the Lecompton constitution with or without the slavery clauses, or to vote against it *in toto*. Stanton was removed from his office as soon as news of his action reached Washington. Outraged by Buchanan's action, Walker resigned his post. In a devastating letter that he gave to the newspapers, Walker charged that the President had been victimized by a southern conspiracy.

It was too late, however, for the Buchanan administration to reverse the flow of events. There was no practical way to rescind the arrangements made by the Kansas legislature for a full plebiscite, and the whole country watched the grotesque situation in which two plebiscites—each boycotted by the opposing political group—were held in the space of two weeks. In the December plebiscite, called for by the Lecompton constitution, 6,116 votes were cast in favor of the constitution with slavery, and 569 without slavery. A legislative committee later determined that at least 2,700 of the ballots were fraudulent. In the January plebiscite called for by the legislature, 10,226 votes against the constitution *in toto*, while 138 were ready to accept it without slavery, and only 24 with slavery.

President Buchanan now found himself in an impossible situation. To accept the result of the full plebiscite would have required a public admission of his error in recommending the acceptance of the Lecompton constitution. In view of his personal quarrel with Douglas such a course of action would have been humiliating to an extreme degree. Moreover, most southerners in the Cabinet and in Congress took the view that the first plebiscite was the only legitimate one. Although Douglas and his supporters urged a face-saving compromise that would provide for a resubmission of the whole constitution to a popular vote, Buchanan chose to follow his southern advisors. In a special message to Congress he urged the immediate admission of Kansas—"at this moment as much a slave state as Georgia and South Carolina."

Buchanan's decision provoked another bitter debate in the Congress that deepened the division in the Democratic party. Southern opinion, particularly in the lower South, was solidified in favor of Buchanan's support of the Lecompton constitution. In the words of John Quitman of Mississippi, the basic issue was "whether any new slave state can be admitted . . . all other questions are mere pretenses, flimsy as the hazy sophistries by which they are attempted to be sustained." Moreover, southerners were strengthened in their resolve by the Dred Scott decision which seemed to place the Constitution and the Bill of Rights on their side. To Douglas and most northern Democrats, the issue was one of fundamental democratic rights—whether the people of a territory should be free to reject a constitution which three-fourths of them abhorred.

After much maneuvering, Congress passed a makeshift bill which proposed to resubmit the entire Lecompton constitution to another vote, coupled with an offer to make favorable grants of land if the people of Kansas accepted the constitution. If they rejected the land grant and the constitution, Kansas would not be allowed to enter the Union until her population reached ninety thousand people. The voters of Kansas indicated their scorn for the implied bribery and blackmail of the makeshift compromise by rejecting the Lecompton constitution, 11,812 to 1,926.

Thus Buchanan's Kansas policy was reduced to a shambles. He had failed to secure the admission of Kansas as a slave state and, in the process, he had succeeded in hardening "geographical divisions" within his own party. Instead of calming "the public mind," he had exasperated it further with his support of the Dred Scott decision and the Lecompton constitution. Important men within the Democratic party were committed to positions from which it would be difficult to retreat. The logic of self-justification would soon force southern Democrats and Douglas Democrats as far apart as southerners and free-soil Republicans.

The Diadem, *1846. Rush Rhees Library. The University of Rochester.*

A House Dividing

The disarray of the Buchanan administration during the bitter con- *The Panic of 1857*
troversy over the Lecompton constitution was matched by the derangement of the national economy. The Panic of 1857 abruptly ended the
10-year boom that had begun in the late 1840's. During the next two
years, a severe depression afflicted the industrial Northeast and the
agricultural Middle West. The South, however, suffered least of all the
sections because the world demand for cotton remained fairly steady.
The southern banking system had fewer suspensions and failures than
that of the North; most of the banking houses in New Orleans rode out
the panic virtually undamaged in sharp contrast to the situation in New
York, Philadelphia, and Boston.

Hence the psychological and political consequences of the economic
crisis were important. The confidence of the South in the strength of its
economic system and its future expandability was increased. Northern
manufacturers, on the other hand, tended to blame a low tariff bill passed
in 1857 as the cause of their difficulty and pressed for a protective tariff to
revive industrial production and reduce unemployment. At the same
time, the farmers of the Middle West renewed their demand for free
land. If eastern manufacturers were to receive the benefit of higher
tariffs, then the agricultural West should have free homesteads along
with internal improvements to help move their crops to market. A
political bargain on this basis was an obvious political strategy for the
new Republican party.

But, for the moment, such possibilities were still latent. The dynamic
element in the political situation was the sharpening of ideological
differences as a result of the stubborn policies of the Buchanan administration. These ideological pressures were brought into dramatic focus by
Stephen A. Douglas' campaign for reelection to the Senate. By the end of
the bitter congressional session in the spring of 1858, the Buchanan
administration was already using all of its political influence to undermine Douglas in Illinois. Furthermore, the Republican party in
Illinois had nominated a formidable candidate, in the person of Abraham
Lincoln, to oppose Douglas for his Senate seat.

Lincoln had come a long way since he had served for a single term as a
Whig Congressman during the Mexican War. Disheartened by his defeat
for reelection, he had turned to a profitable legal career in Illinois,
becoming a counsel for rich railroad and business corporations. Indeed,
the high fees that he earned in such cases enabled him to take time away
from his law business for the senatorial campaign of 1858. Yet, despite
his success in representing banks, insurance companies, and railroads in
the courts, he never forgot his humble origins. He retained an easy-
going and spontaneously democratic manner which enabled him to
communicate with men of all sorts—preachers, lawyers, politicians,
farmers, boatmen, mechanics, and newspapermen. His love of funmak-

ing and story-telling made him particularly effective in dealing with juries or political audiences composed of the social types that he knew so well.

Lincoln's
House Divided
Speech

Although Lincoln had been a cautious and conservative Whig who had endorsed the purposes of the American colonization society in his eulogy of Henry Clay in the capitol at Springfield in 1852, he opened his campaign for the Senate in Illinois with an incisive speech that restated the moral purposes of the Republican party. He attacked the failure of the Democratic party over the previous five years to fulfill its confident promises to put an end to the slavery agitation. Instead, such agitation had constantly increased and would not end, he argued, "until a crisis shall have been reached and passed": "A house divided against itself cannot stand; I believe this government cannot endure permanently half slave and half free."

Lincoln made clear that he did not expect the Union to be dissolved, but that it would have to become "one thing, or all the other." He then put the issue in sharply polarized terms: "Either the opponents of slavery will arrest the further spread of it, and place it where the public mind shall rest in the belief that it is in the course of ultimate extinction; or its advocates will push it forward until it shall become alike lawful in all the States, old as well as new, North as well as South." Thus, Lincoln challenged the legitimacy of the Dred Scott decision as well as the policies of the Buchanan administration but left unanswered the question of how the opponents of slavery were to stop the further spread of it and how the public mind was to be assured that it was on the way toward "ultimate extinction."

Douglas was quick to reply to the challenge of Lincoln's acceptance speech which had been widely reprinted in the newspapers of the country. To an enthusiastic crowd of thirty thousand Chicagoans, he spelled out his fundamental disagreements with Lincoln. He sharply rejected the "house divided" concept as one which would set section against section and threaten the freedom and pluralism of American life. Lincoln's house-divided doctrine could only lead to "a war of extermination" between the North and the South. Furthermore, he condemned Lincoln's attack on the Dred Scott decision as a threat to the maintenance of liberty and lawful order.

The Lincoln-Douglas
Debates

When Lincoln challenged Douglas to debate these and other issues, Douglas agreed to a joint debate at one prominent place in each congressional district of Illinois. The debates immediately acquired a national audience as newspaper reporters from New York and Philadelphia as well as Chicago accompanied the candidates around the state of Illinois. Douglas continued to affirm the right of the people of each state and territory to decide their own local customs and institutions. More particularly, he pressed Lincoln very hard on the question of equality between the white and black races: "Do you wish to turn this beautiful state into a free negro colony, in order that when Missouri abolishes slavery she can send one hundred thousand emancipated slaves into Illinois, to become citizens and voters on an equality with yourselves?"

In the face of such appeals to the deeply-rooted racist attitudes of Illinois audiences, Lincoln hedged his ideas about a Union that would be "all free." At the Ottawa debate, he denied that he had any purpose "to introduce political and social equality between the white and black races." Nevertheless, the natural rights of the black must be recognized: "In the right to eat the bread, without the leave of anyone else, which his own hand earns, he is my equal and the equal of Judge Douglas, and the equal of every living man." At Charleston, forced by Douglas to be even more specific, Lincoln said: "I am not, nor ever have been, in favor of making voters or jurors of negroes, nor of qualifying them to hold office, nor to intermarry with white people, and I will say in addition to this that there is a physical difference between the white and black races which I believe will forever forbid the two races living together in terms of social and political equality." But he refused to budge from his position that the Republic should return to the course that Washington, Jefferson, and Madison had placed it upon, by excluding slavery from the Northwest territory, and by cutting off its source in the slave trade. By containing slavery in the states where it already existed, Lincoln believed that it would be placed on the way to ultimate extinction.

The most momentous of the debates for its political significance, however, was that at Freeport. There, Lincoln raised a question which was aimed directly at the major inconsistency in Douglas's position: "Can the people of a United States territory, in any lawful way, against the wish of any citizen of the United States exclude slavery from its limits prior to the formation of a State constitution?" A direct answer to this question would compel Douglas either to disavow his popular sovereignty principle or to reject the Dred Scott decision.

In a response that came to be known as the Freeport Doctrine, Douglas unhesitatingly reaffirmed his cherished popular sovereignty principle: the people of a territory could by lawful means exclude slavery prior to the formation of a State constitution. The Dred Scott decision, of course, was the law of the land and must be obeyed, but no matter what the Supreme Court said on the "abstract question" of the property rights of slave owners in the territories, slavery could not survive in any territory unless supported by favorable local police regulations. "Those police regulations can only be established by the local legislature, and if the people are opposed to slavery they will elect representatives to that body who will by unfriendly legislation effectually prevent the introduction of it into their midst."

The Freeport Doctrine

Because of an unfair apportionment of seats, Douglas was able to win the senatorial election in Illinois even though the Republican legislative ticket won a plurality of popular votes by a slight margin. His reelection

Discussion gave way to clubs as extremism in party politics grew and passions of men increased. From Nevins and Weitenkampf, A Century of Political Cartoons, *Charles Scribner's Sons, 1944.*

established Douglas as a major contender in the Democratic party for the presidency in 1860, but the Freeport Doctrine exposed a sectional division in the Democratic party that was as significant as the ideological difference between free-soil Republicans and pro-slavery southerners. Indeed, up to that time, no Republican had conceived a practical political strategy for getting around the Dred Scott decision short of a reversal of the court's opinion. But the Freeport Doctrine was an invitation to northern farmers to get into a new territory first in order to control the local "police regulations" before the making of a state constitution. In short, the competitive struggle for Kansas would become the model for future territorial expansion especially in areas where the South chose to try to extend its power and influence.

Subsequent developments revealed the growing disequilibration of the American political system. The Republican gains in the congressional elections of 1858 and Douglas' Freeport Doctrine caused a significant shift toward more extreme positions by the more moderate southern leaders. Extremists like Edmund Ruffin, Robert Barnwell Rhett, and William Yancey had earlier formed a "League of United Southerners" to encourage the idea of a separate southern republic because "no national party can save us." After the elections, important leaders in the South like Governor Wise of Virginia and Jefferson Davis of Mississippi began to give public support to the demand for special congressional protection for slavery in the territories. If Congress would legislate such protection, then there could be no local police regulations unfavorable to the property right in slaves. Paralleling these activities in the South was the development of a plot by New England and New York abolitionists to support John Brown's plan for an armed raid into the South that, it was hoped, would set off a slave revolt.

John Brown's activities in the guerrilla warfare on the plains of "Bleeding Kansas" had made him a hero in abolitionist circles of New England and New York. As early as 1857, he had traveled through the centers of abolitionist strength collecting money and arms for the struggle in Kansas. In 1858, however, Brown conceived of a much bolder plan to strike against the evil of slavery. All over the South, he believed, slaves were eager to escape from bondage and he proposed to lead a raiding party through the mountain country from Maryland and Virginia into Tennessee and Alabama. He apparently believed that slaves would rise up all over the South and struggle to join his guerrilla band in the mountains. Some well-known abolitionists including Gerrit Smith in New York and Theodore Parker, Samuel Gridley Howe, George Stearns, and Thomas Wentworth Higginson in Massachusetts approved Brown's plan. They agreed to furnish funds for it although they did not know just where Brown intended to launch his attack. Indeed, they did not wish to know his specific plans "so as to relieve themselves of responsibility."

In December, 1858, Brown led a small preliminary raid into a border town of Missouri and brought back 11 black slaves, two white prisoners, and some livestock to his farm in Osawatomie. After he had taken the 11 slaves to Canada, the Boston abolitionists raised a considerable sum of money for a new and larger effort. By this time, Brown was already an outlaw; President Buchanan had offered a reward for his capture, and the southern press was denouncing his act. Yet Brown was able to move freely and openly through Chicago, Cleveland, and Detroit where antislavery newspapers praised his daring.

Six months later, Brown struck again, at Harpers Ferry in Virginia where there was a federal arsenal, apparently intending this to be the first step in his grand scheme to conduct raids into the heart of the slaveholding South down the Appalachian mountain chain. Moving at night, Brown and his band of 17 men were able to seize both the armory and arsenal from the surprised watchman; but in the morning their presence became known to the inhabitants of the town when two citizens, including a free black, were killed by gunfire from the arsenal. State militia and citizen volunteers quickly surrounded the armory yard and blocked Brown's escape routes while a detachment of marines commanded by Colonel Robert E. Lee was hurriedly sent by President Buchanan to deal with the attack on federal property. The marines stormed the brick structure in which Brown's small force had taken refuge. Within 36 hours after it began, Brown's effort had been utterly crushed. Ten of his men were killed or fatally wounded, including two of his sons and a black member of his raiding force. He, himself, was wounded and taken prisoner together with five of his associates.

John Brown's Raids

John Brown's
Martyrdom

A wave of anger and hysteria swept the South during the weeks after the raid on Harpers Ferry. Exaggerated rumors of further raids and possible slave uprisings kept much of the South from the Potomac to the Gulf in a state of deep apprehension. Even more traumatic for the South was the discovery that many responsible spokesmen in the North viewed John Brown's act as a crime which had extenuating circumstances. In the words of the New York *Tribune*, Brown and his men "dared and died for what they felt to be right, though in a manner which seems to us fatally wrong." The shock and anger at the evidence of northern sympathy for what was regarded as a conspiracy against southern institutions undoubtedly influenced the Virginia authorities to conduct the speedy trial which resulted in the conviction of Brown and a sentence of death by hanging.

At his trial, Brown behaved with dignity and a clear sense of the symbolic importance of his impending execution. In his statements to the court before he was sentenced, he said: "I did no wrong, but right. Now if it is deemed necessary that I should forfeit my life for the furtherance of the ends of justice, and mingle my blood further with the blood of my children and with the blood of millions in this slave country whose rights are disregarded by wicked, cruel, and unjust enactments, I say, let it be done."

Moderate men, both North and South, pleaded with Governor Wise of Virginia to commute the death sentence and to confine Brown to a prison for the criminally insane. Some antislavery leaders, however, foresaw great meaning in a scaffold scene. Henry Ward Beecher declared during the trial: "Let Virginia make him a martyr . . . His soul was noble; his work miserable. But a cord and gibbet would redeem all that, and round up Brown's failure with a heroic success." Governor Wise, who was just as eager to exploit the hysteria of his own section for his own political ends, refused to stay the execution. And John Brown knew what he had to do; he went to the scaffold with a firmness and dignity that impressed even his most hostile onlookers.

As many had already anticipated, it was easier to put Brown on the scaffold than to get him down again. Special church services, the tolling of bells, and crowded public meetings marked the day of his execution in the North. When John Brown's body reached Philadelphia on the train trip to its final resting place, the station was filled with a spontaneous gathering of poorly dressed blacks who had come to show their respect. His grave in North Elba, New York, became an object of pilgrimage, while popular biographies and lithographed portraits were widely sold throughout the North in the months following the execution. Charles Eliot Norton wrote to an English friend at the time: "I have seen nothing like it. We get up excitements easily enough . . . but this was different. The heart of the people was fairly reached, and an impression has been made upon it which will be permanent and produce results long hence."

The session of Congress that followed John Brown's raid was virtually paralyzed. The House of Representatives wrangled for two months over the election of a Speaker. Sectional antagonism stalemated northern efforts to obtain a tariff law and a Pacific Railroad bill, and southern representatives were equally frustrated in their efforts to get a territorial slave code. A homestead law was passed, but Buchanan vetoed the bill and his veto was upheld primarily with the aid of southern Congressmen who feared that the homestead law would underwrite a free labor system in the territories. Throughout these proceedings, the political atmosphere in Washington was poisonous: members of both houses used insolent and insulting language in their speeches and practically all were armed with deadly weapons. Commenting about his colleagues, Senator Hammond observed, "The only persons who do not have a revolver and a knife are those who have two revolvers."

The Ideology of Free-Soil Republicanism

Because the dramatic events of John Brown's raid, trial, and execution aroused sectional emotions to such a high pitch, a psychological explanation of the crisis which beset the American political system at the end of the 1850's offers tempting possibilities. But it would be quite wrong to assert that Americans of that time were simply experiencing a special form of mass neurosis. The political passions that were so evident were the inevitable accompaniment of ideological politics, for the political climate engendered by ideological politics is very different from the relatively tolerant atmosphere of pragmatic politics.

The rapid growth of the Republican party as a political force must be seen as more than a response to the succession of critical events following the Kansas-Nebraska Act. The Republican party also became a political instrument that produced a strong ideological focus in the politics of the late 1850's. The doctrines of free-soil Republicanism enunciated a relatively coherent cluster of ideas and values that caused those who accepted them to view the South and its system of slavery as a threat to those cherished values.

The view of southern society, which was incorporated into the free-soil Republican ideology, had been nourished by more than two decades of antislavery agitation. Countless pamphlets, newspaper editorials, sermons, and public debates had created a fixed sociological image of the South in the minds of most northerners. A leading example of this antislavery literature was the enormous catalogue of southern sins that Theodore Dwight Weld had gathered together in a volume entitled *American Slavery As It Is* (1839). To document the sinful character of slavery, Weld and his assistants combed through thousands of copies of southern newspapers for evidence of the cruelty and depravity of the slave system. Of all the tracts issued by the American Slavery Society, none sold so well as *Slavery As It Is—The Testimony of a Thousand*

The Moral Argument Against Slavery

Witnesses. At the end of the first year, sales exceeded 100,000 copies, and the book went through several printings in the ensuing decade. Until the appearance of *Uncle Tom's Cabin*, Weld's book held the predominant position in the market for antislavery literature.

Because of its dramatic method of documentation, *Slavery As It Is* became a powerful moral argument, constructed of materials that the South itself had furnished. Weld's impressive array of newspaper clippings and eyewitness statements offered abundant evidence that slaves were overworked, underfed, maimed, beaten, and sometimes killed. In *Slavery As It Is* and other tracts of the American Antislavery Society, the South was depicted as a region dominated by the slaveholding planters whose lives were ruined by affluence, self-indulgence, pride, and power. Sexual virtue was almost unknown—the most attractive of the slave women were prey to the unbridled lusts of their masters.

The Social Ethics of Free-Soil Republicanism

But for free-soil Republicans, the moral depravity of the slave system was only one manifestation of the fundamental deficiency of southern society. Again and again, Republican spokesmen emphasized that slavery was the cause of the South's economic backwardness. In speeches and editorials, statistical comparisons of population growth, agricultural and manufacturing production, commerce and transportation, in the free states and the slave states, were used to demonstrate that the free states of the North were far in the lead in economic development. When Hinton Rowan Helper, a non-slaveholder from North

American Anti-Slavery Almanac, 1846. Rush Rhees Library. The University of Rochester.

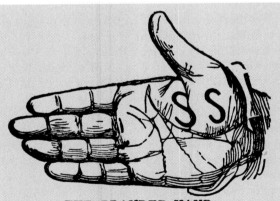

THE BRANDED HAND.

Above we give an exact representation of the *brand*, which was burnt with a hot iron, by an officer of the United States, in the living flesh of a citizen of Massachusetts. Ponder it, fellow-citizens, and as you burn, and blush, and weep, at the disgrace of our country, the indignity done to a worthy neighbor, and the misery of the poor slaves, let the fire burn until your soul is enkindled to the high resolve, that the letters on Jonathan Walker's hand shall be made to read—

SALVATION TO THE SLAVE.

Carolina published his *The Impending Crisis of the South* (1857), the Republicans reprinted it as a campaign document mainly because Helper had amassed an impressive amount of evidence to prove that the slave system was depriving the majority of southern white farmers of the economic and cultural advantages enjoyed by their counterparts in the northern states.

The greatest evil of slavery in the Republican view was its effect on the social ethics of the South. Travellers through the South like Frederick Law Olmsted, whose observations were printed in the *New York Times* and later published in three books, commented on the ignorance and shiftlessness of many of the poor white farmers of the South. Republican spokesmen were fond of making comparisons between the self-reliant and industrious farmers of the North and the lazy and impoverished poor whites of the South. Even the wealthy slaveholders were pictured as wasteful and indolent. Most Republicans shared the view of one Ohio Congressman who declared that as long as the South maintained its system of slave labor it would never be able to build up a "middle class of intelligent farmers, artisans, and mechanics, who constitute the real strength, who make the real wealth, and are justly the pride and glory of the free states."

American Anti-Slavery Almanac, *1844. Rush Rhees Library. The University of Rochester.*

A key idea in the ideology of the free-soil Republicans was the concept of "free labor"—a complex idea which emphasized the dignity of labor and the moral qualities of work. In spirit, the Republican idea of "free labor" was closer to Calvin Colton's conception of the self-made man than to the somewhat narrower Jacksonian conception of "the producing classes." To Republicans, free labor meant the opportunity to achieve economic independence—primarily through the ownership of capital. They believed that northern society was superior to southern society because it had certain social mechanisms which encouraged enterprise and social mobility. The basic constitutency to which they appealed was the middle-class farmers, merchants, manufacturers, and mechanics in the towns and villages of the northern states. These were the people who worked hard, lived in neat houses, built churches and schools, and upheld the moral standards of a Protestant social order.

"Free soil" was a necessary counterpart of the idea of "free labor." To most Republicans the future of America depended on the proper development of the West. If the slave system were allowed to make its way into the undeveloped territories of the West, it would carry with it all the moral degradation and economic backwardness that characterized the South. Only a free labor system could provide the enterprise and virtue needed for the development of the West; and, only if it remained a free-soil country could the nation fulfill its intended destiny.

Free Labor and American Destiny

But the victory of the free labor system could not be won in the West alone. At some point in the future, free-soil Republicans believed there must be a reconstruction of southern society. Some Republicans, like Horace Greeley, believed that the reconstruction of the South could best be accomplished by the migration of northerners into the South. Others believed that northern capitalists and technicians might be able to lead the South into the modernity and mobility that characterized northern society. The South could not expect "the advantages of machinery," one Republican Congressman declared in 1860, "until some Yankees go down and explain the mode and manner of its use."

It is not surprising therefore that a leading Republican like William Henry Seward could speak of an "irrepressible conflict" in 1858. The conflict, he emphasized, was not brought on by "fanatical agitators"; it grew out of opposing and enduring ideas and interests, and "it means," he warned, "that the United States must and will, sooner or later, become either entirely a slaveholding nation, or entirely a free labor nation." And in the free-soil Republican ideology, no solution was acceptable that was not a national solution; no solution would be enduring that did not create a new homogeneity of values in the American social system.

The Southern Counter Culture

Slavery Although only one of four families owned any slaves, southern society and culture was based on slavery as a way of life. The slave labor system underlay the ideals and politics of the antebellum South. In 1860 the slave states had a total population of 12,302,000, of which 8,098,000 were whites, 3,954,000 were black slaves, and 250,000 were free blacks whose status got progressively worse during the decades preceding the Civil War.

The most numerous class of slaveholders did not belong to the planter aristocracy. About 72 per cent of the slaveholders held less than 10 slaves, a figure we might take to establish the "planter class." Fifty per cent of the slaveholders held less than five. The extremely wealthy families who owned a hundred slaves or more accounted for less than 1 per cent of the white population. Yet the small group of planters owning at least 10 slaves owned three-fourths of all slaves, and more than one-half of the slaves lived on plantations with more than 20 slaves. It was these large planters who defined the apex of the status system for the South, shaped opinion, and controlled political power.

Although the dominant image of southern slavery is the large plantation, it is essential to understand that neither the South nor its slave system was monolithic. In South Carolina, in the black belt region of Georgia, and in the delta area of Mississippi there were immense plantations, with blacks vastly outnumbering whites. But slave density was much less in Kentucky, Maryland, and Missouri. If most slaves lived on plantations with twenty or more slaves, many were owned by masters who possessed only one slave and who worked side by side with that slave. Nor were all slaves involved in cotton agriculture, or even agriculture of any kind. Slaves worked in mines and factories; many were skilled workers, either on plantations or in urban trades. Urban slavery was quite important, though it declined toward the end of the period because the price of slaves rose in response to high rural demand. Since alternatives to slave labor existed to a larger degree in the cities than on the plantations, urban slavery declined. But economics does not tell all of this story. Slavery's decline in the cities was also related to a rising fear in the cities that the freedom of movement and association inherent in urban life made the problem of slave control frightfully difficult.

The institution of slavery was full of anomalies. A slave was at once a human being who could steal or murder, and he was a piece of property that could be rented, sold, or inherited. The South's peculiar institution thus contained a morally challenging contradiction that was noted by Frederick Law Olmsted, a northern antislavery intellectual who travelled through the South on the eve of the Civil War. "It is difficult," he wrote, "to handle simply as property, a creature possessing human passions and human feelings . . . while, on the other hand, the absolute necessity of dealing with property as a thing greatly embarrasses a man in any attempt to treat it as a person." If the obvious humanity of the slave could, though it did not always do so, mitigate violence, the definition of the slave as property, ironically, also gave a certain level of protection. An owner would be hesitant about destroying a valuable piece of property.

In the three decades immediately preceding the Civil War, southern leaders tried to present slavery as a "positive good," rather than as the "necessary evil" that Jefferson's generation thought it to be. "It is not enough for them to believe that slavery has been entailed upon us by our forefathers," declared a South Carolina newspaper editor in 1835. "We must satisfy the consciences . . . of our own people. We must satisfy them that slavery is of itself right." With this decision an intellectual blockade went up, isolating the South from the growing anti-slavery thrust of opinion in most of Europe and America. If earlier southern spokesmen often wished slavery might disappear, it was now embraced forever. Along with this growing commitment to slavery as a permanent institution, there was a movement to "reform" the institution to ensure its survival. The idea, writes historian Eugene Genovese, was to "make the South safe for slaveholders by confining the blacks in perpetual slavery and by making it possible for them to accept their fate." The resulting ideology of paternalism reduced the likelihood of eventual freedom for blacks, while it offered some improvement in the material conditions of their lives. By thus assuming some responsibility for the material well-being of the slave, planters sought to achieve a hegemony over the slaves that would legitimize them as a master class.

*The World
of the Slaves*   Yet the world of the slaves was not shaped exclusively by the masters. Within the obvious limits of the slave system, the slaves themselves were able to limit the power of the master. They could often control the work rhythm and the amount of work that could reasonably be expected of a worker. Always, however, the problem of survival with some self-esteem weighed on the mind of the slave. This meant that slaves complied—as they had to—with the master's demands, but much of this apparent cooperation was outward show for the master. In their music, their folk tales, their religion, and even in their everyday relations with whites, slaves covertly mocked their owners. And if the slaves lived with the terrifying thought that at any time a master might whip them or sell their spouses or children, the master too had fears. The master knew that if he went too far the seemingly docile slave could become a vengeful rebel. There was constant fear of slave revolt. The spectre of Toussaint L'Ouverture, the leader of the great slave revolt in Haiti in 1791; Denmark Vesey, who plotted a revolt in Charleston in 1822; and Nat Turner, who organized a revolt in Virginia nine years later, haunted the master class.

Until recently historians believed that slavery had a devastating impact on black slaves—destroying their culture, family life, and human dignity. New research is drastically modifying this position. Historians have discovered the ways in which slave religion, music, folk tales, and family life sustained a vital and evolving culture supportive of human dignity. Within the vicious and terribly constricting limits of the slave system there was, in other words, enough space for slaves to carve out niches of freedom and dignity that allowed the creation of an autonomous and independent Afro-American culture.

Historians have provided striking evidence of the survival of the black family under the incredibly harsh conditions of slavery. Even when families were broken up through sale, non-related friends in the slave community sustained family values by assuming "fictive" roles as uncles and aunts. The family was thus a major instrument of adaptation and of cultural continuity under slavery. This is not to deny, however, the vulnerability of the slave family. The threat of breakup by sale was a constant fear, and planters and their sons used their power to sexually exploit the female adults and children in slave families.

The distinctive Afro-American culture that emerged from the experience of slavery provided a means of resisting complete domination by the white master class. This opposition was not political or violent; slaves had no institutions or opportunities for such opposition. Rather they escaped total domination by embracing a religious world view—transmitted through their religion and music—that united past, present, and future in a sacred and sustaining myth. This mythic world of oral culture, along with the personal ties of family, kinship, and friendship that made up the slave community, gave a measure of dignity and order to their lives.

The Republican attack on southern society helped to shape a southern ideology which defended slavery as the basis of civilization and depicted the North as a society degraded by acquisitiveness and exploitation. But the southern ideology was older than the Republican party; it had its emotional roots in the fear of slave revolts and the anger over the agitation of the abolitionists. For a full generation before the Civil War an enormous amount of intellectual effort in the South went into the justification of southern institutions.

The debate over slavery in the Virginia legislature of 1831 to 1832 can be taken as a starting point for this intellectual effort. The debate took place after the shocking event of a slave insurrection led by Nat Turner and it coincided with the appearance of William Lloyd Garrison's militant abolitionist group in New England.

Following the suppression of the Nat Turner insurrection, two leading newspapers in the state, the Richmond *Enquirer* and the Richmond *Whig,* published editorials and letters from contributors calling upon the legislature to adopt a plan for the general emancipation of slaves. In the legislature, a group of young representatives from the western part of the state attacked the institution of slavery as a violation of the natural rights of man and charged that Virginia's backward economic condition in comparison with northern states was due to the existence of the slave labor system. They proposed the adoption of a plan for the gradual emancipation of slaves with the deportation of the freed blacks to Haiti or Africa.

The planters of the tidewater region of Virginia opposed the adoption of such a plan as violating the rights of property. Furthermore they insisted that the plan for dealing with the large number of freed blacks after manumission was completely impractical. No doubt, many of them were reluctant to give up slavery because of the rich profits that could be made from the sale of slaves to the lower South. Three-fourths of the members of the legislature were slaveholders, but only 18 of them owned any considerable number of slaves; the overwhelming proportion of the non-slaveholders came from the western section of the state where there were comparatively few slaves. When the final vote was taken in January, 1832, the proposal was defeated by a vote of 73 to 58, with the Representatives of the western counties voting solidly in favor of the emancipation resolution.

The Virginia debate was closely watched by other southern states and every informed southerner was given an unusual opportunity to rehearse all the arguments, pro and con, in his own mind. Furthermore, the Virginia debate provided the entire South with a guide for such thinking when Professor Thomas Dew of William and Mary College issued a widely-read summary of the pro-slavery arguments in the legislature.

Thomas Roderick Dew's *Review of the Debates in the Virginia Legislature of 1831 and 1832* was not designed primarily to reply to northern abolitionists, but to convince southerners that slavery was a positive good. Dew cited the long historical experience of mankind to prove that its progress began when captives in war were put to work instead of to death; only then did leisure and culture become possible. It was true in Israel, in Greece, and in Rome that civilization flowered when slavery existed. Indeed, the Scriptures themselves reflected this historical wisdom because they did not condemn the institution of slavery.

Furthermore, Dew argued, slavery had benefitted the black. It had taken him out of the savage conditions of Africa, where starvation, disease, and ignorance abounded, and made him an economically valuable participant in a higher civilization. To free the slaves and to send them back to the horrors of Africa would be one of the worst forms of cruelty, the more so since most of them were American-born and American-reared. To allow them to remain in America after freedom would be equally cruel, because they were not ready for freedom and would soon be exploited by white men who would lack the inducements to sympathy and kind feelings that existed in the slave system. Slaveholding, he asserted, did not debase the white masters as Thomas Jefferson had believed: "Look to the slaveholding population of our country, and you will find them characterized by noble and elevated sentiments by humane and virtuous feelings."

It was not slavery, Dew argued, which had held back southern economic development in comparison with the northern states; rather it was the unfair tariff system imposed by northern manufacturing interests which drained away the productivity of southern agriculture. To free the slaves and send them away would simply bankrupt a society already struggling with the burdens of unfair economic legislation.

It was slavery, moreover, which made a democratic social system possible because it brought all white men "to one common level," at least more so than any other society. "We believe," Dew maintained, "slavery in the United States has accomplished this, in regard to the whites, as nearly as can be expected or even desired in this world. The menial and low offices being all performed by the blacks, there is at once taken away the greatest cause of distinction and separation of the ranks of society."

Dew's review of the debate in the Virginia legislature supplied southern intellectuals with an armory of arguments against the natural right theory of Thomas Jefferson and replaced it with a social theory grounded in history and historical necessity. During the next two decades, the defense of slavery changed more in tone and emphasis than in content as southern indignation over abolitionist propaganda increased. Stung by the attacks on the moral character of southern slaveholders and the aim of slavery, the pro-slavery argument began to stress more heavily the sanction of the Bible, especially as derived from a literal interpretation.

Theory of the Plural Origins of the Races

In the decade of the 1850's, however, pro-slavery arguments began to take a new turn. The origin of races was explored to justify slavery. Dr. Josiah C. Nott, a Mobile physician, and George C. Gliddon, an archaeol-

ogist, published a work entitled *Types of Mankind* in which they presented a theory that black men and white men represented separately created species. *Types of Mankind* was an ingenious effort, based upon anthropological theories popular in the North as well as the South, to escape the logical dilemma imposed on southern slaveholders by the natural rights doctrine of the Declaration of Independence, but it conflicted with the Biblical account of the origin of man. The Richmond *Enquirer* warned that those who accepted Dr. Nott's speculations could not retain the support of Scriptural justifications: "Destroy the Bible, and [you] lay bare the very citadel of our strength. . . . Let us not then allow this shield of strength to be torn from us until we have something to put in its place." Apparently, southerners were more willing to live in contradiction to the Declaration of Independence than to their literal interpretation of the Scriptures.

Southerners, including John C. Calhoun, repudiated the Jeffersonian doctrine of the equality of man. Every society, it was argued, had a "mud sill," a laboring class doing the hard and menial work. In the South white democracy was achieved because this role was assumed by blacks. The most extreme version of this kind of social theory appeared in the writings of George Fitzhugh, a Virginia lawyer and publicist. In his *Sociology for the South, or the Failure of Free Society* (1854) and *Cannibals All: or Slaves Without Masters* (1857) Fitzhugh developed an elaborate comparison between slave and free societies. Modern free societies—like the North and Great Britain—he argued, had legitimized the practice of human exploitation more than any other societies in human history. The economic doctrine of *laissez-faire,* on which free societies were based,

A Sociology for the South

simply meant "every man for himself, and the Devil take the hindmost." The factory masters of England and the North, by their control of machines and raw materials, had complete mastery over their wage workers without any compensating social responsibility. Wage workers in free societies inevitably fell into the condition of paupers when sickness, unemployment, or old age became their lot. This situation was already producing great social unrest and the rapid growth of socialism and all the other wild "isms" of the day.

In contrast to the evils of free society, the slave society of the South was a model of stability and security. The laborers in the slave system were free of all the "corroding cares and anxieties" of sickness, unemployment, and old age. The master had a property in the labor of his slaves, but the slave had "the most invaluable property" in the master's obligation to care for him throughout life. The slave system, indeed, provided the best form of socialism in the sense that society should cooperate for the greatest economic effort and that it should be responsible for the highest social well-being of its weaker elements.

Although Fitzhugh recognized that industrialism and *laissez-faire* capitalism had destroyed the reciprocal rights and obligations of Europe's feudal social order, his sociology for the South cannot be conceived simply as a harking back to the virtues of feudalism. Fitzhugh called the slave system "socialism" rather than feudalism. Furthermore, his social theory was not grounded in a conception of a relatively simple and uncomplicated agrarian order. He was a vigorous advocate of manufactures and internal improvement so that the South could be freed from economic dependence on the North.

Ideology of Expansionism in the South

Indeed, the southern ideology was never wholly defensive. Southern spokesmen looked beyond their own region and imagined a more expansive future for the slave system in the New World. Much of this expansiveness was based upon an assumption that more land had to be brought under cultivation constantly to preserve the value of slaves in declining agricultural areas. The sale of slaves from the old South to the deep South and frontier areas was an important element of the slave economy. Increasingly in the 1850's, the rhetoric of southern representatives in Congress roamed all over Mexico, Central America, the Caribbean, and the Amazon River region, imagining grandiose schemes of expansion that would enable the South to avoid the dangers of surplus slave population. Some of the more intelligent and informed southerners recognized that the slave system would have to be adapted to uses other than the production of cotton and other traditional staple crops. From ancient to modern times, slavery had proved adaptable to mining and they looked, therefore, to the mines of the West and Latin America as profitable possibilities for the expansion of the slave system.

Consequently, it would be wrong to assume that the southern slave system had reached the natural limits of expansion and the South needed to be given a little time to work out some kind of alternative labor system. Planter capitalism was still essentially dynamic in the 1850's, and much of its self-propelling energy was being channeled even more insistently toward the exploitive use of new lands and new resources. The southern ideology, therefore, included a drive for profit as well as a defense of southern race relations, or southern pride and honor.

But we need to ask a further question about the southern ideology. How deeply did it penetrate the southern consciousness? Why should the people of the South, three-fourths of whom owned no slaves, be willing to uphold a permanent future for the slave system? The question acquires added significance when we remember that the southern states had also shared in the movement toward political democracy that took place in the Jacksonian generation.

During the 1830's and 1840's, constitutional reforms that provided a broader and more equitable distribution of political power were instituted in many of the southern states. These changes included a broadening of the suffrage, the abolition of property qualifications for officeholding, and the reapportionment of seats in the legislatures so as to provide a fairer basis of representation for interior counties, particularly in the seaboard states. Everywhere, except in Virginia and South Carolina, politics became vigorous and noisy, and a new breed of officeholders filled places of political power. Yet this democratic upheaval was not accompanied by a broader ferment of humanitarian and social reform such as that which took place in the North. There was some agitation for common schools, and for improved prisons and asylums, but very little was accomplished. Once the political reforms had been achieved, the reformers seemed to lose sight of broader social goals.

To a certain extent, the rise of the abolitionist movement in the North checked the reformist spirit in the South. Indeed, many of the new political leaders became the loudest defenders of slavery. Undoubtedly, these new champions of slavery in southern legislatures reflected the feelings of non-slaveholding whites who found intangible rewards in the system. The existence of black slavery allowed them a concrete sense of membership in a superior caste. Furthermore, the small but growing class of white urban workingmen resented the competition of slave workers and free blacks in southern factories. But, most of all, the "poor whites" of the South—the disease-ridden, illiterate, and poverty-striken farmers in the back country districts—supported slavery as a way to preserve some sense of status in their otherwise miserable social condition. The northern traveller, Frederick Law Olmsted, noted in his *A Journey in the Back Country* (1860) that these back country whites ". . . more than any other portion of the community . . . hate and despise the Negro."

Yet the poor whites did not comprise a significant element in southern politics. The new politicians of the South, like their counterparts in the

Non-Slaveholders and the Southern Ideology

North, represented the more ambitious portion of the non-slaveholding whites—the lawyers, small businessmen, yeoman farmers who were in hot pursuit of the main chance that would enable them to rise in the world. And in the southern social system, the main economic rewards and the most significant symbols of prestige were attached to the plantation and to the ownership of slaves. If the democratic reformers of the South had been completely blocked in their efforts to gain access to power, they might have been willing to destroy the existing system of wealth and status. But, having obtained a share of political power, they were willing to accept the legitimacy of the slave system.

It must be remembered also that the southern whites, slaveholders and non-slaveholders alike, shared deep fears about the danger of slave insurrections. The bloody and successful black revolution in Haiti in the 1790's left an unforgettable imprint in the southern consciousness. In almost every decade of the nineteenth century, southerners were alarmed by rumors of slave conspiracies in their midst. To be sure, actual slave revolts were rare, but the Denmark Vesey plot of 1822 and the Nat Turner insurrection of 1831 convinced them that the possibility of servile revolts was real. Furthermore, experiences with refractory or runaway slaves were common enough to demonstrate that there were many slaves who did not conform to the cultural fiction of submissive, childlike Sambos that had been developed by southern apologists for slavery. In the mid-1850's, when a major political party in the North seemed to be arrayed against their social system, these forebodings among southerners reached a high pitch of intensity.

From The National Atlas of the United States of America. *United States Department of the Interior Geological Survey.*

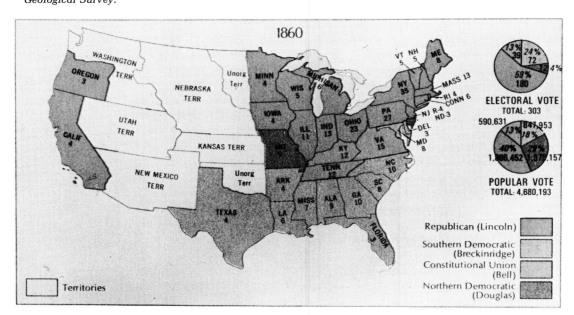

The southern ideology, therefore, did not find its expression through the institution of a political party. It was part of the total fabric of the southern social system, intertwining both the leaders and the led. To a significant degree, the South was becoming a counter-culture, sharing some of the values of the American social system, but challenging others with seriousness and passion. The challenges threatened explosive consequences because the southern ideology was not merely defensive. The economic requirements of the slave system were driving the slaveholding planters and their non-slaveholding supporters into a compulsive expansionism that brought them into direct conflict with equally dynamic northern interests.

The Four-Party Election

The presidential campaigns of 1860 were conducted in a highly charged atmosphere resulting from the pronounced ideological focus that had developed in the politics of the 1850's. This was evident as soon as the Democratic party assembled for its national convention at Charleston, South Carolina, near the end of April. Northern delegates must have regretted the location of the convention because, from the start, the people of the city seemed to be particularly hostile to northern men and ideas.

The Rupture of the Democratic Party

The majority of the delegates, mostly from the Northeast and the Northwest, were committed to support Douglas for the presidential nomination. But Douglas' Free Doctrine was completely unacceptable to southern delegates who were demanding a federal law to protect slave property in the territories. After a bitter battle on the floor of the convention over the platform, most of the delegates of the eight states of the lower South walked out when it became apparent that the convention majority would never endorse a slave code for the territories in the platform. Their withdrawal made it impossible for Douglas to obtain two-thirds of all the delegate votes accredited to the convention. Since no other candidate could muster a significant number of votes, the convention adjourned without any nomination for the presidency.

Two months later the Democratic convention reconvened in Baltimore, where Douglas was able to receive the nomination because the convention accredited new delegates to replace those who had bolted from southern state delegations. At this point, additional southerners left the party to join in a convention of southern democrats that proceeded to nominate John C. Breckenridge of Kentucky for the presidency on a platform which demanded equal protection of property rights for slaveholders in the territories. Thus, the rupture of the Democratic party left the American political system without any broad national party coalition to mediate conflicting sectional demands. The political struggle had become so dangerously polarized that not even the pragmatic politics of the Freeport Doctrine had any broad appeal as a tension-managing strategem.

The Republicans Nominate Lincoln

The Republicans went to their national convention in Chicago after the Democratic fiasco in Charleston with a spirit of complete confidence in the possibility of victory for their new party. The leading candidate for the nomination when the convention assembled was William H. Seward of New York, but many delegates thought that his views on the "irrepressible conflict" between slave and free states were too extreme. After several ballots the nomination went to Abraham Lincoln whose views on slavery seemed more moderate; apparently the phrase "house divided" sounded less contentious than "irrepressible conflict," and it had the added advantage of being a Biblical metaphor.

The Republican platform reflected a more moderate spirit than that adopted four years earlier. The party strategists were determined to put together a broad coalition of groups that would undermine the entrenched position of the Democratic party in key northern states like Pennsylvania, Indiana, and Illinois. Hence the platform was a carefully constructed combination of moral and material demands. True to the original moral idealism of the party, the platform condemned the Lecompton constitution and demanded the admission of Kansas with the free-soil constitution ratified by the clear majority of her people. Another plank declared that freedom was the "normal condition" of any of the territories of the United States and characterized the claim that the Constitution protected slavery everywhere in the territories as "a dangerous political heresy." An appeal to the material concerns of interest groups in the North was carried in the planks calling for protective tariffs, internal improvements, a federally subsidized railroad, and free homesteads.

The Constitutional Union Party

The disruption of the Democratic party, and the evident determination of the Republican party to adhere to a free-soil program despite the Dred Scott decision, led to the organization of a fourth party that sought to overcome the rampant spirit of sectionalism. A group of leaders, most of them old line Whigs who hoped to revive the compromise tradition associated with the leadership of Henry Clay, met in Baltimore to form the Constitutional Union party. Most of the leaders of this movement, like John Bell of Tennessee and John Crittenden of Kentucky, came from the border states; but General Winfield Scott was known to sympathize with the effort, and in Massachusetts Edward Everett, Amos A. Lawrence, and Robert C. Winthrop added their prestige to the party. The convention chose John Bell of Tennessee as the Constitutional Union party's candidate for the presidency and Edward Everett as his running mate. The party platform consisted of a brief declaration "that it is both the part of patriotism and of duty to recognize no political principles other than the Constitution of the country, the union of the states, and the enforcement of the laws."

Thus, within a few short months, the party system that men had known for a full generation seemed to be totally annihilated. Everywhere men sensed a general loss of orientation and a lack of faith in the possibility of political solutions for the developing political crisis. Alexander H. Stephens of Georgia gloomily predicted that "men will be cutting one another's throats in a little while. In less than twelve months we shall be in a war, and that the bloodiest in history."

Lincoln made no major speech during the campaign, pursuing a cautious strategy based on the conviction that the rupture of the Democratic party insured a Republican victory. Even when the southern press began to quicken the alarmist mood of its section by distorted accounts of Lincoln's views, he took the position that any honest seeker of his opinions would find repeated assurances in his earlier speeches that he would never molest the institution of slavery within the states. Breckenridge, likewise, made no attempt to conduct an active campaign; he was concerned mainly to win a solid southern vote that might throw the election into the electoral college. The Bell-Everett forces seemed strangely irrelevant with their emphasis on the Constitution as a symbol of national consensus particularly in view of the continuing controversy over the Dred Scott decision. Of all the candidates, only Stephen A. Douglas campaigned energetically, travelling widely and speaking vigorously to large crowds everywhere he went.

The Election of 1860

Throughout the country men had the sensation of watching a more fundamental drama than the outward show of political parades, posters, and circulars. The electoral contest was only one scene in a far more fateful dialogue which would determine whether the Republic would be torn apart. During the campaign, indeed, southern governors were exchanging ideas on possible ways and means of secession. And if Lincoln and the Republican managers refused to take the secessionist talk seriously, Douglas did. He realized very early in the contest that Lincoln and the Republicans would be victorious; hence, he campaigned mainly to prevent secession. The most dramatic part of his campaign was his speaking tour into the South, the lower South as well as the border states. Behind his energetic speech-making lay the conviction that a widespread conspiracy was being formed to organize some kind of *coup d' état* as early as November and December. Thus, everywhere in the South he denounced disunion and secession: "I think the President of the United States, whoever he may be," he declared in one of his southern speeches, "should treat all attempts to break up the Union by resistance to its laws as Old Hickory treated the nullifiers in 1832."

It is possible that Douglas' vigorous campaigning may have affected the result in the South. At any rate, the Breckenridge vote was mainly confined to the lower South, while Virginia, Kentucky, and Tennessee went for Bell, and Missouri for Douglas. Furthermore, Douglas could take some comfort in his large popular vote, which was 1,376,957 (29.4 per cent) as compared to 1,866,452 (39.9 per cent) cast for Lincoln. Breckenridge received 899,781 votes (18.1 per cent) and Bell only 588,879

(12.6 per cent). Despite the fact that he had received less than 40 per cent of the popular votes, Lincoln won a decisive majority in the electoral college since his votes were concentrated in the more populous states of the North. In the electoral college count, Lincoln received 180 votes to 72 for Breckenridge, 39 for Bell, and 12 for Douglas.

Although Lincoln received some popular votes in the border states, he had not received a single ballot in the lower South which then constituted one-third of the states in the Union. One might say, therefore, that a President-elect who was totally rejected by the voters of one-third of the states and who had received only a little more than one-third of the total votes cast could not make a very strong claim to the legitimacy of his position even though the election had been constitutional and legally fair. And certainly one could argue that there was no clear national mandate for Lincoln and the tenets of the Republican party. Yet there was a central meaning to the result that was clear enough. Presumably a majority of the nation's voters had decided that slavery must be circumscribed and contained: Lincoln's 1,866,452 supporters wished to contain the institution by congressional refusal to recognize it in the territories; undoubtedly, a large portion of the 1,375,957 adherents of Douglas hoped to contain it by the local option type of popular sovereignty suggested by the Freeport Doctrine. In a sense, the election results seemed to endorse Lincoln's repeated assertion during his debates with Douglas that the future of slavery should be placed in the course of "ultimate extinction."

The Secession Crisis

The Secession Movement in the South

As soon as Lincoln's election was certain, the lower South was aflame with fire-eating politics. Mass meetings were held in the leading cities of Georgia, Alabama, and Mississippi to demand immediate secession. The South Carolina legislature, assembled to choose presidential electors, was ready to offer vigorous leadership to the secessionist forces elsewhere in the South. On November 13, the legislature adopted a bill calling for the election of delegates to a special convention which was to be convened on December 17. Before November ended, Georgia, Florida, Alabama, and Mississippi had also authorized the election of conventions to meet early in January. The dramatic surge of such organized secessionist activity took men by surprise, both North and South. Indeed, men of Union sympathies in the South seemed to be demoralized and impotent in the face of the explosive manifestations of secessionist feeling. Alexander H. Stephens was pre-eminent as a southern Unionist, yet even he declared that if Georgia seceded he would follow the will of his constituency.

Rational men in the South found it difficult to hold back the tide. In previous years they had been able to effectively oppose the clamor of southern fire-eaters because they could easily be identified as reckless extremists. But now it was difficult to resist hard-headed assessments of the South's future in the light of the Republican victory. To be sure, intelligent men in the South knew that Lincoln had promised not to touch the institution of slavery in the South and that he could not constitutionally interfere with slavery in the states anyway. But they now perceived that the movement of political forces in the Republic would move inexorably to circumscribe and contain slavery and, in their imaginations, they foresaw disaster in the restriction of their expansionist dreams. Senator Johnson of Arkansas, in an address to his constituents, warned that if slavery were limited to its existing domain, it would be filled by the natural multiplication of blacks until the pressure of the blacks became intolerable. Eventually, he warned, a conflict for racial supremacy would take place and either the blacks would be exterminated, or the white man forced to abandon an Africanized domain. Thus many southerners were predisposed to believe that their future would be safer against a revolution of their social system outside the Union than in it.

Secessionist opinion in the South may also have been encouraged by the uncertainty and confusion of northern attitudes. The overwhelming majority of northern newspapers disliked slavery, but also believed in respecting the rights of southern states. There was a general reluctance to entertain the idea of coercing southern states to remain in the Union. Even a newspaper of strong antislavery sentiments like Greeley's *Tribune* editorialized: "Whenever a considerable section of our Union shall deliberately resolve to go out, we shall resist all coercive measures designed to keep it in. We hope never to live in a republic whereof one section is pinned to the residue by bayonets . . ." Hence there was a widespread belief in the South that secession probably would be bloodless and peaceable.

Buchanan, whose presidential term would end in three months, was in a quandary. The prevailing opinion expressed in leading newspapers seemed to suggest that the country desired caution and conciliation. Yet the one clear precedent in the history of the American presidency was Andrew Jackson's threat of force against the South Carolina nullifiers. Large numbers of Constitutional Unionists and Democrats were pressing for some kind of bold action, like a convention of the states, as a device for conciliation and compromise. But Buchanan was unwilling and perhaps unable to provide the energetic leadership that might have served as a focus for national interest and Union sentiment. Instead he decided to shift responsibility to Congress—a body which had been hopelessly deadlocked since the elections of 1858.

Buchanan's Cautious Policy

Hence when Congress convened, Buchanan's message on the state of the Union declared that secession was unconstitutional, but that there was no power in Congress or the Executive to compel a state to remain in the Union. "The fact is," he asserted, "that our Union rests upon public opinion, and can never be cemented by the blood of its citizens shed in civil war . . ." He blamed the crisis on the antislavery agitation in the North which had made southerners unsure of their continued safety in the Union. The only remedy for the crisis that he could suggest was the adoption by Congress of an explanatory amendment to the Constitution that would guarantee the right of property in slaves where it existed and extend the same protection to slave property in all territories until they were admitted as states. At the same time, President Buchanan refused to take any preparatory measures to secure federal forts and property in Charleston before the South Carolina convention met to consider the question of secession, despite urgent requests for reenforcements from Major Anderson who was in command of the small garrisons in the forts of Charleston harbor.

The secession of South Carolina on December 20 was followed within a matter of days by the seizure of Fort Moultrie and the retirement of Major Anderson's small force to Fort Sumter in Charleston's outer harbor. After several contentious Cabinet meetings, Buchanan decided to send troops, ammunition, and stores to Fort Sumter. These reinforcements, as it turned out, never reached Charleston; an unarmed steamer, *Star of the West,* carrying two hundred troops and supplies, attempted to enter the harbor but was driven off by shore batteries. Thereafter, Buchanan continued to assert the right of the government to maintain the forts and other property of the government; in actuality, however, his administration managed to hold on to only a few small forts like Sumter in South Carolina and Pickens in Florida. Elsewhere the seceding states were able to seize forts, arsenals, and other federal property with impunity.

The Failure of Broker Politics   Meanwhile, both houses of Congress created special committees representing both sections, Republicans as well as Democrats, to deal with the crisis. A Committee of Thirteen in the Senate became the source of a compromise plan that caught national attention. Senator Crittenden of Kentucky, who put forth the plan, proposed six amendments to the Constitution. One would have extended the old Missouri Compromise line of 36°30′ to California, prohibiting slavery in all territories north of the line, but protecting the slave property south of it. Another amendment would have forbidden Congress to abolish slavery in any place of national jurisdiction within a slave state. A related amendment stipulated that there could be no abolition of slavery in the District of Columbia so long as either Virginia or Maryland legalized slavery, and such abolition must have the consent of the people of the District and provide for compensation to slave owners. Another would have prohibited federal laws that interfered with the interstate transportation of slaves. The remaining amendments would have authorized Congress to furnish compensation to the owners of fugitive slaves rescued by force and prevented any future changes in the Constitutional clauses that protected slavery.

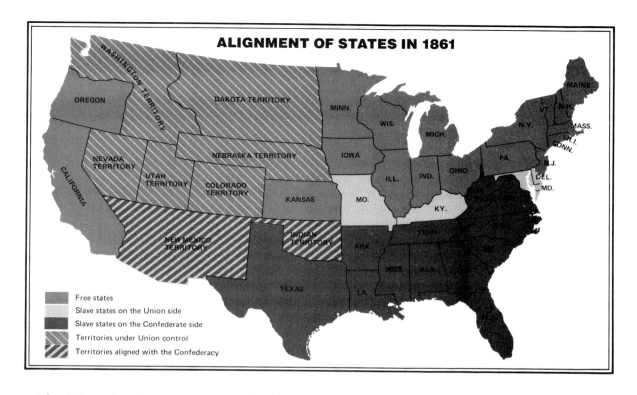

ALIGNMENT OF STATES IN 1861

Free states
Slave states on the Union side
Slave states on the Confederate side
Territories under Union control
Territories aligned with the Confederacy

The Crittenden plan received considerable support in the North and in the border states; favorable resolutions from those areas and petitions began pouring into Congress. In view of the secessionist fever that was sweeping the lower South, it was uncertain how the people of that area would respond; yet the amendments were clearly favorable to southern interests. But the plan failed primarily because the five Republicans on the Committee of Thirteen refused to support it. They followed the lead of President-elect Abraham Lincoln, whose letters to congressional leaders emphasized that there should be no compromise on the question of extending slavery; the new territories of the West must be given a clean bed, with no snakes in it. Lincoln, however, was ready to concede all the other points—he had no idea of recommending the abolition of slavery in the District of Columbia, or of interfering with the interstate slave trade; and he had repeatedly affirmed that he had no intention of interfering with slavery in the states where it already existed.

This was a fateful decision and one which probably prevented any possibility for compromise within the Congress. To Lincoln, the containment of slavery was the central tenet of the Republican party. To yield that purpose would be to reverse the course of history and to undo the ideological consensus that had taken its start from the Wilmot Proviso and gathered more support with the Free-Soil party, and reached its fruition with the formation of the Republican party and the tremendous mobilization of editors, orators, pamphleteers, and intellectuals associated with the party effort. To accept the Missouri Compromise line would simply encourage the South to redouble its efforts to expand their system south of that line into lower California, Central America, or Cuba. "There is no possible compromise upon it but which puts us under again, and leaves us all our work to do over again," Lincoln emphasized. "The tug has to come, and better now than at any time hereafter."

In the House of Representatives, a Committee of Thirty-Three actually succeeded in getting three propositions adopted by that House: one which called for the repeal of personal liberty laws and a faithful execution of the Fugitive Slave Act; the second, a constitutional amendment providing that the Constitution should never be altered in such a way as to abolish or interfere with the domestic institutions of any state; and a third which granted fugitive slaves a jury trial in the state from which they had fled. But most southern members systematically absented themselves from the Committee and made clear that no adjustment would satisfy them which did not fix in the Constitution an obligation to protect and extend slavery.

One last effort was made to find a broad political basis for compromise. At the urging of its governor, Virginia invited all states to send delegates to a national Peace Convention in Washington. Twenty-one states sent delegates to a convention early in February which was presided over by the venerable ex-President John Tyler and which included an aging David Wilmot as one of its prominent delegates. The Peace Convention agreed to resolutions resembling the Crittenden compromise, but their work was futile in view of the fact that eight states of the lower South boycotted the gathering; they were too busy forming a new confederacy.

The Southern Confederacy Within six weeks after South Carolina's secession on September 20, five other southern states had taken similar action—Georgia, Florida, Alabama, Mississippi, and Louisiana—although not without opposition especially in Georgia. All the political and psychological advantages were on the side of the secessionists: effective use of appeals to solidarity and local tradition, superior organization, the driving energy of their leaders, and success in making action so rapid that the opposition could not mobilize. On February 4, 1861, the very day that the Peace Convention opened in Washington, delegates from six states met in Montgomery, Alabama, to organize a new southern republic. The convention chose Jefferson Davis as President and Alexander Stephens as Vice-President and adopted a constitution for their new government styled "The Confederate States of America."

In its formal structure, the Confederate constitution resembled that of the United States; the main differences were in the emphasis upon state rights and the careful guarantee of slavery which was named without the circumlocutions used by the framers of the Constitution of 1787. The preamble stressed that each state acted "in its sovereign and independent character" to form the confederacy. The Confederate constitution and the laws and treaties made under it were declared to be the "supreme law of the land" but any federal officer acting within the limits of any state might be impeached by the state legislature. A provision for a supreme court was carried over from the United States constitution without change in wording—but in point of fact no supreme court was actually created during the life of the Confederacy. The distribution of power and the restrictions upon state powers were similar to those of the federal Constitution except that the central government was forbidden to pass any law denying the right of property in slaves.

The decentralist emphasis of the Confederate constitution was carried forward by the provision that, with certain exceptions, Congress was not to appropriate money except by a two-thirds vote of both houses. The precise purpose of each appropriation was to be specified and the President was given authority to veto particular items of an appropriation bill without vetoing the entire bill. Protective tariffs were prohibited and no bounties were to be paid out of the Treasury for any purpose. These mechanisms were obviously designed to require the kind of limited fiscal policies that were appropriate to an agrarian economy and to discourage those that were associated with the industrializing process of the North. The President was limited to a single term of six years and cabinet members might be granted seats in either house of Congress; but there was too little experience in the history of the Confederacy to indicate how this might have translated itself into a new structure of party politics. It is quite possible that the presidential politics of the Confederacy over the long run might have moved back to something like the one-party situation under the Jeffersonians.

Lincoln and the Problem of Coercion

Although Lincoln had told Republican Congressmen that he believed that the "tug" over the question of the containment of slavery could not be postponed, there was still the question of how such a policy might be carried out. Within the cabinet that the President-elect had selected, two rival approaches were being proposed. Secretary of State William H. Seward, with the support of Charles F. Adams who was to be ambassador to England, advocated a firm but conciliatory policy toward the South in the hope of holding the border states and eventually rebuilding the Union. The other group led by the Secretary of the Treasury, Salmon Chase and militant Republicans in the Congress like Charles Sumner and Benjamin Wade favored an ironhanded policy toward the seceded states.

Lincoln's inaugural address took a middle ground with a carefully-worded combination of firmness and conciliation. He denied the right of any state "upon its own mere motion" to leave the Union. "The Constitution, the Union, these states is perpetual," he declared, and all resolves and ordinances to break the constitutional compact are "legally

Lincoln's Play for Time

void" and all acts of violence within any state against the authority of the United States, "are insurrectionary or revolutionary, according to circumstances." He announced his intention to use the power confided in him to "hold, occupy, and possess the property and places belonging to the government, and to collect the duties and imports." But he was also careful to emphasize that "beyond what may be necessary for these objects, there will be no invasion, no using of force against or among the people anywhere."

Lincoln appealed for patience to the people of the South: "Nothing valuable can be lost by taking time." He reminded them that their domestic institutions and the laws of their own framing were protected by the Constitution and that "the new administration will have no immediate power, if it would, to change either." Then he ended with an appeal to the traditional ties of consensus that had bound the Republic together: "We are enemies, not friends. We must not be enemies. Though passion may have strained, it must not break our bonds of affection. The mystic chords of memory, stretching from every battlefield and patriot grave to every living heart and hearthstone all over this broad land, will yet swell the chorus of the Union when again touched, as surely they will be, by the better angels of our nature."

Lincoln apparently shared the hope of many that the secessionist movement in the South had been caused by a temporary emotional reaction following Lincoln's election and that a counter-reaction might soon take place. Seward and Adams believed that the new southern confederacy was too weak to be viable. And there seemed to be no disposition on the part of other southern states to join it after Texas had brought the number of member states to seven. In Delaware, Maryland, Kentucky, North Carolina, and Tennessee the legislatures rejected all movements toward secession; Virginia, Arkansas, and Missouri elected special conventions, but they were in the control of conservatives who preferred to play a waiting game.

Indeed, Lincoln was so encouraged by these developments that he was tempted to recede from his announced intention to "hold, occupy, and possess the property and places belonging to the government." He toyed with the idea of evacuating Fort Sumter and to remain "firm" only at Fort Pickens where the symbolic retention of authority would seem less threatening to the South. He is reported to have told some visiting representatives of the Virginia convention that he would evacuate Sumter if they would break up their secessionist convention. "A state for a fort," he is supposed to have remarked to one of his presidential assistants, "is no bad business."

Pressures on Lincoln   But Francis P. Blair, the stalwart Jacksonian, when informed by his son Montgomery Blair (who was serving in Lincoln's cabinet as Postmaster General) of this possibility, went to the White House in person to tell the President: "If you abandon Sumter, you will be impeached." Blair's views were those of a man devoted to the memory of "Old Hickory," but they coincided with a hardening of sentiment in the North.

Northern businessmen who had called for compromise at the start of the secession crisis because of their heavy investments in the South were led to reconsider their position in the face of the problems posed by the creation of a southern confederacy. Those to whom southerners owed money feared they would be repaid in depreciated paper money and that the Confederacy would develop foreign trade policies that would be detrimental to their interests. Holders of government securities feared that their investments would be jeopardized by the success of the secessionist movement. In short, northern businessmen had calculated the consequences of disunion and decided that they would be intolerable. Similarly, the agricultural and mercantile interests of the West were appalled by the prospect that they would lose their freedom to navigate the Mississippi. To be sure, the West now had railroads that connected it with eastern seaports, but westerners feared that they would become the economic vassals of the seaboard states if the flexibility of alternative routes of commerce should be taken away. Stephen A. Douglas declared, "We can never consent to be shut up within the circle of a Chinese wall, erected and controlled by others without our permission." Even Clement Vallandigham of Ohio, who was to become a leading peace Democrat during the Civil War, proclaimed ". . . if we cannot secure a maritime boundary upon other terms, we will cleave our way to the sea-coast with the sword."

Undoubtedly Lincoln was sensitive to such attitudes, particularly in his own section, and he was also aware of pressures within his own party against too much softness toward the South. Not only the radical antislavery men in the party but also the more pragmatic politicians were fearful of a compromise that would make too many concessions to the South. "Beware of compromise" was the warning of one Ohio politician. "It killed Clay and Webster. It killed the Old Whig Party, and if you are not careful it will slaughter the present generation of politicians."

On March 29, finally yielding to pressures for stronger measures, Lincoln ordered a supply expedition to be fitted out for Fort Sumter. It was an agonizing decision that increased the likelihood of civil war, and Lincoln made it in the deepest agony of spirit. On the day after he issued the order he had a severe headache and "keeled over," as Mrs. Lincoln reported to a friend.

Lincoln's Fort Sumter Decision

Although Lincoln knew that the risk of war was now very great, it would be wrong to argue, as one distinguished southern historian has done, that Lincoln deliberately maneuvered the Confederates into firing the first shot. Lincoln had carefully refrained from any other provocative actions or belligerent statements against the South from the day of his inauguration. In the context of his public statements and his cautious policies, Lincoln's action did little more than signal an intention to maintain the *status quo.* He directed a clerk in the State Department to proceed to South Carolina to inform Governor Pickens that "I am directed by the President of the United States to notify you to expect an attempt will be made to supply Fort Sumter with provisions only; and that if such attempt be not resisted, no effort to throw in men, arms or ammunition, will be made, without further notice, or in case of an attack upon the Fort."

To the Confederate leaders, however, Lincoln's decision to reprovision Sumter seemed to be a threat and a breach of the assurances in his inaugural address. After an anxious cabinet discussion at Montgomery, the Secretary of War, L. P. Walker, directed General Beauregard, who commanded the Confederate forces at Charleston, to demand the evacuation of the fort and, if refused, to "reduce it." When Beauregard's emissaries visited Fort Sumter under a flag of truce, Major Anderson refused the demand to surrender, but also remarked that his garrisons would be "starved out in a few days." On the basis of this information, the Confederate authorities in Montgomery were reluctant to fire the shots that would start a war. The Confederate Secretary of War sent a telegram to Beauregard instructing him not to "needlessly" bombard Fort Sumter, but to obtain assurances from Major Anderson that he would not fire unless fired upon and an understanding about the time of his evacuation. On the night of April 11, Major Anderson indicated his willingness to negotiate such an agreement provided, however, that he did not receive contrary instructions or additional supplies from his superiors in Washington.

The Confederate Attack on Fort Sumter

Without waiting to transmit this conditional response their superior for further instructions, Beauregard's emissaries served notice on Anderson that the Confederate batteries would open fire in one hour. It seems incredible that Beauregard should have given his young officers so much discretion, but at any rate, they gave the order for the firing of the signal gun that was to begin the bombardment. To be sure, before the negotiations with Anderson began, word had come of the arrival in the outer harbor of the reprovisioning expedition but, even so, it seems strange that neither General Beauregard nor the Confederate government at Montgomery should have taken a more direct hand in the final decision to begin the cannonading of Sumter.

At 4:30 A.M., April 12, the bombardment began, and after 40 hours, in which great damage had been done and his ammunition was exhuasted, Anderson surrendered the fort. He and his garrison were permitted to return to the North; the relief expedition served as the means of transporting Anderson and his men back to a hero's welcome.

The Sumter incident ended the waiting game that had been played by both governments and the upper South. On April 15, President Lincoln issued a proclamation calling forth "the militia of the several states of the Union . . . to the aggregate number of seventy-five thousand . . . in order to subdue combinations too powerful to suppress by the ordinary course of judicial proceedings or by the powers vested in the marshalls by law." In the same proclamation, the President summoned Congress to meet in special session on July 4. The secession of Virginia and the upper South followed this appeal to arms and Lincoln, therefore, faced a larger body of seceding states. The "tug" had finally come, and Lincoln had been forced to the use of ultimate measures of coercive power in his effort to keep the Republic intact.

From Harper's Weekly, c. 1870.

The Military Suppression of Southern Secession

By the time Congress had met in special session, Lincoln was obviously hopeful that the forces already mobilized by the federal government could be used to bring about a rapid capitulation by the Confederate leaders. In mid-summer of 1861, the border states were still in the Union; Unionist sentiment was strong enough in Kentucky and Missouri to prevent the passage of secessionist ordinances, and the same was true in Maryland even though the Sixth Massachusetts regiment was mobbed by riotous pro-southern citizens as it had passed through Baltimore near the end of April. With the support of federal troops, a Unionist government was set up at Wheeling in the western mountains of Virginia, and when the Confederate Congress voted to move the capitol from Montgomery to Richmond, the seat of Confederate power seemed to lie within easy reach of a swift offensive by the forces of the federal government.

Lincoln's chief of staff in the regular army was General Winfield Scott, the commander of the brilliant campaign against Mexico City in the Mexican War, but he was so old and obese that he could no longer mount a horse. Scott did not favor any of the grandiose plans for quick offensives that were being urged by excited Congressmen in the week after Fort Sumter. He proposed instead a grand strategy that came to be known as the "anaconda plan"—a scheme for strangling southern resistance by establishing a tight naval blockade of the southern coastline, and then moving an army down the Mississippi River to seize and hold it from Cairo, Illinois, to New Orleans. Then by coordinated military pressures from the Mississippi valley and Virginia, he hoped to bring the South to the point of collapse. He believed that this slow, steadfast, strangulation would bring the South to submission by the spring of 1862.

Strategic Conceptions of the War

The economic advantages of the North were bound to be weighty in following an anaconda strategy. There were twenty-two million people in the 19 free states and four border states that supported the Union compared to nine million people in the Confederacy, of whom 3.5 million were blacks, mostly slaves. Hence the North had a much larger reservoir of manpower to draw upon, not only for military needs, but also to carry on agricultural and industrial activities. Furthermore, there was much more balance, diversity, and depth in the economy of the North in contrast to the South. According to the census of 1860, the North had (in round numbers) 110,000 manufacturing establishments with 1,300,000 workers; the total in the Confederacy was about 18,000 with 110,000 workers. The value of the product of manufacturing in all the southern states was only one-third as great as that of the state of Massachusetts alone. Of the 31,256 miles of railroads in the United States in 1860, the South contained only 9,283, or less than a third. The southern states also had about half the number of horses, donkeys, and mules that were

available in the northern states. The number of iron furnaces, forges, and rolling mills in the North exceeded that of the southern states by a ratio of almost ten to one; in addition, the southern states manufactured only 3 per cent of the firearms produced in 1860.

The secessionists might have been able to offset the tremendous economic advantages of the North by pursuing a strategy of protracted guerilla warfare, but the southern social structure made such a strategy impossible. One cannot fight a guerilla war and expect to keep 3,500,000 slaves in subjection. Hence the secessionist movement lacked the revolutionary character that would have enabled it to use dispersed forces of fighting men even to the extent that this was true in the American Revolution. The South had to meet the armies of the North on the conventional battlefield with the conventional tactics of massed armies. And in that kind of warfare, the strongest battalions in the long run are those with the longest supply trains and the greatest amount of fire power.

The Illusion
of a Quick Victory

Whatever its merits, Scott's grand strategy lacked popular appeal. Public opinion in the North was being whipped up to demands for quick military victories. Greeley's *Tribune* began to reiterate the demand in each issue: "Forward to Richmond! Forward to Richmond! The Rebel Congress must not be allowed to meet there on the 20th of July!" Impatient Congressmen were shouting demands for an early offensive against Richmond and for hanging the traitorous leaders of the Confederacy as soon as they were caught. General McDowell, who was in command of the principal force of 30,000 troops around Washington, had no wish to lead an offensive until his raw troops were better trained and his supply trains were more adequately organized. But Lincoln decided that the risk was worth taking: "You are green, it is true," he told McDowell, "but they are green also; you are green alike." A victory by 30,000 untrained federal troops over 20,000 untrained Confederate troops stationed at Manassas on the road to Richmond might lead to a quick collapse of the whole secessionist movement.

The idea of a short war died quickly on July 21 when McDowell's forces were defeated at Bull Run by the Confederates who had been reinforced by the rapid shift of Confederate forces from the Shenandoah valley to the main body of troops under General Beauregard's command at Manassas Junction. The defeat turned into a rout when panic swept through the Union regiments and McDowell's army disintegrated into a disorderly mob that ran pell-mell down the main highway to Washington. Fortunately for the Union cause, the Confederate forces were almost as much disorganized by victory as the Union forces were by defeat. They failed to follow up their advantage with a rapid counteroffensive which might easily have led to the capture of Washington. Hence the armed struggle became a protracted war of four years in which Lincoln adopted strategic conceptions similar to Scott's anaconda policy: to strengthen the naval blockade of the South; to launch offensives in the West down the Mississippi from Cairo, and into East Tennessee from Cincinnati; and to build up large forces in Virginia for continued pressure against the Confederate forces guarding the approaches to Richmond.

In the next four years, while the Union navy hampered the flow of supplies from abroad, Union armies fought to penetrate the vitals of the Confederacy. In the spring of 1862, an army led by General Ulysses S. Grant won control of western Tennessee, while Admiral Farragut captured New Orleans and moved up the river as far as Vicksburg. By concentrating their forces in that city, the Confederates in the South were able to hold out for another year, but on July 4, 1863, General Grant's army, aided by naval forces under David Porter, compelled the city to surrender. This meant that the federal government now had control of the entire Mississippi River cutting off the three Western states of Arkansas, Louisiana, and Texas from the main body of the Confederacy.

Military Campaigns in the West

Grant's victory at Vicksburg enabled him to come to the support of the Union military offensive in East Tennessee. The focal point of this campaign was Chattanooga, a vital transportation center. As long as the Confederates held it they could threaten Kentucky and Ohio by rapid advances up the valley of the Tennessee and, from the same point, they could prevent the Union armies from moving south into Georgia or Alabama. In 1862, Union forces under General Buell had advanced into eastern Tennessee but had won no decisive victories. In the summer of 1863, General Rosecrans, who had replaced Buell, captured Chattanooga, but was bottled up in the city by a Confederate counteroffensive. Coming east from the siege of Vicksburg, General Grant was put in command of all forces in the West and, in November of 1863, he won a decisive victory at Chattanooga over the Confederate army commanded by General Bragg. Soon afterwards, Grant was summoned to Washington to become General-in-Chief of all the Union armies. The western army was placed under the command of General William T. Sherman who prepared to invade Georgia from his base in eastern Tennessee.

Military Campaigns in the East

Unlike the successful campaigns in the West which tore deep holes into Confederate territory, the Union campaigns against Richmond were stalemated. McDowell's successor, George B. McClellan, trained and organized an army of over 100,000 men into a superb fighting force. But he proved to be indecisive in battle and his campaign against Richmond up the peninsula between the York and James Rivers in the spring and summer of 1862 was unsuccessful. Further invasions of Virginia led by a succession of new commanders—Pope, Burnside, and Hooker—were easily defeated by the Confederate forces under General Lee. In most of these campaigns the Union army was prevented from concentrating larger forces because the brilliant maneuvering and fighting of a small army under the command of General "Stonewall" Jackson in the Shenandoah valley kept Washington in a continual state of nervousness. Lee made two counterthrusts into the North but was checked at Antietam in September, 1862, and more decisively at Gettysburg in July of 1863, where he suffered heavy losses.

When Grant took command of the Army of the Potomac in the spring of 1864, he began a relentless offensive against Lee's forces counting on his superiority in manpower of two to one to bring Lee to his knees. In May and June of 1864, after a series of hard fought battles (the Wilderness, Spottsylvania, Cold Harbor), he reached the area east of Richmond where McClellan had been two years earlier. But Lee's army was still unbeaten and Grant's losses had been so heavy that northern public opinion became increasingly disheartened. In the deep South, however, General Sherman began his invasion of Georgia, where Atlanta fell in September, and Savannah in December, 1864. While Sherman advanced northward into South Carolina, Grant methodically extended his lines in the hope of surrounding Richmond and starving Lee's troops into submission. In April, Lee evacuated Richmond to escape the trap, hoping to continue the fight in the mountains, but Union forces under General Philip Sheridan cut off his line of retreat. On April 9, 1865, Lee met with Grant at Appomattox Court House and agreed to terms of surrender. Two weeks later, General Joseph Johnston surrendered his forces to General Sherman near Raleigh, North Carolina.

The Raising of Large Armies

Needless to say, four years of warfare on such a scale required the raising of large armies far beyond anything imagined by Lincoln in his first appeal to arms after the fall of Fort Sumter. Because of the lack of reliable records, it is not possible to say with any degree of statistical accuracy how many men served in the Union army. Since the regular federal army and the state militias were expanded by volunteer enlistments throughout the war, and since many enlistments were for specified periods of time rather than for the duration, one can only conjecture about the numbers of men actually in the field when the war moved into the massive and prolonged campaigns in the East and West. T. L. Livermore, who has made elaborate calculations in his *Numbers and Losses in the Civil War,* estimates that there were 2,898,304 enlistments in the Union army. But since many men enlisted several times for specified periods ranging from three months to three years, we must assume that the actual number of men under arms in any month of the war was far less than such an estimate would suggest. Also, some deduction should be made for "bounty-jumpers." In 1861, the federal government offered a bounty of $100 to each volunteer, later raised to $300 for new recruits, and $400 for reenlistments. Since there were many "bounty-jumpers"—men who enlisted, collected their bounties, and then deserted, sometimes repeating the process—estimates based on total enlistments tend to rest on shaky grounds.

Since the official records of the Union army indicate that the actual number of federal men in the field at the end of April, 1865, amounted to about 1,000,000, it seems safe to conclude that this is probably the highest total ever reached during the Civil War. Equivalent estimates place the highest total in the Confederate forces at about 600,000 to 700,000 men, with perhaps double the number of enlistments for the entire period of the war.

When we remember that there were about 360,000 deaths from all causes in the Union army and about 250,000 in the Confederate forces, and nearly as many on both sides who suffered battle wounds, it is understandable that neither government could continue to rely on militia drafts and "voluntary" enlistments to replace the casualties and to recruit additional men for the ever-expanding demands of the military

*Resistance
to Conscription*

*Patients in the ward of
Harewood Hospital,
Washington, D.C., 1864.
From the Brady Collection.
Library of Congress.*

campaigns. Both sides were forced to resort to conscription. In March, 1863, the federal Congress adopted a law which made all citizens between 20 and 45 liable to military service. Exemptions were granted to the physically and mentally unfit, and to only sons of dependent widows or infirm parents. Conscription was only to be used, however, when volunteer enlistments failed to make up the quotas of men assigned to the states. The Conscription Act also retained some unfortunate provisions that perpetuated the inequities of the militia system of many states. If a drafted man hired a fit substitute, he was exempted from service; such an exemption could also be bought outright for $300—the amount of the bounty for new enlistments. The conscription legislation of the Confederacy also permitted the hiring of a substitute and, in addition, outright exemptions were granted to slaveowners and overseers on the basis of one to every 20 slaves.

The inequities of the Conscription Act of 1863 as well as its compulsive features aroused great opposition. Evasion and obstruction of the law was widespread and popular disaffection often led to violence. In many counties of the North it became extremely hazardous for draft officers to serve notices or to make an arrest for resistance to the draft. Some draft officers were mobbed, and some were shot in the performance of their duties. Secret societies were organized in the Middle West to encourage resistance to the draft and there was rioting in such eastern cities as Troy, Albany, and Newark.

It was in New York City, however, that the bloodiest disturbances occurred. Several of the leading newspapers there were highly critical of Lincoln's policies and tended to blame his administration for the bloody prolongation of the war. Furthermore, the Democratic governor of the state, Horatio Seymour, openly questioned the constitutionality of the conscription law. In New York City, Tammany Democrats led by Mayor Fernando Wood worked actively against the war policies of the federal government, gaining much popular support from Irish workers who were hostile to the blacks and to the Yankeee reformers who were promoting the black's struggle for equality. The calling into service of the first drafted men on July 11, 1863, brought these disaffected feelings to the point of explosion. For three days there was serious rioting in the city; the mob engaged in pitched battles with the police, and looted houses and jewelry stores. Blacks were also the special victims of the rioter's fury: an indeterminate number were lynched. The police, militia, and a company from West Point finally stopped the rioting in a bloody week in which more than a thousand white rioters were killed.

The Conscription Act eventually provided the formidable battalions that Grant and Sherman were to use in the final campaigns of the war largely because it stimulated the voluntary enlistment of tens of thousands of young men who wished to avoid being stigmatized as conscripts. Yet the Lincoln administration had to pay a high political price in order to throw more men and material into the grinding purposes of the

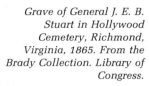

Grave of General J. E. B. Stuart in Hollywood Cemetery, Richmond, Virginia, 1865. From the Brady Collection. Library of Congress.

anaconda strategy. The disaffection and violence that greeted the enforcement of the Conscription Act of 1863 was more than an outraged response to the idea of conscription. It also brought to the surface weariness over the ever-mounting list of battlefield casualties, increasing agitation for peace by negotiation, and deep-seated feelings of race prejudice among unskilled workers and immigrants.

Wartime Dissent

The opposition to military conscription was only one aspect of a persistent pattern of dissent which the Lincoln administration faced throughout the Civil War. Some of this dissent stemmed from Lincoln's use of extraordinary and arbitrary war powers, but the more significant forms of dissent grew out of disillusionment with the war itself—a disillusionment that was fed by repeated military setbacks particularly in the campaigns against Richmond.

Lincoln's use of presidential authority had been somewhat groping and uncertain in the weeks before the bombardment of Fort Sumter, but, once he issued his proclamation of insurrection, he developed a conception of his war powers that ranged far beyond any previously-established precedents. Instead of calling Congress into special session immediately, he set a convening date far ahead to July 4 and, during the intervening 80 days, assumed powers that were virtually dictatorial. By executive proclamation on May 3, 1861, he ordered the regular army increased by 22,714 officers and men, the navy by 18,000, and called for 42,034 volunteers to serve in the Union army. All this was done in spite of the clear language of the Constitution which delegates to Congress the power "to raise and support armies." He also spent two million dollars for these purposes, and pledged the government's credit for amounts up to a quarter of a billion dollars without statutory authority. When Congress finally convened in special session, Lincoln invited the members of both houses to grant him retroactive authority for what he had done, and Congress complied by passing an act providing "that all the acts, proclamations and orders of the President respecting the army and navy of the United States, and calling out or relating to the militia or volunteers from the United States, are hereby approved and in all respects made valid . . . as if they had been issued and done under the previous express authority and direction of the Congress of the United States."

Lincoln's Use of War Powers

Lincoln's use of his presidential war powers frequently evaded the restraints that were reasonably explicit in the Bill of Rights and implicit in the tradition of Anglo-Saxon jurisprudence. This was particularly true of his use of martial law and arbitrary arrest. Shortly after the fall of Fort Sumter, the President issued proclamations suspending the writ of *habeas corpus* in specified areas where he believed the national authority was endangered. Hundreds of arrests were made on the basis of these orders; prisoners were not told why they were arrested, and often the federal marshals and military authorities acted without sufficient investigation or evidence to provide a reasonable basis for definite charges.

The President's policy was immediately challenged in the federal courts, largely through the direct intervention of Chief Justice Taney in the case known as *ex parte Merryman*. John Merryman, an officer in a Maryland secessionist military organization that was suspected of having destroyed some railroad bridges, was arrested in May, 1861, by order of the Union general in command of the district. Taney issued a writ directing the military authorities to produce Merryman in the federal Circuit Court at Baltimore for a hearing on the causes of his imprisonment. Failing to secure compliance with his writ, Taney wrote an opinion which strenuously denied the legality of Lincoln's suspending order and had a copy transmitted to the White House. The Chief Justice argued that the provision concerning the suspension of *habeas corpus* appears in that section of the Constitution that pertains to legislative powers; hence the President's proclamation had been an act of executive usurpation.

Lincoln undoubtedly felt the sting of Taney's admonition that a public officer sworn "to take care that the laws.shall be faithfully executed" should not himself violate them. His message to the special session of Congress that met on July 4, 1861, attempted to justify his action: "The whole of the laws which I was sworn to [execute] were being resisted . . . in nearly one-third of the states. Must I have allowed them to finally fail of execution? Are all the laws but one to go unexecuted, and the government itself go to pieces, lest that one be violated?"

At any rate, the Congress was not disposed to quarrel with Lincoln over the question. The Republican majorities in both houses were even more eager than the President to pursue relentlessly the war against all rebels and disloyal persons. In March, 1863, the Congress adopted a Habeas Corpus Act which declared "that during the present rebellion the President of the United States, whenever in his judgment, the public safety may require it, is authorized to suspend the privilege of the writ of *habeas corpus* in any case throughout the United States or any part thereof."

Political Resistance to the War

Meanwhile, the opposition to heavy militia drafts in 1862 was becoming part of a growing political resistance to the war itself. Much of this opposition was centered in the Democratic party, particularly in the Middle West, and took the form of open public criticism by Democratic leaders and Democratic newspaper editors. But Republic governors in the Middle West were also convinced that there were large numbers of secret, semi-treasonable, organizations that were ready to give aid to the Confederacy by discouraging enlistments, by spying, and by various acts of guerrilla warfare. There were such secret organizations as the Knights of the Golden Circle in the states north of the Ohio River, some of which were engaging in questionable activities; but the Republican governors exaggerated their strength and the nature of their activities. Much of the political opposition to the war was entirely legitimate and based on a desire to negotiate an end to the bloody fratricidal conflict.

On September 24, 1862, therefore, President Lincoln issued a new proclamation stipulating that "all persons discouraging volunteer enlistments, resisting militia drafts, or guilty of any disloyal practice affording aid and comfort to rebels against the authority of the United States, shall be subject to martial law, and liable to trial and punishment by court martial and military commissions." He also authorized the suspension of the writ of *habeas corpus* in all such cases. The arrests made under this order exceeded thirteen thousand; many of those arrested were Democratic newspaper editors or other Democrats of local importance.

Such stern measures failed to stem the growth of opposition; in fact they may have helped to increase it. In the fall elections of 1862, the Democrats captured a majority of the congressional seats and many state legislative seats in such states as Ohio, Indiana, Illinois, and Wisconsin. Within this surging tide of Democratic strength there developed a peace movement whose most dynamic spokesman was Congressman Clement Vallandigham of Ohio.

On January 19, before a packed House of Representatives, Vallandigham attacked the war openly, accusing the Lincoln administration of having abandoned the "war for the Union" in favor of "war for the Negro." But most of all he emphasized the futility of the effort to conquer the South: "Defeat, debt, taxation, sepulchers, these are your trophies." He urged a unilateral withdrawal from the war by the Union government in the hope that time might pave the way for some basis of reunion: "Stop fighting. Make an armistice—no formal treaty. Withdraw your army from the seceded states—Declare absolute free trade between North and South—Let time do his office—drying tears, dispelling sorrows, mellowing passion, and making herb and grass and tree to grow again upon the hundred battlefields of this terrible war."

The Peace Democrats

Vallandigham enjoyed complete immunity when he made such statements in the chamber of the House of Representatives, but he encountered military arrest on a speaking campaign in Ohio after the end of the congressional session. He was particularly outraged by a general order issued by General Burnside, the military commander of "the Department of the Ohio," which declared that "the habit of declaring sympathies for the enemy will no longer be tolerated—Persons committing such offenses will be at once arrested, with a view to being tried [as spies or traitors] or sent beyond our lines into the lines of their friends." In a speech to a large crowd at Mount Vernon, Ohio, Vallandigham attacked Burnside's general order as "a base usurpation of arbitrary authority" and denounced the war as one "for the purpose of crushing our liberty and erecting a despotism—a war for the freedom of the blacks and the enslavement of the whites." He also charged that the war could have been ended months earlier and that "peace might have been honorably obtained by listening to the proposed intermediation of France." By General Burnside's order, Vallandigham was placed under military arrest, denied *habeas corpus,* and sentenced to prison by a military court.

This was a severe test of Lincoln's policy of arbitrary arrest and one that clearly embarrassed him. Vallandigham had become the recognized leader of the peace movement in the preceding session of Congress and, consequently, one of the most rapidly rising leaders in the Democratic party. The Democratic press throughout the country denounced the arrest; mass protest meetings were held in cities of the Middle West and in such eastern cities as New York and Philadelphia. Although Lincoln told General Burnside that he regretted the necessity for the arrest, he was unwilling to disavow the extended policy of arbitrary arrest that he had instituted. Instead, he used his pardoning power to commute the prison sentence imposed on Vallandigham by the military court to banishment behind the Confederate lines.

But banishment failed to eliminate the political problems that were aggravated by Vallandigham's arrest. Meeting only a few weeks after Vallandigham's banishment, the Democrats of Ohio nominated their exiled leader for the governorship of Ohio in a wildly-enthusiastic convention which adopted resolutions condemning the policy of arbitrary arrest as "a palpable violation of the provisions of the Constitution of the United States." Meanwhile Vallandigham escaped from the South to Canada. From across the border, he proceeded to encourage his supporters with addresses and letters that were widely reprinted in northern newspapers. The Lincoln administration had to use strenuous means to defeat the aroused Democrats of Ohio: Union Leagues were organized by Republican partisans to combat "rebel sympathizers" with arms if necessary; leading members of the administration were sent into Ohio to support the Republican ticket with speeches; and government clerks were given special furloughs to go home and vote.

After his defeat in the Ohio gubernatorial contest, Vallandigham took the bold step of returning to Ohio, first in disguise and then openly throwing himself into the political campaign of 1864. Lincoln's common sense prevented him from making a second arrest; indeed such an action might have triggered violent resistance by Vallandigham's supporters in the Middle West. Thus Vallandigham was able to play an important role in the national Democratic convention where he used his prestige and influence to get a peace plank included in the party platform. This platform resolution declared that after "four years of failure to restore the Union by the experiment of war, during which, under the pretense of a military necessity or a war power higher than the Constitution, the Constitution itself has been disregarded in every part, and public liberty and private right alike trodden down . . . justice, liberty, and the public welfare demand that immediate efforts be made for a cessation of hostilities, with a view to the ultimate convention of the states, or other peaceable means, to the end that, at the earliest practicable moment, peace may be restored on the basis of the federal Union of the states."

Vallandigham's peace plank, however, proved to be an albatross around the neck for the Democratic party. The national convention nominated General George B. McClellan as its presidential candidate hoping to capitalize on the popular resentment that still lingered after Lincoln's dismissal of McClellan from his post as General-in-Chief of the Army of the Potomac. McClellan, however, could not accept the peace plank as stated. In his letter accepting the nomination he stated categorically that "the Union is the one condition of peace . . . the Union must be preserved at all hazards. I could not look upon the faces of my gallant comrades . . . who have survived so many bloody battles, and tell them that their labors and the sacrifices of so many of our slain and wounded brethren have been in vain . . . A vast majority of our people . . . would, as I would, hail with unbounded joy the permanent restoration of peace . . . without the effusion of another drop of blood; but no peace can be permanent without Union."

McClellan's letter removed the peace issue from the campaign, but it probably also made it easier for Republicans to stigmatize the peace plank in the Democratic platform as "the Copperhead plank," using the popular term of opprobrium that was widely applied to rebel sympathizers in the North. Furthermore, no intelligent voter could accept the thesis by autumn of 1864 that the war had been a failure; victory had not yet been achieved, but it was clear that the South was fighting with its back to the wall. The political dynamics associated with military success put the peace movement on the defensive, and the collapse of the Confederacy gave added saliency to the issues of emancipation and social reconstruction.

The Civil War and World Politics

Internal political opposition to the war was ultimately weakened by the military successes of the Union armies. In an analogous fashion, the Lincoln administration was able to forestall disastrous outcomes in foreign policy. Civil wars have a way of attracting foreign interventions and Lincoln's main problem was to prevent any European government from giving military or political support to the Confederacy. Thus his ultimate diplomatic success depended upon the ability of the Union armed forces to suppress the rebellion and to restore the American Union.

At the start of the war, the leaders of the Confederacy were confident that they could obtain recognition of their independence from England and France and possibly other forms of cooperation. They assumed that these two leading European countries were so dependent on southern cotton that they would have no choice but to pursue diplomatic policies

Confederate Hopes for European Support

that would keep the avenues of commerce open between the ports of the Confederacy and those of Western Europe. It was taken for granted that the French and English, but especially Napoleon III, would be eager to encourage the dissolution of the upstart republic across the Atlantic.

There seemed to be some basis for these Confederate illusions at the start of the war because the Lincoln administration instituted a full-scale naval blockade of the South as part of the anaconda strategy. This greatly disrupted the flow of cotton to British and French ports and raised some thorny questions about the legality and effectiveness of the naval blockade of the extended coastline of the Confederate states particularly for British commerce. But England's position in world politics depended on the use of sea power and naval blockades; hence there was little disposition on the part of the British government to create precedents that might jeopardize the future use of its own sea power.

The Problem of English Neutrality

This is not to say that the position of the Lincoln administration in regard to England was an easy one. It was crucial to prevent any form of English involvement—diplomatic recognition and aid in circumventing the blockade would probably have assured a victory for southern independence. At the outbreak of the conflict there was some danger of English involvement because of the considerable sympathy for the southern cause among upper-class Englishmen. According to Henry

Wharf, federal artillery, and anchored schooners, City Point, Virginia. From the Brady Collection. Library of Congress.

Adams "the great body of the aristocracy" in England was "anxious to see the United States go to pieces." There were, however, other segments of British opinion that favored the Union cause. Leaders of the principal British humanitarian and antislavery societies found it almost impossible to sympathize with the Confederacy, and the leaders of the British trade unions were firmly on the side of the North because they sensed that their own repressive upper classes were moved by a desire to see democratic aspirations and institutions discredited. British mercantile and manufacturing groups were somewhat divided in their attitudes; some were fearful of the American economic challenge to the pre-eminence of British manufacturers, others had strong economic ties to northern mercantile and banking houses and were ideologically closer to northern conceptions of social development.

For the important post of minister to England, Lincoln chose Charles Francis Adams, the son of a former President and Secretary of State. Adams was able to establish an effective relationship with leaders of British opinion that enabled him to cope successfully with the major problems that he had to confront in carrying out his mission.

Adams' skillful efforts were nearly wrecked by an overzealous naval commander in the early months of the war. On November 8, 1861, a British merchant ship, the *Trent,* which had received as passengers at Havana the two commissioners that the Confederate government had selected for the most important foreign capitals was stopped and boarded by a search party from the United States warship, the *San Jacinto.* By the order of Captain Wilkes of the *San Jacinto,* the two envoys and their secretaries were removed from the British vessel and taken to Fort Warren in Boston harbor as political prisoners. The news of the seizure caused a great sensation on both sides of the Atlantic. In the Union states, Captain Charles Wilkes was hailed as a hero; in England there was universal indignation at what was considered an unlawful use of the right of search and seizure. Prime Minister Palmerston is reported to have shouted in a Cabinet meeting, "You may stand for this, but damned if I will."

The American minister to England was greatly depressed at the prospect of the calamitous consequences which seemed likely to follow from Captain Wilkes' unauthorized action, while his son and secretary, Henry Adams, sent off letters to his family and friends in America castigating "the bloody set of fools" who were applauding Wilkes. Lincoln recognized that large stakes were involved and, in a Christmas day meeting of his Cabinet, it was decided that war with England must be avoided. As a result, the Secretary of State was authorized to send a letter to the British Government promising to release the two envoys. The British Cabinet also took a reasonable course. It decided not to issue an ultimatum; an apology was demanded, but even that demand was given up when it was decided to accept, in lieu of an apology, the assurance of the American government that Wilkes had acted without authorization.

This settlement was important because it dissipated much of the widespread anti-American feeling that had temporarily united all segments of British public opinion. After the Confederate armies had successfully thwarted McClellan's peninsular campaign against Richmond in the summer of 1862, the British Foreign Secretary, Lord John Russell, seriously considered the possibility of launching a joint mediation of the American Civil War by England, France, and Russia. Such a mediation, of course, would be premised on the recognition of the independence of the southern states, and Adams was under instructions to break relations if this should happen; Adams, therefore, made it unmistakably clear that mediation was unacceptable to the Lincoln administration. Furthermore, Lincoln's decision in 1862 to issue an Emancipation Proclamation brought an immediate and impressive response from the more liberal sectors of British public opinion. Crowded public meetings were held in the leading commercial and industrial towns where humanitarian reformers, labor leaders, and middle-class leaders joined together in adopting resolutions favorable to the Union cause. The two great leaders of middle-class liberalism in England, Richard Cobden and John Bright, rallied these forces so effectively that Palmerston and Russell decided to abandon the mediation scheme.

The Problem of the Confederate Blockade Runners

This was the improving political context within which Adams effectively worked to prevent the building of raiding cruisers and blockade runners for the Confederacy in England. The English neutrality law forbade the building or arming of vessels for warlike operations in a war in which England was neutral. Yet, by subterfuge, two cruisers were built on contract for the Confederate navy in Liverpool during 1862. In March, 1862 the *Florida,* not yet supplied with war equipment, departed from Liverpool and later turned up at Nassau where she was equipped with English-supplied arms and other materials; in July, 1862, the *Alabama* departed from Liverpool to a rendevous off the Azores where it was equipped for raiding operations against northern commerce. Both of these Confederate cruisers carried on effective commerce-destroying operations against merchant ships of the United States; indeed for the next two years, the *Alabama* became the scourge of northern shipping, burning prizes at sea when they could not safely be taken into neutral ports.

Adams had protested the building of these ships and had presented evidence of their true purpose to the British government, but the response of the British authorities was so dilatory that the order to detain the *Alabama* in Liverpool came too late to prevent the departure of the ship. The Lincoln administration angrily charged that the British government had connived in these violations of its neutrality legislation, while Congress passed a sweeping privateering bill which would allow privateers to harass British merchantmen on the possibility that they might be blockade-runners. Matters reached a crisis in the late summer of 1863 when two iron-clad ships—"the Laird rams"—were nearing completion in the Laird shipyard at Liverpool. These ships would have overmatched most of the ships in the Union navy, and the Confederate government exultantly hoped that they would be able to break the blockade at any point where they chose to operate.

On September 5, 1863, Adams warned Lord John Russell against the expected delivery of the rams saying: "It would be superfluous in me to point out to your lordship that this is war." The British Foreign Secretary, however, did not need this letter to persuade him to stop the departure of the iron-clads. He realized fully that the Laird rams presented a serious threat to the United States and as such would be a cause of war. Although, under English law it was difficult to move against the Laird firm because the "rams" were ostensibly being built for the viceroy of Egypt, the British decided to take them over in a forcible purchase.

At this point, one can say that the main stakes had been won by the United States in the diplomacy of the Civil War. English recognition of the Confederacy and a joint mediation of the conflict had been forestalled, and the further building of naval cruisers for the Confederacy had been stopped. The anaconda strategy was, therefore, protected against the most serious form of external interference. Hence the stopping of the Laird rams must be ranked with the Union victories at Vicksburg and Gettysburg as a crucial aspect of the turning point which had been reached in the Civil War in 1863. The South had no way of escaping the iron ring that was closing in upon it.

The diplomatic successes in London had an important bearing on the role of France. Napoleon III was clearly sympathetic to the Confederacy and, almost from the beginning of the American conflict, the French emperor was ready to recognize the Confederacy and break the blockade if the British would act with him. Although there was a strong undercurrent of antislavery feeling in France, the most influential voices in France were those which complained of the economic damage to the French cotton and exporting industries caused by the Union blockade. Hence, as early as October, 1861, Napoleon made proposals to England for a joint effort to break the blockade.

The British, however, were extremely suspicious of Napoleon; indeed, most British leaders regarded him as a potentially dangerous adventurer. These suspicions were confirmed by Napoleon's behavior in the joint action taken by the two countries in company with Spain in Mexico. The civil war which was raging in the United States was matched by political instability and internal warfare in Mexico. In the spring of 1861, Benito Juarez, a full-blooded Indian, had been elected President of the Mexican Republic after three years of bloody internal war known as the "War of Reform." Juarez' Liberal party was pledged to the separation of church and state, the confiscation of church property, the dividing of huge landed estates, the improvement of schools, and the building of railroads; the general purpose was to begin the task of modernizing Mexico

The Problem of French Intervention in Mexico

with a public administration free from the reactionary repressions of the church oligarchy and ambitious generals.

Juarez faced a difficult situation because the national treasury was bankrupt. To gain a financial breathing spell, in July, 1861, the Mexican Congress approved a decree issued by Juarez suspending foreign debts for two years. European creditors, who had made large loans to the previous governments of Mexico, brought pressure on their governments to take action; on October 31, 1861, a convention was agreed to by France, England, and Spain to set up a joint expedition that would force payment of such claims.

In the next three months, the three nations sent ten thousand troops to Vera Cruz where they soon discovered that a forcible collection of the debts would require a costly military campaign into the interior against the capitol city. They also learned that Juarez was willing to make reasonable arrangements for the future payment of debts owed to foreign creditors. Satisfied with these concessions, England and Spain withdrew their forces in May, 1862. The French, however, continued to make impossible financial demands on the Mexican government and sent in additional forces which reached a total of thirty-five thousand men by the end of the year.

It was clear to the British government, therefore, that Napoleon had deceived them as to his full intentions. Indeed, he had conceived of the possibility of establishing a satellite government in Mexico before the joint convention of 1861 and had even made preliminary overtures to the Archduke Maximillian of Austria several weeks earlier concerning the possibility of becoming the head of a French-supported puppet regime.

After several military reverses, French forces occupied Mexico City on June 7, 1863. A hand-picked Assembly of Notables made up of clericals and other Mexican reactionaries met and voted to offer the throne of the "empire of Mexico" to Archduke Maximilian of Austria. A dubious plebiscite was held to persuade the Archduke that the invitation was supported by the Mexican people and, on April 10, 1864, Maximillian accepted the call. On the same day he signed the convention of Miramar, by which France guaranteed full military support for his regime. Maximilian's decision was a miscalculation that was to have fatal consequences. The French conquest of Mexico was in no sense complete; Juarista bands continued to oppose the foreign intervention with ceaseless guerrilla warfare in a country where the terrain is admirably suited for such operations.

Furthermore, Napoleon III was unable to win any further diplomatic advantages from his Mexican adventure. He hoped to rally European support for the independence of the Confederacy and thus widen the French sphere of influence in the New World. In February, 1863, the French government actually made an offer of mediation to the United States, but Secretary of State Seward firmly rejected it. Napoleon then encouraged the building of iron-clad ships in France to help the Confederacy break out of the blockade. With the specific authorization of the French minister of Marine, contracts were made with Confederate agents for the construction of four cruisers and two iron-clad rams at Nantes and Bordeaux. The vessels were not completed, however, until 1864 and, by that time, the military situation was so favorable to the North that Napoleon, unwilling to risk war with the United States, arranged to have the cruisers sold to Denmark and Prussia.

Meanwhile the Confederacy and Maximilian's government were seeking to establish close and cordial relations—both realizing that neither regime could succeed without the success of the other. But the advance of the Union armies destroyed such hopes for political collaboration. The collapse of the Confederacy left Maximilian to face the growing power of the Juaristas alone, because the United States began to apply strong pressure on Napoleon to withdraw the French troops from Mexico. The presence of fifty-thousand Union army veterans on the Texas border gave added weight to these demands and, in April, 1866, the French government announced its intention to conduct a phased withdrawal of its troops. Within a year, Maximilian's empire had collapsed and the Archduke was executed by a Mexican firing squad.

The successes of American diplomacy during the nation's greatest crisis are a tribute to the patience and firmness of Lincoln's foreign policy; but it must be remembered that the uncertainties of world politics at the time gave the United States more leverage than it might otherwise have had. The reasonably stable European order created largely by the efforts of Metternich after the Congress of Vienna had been overthrown by the Crimean War and the unification of Italy. Hence the great powers of Europe were trying to find their way in a new atmosphere of international suspicion and hostility. Although the British had given moral support to the unification of Italy which was accomplished with the help of French troops, they distrusted French intentions especially after Napoleon annexed Savoy and left an occupying force in Rome. Napoleon's efforts to develop an entente with Alexander of Russia also alarmed the English, whose anti-Russian feelings remained strong after the Crimean War. The Austrians were bitter about their losses in the Italian War of Unification, and the Prussians were resentful of Austrian hegemony in the German Confederation. Furthermore, the Polish uprising against Russian rule in 1863 aroused public sympathy in England and France and led to a joint protest by England, France, and Austria over the ruthless measures being used to crush the Polish liberation movement. The potentially explosive tensions created by these events made European leaders more cautious in dealing with "the American question," and thus, indirectly, strengthened the position of the Lincoln administration in the difficult diplomacy of the Civil War years.

The Politics of Emancipation

Despite his decision to use armed force against the seceding states of the South, Lincoln continued to pursue cautious and conservative war aims. He was particularly anxious to keep the border states in the Union by reiterating his purpose not to interfere "directly or indirectly . . . with the institution of slavery in the states where it exists." To him the overriding purpose of the conflict was to restore as quickly as possible the seceding states to their normal relationship to the Union. His message to the special session of Congress on July 4, 1861, made no mention of slavery. He emphasized instead that the war was essentially "a people's contest" and that "it is now for them to demonstrate to the world that those who can fairly carry an election can also suppress a rebellion; that ballots are the rightful and peaceful successors of bullets; and that when ballots have fairly and constitutionally decided, there can be no successful appeal back to bullets; that there can be no successful appeal, except to ballots themselves, at succeeding elections."

Many members of Lincoln's own party, however, saw the war in other terms—particularly as an opportunity to move more rapidly toward the destruction of the institution of slavery. And as the conflict progressed, a persistent and substantial form of radical politics began to emerge despite the surface unity of party support for measures needed ultimately to win the war.

These efforts to convert the war to more radical purposes were held back initially by the defeat at the battle of Bull Run. In the immediate aftermath of that disaster, both houses of Congress adopted the famous Crittenden resolution stating that "this war is not waged . . . in any spirit of oppression or subjugation, or of overthrowing or interfering with the rights or established institutions" of the seceded states. But the public realization that the war would be long and bitter was accompanied by growing support for efforts to give the war a more radical character. On August 6, 1861, both houses of Congress adopted a Confiscation Act that provided for the confiscation of all property, including slaves, used in aid of the rebellion. In the House of Representatives, Thaddeus Stevens of Pennsylvania linked the adoption of the bill to the revolutionary purpose of liberating slaves: "If their whole country must be laid waste and made a desert to save this Union from destruction, so let it be. I would rather, Sir, reduce them to a condition where their whole country is to be re-peopled by a band of freemen, than to see them perpetuate the destruction of this people through our agency . . . I warn southern gentlemen, that if this war is to continue, there will be a time when . . . every bondman in the South belonging to a rebel . . . shall be called upon to aid us in a war against their masters. . . ."

The Confiscation Act of 1861 was never really applied partly because the law was vague about the method of enforcement and partly because of legal uncertainties about federal authority in the rebellious states. Two Union army generals, however, attempted to break through the legal entanglements by the use of martial law. On August 30, 1861, General John Fremont proclaimed martial law throughout the state of Missouri and announced to all persons in rebellion against the authority of the United States that their property was confiscated and their slaves were freed. Fearful of the effect that such a drastic policy of military emancipation might have on the border states, Lincoln promptly overruled Fremont's order and, when Fremont began to engage in defiant political criticism, Lincoln removed him from his command. In May, 1862, he overruled a similar order issued by General Hunter freeing "persons" in the sea islands of South Carolina "heretofore held as slaves."

Lincoln's repudiation of Fremont aroused a storm of criticism inside and outside of Congress. The more radical members of his party, like Benjamin Wade and Charles Sumner of Massachusetts in the Senate and Thaddeus Stevens in the House, were bitter in their denunciation of the President. Furthermore, the Fremont episode helped to crystallize a body of public opinion committed to emancipation as an objective of the war. Indeed, the dismissal of Fremont became the occasion for a decisive change in the strategy of the Garrisonite abolitionists. They had remained totally outside of the political system in the ante-bellum years, but now they were ready to become involved in the political process. After Lincoln's call for troops following the firing on Fort Sumter, Garrison announced that, although he had been a pacifist as well as an abolitionist, he believed that if the Civil War would end in the total abolition of slavery "it will bring inconceivable national blessings." The Fremont episode, however, revealed that this outcome could come about only through a massive program of public education and intense political activity.

Contrabands on Mr. Foller's farm, Cumberland Landing, Virginia, 1862. From the Brady Collection. Library of Congress.

Accordingly, a group of prominent Massachusetts abolitionists including Garrison and Wendell Phillips joined with antislavery Republicans to form an Emancipation League. Their purpose was to inaugurate a propaganda campaign to arouse public opinion throughout the North in favor of emancipation. The new Emancipation League quickly won the support of Greeley's *Tribune* and the *New York Independent*, the largest political-religious weekly in the country whose new editor-in-chief was Henry Ward Beecher. These two newspapers were strategic centers for the distribution of emancipation articles and editorials to smaller newspapers throughout the country. Emancipation associations modelled on the Boston organization multiplied rapidly and, in November, 1861, a National Emancipation Association was formed in New York City to act as a clearing house for petitions sent to the national government.

This strengthened the position of the congressional radicals, a well-organized emancipationist constituency in the North. On April 16, 1862, Lincoln signed a measure for compensated emancipation of all slaves in the District of Columbia; on June 19, Congress prohibited slavery in all the territories of the United States; and on July 17, a second, more drastic Confiscation Act was signed by a reluctant President. Indeed, this act was the entering wedge of a general policy of emancipation because it provided that "all slaves of persons . . . hereafter . . . engaged in rebellion against the government of the United States . . . shall be forever free of their servitude, and not held again as slaves." To become effective, however, the provisions of the act required a judicial determination as to the fact of ownership by a particular person and of the rebellious character of that person.

Horace Greeley chose this moment for a direct confrontation with the President on his war aims. The *Tribune* of August 19, 1862, carried an editorial entitled *The Prayer of Twenty Millions* in the form of an open letter to President Lincoln. In a truculent manner, Greeley declared that "all attempts to put down the rebellion and at the same time uphold its inciting cause are preposterous and futile . . . every hour of deference to slavery is an hour of added peril to the Union." Sensing the growth of emancipationist sentiment, Lincoln took the unusual step of replying publicly to Greeley in a statement that was reprinted everywhere in the North. "My paramount object in this struggle," Lincoln emphasized, "is to save the Union, and is not either to save or destroy slavery. If I could save the Union without freeing any slave I would do it, and if I could save the Union by freeing some and leaving others alone I would also do that. What I do about slavery, and the colored race, I do because I believe it helps to save the Union; and what I forbear, I forbear because I do not believe it would help to save the Union."

Lincoln's Emancipation Policy   Lincoln's reply was more than a rebuke to Greeley; it was also a carefully-worded effort to prepare the way for his cautious approach to a limited policy of presidential emancipation. A draft of an emancipation proclamation was already being considered within the Cabinet and

Lincoln was waiting for a favorable moment to issue it. He chose to make a public announcement on September 22 after the Union victory at the battle of Antietam in the form of a preliminary proclamation which stipulated that after the first day of January, 1863, "All persons held as slaves within any State, or designated part of a State, the people whereof shall then be in rebellion against the United States, shall be then, thenceforward, and forever free." Lincoln's proclamation, in one sense, did little more than follow the course already developed in the confiscation acts of Congress; on the other hand, it was potentially a more sweeping measure because it did not require any complex and uncertain judicial processes to determine whether any black had indeed been the property of a person engaged in rebellion. Yet it must also be recognized, as many of Lincoln's critics at the time did, that the Proclamation at the moment of its issuance did not free a single slave; it "emancipated" only those beyond the power of the federal government, and left those within Union lines in their state of servitude.

Lincoln's preferred course of action toward the problem of emancipation had already been outlined to Congress in proposals for a gradual policy of "compensated emancipation." He hoped that the states themselves might be encouraged to emancipate slaves with the help of federal grants-in-aid to compensate owners. In July, 1862, he had actually invited border state representatives to a conference at the White House in an effort to win support for his scheme. The results of the conference were disappointing; the border state representatives generally resisted the idea. Even after the Emancipation Proclamation took effect, Lincoln pressed Congress to adopt a measure of financial aid to Missouri to encourage the development of such a policy, but the House and Senate were unable to agree on the terms of compensation.

Lincoln also urged proposals for the colonization of freed blacks in the West Indies of Africa. He said to a group of blacks who came to the White House in August, 1862: "You and we are different races. We have between us a broader difference than exists between almost any other two races. Whether it is right or wrong I need not discuss, but this physical difference is a very great disadvantage to us, as I think your race suffers very greatly, many of them by living among us, while ours suffer from your presence. In a word we suffer on each side . . . It is better for us both to be separated." Hence he urged the deputation of blacks to consider the possibility of establishing a colony in Central America or the Caribbean, promising to aid them with government funds. Lincoln actually provided government support for a scheme to colonize a group of freed slaves on a small island off the coast of Haiti but the disastrous failure of this venture within a year demonstrated that colonization was an illusory policy.

Emancipationist leaders took the view that black freedmen must be absorbed into American society. Hence they urged the national government to create a bureau to assist the freedmen in making the transition

The Freedmen's Aid Societies

from slavery to freedom. A Freedmen's Bureau was not created by Congress until March, 1865, but in the preceding three years the emancipationists mobilized numerous voluntary efforts to demonstrate that the freedmen were capable of a productive, self-reliant, and virtuous life within the American social system.

The most spectacular demonstration of this kind was a social experiment with the freed blacks on the sea islands of Port Royal Sound, captured early in the war by a Union fleet. With the arrival of the Union forces, most of the white population fled to the South Carolina mainland, leaving behind their cotton plantations and eight thousand slaves. The Lincoln administration agreed to permit an experiment in free labor in which the former slaves would raise cotton under the supervision of civilian volunteers and be permitted to acquire title to small plots of land. Freedmen's aid societies organized in the leading cities of the North furnished the first group of superintendents and teachers who were sent to the sea islands. Despite many discouragements and difficulties, their patient work resulted in considerable success in the educational and agricultural operations.

As the war progressed, freedmen's aid societies and church groups sent teachers and missionaries into other areas of the South in ever-increasing numbers. By the end of the war, there were nearly a thousand such volunteer workers in the South. Thus, when the Freedman's Bureau was finally legislated into existence, it was able to draw upon a considerable amount of organized experience in educational and relief activities.

Black Soldiers in the Civil War

The commitment of the emancipationists to the goal of absorbing the freed slaves into American society was also underscored in the demand for the use of black troops in the war. Blacks had fought in the American Revolution and had helped Andrew Jackson win his victory at New Orleans in 1815, but federal and state laws had gradually eliminated them from the United States army and the state militias before 1860. Nevertheless, soon after Lincoln's first call for troops, Boston, New York, and Philadelphia blacks began to recruit militia units; the black Abolitionist, Frederick Douglass, urged blacks throughout the North to do likewise: "Once let the black man get upon his person the brass letters, *U.S.*; let him get an eagle on his button, and a musket on his shoulder and bullets in his pocket, and there is no power on earth which can deny that he has earned the right to citizenship in the United States."

At this point, the Lincoln administration was not willing to use black troops; such a policy would give the war a revolutionary character that Lincoln was anxious to avoid. As the war dragged on in 1862, some antislavery Union generals made limited efforts to enroll black soldiers but they were not sustained by the Lincoln administration. "To arm the Negroes," Lincoln said to a delegation at the White House in 1862, "would turn 50,000 bayonets from the loyal Border States against us that were for us."

Regardless of Lincoln's policies, blacks were a part of the crew of the U.S.S. Monitor. From the Brady Collection. Library of Congress.

As the Lincoln administration moved cautiously toward the announcement of an emancipation policy, such an attitude could not be maintained with any degree of consistency. Even before the Emancipation Proclamation took effect in January, 1863, the War Department authorized the raising of black troops and, significantly, the first black regiment was recruited from volunteers on the sea islands of South Carolina. Thomas Wentworth Higginson of Massachusetts, a committed emancipationist, was appointed colonel of this "First Regiment of South Carolina Volunteers."

Other black regiments, recruited in both the North and the South, were used in major military engagements in the summer of 1863. By that time, Lincoln had become a staunch defender of the policy of using black troops saying: "The emancipation policy, and the use of colored troops, constitute the heaviest blow yet dealt to the rebellion." When the Confederate President charged that Lincoln's policy was designed "to excite servile war within the Confederacy" and proclaimed that "slave soldiers and the Federal commissioned officers serving with them" should be treated as outlaws and executed as felons, Lincoln issued an order of counter-retaliation proclaiming that a rebel soldier would be executed for every Union soldier killed in violation of the laws of war. Despite some atrocities committed by overzealous Confederate troops and commanders, countering retaliatory proclamations prevented any wholesale use of uncivilized practices arising from the employment of black soldiers in the Union army. By the end of the war, there were 178,895 such soldiers in the Union army, representing a significant portion of the manpower mobilized for the final campaign of the war.

Throughout the war, black soldiers were discriminated against in the matter of pay and bounties. Higginson and other officers were outraged to discover that the War Department had ruled that black soldiers should be paid only three-fifths as much as white soldiers. Indignant newspaper editors, governors, and congressmen joined the effort to eliminate this unfortunate parallel to "the three-fifths compromise." Thaddeus Stevens in the House of Representatives and Charles Sumner in the Senate led the fight to eliminate the degrading distinctions in pay. On June 15, 1864, Congress finally enacted a law that gave partial justice to black soldiers: equal pay was given to them but was made retroactive to the time of enlistment only for soldiers who had been free men on April 19, 1861; for all others, namely former slaves fighting for their own freedom, the law was made retroactive to January 1, 1864.

The Struggle for Equal Rights   The fight for equal pay quickly merged with a struggle to obtain equal rights for blacks in all respects. It was recognized that this would require changes in the social order in the North as well as in the South once the war was won. Northern blacks had been denied equal civil and political rights, excluded from white schools and churches, and forced into menial occupations and wretched slums. Free blacks had made the most gains in New England where they enjoyed full political rights in all states except Connecticut; and the combined efforts of free blacks and abolitionists had brought about the desegregation of most public schools and the abolition of Jim Crow regulations on New England stage coaches, horse cars, and railroads.

Taking advantage of the shift in public opinion following the Emancipation Proclamation, the emancipationists began an organized effort to abolish all forms of segregation and discrimination throughout the nation. The leading streetcar companies of New York were compelled to end their discrimination against blacks in 1864. In the following year, Massachusetts enacted a comprehensive law forbidding discrimination because of race in restaurants, inns, theaters, and other public accommodations. Blacks were allowed to testify against white men as a result of changes in the legal codes of California (1863) and Illinois (1865).

Everywhere, emancipationists began to raise demands for equal suffrage—a revolutionary conception even in the North where blacks could vote in only five states. More than any other single factor, the performance of black soldiers helped to win the respect of northern public opinion and to revolutionize conceptions of political and social change. In this respect, the employment of black soldiers was one of the most revolutionary features of the war and the consequences of that policy shaped the far-reaching political struggle over the reconstruction of the Republic.

The Politics of Reconstruction

The reconstruction of the South became a central political question almost from the very first moments of the Civil War. Indeed, the idea of reconstructing the South had already been an important component of the free-soil Republican ideology. But the Civil War presented new and revolutionary political opportunities for the social regeneration of a society that was viewed as morally degraded and economically backward.

Much of the debate over war aims and reconstruction in the first years of the war tended to focus on the question of emancipation; but by 1863 the radical emancipationists were ready to articulate a more sweeping conception of social reconstruction that was consonant with the ideology of free-soil Republicanism. Wendell Phillips, the most eloquent spokesman for these views, declared in one of his more notable speeches: "I hold that the South is to be annihilated. I do not mean the geographical South . . . [I] mean the intellectual, social, and aristocratic South—the thing that represented itself by slavery and the bowie-knife, by bullying and lynch law, by ignorance and idleness."

Conflicting
Conceptions
of Reconstruction

Phillips held forth a vision of a nation which would be integrated in a totalist sense . . . a nation in which there would be "no Yankee, no Buckeye, no Hoosier, no Sucker, no native, no foreigner, no black, no white, no German, no Saxon; . . . only American citizens, with one law impartial overall." And the means to reach such ends seemed reasonably clear to Phillips: "Never will this nation be a unit until every class God has made, from the lakes to the Gulf, has its ballot to protect itself . . . The Negro has earned land, education, rights. Before we leave him, we ought to leave him on his own soil, in his own house, with the right to the ballot and the schoolhouse within reach." Significantly, Phillips also argued that this social revolution must be accomplished primarily by the black freedmen: "I want the blacks as the very basis of the effort to regenerate the South . . . We want the four million of blacks—a people instinctively on our side, ready and skilled to work; the only element in the South that belongs to the nineteenth century."

Such ideas had little chance of being accepted by the Lincoln administration. Lincoln was too much of a practical politician to believe that it was within the power or right of the government to significantly change existing social arrangements; for him, reconstruction was to be essentially a work of restoration (with emancipation of the slaves) but not revolutionary social change.

Lincoln announced a general policy of reconstruction in a proclamation issued on December 8, 1863. He offered pardon and restoration of all rights except property in slaves to any adherents of the Confederacy (with the exception of specified classes of civil and military officers) who would take an oath to support the Constitution of the United States. Whenever one-tenth of the voters qualified in the election of 1860 should take such an oath, they might then establish a state government that would receive presidential recognition. This 10 per cent of white oath-takers would be the "tangible nucleus" with which Lincoln hoped to carry on the work of reconstruction—not the black freedmen to whom the radical emancipationists looked as the basis of a program of social reconstruction. Lincoln agreed that a nucleus of only 10 per cent of the voters was a makeshift, but he hoped that it would be the starting point for a more widespread return to loyalty and cooperation by the southern people. Such a government, he later argued, "is only to what it should be as the egg is to the fowl, and we shall sooner have the fowl by hatching the egg than smashing it."

The announcement of Lincoln's reconstruction policy crystallized radical opposition to the President. The *Anti-Slavery Standard* likened the idea of entrusting the freedmen to such white minorities to the giving of "lambs to the nurture and admonition of wolves." And on this issue the radical emancipationists found widespread support in Congress. Under the leadership of such men as Henry Winter Davis, Thaddeus Stevens, and George Julian in the House, and Charles Sumner, Benjamin Wade, and Zachariah Chandler in the Senate, Congress enacted the Wade-Davis Bill on July 2, 1864, which outlined more severe conditions of reconstruction. The Wade-Davis bill provided that each Confederate state was to be administered temporarily by a military governor who would "as speedily as may be" enroll all the qualified white male citizens (with the exception of specified classes of civil and military officers) and request each to take an oath to support the Constitution of the United States. Only when a majority of those enrolled had taken the oath of allegiance could the governor authorize the election of delegates to a state convention which must abolish slavery and repudiate the Confederate debt and disenfranchise all persons who had held significant civil or military offices "under the usurping power."

Since Congress passed the bill on the last day of its session, Lincoln was able to kill it with a pocket veto. But he said that he was not "inflexibly committed to any single plan of restoration" and that any state that chose to adopt the congressional plan in preference to his own would have his support. Wade and Davis responded with a manifesto in which they instructed the President "to confine himself to his executive duties . . . and leave political reorganization to Congress." Furthermore the Wade-Davis manifesto accused the President of using his reconstruction policy as a means of holding the electoral votes of the rebel states "at the dictation of his personal ambition."

Presidential Politics
in 1864

The Wade-Davis manifesto revealed the depth of the intra-party struggle that had been festering ever since the President issued his proclamation of amnesty and reconstruction. Indeed, the radical Republican leaders were ready for an open effort to deny Lincoln the party's nomination in 1864. In February of 1864, an attempt was made to rally support for Secretary of the Treasury Chase as a candidate with more suitable qualities than the President. The movement backfired, however, when Chase's supporters, led by Senator Pomeroy, distributed a statement known as "the Pomeroy circular" which declared that the election of Lincoln was virtually impossible and that a change of administration was necessary. Local Republican leaders all over the North who had not been informed of these congressional maneuvers protested vigorously and the Chase movement collapsed.

More serious and more sustained was a movement to put forth General John C. Fremont as a Republican rival to Lincoln. On May 31, some of the more disaffected radical Republicans and their emancipationist allies gathered in a convention to nominate Fremont for the presidency and to frame a platform calling for a radical program of reconstruction. Fremont took his nomination seriously, but many Radical Republican leaders—especially those who had stayed away from the Cleveland convention—hoped that the Fremont movement would scare the regular Republican convention into adopting a radical platform and possibly dropping Lincoln at the last moment in favor of another candidate, perhaps Chase rather than Fremont.

But Lincoln and his party managers made effective use of their control of patronage and party committees to build up an overwhelming majority of Lincoln delegates to the "Union Republican" national convention. On the first ballot only the Missouri delegation cast its votes against Lincoln, and the convention proceeded to make a bid for a broader consensus by nominating Andrew Johnson, a war Democrat, for Vice-President. After calling for unity in the effort to win the war, the party platform denounced slavery as the cause of the war, demanding its "utter and complete extirpation" by constitutional amendment. The platform, however, was completely silent on the question of reconstruction.

The election campaign of 1864 took place in an atmosphere of discontent and frustration. There was growing war-weariness as Grant's campaigns against Lee seemed to be piling up never-ending reports of heavy casualties. The peace movement attained special prominence when Horace Greeley, who had generally been associated with the radical emancipationists, thought that he had evidence that there were two emissaries of Jefferson Davis in Canada, with full power to negotiate a settlement. Lincoln responded by making Greeley his appointed intermediary to meet with the southern "commissioners." Greeley made the contact only to find that the supposed commissioners had no credentials. Lincoln also gave his tentative support to two other amateur peacemakers who visited Richmond to confer with President Davis, but the mission simply exposed the unyielding demand of the Confederate government for a recognition of southern independence.

The futility of the peace efforts combined with the frustration over Grant's inability to win a decisive battle against Lee's army led to a last-minute effort within the Republican party to dump their chosen nominee. Leading Republicans actually circulated confidential letters suggesting another convention to meet in September for the purpose of choosing a new candidate. Lincoln, himself, began to lose hope in his own re-election and prepared a memorandum at the end of August in which he wrote, " . . . it seems exceedingly probable that this adminis-tration will not be re-elected. Then it will be my duty to so cooperate with

Long Abraham Lincoln a little longer. Harper's Weekly, *1865.*

Long Abraham Lincoln a Little Longer.

the President-elect, so as to save the Union between the election and the inauguration . . . "

In the last analysis, however, the Democrats were more disorganized by their peace plank than the Republicans by the intra-party disputes over Lincoln's candidacy. The fall of Atlanta and General Sherman's forward movement through Georgia to the seacoast brightened the prospects for victory in the war. Fremont withdrew from the contest and even the most radical Republicans, concerned over the prospect of an electoral victory for McClellan, decided that it was expedient to support the President's re-election. Lincoln won the election with a popular majority of 400,000 votes and an electoral college count of 212 to 21.

Congress Opposes Lincoln's Reconstruction Procedures

Lincoln's re-election, however, did not weaken the resolve of the radical Republican leaders to assert the paramount authority of Congress in the matter of reconstruction. This was made clear when the joint session of the Congress refused to include in the electoral count of 1864 any of the electoral votes from southern states that had been reconstructed under Lincoln's 10 per cent plan—Tennessee, Louisiana, Arkansas, and Virginia. Indeed, in the joint resolution that excluded these states from the electoral count, Congress again asserted the invalidity of the President's reconstruction procedures.

As a practical politician, Lincoln knew that he would have to make concessions to the radicals in his own party. In his last public address three days before his assassination, the President reaffirmed his position that "the seceded states, so called, are out of their proper practical relation with the Union; and that the sole object of the government, civil and military, in regard to those states is to again get them into that proper, practical relation." He admitted that governments already restored to such a practical relation by his plan of reconstruction did not have a satisfactory basis of popular support not only because of the minority of whites involved but also because of the absence of any political participation by black freedmen. Hence he announced his willingness to see the elective franchise granted to "the very intelligent" among the freedmen and to "those who serve our cause as soldiers." We will never know whether Lincoln would have been able to win support for a moderate policy of reconstruction by cautious concessions, even as he had won a measure of control over the emancipation policy by his limited Emancipation Proclamation. His assassination on April 14, 1865, removed his experienced hand from the levers of politics.

Andrew Johnson's Reconstruction Policies

Although Lincoln's assassination created a popular clamor for vengeance against the South, there was little likelihood that the new President, Andrew Johnson, would pursue a policy of reconstruction that would differ greatly from Lincoln's. Johnson had been a firm supporter of the Crittenden resolution in 1861 which announced that the war was not being waged for any purpose of subjugation. He was also a firm advocate of policies that would preserve the "dignity and equality and rights" of the states within the Union. Therefore, in the long months between the assassination and the assembling of Congress in December of 1865, Johnson proceeded to develop a policy of executive reconstruction that was consistent with the guidelines already established.

In a proclamation issued on May 29, 1865, Johnson offered amnesty and pardon to all persons who had taken part in the rebellion against the United States provided they would take an oath to support the federal Constitution. In addition to the classes of civil and military officers excepted by Lincoln, the new President's proclamation also excepted all persons whose taxable property exceeded $20,000. Apparently Johnson, who had risen from the ranks of the poor white class in Tennessee, shared the radical Republican hostility toward the planter aristocracy of the South.

On the same day, another presidential proclamation appointed a provisional governor for North Carolina and outlined a procedure for the restoration of normal constitutional relations with the federal government that became the model for the reconstruction of other states in the South. The provisional governor was instructed to call a convention to be chosen by qualified voters who had taken the amnesty oath; no one might serve as a delegate to such a convention who had not taken the prescribed oath. Once the convention assembled, it would have the right to prescribe permanent voting and officeholding qualifications in the exercise of "a power the people of the several states have faithfully exercised from the origin of the government to the present time." Those taking the amnesty oath were required to abide by all laws and proclamations made during the war with reference to the emancipation of slaves but no further conditions were imposed on the states other than the resumption of federal functions—the collection of taxes and custom duties, the reopening of post offices and postal routes, and the holding of courts by federal judges to hear all cases within the jurisdiction of the federal courts.

In the procedures recommended to the southern states by Johnson, nothing was said about the enfranchisement of black freedmen even though the Thirteenth Amendment was moving rapidly toward adoption by the requisite number of states and something would have to be decided about their political rights. Johnson personally encouraged some of his provisional governors to suggest the possibility of extending the vote to those blacks who could read or write or who owned property; but it was clear from his proclamations that he believed the establishment of voter qualifications was a matter strictly within the Constitutional sphere of authority reserved to the states.

Radicalism at High Tide

When Congress reassembled in December of 1865, Johnson had already recognized the governments established according to Lincoln's reconstruction policy in Arkansas, Louisiana, Tennessee, and Virginia, and those established in seven other states on the basis of his own proclamations. Throughout, he displayed a generous spirit by granting thousands of special pardons in answer to petitions from persons in the excepted classes. Hence when Congress met, the President was fully convinced in his own mind that the majority of southerners were ready to accept their responsibilities within the Union and that the delegations of southern Congressmen arriving in Washington were rightfully entitled to their seats in the national legislature.

Congressional Opposition to Johnson's Reconstruction Policies

But the Republican majority in the Congress was of another mind. They were not convinced that the South was reconstructed or that southerners had really accepted the meaning of their defeat in their minds and hearts. Radical Republicans were already committed to the revolutionary purposes of social reconstruction in the South and many had worked closely with radical emancipationists in a massive campaign organized during the summer and fall of 1865 in behalf of black suffrage.

Large numbers of moderate Republicans were also disturbed about the course of reconstruction in the South under the state governments sponsored by President Johnson. They noted that several southern states had used evasive language in repealing their ordinances of secession. The South Carolina convention raised objections to ratifying the Thirteenth Amendment, and Mississippi refused to ratify on the grounds that it had already been accomplished within her boundaries by state action. No southern convention accepted Johnson's suggestion that suffrage might be given to literate and propertied blacks. Furthermore, the elections held in the southern states under Johnson's program gave ample evidence that the power structure within the South remained essentially unchanged. In Alabama, three-fourths of the members of the legislature had been officers or privates in the Confederate army; candidates lacking such records were denounced as "traitors to the South" and overwhelmingly defeated. The newly-chosen governor of South Carolina had been a Confederate Senator, the governor of Mississippi had been a brigadier-general in the Confederate army, and a Confederate major-general was a member of the Alabama congressional delegation that arrived in Washington for the opening of Congress.

The Southern "Black Codes"

Even more alarming was the enactment of "black codes" to regulate the black population adopted by the newly-elected legislatures under the Johnson program of reconstruction. Faced with a disorganized and scattered labor force as a result of the rapid process of wartime emancipation, the southern whites who controlled the legislature sought to develop new institutional forms that would adjust race relations on the basis of the continued subservence of the blacks. The legal codes adopted by the southern states varied somewhat in their severity but they generally attempted to create legal definitions and special forms of control for nearly every significant aspect of the freedmen's economic and social life. Marriages between blacks and mulattoes were given full

technology and art

Americans have long been identified with technological innovation. Yankee ingenuity reached mythic proportions in the nineteenth century when the inventive skill of Americans produced new gadgets, machines, and processes at a prodigious rate. By the 1850's, so many patents had been registered in the United States patent office that the Commissioner of Patents wondered whether there was much left to be invented. In fact, the rate only accelerated as Americans moved into the second half of the nineteenth century.

Because labor in the United States was scarcer and thus often more costly than in Europe, American capitalists were encouraged to invest in labor-saving technologies. Yet there was more to the inventive impulse of nineteenth-century Americans than this. Looking at the hundreds of models and drawings of inventions that survive, one cannot avoid a feeling that the simple fun of tinkering with gadgetry played an important role in the American romance with machinery. These new machines and tools were of infinite variety. Some were elaborate . . .

Engraving in The Pennsylvania Magazine. *Philadelphia, 1775. Rare Book Division. The New York Public Library. Astor, Lenox and Tilden Foundations.*

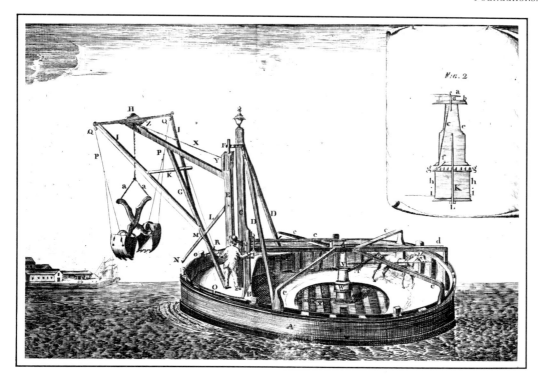

FOOT CORN PLANTER.

. . . while others were relatively simple but clever labor-saving tools.

*There is an important sense in which technological innovation,
particularly major developments like factories, railroads, and steam
engines, raised important and difficult cultural issues. While
technology is usually discussed in labor-saving and economic terms,
it can also become a part of larger dialogues concerning aesthetic
and moral issues.*

*Technology, especially the steam engine and the railroad, brought
vast new power to American economic life and stimulated growth,
but did this development mean less beauty in the landscape and in
life? Or is there a kind of beauty distinctive to a machine civilization? Could nineteenth-century Americans easily accommodate the
machine to traditional artistic and aesthetic conventions? Did machine technology seem to be a proper part of a romantic landscape
painting?*

The Lackawanna Valley
*(1855), George Inness.
National Gallery of Art,
Washington. Gift of Mrs.
Huttleston Rogers.*

What is an appropriate architecture for a machine civilization? Could traditional designs serve the new age? Did the steam engine for the Philadelphia Water Works, with its smoke stack spewing forth, belong in a classical temple? Could new technologies be contained within traditional architectural forms?

The Water Works by William Birch. Prints Division. The New York Public Library. Astor, Lenox and Tilden Foundations.

Vernacular design. *From Woollett's* Old Homes Made New, *New York, 1878.*

Cultivated taste. *From Woollett's* Old Homes Made *New, New York, 1878.*

If one looks closely at the arts of design in nineteenth-century America, it appears that there are two aesthetic traditions. One is formal and traditional, deriving from Euro-American high culture; the other, which some scholars call the "vernacular," was a severely functional tradition of design that was more obviously expressive of the technological and industrial civilization Americans were building. When Americans built machines, factories, or ships, they adapted design to the proposed function, without worrying much about conventional notions of art. To many, however, the products of this vernacular tradition were not truly art—or beautiful—and they felt compelled to decorate them—whether houses or machines.

Art and engineering were thus separated, and art became decoration unrelated to structure and function. Cast-iron buildings, forerunners to the modern skyscraper developed in the 1850's, did not express the materials and engineering techniques that made them and later skyscrapers possible; rather they imitated classical or Renaissance designs in their facades.

Haughwout Store, *1857, New York City. From D. D. Badger,* Architectural Iron Works of New York, *New York, 1865.*

This same combination of technological innovation and decorative or derivative aesthetic convention is apparent in the Victorian Gothic House. While its structure was based upon the innovative balloon frame construction that required less skill to construct and thus made mass production of houses possible, this revolutionary structural invention was smothered in decoration.

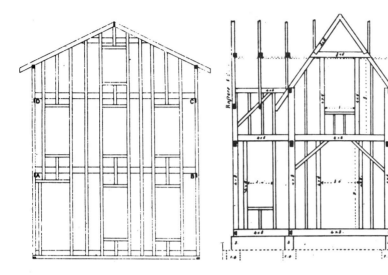

Balloon frame. From James H. Monckton, The National Carpenter and Builder, *New York, 1873.*

Traditional frame, with mortise and tenon joints. From William H. Ranlett, The Architect, A Series of Original Designs, *New York, 1847.*

The Lace House *Denver Public Library, Western History Department. Photo by Karl Arndt.*

The western riverboat was a distinctively American creation. For many foreign visitors, it seemed an apt symbol of the restless persistence with which Americans used technology to wrest economic opportunity out of a formidable geography.

The design of the western riverboat also symbolized the American paradox of linking traditional aesthetics and revolutionary engineering. Driven by powerful steam engines and riding hulls innovatively designed to meet the unique demands of river navigation, the boat's interior space was decorated in a traditional aesthetic reminiscent of a first-class hotel and the smoke stack was often topped off with Gothic decoration.

Steamboat docked at New Orleans. *The Art Collection, Tulane University, New Orleans.*

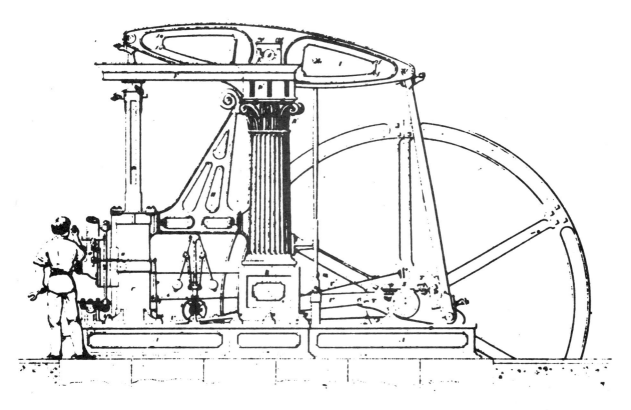

Even more striking than the riverboat are the many instances of machines that Americans felt needed classical decoration. Here, a steam engine is given a Corinthian frame.

Steam Engine. *From Oliver Byrne,* The American Engineer, Draftsman and Machinists's Assistant, *Philadelphia, 1853.*

Steamer Wooding Up on the Mississippi River *in Volume 10 of Ballou's Pictorial, 1856.*

Yacht America, 1851.
*Courtesy of the New-York
Historical Society, New
York City.*

*Gradually, however, Americans began to recognize beauty in the
machine and in the vernacular style. Decoration could be dispensed
with. By the end of the century this aesthetic principle would be
called functionalism. In the 1840's, the sculptor and critic Horatio
Greenough had noted the connection between the useful and the
beautiful in the work of American ship builders. "Observe the grace-
ful bend of her body. . . . What Academy of Design . . . what imitation of the Greeks produced this marvel of construction? Here is the
result of the study of man upon the great deep, where Nature spake
the laws of building."*

"The men who have reduced locomotion to its simplest elements are nearer to Athens at this moment," Greenough continued, "than they who would bend the Greek temple to every use. . . . The slender harness, and tall gaunt wheels, are not only effective, they are beautiful for they respect the beauty of a horse, and do not uselessly tax him."

In Full Stride by an unknown American artist, c. 1840. Philadelphia Museum of Art. The Edgar William and Bernice Chrysler Garbisch Collection '65-209-4

Corliss machine. The
Library of Congress.

Could the machine be beautiful without embellishment? At the Centennial Celebration held at Philadelphia in 1876, visitors saw the American-made Corliss machine, the world's most powerful engine. Its power was marvellous, its operation awesome, but visitors were also struck by its unadorned beauty. Was engineering producing art?

Merchant's Cotton Mill on the Appomattox River near Campbell's Bridge, Petersburg, Virginia. May, 1865. by T. H. O'Sullivan. From the Brady Collection. Library of Congress.

Factory buildings, beginning with the early cotton mills, emerged out of a vernacular tradition emphasizing use rather than beauty.

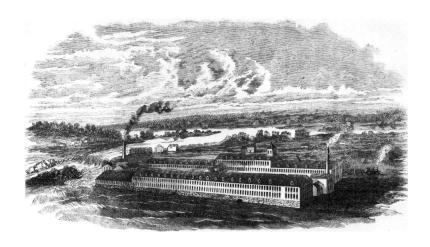

John Russell Manufacturing Company. Green River Works, Massachusetts. Collection of j mara gutman.

As time went on, factories became larger and seemed to represent a functional aesthetic of their own. If machines could go unadorned, might the utilitarian buildings of a machine civilization do the same? If functionalism were acceptable—and less expensive—in factories and warehouses, was it legitimately architecture? Or was it mere engineering?

WESTERN UNION TELEGRAPH COMPANY.

BROADWAY, NEW YORK.

Was architecture without ornamentation possible? For many, artistic embellishment, from whatever historical source, made architecture. It was this that distinguished it from engineering. The Western Union Building constructed during the 1870's in New York represented this high Victorian ideal.

At the same time, however, a new aesthetic that united art and engineering was finding expression in the spectacular and technologically daring Brooklyn Bridge, begun in 1867 and completed in 1883. Here was a utilitarian architecture of great beauty. "It is," Montgomery Schuyler wrote at the time, "an organism of nature. There was no question in the mind of the designer of 'good taste' or of appearance. His work is beautiful, as the work of a ship-builder is unfailingly beautiful in the forms and outlines in which he is only studying 'what the water likes' without a thought of beauty."

George B. Post, *Western Union Building, New York City, 1865. Museum of the City of New York.*

Brooklyn Bridge. *The Harry T. Peters Collection, Museum of the City of New York.*

PUBLISHED BY CURRIER & IVES   COPYRIGHT 1881, BY CURRIER & IVES, N.Y.   115 NASSAU ST. NEW YORK

THE GREAT EAST RIVER SUSPENSION BRIDGE.
CONNECTING THE CITIES OF NEW YORK AND BROOKLYN.

The Bridge crosses the river by a single span of 1595 ft. suspended by four cables 15½ inches in diameter. The approach on the New York side is 2492 ft., the approach on the Brooklyn side is 1901 ft. Total length 5988 ft. From high water to roadway, 120 ft. From roadway to top 157 ft. From high water to centre of span, 135 ft. Width of bridge, 85 ft. Total height of Towers, 277 ft.

What was developed by anonymous builders and craftsmen and by great engineers like John and Washington Roebling, builders of the Brooklyn Bridge, in their designs for machines, factories, and bridges eventually found formal expression as an urban aesthetic appropriate to a utilitarian and technological society. The functional aesthetic of Louis Sullivan's skyscraper united art and engineering in a modern architecture. "Form," Sullivan declared, "follows function."

legal status but intermarriage of whites with blacks or mulattoes was prohibited, and all persons of black blood were deemed to be blacks even though there may have been one or more white ancestors in the preceding generations. Black freedmen were given the right to sue and be sued, to acquire property and to dispose of it by sale or descent although in some cases they were not allowed to rent or lease land except in incorporated cities and towns. Regulations for labor contracts involving blacks and black apprentices included severe penalties for any who left their legal employment. Civil officers, and often any white citizen, could arrest and return such "vagrant" persons and were entitled to receive a specified reward to be paid by the employer out of the fugitive's wages.

Special punishments were provided for any black who, quoting the language of the Mississippi code, committed "riots, routs, affrays, trespasses, malicious mischief, cruel treatment to animals, seditious speeches, insulting gestures, languages, or acts, or assaults on any person, disturbance of the peace, exercising the function of a minister of the gospel without a license from some regularly organized church, vending spirituous or intoxicating liquors, or committing any other misdemeanor, the punishment of which is not specifically provided for by law. . . . " In the implementation of such laws the blacks were not to be judged by their peers since the codes, for the most part, did not allow them to serve on juries. The black codes varied somewhat in the right to testify: in some states, it was restricted to cases in which persons of color were concerned; in others, testimony could be given in cases involving whites.

The growing criticism of the character of the southern governments in the North tended to increase the political leverage of the radical Republicans. Consequently, when the Congress assembled in December, 1865, it refused to seat the Congressmen elected by the Johnson-reconstructed states and sought to take control over reconstruction policy by creating a Joint Committee on Reconstruction. In repeated arguments, the radical Republicans attacked the restorationist theory of reconstruction followed by Lincoln and Johnson.

Charles Sumner expounded a theory that the southern states had committed "state suicide" and were, in effect, in the status of organized territories subject to the regulations of Congress. These territories might come back to statehood only by fulfilling conditions that Congress might impose; and Sumner repeatedly emphasized that black suffrage should be one of those conditions. Thaddeus Stevens developed a harsher version of this theory by arguing that the southern states had left the Union and now had only the status of "conquered provinces." Therefore Congress would have more freedom to act than it possessed in any organized territory. In one of his most radical speeches Stevens called for a "thorough" policy that would confiscate the property of all rebels and distribute all such property as well as the remaining public lands of the states to the black freedmen. Specifically he proposed that each head of a

*Radical Theories
of Reconstruction*

freedman's family should receive 40 acres, with further gifts of money and buildings. He favored black suffrage as "a punishment to traitors" but he bluntly declared, "Forty acres . . . and a hut, would be more valuable . . . than the . . . right to vote."

The majority of Republicans ultimately came to accept a more complex theory developed by Congressman Samuel Shellabarger of Ohio. He argued that the states were indestructible—no state ever was or could be out of the Union—but that, by engaging in rebellion, the southern states had forfeited their rights. Hence the key to reconstruction was to be found in the Constitutional authority of the United States "to guarantee to each state a republican form of government." In short, the southern states were in a state of "suspended animation" within the Union until Congress determined whether such states had reestablished a republican form of government. The "forfeited rights" theory was eventually upheld in the case of *Texas* v. *White* (1869) when the Supreme Court ruled that the reconstruction of the South was primarily a political question and consequently one that must rest upon the power of Congress.

Congressional Reconstruction in 1866

The "forfeited rights" theory became the basis of the first phase of the congressional reconstruction. This consisted of measures to undo the "black codes" and to establish more effective guarantees of the civil rights of black freedmen. The first step in this effort was the passage of a bill in February, 1866, to extend the life and to enlarge the powers of the Freedmen's Bureau. Much of the work of this agency during its first year of operation had emphasized humanitarian services: feeding displaced freedmen, finding jobs and shelter, providing medical aid, establishing schools, and establishing some on public lands under the homestead law. The new law empowered the Bureau "to extend military protection and jurisdiction over all cases involving discrimination against persons on account of race, color, or previous condition of slavery." Heavy penalties were provided against any persons who, by reason of state or local law, deprived any freedmen of his civil rights.

Johnson vetoed the new Freedmen's Bureau Bill, arguing that state courts were functioning adequately in the South and that the bill would provide for a dangerous extension of military jurisdiction in time of peace. In his veto message the President also bluntly challenged the right of Congress to pass any legislation affecting the South without the elected representatives of the southern states being present to vote on it.

Although by only a few votes, the Republican majority was unable to muster the necessary two-thirds majority to override the veto, the House of Representatives adopted a resolution introduced by Thaddeus Stevens which emphatically declared that "no senator or representative shall be admitted to either branch of Congress from any of [the states which have been declared to be in insurrection] until Congress shall have declared such state entitled to such representation." The lines were clearly drawn for a struggle over power and policy between the President and the

Congress, and Johnson gave the struggle an intense personal and emotional character when he charged, in a tactless Washington's Birthday speech, that radicals like Stevens, Sumner, and Phillips had "incited" the assassination of Lincoln in order to remove the primary obstacle to their lust for "place and power."

Johnson's wild charges alienated moderate as well as radical Republicans. The Republican majority immediately rallied to give virtually unanimous support to a civil rights bill that had been introduced by Senator Lyman Trumbull of Illinois, a leading Republican moderate. This measure declared that all persons born in the United States, excluding Indians not taxed, were citizens of the United States, and such citizens, regardless of race, color, or previous condition of servitude, were entitled to equal rights and "the full and equal benefit of laws . . . as is enjoyed by white citizens" no matter what contrary laws or regulations were in existence in the states. Any person, "under the color of any [local] law, statute, ordinance, regulation, or custom" who attempted to deprive any citizen of his equal rights was subject to punishment by fine and imprisonment, and federal courts were given exclusive jurisdiction over such cases.

Johnson promptly vetoed the Civil Rights Act with a strongly-worded message which charged that the bill established "for the security of the colored race safeguards which go infinitely beyond any that the general government has ever provided for the white race." He also claimed that the measure exceeded all constitutional bounds by creating "an absorption and assumption of power by the general government, which, if acquiesced in, must sap and destroy our federative system of limited powers and break down the barriers which preserve the rights of the states." The President's tongue-lashing was more effective than any party discipline in consolidating the Republican majority in Congress. On April 9, 1866, the Republican moderates and radicals were firmly united in passing the Civil Rights Act over the Presidential veto, and soon afterwards they overrode a veto of a second version of the Freedmen's Bureau Act.

This legislation, therefore, created the means to intervene in the southern states with federal authority in all matters affecting the civil rights of all citizens regardless of race. Yet the President's constitutional objections raised a serious problem for the future. Some day, the 11 southern states would be readmitted to the Union and, when readmitted, southerners, aided by their northern allies, would be able to repeal all the special guarantees of civil rights by simple legislative enactment. This possibility seemed all the more real since the abolition of slavery nullified the old three-fifths clause of the Constitution; hence, the southern states would be coming back into the Union with increased representation—amounting to approximately 15 House seats. Furthermore, in April, 1866, in the midst of the quarrel between Congress and the President over the Civil Rights Act, the Supreme Court rendered its notable decision in the case of *ex parte Milligan*. The Court ruled unanimously that the military commission authorized by President Lincoln to try the case of Milligan, who had been subjected to arbitrary arrest in 1864, was invalid. Speaking for the Court, Justice David Davis, stated that "martial rule can never exist where the [civil] courts are open, and in the proper and unobstructed exercise of their jurisdiction." Such reasoning seemed to lend support to Johnson's constitutional arguments.

The Fourteenth Amendment

The significance of the Court's action was not lost on the Republican majority; even while Congress was overriding the President's veto of the Civil Rights Act, the Joint Committee on Reconstruction was preparing a sweeping constitutional amendment to give its radical program a more durable legal foundation. This complex amendment contained provisions concerning civil rights, representation, suffrage, and the disfranchisement of Confederate leaders. Since these were fundamental questions of great import to the restructuring of the American political system, the drafting of the amendment produced intense bargaining and debate between the moderate and radical groups in the Republican party. In its final form it was a compromise not entirely satisfactory to either group; indeed Stevens and Sumner voted for it with emphatic protests about its inadequacies. Yet, for all its vagueness and ambiguity, the Fourteenth Amendment was to become the most important amendment in all of our constitutional history.

The first section of the Fourteenth Amendment repeated the definition of citizenship already embodied in the Civil Rights Act and forbade any state to "deprive any person of life, liberty, or property without due process of law; nor deny to any person within its jurisdiction the equal protection of the laws." Since the guarantee to property in this section was later used by the courts to protect the rights of corporations, some historians have argued that there was conspiratorial intent to make the Fourteenth Amendment a protective shield for corporations in American economic development. Yet the contemporary evidence indicates overwhelmingly that the framers of the Fourteenth Amendment were thinking only of the life, liberty, and property of "natural persons." Furthermore, the evidence is also clear that corporations in 1865 were in no great need of special protection; they had already won established strongholds of power in many state governments.

The second section of the Fourteenth Amendment was especially unsatisfactory to the radical Republicans. It wrote into the Constitution a new formula of representation, eliminating the irrelevant three-fifths ratio for black slaves that had been part of the original constitutional compromise. In addition this section contained a weak provision regarding black suffrage. Radical leaders like Sumner and Stevens wanted positive guarantees of black suffrage, but moderate Republicans were well aware that most northern states had not yet given blacks the right to vote and they were not ready to impose suffrage upon them. Hence the second section of the Fourteenth Amendment provided that when a state denied suffrage to any of its citizens "except for . . . rebellion, or other crime" there should be a proportionate reduction of its representation in the lower house. Such a penalty would have been difficult to enforce; indeed it never was enforced against any southern state.

The third section of the Fourteenth Amendment disqualified from holding any office, state or federal, all those who had engaged in insurrection or rebellion against the United States after having previously taken the oath to support the Constitution as a member of Congress, or any state legislature, or as an executive or judicial officer of any state or the United States. Such disabilities could be removed only by a two-thirds vote of Congress—thus depriving the President of the use of his pardoning power for such cases. The final section of the act imposed economic disabilities upon the South by declaring illegal and void all debts incurred in the rebellion against the United States and invalidating any and all claims for the loss or emancipation of slaves. At the same time the validity of the debt of the United States including the payment of pensions for services in suppressing the insurrection was affirmed and, therefore, made equally binding on citizens of southern states.

Congress adopted the amendment in June, 1866, and offered it to the states for ratification. Although the President's approval is not required for constitutional amendments, Johnson took the opportunity to challenge the validity of any amendment prepared without the representation of southern states. The President's public disapproval was taken as a cue by southern states to reject the amendment; all the seceded states, except Tennessee, rejected the amendment in the ensuing eight or nine months. This was enough to defeat ratification since two border states, Kentucky and Delaware, also opposed the amendment.

Meanwhile, the problem of reconstruction became the central issue in the campaign of 1866 for the choice of a new Congress. It was an unusual campaign because, contrary to custom, President Johnson decided to throw himself vigorously into the contest with a "swing around the circle," making speeches in many key cities in the Northeast and Middle West. His speeches were made in the stump-speaking style that was appropriate for back country politics but undignified for one who held the high office of President. He often lashed back at hecklers with intemperate language that embarrassed his supporters and gave more political ammunition to his enemies.

The Congressional Elections of 1866

Despite the view of some historians that there were economic issues before the country—currency, national banks, and tariffs—that might have made a significant difference in the campaign if they had been properly managed, the evidence clearly indicates that the overriding issue of the campaign was the question of reconstruction. It seems very unlikely that Johnson could have managed any of the economic issues to his advantage, since there was intense intra-party jockeying on such questions in both the Democratic and Republican parties. But the President had no intention of trying to exploit such issues; more than

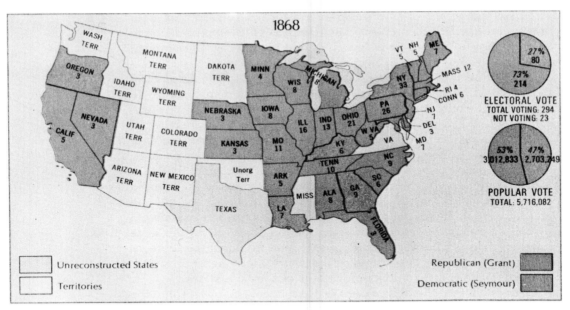

1868

ELECTORAL VOTE
TOTAL VOTING: 294
NOT VOTING: 23

27% 80

73% 214

POPULAR VOTE
TOTAL: 5,716,082

53% 3,012,833   47% 2,703,249

Unreconstructed States

Territories

Republican (Grant)

Democratic (Seymour)

From The National Atlas of the United States of America. *United States Department of the Interior Geological Survey.*

anyone else, he saw to it that reconstruction policy should be presented as the central issue of the campaign.

When the election returns were counted, the Republicans had obtained more than a two-thirds majority in both houses of Congress, carrying every Union state except Delaware, Maryland, and Kentucky. In every state where a governorship was contested, the Republicans were victorious and they carried every state legislature as well. Furthermore, Johnson's dramatic intervention in the campaign had polarized the issues relating to reconstruction so sharply that the electoral victory quickly became an irresistible force for the furtherance of a radical reconstruction program. And with more than a two-thirds majority, there was little to fear from presidential vetoes.

The Goals of Radical Reconstruction

The election of 1866, indeed, was the culmination of a process which had given sharper definition to the Republican policy of reconstruction. The pattern of events and the bitter political battles with President Johnson had moved the party toward radical conceptions. Even though cautious politicians and moderate men within the Republican party had been driven by events to go further than they intended, we must recognize that ideas of racial equality and equal rights had become living ideas in 1866 with as much urgency for many Americans as has become the case in our own time.

In many respects the idea of equal rights which was given expression in the congressional enactments of 1866 was a logical extension of the ideology of free-soil Republicanism. There were, to be sure, serious weaknesses in the Republican reconstruction program. The Fourteenth

Amendment offered broad guarantees of civil rights, but provided weak protection for black suffrage. It imposed serious political disabilities on the old ruling elites of the South, but nothing in the amendment opened the way toward the confiscation of lands and their redistribution to black freedmen.

Many historians, indeed, are reluctant to apply the term "radical" to any aspect of Reconstruction policy. But if we remember that the majority of Americans in the middle of the nineteenth century believed that both science and historical experience demonstrated the inferiority of the black, the guarantees of equal rights in the Fourteenth Amendment represented a tremendous stride toward the conception of a biracial society based upon a principle of equality. To be sure, such legal guarantees of equality would need to be supported by other political and social arrangements. There are some historians, therefore, who question the radicalism of Republican reconstruction policy because it failed to develop concepts of social planning and sustained governmental assistance that would have given the legal rights of the black freedmen a more secure social basis. A radical emancipationist like Wendell Phillips, for example, opposed any lengthy policy of freedmen's aid that would hold the black up before the country as "a chronic pauper." At another time Phillips declared that he asked "nothing more for the Negro than I ask for the Irishman or German who comes to our shores." Even Frederick Douglass, the black abolitionist, took the view that the proper policy toward the freedmen was "to do nothing with them . . . They have been undone by your doings, and all they ask and really need . . . is just to let them alone."

But we must be careful not to invoke twentieth-century conceptions of social planning in our interpretations of the process of reconstruction. The idea of social change that ruled the minds of even the most radical Republicans was one which looked to the creation of legal institutions that would define and protect the rights of citizens in their lives and callings. To be sure, the radical Republicans had their private prejudices—they were, as all of us are, imperfect men—but the best of them believed that public discrimination could be and should be legislated out of existence. Thaddeus Stevens said, "Show me . . . anything created and regulated by law, and I will show you what must be opened to all without distinction of color." By requiring courts and public authorities to uphold equal rights, the black freedman would be able to take his place in the American social system as an industrious and self-reliant individual.

The magnitude of the Republican victory in 1866 opened the way to social changes of that kind. Many Republican moderates undoubtedly would have been willing to stop with the reconstruction measures of 1866, but the rejection of the Fourteenth Amendment by the southern states left them no alternative except to pursue more drastic policies. The major measure enacted into law by the new Congress was the Military Reconstruction Act of March 2, 1867. Although some concessions were

The Measures of Radical Reconstruction

made to moderate viewpoints, the bill was essentially the product of the radical leaders' imagination. The law provided that the 10 states still designated as unreconstructed (not including Tennessee, which had ratified the Fourteenth Amendment) were to be divided into five military districts and placed under federal commanders who could make arrests, conduct trials, and carry on all civil functions necessary to protect all persons in their rights of life and property. In addition, such federal commanders were to direct the processes of constitution-making, and to require that such constitutions should be framed by delegates elected by male citizens at least 21 years of age of whatever race, color, or previous condition. All persons disqualified by the provisions of the Fourteenth Amendment were to be excluded from voting, and the new constitutions must contain the same disqualifications as well as a full elective franchise for blacks. When the qualified voters of any state had ratified such a constitution, and when a duly-elected legislature had ratified the Fourteenth Amendment, and when that Amendment had become a part of the federal Constitution, the state would become entitled to representation in Congress.

Following the passage of the Military Reconstruction Act, the radicals stepped up their agitation for a program of land reform in the South as an act of justice to the black freedmen. But they were fighting a battle against very great odds. President Johnson's amnesty proclamation had undermined all hopes for a wholesale confiscation of the lands of ex-Confederates, since it restored property rights to most rebels who would take an oath of allegiance; and his generous use of pardoning power for the excepted classes of Confederate leaders quickly removed their lands as a possible resource for the Freedmen's Bureau's resettlement activities. Furthermore, the Republican majority was reluctant to embark upon a policy that would disturb existing legal definitions of property rights.

The Republican majority preferred the approach to the problem of black land ownership that was taken with the adoption of a southern homestead act, which extended the provisions of the Homestead Law of 1862 to the public lands within Alabama, Arkansas, Florida, Louisiana, and Mississippi. For a limited period this law gave black freedmen first chance at the land, but the results were disappointing. Most of the public lands left in the southern states were of inferior quality and few freedmen had the necessary capital and farm implements to make a go of it on such lands.

Confronted by a President they did not trust, the Republican majority also enacted measures to limit the President's authority over the administrators of reconstruction policy. The Tenure of Office Act of March, 1867, declared that the President would be guilty of "high misdemeanors" if he removed without the Senate's consent any officeholder who had been appointed with the Senate's advice and consent. According to this law cabinet members were to hold office during the term of the

President by whom they were appointed and one month thereafter. On the same day, Congress enacted a Command of the Army Act, which required that all orders issued by the President or Secretary of War should be channeled through the General of the Army, who could not be removed, suspended, or relieved from his command without the consent of the Senate. It was believed by the radicals that General Grant was more sympathetic to their purpose than the President.

Johnson fought back against what he believed to be unconstitutional invasions of his presidential powers. Because Secretary of War Stanton had allied himself with the radical Republicans, the President suspended him from office and authorized General Grant to act in his place temporarily. He also dismissed Generals Sheridan and Sickles from their commands in southern military districts and replaced them with conservative generals. These efforts to control military reconstruction were unavailing, however. Grant's loyalty was questionable in view of his flirtations with radical politicians, and he embarrassed the President by withdrawing as head of the War Department when the Senate refused to confirm Stanton's suspension. Johnson then appointed General Lorenzo Thomas to the post but Stanton refused to surrender his office; he continued to conduct official business there, while General Thomas merely attended cabinet meetings.

As the new session of Congress assembled in December of 1867, impeachment emerged as the main political issue. The radical Republicans were convinced that their reconstruction policy could not be properly consummated as long as Andrew Johnson remained in the White House. They were particularly provoked by his public praise of a general he had appointed to a southern military district for issuing an order that proclaimed the supremacy of civil over military government in direct defiance of congressional reconstruction legislation.

The Impeachment of Andrew Johnson

Accordingly, the House of Representatives voted on February 24, 1868, to impeach Andrew Johnson "of high crimes and misdemeanors in office." But, in drawing up the articles of impeachment which would substantiate the charge of high treason, the House leaders found little that they could use except the apparent violation of the Tenure of Office Act through the attempted removal of Stanton, and Johnson's assertion of authority over the commanders of military districts in the South in flagrant disregard of the Command of the Army Act. Other articles accused the President of delivering "inflammatory and scandalous harangues" designed to bring Congress into disrepute.

As the trial proceeded in the Senate, the President's lawyers skillfully demonstrated the flimsiness of the charges that the President had committed any "high crimes." After all, the President is clearly designated by the Constitution as commander-in-chief of the army; and the removal of Stanton was clearly not a violation of the Tenure of Office Act since he had been appointed by Lincoln and had served more than one month beyond the term of the President by whom he had been appointed. The radicals tried very hard to persuade the Senate that impeachment should be construed as a political rather than as a legal process subject to the usual rules of evidence and definition. They convinced a majority of the Senate but not the two-thirds necessary to convict the President. Seven moderate Republicans voted with the Democrats to produce the same division on each of the articles—35 to 19 for conviction—one short of a two-thirds majority.

The Election of 1868

The Republicans, then, turned to the normal processes of politics to obtain a more satisfactory candidate. In the election of 1868, the Republican national convention nominated General Grant, the war hero, as the party's standard bearer. The party platform defended congressional reconstruction policies and denounced the "treachery" of Andrew Johnson. The Democrats nominated Horatio Seymour, the war governor of New York, who had often opposed the war policy of the Lincoln administration. In the savage campaign that followed, the Republicans portrayed the Democratic party as a treasonous political organization not fit to be trusted with the tasks of reconstruction.

When the votes were cast, Grant received 52.7 per cent of the popular vote and carried the electoral college, 214 to 80. But, without the votes of 450,000 black freedmen, he would have been a minority president. The future of the Republican party seemingly required a continuing political base in the South. After the election, therefore, the Republican Congress adopted the Fifteenth Amendment which stated that "the right of citizens of the United States to vote shall not be denied or abridged by the United States or by any State on account of race, color, or previous condition of servitude." The timing of the new suffrage amendment suggests that conceptions of power rather than of rights were beginning to predominate in the Republican program of reconstruction.

Reconstruction in the South

By 1868, six of the unreconstructed states had met the requirements of the radical program of reconstruction and were readmitted to the Union. Opposition by conservative whites to the radical terms of reconstruction in Georgia, Mississippi, Virginia, and Texas delayed their readmission to the Union for another two years. By 1870, black freedmen had been catapulted into enfranchisement in all 10 states and constituted a force to be reckoned with in the politics of the reconstructed South. The Fifteenth Amendment, approved by Congress in 1869 and ratified in 1870 by enough states including the reconstructed southern states, ostensibly protected the freedmen's right to vote against any attempts to deny or abridge it.

The Political Role of the Black Freedmen

Black suffrage and the possibility of a share in political power had become a reality, but the use of such opportunities depended upon collaborative relationships with white groups in the reconstructed states.

According to the 1860 census figures, blacks were in a majority only in South Carolina and Mississippi, and even if one accepts the high estimate that 150,000 whites throughout the South were disfranchised by the Fourteenth Amendment, such disqualifications could add a black majority only in the state of Louisiana. Thus the majority of voters in the South was always white and the creation of radical governments would always need some support from southern whites.

Furthermore, the freedmen lacked the political experience that would have provided them with any considerable cadre of political leaders. Even in the most favorable moments of political reconstruction in the South, blacks never filled state offices in proportion to their numbers within the population. Only in South Carolina did they have a legislative majority; no black was ever elected governor, though they became lieutenant governors in South Carolina, Mississippi, and Louisiana. Only 14 blacks were elected to the national House of Representatives, and two to the United States Senate during the Reconstruction period. Yet when we think of the time scale involved, it should be recognized that this was a much more rapid access to high office than was to be achieved by many immigrant groups after their enfranchisement. The greater number of black officeholders held minor offices as sheriffs, justices of the peace, members of county board of supervisors, or members of state legislatures—particularly in such states as South Carolina, Mississippi, and Louisiana. As Vernon Wharton has observed in his study of the black in Mississippi, many of these local officials were generally dominated by white Republicans, either natives or northerners.

Thus the development of politics in the reconstructed states took place in a complex pattern of relationships among blacks, white southerners willing to ally themselves with blacks, and northern whites ("carpetbaggers") who had gone South to participate in the opportunities of reconstruction. According to southern legend, the southern whites who were willing to ally themselves with blacks were "scalawags"—men of lowly social origins and questionable characters in quest of political booty and personal advancement. Undoubtedly, there were such political types in southern politics—they were, indeed, a familiar type everywhere in the American political system. But large numbers of the southern whites who were willing to cooperate with black voters in the reconstruction of the South were planters and merchants who had been pre-war southern Whigs. They were anxious to develop the southern economy in the direction already taken by the North and, since many of them were former slaveholders, they were accustomed to dealing with blacks —albeit with a somewhat paternalistic style. The northern whites included many who had gone South looking for the main chance, but others were radical emancipationsits who were committed to the radical vision of social reconstruction and who were anxious to serve as teachers, Freedmen's Bureau representatives, or in any other way that might create an acceptable social order based on equal rights. Of course, they

The Political Role of Carpetbaggers and Scalawags

were much more radical in temperament and tactics than the Whiggish "scalawags."

Indeed many of the southern Whigs found it difficult to establish a satisfactory relationship with the radical Republicans. They resented the growing influence of northern carpetbaggers among the blacks and they soon found themselves elbowed aside from posts of leadership within the Republican party. Some efforts were made by southern Whigs to establish a third party which would appeal to blacks while avoiding some of the extravagances of the carpetbagger governments. The most ambitious of these attempts was the "Unification Movement" of 1873 in Louisiana which promised to guarantee black political rights and to end discrimination in education, employment, and land ownership. But the movement failed because the blacks felt that the radical carpetbaggers could and would offer them more; furthermore the "Unification Movement " had little chance of attracting the majority of the whites because they were unwilling to support broad concessions of political rights to the blacks. Frustrated in their efforts to win power within the Republican party, or to start up a third party, the Whiggish planters and businessmen drifted into the Democratic party.

Economic Forces in Southern Reconstruction

Beneath these complex political developments lay the rivalry of economic groups seeking to win control of profitable opportunities in the post-war development of the South. There was acute competition for such favors as public printing contracts, contracts for hiring prison labor, or for marketing public bonds. The most intense of these economic rivalries involved grants of land and money to railroads. Railroad building was a crucial aspect of the modernization of the South after the Civil War, not only because of the opportunities for profit in railroad speculation but also because the new transportation systems were linked to the control of other strategic economic resources. Thus in Alabama, where the political history of reconstruction is usually pictured as a contest between white conservatives and a radical coalition of carpetbaggers and blacks, the underlying rivalry of railroad interests was more crucial in shaping the economic and social future of the state. The stakes were very high because the principal rivals for state favors wanted rail access to the rich ore deposits of the Birmingham area. This rich prize also attracted important outside capital—one group of railroad promoters was financed by August Belmont and Democratic capitalists of New York, while another was backed by Jay Cooke, a leading northern Republican financier.

The fraud and graft associated with this competition for railroad charters and state subsidies for railroad building contributed to the legend of corruption that was used so effectively against the radical Republican governments in the South by the conservative white "redeemers." But the political operations associated with the southern railroads during the Reconstruction era were part of the general pattern that prevailed everywhere in the American economy as it entered upon a cyclonic period of development. The forces of an expanding capitalism, eager to secure quick results in growth and profits, created enormous pressures on the political system at all levels. Furthermore, it is impossible to distinguish between radical Republicans and conservative Democrats in their willingness to respond to such pressures in the southern states. The political victory of redeemer movements often marked the victory for another set of railroad promoters.

The "black legend of Reconstruction" developed by white "redeemers" also included the charge that the radical regimes left the southern states saddled with huge debts that were the result of financial extravagance and fraud. There certainly were crude instances of bribery and graft in the South during this period, yet they are relatively modest in comparison with the unrestrained looting of the Tweed Ring in New York, or the Whiskey Ring during the Grant administration. Indeed, all parties shared in the looting without distinction as to race, class, or previous condition. "Why damn it," said Henry Clay Warmouth, the carpetbagger governor of Louisiana, "everybody is demoralizing down here. Corruption is the fashion." Furthermore, it must be remembered that the larger portion of the state debts consisted of bonds issued by the state government to support railroad construction, bonds that were secured by liens on the property of the railroads.

Railroad building increased in the South after the Civil War. Freight train on Orange and Alexandria Railroad, Culpepper Court House, Virginia, 1862. From the Brady Collection. Library of Congress.

It is true that state expenditures in the South increased markedly in the reconstruction period but that was partly the result of greatly increased appropriations for public education, public works, and other social services in which the ante-bellum South had been laggard compared to the North. In South Carolina the number of children attending public schools increased from 30,000 to 123,000 between 1868 and 1876, with more than half of the larger total composed of black pupils. These changes in the scale of public services manifested the modernizing of southern state governments that was bringing them in step with the growth of public services in the rest of the country.

Similar changes can be seen in the framing of new constitutions for the southern states. In addition to clauses granting blacks the same civil and political rights as white men, there were changes which eliminated undemocratic features that had persisted in the southern political system in the ante-bellum years. Inequitable systems of apportionment that had discriminated against back country districts were corrected, and in the older South, many offices that had been appointive were made elective—thus reducing the power of the county courthouse oligarchies. Tax systems, penal codes, and judicial systems were also reformed.

Hence the achievements of reconstruction politics in the southern states were many and lasting, but the radical Republicans were unable to develop a permanent political base. Their power rested on the black vote, Republican control of the national government, and the presence of federal troops in the South. And since the carpetbaggers were unable to establish a stable alliance with Whiggish planters and merchants, they became increasingly vulnerable to attacks by a hostile white majority.

*The Restoration
of White
Supremacy*

In the states where the whites constituted a large majority, the overthrow of the radical Republican governments was easily accomplished by the normal process of organizing and winning elections. Their success was facilitated by the willingness of Congress to enact an amnesty act, in 1872, that restored political rights to all but 500 of 150,000 ex-Confederates who had composed the old leadership structure of the South. Tennessee, Virginia, and North Carolina passed under conservative control by 1870; Georgia followed in 1871. But in states where blacks made up a majority of the population, or where the population differences between the races were not great, the struggle was prolonged, bitter, and frequently violent because organized white groups used tactics of terror and intimidation.

The most sensational of the organized methods of intimidation and violence was the activity of secret terroristic societies like the Ku Klux Klan or the Knights of the White Camelia. The Klan was the most notorious of these, attracting widespread attention because of its weird rituals, outlandish titles—"Grand Dragons," "Titans," "Cyclops"—and the white robes and hoods worn by Klansmen. Riding at night they intimidated blacks and punished scalawags: they often whipped, tortured, and even killed their victims. Such crude uses of violence, however, strengthened the political position of the radical Republicans because it shocked northern opinion and led to congressional legislation designed to stamp out terrorism.

Two national "force bills," passed in 1870 to 1871, provided heavy penalties of fine and imprisonment for anyone who tried to hinder or prevent citizens from voting by force or intimidation; the President was empowered to use federal troops to enforce the acts. In 1871, Congress passed a third force act aimed particularly at secret terroristic societies. In great detail, the law defined such groups as conspirational and their actions as tantamount to rebellion; in addition, the President was authorized to suspend the writ of *habeas corpus* for the suppression of such "armed combinations." On the basis of this act, nine counties in South Carolina were put under virtual martial rule and the *habeas corpus* process suspended; hundreds of arrests were made and sentences of fines and imprisonment were imposed on 82 persons. But any sustained use of the first two force bills was greatly weakened by the Supreme Court's decision in *United States* v. *Reese* (1876) that the Fifteenth Amendment did not give the federal government unlimited power of intervention to unlimited guarantee the right of suffrage.

By using methods of intimidation that would not provoke federal intervention, most of the southern states had been restored to white control by 1876: Arkansas, Alabama, and Texas were "redeemed" in 1874, and Mississippi followed in 1875. In that year, only Louisiana, South Carolina, and Florida had radical governments and it was probably only a matter of time—a short time—before these remnants of radical political rule would be swept away.

To be sure, the radical reconstructionists, with few exceptions, never conceived of military reconstruction as being anything more than a temporary stage—they were attempting to make a democratic, not a totalitarian, revolution. Hence they hoped to see the social changes that they had imposed in the South established as quickly as possible within a framework of legitimacy; the law court and the ballot box, rather than the bayonet and arbitrary arrest, were to be the main weapons to defend the new social arrangements. It was not an unrealistic conception but one which had a chance of success only if supported by a sustained effort to maintain a political base in the South. It seems questionable to assume, as many historians do, that the crucial fault in the radical reconstruction program was the failure to give the black freedmen his 40 acres and a mule. Such small property ownership could not have protected them from the inexorable economic pressures that would force a high proportion of southern farmers into the harsh conditions of tenancy and sharecropping. What was needed was a continued political activity in the South, even as a minority party, in order to maintain a political environment in which access to the ballot box and to due process of law could be defended. Minority power is not necessarily ineffectual and the radical Republicans might have been able to make effective use of

The Waning of Radicalism

minority power in the South particularly if they had the continued support of a united national party in control of the federal government.

One of the many ironies in the reconstruction story is that some of the radical Republicans took the first steps toward destroying the political alliances on which the Republican political position in the South depended. During the first Grant administration a new set of leaders won a dominant position in the presidential circle. These were men who were most responsive to the economic pressures created by the cyclonic growth of American capitalism after the Civil War. They helped to make Congress, the state legislatures, and state political machines the willing collaborators of railroad, oil, textile, and steel interests that wanted government favors. The older crusading radicals found this new Republican leadership appalling, particularly as evidence of corruption began to come to light. "Like all parties that have an undisturbed power for a long time," wrote Senator James Grimes of Iowa, "[the Republican party] has become corrupt, and I believe it is today the most corrupt and debauched political party that has ever existed."

The revulsion against these tendencies in the Republican party caused some of the old radicals to repudiate Grant in 1872 and to form the so-called Liberal Republican party that nominated Horace Greeley for the presidency. In varying ways, old radicals like Carl Schurz, George Julian, Charles Sumner, and Theodore Tilton gave moral and political support to the Liberal Republican movement. Many of the Liberal Republicans were particularly disillusioned with the carpetbag governments in the South because of their corruption, and they were deeply disappointed that "the black freedmen," as Carl Schurz stated, "are blindly following the lead of unscrupulous and rapacious demagogues."

The kind of dignity Washington wanted for the Chief Executive came first in the development of the city named after him, this printed 50 years later. The I. N. Phelps Stokes Collection of American Historical Prints. Prints Division. The New York Public Library.

Although the Grant Republicans won the election of 1872, the party schism, combined with the recovery of the national Democratic party, undermined the effectiveness of the Republican party in the South. Factional quarrels in Congress set off feuds and division within the Republican party organizations in the South that weakened them in the face of the gathering strength of the white conservatives.

Hence the end of federal intervention was a foregone conclusion by the time of the presidential election of 1876. The Republicans nominated Rutherford Hayes, who had established a reputation for personal moral rectitude as governor of Ohio, and who was conciliatory in his attitude toward southern whites. Indeed, many of his political advisers were pressing him to attract the support of old line southern Whigs by promises of federal aid for internal improvements—clearing rivers and harbors along the Mississippi River and subsidizing large railroad projects. Without committing himself to any specific bargains, Hayes indicated his sympathy for a policy of internal improvements. When he failed to win a majority of the electoral votes in the disputed election of 1876, his supporters in Congress had to offer assurances that Hayes would remove federal troops from the South and include southerners in the distribution of federal patronage; in return they were assured of southern acquiescence was expected in the decision of the electoral commission concerning the disputed electoral votes of South Carolina, Louisiana, and Florida.

The Compromise of 1877

The "Compromise of 1877" that brought Hayes to the presidency with a promise to withdraw remaining federal troops in the South signified a symbolic ending to radical reconstruction. There was no immediate abandonment of black political and civil rights, however, for they continued to vote in large numbers in many parts of the South for nearly two decades. Indeed they continued to hold minor offices and to keep at least one black representative in Congress until the end of the century. Yet, what was lacking was any effective political connection between blacks and the Republican party. Some of the Republican carpetbaggers in the South tried desperately to build a new political base in alliance with the poorer farmers who supported agrarian political movements as a means of expressing their social discontents. But such "radicalism" alienated even the liberal Republicans of the North who were, by and large, committed to "sound money" principles. Ironically, southern conservatives—especially those of paternalistic Whig backgrounds— were able to rally large numbers of black voters against these discontented lower-class whites who were not noted for their love of the blacks.

On the eve of these changes, old Republican radicals chose to devote most of their energy to the enactment of a civil rights law that would strengthen the possibilities for equality and justice through legal processes. The new civil rights law was Charles Sumner's brainchild, even though he did not live to see the measure finally adopted. From the beginning of radical reconstruction, Sumner had believed that the

The Fate of the Civil Rights Act of 1875

political and civil rights of the black could never be fully effective unless all forms of racial segregation were outlawed. He battled incessantly to desegregate the schools of the District of Columbia, and he urged his colleagues to subsidize biracial public schools. Above all, he fought for the adoption of a comprehensive Civil Rights Act that would proscribe all forms of segregation.

In 1875, the year after Sumner's death, Congress finally passed a Civil Rights Act whose preamble declared that "it is essential to just government [that] we recognize the equality of all men before the law, and hold that it is the duty of government in its dealings with the people to mete out equal and exact justice to all, of whatever nativity, race, color, or persuasion, religious and political." The act therefore declared that all persons, regardless of race or color, should be guaranteed "the full and equal enjoyment of the accommodations, advantages, facilities, and privileges of inns, public conveyances on land or water, theatres and other places of public amusement." It also prohibited the discrimination on account of race for jury services but failed to include any reference to public education—thus defeating one of Sumner's most cherished hopes.

The Civil Rights Act was the last radical effort to create a legal environment that was inimical to racial discrimination. There is no way of knowing whether such legal sanctions could have affected the dynamics of racial adjustment because the act was invalidated by the Supreme Court in 1883. In the civil rights cases of that year the Court ruled that the Civil Rights Act was void because the Fourteenth Amendment was "prohibitory upon the states" but not upon private individuals. By declaring that no state could "abridge the privileges and immunities of citizens," or deny them the "equal protection of the laws," the amendment only prohibited invasion of private rights by state action. "Individual invasion of individual rights," the majority opinion declared, "is not the subject matter of the amendment." In effect, this opinion served notice that the federal government could not lawfully protect the black against discrimination which might be exercised against him by quasi-public accommodations or facilities that were privately-owned. The Court, however, did not invalidate that part of the Act which prohibited the exclusion of blacks from jury service, nor did the decision foreclose the possibility of legislation barring segregation in public schools.

The Supreme Court decision had far-reaching implications, for it removed important legal and psychological barriers that might have impeded the development of a rigid pattern of racial segregation in the American social system. The failure of the Civil Rights Act also underscored the tragic error of the liberal Republicans in abandoning a political base in the South. Without a friendly judiciary, organized political action was the only hope of achieving the construction of a social order in which blacks could enjoy access to the opportunities of American life in a way that might be roughly parallel to the experience of immigrants.

Selected Bibliography

The books cited in this section of the bibliography are designed to direct the reader to useful reference works and to comprehensive studies of special aspects of American history.

The most comprehensive bibliographic guide for works of history is Frank Freidel, ed., *The Harvard Guide to American History* (1974). Allen Johnson and Dumas Malone (eds.), *Dictionary of American Biography* (21 vols., 1928–1944) is an indispensable source for biographical information on the lives of leading Americans. Richard B. Morris (ed.), *Encyclopedia of American History* (1965) is a useful encyclopedic work. *The National Atlas of the United States of America* (1970) is a valuable compendium of maps and charts. *The American Heritage Pictorial Atlas of American History* (1966) is a superb collection of historical maps. Indispensable for theories and concepts of the social sciences is the new *International Encyclopedia of the Social Sciences* (17 vols., 1968). A brief *Dictionary of the Social Sciences* (1964) edited by Julius Gould and William L. Kolb is also very useful.

For constitutional history, A. H. Kelly and W. A. Harbison, *The American Constitution, Its Origins and Development* (4th ed., 1970) is excellent for its comprehensive treatment and extended bibliography. Also useful is A. T. Mason and William Beany, *The Supreme Court in a Free Society* (1959).

For political parties, W. E. Binkley, *American Political Parties: Their Natural History* (1963) is a standard work which should be supplemented by William N. Chambers and Walter Dean Burnham (eds.), *The American Party Systems; stages of political development* (1967).

For political ideas, Richard Hofstadter's *The American Political Tradition* (1948) and Louis Hartz, *The Liberal Tradition in America* (1955) provide provocative interpretations. One should also consult Allen Guttmann, *The Conservative Tradition in America* (1967), and Russell Kirk, *The Conservative Mind, from Burke to Santayana* (1954).

For diplomatic history, Alexander De Conde, *A History of American Foreign Policy* (1963) and R. W. Leopold, *The Growth of American Foreign Policy* (1962) are good recent works. Two older texts, Thomas A. Bailey, *A Diplomatic History of the American People* (8th ed., 1969) and J. W. Pratt, *A History of United States Foreign Policy* (2nd ed., 1965) are also useful.

For economic history, the eight volumes in Henry David et al. (eds.), *The Economic History of the United States* (1945–1962) are indispensable. E. C. Kirkland, *A History of American Economic Life* (1951) and R. M. Robertson, *History of the American Economy* (1964) are good one-volume studies. J. G. Rayback, *A History of American Labor* (1959) is a useful one-volume study of labor. For manufactures consult V. S. Clark, *History of Manufacturers in the United States* (3 vols., 1929). Paul F. Studentski and H. E. Krooss, *Financial History of the United States* (1963) is very useful for financial and monetary history. The best study of westward expansion in all its aspects is R. A. Billington, *Westward Expansion* (1967). Joseph Dorfman, *The Economic Mind in American Civilization* (5 vols., 1946–1959) is a comprehensive analysis of economic ideas.

For immigration, consult Carl Wittke, *We Who Built America* (1940) and Marcus L. Hansen, *The Atlantic Migration, 1607–1860* (1940), as well as Oscar Handlin, *Immigration as a Factor in American History* (1959). John H. Franklin, *From Slavery to Freedom: A History of American Negroes* (1956) and Benjamin Quarles, *The Negro in the Making of America* (1964) are comprehensive works on the historical experience of blacks in Africa and America.

For intellectual and cultural history, Vernon L. Parrington, *Main Currents in American Thought* (3 vols., 1927–1930) is a classic work. Merle Curti, *The Growth of American Thought* (1964) is very useful on popular thought. R. E. Spiller et al., *Literary History of the United States* (3 vols., 1943) is a comprehensive survey of literature with a rich bibliography. Herbert W. Schneider, *A History of American Philosophy* (1946), and Joseph Blau, *Men and Movements in American Philosophy* (1952) are good studies of philosophic ideas. Oliver Larkin, *Art and Life in America* (1949) and James Burchard and Albert Bush Brown, *The Architecture of America, A Social and Cultural History* (1966) are comprehensive histories that locate art and architecture in the social history of America. Frank Luther Mott's *A History of American Magazines* (4 vols., 1930–1957) is a useful survey of magazine literature and art. His *American Journalism* (1962) is an excellent survey of newspaper history.

References by
Chapters

The works cited under the following chapter headings include the principal books from which I have taken my factual data and many of my interpretations. But the major purpose of the listing is to aid those who might wish to discover more about points of interpretation that are obviously problematic or events that are passed over lightly. Significant recent books are cited together in the supplemental bibliography for the second edition at the end of the chapter references.

1. The European Discovery of America

The study of European conceptions of the Atlantic and the New World has had a stimulating revival in recent years with the publication of *The*

Vinland Map and *Tartar Relation* (1965) by the Yale University Library, with valuable commentaries by Raleigh A. Skelton, Thomas E. Marston, and George D. Painter. Samuel Eliot Morison, *The European Discovery of America: The Northern Voyages, A.D. 500–1600* (1971) provides an authoritative account of early European geographical conceptions of the Atlantic as well as the early voyages across the North Atlantic. William Babcock's *Legendary Islands of the Atlantic* (1922) and John Kirtland Wright's *The Geographical Lore at the Time of the Crusades* (1925) are still useful. A fascinating recent study of European geographical conceptions is Vincent H. Cassidy's *The Sea Around Them* (1968). The part played by the myth of the New World in European thought has recently been reexamined by the distinguished Mexican historian, Edmundo O'Gorman, in his book entitled *The Invention of America* (1961), and by the English historian J. H. Elliott in his *The Old World and the New, 1492–1650* (1970).

The gathering forces of European expansion, political and cultural, are brilliantly summarized by W. H. McNeil in *The Rise of the West* (1963). Robert R. Reynolds' *Europe Emerges: Transition Toward an Industrial World-Wide Society, 600–1750* (1961) provides an excellent analysis of the economic bases of European expansion. On the Portuguese explorations, Edgar Prestage's *The Portuguese Pioneers* (1933) provides a general survey, but even more useful are Samuel E. Morison's *Portuguese Voyages to America before 1500* (1940), and Elaine Sanceau's *The Land of Prester John, A Chronicle of Portuguese Exploration* (1944). Samuel E. Morison's two-volume study of Columbus, *Admiral of the Ocean Sea* (1942) provides an indispensable introduction to Spanish exploration. John Bartlett Brebner's *The Explorers of North America* (1933) is very useful for inland explorations. Frederick A. Pohl's *Amerigo Vespucci, Pilot Major* (1944) contains useful information on the voyages of Vespucci and the naming of America.

William H. Prescott's classic accounts of the conquistadors, *History of the Conquest of Mexico* (3 vols., 1843) and *History of the Conquest of Peru* (2 vols., 1847) are still fascinating to read and are available in many modern editions. Both histories also contain valuable descriptions of the high Indian cultures in Mexico and Peru. A first-hand account of the conquest of Mexico is Bernal Diaz del Castillo's *The Discovery and Conquest of Mexico,* as edited by I. A. Leonard (1956). This should be read in conjunction with M. Leon Portilla's *The Broken Spears, The Aztec Account of the Conquest of Mexico* (1962). Good studies of the Spanish empire in its various aspects are E. Dwight Salmon's *Imperial Spain* (1931), Frederick A. Kirkpatrick's *The Spanish Conquistadores* (1939), Lesley B. Simpson's *The Encomienda in New Spain* (1950), and John H. Parry's *The Spanish Seaborne Empire* (1960). Spain's French and Dutch rivals in the New World are satisfactorily described in George M. Wrong's *The Rise and Fall of New France* (2 vols., 1928) and Charles R. Boxer's *The Dutch Seaborne Empire: 1600–1800* (1965). Francis Parkman's classic work, *Pioneers of France in the New World* (1865 and later editions), deserves to be read as much as the works of his contemporary, W. H. Prescott.

On the background of English expansion, Wallace Notestein's *The English People on the Eve of Colonization, 1603–1630* (1951) and Carl Bridenbaugh's *Vexed and Troubled Englishmen, 1500–1642* (1968) are virtually indispensable. William Haller's *The Rise of Puritanism* (1938) is still the most thorough account of English Puritanism. A brief and perceptive book on the same subject is Alan Simpson's *Puritanism in Old and New England* (1955). For social and economic developments in England, Ralph A. Tawney's *The Agricultural Problem in the Sixteenth Century* (1917) is still useful despite the controversy it has provoked among modern historians. Mildred Campbell's *The English Yeoman Under Elizabeth and the Early Stuarts* (1942) should also be consulted. John U. Nef's *Industry and Government in France and England, 1540–1690* (1940) is valuable on industrial and commercial developments. Christopher Hill's *The Century of Revolution, 1603–1714* (1961) contains an excellent analysis of social, economic, and political developments in England.

A. L. Rowse's *The Expansion of Elizabethan England* (1955) and *The Elizabethans and America* (1959) are highly readable accounts of the English enterprisers who risked their reputations and their fortunes in the New World. James A. Williamson's *The Age of Drake* (1938) and David B. Quinn's *Raleigh and the British Empire* (1947) portray the adventurous spirit of English explorations. On the earliest settlements, Wesley Frank Craven's *The Southern Colonies in the Seventeenth Century, 1607–1689* (1949) is an excellent starting point particularly for Jamestown and Virginia. Thomas J. Wertenbaker has written a social history of the founding of the colonies in three books—*The Founding of American Civilization: The Middle Colonies* (1938), *The Old South* (1942), and *The Puritan Oligarchy* (1947). The first three volumes of Charles M. Andrews' *The Colonial Period of American History* (1934–1937) are particularly valuable for their careful and thorough scrutiny of charters, legislative and court records. On Plymouth colony, Samuel Eliot Morison's edition of William Bradford's *Of Plymouth Plantation* (1952) allows us to see the experience of the Pilgrims through the eyes of their governor. George F. Willison's *Saints and Strangers* (1945) is a useful modern account of the Plymouth venture; and John P. Demos, in *A Little Commonwealth* (1970), develops a fascinating analysis of family and society in Plymouth colony.

2. Society-Building in a Virgin Land

Accounts of the "great migration" to the colonies may be found in Arthur P. Newton's contribution to Volume I of the *Cambridge History of* the British Empire (1929) and in the opening chapters of Marcus L. Hansen's *The Atlantic Migration, 1607–1860* (1940). For estimates of population growth and distribution during the seventeenth century, one should consult Evarts B. Greene and Virginia Harrington, *American Population Before the Federal Census of 1790* (1932) and Stella Sutherland, *Population Distribution in Colonial America* (1936).

The land tenure systems of the seventeenth-century colonies are described in Marshall Harris, *Origin of the Land Tenure System in the United States* (1953). The first three volumes of Charles M. Andrews, *The Colonial Period of American History* (1934–1937) also contain much useful information about patterns of land tenure; the same is true of Thomas J. Wertenbaker's three volumes on *The Founding of American Civilization* (1938–1947) and Wesley Frank Craven's *Southern Colonies in the Seventeenth Century* (1949). Richard Morris analyzes some of the changes in English property law in the colonies in his *Studies in the History of American Law* (1930). Beverly Bond's *The Quit-Rent System in the American Colonies* (1919) is useful for an understanding of some of the quasi-feudal aspects of land tenure.

The diversifying patterns of seventeenth-century economic activity are examined in such works as the following: Bernard Bailyn, *The New England Merchants in the Seventeenth Century* (1955); Richard Pares, *Merchants and Planters* (1960); Charles B. Judah, *The North Atlantic Fisheries and British Policy to 1713* (1933); Carl Bridenbaugh, *The Colonial Craftsman* (1950); Percy W. Bidwell and John I. Falconer, *History of Agriculture in the Northern United States, 1620–1860* (1925); and Lewis G. Gray, *History of Agriculture in the Southern United States* (2 vols., 1933).

Recent views on the social structure of seventeenth-century America may be found in the excellent collection of essays edited by James M. Smith, *Seventeenth Century America, Essays in Colonial History* (1959). Analyses of social classes and social attitudes also may be found in Carl Bridenbaugh, *Cities in the Wilderness, The First Century of Urban Life in America, 1625–1742* (1938); Thomas J. Wertenbaker, *The Planters of Colonial Virginia* (1922); and two works by Louis B. Wright, *The First Gentlemen of Virginia* (1940) and *The Atlantic Frontier* (1947). Abbot E. Smith's *Colonists in Bondage: White Servitude and Convict Labor in America, 1607–1776* (1947) depicts the conditions of lower orders in the population. Illuminating chapters on the origins and rationale of black slavery and race prejudice can be found in John Hope Franklin, *From Slavery to Freedom: A History of American Negroes* (1947); Stanley Elkins, *Slavery: A Problem in American Institutional and Intellectual Life* (1959); and Winthrop Jordan, *White Over Black: American Attitudes Towards the Negro, 1550–1812* (1968). Wilcomb E. Washburn has an excellent essay on Indian-white relations in Smith's collection of essays on *Seventeenth Century America*, and one should also consult his recent work entitled *Red Man's Land, White Man's Law* (1971).

3. The Political Culture of Seventeenth-Century America

John A Pomfret, *Founding the American Colonies, 1583–1660* (1970), provides a well-rounded account of the development of political and social institutions in the seventeenth century. The opening chapters in Daniel Boorstin, *The Americans, The Colonial Experience* (1958) contain some provocative ideas about the political cultures formed by Puritans, Quakers, and Virginians in the New World.

Wesley Frank Craven's *The Southern Colonies in the Seventeenth Century* (already cited) is indispensable for political developments in Virginia, Maryland, and the Carolinas. The first volume of Richard Morton's *Colonial Virginia* (1960) also is useful for Virginia, as is Elizabeth Baer's *Seventeenth Century Maryland* (1949) for Maryland.

The political history of Puritan New England has aroused considerable controversy among historians. As a result, many excellent works are available on Puritan political culture. Two older works that are still useful are James T. Adams, *The Founding of New England* (1921) and Samuel E. Morison, *The Builders of the Bay Colony* (1930). The first volume of Charles M. Andrews' *Colonial Period of American History* is valuable for the earlier years of Massachusetts Bay Colony and Thomas J. Wertenbaker carries the story further in *The Puritan Oligarchy* (1947). Edward S. Morgan's *The Puritan Dilemma: The Story of John Winthrop* (1958) is a biography that contains a very perceptive analysis of the political and legal institutions created by the Puritans. Ola Winslow's *Master Roger Williams* (1957) and Samuel H. Brockunier's *The Irrepressible Democrat: Roger Williams* (1940) develop different approaches to one aspect of the turmoil in the early years of the Bay Colony. Perceptive analyses of the antinomian controversy may be found in Larzer Ziff, *The Career of John Cotton: Puritanism and the American Experience* (1962) and Emery Battis, *Saints and Sectaries: Anne Hutchinson and the Antinomian Controversy in Massachusetts Bay Colony* (1962).

The works of Andrews and Wertenbaker (already cited) on the founding of the seventeenth-century colonies are valuable for developments in the middle colonies. The first two volumes of Alexander C. Flick (ed.), *History of the State of New York* (10 vols., 1933–1937) provide a reliable history of the political life of New York colony under the Dutch and the English. A good modern work on Pennsylvania is Edwin B. Bronner's *William Penn's "Holy Experiment," The Founding of Pennsylvania, 1681–1701* (1962).

For conceptions of authority and the religious basis of authority, one should consult Perry Miller's works on the intellectual history of the Puritans. Particularly useful is his excellent anthology of Puritan writing edited in collaboration with T. H. Johnson, *The Puritans* (1938). Other works by Miller that should be consulted are *Orthodoxy in Massachusetts, 1630–1650* (1933); *The New England Mind: The Seventeenth Century* (1939); and *The New England Mind, From Colony to Province* (1953).

Michael Walzer's *The Revolution of the Saints; A Study of the Origins of Radical Politics* (1965) is valuable for an understanding of the political conceptions of English Puritanism at the time the New England colonies were established. Edward S. Morgan's *The Puritan Dilemma* (already cited) contains a very perceptive analysis of Winthrop's conceptions of authority. An excellent examination of Quaker ideas may be found in Frederick B. Tolles, *Meeting House and Counting House: Quaker Merchants of Colonial Philadelphia* (1948) and his *Quakers and the Atlantic Culture* (1960). Louis B. Wright's *The First Gentlemen of Virginia* (already cited) contains some excellent chapters on the intellectual life of the planter elite.

An excellent account of Bacon's rebellion may be found in Wilcomb E. Washburn's *The Governor and The Rebel* (1957). Washburn's account is less favorable to Bacon than Thomas J. Wertenbaker's earlier book on Bacon's rebellion entitled *Torchbearer of the Revolution* (1940). The insurrection in New York colony at the time of the Glorious Revolution is examined in Jerome A. Reich's *Leisler's Rebellion, A Study of Democracy in New York, 1664–1720* (1953). Viola F. Barnes' *The Dominion of New England* (1928) is still the best account of the political turmoil in New England under Governor Andros.

The development of England's new imperial regulations in the last half of the seventeenth century may be traced through several important special studies: Lawrence A. Harper, *The English Navigation Laws, A Seventeenth Century Experiment in Social Engineering* (1939); Maurice Ashley, *Financial and Commercial Policy under the Cromwellian Protectorate* (1934); and M. G. Hall, *Edward Randolph and the American Colonies, 1676–1703* (1960). G. L. Beer's older study, *The Old Colonial System* (2 vols., 1912) is still useful. The same is true of James A. Williamson's chapters in Volume I of the *Cambridge History of the British Empire* (1963).

4. Learning and Literature in Seventeenth-Century America

Lawrence Cremin's *American Education: The Colonial Experience, 1697–1783* (1971) is the most complete and up-to-date study of colonial education available. Bernard Bailyn's *Education in the Forming of American Society* (1960) is a fascinating exploration of education in the colonial social order. The first five chapters of Newton Edwards and Herman Richey, *The School in the American Social Order* (1963 ed.) provide a good general account of colonial educational institutions and practices. Samuel Eliot Morison's *Harvard College in the Seventeenth Century* (2 vols., 1936) is an indispensable work on higher education. The opening chapters in Richard Hofstadter's *Academic Freedom in the Age of the College* (1955) provide an excellent brief analysis of conceptions and practices of higher education at the time the first colonial colleges were founded. There is a very useful section on Puritan education in the Miller and Johnson anthology on *The Puritans*.

Perry Miller's two volumes on *The New England Mind* occupy a commanding position among works on Puritan intellectual life, but Samuel Eliot Morison's *The Intellectual Life of Puritan New England* (1956 ed.), formerly entitled *The Puritan Pronaos,* is still the liveliest account of Puritan thought and literature. Both Miller and Morison contain chapters on the Salem witchcraft episode and the scientific interest of the Puritans. Marion L. Starkey's *The Devil in Massachusetts* (1950) presents a full and accurate account of the Salem witchcraft trials. Richard H. Shryock and Otho Beall, Jr., have extended our knowledge of colonial science and medicine with their volume on *Cotton Mather: The First Significant Figure in American Medicine* (1954).

The literature of seventeenth-century America is competently surveyed and analyzed in the opening sections of Robert Spiller, et al. (eds.), *Literary History of the United States* (3 vols., 1948). But Moses Coit Tyler's *History of American Literature, 1607–1763* (2 vols., 1878–1879) is a masterpiece that no modern student can afford to ignore. Kenneth Murdock's *Literature and Theology in Colonial New England* (1949) is an excellent brief study of the literary achievement of the New England Puritans. Louis B. Wright's *The First Gentlemen of Virginia* (1940) contains some excellent chapters on literature and learning in Virginia and we are indebted to him for an excellent modern edition of Robert Beverly's *The History and Present State of Virginia* (1947). The best biography of Cotton Mather is still the one published in 1891 by Barrett Wendell under the title, *Cotton Mather, the Puritan Priest,* but it should be supplemented by the relevant chapters in Perry Miller's *The New England Mind, From Colony to Province.* Of course, no one should miss the chance to sample Cotton Mather's *Magnalia Christi Americana,* now available in several reprints (1967). A good sampling of Mather's writings is available in Kenneth Murdock's *Selections from Cotton Mather* (1926).

5. The Course of Empire

Two recent books provide useful accounts of the imperial wars between England and France: Edward P. Hamilton, *The French and Indian Wars* (1962), and Howard Peckham, *The Colonial Wars, 1689–1762* (1964). Francis Parkman's classic history of *France and England in North America* (9 vols., 1869–1892) is still worth reading, but the highlights of his many volumes can be sampled in *The Parkman Reader* (1955) edited by Samuel Eliot Morison. John B. Brebner's *New England's Outpost: Acadia Before the Conquest of Canada* (1927) is a useful book on one of the focal points of conflict, and George M. Waller's *Samuel Vetch: Colonial Enterprises*

(1960) explores British policies during Queen Anne's War. Richard Pares, *War and Trade in The West Indies, 1739–1763* (1936) examines another focal point of conflict. Lawrence Henry Gipson's two volumes on "The Great War for Empire" (vols. 6 and 7 of his *The British Empire Before the American Revolution,* 14 vols., 1936–1968) are superb works of scholarship. Walter L. Dorn's *Competition For Empire, 1740–1763* (1940) is a good single-volume study of the European background of Anglo-French rivalry.

The fourth volume of Charles M. Andrews' *The Colonial Period of American History* (1938) contains an excellent account of England's commercial and colonial policy after the reorganizing legislation of 1696. Also useful is an older work by Oliver M. Dickerson, *American Colonial Government, 1696–1765, a Study of the British Board of Trade in its Relations to the American Colonies, Political, Industrial, Administrative* (1912). Two books by Leonard W. Labaree provide a comprehensive analysis of royal government in the colonies: *Royal Government in America* (1930) and *Royal Instructions to British Governors, 1670–1776,* (2 vols., 1935). Good studies of royal governors may be found in Leonidas Dodson, *Alexander Spotswood* (1932), and John Schutz's *Thomas Pownall* (1951) and *William Shirley* (1961).

Lawrence Henry Gipson's volumes on *The British Empire Before the American Revolution* (1936–1968) are a storehouse of information on colonial economic life—agriculture, commerce, and manufacturing—as it was affected by British mercantilism. The activities of enterprising colonial merchants are explored in Byron Fairchild, *Messrs. William Pepperell: Merchants at Piscataqua* (1954); James B. Hedges, *The Browns of Providence Plantations: Colonial Years* (1952); and Frederick B. Tolles, *Meeting House and Counting House: The Quaker Merchants of Colonial Philadelphia, 1682–1763* (1948). William B. Weeden's *Economic and Social History of New England, 1620–1789* (2 vols., 1890) remains a basic work on economic developments in New England.

The opening chapters of Marcus L. Hansen, *The Atlantic Migration, 1607–1860* (1940) and Carl Wittke, *We Who Built America: The Saga of the Immigrants* (1939) provide useful surveys of immigration to the English colonies in the eighteenth century. The Scotch-Irish are reexamined in James G. Leyburn's recent work, *The Scotch Irish: A Social History* (1962). Frederick Klees' *Pennsylvania Dutch* (1950) is also useful, as is an early description of german migrants to Pennsylvania by Gottlieb Mittelberger, *Journey to Pennsylvania,* recently edited (1960) by Oscar Handlin and John Cleve. Recent studies of Scotch emigrants are available in Ian C. C. Graham, *Colonists from Scotland: Emigration to North America, 1707–1783* (1956) and Duane Meyer, *The Highland Scots of North Carolina, 1732–1776* (1961).

The religious ferment associated with the great awakening is well presented in such works as Edwin S. Gaustad, *The Great Awakening in New England* (1957); Charles H. Maxson, *The Great Awakening in the*

Middle Colonies (1920); Wesley M. Gewehr, *The Great Awakening in Virginia, 1740–1790* (1930); and Leonard J. Tinterud, *The Forming of an American Tradition* (1958). William Warren Sweet's *Religion in Colonial America* (1942) provides a comprehensive survey of religion in eighteenth-century America along with chapters on the Great Awakening. An excellent collection of documents has been edited by Alan Heimert and Perry Miller, *The Great Awakening, Documents Illustrating the Crisis and Its Consequences* (1966). Alan Heimert also develops a provocative thesis about the influence of the Great Awakening in his *Religion and the American Mind: From the Great Awakening to the Revolution* (1966).

Useful material on social structure and social conflicts may be found in James T. Adams, *Revolutionary New England, 1691–1776* (1923); George A. Billias, *The Massachusetts Land Banks of 1740* (1959); and Carl Bridenbaugh, *Cities in Revolt, 1743–1776* (1955). A very perceptive study of community conflict is provided by Michael Zuckerman's recent book, *Peaceable Kingdoms, New England Towns in the Eighteenth Century* (1970). Richard Hofstadter's *America at 1750: A Social Portrait* (1971) provides a fascinating examination of the social order of mid-eighteenth-century America.

An excellent study of the rise of the assemblies is available in Jack P. Greene, *The Quest for Power, The Lower Houses of the Assembly in the Southern Royal Colonies, 1689–1776* (1963). Mary P. Clarke's *Parliamentary Privilege in the American Colonies* (1943) is an authoritative study of the assemblies' efforts to enlarge their privileges. Robert R. Brown has explored the franchise and representation in his *Middle Class Democracy and the Revolution in Massachusetts, 1691–1780* (1955) and, with Katherine Brown, *Virginia, 1705–1786; Democracy or Aristocracy?* (1964). The early chapters of Chilton Williamson's *American Suffrage, From Property to Democracy, 1760–1860* (1960) provide a good survey of eighteenth-century suffrage and political practices.

6. Children of the Enlightenment

The works of Cremin, Hofstadter, Edwards, and Richey, already cited, should be consulted for educational developments in the eighteenth century. Also useful are Robert Middlekauf's *Ancients and Axioms: Secondary Education in the Eighteenth Century* (1963) and the early chapters in Frederick Rudolph's *The American College and University* (1962).

General accounts of the influence of the Enlightenment in America may be found in Max Savelle's *Seeds of Liberty* (1948), Michael Kraus' *Atlantic Civilization: Eighteenth Century Origins* (1949), and Louis B. Wright's *The Cultural Life of the American Colonies, 1607–1763* (1957). Perry Miller's *Johnathan Edwards* (1949) contains a very sophisticated analysis of the influence of Locke on Edwards. Benjamin Franklin, of course, will always be a focus of interest for students of the American Enlightenment; Franklin's intellectual life is ably presented in Carl Van Doren's *Benjamin Franklin* (1938), Verner Crane's *Benjamin Franklin* (1956), and A. O. Aldridge's *Benjamin Franklin: Philosopher and Man* (1965). The early chapters of Dumas Malone's *Thomas Jefferson and the Rights of Man* (1948) also contain perceptive analyses of the way in which European ideas were received by Jefferson and other men of learning. The first volume of Page Smith's *John Adams* (1963) is also useful for the same purpose. Adrienne Koch has edited a valuable anthology of American thought in the eighteenth century under the title, *The American Enlightenment: The Shaping of the American Experiment and a Free Society* (1965).

Brooke Hindle has written a comprehensive and thorough study of *The Pursuit of Science in Revolutionary America, 1735–1789* (1956). Dirk Struik's *Yankee Science in the Making* (1948) is also useful, as is Richard Shryock's *Medicine and Society in America, 1660–1860* (1960). I. Bernard Cohen provides a superb study of scientific thought and experimentation in *Franklin and Newton: An Inquiry into Speculative Experimental Science and Franklin's Work in Electricity as an Example Thereof* (1956). This should be compared with the chapters on science in Daniel J. Boorstin's *The Americans: The Colonial Experience* (1958).

Colonial conceptions of law and government in the eighteenth century are well presented in Clinton Rossiter's *Seedtime of the Republic* (1953). Caroline Robbins, *The Eighteenth Century Commonwealthman* (1959), provides a valuable study of the development and transmission of English liberal thought in the eighteenth century. Benjamin Wright has examined conceptions of natural law in his *American Interpretations of Natural Law: A Study in the Historical Process of Political Thought* (1931).

7. America's Revolution

Volumes 9 to 12 of Lawrence Henry Gipson's *The British Empire Before the American Revolution* (1956–1965) are invaluable for an understanding of political developments after 1763 on both sides of the Atlantic. Gipson's *The Coming of the Revolution, 1763–1775* (1954) is an excellent single-volume summary of his monumental researches. John C. Miller's *Origins of the American Revolution* (1959) is a lively and thorough analysis of the developing political conflict that led to the Revolution. Bernhard Knollenberg's *Origin of the American Revolution* (1960) is another well-written recent study. The earlier chapters in Edmund S. Morgan's *The Birth of the Republic: 1763–1789* (1953) are a useful, short summary that are influenced by his special study (with Helen M. Morgan) of the Stamp Act crisis in *The Stamp Act: Prologue to Revolution* (1953).

For British politics on the eve of the Revolution, one should consult

Lewis Namier's *England in the Age of the American Revolution;* Richard Pares, *King George III and the Politicians* (1953); and Eric Robson, *The American Revolution, 1763–1783* (1955). Max Beloff has edited a fine collection of British and American documents entitled *The Debate on the American Revolution, 1761–1783* (1949).

There are many biographical studies of American political leaders which are of value such as the following: Page Smith, *John Adams* (2 vols., 1962); John C. Miller, *Sam Adams: Pioneer in Propaganda* (1936); Dumas Malone's *Thomas Jefferson, the Virginian* (1948); Carl Van Doren, *Benjamin Franklin* (1938); and Robert Meade, *Patrick Henry, Patriot in the Making* (1957). The role of colonial merchants in the Revolution is presented in Arthur M. Schlesinger's *The Colonial Merchants and the American Revolution, 1763–1776* (1918). Alice M. Baldwin's *The New England Clergy and the American Revolution* (1928) is an early examination of the role of the clergy. Carl Bridenbaugh's *Mitre and Sceptre: Transatlantic Faiths, Ideas, Personalities and Politics 1689–1775* (1962) and Alan Heimert's *Religion and the American Mind: From the Great Awakening to the Revolution* (1966) have reopened the problem of the role of the clergy and the impact of religious questions on the coming of the Revolution.

The role of ideology in the coming of the Revolution is ably presented by Bernard Bailyn in his *Ideological Origins of the American Revolution* (1967), which was originally written as an introductory essay for an anthology entitled *Pamphlets of the American Revolution 1763–1783* (1965). Bailyn's essay on ideological origins should be supplemented by the opening chapters in Gordon Wood's *The Creation of the American Republic, 1770–1787* (1969). Carl Becker's *The Declaration of Independence* (1922) is still a very useful study of the making of the Declaration, but his analysis of the ideological background has been superseded by the works of Bailyn and Wood. Two recent studies have enriched our understanding of the intellectual origins of American revolutionary thought: H. Trevor Colburn, *The Lamp of Experience: Whig History and the Intellectual Origins of the American Revolution* (1965) and Richard Gummere, *The American Colonial Mind and the Classical Tradition: Essays in Comparative Culture* (1963).

For accounts of the military, political and diplomatic aspects of the Revolution, John C. Miller, *Triumph of Freedom 1775–1783* (1948); Willard M. Wallace, *Appeal to Arms* (1951); and John R. Alden, *The American Revolution* (1959); are valuable. Paul H. Smith's *Loyalists and Redcoats: A Study in British Revolutionary Policy* (1964) is valuable for British efforts to use Loyalists in the war. Henry S. Commager and Richard B. Morris (eds.), *The Spirit of Seventy-Six* (2 vols., 1958), is an excellent anthology of eye witness and participant accounts covering military and civilian aspects of the war. George F. Scheer and Hugh Rankin have edited a shorter collection of source materials entitled *Rebels and Redcoats* (1957). Samuel F. Bemis' *The Diplomacy of the*

American Revolution (1935) is a detailed account which should be supplemented by Felix Gilbert's perceptive analysis of the basic ideas of American foreign policy in his *The Beginnings of American Foreign Policy; To the Farewell Address* (1961). Richard B. Morris has written the most recent study of the Peace of Paris in a book entitled *The Peacemakers: The Great Powers and American Independence* (1965).

8. Building a New Constitutional Order

Gordon Wood's *The Creation of the American Republic, 1776–1787* (1969) is an indispensable work on the shaping of a republican ideology and the formal and informal institutions created during the revolutionary decade. Revolutionary politics is largely state politics and Allan Nevins' *The American States during and after the Revolution, 1775–1789* (1924) is still the most thorough account of state politics and state constitution-making. Elisha P. Douglass emphasizes ideological differences in his *Rebels and Democrats: The Struggle for Equal Political Rights and Majority Rule during the American Revolution* (1955). Fletcher M. Green has provided an authoritative survey of southern states in his *Constitutional Development in the South Atlantic States, 1766–1860* (1930). Jackson T. Main's *The Upper House in Revolutionary America, 1763–1788* (1967) is a valuable contribution to our understanding of changes in the Revolutionary legislatures. For good accounts of the radical politics of Pennsylvania see J. Paul Selsam, *The Pennsylvania Constitution of 1776: A Study of Revolutionary Democracy* (1936) and David Hawke, *In the Midst of a Revolution* (1961). Robert J. Taylor (ed)., *Massachusetts, Colony to Commonwealth, Documents on the Formation of Its Constitution* (1961) is useful for the Massachusetts constitution of 1780.

For social development during the Revolutionary period one should consult J. Franklin Jameson's *The American Revolution Considered as a Social Movement* (1926) and E. B. Greene's *The Revolutionary Generation, 1763–1790* (1943) even though they frequently overstated the degree of social change. On developments relating to slavery during the Revolutionary generation, the relevant chapters in Winthrop Jordan's *White Over Black* (1968) and Donald L. Robinson's *Slavery in the Structure of American Politics, 1765–1820* (1971) are indispensable. On social conditions and social structure, Jackson T. Main's *The Social Structure of Revolutionary America* (1965) is a good recent analysis.

On the national government during the Revolutionary generation, E. C. Burnett's *The Colonial Congress* (1941) is a thorough study of the activities of that body. Merrill Jensen's *The Articles of Confederation* (1940) has produced much controversy among historians, but his analysis of the debates over the Articles is useful. Jensen's *The New Nation: A History of the United States During the Confederation, 1781–1789* (1950) is the most fully-rounded recent work on the Confederation in the

1780's. Good studies of states during the Confederation period are Richard J. McCormick's *Experiment in Independence: New Jersey in the Critical Period, 1781–1789* (1950) and Thomas C. Cochran's *New York in the Confederation* (1932). Marion L. Starkey has written a good account of Shays Rebellion in her *A Little Rebellion* (1955) but one should also consult Robert S. Taylor's *Western Massachusetts in the Revolution* (1954). Robert E. East, *Business Enterprise in the American Revolutionary Era* (1938) is a comprehensive analysis of business activities, and E. James Ferguson develops a useful analysis of financial affairs in his *The Power of the Purse, A History of American Public Finance, 1776–1790* (1961).

Two good brief books on the making of the Constitution are Robert L. Schuyler, *The Constitution of the United States* (1923) and Clinton Rossiter, *1787—The Grand Convention* (1966). The debate over Charles Beard's *An Economic Interpretation of the Constitution of the United States* (1913), which reached a high point with Robert S. Brown's *Charles Beard and the Constitution: A Critical Analysis of "An Economic Interpretation of the Constitution"* (1956) has faded away enough to allow historians to reexamine the restrictive aspects of the Constitution and the social contexts in which they were formed. Forrest McDonald's *We the People: The Economic Origins of the Constitution* (1958) reexamines occupational and capital-forming groups without allowing them to disappear from the social landscape. Jackson T. Main's *The Antifederalists: Critics of the Constitution, 1781–1788* (1961) attempts to restore a social and economic basis for the debate over the Constitution. Stoughton Lynd has attempted to do the same in his collection of essays entitled *Class Conflict, Slavery and the United States Constitution* (1968). For a very deft analysis of feelings of social distinction in the controversy over the Constitution, one should consult Robert A. Rutland's *The Ordeal of the Constitution: The Anti-Federalists and the Ratification Struggle of 1787–1788* (1966). The interplay of political and social forces can be explored in such studies as R. L. Brunhouse, *The Counter-Revolution in Pennsylvania, 1776–1790* (1942); S. B. Harding, *The Contest over Ratification of the Federal Constitution in the State of Massachusetts* (1896); and C. E. Miner, *Ratification of the Federal Constitution by the State of New York* (1921).

For the underlying political science of the Constitution, no one should neglect *The Federalist* papers written by Hamilton, Madison, and Jay and available in many editions. Max Farrand has edited an indispensable record of the debates in the Philadelphia Convention, *Records of the Federal Convention* (4 vols., 1911–1937), and one can pursue the debates into the states in Jonathan Elliott (ed.), *The Debates in the Several State Conventions on the Adoption of the Federal Constitution* (1941). The opening chapters of Louis Hartz, *The Liberal Tradition in America* (1955) dismiss the political ideas of the Federalists as largely irrational and irrelevant, but Gordon Wood's thorough study of the political science of the Federalists in *The Creation of the American Republic* (1969) seem more likely to shape present and future interpretations. In addition, no serious student of the constitutionalism of the American revolutionary generation can afford to ignore the chapters on America in Robert R. Palmer's superb study, *The Age of Democratic Revolution: A Political History of Europe and America, 1760–1800* (2 vols., 1959, 1965).

9. The Federalists

John C. Miller's *The Federalist Era, 1787–1801* (1960) is a balanced synthesis of the decades when the Federalists controlled the new national government. Also valuable on the organization and administration of the government is Leonard D. White's *The Federalists* (1948). Claude G. Bowers' *Jefferson and Hamilton* (1925) is a lively account of the party battles of the decade, written with a pronounced Jeffersonian bias. Joseph C. Charles, *Origins of the American Party System* (1956) is a valuable brief account of the formation of parties, but the earlier chapters in William N. Chambers, *Political Parties in a New Nation* (1963) should also be consulted. Richard Hofstadter's *The Idea of a Party System* (1969) is a fascinating study of the evolving ideas of parties and party conflict in the formative years of the Republic.

Biographical studies of the Federalist leaders are also helpful for an understanding of ideas and institutions in these nation-building years. Douglas Southall Freeman's *George Washington, Patriot and President, 1784–1793* (1954), the sixth volume of his massive biography, and *George Washington, First in Peace, 1793–1799* (volume 7, 1957), written by Freeman's research associates John A. Carroll and Mary W. Ashworth after his death, are rich in biographical detail. Marcus Cunliffe's *George Washington: Man and Monument* (1958) is a brief and perceptive study. John C. Miller's *Alexander Hamilton: Portrait in Paradox* (1959) is a good study of Hamilton's political ideas and policies while Broadus Mitchell's *Alexander Hamilton* (2 vols., 1957, 1962) is particularly strong on the economic aspects of Hamilton's program. Manning J. Dauer, *The Adams Federalists* (1953) and Stephen G. Kurtz, *The Presidency of John Adams: The Collapse of Federalism 1795–1800* (1958) are excellent. One can follow the story of the Federalists after they lost power in David Fischer's *Revolution of American Conservatism* (1965) and Shaw Livermore's *Twilight of Federalism* (1962).

On the French Revolution and foreign policy L. M. Sears, *George Washington and the French Revolution* (1960) and Alexander De Conde, *Entangling Alliance* (1958) are useful. Paul A. Varg, *Foreign Policy of the Founding Fathers* (1963) and Gilbert Lycan, *Alexander Hamilton and Foreign Policy* (1971) examine the effect of disagreements over foreign policy on the formation of parties. Samuel F. Bemis has provided thorough studies of two key treaties of the period in his *Jay's Treaty* (1923) and *Pinckney's Treaty* (1960).

The Whiskey Rebellion is well-presented in Leland D. Baldwin's *Whiskey Rebels: The Story of a Frontier Uprising* (1939). E. P. Link's *Democratic-Republican Societies, 1790–1800* (1942) examines the influence of French revolutionary ideas in political clubs organized to oppose Federalist parties. The Alien and Sedition Acts are perceptively examined in two books: James M. Smith's *Freedom's Fetters* (1956) and John C. Miller's *Crisis in Freedom* (1952). Leonard Levy's *Legacy of Suppression* (1960) reexamines the whole question of freedom of press and speech in the formative years of the Republic.

10. The Jeffersonians

Comprehensive and brief accounts of the Jeffersonian period are available in Morton Borden's recent work, *Parties and Politics in the Early Republic, 1789–1815* (1967), and in Marshall Smelser's *The Democratic Republic 1801–1815* (1968). One should also read James S. Young's perceptive analysis of the Jeffersonian political leadership in *The Washington Community, 1800–1829* (1966). Leonard D. White's *The Jeffersonians, A Study in Administrative History* (1951) is an indispensable work on the organization and administrative methods of the Jeffersonians. Henry Adams' classic work on the *History of the United States During the Administrations of Jefferson and Madison* (9 vols., 1888–1891) is still valuable for many aspects of Jeffersonian thought and policy.

Biographies of Jeffersonian leaders also help our understanding of the period. Merrill Peterson's *Thomas Jefferson and the New Nation* (1970) is an excellent recent biography. Nathan Schachner's *Thomas Jefferson, a Biography* (2 vols., 1951) is thorough and complete on the presidential years. Two older works are also valuable: Albert J. Nock's *Thomas Jefferson* (1926) and Gilbert Chinard's *Thomas Jefferson, The Apostle of Americanism* (1929). Alexander Balinky's *Albert Gallatin: Fiscal Theories and Policy* (1958) is an excellent analysis of Gallatin's fiscal policies. Irving Brant's volumes on Madison as secretary of state and president are excellent: *James Madison, Secretary of State 1800–1809* (1953); *James Madison, The President 1809–1812* (1956); and *James Madison, Commander-in-Chief 1812–1836* (1961).

There are several useful studies of the Jeffersonian party and the evolving party system: Noble Cunningham, *The Jeffersonian Republicans: The Formation of Party Organization, 1789–1801* (1957) and *The Jeffersonian Republicans in Power: Party Operations, 1801–1809* (1963). See also William N. Chambers, *Political Parties in a New Nation, 1776–1809* (1963).

On Jefferson's foreign policies one should consult these books: E. W. Lyon, *Louisiana in French Diplomacy, 1759–1804* (1934); Bradford Perkins, *First Rapprochement: England and the United States, 1795–1805* (1955); L. M. Sears, *Jefferson and the Embargo* (1927); and J. F.

Zimmerman, *Impressment of American Seamen* (1925). On the coming of the War of 1812, Julius W. Pratt's *Expansionists of 1812* (1925) emphasizes the pressures of western and southern expansionists while A. L. Burt, *The United States, Great Britain and British North America* (1940) emphasizes the issues of impressment and neutral commerce. Also valuable on the causes of the war are Reginald Horsman, *The Causes of the War of 1812* (1962) and Bradford Perkins, *Prologue to War: England and the United States, 1805–1812* (1961).

Francis F. Beirne, *The War of 1812* (1949) and Harry L. Coles, *The War of 1812* (1965) are good brief accounts of the war. James M. Banner's *To the Hartford Convention: The Federalists and the Origins of Party Politics in Massachusetts 1789–1815* (1970) is an excellent recent study of the Hartford Convention. The Treaty of Ghent is examined in Fred L. Engleman, *The Peace of Christmas Eve* (1962), but one should also consult relevant chapters in Samuel Flagg Bemis, *John Quincy Adams and the Foundations of American Foreign Policy* (1949). The Bemis book is also valuable on the diplomatic developments leading to the Monroe Doctrine, but one should also consult Dexter Perkins, *The Monroe Doctrine, 1823–1826* (1927) and Arthur P. Whitaker, *The United States and the Independence of Latin America 1800–1830* (1941).

George Dangerfield's two works on the period after the War of 1812 contain valuable analyses of the politics of Republican nationalism: *The Era of Good Feelings* (1952) and *The Awakening of American Nationalism, 1815–1828* (1965). Paul C. Nagel explores the intellectual bases of American nationalism in *One Nation Indivisible: The Union in American Thought, 1776–1861* (1964). Charles M. Wiltse's *John C. Calhoun, Nationalist, 1782–1828* (1944) is very useful and one should also consult W. P. Cresson's *James Monroe* (1946) and Glyndon G. Van Deusen's *The Life of Henry Clay* (1937).

11. The Genteel Republic

Jefferson's political ideas and his philosophic outlook are analyzed by Charles M. Wiltse in *The Jeffersonian Tradition in American Democracy* (1935) and Adrienne Koch, *The Philosophy of Thomas Jefferson* (1943). Charles Syndor's *Gentleman Freeholders; political practices in Washington's Virginia* (1952) is excellent on the social structure that produced leaders like Jefferson. Karl Lehmann's *Thomas Jefferson, American Humanist* (1947) is a good study of Jefferson's ideas on art, architecture, and learning. Edward T. Martin's *Thomas Jefferson, Scientist* (1952) explores Jefferson's scientific interests. Merrill Peterson's *The Jeffersonian Image in the American Mind* (1960) is a very perceptive analysis of the changing and enduring influence of the Jeffersonian tradition on American thought. Saul Padover's *The Complete Jefferson* (1943) is an excellent collection of Jeffersonian addresses and writings on politics, science, morals, manners, and education. Jefferson's educational ideas are perceptively analyzed in the relevant chapters of R. Freeman Butts and Lawrence A. Cremin, *A History of Education in American Culture* (1953). Developments in public, private, and philanthropic education in the Jeffersonian era are succinctly described in Edwards and Richey, *The School in the American Social Order* (1947).

The first volume of Robert Spiller et al., *Literary History of the United States* (1948) contains some very useful essays on literature and the literary market place in the opening decades of the nineteenth century. Van Wyck Brooks, *The World of Washington Irving* (1944) is a comprehensive account of the activities of artists, writers, and intellectuals for the same period. Frank L. Mott's *A History of American Magazines* (Volume I, 1938) is a storehouse of information on magazines that contain a lengthy account of Dennie's *Portfolio.* H. Milton Ellis has done a full-length biography of Dennie in *Joseph Dennie and His Circle: A Study of American Literature from 1792 to 1812* (1915). Stanley T. Williams, *The Life of Washington Irving* (2 vols., 1935) is a detailed study. On Joel Barlow's career and contribution consult Leon Howard, *The Connecticut Wits* (1943). There is a perceptive assessment of Charles Brockden Brown in Richard B. Lewis, *The American Adam* (1955).

There is a very useful chapter on the historical writing of the early Republic in Harvey Wish, *The American Historian, A Social and Intellectual History of the Writing of the American Past* (1960). The Washington image is examined by William Alfred Bryan in *George Washington in American Literature, 1775–1865* (1952). Also useful on the same subject is C. M. Garland's *Washington and His Portraits* (1931). Marcus Cunliffe has edited a modern edition of Parson Weems, *The Life of Washington* (1962).

12. The Market Revolution

Two excellent brief studies of American economic growth in the pre-Civil War decades are Douglas C. North, *The Economic Growth of the United States, 1790–1860* (1961) and Stuart Bruchey, *The Roots of American Economic Growth, 1607–1861, An Essay in Social Causation* (1965). The early chapters in Peter d'A. Jones, *The Consumer Society, A History of American Capitalism* (1965) are particularly useful for an understanding of the development of the national market economy. W. B. Smith and A. H. Cole, *Fluctuations in American Business, 1790–1860* (1935) is valuable for cyclical patterns in economic growth. For the major panics of the period see M. N. Rothbard, *The Panic of 1819, Reactions and Policies* (1962); R. C. McGrane, *The Panic of 1837* (1924); and George W. Van Vleck, *The Panic of 1857* (1943).

George Rogers Taylor, *The Transportation Revolution, 1815–1860* (1951) is an excellent analysis of the transformation of the national economy that accompanied the development of roads, canals, steam-boats, and railroads. Also useful is Carter G. Goodrich, *Government Promotion of American Canals and Railroads, 1800–1860* (1960). John G. B. Hutchins, *The American Maritime Industries and Public Policy, 1789–1914* (1941) contains some excellent chapters on American commerce and shipping in this period.

Paul W. Gates, *The Farmer's Age* (1960) is a comprehensive account of the regional changes in agriculture during the first half of the nineteenth century. Roy F. Robbins, *Our Landed Heritage: The Public Domain, 1776–1936* (1942) contains useful chapters on public land policies. A very useful work on agricultural technology is Leo Rogin, *The Introduction of Farm Machinery in its Relation to the Productivity of Labor in the Agriculture of the United States During the Nineteenth Century* (1931).

Caroline A. Ware's *The Early New England Cotton Manufacture* (1931) is an outstanding study of a strategic sector in American manufacturing development. A. H. Cole, *The American Wool Manufacture* (2 vols., 1926) is also valuable. J. W. Oliver's *History of American Technology* (1956) and Roger. Burlingame's *The March of the Iron Men* (1938) are useful for the role of invention in industrial development. A more sophisticated analysis is presented in H. J. Habakkuk, *American and British Technology in the Nineteenth Century* (1962).

The development of corporations is examined in E. M. Dodd, *American Business Corporations Until 1860* (1954) and Joseph S. Davis, *Essays in the Earlier History of American Corporations* (1917). Two excellent studies of the public policies of states affecting corporations are Oscar and Mary Handlin, *Commonwealth, A Study of the Role of Government in the American Economy: Massachusetts 1774–1861* (1947) and Louis Hartz, *Economic Policy and Democratic Thought, Pennsylvania 1776–1860* (1948).

Norman Ware's *The Industrial Worker 1840–1860* (1924) is a good brief account of the condition of labor, but one should also. consult the first volume of John R. Commons et al., *History of Labor in the United States* (4 vols., 1918–1935). The first volume of Philip S. Foner's. *History of the Labor Movement in the United States* (1947) is also useful.

13. The Emergence of Democratic Politics

George Dangerfield's *The Era of Good Feelings* (1952) is an excellent general account of the new currents of politics in the 1820's. The later chapters in James S. Young's *The Washington Community, 1801–1828* (1966) contain a very perceptive analysis of the fragmentation of the Jeffersonian Republicans under Jefferson's presidential successors. Paul Goodman and Richard McCormick have contributed excellent essays on party development during this period to William N. Chambers and Walter D. Burnham (eds.), *The American Party Systems, Stages of Political Development* (1967). Richard McCormick's *The Second American*

Party System: Party Formation in the Jacksonian Era (1966) examines the changes in politics and the party system in greater detail.

Glover Moore, *The Missouri Controversy 1819–1821* (1953) is a good analysis of the sectional politics behind the Missouri Compromise. Murray Rothbard's *The Panic of 1819: Reactions and Policies* (1962) is very useful for an understanding of the conflicts in the states over proposals for restrictions on banks and the relief of debtors. Edward S. Corwin's *John Marshall and the Constitution* (1919) and the third volume of Albert J. Beveridge's *The Life of John Marshall* (4 vols., 1916) contain valuable analyses of Marshall's controversial decisions on the contract clause and the National Bank. Charles G. Haines, *The Role of the Supreme Court in American Government and Politics, 1789–1835* (1944) is also valuable for the political controversies associated with the Supreme Court. Eugene T. Mudge, *The Social Philosophy of John Taylor of Caroline* (1939) is a good study of a leading critic of Marshall's nationalist doctrines. The final chapters in Norman K. Risjord's *The Old Republicans* (1965) are particularly valuable on the transformation of old Republicanism into self-conscious southern sectionalism.

Samuel Flagg Bemis, *John Quincy Adams and The American Union* (1956) is a thorough study of the political events of the Adams administration. For the battles over Clay's "American System," Glyndon Van Deusen's *The Life of Henry Clay* (1937), and Clement Eaton's *Henry Clay and the Art of American Politics* (1957) should be consulted. Charles M. Wiltse's *John C. Calhoun, Nullifier 1829–1840* (1949) is excellent for the controversy over the tariff of 1828.

14. Jacksonian Democracy

Glyndon G. Van Deusen, *The Jacksonian Era* (1959) and Charles M. Wiltse, *The New Nation, 1800–1845* (1961) contain excellent general accounts of the Jacksonian era based on modern scholarship. Although his interpretation has been the subject of much controversy, Arthur M. Schlesinger, Jr., *The Age of Jackson* (1945) is rich in detail as well as in provocative insights. Marvin Meyers, *The Jacksonian Persuasion* (1957) provides an excellent analysis of the ideological aspects of Jacksonian democracy, but one should also read Lee Benson's *The Concept of Jacksonian Democracy: New York as a Test Case* (1961) for further insights into differences in the ideas and policies of Whigs and Democrats. John William Ward's *Andrew Jackson, Symbol for An Age* (1955) provides a valuable analysis of Jacksonian symbols. The institutions and ideas of American society in the Jacksonian generations are very perceptively analyzed by Alexis de Tocqueville in his classic work, *Democracy in America,* available in an excellent edition edited by Phillips Bradley (2 vols., 1945).

Valuable for their examination of Jacksonian politics and the party system are Robert V. Remini, *The Election of Andrew Jackson* (1963) and Richard McCormick, *The Second American Party System: Party Formation in the Jacksonian Era* (1966). Two excellent studies of the new style politicians of the period are Robert Remini's *Martin Van Buren and the Making of the Democratic Party* (1959) and Glyndon Van Deusen's *Thurlow Weed, Wizard of the Lobby* (1947). The development of the Whig party is explored in various aspects by Arthur C. Cole, *The Whig Party in the South* (1913); E. M. Carroll, *Origins of the Whig Party* (1925); and G. R. Poage, *Henry Clay and the Whig Party* (1936). The election of 1840 is described in detail in R. G. Gunderson's *The Log Cabin Campaign* (1957). Joel H. Silbey's *The Shrine of Party* (1967) is an excellent study of Whig-Democratic voting patterns in Congress. Walter Hugins' *Jacksonian Democracy and the Working Class: A Study of the New York Workingmen's Movement, 1829–1837* (1960) and D. T. Miller's *Jacksonian Aristocracy: Class and Democracy in New York, 1830–1860* (1967) explore some of the complex relationships between parties and social structure. Edward Pessen (ed.), *New Perspectives on Jacksonian Parties and Politics* (1969) is a very useful selection that points up the unresolved problems of interpretation regarding Jacksonian politics.

There are several good studies that focus on the bank issue and related economic questions. The relevant chapters in Bray Hammond's *Banks and Politics in America from the Revolution to the Civil War* (1957) are excellent. W. B. Smith, *The Economic Aspects of the Second Bank of the United States* (1953) is also useful. Jean A. Wilburn's *Biddle's Bank: The Crucial Years* (1967) is an important recent reexamination. Thomas P. Govan, *Nicholas Biddle, Nationalist and Public Banker 1786–1844* (1959) is a useful study of Biddle's career. Peter Temin's *The Jacksonian Economy* (1969) challenges many widely-held assumptions about economic affairs in the Jacksonian period.

An excellent recent study of the nullification controversy is William W. Freehling's *Prelude to Civil War* (1966). Charles S. Sydnor's *The Development of Southern Sectionalism 1819–1848* (1948) locates the nullification movement in the unfolding development of southern history. C. S. Boucher *The Nullification Controversy in South Carolina* (1916) and Frederic Bancroft, *Calhoun and the South Carolina Nullification Movement* (1928) are also useful.

Biographical studies of political leaders during the Jacksonian era are helpful for an understanding of the relationship between leaders and their constituencies. Marquis James, *Andrew Jackson, Portrait of a President* (1937) and James S. Bassett, *The Life of Andrew Jackson* (2 vols., 1925) are good studies of Jackson. Other good biographies of key Jacksonian leaders are Charles G. Sellers, *James K. Polk, Jacksonian 1795–1843* (1957); William N. Chambers, *Old Bullion Benton: Senator From the West* (1956); and Carl B. Swisher, *Roger B. Taney* (1936). For Whig leaders consult the biographies of Clay by Van Deusen and Eaton; also refer to Richard N. Current, *Daniel Webster and the Rise of National*

Conservatism (1955) and V. P. Chitwood, *John Tyler, Champion of the Old South* (1939).

15. The Ferment of a Democratic Culture

William Warren Sweet, *Revivalism in America* (1944); Whitney R. Cross, *The Burned-Over District* (1950); Bernard A. Weisberger, *They Gathered at the River* (1958); William J. McLoughlin, *Modern Revivalism: from Charles Grandison Finney to Billy Graham* (1959); and Perry Miller, *The Life of the Mind in America from the Revolution to the Civil War* (1965) are valuable for an understanding of Protestant revivalism. The relationship between revivalism and reform is explored in Charles C. Cole, Jr., *The Social Ideas of Northern Evangelists, 1826–1860* (1954) and T. L. Smith, *Revivalism and Social Reform in Mid-Nineteenth Century America* (1957). The relationship between revivalism and social control is examined in C. S. Griffin, *Their Brothers Keepers; Moral Stewardship in the United States, 1800–1865* (1960); Ray A. Billington, *The Protestant Crusade* (1938); and John R. Bodo, *The Protestant Clergy and Public Issues, 1812–48* (1954).

A good general account of the many reform movements of the first half of the nineteenth century may be found in Alice F. Tyler, *Freedom's Ferment: Phases of American Social History to 1860* (1940). Arthur Bestor's *Backwoods Utopias: The Sectarian and Owenite Phases of Communitarian Socialism in America, 1663–1829* (1950), Charles Nordhoff's *The Communistic Societies of the United States* (1875), and William Wilson's *The Angel and the Serpent* (1964) are useful for the utopians, but one should also consult the relevant chapters in volume I of Donald Egbert and Stow Persons, *Socialism and American Life* (1952). R. B. Flanders, *Nauvoo, Kingdom on the Mississippi* (1965) is an excellent study of the Mormons. John A. Krout, *The Origins of Prohibition* (1925) is valuable for the temperance reformers, but one should also consult Joseph Gusfield, *Symbolic Crusade* (1963).

Works on the abolitionists are numerous and stimulating. D. L. Dumond, *Antislavery* (1961) and Louis Filler, *The Crusade Against Slavery* (1960) are comprehensive studies of the antislavery movement. Gibert H. Barnes, *The Antislavery Impulse 1833–1844* (1933) emphasizes the efforts of the moderate abolitionists. John L. Thomas, *The Liberator, William L. Garrison* (1963) and Aileen Kraditor, *Means and Ends in American Abolitionism: Garrison and His Critics on Strategy and Tactics, 1834–1850* (1959) focus on Garrison and the radical abolitionists. Benjamin Quarles, *Black Abolitionists* (1969), is valuable on the role of blacks in the abolitionist movement. Martin Duberman (ed.), *The Antislavery Vanguard* (1965) is an excellent collection of essays on the antislavery movement. Stanley Elkins, *Slavery, A Problem in American Institutional and Intellectual Life* (1959) contains a critical evaluation of the role of the abolitionists. L. F. Litwack's, *North of Slavery: The Negro in the Free States, 1790–1860* (1961) is a perceptive study of race prejudice in the North.

Among the more useful books on education and educational reform are the following: S. L. Jackson, *America's Struggle For Free Schools: Social Tension and Education in New England and New York 1827–1842* (1941); Merle Curti, *The Social Ideas of American Educators* (1935); Rush Welter, *Popular Education and Democratic Thought* (1962); and Lawrence Cremin, *The American Common School* (1951). Carl Bode's *The American Lyceum* (1956) is excellent. There are excellent chapters on higher education in Richard Hofstadter, *Academic Freedom in the Age of the College* (1955), and Frederick Rudolph, *The American College and University* (1962).

Although superseded by later scholarship, Vernon L. Parrington's *The Romantic Revolution in America, 1800–1860* (1927) is still a fascinating work to read on the literary contributions of the Jacksonian generation. F. O. Matthiessen's *American Renaissance* (1941) is a brilliant study of the remarkable burst of literary genius in this period. R. W. B. Lewis, *The American Adam* (1955) emphasizes the theme of innocence, and Leo Marx, *The Machine in the Garden* (1964) examines the theme of pastoralism in the writings of the period. Charles Feidelson's *Symbolism and American Literature* (1953) is also valuable. For individual authors consult the following: James Grossman, *James Fenimore Cooper* (1949); R. L. Rusk, *The Life of Ralph Waldo Emerson* (1949); Henry S. Canby, *Thoreau* (1939); Mark Van Doren, *Nathaniel Hawthorne* (1949); Newton Arvin, *Herman Melville* (1950); Edward H. Davidson, *Poe: A Critical Study* (1957); and G. W. Allen, *The Solitary Singer: A Critical Biography of Walt Whitman* (1955). David Levin, *History As Romantic Art* (1959) is an excellent study of the romantic historians of the Jacksonian generation.

16. The Disruption of the Party System

Albert K. Weinberg, *Manifest Destiny* (1935) and Frederick Merk, *Manifest Destiny and Mission in American History* (1963) are excellent analyses of the ideology of manifest destiny. Frederick and L. B. Merk have also examined the expansionism of the 1840's in *The Monroe Doctrine and American Expansionism, 1843–1849* (1966). Henry N. Smith's *Virgin Land* (1950) is a fascinating analysis of the symbols of empire and agrarianism in American thought. Ray A. Billington, *The Far Western Frontier* (1956) is a comprehensive account of western expansion.

American penetration into Texas is examined in E. C. Barker, *Mexico and Texas 1821–1835* (1928) and W. C. Binkley, *The Texas Revolution* (1952). Norman A. Graebner, *Empire on the Pacific* (1955) explores the commercial motives in the new expansionism. The Oregon question and its settlement is examined in M. C. Jacobs, *Winning Oregon* (1938).

For Polk and the Mexican War, Charles Seller's *James K. Polk: Continentalist, 1843–1846* (1966) is an indispensable introduction. Polk's presidential administration is fully covered by E. I. McCormac's *James K. Polk* (1922). J. W. Schmitz, *Texas Statecraft, 1836–1845* (1945) is a good analysis of negotiations for the annexation of Texas, and G. L. Rives, *The United States and Mexico, 1821–1848* (1913) provides a comprehensive account of relations with Mexico. Three recent studies contain good brief accounts of the Mexican War: A H. Bill, *Rehearsal For Conflict: The War With Mexico, 1846–1848* (1947); R. S. Henry, *The Story of the Mexican War* (1950); and O. A. Singletary, *The Mexican War* (1960).

On the political crisis created by the Mexican War, Allan Nevins, *Ordeal of the Union* (2 vols, 1947) is a superb study which examines the successive moments of crisis from the Wilmot Proviso to the Kansas–Nebraska Act. Holman Hamilton's *Prologue to Conflict: The Crisis and Compromise of 1850* (1964) is an excellent analysis. The politics of these crisis years can also be studied in the following political biographies: C. B. Going, *David Wilmot, Free Soiler* (1924); George F. Milton, *The Eve of Conflict: Stephen A. Douglas and the Needless War* (1934); Charles M. Wiltse, *John C. Calhoun: Sectionalist, 1840–1850* (1951); Richard Current, *Daniel Webster and the Rise of National Conservatism* (1955); Glyndon Van Deusen, *The Life of Henry Clay* (1937); Holman Hamilton, *Zachary Taylor* (2 vols. 1941, 1951); Roy F. Nichols, *Franklin Pierce* (1931); and Glyndon Van Deusen, *William Henry Seward* (1967).

Useful for an understanding of party disruption are these books: T. C. Smith, *The Liberty and Free Soil Parties in the Northwest* (1897); J. M. White, *The Secession Movement in the United States, 1847–1852* (1961); and Avery O. Craven, *The Growth of Southern Nationalism, 1848–1861* (1953). The role of the Know-Nothing party can be studied in the relevant chapters of Ray A. Billington's *The Protestant Crusade* (1938) and R. J. Rayback's *Millard Fillmore, Biography of A President* (1959). W. D. Overdyke's *The Know-Nothing Party in the South* (1850) and Sister M. E. Thomas' *Nativism in the Old Northwest, 1850–1860* (1936) are good regional studies. The controversy over Kansas and Nebraska is scrutinized by J. C. Malin in *The Nebraska Question, 1852–1854* (1953) and Alice Nichols, *Bleeding Kansas* (1954). The politics of expansion in the Pierce administration can be studied in Basil Rauch's *American Interests in Cuba, 1848–1855* (1948) and E. S. Wallace's lively account of filibustering, *Destiny and Glory* (1957).

17. The Polarization of Politics

Allan Nevins, *The Emergence of Lincoln* (2 vols. 1950) is unmatched for its thorough and perceptive account of the critical years 1854 to 1861. Roy

F. Nichols, *The Disruption of American Democracy* (1948) is an excellent analysis of the disruptive forces in party politics. Avery O. Craven, *The Coming of the Civil War* (1942) provides a good analysis of political tensions and psychological aspects of the sectional conflict. The early chapters in J. J. Randall and David Donald, *The Civil War and Reconstruction* (1961 ed.) provide an excellent brief analysis of the events leading to the Civil War.

The origin and development of the Republican party is adequately presented in A. W. Crandall, *The Early Years of the Republican Party, 1854–1856* (1930) and J. A. Isely, *Horace Greeley and The Republican Party, 1853–1861* (1947). Two excellent biographies are also helpful for an understanding of the new party: Martin B. Duberman's *Charles Francis Adams* (1961) and David Donald's *Charles Sumner and the Coming of the Civil War* (1960). Don E. Fehrenbacher's *Prelude to Greatness, Lincoln in the 1850's* (1962) is a fine analysis of Lincoln's emergence as a national leader. H. V. Jaffa's *Crisis of the House Divided* (1959) is an incisive analysis of the Lincoln-Douglas debates. The free-soil ideology of the Republican party is brilliantly analyzed by Eric Foner in *Free Soil, Free Labor, Free Men: the Ideology of the Republican Party Before the Civil War* (1970).

Comprehensive accounts of southern civilization and sectional consciousness may be found in Clement Eaton's *The Growth of Southern Civilization, 1790–1860* (1961) and *Freedom of Thought in the Old South* (1940). J. T. Carpenter's *The South as a Conscious Minority* (1930) and Avery O. Craven's *The Growth of Southern Nationalism, 1848–1861* (1953) are good analyses of southern sectionalism. William R. Taylor's *Cavalier and Yankee: The Old South and American National Character* (1961) is a fascinating study of literary symbols and myths relating to the South. R. G. Osterweis, *Romanticism and Nationalism in the Old South* (1949) explores themes of cultural nationalism in southern literary and intellectual life. The slave system is examined in John Hope Franklin's *From Slavery to Freedom: A History of American Negroes* (1956), Kenneth Stampp's *The Peculiar Institution: Slavery in the Ante-Bellum South* (1956), and Stanley Elkins, *Slavery, A Problem in American Institutional and Intellectual Life* (1959). Herbert Aptheker, *American Negro Slave Revolts* (1943) is the only thorough book on the subject. Pro-slavery thought on the South may be studied in W. J. Jenkins, *Pro-Slavery Thought in the Old South* (1935) and Harvey Wish, *George Fitzhugh, Propagandist of the Old South* (1943). Two works by Eugene Genovese explore the relationship between consciousness and social reality in the ante-bellum South: *The Political Economy of Slavery* (1965) and *The World the Slaveholders Made* (1969).

For the Dred Scott case, see Vincent Hopkins, *Dred Scott Case* (1951) and the relevant chapters in Carl B. Swisher, *Roger B. Taney* (1935). Allan Nevins provides a richly-detailed account of John Brown in the second volume of his *The Emergence of Lincoln* (1950), but one should also read Stephen B. Oates, *To Purge This Land With Blood; a biography of John Brown* (1970).

For the election of 1860 and the secession crisis Kenneth M. Stampp, *And The War Came: The North and the Secession Crisis 1860–1861* (1950) and David Potter, *Lincoln and His Party in the Secession Crisis* (1942) are indispensable. The secession movement in the South is examined in the following: D. L. Dumond, *The Secession Movement, 1860–1861* (1931); Ulrich B. Phillips, *The Course of the South to Secession* (1939); and R. A. Wooster, *The Secession Conventions of the South* (1962). Richard N. Current, *Lincoln and the First Shot* (1963) is an admirable study of Lincoln's decision-making in the events that culminated in the bombardment of Fort Sumter.

18. The Civil War and the American Social System

An indispensable starting point for a study of the Civil War is David Donald's *The Divided Union* (1961) which revises J. G. Randall's *The Civil War and Reconstruction* (1937) to take account of recent scholarship. Allan Nevins, *The War for the Union* (2 vols. 1959–1960) analyzes the first two years of the war with a richness of detail and a breadth of conception acquired in the writing of his multi-volumed study of the coming of the Civil War. Bruce Catton's *This Hallowed Ground* (1956) is good on military events and there are some very perceptive essays on military aspects in David Donald (ed.), *Why the North Won the Civil War* (1960). Useful for an understanding of the military policies of the Lincoln administration are T. Harry Williams, *Lincoln and His Generals* (1952) and Robert V. Bruce, *Lincoln and the Tools of War* (1956). Frank E. Vandiver's *Revel Brass* is a good brief analysis of the South's command system. Fred A. Shannon's *Organization and Administration of the Union Army, 1861–1865* (2 vols., 1928) is an admirable and thorough study. Jack F. Leach, *Conscription in the United States* (1952) contains a good account of conscription in the North, and A. B. Moore, *Conscription and Conflict in the Confederacy* (1924) does the same for the South. Benjamin Quarles, *The Negro in the Civil War* (1953) is a comprehensive treatment, but D. T. Cornish, *The Sable Arm: Negro Troops in the Union Army 1861–1865* (1958) should also be consulted.

There are several useful studies of the Confederacy and its government. Clement Eaton, *A History of the Southern Confederacy* (1954) is excellent and comprehensive. C. P. Roland's *The Confederacy* (1960) is a brief work which makes use of recent scholarly studies. E. Merton Coulter, *The Confederate States of America, 1861–1865* (1950) is richly detailed on political, economic, and social aspects. Hudson Strode, *Jefferson Davis, Confederate President* (1959); Rembert W. Patrick, *Jefferson Davis and His Cabinet* (1964); and Wilfred B. Yearns, *The Confederate Congress* (1960) are useful on the organization and activities of the Confederate government. Charles Ramsdell's *Behind the Lines in the Southern Confederacy* (1944) and Bell I. Wiley's *The Plain People of the Confederacy* (1943) and *Southern Negroes, 1861–1865* (1938) are valuable for social history.

Diplomatic aspects of the Civil War for the South are competently analyzed by F. L. Owsley's *King Cotton Diplomacy* (1931). Martin B. Duberman, *Charles Francis Adams* (1961) and E. D. Adams, *Great Britain and the American Civil War* (2 vols., 1925) are useful for relations with England. Henry Blumenthal, *France and the United States, Their Diplomatic Relations 1789–1914* (1970) contains a good analysis of relations with France for both the North and the South. Donaldson Jordan and Edwin J. Pratt examine the responses of European powers to the American Civil War in their *Europe and the American Civil War* (1931).

The politics of the first years of the Lincoln administration is thoroughly explored in J. G. Randall, *Lincoln, the President: Springfield to Gettysburg* (4 vols., 1945–1955; volume 4 completed by Richard Current). B. P. Thomas, *Abraham Lincoln* (1952) contains a comprehensive treatment of the presidential years. Special aspects of wartime politics are explored in T. Harry Williams, *Lincoln and the Radicals* (1941) and H. B. Hesseltine, *Lincoln and the War Governors* (1948). James M. McPherson, *The Struggle for Equality, Abolitionists and the Negro in the Civil War and Reconstruction* (1964) and Hans L. Trefousse, *The Radical Republicans, Lincoln's Vanguard for Racial Justice* (1969), are excellent on the politics of emancipation. G. M. Frederickson, *The Inner Civil War: Northern Intellectuals and the Crisis of the Union* (1965) is a fine analysis of the impact of the war on the attitudes of intellectuals. Opposition to the war in the North is examined in Wood Gray, *The Hidden Civil War* (1942); F. L. Klement, *The Copperheads in the Middle West* (1960); and J. G. Randall, *Constitutional Problems Under Lincoln* (1926).

There are several recent works that provide excellent comprehensive analyses of Reconstruction: Kenneth M. Stampp, *The Era of Reconstruction* (1965); David Donald, *The Politics of Reconstruction* (1965); John Hope Franklin, *Reconstruction, After the Civil War* (1962); W. R. Brock, *An American Crisis* (1963); and R. W. Patrick, *The Reconstruction of the Nation* (1967). Preliminary efforts at reconstruction are examined in W. L. Rose, *Rehearsal for Reconstruction, The Port Royal Experiment* (1964) and W. B. Hesseltine, *Lincoln's Plan For Reconstruction* (1960). Herman Belz, *Reconstructing the Union: Theory and Policy During the Civil War* (1969) provides a good analysis of the evolving theories of reconstruction. Three useful studies of the troubled politics of Johnson's presidency are Howard K. Beale, *The Critical Year: A Study of Andrew Johnson and Reconstruction* (1930); LaWanda and J. H. Cox, *Politics, Principle and Prejudice, 1865–1866* (1963); and Eric L. McKitrick, *Andrew Johnson and Reconstruction* (1960). For special studies of the Reconstruction amendments consult J. B. James, *The Framing of the Fourteenth Amendment* (1956); Jacobus TenBroek, *Equal under Law* (1965); and William

Gillette, *The Right to Vote, Politics and the Passage of the Fifteenth Amendment* (1965). S. I. Kutler, *Judicial Power and Reconstruction Politics* (1968) is a significant analysis of the role of the courts.

On Reconstruction in the South, conflicting views of the political roles of whites and blacks are presented in E. M. Coulter, *The South During Reconstruction, 1865–1877* (1947) and William E. B. DuBois, *Black Reconstruction* (1935). Good special studies of the role of black freedmen are Vernon L. Wharton, *The Negro in Mississippi, 1865–1890* (1947) and Joel R. Williamson, *After Slavery: The Negro in South Carolina During Reconstruction* (1966). G. R. Bentley's *A History of the Freedmen's Bureau* (1955) is useful, but it should be supplemented by William S. McFeely's *Yankee Stepfather, General O. V. Howard and the Freedmen* (1968). J. E. Sefton, *The United States Army and Reconstruction* (1967) is a significant analysis of the role of the army. Good studies of the politics of "reconstruction" and "redemption" in the South can be found in these books: Francis B. Simkins and Robert Woody, *South Carolina During Reconstruction* (1932); Garnie W. McGinty, *Louisiana Redeemed; The Overthrow of Carpet-bag Rule, 1876–1880* (1941); and Thomas B. Alexander, *Political Reconstruction in Tennessee* (1950). Southern white efforts to intimidate black freedmen are described in Stanley Horn's *Invisible Empire: The Story of the Ku Klux Klan, 1866–1871* (1939). C. Vann Woodward, *Reunion and Reaction: The Compromise of 1877 and the End of Reconstruction* (1951) is a fascinating study of economic motives in the ending of reconstruction.

Supplemental Bibliography for the Second Edition

European responses to the New World are considered in a collection of fine original essays, Fredi Chiappelli, ed. *First Images of America: The Impact of the New World on the Old* (1976). *The European Discovery of America: The Southern Voyages* (1974), by Samuel Eliot Morison, who retraced the routes of the early explorers in his own boat, matches the excellence of his earlier volume on the northern voyages. James Lang, *Conquest and Commerce: Spain and England in the Americas* (1975) is useful for making comparisons. *American Slavery, American Freedom* (1975), by Edmund S. Morgan is a brilliant investigation of the simultaneous development of freedom and slavery in colonial Virginia. In *The Indian in America* (1975) Wilcomb Washburn offers the best one-volume history. Gary B. Nash probes the cultural interaction of native Americans, Europeans, and Africans with care and insight in his *Red, White and Black* (1974), while Francis Jennings offers a view of European colonization from a perspective sympathetic to tribal cultures in *The Invasion of America* (1975). The early history of Afro-Americans and their role in developing the new economy and society in South Carolina is the subject of Peter H. Wood's *Black Majority: Negroes in Colonial South Carolina* (1974). There is a very informative comparison of the developing patterns of race relations in Brazil and the United States in Carl N. Degler, *Neither Black Nor White: Slavery and Race Relations in Brazil and the United States* (1971).

Michael Kammen explores the colonial origins of the American "character" in *People of Paradox* (1972) and Sacvan Bercovitch, *The Puritan Origins of the American Self* (1975) offers a sophisticated analysis of literary presentations of national selfhood. Sydney Ahlstrom's *Religious History of the American People* (1972) is a comprehensive and reliable guide to all periods of American religious history.

Robert Middlekauff, *The Mathers: Three Generations of Puritan Intellectuals* (1971) and David D. Hall, *The Faithful Shepherd: A History of the New England Ministry in the Seventeenth Century* (1972) reassess Puritan intellectual history by stressing the pastoral context of ministerial writings. Other recent books have provided new views of Puritan New England by focusing upon the social history of New England towns: Kenneth A. Lockridge, *A New England Town: The First Hundred Years* (1970), Philip J. Greven, Jr., *Four Generations: Population, Land, and Family in Colonial Andover, Massachusetts* (1970), Michael Zuckerman, *Peaceable Kingdoms: New England Towns in the Eighteenth Century* (1970), Edward M. Cook, Jr., sketches a typology of towns in the eighteenth century and relates these types to political style in *Fathers of the Towns* (1976).

Henry May offers a lucid guide to the various dimensions of *The Enlightenment in America* (1976), and Lawrence Cremin provides a comprehensive history of education, including much recent research on the family and other educational institutions besides the schools, in his *American Education: The Colonial Experience, 1607–1783* (1970). Wilson Smith's *Theories of Education in Early America, 1655–1819* (1973) is a fine anthology of documents articulating educational ideas. The changing character of intellectual life between 1750 and 1870 is sketched in Daniel Calhoun's imaginative psychological history *The Intelligence of a People* (1973).

The colonial population records are analyzed in Robert V. Wells, *The Population of the British Colonies in America Before 1776* (1975). James A. Henretta synthesizes a wide range of demographic, economic, and social data in a fascinating study of *The Evolution of American Society, 1700–1815* (1973). Richard Hofstadter summarizes and judiciously comments on recent scholarship in *America at 1750: A Social Portrait* (1971). The connection between social change, ideology, and the revolution is illuminated in Henretta's book noted above, and in Robert A. Gross, *The Minutemen and Their World* (1976), a study of the rural town of Concord during the Revolution, and in Eric Foner, *Tom Paine and Revolutionary America* (1976), where Paine's thought is related to the social context of Philadelphia's artisan world. Stephen G. Kurtz and James H. Hutson, eds. *Essays on the American Revolution* (1973) and Alfred F. Young, ed. *The American Revolution: Explorations in the History of American Radicalism* (1976) both contain stimulating original essays. The character of politics in New York is brilliantly explained in Patricia U. Bonomi, *A Factious People: Politics and Society in Colonial New York* (1971), and Pauline Maier describes the developing pattern of opposition from colony to colony in *From Resistance to Revolution* (1972). Recent studies of loyalists include Mary Beth Norton, *The British Americans: The Loyalist Exiles in England* (1972) and Bernard Bailyn, *The Ordeal of Thomas Hutchinson* (1974).

Peter Shaw offers a compelling portrait of John Adams in *The Character of John Adams* (1976), while Merrill Peterson's *Thomas Jefferson and the New Nation: A Biography* (1970) is a reliable guide to Jefferson's career. Gerald Stourzh uses Alexander Hamilton to explore the political ideas of the Revolutionary era in *Alexander Hamilton and the Idea of Republican Government* (1970), while J.G.A. Pocock places American republican thought into a broad cultural and historical context in *The Machiavellian Moment* (1975). Wilson Carey McWilliams has written an impressive commentary on American political theory in *The Idea of Fraternity in America* (1973). David Brion Davis skillfully probes the inter-relationships of social change, revolution, and the emergence of antislavery thought in *The Problem of Slavery in the Age of Revolution, 1770–1823* (1975).

John R. Howe provides a well-organized account of the transition from the eighteenth to the nineteenth century in *From the Revolution Through the Age of Jackson* (1973). Richard Buel, Jr., *Securing the Revolution* (1972) and James M. Banner, *To the Hartford Convention* (1970) show that many of the ideological issues of the Revolution held the attention of political leaders until 1815.

The literature on the development of the West is carefully summarized in Ray A. Billington, *Westward Expansion* (1974). Indian policy under Jefferson and Jackson may be studied in Bernard W. Sheehan, *Seeds of Extinction: Jeffersonian Philanthropy and the American Indian* (1973), and in Ronald N. Satz, *American Indian Policy in the Jacksonian Era* (1975). Michael P. Rogin offers a provocative and highly critical interpretation in *Fathers & Children: Andrew Jackson and the Subjugation of the American Indian* (1975). The cultural meaning of Indians and the frontier is brilliantly analyzed in a demanding book by Richard Slotkin, *Regeneration Through Violence: The Mythology of the American Frontier* (1973).

The "new politics" of the Jacksonian era is the subject of Richard Hofstadter's *The Idea of a Party System: The Rise of Legitimate Opposition in the United States, 1740–1840* (1969) and Ronald Formisano's *The Birth of Mass Political Parties: Michigan, 1827–1861* (1971). The violent opposition to abolitionism in the North is studied with great insight by Leonard L. Richards in *"Gentlemen of Property and Standing": Anti-Abolition Mobs in Jacksonian America* (1970).

The development of educational systems during the early nineteenth century is the subject of two recent books: Carl F. Kaestle, *The Evolution of an Urban School System: New York City, 1790–1850* (1973), and Stanley K. Schultz, *The Culture Factory: Boston Public Schools, 1789–1860* (1973). These books reveal a critical approach to educational reform and thus follow the tradition established in Michael B. Katz's pathbreaking book, *The Irony of Early School Reform: Educational Innovation in Mid-Nineteenth Century Massachusetts* (1968). David Rothman offers a provocative analysis of the development of institutions for the care of poor and dependent persons in *The Discovery of the Asylum* (1971). In a less exciting but a carefully argued book, Gerald Grob considers *Mental Institutions in America: Social Policy to 1875* (1973). Carroll Smith Rosenberg studies the evangelical basis of urban reform in antebellum New York in *Religion and the Rise of the American City* (1971), while Jay P. Dolan offers an extremely effective portrait of antebellum urban Catholics in *The Immigrant Church: New York's Irish and German Catholics, 1815–1865* (1975). Edward Pessen documents the existence of an extremely wealthy urban elite in the age of the common man in his *Riches, Class and Power Before the Civil War* (1973).

Rowland Berthoff offers a comprehensive account of American social history in *An Unsettled People: Social Order and Disorder in American History* (1971). The significance of the city for American social and cultural life is the subject in Thomas Bender, *Toward an Urban Vision: Ideas and Institutions in Nineteenth-Century America* (1975). The best of several recent surveys of American urban history is Sam Bass Warner's *The Urban Wilderness* (1972). Dolores Hayden presents an imaginative account of utopian communities in *Seven American Utopias* (1976) that emphasizes the physical design of utopia; the social dimension is considered in Rosabeth Moss Kanter, *Commitment and Community* (1972). Most of the recent literature on the history of women is in journal articles, but Kathryn Kish Sklar's book length study of *Catherine Beecher* (1973) throws a broad shaft of light on the history of women in the nineteenth century. Ann Douglas, *The Feminization of American Culture* (1977) and Nancy F. Cott, *The Bonds of Womanhood: "Woman's Sphere" in New England, 1780–1835* (1977) are also illuminating.

The study of slavery has produced some of the best historical writing being published today. Eugene Genovese, *Roll, Jordan Roll: The World the Slaves Made* (1974) is a comprehensive account of slavery that is particularly interested in the legitimization and exercise of power in a slave society. The persisting strength of the Afro-American family is the subject of Herbert G. Gutman, *The Black Family in Slavery and Freedom, 1750–1925* (1976). *The Slave Community* (1972) by John Blassingame probes the relations among slaves. Black culture is imaginatively and effectively interpreted in Lawrence W. Levine, *Black Culture and Black Consciousness: Afro-American Folk Thought from Slavery to Freedom* (1977). *Time on the Cross* (1974) by Robert W. Fogel and Stanley Engerman is a controversial analysis of slavery based upon quantitative research; it has been sharply and effectively criticized in Herbert G. Gutman, *Slavery and the Numbers Game* (1975). The free blacks in the South have been studied by Ira Berlin in *Slaves Without Masters* (1975). Race and slavery are the themes of two fine recent books: C. Vann Woodward, *American Counterpoint* (1971) and George M. Fredrickson, *The Black Image in the White Mind* (1971).

David Potter's *The Impending Crisis, 1848–1861* (1976) is a very good account of the drift toward war. Lincoln and Douglas are both the subject of recent biographies: Stephen B. Oates, *With Malice Toward None: The Life of Abraham Lincoln* (1977), and Robert W. Johannson, *Stephen A. Douglas* (1973).

Appendix

The Constitution of the United States of America

We the people of the United States, in order to form a more perfect union, establish justice, insure domestic tranquility, provide for the common defense, promote the general welfare, and secure the blessings of liberty to ourselves and our posterity, do ordain and establish this Constitution for the United States of America.

ARTICLE I

Section 1. All legislative powers herein granted shall be vested in a Congress of the United States, which shall consist of a Senate and House of Representatives.

Section 2. 1. The House of Representatives shall be composed of members chosen every second year by the people of the several States, and the electors in each State shall have the qualifications requisite for electors of the most numerous branch of the State legislature.

2. No person shall be a representative who shall not have attained to the age of twenty-five years, and been seven years a citizen of the United States, and who shall not, when elected, be an inhabitant of that State in which he shall be chosen.

3. Representatives and direct taxes[1] shall be apportioned among the several States which may be included within this Union, according to their respective numbers, which shall be determined by adding to the whole number of free persons, including those bound to service for a term of years, and excluding Indians not taxed, three fifths of all other persons.[2] The actual enumeration shall by made within three years after the first meeting of the Congress of the United States, and within every subsequent term of ten years, in such manner as they shall by law direct. The number of representatives shall not exceed one for every thirty thousand, but each State shall have at least one representative; and until such enumeration shall be made, the State of New Hampshire shall be entitled to choose three, Massachusetts eight, Rhode Island and Providence Plantations one, Connecticut five, New York six, New Jersey four, Pennsylvania eight, Delaware one, Maryland six, Virginia ten, North Carolina five, South Carolina five, and Georgia three.

4. When vacancies happen in the representation from any State, the executive authority thereof shall issue writs of election to fill such vacancies.

5. The House of Representatives shall choose their speaker and other officers; and shall have the sole power of impeachment.

Section 3. 1. The Senate of the United States shall be composed of two senators from each State, chosen by the legislature thereof,[3] for six years; and each senator shall have one vote.

---

[1] Altered by the 16th Amendment.
[2] Altered by the 14th Amendment.
[3] Superseded by the 17th Amendment.

---

2. Immediately after they shall be assembled in consequence of the first election, they shall be divided as equally as may be into three classes. The seats of the senators of the first class shall be vacated at the expiration of the second year, of the second class at the expiration of the fourth year and of the third class at the expiration of the sixth year, so that one third may be chosen every second year; and if vacancies happen by resignation, or otherwise, during the recess of the legislature of any State, the executive thereof may make temporary appointments until the next meeting of the legislature, which shall then fill such vacancies.[4]

3. No person shall be a senator who shall not have attained to the age of thirty years, and been nine years a citizen of the United States, and who shall not, when elected, be an inhabitant of that State for which he shall be chosen.

4. The Vice President of the United States shall be President of the Senate, but shall have no vote, unless they be equally divided.

5. The Senate shall choose their other officers, and also a president pro tempore, in the absence of the Vice President, or when he shall exercise the office of the President of the United States.

6. The Senate shall have the sole power to try all impeachments. When sitting for that purpose, they shall be on oath or affirmation. When the President of the United States is tried, the chief justice shall preside: and no person shall be convicted without the concurrence of two thirds of the members present.

7. Judgment in cases of impeachment shall not extend further than to removal from office, and disqualifications to hold and enjoy any office of honor, trust or profit under the United States: but the party convicted shall nevertheless be liable and subject to indictment, trial, judgment and punishment, according to law.

Section 4. 1. The times, places, and manner of holding elections for senators and representatives, shall be prescribed in each State by the legislature thereof: but the Congress may at any time by law make or alter such regulations, except as to the places of choosing senators.

2. The Congress shall assemble at least once in every year, and such meeting shall be on the first Monday in December, unless they shall by law appoint a different day.

Section 5. 1. Each House shall be the judge of the elections, returns and qualifications of its own members, and a majority of each shall constitute a quorum to do business; but a smaller number may adjourn from day to day, and may be authorized to compel the attendance of absent members, in such manner, and under such penalties as each House may provide.

---

[4] Altered by the 17th Amendment.

2. Each House may determine the rules of its proceedings, punish its members for disorderly behavior, and, with the concurrence of two thirds, expel a member.

3. Each House shall keep a journal of its proceedings, and from time to time publish the same, excepting such parts as may in their judgment require secrecy; and the yeas and nays of the members of either House on any question shall, at the desire of one fifth of those present, be entered on the journal.

4. Neither House, during the session of Congress, shall, without the consent of the other, adjourn for more than three days, nor to any other place than that in which the two Houses shall be sitting.

Section 6. 1. The senators and representatives shall receive a compensation for their services, to be ascertained by law, and paid out of the Treasury of the United States. They shall in all cases, except treason, felony, and breach of the peace, be privileged from arrest during their attendance at the session of their respective Houses, and in going to and returning from the same; and for any speech or debate in either House, they shall not be questioned in any other place.

2. No senator or representative shall, during the time for which he was elected, be appointed to any civil office under the authority of the United States, which shall have been created, or the emoluments whereof shall have been increased, during such time; and no person holding any office under the United States shall be a member of either House during his continuance in office.

Section 7. 1. All bills for raising revenue shall originate in the House of Representatives; but the Senate may propose or concur with amendments as on other bills.

2. Every bill which shall have passed the House of Representatives and the Senate, shall, before it become a law, be presented to the President of the United States; If he approves he shall sign it, but if not he shall return it, with his objections, to that House in which it shall have originated, who shall enter the objections at large on their journal, and proceed to reconsider it. If after such reconsideration two thirds of that House shall agree to pass the bill, it shall be sent, together with the objections, to the other House, by which it shall likewise be reconsidered, and if approved by two thirds of that House, it shall become a law. But in all such cases the votes of both Houses shall be determined by yeas and nays, and the names of the persons voting for and against the bill shall be entered on the journal of each House respectively. If any bill shall not be returned by the President within ten days (Sundays excepted) after it shall have been presented to him, the same shall be a law, in like manner as if he had signed it, unless the Congress by their adjournment prevent its return, in which case it shall not be a law.

3. Every order, resolution, or vote to which the concurrence of the Senate and the House of Representatives may be necessary (except on a question of adjournment) shall be presented to the President of the United States; and before the same shall take effect, shall be approved by him, or being disapproved by him, shall be repassed by two thirds of the Senate and House of Representatives, according to the rules and limitations prescribed in the case of a bill.

Section 8. The Congress shall have the power

1. To lay and collect taxes, duties, imposts, and excises, to pay the debts and provide for the common defense and general welfare of the United States; but all duties, imposts, and excises shall be uniform throughout the United States;

2. To borrow money on the credit of the United States;

3. To regulate commerce with foreign nations, and among the several States, and with the Indian tribes;

4. To establish an uniform rule of naturalization, and uniform laws on the subject of bankruptcies throughout the United States;

5. To coin money, regulate the value thereof, and of foreign coin, and fix the standard of weights and measures;

6. To provide for the punishment of counterfeiting the securities and current coin of the United States;

7. To establish post offices and post roads;

8. To promote the progress of science and useful arts, by securing for limited times to authors and inventors the exclusive right to their respective writings and discoveries;

9. To constitute tribunals inferior to the Supreme Court;

10. To define and punish piracies and felonies committed on the high seas, and offenses against the law of nations;

11. To declare war, grant letters of marque and reprisal, and make rules concerning captures on land and water;

12. To raise and support armies, but no appropriation of money to that use shall be for a longer term than two years;

13. To provide and maintain a navy;

14. To make rules for the government and regulation of the land and naval forces;

15. To provide for calling forth the militia to execute the laws of the Union, suppress insurrections and repel invasions;

16. To provide for organizing, arming, and disciplining the militia, and for governing such part of them as may be employed in the service of the United States, reserving to the States respectively, the appointment of the officers, and the authority of training the militia according to the discipline prescribed by Congress;

17. To exercise exclusive legislation in all cases whatsoever, over such district (not exceeding ten miles square) as may, by cession of particular States, and the acceptance of Congress, become the seat of the government of the United States, and to exercise like authority over all places purchased by the consent of the legislature of the State in which the same shall be, for the erection of forts, magazines, arsenals, dockyards, and other needful buildings; and

18. To make all laws which shall be necessary and proper for carrying into execution the foregoing powers, and all other powers vested by this Constitution in the government of the United States, or any department or officer thereof.

Section 9. 1. The migration or importation of such persons as any of the States now existing shall think proper to admit, shall not be prohibited by the Congress prior to the year one thousand eight hundred and eight, but a tax or duty may be imposed on such importation, not exceeding ten dollars for each person.

2. The privilege of the writ of habeas corpus shall not be suspended, unless when in cases of rebellion or invasion the public safety may require it.

3. No bill of attainder or ex post facto law shall be passed.

4. No capitation, or other direct, tax shall be laid, unless in proportion to the census or enumeration hereinbefore directed to be taken.[5]

5. No tax or duty shall be laid on articles exported from any State.

6. No preference shall be given by any regulation of commerce or revenue to the ports of one State over those of another: nor shall vessels bound to, or from, one State be obliged to enter, clear, or pay duties in another.

7. No money shall be drawn from the treasury, but in consequence of appropriations made by law; and a regular statement and account of the receipts and expenditures of all public money shall be published from time to time.

8. No title of nobility shall be granted by the United States: and no person holding any office of profit or trust under them, shall, without the consent of the Congress, accept of any present, emolument, office, or title, of any kind whatever, from any king, prince, or foreign State.

Section 10. 1. No State shall enter into any treaty, alliance, or confederation; grant letters of marque and reprisal; coin money; emit bills of credit; make any thing but gold and silver coin a tender in payment of debts; pass any bill of attainder, ex post facto law, or law impairing the obligation of contracts, or grant any title of nobility.

2. No State shall, without the consent of the Congress, lay any imposts or duties on imports or exports, except what may be absolutely necessary for executing its inspection laws: and the net produce of all duties and imposts laid by any State on imports or exports, shall be for the use of the treasury of the United States; and all such laws shall be subject to the revision and control of the Congress.

3. No State shall, without the consent of the Congress, lay any duty of tonnage, keep troops, or ships of war in time of peace, enter into any agreement or compact with another State, or with a foreign power, or engage in war, unless actually invaded, or in such imminent danger as will not admit of delay.

ARTICLE II
Section 1. 1. The executive power shall be vested in a President of the United States of America. He shall hold his office during the term of four years, and, together with the Vice President, chosen for the same term, be elected, as follows:

2. Each State shall appoint, in such manner as the legislature thereof may direct, a number of electors, equal to the whole number of senators and representatives to which the State may be entitled in the Congress: but no senator or representative, or person holding an office of

trust or profit under the United States, shall be appointed an elector.

The electors shall meet in their respective States, and vote by ballot for two persons, of whom one at least shall not be an inhabitant of the same State with themselves. And they shall make a list of all the persons voted for, and of the number of votes for each; which list they shall sign and certify, and transmit sealed to the seat of the government of the United States, directed to the president of the Senate. The president of the Senate shall, in the presence of the Senate and House of Representatives, open all the certificates, and the votes shall then be counted. The person having the greatest number of votes shall be the President, if such number be a majority of the whole number of electors appointed; and if there be more than one who have such majority, and have an equal number of votes, then the House of Representatives shall immediately choose by ballot one of them for President; and if no person have a majority, then from the five highest on the list the said House shall in like manner choose the President. But in choosing the President, the votes shall be taken by States, the representation from each State having one vote; a quorum for this purpose shall consist of a member or members from two thirds of the States, and a majority of all the States shall be necessary to a choice. In every case, after the choice of the President, the person having the greatest number of votes of the electors shall be the Vice President. But if there should remain two or more who have equal votes, the Senate shall choose from them by ballot the Vice President.[6]

3. The Congress may determine the time of choosing the electors, and the day on which they shall give their votes; which day shall be the same throughout the United States.

4. No person except a natural born citizen, or a citizen of the United States, at the time of the adoption of this Constitution, shall be eligible to the office of President; neither shall any person be eligible to that office who shall not have attained to the age of thirty-five years, and been fourteen years a resident within the United States.

5. In case of the removal of the President from office, or of his death, resignation, or inability to discharge the powers and duties of the said office, the same shall devolve on the Vice President, and the Congress may by law provide for the case of removal, death, resignation or inability, both of the President and Vice President, declaring what officer shall then act as President, and such officer shall act accordingly, until the disability be removed, or a President shall be elected.

6. The President shall, at stated times, receive for his services a compensation, which shall neither be increased nor diminished during the period for which he shall have been elected, and he shall not receive within that period any other emolument from the United States, or any of them.

7. Before he enter on the execution of his office, he shall take the following oath or affirmation:—"I do solemnly swear (or affirm) that I will faithfully execute the office of President of the United States, and will to the best of my

---

[5] Superseded by the 16th Amendment.

[6] Superseded by the 12th Amendment.

ability, preserve, protect, and defend the Constitution of the United States.''

Section 2. 1. The President shall be commander in chief of the army and navy of the United States, and of the militia of the several States, when called into the actual service of the United States; he may require the opinion, in writing, of the principal officer in each of the executive departments, upon any subject relating to the duties of their respective offices, and he shall have power to grant reprieves and pardons for offenses against the United States, except in cases of impeachment.

2. He shall have power, by and with the advice and consent of the Senate, to make treaties, provided two thirds of the senators present concur; and he shall nominate, and by and with the advice and consent of the Senate, shall appoint ambassadors, other public ministers and consuls, judges of the Supreme Court, and all other officers of the United States, whose appointments are not herein otherwise provided for, and which shall be established by law: but the Congress may by law vest the appointment of such inferior officers, as they think proper, in the President alone, in the courts of law, or in the heads of departments.

3. The President shall have power to fill up all vacancies that may happen during the recess of the Senate, by granting commissions which shall expire at the end of their next session.

Section 3. He shall from time to time give to the Congress information of the state of the Union, and recommend to their consideration such measures as he shall judge necessary and expedient; he may, on extraordinary occasions, convene both Houses, or either of them, and in case of disagreement between them with respect to the time of adjournment, he may adjourn them to such time as he shall think proper; he shall receive ambassadors and other public ministers; he shall take care that the laws be faithfully executed, and shall commission all the officers of the United States.

Section 4. The President, Vice President, and all civil officers of the United States, shall be removed from office on impeachment for, and conviction of, treason, bribery, or other high crimes and misdemeanors.

ARTICLE III

Section 1. The judicial power of the United States shall be vested in one Supreme Court, and in such inferior courts as the Congress may from time to time ordain and establish. The judges, both of the Supreme and inferior courts, shall hold their offices during good behavior, and shall, at stated times, receive for their services, a compensation, which shall not be diminished during their continuance in office.

Section 2. 1. The judicial power shall extend to all cases, in law and equity, arising under this Constitution, the laws of the United States, and treaties made, or which shall be made, under their authority;—to all cases affecting ambassadors, other public ministers and consuls;—to all cases of admiralty and maritime jurisdiction;—to controversies to which the United States shall be a party;[7]—to controversies between two or more States;—between a State and citizens of another State;—between citizens of different States;—between citizens of the same State claiming lands under grants of different States, and between a State, or the citizens thereof, and foreign States, citizens or subjects.

2. In all cases affecting ambassadors, other public ministers and consuls, and those in which a State shall be party, the Supreme Court shall have original jurisdiction. In all the other cases before mentioned, the Supreme Court shall have appellate jurisdiction, both as to law and fact, with such exceptions, and under such regulations as the Congress shall make.

3. The trial of all crimes, except in cases of impeachment, shall be by jury; and such trial shall be held in the State where the said crimes shall have been committed; but when not committed within any State, the trial shall be at such place or places as the Congress may by law have directed.

Section 3. 1. Treason against the United States shall consist only in levying war against them, or in adhering to their enemies, giving them aid and comfort. No person shall be convicted of treason unless on the testimony of two witnesses to the same overt act, or on confession in open court.

2. The Congress shall have power to declare the punishment of treason, but no attainder of treason shall work corruption of blood, or forfeiture except during the life of the person attainted.

ARTICLE IV

Section 1. Full faith and credit shall be given in each State to the public acts, records, and judicial proceedings of every other State. And the Congress may by general laws prescribe the manner in which such acts, records and proceedings shall be proved, and the effect thereof.

Section 2. 1. The citizens of each State shall be entitled to all privileges and immunities of citizens in the several States.[8]

2. A person charged in any State with treason, felony, or other crime, who shall flee from justice, and be found in another State, shall on demand of the executive authority of the State from which he fled, be delivered up to be removed to the State having jurisdiction of the crime.

3. No person held to service or labor in one State under the laws thereof, escaping into another, shall, in consequence of any law or regulation therein, be discharged from such service or labor, but shall be delivered up on claim of the party to whom such service or labor may be due.[9]

Section 3. 1. New States may be admitted by the Congress into this Union; but no new State shall be formed or erected within the jurisdiction of any other State; nor any State be formed by the junction of two or more States, or parts of States, without the consent of the legislatures of the States concerned as well as of the Congress.

2. The Congress shall have power to dispose of and make all needful rules and regulations respecting the

---

[7] Cf. the 11th Amendment.

[8] Superseded by the 14th Amendment, Sec. 1.

[9] Voided by the 13th Amendment.

territory or other property belonging to the United States; and nothing in this Constitution shall be so construed as to prejudice any claims of the United States, or of any particular State.

Section 4. The United States shall guarantee to every State in this Union a republican form of government, and shall protect each of them against invasion; and on application of the legislature, or of the executive (when the legislature cannot be convened) against domestic violence.

ARTICLE V

The Congress, whenever two thirds of both Houses shall deem it necessary, shall propose amendments to this Constitution, or, on the application of the legislatures of two thirds of the several States, shall call a convention for proposing amendments, which in either case, shall be valid to all intents and purposes, as part of this Constitution, when ratified by the legislatures of three fourths of the several States, or by conventions in three fourths thereof, as the one or the other mode of ratification may be proposed by the Congress; Provided that no amendment which may be made prior to the year one thousand eight hundred and eight shall in any manner affect the first and fourth clauses in the ninth section of the first article; and that no State, without its consent, shall be deprived of its equal suffrage in the Senate.

ARTICLE VI

1. All debts contracted and engagements entered into, before the adoption of this Constitution, shall be as valid against the United States under this Constitution, as under the Confederation.

2. This Constitution, and the laws of the United States which shall be made in pursuance thereof; and all treaties made, or which shall be made, under the authority of the United States, shall be the supreme law of the land; and the Judges in every State shall be bound thereby, any thing in the Constitution or laws of any State to the contrary notwithstanding.

3. The senators and representatives before mentioned, and the members of the several State legislatures, and all executive and judicial officers, both of the United States and of the several States, shall be bound by oath or affirmation to support this Constitution; but no religious test shall ever be required as a qualification to any office or public trust under the United States.

ARTICLE VII

The ratification of the conventions of nine States shall be sufficient for the establishment of this Constitution between the States so ratifying the same.

Done in Convention by the unanimous consent of the States present the seventeenth day of September in the year of our Lord one thousand seven hundred and eighty-seven, and of the independence of the United States of America the twelfth. In witness whereof we have hereunto subscribed our names.

[Names omitted]

*   *   *

Articles in addition to, and amendment of, the Constitution of the United States of America, proposed by Congress, and ratified by the legislatures of the several States, pursuant to the fifth article of the original Constitution.

AMENDMENT I [First ten amendments ratified December 15, 1791]

Congress shall make no law respecting an establishment of religion, or prohibiting the free exercise thereof; or abridging the freedom of speech, or of the press; or the right of the people peaceably to assemble, and to petition the government for a redress of grievances.

AMENDMENT II

A well regulated militia, being necessary to the security of a free State, the right of the people to keep and bear arms, shall not be infringed.

AMENDMENT III

No soldier shall, in time of peace be quartered in any house, without the consent of the owner, nor in time of war, but in a manner to be prescribed by law.

AMENDMENT IV

The right of the people to secure in their persons, houses, papers, and effects, against unreasonable searches and seizures, shall not be violated, and no warrants shall issue, but upon probable cause, supported by oath or affirmation, and particularly describing the place to be searched, and the persons or things to be seized.

AMENDMENT V

No person shall be held to answer for a capital, or otherwise infamous crime, unless on a presentment or indictment of a grand jury, except in cases arising in the land or naval forces, or in the militia, when in actual service in time of war or public danger; nor shall any person be subject for the same offense to be twice put in jeopardy of life or limb; nor shall be compelled in any criminal case to be a witness against himself, nor be deprived of life, liberty, or property, without due process of law; nor shall private property be taken for public use, without just compensation.

AMENDMENT VI

In all criminal prosecutions, the accused shall enjoy the right to a speedy and public trial, by an impartial jury of the State and district wherein the crime shall have been committed, which district shall have been previously ascertained by law, and to be informed of the nature and cause of the accusation; to be confronted with the witnesses against him; to have compulsory process for obtaining witnesses in his favor, and to have the assistance of counsel for his defense.

AMENDMENT VII

In suits at common law, where the value in controversy shall exceed twenty dollars, the right of trial by jury shall be preserved, and no fact tried by a jury shall be otherwise reëxamined in any court of the United States, than according to the rules of the common law.

AMENDMENT VIII

Excessive bail shall not be required, nor excessive fines imposed, nor cruel and unusual punishments inflicted.

AMENDMENT IX

The enumeration in the Constitution of certain rights shall not be construed to deny or disparage others retained by the people.

AMENDMENT X

The powers not delegated to the United States by the Constitution, nor prohibited by it to the States, are reserved to the States respectively, or to the people.

AMENDMENT XI [Ratified January 8, 1798]

The judicial power of the United States shall not be construed to extend to any suit in law or equity, commenced or prosecuted against one of the United States by citizens of another State, or by citizens or subjects of any foreign State.

AMENDMENT XII [Ratified September 25, 1804]

The electors shall meet in their respective States, and vote by ballot for President and Vice President, one of whom, at least, shall not be an inhabitant of the same State with themselves; they shall name in their ballots the person voted for as President, and in distinct ballots, the person voted for as Vice President, and they shall make distinct lists of all persons voted for as President and of all persons voted for as Vice President, and of the number of votes for each, which lists they shall sign and certify, and transmit sealed to the seat of the government of the United States, directed to the President of the Senate;—The President of the Senate shall, in the presence of the Senate and House of Representatives, open all the certificates and the votes shall then be counted;—The person having the greatest number of votes for President, shall be the President, if such number be a majority of the whole number of electors appointed; and if no person have such majority, then from the persons having the highest numbers not exceeding three on the list of those voted for as President, the House of Representatives shall choose immediately, by ballot, the President. But in choosing the President, the votes shall be taken by States, the representation from each State having one vote; a quorum for this purpose shall consist of a member or members from two thirds of the States, and a majority of all the States shall be necessary to a choice. And if the House of Representatives shall not choose a President whenever the right of choice shall devolve upon them, before the fourth day of March next following, then the Vice President shall act as President, as in the case of the death or other constitutional disability of the President. The person having the greatest number of votes as Vice President shall be the Vice President, if such number be a majority of the whole number of electors appointed, and if no person have a majority, then from the two highest numbers on the list, the Senate shall choose the Vice President; a quorum for the purpose shall consist of two thirds of the whole number of Senators, and a majority of the whole number shall be necessary to a choice. But no person constitutionally ineligible to the office of President shall be eligible to that of Vice President of the United States.

AMENDMENT XIII [Ratified December 18, 1865]

Section 1. Neither slavery nor involuntary servitude, except as a punishment for crime whereof the party shall have been duly convicted, shall exist within the United States, or any place subject to their jurisdiction.

Section 2. Congress shall have power to enforce this article by appropriate legislation.

AMENDMENT XIV [Ratified July 28, 1868]

Section 1. All persons born or naturalized in the United States, and subject to the jurisdiction thereof, are citizens of the United States and of the State wherein they reside. No State shall make or enforce any law which shall abridge the privileges or immunities of citizens of the United States; nor shall any State deprive any person of life, liberty, or property, without due process of law; nor deny to any person within its jurisdiction the equal protection of the laws.

Section 2. Representatives shall be apportioned among the several States according to their respective numbers, counting the whole number of persons in each State, excluding Indians not taxed. But when the right to vote at any election for the choice of electors for President and Vice President of the United States, representatives in Congress, the executive and judicial officers of a State, or the members of the legislature thereof, is denied to any of the male inhabitants of such State, being twenty-one years of age, and citizens of the United States, or in any way abridged, except for participating in rebellion, or other crime, the basis of representation therein shall be reduced in the proportion which the number of such male citizens shall bear to the whole number of male citizens twenty-one years of age in such State.

Section 3. No person shall be a senator or representative in Congress, or elector of President and Vice President, or hold any office, civil or military, under the United States, or under any State, who having previously taken an oath, as a member of Congress, or as an officer of the United States, or as a member of any State legislature, or as an executive or judicial officer of any State, to support the Constitution of the United States, shall have engaged in insurrection or rebellion against the same, or given aid or comfort to the enemies thereof. But Congress may by a vote of two thirds of each House, remove such disability.

Section 4. The validity of the public debt of the United States, authorized by law, including debts incurred for payment of pensions and bounties for services in suppressing insurrection or rebellion, shall not be questioned. But neither the United States nor any State shall assume or pay any debt or obligation incurred in aid of insurrection or rebellion against the United States, or any claim for the loss or emancipation of any slave; but all such debts, obligations, and claims shall be held illegal and void.

Section 5. The Congress shall have power to enforce, by appropriate legislation, the provisions of this article.

AMENDMENT XV [Ratified March 30, 1870]
Section 1. The right of citizens of the United States to vote shall not be denied or abridged by the United States or by any State on account of race, color, or previous condition of servitude.
Section 2. The Congress shall have power to enforce this article by appropriate legislation.

AMENDMENT XVI [Ratified February 25, 1913]
The Congress shall have power to lay and collect taxes on incomes, from whatever source derived, without apportionment among the several States, and without regard to any census or enumeration.

AMENDMENT XVII [Ratified May 31, 1913]
The Senate of the United States shall be composed of two senators from each State, elected by the people thereof, for six years; and each senator shall have one vote. The electors in each State shall have the qualifications requisite for electors of the most numerous branch of the State legislature.

When vacancies happen in the representation of any State in the Senate, the executive authority of such State shall issue writs of election to fill such vacancies: *Provided,* That the legislature of any State may empower the executive thereof to make temporary appointments until the people fill the vacancies by election as the legislature may direct.

This amendment shall not be so construed as to affect the election or term of any senator chosen before it becomes valid as part of the Constitution.

AMENDMENT XVIII[10] [Ratified January 29, 1919]
After one year from the ratification of this article, the manufacture, sale, or transportation of intoxicating liquors within, the importation thereof into, or the exportation thereof from the United States and all territory subject to the jurisdiction thereof for beverage purposes is thereby prohibited.

The Congress and the several States shall have concurrent power to enforce this article by appropriate legislation.

This article shall be inoperative unless it shall have been ratified as an amendment to the Constitution by the legislatures of the several States, as provided in the Constitution, within seven years from the date of the submission hereof to the States by Congress.

AMENDMENT XIX [Ratified August 26, 1920]
The right of citizens of the United States to vote shall not be denied or abridged by the United States or by any State on account of sex.

Congress shall have the power to enforce this article by appropriate legislation.

AMENDMENT XX [Ratified January 23, 1933]
Section 1. The terms of the President and Vice President shall end at noon on the 20th day of January, and the

terms of Senators and Representatives at noon on the 3d day of January, of the years in which such terms would have ended if this article had not been ratified; and the terms of their successors shall then begin.
Section 2. The Congress shall assemble at least once in every year, and such meeting shall begin at noon on the 3d day of January, unless they shall by law appoint a different day.
Section 3. If, at the time fixed for the beginning of the term of President, the President-elect shall have died, the Vice President-elect shall become President. If a President shall not have been chosen before the time fixed for the beginning of his term, or if the President-elect shall have failed to qualify, then the Vice President-elect shall act as President until a President shall have qualified; and the Congress may by law provide for the case wherein neither a President-elect nor a Vice President-elect shall have qualified, declaring who shall then act as President, or the manner in which one who is to act shall be selected, and such person shall act accordingly until a President or Vice President shall have qualified.
Section 4. The Congress may by law provide for the case of the death of any of the persons from whom the House of Representatives may choose a President whenever the right of choice shall have devolved upon them, and for the case of the death of any of the persons from whom the Senate may choose a Vice President whenever the right of choice shall have devolved upon them.
Section 5. Sections 1 and 2 shall take effect on the 15th day of October following the ratification of this article.
Section 6. This article shall be inoperative unless it shall have been ratified as an amendment to the Constitution by the legislatures of three-fourths of the several States within seven years from the date of its submission.

AMENDMENT XXI [Ratified December 5, 1933]
Section 1. The Eighteenth Article of amendment to the Constitution of the United States is hereby repealed.
Section 2. The transportation or importation into any State, Territory, or possession of the United States for delivery or use therein of intoxicating liquors in violation of the laws thereof, is hereby prohibited.
Section 3. This article shall be inoperative unless it shall have been ratified as an amendment to the Constitution by conventions in the several States as provided in the Constitution, within seven years from the date of the submission thereof to the States by the Congress.

AMENDMENT XXII [Ratified March 1, 1951]
No person shall be elected to the office of the President more than twice, and no person who has held the office of President, or acted as President, for more than two years of a term to which some other person was elected President shall be elected to the office of the President more than once.

But this article shall not apply to any person holding the office of President when this article was proposed by the Congress, and shall not prevent any person who may be holding the office of President, or acting as President, during the term within which this article becomes operative from holding the office of President or acting as President during the remainder of such term.

[10] Repealed by the 21st Amendment.

This article shall be inoperative unless it shall have been ratified as an amendment to the Constitution by the legislatures of three-fourths of the several States within seven years from the date of its submission to the States by the Congress.

AMENDMENT XXIII [Ratified March 29, 1961]
Section 1. The District constituting the seat of Government of the United States shall appoint in such manner as the Congress may direct:

A number of electors of President and Vice President equal to the whole number of Senators and Representatives in Congress to which the District would be entitled if it were a State, but in no event more than the least populous State; they shall be in addition to those appointed by the States, but they shall be considered, for the purposes of the election of President and Vice President, to be electors appointed by a State; and they shall meet in the District and perform such duties as provided by the twelfth article of amendment.
Section 2. The Congress shall have power to enforce this article by appropriate legislation.

AMENDMENT XXIV [Ratified January 23, 1964]
Section 1. The right of citizens of the United States to vote in any primary or other election for President or Vice President, for electors for President or Vice President, or for Senator or Representative in Congress, shall not be denied or abridged by the United States or any State by reason of failure to pay any poll tax or other tax.
Section 2. The Congress shall have power to enforce this article by appropriate legislation.

AMENDMENT XXV [Ratified February 10, 1967]
Section 1. In case of the removal of the President from office or of his death or resignation, the Vice President shall become President.
Section 2. Whenever there is a vacancy in the office of the Vice President, the President shall nominate a Vice President who shall take office upon confirmation by a majority vote of both Houses of Congress.
Section 3. Whenever the President transmits to the President pro tempore of the Senate and the Speaker of the House of Representatives his written declaration that he is unable to discharge the powers and duties of his office, and until he transmits to them a written declaration to the contrary, such powers and duties shall be discharged by the Vice President as Acting President.
Section 4. Whenever the Vice President and a majority of either the principal officers of the executive departments or of such other body as Congress may by law provide, transmit to the President pro tempore of the Senate and the Speaker of the House of Representatives their written declaration that the President is unable to discharge the powers and duties of his office, the Vice President shall immediately assume the powers and duties of the office as Acting President.

Thereafter, when the President transmits to the President pro tempore of the Senate and the Speaker of the House of Representatives his written declaration that no inability exists, he shall resume the powers and duties of his office unless the Vice President and a majority of either the principal officers of the executive departments or of such other body as Congress may by law provide, transmit within four days to the President pro tempore of the Senate and the Speaker of the House of Representatives their written declaration that the President is unable to discharge the powers and duties of his office. Thereupon Congress shall decide the issue, assembling within forty-eight hours for that purpose if not in session. If the Congress, within twenty-one days after receipt of the latter written declaration, or, if Congress is not in session, within twenty-one days after Congress is required to assemble, determines by two-thirds vote of both Houses that the President is unable to discharge the powers and duties of his office, the Vice President shall continue to discharge the same as Acting President; otherwise, the President shall resume the powers and duties of his office.

Index

About the Authors

Esteemed educator Edwin Rozwenc was Dwight Morrow Professor of History and chairman of the Department of American Studies at Amherst College for many years until his death in 1974. He also taught for several years at Cornell and Clark Universities and became a fellow of the Foundation for the Advancement of Education in 1954. Professor Rozwenc is the author of *Cooperatives Come to America*; co-author of *Restless Americans: The Challenge of Change in America*, and *The People Make a Nation*; and editor of a long list of books, including *Causes of the American Civil War*, *New Deal: Evolution and Revolution*, and *Reconstruction in the South*. He received his B.A. from Amherst College in 1937, M.A. from Columbia University in 1938, and Ph.D. from Columbia University in 1941.

Thomas Bender is Samuel Rudin Professor of the Humanities and professor of history at New York University. A distinguished historian, Professor Bender won the Frederick Jackson Turner Prize of the Organization of American Historians for his book *Toward an Urban Vision* (1975). He is also the author of *Community and Social Change in America* (1978) and has written for several historical journals and magazines, including *New York History*, *New England Quarterly*, *Journal of American History*, and *American Historical Review*. He received his B.A. from the University of Santa Clara in 1966, M.A. from the University of California, Davis, in 1967, and Ph. D. from the University of California, Davis, in 1971.

A Note on the Type

The text of this book was set by means of modern computer composition in a text type called PALATINO. The display types are MICHELANGELO and POST ROMAN BOLD. MICHELANGELO is a companion titling to PALATINO and both are contemporary creations of the German type designer Hermann Zapf. PALATINO is distinguished by broad letters and vigorous, inclined serifs typical of the work of a sixteenth century Italian master of writing. MICHELANGELO expresses the simplicity and clarity of the classic form. Both PALATINO and MICHELANGELO reflect the early Venetian scripts influencing Zapf's creations. POST ROMAN BOLD, a display roman with slight variation of colour, designed by Herbert Post, distinguishes itself by capitals almost without serifs, most of them wide, and a lower case of small, strong, horizontal serifs and short descenders.

This book was composed by Black Dot, Inc., Crystal Lake, Illinois, printed and bound by R. R. Donnelley & Sons, Co., Crawfordsville, Indiana.